A GOVERNOR'S TRYST WITH HARYANA

A GOVERNOR'S TRYST WITH HARYANA

H.A. Barari

GYAN PUBLISHING HOUSE
New Delhi-110002

A GOVERNOR'S TRYST WITH HARYANA

Rs. 790

ISBN : 81-212-0919-6

Published in 2007 in India by
Gyan Publishing House
5, Ansari Road, Darya Ganj, New Delhi-110002
Phones : 23282060, 23261060, Fax : (011) 23285914
E-mail : books@gyanbook . com
Website : http : //www. gyanbooks. com

Laser Type Setting at : Master Computer's, Delhi
Printed at : Salasar Imaging System, Delhi

Dedicated to the people of Haryana
whose unbounded love lighted up
my days spent with them

Contents

Preface 11

1. **Through My Paces** 15
2. **A Flashback to Haryana's Past** 21
3. **Further on Haryana's History : Its Saga of Rebellion and Resistance : the 1857 Struggle for Independence First Started Here : Haryana's Rich Spiritual and Cultural Heritage** 53
4. **Getting into My Stride** 79
5. **In the Holy Land of Kuru** 89
6. **Governor or Jack of All Trades?** 121
7. **Governor As Patron of Ngo's: on Panipat, Rohtak, Pehowa and Other Places** 143
8. **Visits to Simla, Ambala and Baba Ka Ladhana: Sher Shah, A Haryanvi? The Battles of Panipat: Himu, the Emperor of Delhi and Hero of Panipat** 179
9. **Teej, the Joyous Festival of Home-coming: Bhiwani's Links With Harappan Civilisation: Hissar, the Town of Emperor Feroze Shah Tughlak: the Emperor's Romance With A Peasant Girl: Sher Shah Suri Born At Hissar? 1857 Uprising: Heroic Roles of Hissar and Hansi: Agroha: the Original Home of the Aggarwals** 211

10. **Sirsa Where Prithviraj was Captured by Mohd. Ghori: Akbar at Kurukshetra During A Solar Eclipse: I Swim Across Sannihit Tank on A Solar Eclipse: Jyotisar Where Krishna Revealed the Gita: the Ancient Temples of Bhadrakali and Katyayani** 237

11. **Thanesar, the Place of Lord Shiva, Harshavardhana and Sufi Saints, Sheikh Chilli and Qutb Jalaluddin** 253

12. **Rewari and Rao Tula Ram: Haryana's World Class Cricketers: Annual Governors' Conference in Delhi: Prime Minister Helps Flood-afected Haryana, Punjab: Ch. Devi Lal's Pre-election Political Moves: Gurgaon, the Village of the Guru: The Revolutioaries of Mewat** 275

13. **Kunti, Karna and Karnal: Karva Chauth, Dhan Teras and Diwali: Sonepat or Swarnprasth of Mahabharata: SOS Village, Faridabad: Surdas, Blind Poet of Sihi** 291

14. **Haryana's Torch-bearers of Vedanta: Gaudapada, Teacher of Adi Shankaracharya's Teacher: Totapuri, Baba of Ladhana, Guru of Sri Ramakrishna** 313

15. **I Take to Golf: 1857 Uprising: Raja Nahar Singh's Double Game: the Surajkund Crafts Mela: Plight of Bonded Labourers: Relics of Indus Valley Civilisation Unearthed in Haryana: Vedic Civilisation Pre-Harappan? Aryan Invasion of India A Myth? Aryan Roots of the Persians: Vedic Mathematics: Excavations at Rakhigarhi and Other Harappan Sites in Haryana: Indus Valley or Saraswati Valley Civilisation? Was Lord Rama Born at Banwali in Haryana?** 331

16. **Seminar on the Gita: A Preceptor Blesses his Pupil: Cricket Match between Punjab and Haryana: 40th Anniversary of our Independence: Hindu Scriptures and Qoran–Similarity of their Spiritual Concepts: Yamunanagar, Sugh, Kalesar, Bilaspur, Kapal Mochan: Tajewala and Firoz Shah's West Yamuna Canal: Motilal Nehru School of Sports, Rai: Generals as Vice-chancellors of Universities: Teej Again: Kaithal and the Pandavas: Kalayat and Sage Kapil** 355

17. **In Gujarat, the Land of Pilgrimages** 383

18. **A New Political Dispensation** 405

19. **Haryana on the Road to All-round Progress** 425

Index 429

Preface

In less than a year of my retirement from the highest police job in India, namely that of the Director, Intelligence Bureau, I was sworn in as the Governor of Haryana on February 22, 1988, an assignment that came to an abrupt end in February 1990—a span of about two years despite the constitutional provision of a five-year tenure. Howsoever brief, this sojourn in Haryana gave me a golden opportunity of delving deep into the history and culture of a state which should attract notice not only for its rich and ancient heritage but also by virtue of the fact that it surrounds the national capital region of Delhi on all sides except the east.

People elsewhere ridicule Haryana and make it the butt of jokes because of their misconception that its people are a rough and tough lot who are steeped in the prejudices of their castes and clans. They poke fun at the follies and foibles of some typical Haryanvi characters such as Tau (village elder) and Taei (elderly lady), Chhorra (son or boy) and Chorri (daughter or girl), Pali (shepherd) and Phoji (a serviceman of low rank) with a view to projecting them as figures of rustic tomfoolery. But this is an utter travesty of truth and an inversion of the reality. It is my firm conviction that most people outside Haryana are not fully conversant with the greatness of its cultural and spiritual heritage as well as the pivotal role its people played in the different phases of our country's history and even in pre-historic times. There is a view that Haryana's civilisational evolution was set in motion three crore years ago! The Siswal Civilisation that flourished here was followed by the Indus Valley Civilisation and the Vedic Civilisation of the Aryans that initially revolved around the sacred Saraswati river of Haryana.

Haryana is the land that was cultivated by its King Kuru in days of yore with a golden plough. Shorn of its mythical symbolism, this implied that Kuru had instilled in the people of this tract the habit of hard work and a host of moral values, ensuring that they enjoyed economic prosperity and lived a life of moral rectitude.

Dushyanta, a ruler of Haryana, and Shakuntala gave birth to a son, Bharata, who also became the ruler of Haryana and gave his name to our country. The Pandavas ruled over Haryana from their capital at Indraprastha (or present-day Delhi). Ever since, the people of Haryana have looked upon Delhi as their capital—a linkage that was drastically diluted by the British rulers in the 19th century as part of the punitive administrative changes introduced in the wake of the 1857 freedom struggle. Kurukshetra in Haryana is one of our country's holiest pilgrimages, apart from being the battle ground where the Pandavas and the Kauravas fought the Mahabharata war.

It was in Haryana that the Mahabharata, several Puranas and the Smritis were composed and the message of the Gita was revealed. It was here that Karna, the epic hero of the Mahabharata, was born. Many of the well-known sages of ancient India had their hermitages in Haryana. Claims have been put forward that both Lord Rama and Sita were born at places in Haryana though this question calls for a deeper probe. Lord Buddha had visited several places in Haryana and held discourses to spread his new religion. Haryana has been the home of many Sufi saints. In the context of Haryana's ancient spiritual heritage, it is worth mentioning that Gaudapada, the preceptor of Adi Shankaracharya's teacher, was a man from a place near Kurukshetra. Centuries later, their Vedantic tradition was kept alive by another saint from Haryana namely, Totapuri, Baba of Ladhana, who had initiated Sri Ramakrishna Paramahansa into Vedanta Sadhana at Dakshineswar near Kolkata.

Several leading figures of Indian history were from Haryana. There is some evidence to show that Chandragupta Maurya, the Gupta Emperor of India, belonged to Haryana. Harshavardhana, the seventh century Pushpabhuti ruler of India, was from Thanesar in Haryana. Sher Shah Suri, the 15th century Emperor of Delhi, was born at Narnaul in Haryana. Himu, the hero of Haryana had occupied the throne of Delhi, albeit for a brief interlude, and proclaimed himself as Maharaja Vikramaditya in the sixteenth century A.D.

Many cataclysmic developments that changed the course of India's history in the medieval period took place on the soil of Haryana. In view of its strategic location close to the western frontier of India, Haryana had to face the onslaught of Muslim marauders and invaders all through this period. In the 11th century A.D., Mahmud of Ghazni as well as his successors, Masud and Madud, launched several attacks on Haryana, causing untold suffering to its people. Towards the end of the 12th century A.D., Muhammad Ghori of Afghanistan, invaded

India twice and in the battles fought at Tarain in Haryana he lost to Prithviraj Chauhan on the first occasion, but defeated the latter the next year, which marked a watershed in India's history and the advent of Muslim rule in India. The invasion of Taimur, the Turkish ruler of Samarqand, in 1398 A.D. wrought havoc on the people of Haryana. The latter again suffered badly at the hands of Nadir Shah, the ruler of Persia, who indulged in loot and plunder during his invasion in 1739 A.D. The three battles fought at Panipat in Haryana in 1526 A.D., 1556 A.D. And 1761 A.D. decided our country's destiny at critical junctures of our history.

The people of Haryana fought bravely to keep the foreign invaders out and even if they failed to stop them, they continued to resist them, organising rebellious movements against foreign rule. Even after the advent of the British, the people of Haryana did not meekly accept the rule of the latter. In the 1857 freedom struggle against the British that engulfed the greater part of northern India, it was some Sepoys of Haryana, who fired the first salvo at Ambala at 9 a.m. On May 6, 1857. About nine hours before their brethren joined the struggle the same evening at Meerut.

Haryana has a rich cultural heritage encompassing such diverse fields as art, music and literature. The blind poet-musician Surdas of Sihi and Kalla Khan, the famous Khayal singer of Rewari are two of Haryana's all-time greats in this sphere. Haryana has contributed many famous Ragas to India's classical music. Haryana has produced many great stalwarts in Sanskrit, Hindi and Urdu literatures. Haryana is regarded as the birth-place of Urdu language.

There is hardly a town, village, river, field, tree nor even an ordinary pebble or a clod of earth in Haryana that does not have a story or an anecdote woven around it which may be full of significance—historical, cultural, religious or mythological. The famous lines of the English poet William Wordsworth readily come to mind:

To me the meanest flower that blows can give
Thoughts that do often lie too deep for tears.

The dynamic people of Haryana have achieved a high rate of economic growth, thanks to the remarkable capacity for hard work of its people, both men and women—a virtue they have probably inherited from the example set for them by their King Kuru. Women work in the fields as vigorously as men, often driving their tractors and engaging in other back-breaking agricultural operations. Traces of the moral streak imbibed by the people from King Kuru can still be found in certain practices in Haryana such as vegetarianism, abstention from alcoholic drinks, avoidance of cruelty towards birds and beasts etc., though, as everywhere else, these practices are fast yielding place to new socio-ethical mores.

Signs of Haryana's economic progress are there for all to see. There are good roads, piped water is available in all villages and the people at large still use nothing but pure Ghee in the preparation of their food. I saw no beggar in Haryana. Gurgaon and, to some extent, Faridabad with their glittering housing complexes, shopping malls and state-of-the-art casinos represent the modern face of the state. It has the second highest per capita income in the country, coming next to only Punjab.

I shall consider my labour amply rewarded if this book helps to stimulate some interest among people across our country in Haryana's undoubtedly great and ancient heritage and the strides it has made in recent years in several fieldsWhile I was the Governor of Haryana, I simultaneously held the office of the Governor of Himachal Pradesh for a short while in 1989-1990. I also went on an official visit to Gujarat in October 1989. Apart from addressing the State's Chamber of Commerce, I visited some of the holy places of this State. I have, therefore, devoted some pages to certain matters pertaining to Himachal Pradesh and Gujarat that I consider worth mentioning.

I wish to place on record the valuable assistance rendered in the writing of this book by my wife Anita, but for whose constant encouragement and unstinted support I would not have been able to bring this project to fruition. My thanks are also due to Dr. Sukhbir Singh I.A.S. (retd.), Aparajit Chattopadhyay of the Jawaharlal Nehru University, Delhi, and Smt. Sumita Bhattacharya for their valuable help and suggestions.

New Delhi **H.A. Barari**
March, 2006

1

Through My Paces

It was late at night on February 13, 1988 that Prime Minister Rajiv Gandhi telephonically informed me of the decision to appoint me as the Governor of Haryana. No sooner had I put down the receiver than my telephone began to ring almost incessantly. The first person to congratulate me was Sardar Buta Singh, Union Home Minister, with whom I had developed a close personal rapport by virtue of having been the Director of the Intelligence Bureau till my retirement on March 31, 1987.

For the next few days, I was overwhelmed by a steady stream of congratulatory telephone calls, telegrams and letters. These came from all over the country and even from some, who hailed from my native village Shyamsiddhi of Dhaka district (now in Bangladesh). Many of the messages were, of course, from police and intelligence officers, serving as well as retired. Many among them, who had the privilege of having known my father-in law, the late B.N. Mullik—the patron-saint of India's police and the Intelligence Bureau—wished he was alive to see me as a Governor. One of them wrote: "The entire police force of the country should feel proud of your achievement. In fact, it should raise their morale. How we wish that Mr. Mullik was amidst us today to share our joy and to bless you." Wrote another veteran police officer: "Today Mr. And Mrs. Mullik would be so happy in their heavenly home. The plant they had nurtured has flowered."

Another person not connected with the police, who wrote in the same strain to my wife, Anita, was Ven. Saddhananda Thera, Bhikkhu-In-Charge, Orissa Centre, Bhubaneswar. To quote: "May Lord Buddha bless you and all the members of your noble family. Please convey my hearty congratulations to Mr. Barari on his elevation to the highest rank as the Governor of Haryana. I am indeed very happy and proud that the son-in-law of my late benefactor, Shri B.N. Mullik, has achieved the highest goal that a government officer can aspire for. With blessings of Lord Buddha."

Emotional letters came from my close relatives. My eldest brother, H.M. Barari, while offering me his blessings, also wrote how my octogenarian, bed-ridden mother had reacted: "The other day, when I conveyed to mother the news of your gubernatorial appointment, she was so glad that she remained speechless for a while. Then she shed tears of joy and remembered our revered father, as, according to her, he would have been the happiest man in the world." As I read this letter, my eyes got suffused.

A tribute that moved me very much was paid by my teacher of long years ago, Krishna Bandhu Goswami, who had taught me Sanskrit at my village school in the Dhaka district of pre-partition Bengal in the early 1940's. He composed a Bengali poem 1 in my honour, which, translated into English would read somewhat as below:

"Very dear one,
Hari Ananda,
Be happy, live in happiness;
Take care;
Let your speech be brightened up by your smile;
This is all that I pray for to God;
Apart from this,
No other thought comes to my mind.
With blessings from
Krishna Bandhu Goswami"

For a school teacher to remember his pupil after the lapse of more than four decades and convey his blessings to the latter with a few lines of self-composed poetry is the acme of preceptorial affection. When I left school in 1945, this teacher was just a Matriculate, though he was a great scholar in Sanskrit. But now from the many degrees including a doctorate appended to his name at the letter-head, I realised what a lot of effort he must have put in after moving over to post-partition West Bengal to improve his academic background and then become a lecturer at a government college at Maldah.

Some newspapers of West Bengal carried reports reflecting a certain measure of happiness that a person hailing from the State had been appointed as a Governor. The Bengali daily Ananda Bazar Patrika reported that mine was the first case of an officer of the Indian Police Service having been appointed as Governor straightway without being put through the intermediate stage as a Lt. Governor or some such functionary. Another significant fact mentioned in the press reports was that Haryana where I was being sent as Governor was that it was a politically sensitive State in the country's heartland where the government was led by a stalwart of the non-Congress opposition, namely Chaudhuri Devi Lal of the Lok Dal.

On February 21, 1988, Anita and I took off in the small Beechcraft plane of the Haryana Government for Chandigarh, the joint capital of Punjab and Haryana, where I was to be sworn in as the Governor of Haryana the next day. This marked the beginning of our ceremonial life in which protocol held great sway. Captain Viswanathan, the smart and celebral A.D.C., was with us in the plane and was already briefing us about the many do's and don't's. As we alighted at the Chandigarh airport, we were met by Smt.Komal Anand I.A.S., Secretary to the Governor and some Ministers of Haryana among whom were Smt. Kamala Verma, Minister for Health and Smt. Sushma Swaraj, Minister for Food. Also to greet us on arrival were many officials such as Secretaries to the Government of Haryana and police officers of various ranks including the Director-General, H.R. Swan. After inspecting the ceremonial guard of honour, which for the first time for me gave me the 'National Salute', I left along with Anita for the Haryana Raj Bhawan. We drove along the roads of the city beautiful, as Chandigarh is called, soaking in its crisp, pollution-free air and fully relishing our just acquired exalted status and the display of public adulation.

At Raj Bhawan, we were introduced to some members of the staff ably commanded by a seasoned Comptroller of Governor's Household, Daryao Singh by name. I was told that it was the constant endeavour of the staff of about 250 persons to keep the wheels of Raj Bhawan moving as effectively as was generally expected. In retrospect, I can say that the staff never failed me.

As Governor, I had two Aides-de-camp (A.D.C's), one of whom was an I.P.S. Officer R.K. Vachher by name, the other being Captain Vishwanathan, who belonged to the Ordnance Corps of the Indian Army. Both of them were exceptionally competent, besides being personally graceful and very helpful to me and my wife. Captain Vishwanathan, who had virtually put me through my paces in the initial stage in so far protocol was concerned, completed his term as A.D.C. On May 31, 1988, before proceeding to report back to the Indian Army. His place was later taken by Captain Ravi Bhatia, another bright officer of the Indian Army.

My wife and I both felt very sad to have to part with Vishwanathan. We hosted a farewell lunch for him at Raj Bhawan and presented him with a memento to remember us by. He was a bachelor and got married a few years later in Delhi. By then I had ceased to be a Governor, but being in Delhi, my wife and I attended his wedding. And then tragedy struck: Vishwanathan died prematurely on November 15, 1995 in an accident while he was leading the Ordnance Odyssey Motor Cycle Rally. It was for me and my wife a great personal loss.

Among the first to call on me and my wife after I took over as the Governor were my friend and I.P.S. batch-mate J.F. Ribeiro and his wife. The famous super-cop was then the Director-general of Police, Punjab. What he told me many on the personal net gave me a valuable insight into the political, and more importantly, the social scene in Punjab, Haryana and Chandigarh. From Ribeiro and also from the turn-out of police officers at the airport to receive us, I gathered the distinct impression that police officers in general were very happy to have one of their tribe as the first citizen of a state like Haryana.

On February 22, 1988, I was sworn in as the Governor of Haryana at a ceremony held on the lawns of Raj Bhawan. Before that, Devi Lal, Chief Minister, formally called on me, when we exchanged pleasantries. I had not seen him before, though I had heard a lot about him—on the professional net and even otherwise. To me, he appeared to be a benevolent kind of man, who wanted to do good to the ordinary man, though he had many hang-ups about which more later. After the swearing-in ceremony, there was a tea party where I had the opportunity of meeting people from various walks of life including Ministers, officials, academicians and journalists.

Devi Lal and I were seated next to each other, when some journalists asked me questions on various issues. One of them enquired about my reaction to the apprehension reportedly voiced by Devi Lal that I, a former Director of the Intelligence Bureau, had been sent to Haryana by the Congress Government at the Centre to topple his government. A journalist also drew my attention to Devi Lal's statement to the press that before my appointment as Governor he had not been consulted as required by the Constitution of India.

I told the journalists that I had not seen Devi Lal's statements and that, in any case, the Governor's relationship with the Chief Minister should be judged by developments that took place after my swearing-in rather than by what statements might have been issued by the Chief Minister before my arrival in Haryana. Of course, I stated emphatically that Union Home Minister, Sardar Buta Singh had discussed the matter pertaining to my appointment with Devi Lal, which amounted to consultation with the State Government in the accepted sense of the term. I made it clear that consultation did not mean the State Government's acceptance of or concurrence with the views of the Central Government.

I also told the journalists within the hearing of Devi Lal that the Centre had not given me nor was it competent to give me any assignment to topple the State Government. I told everybody that in any case nobody could throw out a Ministry if it enjoyed the support of a majority in the State Assembly.

My swearing-in was widely reported in the press in different parts of the country. One of the Delhi newspapers, the National Herald, while reporting the event on February 28, 1988 commented that it augured well for harmonious relations between Punjab and Haryana because S.S. Ray, the Governor of Punjab, and I were both Bengalees. It also envisaged that, in view of our common interest in tennis, a meeting of the two Governors on the tennis ground was quite on the cards. The press report in question is reproduced below:

National Herald-24.2.88

Of Governors and tennis

Herald News Service

Chandigarh, Feb. 22. Over the years, the relations between neighbouring Punjab and Haryana states have been viewed keeping in view subjects ranging from the construction of the controversial Satluj-Yamuna, Link Canal, sharing of river waters, transfer of Chandigarh to Punjab and other territorial disputes.

But with the appointment of Mr. Hari Anand Barari as the Governor of Haryana on Monday, another subject tennis has been added to this list.

Though the Haryana Chief Minister, Mr. Devi Lal, is not a happy man with appointment of a former director of the Intelligence Bureau as the Governor of the State, the Punjab Governor, Mr. S.S. Ray, is a happy man for the reason that he has found another Bengali across the wall to play tennis. The Raj Bhavan of Punjab and Haryana are next door in Sector 6 here.

Even when the Punjab state is passing through a phase of unprecendented terrorism, the Governor, Mr. S.S. Ray, frequently finds time to make his way to tennis court built within the Punjab Raj Bhavan. Even when he is on tour, the tennis courts in the districts are spruced up for "Governors game".

The bio-data of Mr. Barari distributed to newsmen at his swearing in ceremony says that he is fond of tennis.

No other hobbies.

The Secretary to Haryana Governor, Mrs. Komal Anand, said that a tennis court would soon be laid out in the Raj Bhavan once the Governor settles down. The original tennis court was turned into a huge lawn as the former Governor Mr. S.M.H. Burney, was not at all a sports enthusiast.

This is for the first time that the Governors of the two states are hailing from the same state—West Bengal and are fond of the same game-tennis. Though Mr Ray has shown his hand at tennis at few of the tournaments held in the state, the credentials of Mr. Barari on the field are not yet known. But off the field.

Mr. Barari has made a mark as Chief of Intelligence Bureau. "A meeting of the two Governors" on the field is on the cards once Mr. Barari has a practising session," a senior official of the Haryana Raj Bhavan said.

Meanwhile the Punjab Governor XI takes on the Haryana Governor XI in a cricket match some time next month.

Note

1\.

Dr. Krishna Bandhu Goswami
M. A. (Double) Ph. D., B. T., Kavyatirtha, Saraswati,
Ex Asstt. Teacher, Maldah Zilla School.
Ex Lecturer, Govt. T. T. College, Maldah.
Adhyaksha, Abhoya Chatuspathi.
Moral Instructor, Maldah District Jail.

KUTUBPUR
OMKARDHAM
MALDAH-732 101

Date 26-3-88

সুপ্রিয়,

হরি আনন্দ

সুখী হও সুখে থাকো
থেকো সাবধানে,
উঠিয়া ফুটুক হাসি
তোমার বয়ানে।
ইহাই প্রার্থনা মোর
বিভুর চরণে,
ইহা বিনা অন্যচিন্তা
নাহি আসে মনে।

আশীর্বাদান্তে—

(কৃষ্ণবন্ধু গোস্বামী)

2

A Flashback to Haryana's Past

As I was settling down, people from different walks of life started calling on me at Raj Bhawan. Asked by many of them how I felt being the Governor of Haryana, I used to reply that I felt privileged to have got the opportunity of serving the people of a state where the battle of the Mahabharata was fought and the message of the Geeta was revealed and which counted among its pilgrimages Kurukshetra, besides many other places associated with our country's ancient history and culture.

My tryst with Haryana and its pilgrimages and well-known historical sites had begun forty years ago in 1949, when, as an undergraduate student of Kolkata's Presidency College, I had paid a visit to some of these places. Ever since, I had kept up my studies about Kurukshetra, the Mahabharata and the Geeta. Now, as the Governor of Haryana, I was in a position to gain easy access to the vast mass of literature on this subject and interact directly with several scholars. Visits to many of the places that figure in Haryana's history, legends and myths helped to concretise my perception.

I had flown over the territory of Haryana on several occasions in the past on professional errands. And this time round, on February 21, 1988, when I flew from Delhi to Chandigarh in a special aircraft along with my wife, Anita, to take up my gubernatorial assignment, I intently looked down to see if I could identify some of the spiritually and historically significant places of Haryana about which I had read and heard so much.

Though Haryana came into being as a State of the Indian Union on November1, 1966, it had an identity of its own even in ancient times. Historians have expressed different views about the origin of the name 'Haryana'. References to this tract in ancient literature such as the Brahmanas and the Atharva Veda testify to its antiquity. A verse in the Rig Veda [1] describes this region as 'Harayana' in view of its all-round prosperity. According to G.C. Awasthi, author of Veda-Dharatala, Varuraja, who ruled over this tract, had used the word 'Haryana' as an adjective to describe this region.[2]

The Mahabharata mentions the Haryana region as 'Bahudhanyaka' *i.e.*, a country full of greenery and vegetation. Rohitaka (I, e, modern Rohtak), an important place of Haryana, was then under the rule of the Yaudheyas, whose coins also used the word 'Bahudhanyaka' for this region. Nakula, one of the five Pandava brothers, had conquered the Yaudheyas' territory and taken over the ten forts of the latter. This is the reason why, according to Acharya Bhagawan Dev, this region came to be known as 'Dasharna' (*i.e.*, a country of ten forts).[3]

The Skanda Purana (Kumarika Khand) also called this tract 'Hariala' in view of its greenery. To quote: "Hariale Cha Gramanam Lakshapanchaka Sammitam" (In Hariala, there are five lac villages).[4] the name Haryana may be a corruption from the word 'Hariala'. In fact, this was a densely forested area which presented an ever verdant look. Little wonder that poet Banabhatta, a contemporary of Harshavardhana, had waxed so eloquent about the beauty of Shrikanta Janapada, the name by which Haryana was then known. It was the same realization that had led Rahul Sankirityayana, the eminent scholar, to give the name 'Hari-dhanyaka' to this region by slightly modifying the appellation 'Bahudhanyaka' that figures in the Mahabharata. Dr. M.S. Randhawa and Devi Shankar Prabhakar were of the view that the word Haryana was derived from the conjunction of the two words—Hari (Lord Krishna) and Aranya (forest)—words that signified the association of Lord Krishna with this region as well as the presence here of extensive forests.[5]

Some others have also linked the name of Haryana with Hari or Lord Vishnu, as the rulers of ancient Haryana belonged to a dynasty called 'Harivansham'.[6] Some have traced the name Haryana to the time when Hari's (Krishna's) chariot ('Ayana') came here on the eve of the battle of Kurukshetra, a slightly different version being that the name refers to Hari's 'Ana' (coming). Dharnidhar, author of Akhand Prakash says that this name originated from 'Haribanka' associated with the worship of Hari (Lord Indra).[7]. According to some, this region was called Haryana because it was the place where Har or Lord Shiva resided or where Har's 'Yana' (or vehicle) used to ply. It is true that in Haryana the Shaivites have all along been present in great strength.

Another view associates the name of Haryana with King Harish Chandra of Oudh. It was the Jaina poet Pushpadant hailing from a place near Rohtak, who used the term 'Haryanu' for the first time in his book 'Mahapurana' composed in the latter half of the 10th century A.D.[8] the word Haryana figured in a verse in the Apabhramsha language composed by the famous Jaina poet Shridhar in V.S. 1189 where he described himself as a 'Haryanabasi' (a resident of Haryana). The Delhi Museum Inscription of 1328 A.D. also mentioned the word Haryana and said that it was heaven on earth and that it included Delhi (Dhillika) that had been founded by the Tomaras in it.[9] the Palam Baoli Inscription of V.S. 1333 calls this territory 'Hariyananka', a country full of greenery and vegetation.[10] the Lander Inscription (Jodhpur) of V. S. 1373 described Haryana as 'Haritanaka', whereas the Sarahan Inscription of V.S. 1384 and the Badayun Inscription of the 13th century mentioned the word Haryana.

During British rule, several western authors as well as the Imperial Gazetteer of India cited the greenery of this region as the ground on which it came to be called Haryana. Maharaj Krishan, author of 'Tarikh-I-Zillah Rohtak', has expressed the view that this name was derived from 'Harana' (robbery) for which this region was said to have earned notoriety once upon a time! Another scholar, Dr. H.R. Gupta, has put forward his view that Hayana was a corrupt form of the word 'Aryana', the home of the Aryans.

According to Dr. Buddha Prakash, the word 'Haryana' is traceable to 'Abhirayana', the precursors of the latter-day 'Ahirs'. He traces the probable etymology as follows: Abhirayana = Ahirayana = Hirayana = Hariyana.[11] He thinks that since in the post-Mahabharata period, the Abhiras, the modern Ahirs, became prominent in this region, it came to be known by their name. Dr. K.C. Yadav, who has gone into this matter in some depth, regards this view as more reasonable from the point of view of both historical evidence and philology. He mentions the fact that according to the Kamasutra, this region was named after its Ahira inhabitants and included the Shrikanta Janapada and Kurukshetra were parts of it.[12] However, at a later date, in his Hindi book on the history of Haryana, Dr. Yadav expresses his agreement with the view of Sir Jadunath Sarkar, the well-known historian, that the name Haryana is traceable to the greenery of this region.[13] I am inclined to agree with this view.

Now I would mention something which had not struck anyone nor even me before I was appointed as the Governor of Haryana. It was after I took over this assignment that I suddenly became aware of it one fine morning. My own name 'Hariananda' includes in it the word 'Hariana', the name of the State! It was a strange coincidence. During my tenure in Haryana, I mentioned this fact in some of my public speeches saying that the State I was deputed to serve was a part and parcel of my name and of my very being. Did my father, who had given me this name in my childhood, when the State of Haryana had not even come into existence in its present form, have any premonition that some day I would become the Governor of the as yet unborn State of Haryana? I do not know.

According to Dr. Hari Ram Gupta, Haryana was the abode of early man.[14] Haryana and Punjab were separated in ancient times from the rest of India by sea, which then existed where present-day Rajasthan and Sind are located and covered a large part of the Ganges basin, extending as far as Assam. Dr. Gupta refers to certain discoveries made by Dr. Guy E. Pilgrim in the Shivalik hills which led him to conclude that one and a half crore years ago, early man lived in the Pinjore region of Haryana around Chandigarh. He also refers in this context to the view of Dr. S.A.Q. Hussain, who puts the age of this early man here at three crore years.[15] Dr. K.C. Yadav, however, does not consider it reasonable to assume that early man lived here earlier than 10 to 15 lakh years ago.[16]

This early man of Haryana used stone implements. Dr. Yadav has mentioned the names of several places in Haryana where many of the stone implements used in the Old Stone Age (Palaeolithic Age), Middle Stone Age (Mesolithic Age) and New Stone Age (Neolithic Age) have been discovered. The New Stone Age was followed by the Early Historical Age. Traces of human settlements dating back to this period have been found at Siswal in the Hisar district and at several other places of Haryana. This ancient civilization is now called the Siswal Civilization, which was predominantly agriculture-based.[17]

Haryana next passed through the stage of the Indus Valley Civilisation, whose traces first came to notice at Harappa and Mohenjodaro (now in Pakistan) in the 19th and 20th centuries respectively. Traces of this civilisation have been found at many places in Haryana. Many scholars think that this was identical with the Aryan Civilisation. In their view, the Aryans first settled down in the rural areas and later, when they shifted to the towns, their civilization came to be characterised as the Indus Valley Civilisation. Dr. K.C. Yadav has cited several reasons for not accepting this view.[18] I do not want to go any further into this question which has generated quite some controversy of late.

Where did the Aryans, the progenitors of the Vedic civilization that flourished in Haryana, come from? There are three views in this regard namely that they came (a) from within India, (b) from outside

India but from somewhere in Asia and (c) from Europe. Dr. K.C.Yadav is of the view that the Aryans were from within India—either from the distant north western region or from the sub-Himalayan Terai region. Around 2000 B.C., they are said to have left their original home for some reason and proceeded in different directions—some towards Iran, Afghanistan etc., some further west towards the other countries of Asia, some towards Europe and some lower down towards Punjab and Haryana. The members of the last group were fascinated by the Saraswati and Drishadwati rivers and the all-pervasive greenery of Haryana where they decided to settle down. This marked the beginning of the Vedic civilization of the Aryans. Some scholars have characterised this civilization as the Painted Grey Earthenware Civilisation whose traces have been discovered at many places in Haryana.

It has sometimes been alleged that archaeologists with a fundamentalist pro-Hindu mind-set have been discounting the Aryan invasion theory and seeking to project the Harappan and Vedic civilizations as two sides of the same coin, both being treated as indigenous, with a view to propagating the indigenousness of Hinduism as contrsted with Christianity and Islam which originated outside India. Many archaeologists professing to be secular have opposed these views and looked askance at projects undertaken during the BJP-led NDA regime to develop and glorify the basin of the Saraswati river which occupied a pride of place in the Rigveda. I reserve my comments on the validity or otherwise of these opposing strands of thinking.

Historians have expressed divergent views about the time when Vedic civilization thrived. The generally accepted view is that this civilization began to make its presence felt around 1500 B.C. And that it was in Haryana that it all began. A little later, it spread to Punjab. This phase is generally called the Early Vedic Period. In the Later Vedic Period that followed, this civilization spread to Aryvarta or the Indo-Gangetic plains of northern India and still later to the rest of India.

The Rigveda and the archaeological excavations of more recent times throw considerable light on various aspects of the early Vedic civilization of Haryana whose fertile soil and ever-flowing rivers helped the Aryans to usher in an era of economic prosperity and social well-being. There was a conflict between the Aryans and the non-Aryans called 'Dasyus' or 'Dasas', who included the local 'Panis' belonging presumably to modern Panipat. The Rigveda speaks of this conflict.

The earliest name by which the Haryana region was known was Brahmavarta, the territory between the Saraswati and Drishadwati rivers. According to Manu, the Brahmins of Brahmavarta were highly accomplished from whom men from all over the world could take lessons for improving their character.[19] Some scholars have said that Brahmavarta formed part of a bigger territory known as Sapta-Sindhu *i.e.*, The region between the Indus and Sutlej and Saraswati rivers. Dr. K.C. Yadav does not agree with this view because, as he says, there was no territory called Sapta-Sindhu. According to Dr. Yadav, the term Sapta-Sindhu did not refer to any specific territory but was an adjectival term signifying location on the banks of rivers.[20]

Some of the other names of Haryana were Uttaravedi, Brahmavedi, Kurukshetra, Samantapanchaka, Sarvapanchaka etc. The old scriptures mention the names of many forests in this region such as Kamyakavana, Aditivana, Vyasavana, Phalakivana, Suryavana, Madhuvana, Prithuvana (modern Pehova) and Shalavana (modern Salon). There are numerous sacred ponds and pilgrimages in Haryana.

According to tradition, the first powerful king of Haryana was Manu Vaivaswat, son of Vaivaswat and the seventh of the fourteen Manus. In fact, he is said to be the first traditional king of India, who ruled around 3110 B.C. He has been described as the originator of the human race and of all the dynasties mentioned in the Puranas, who framed the rules and the laws of government and collected a sixth of the produce of the land as a tax to meet administrative expenses.[21] Vaivaswat had nine sons apart from the eldest child who had a dual personality as the male Ila and the female Ila.

Dr. K.C. Yadav, however, says that Vaivaswat had only four sons—Ikshwaku, Pramshu, Saudyumna and Sharyati.[22] Only the last two sons of Vaivaswat had a Haryana connection. Sudyumna was the ruler of the territory below the Sutlej that included Ambala and the northern part of Kurukshetra district. Sharyati ruled over some other parts of Haryana extending up to Rajasthan. His capital might have been located somewhere near Narnaul. After Sudyumna, his son Pururavas, who became the king of Haryana, was a powerful ruler. His uncle Sharyati, who presumably had no issue, gave his territory to him with the result that he had an extensive domain that included the whole of Haryana.

The Devi-Bhagawata Purana has given interesting accounts about Sudyumna as well as Pururavas and his spouse Urvashi, who was a celestial nymph. There are divergent accounts of the love affair of Urvashi and Pururavas in many of the Puranas, Satapatha Brahmana, Kathasaritsagara and other ancient texts. The themes of Ila and Pururavas also figure in the Ramayana (Uttarkanda).

The Devi-Bhagawata describes Sudyumna as a truthful king, who had complete control over his senses. Once he went a-hunting to a forest on horse-back accompanied by a large retinue of his functionaries. The forest is said to be very beautiful with a variety of trees, creepers, fruits, flowers, bees, birds etc. It may have been one of the many forests whose description one reads in books on Srikantha Janapada or ancient Haryana.

As soon as King Sudyumna arrived at a certain spot in the forest, he became transformed into a girl! His horse also turned into a mare! the king was surprised by this development and was overwhelmed with grief and shame. How did this happen? the Devi-Bhagawata says that once Sanaka and some other sages went to pay obeisance to Lord Shiva. Just then, his spouse, Ambika, happened to be in the nude and sitting on the lap of Shiva, preparing for their sexual union. Feeling ashamed of being seen in that state by the sages, Ambika left the place at once and covered her body with clothes. The sages also felt embarrassed and disappeared from that spot as soon as they could in order not to hamper the divine couple's amorous exploits. Lord Shiva told Ambika not to lose her sleep over this matter and ordained that from then on, any man, who entered that forest, would turn into a woman!

Smitten by a sense of shame, King Sudyumna did not return to his capital. In his new incarnation as a woman, the king was given the name of Ila (meaning worshipable) by his ministers. At this stage, Budha, son of the Moon, came to that forest and chanced to see Ila (*i.e.*, The female form of Sudyumna). Both felt so deeply attracted to each other that they engaged in the sexual act then and there.[23] Their union resulted in the birth of a son by name Pururavas, who was endowed with great strength and vigour.

Though transformed into a girl, Sudyumna continued to pine for getting back his male form and returning to his capital as the king of Haryana. Through meditation, he tried to draw the attention of sage Vashistha, the preceptor of his family. Vashistha took note of the king's plight and, by means of his penance, he succeeded in pleasing Lord Shiva. Vashistha then appealed to Lord Shiva to restore Sudyumna's manhood. Lord Shiva granted the king's wish, but also decreed that King Sudyumna would become a man for a month and a woman for the next month and so on in a continuous cycle of alternative sexual transformations. The Ramayana (Uttarkand, chapter 87), however, says that the king got this favour by the grace of Parvati.

King Sudyumna returned to his capital after regaining his manhood and started discharging his royal functions. But, during the month he got transformed into a woman, he did not go out and confined himself to the inner precincts of his palace so as to avoid being seen by his people. This did not fully take care of the king's difficulties as he failed to remain in direct touch with his people and get to know of their problems at first hand. Eventually, Sadyumna was able to divest himself of his female form and get back his manhood on a permanent basis as a sequel to an Ashwamedha sacrifice that he performed (Ramayana, Uttarkand, chapter 90).

After the lapse of some time, as his son Pururavas grew up, Sudyumna handed over his kingdom and his capital city of Pratisthan to the former and retired to a forest. There he met sage Narada, under whose guidance he began to proceed along a certain spiritual path that eventually won for him the grace of Devi Bhagawati, who appeared before him and granted him emancipation through his absorption into her divine essence.[24].

Chapter XIII of the Devi-Bhagawata narrates the story of King Pururavas of Haryana and Urvashi, an Apsara or a nymph of heaven, whom he married in circumstances that bear recounting. According to this Purana, Pururavas was endowed with many qualities and ever eager to minister to the welfare of his people.[25] Nobody ever knew of what his plans were, but he himself always came to know what the others were up to. Highly religious-minded, he performed many sacrifices and provided all facilities to his people for the observance of their religious rites.

Hearing of his physical charm, wealth, prowess, character and bearing, Urvashi began to cherish him and sought his hand.[26] This suited her well because, under a curse pronounced by a Brahmin, she was required to go down to and live on the earth.

Urvashi, whom Rabindranath Tagore has described in his eponymous poem as the symbol of eternal youth (Anantayouvana) and the enchantress of the world (Bhuvana-mohini), was one of the Apsaras mentioned in the Rig Veda. In the Puranas, the Apsaras are described as the camp followers of Lord Indra, who danced for the gods. Of them, Urvashi was the best. In the Vedas, however, the Apsaras were not corporeal figures, but symbolized some particular ideas. Many scholars are of the view that the Apsaras had some connection with water (Apas in Sanskrit) and that the water vapour produced by the impact of the sun's rays on the water was the sutff that Apsaras were made of. The source behind the idea of the Apsara was the sun. Urvashi, the Apsara, was thus closely linked with the sun. In the Vedas, Urvashi symbolized the first rays of the sun at dawn or 'Usha'. In the story of

Urvashi and Puru-ravas, Urvashi symbolizes Usha (dawn) and Puru-ravas the sun. Urvashi herself tells Puru-ravas that she had come to him like Usha or dawn.

About the birth of Urvashi, the Bhagavata Purana says that once while Lord Narayana was engaged in deep penance at Badarikashrama, Lord Indra, concerned over the likelihood of losing his position as the Lord of heaven, deputed Kamadeva and the Apsaras there in order to create a situation bad enough to make it impossible for Narayana to continiue his penance. However, all this failed to distract Narayana. Impressed by Narayana's extraordinary control over his senses, the gods started singing his praise. Narayana created some women of outstanding beauty out of his thigh (Uru) and asked the gods to take any one of them. The gods accepted Urvashi, one of the women thus created by Narayana. Because she was created out of Narayana's thigh (Uru), she was called Urvashi.

A different story is told by the Padma Purana about how Urvashi came into being. Once Lord Vishnu was engaged in penance on top of the Gandhmadana mountain. Perturbed by this, Lord Indra sought to disturb Vishnu's penance by sending there Madan (Kamadeva) and his troupe of Apsaras. When they failed to make Vishnu give up his penance, Kamadeva created Urvashi out of his thigh. Urvashi succeeded in bringing about the termination of Vishnu's penance. Greatly pleased over this, Indra offered to marry Urvashi and the latter agreed. Later, another god, Mitravaruna wanted to marry her, but she refused to oblige him. Displeased over this, Mitravaruna pronounced a curse as a result of which Urvashi would now be eligible for marriage with human beings. This paved the way for her marriage with King Puru-ravas whereafter they lived in marital bliss for a long time.

But before she married Pururavas, she laid down certain conditions one of which was that the king was to offer protection to a pair of lambs of which she was specially fond. Another condition was that her food would consist exclusively of clarified butter (Ghee).[27] I am reminded here of the fact that, unlike in many other parts of our country, the people of Haryana take a lot of pure Ghee (Sanadh-Ka-Ghee in Haryana parlance). Women in Haryana are given pure Ghee in ample quantities as part of their meal when they become pregnant as well as after child-birth.. It appears to me that this tradition of Haryana dates back to ancient times.

Urvashi also stipulated that she would not like to see Pururavas in the nude except at the time of their sexual union.[28]. She made it clear that should the king fail to comply wuth any of these conditions, she would leave him.

Pururavas accepted these conditions and the two lived happily for many years. The king was so deeply in love with Urvashi that he did not leave her company even for a moment and forgot his multifarious duties. In course of time, Lord Indra decided to get Urvashi back to heaven. With that end in view, he sent some Gandharvas to the earth, who, under Indra's instructions, stole the two lambs of Urvashi. Now Urvashi told the king that she was leaving him because this was a breach of their agreement which had badly shaken her faith in the king. She lamented that even after her lambs were stolen, the king was making no effort to retrieve them but was simply lying on bed like a woman. She even charged the king with being impotent (Napumsak).[29].

On being thus reviled by Urvashi, King Pururavas perked himself up and rushed out in a nude state to look for the lambs. At that very moment, the Gandharvas managed to get lightning flashes focused on the king with the result that he was seen by Urvashi in a state of complete nudity. As this was a violation of another term of their agreement, Urvashi deserted the king, who began to weep in grief. He roamed about from place to place and at last he chanced to see Urvashi in Kurukshetra on the banks of the Brahmosarovara.

Highly pleased to see Urvashi, Pururavas made a fervent appeal to the former to come back and asserted that he was guiltless. To paraprase in English prose the relevant lines in Sanskrit from the Devi-Bhagawata: Oh goddess with beautiful thighs, here is my body which had once given you enormous sensuous pleasure—the body which you have brought to this place where it will now fall down *i.e.*, perish. If you leave this body here, it will be feasted upon by the tiger and the crow.[30]. In other words, Pururavas said that he was going to commit suicide if Urvashi did not come back!

Urvashi replied: "Oh king, I look upon you as a fool. Where is all your knowledge gone? Do you not know that the friendship of a woman, like that of a hyena, does not last long? Kings should not trust women and thieves. Go home and be happy. Do not grieve unnecessarily." [31].

The Rig Veda (X.95) beautifully describes the dialogue between the two that is said to have taken place at Brahmsarovar in Kurukshetra before their separation. Mortal Puru-ravas tries his best to persuade Urvashi, the ethereal nymph, to continue to live with him. But Urvashi does not agree because the lure of paradise is too much for the fickle female. She leaves her mortal lover and her last words (verse 15) are cruel and cynical, though not unsympathetic: [32]

"Puru-ravas, do not die, do not perish
Let not the cruel wolves devour you;
The friendship pf women is never indeed firm,
For they are hyenas in heart."

This is one of those typical dialogue-hymns which have been described as dramas in embryo, not necessarily for the stage.[33]

It was this theme that inspired poet Rabindranath Tagore to pen his famous poem 'Urvashi' in Bengali, bringing out the pathos and poignancy of the feelings of mortals on earth through the ages ever since Puru-ravas got jilted by Urvashi. Tagore described her as 'cruel' and 'deaf' since she was not going to return to the earth despite all the entreaties that were made. In the English version of his poem, however, Tagore paints a slightly better picture of Urvashi when he says:

"Woman are you, to ravish the soul of Paradise.

....

Like the dawn, you are without veil, Urvashi, and without shame.

....

Were you ever small, timid or in bud, Urvashi, O Youth everlasting?

....

Adored are you of all men in all ages, Urvashi, O endless wonder!

The world throbs with youthful pain at the glance of your eyes, the ascetic lays the fruit of his austerities at your feet, the songs of poets hum and swarm round the perfume of your presence. Your feet, as in careless joy they flit on, wound even the heart of the hollow wind with the tinkle of golden bells.

You are the first break on the crest of heaven's slumber, Urvashi, you thrill the air with unrest.

...."

Poet Kalidasa's treatment of the theme of love between Pururavas, King of Haryana, and Urvashi is worth going into. He gives the title 'Vikramorvasiya" to his famous Sanskrit drama on this theme, because it shows how the king used his valour (Vikram) to win Urvashi. He does not stick to any of the several versions of this story that figures in the ancient texts, but takes the basic facts from them and introduces some new events and situations in order to create a drama, which, while being faithful to the mythological story, boldly departs from it and thus puts in place something original.

Proof of the valour of King Pururavas is provided by Kalidasa at the very beginning of Vikramorvasiya as he rescues Urvashi, the nymph, and her companion, Chitralekha, abducted by a demon, and brings them back. Urvashi is shown to be in an unconscious state in the arms of Chitralekha and when she regains her consciousness, both she and Pururavas at once fall in love with each other. Several verses of Vikramorvasiya are devoted to describing how each of them was enamoured of the qualities of the other. The King says of Urvashi:

"Behold, her heart (fluttering) like a flower on its stem does not yet forego its tremor, which is indicated by the sandal-smearings rising up between her two breasts." (chapter I, 6).

Further on:

"That my shoulder should have rubbed the shoulder of that lovely damsel in the joltings of the chariot so as to thrill me (with joy) looks as if love hath sprouted." (chapter I, 11).

Pururavas reverts to the same point elsewhere:

"This shoulder that was pressed by hers owing to the jolting of the chariot is the only limb that exists with reason; the rest is a mere burden to the earth." (chapter III, 11).

Kalidasa uses some similes to describe the beauty of Urvashi. He compares Urvashi's arching brow with the rippling wave of a mountain stream and her stumbling gait with the meandering course of the stream (Vikramorvasiya, IV, 28). The love story is developed by Kalidasa with great finesse and one of the tools employed by him is a love letter to the King penned by Urvashi with which the former is highly pleased. Apart from being passionate in love, Pururavas is described by Kalidasa as a valiant king, whose help Lord Indra sought to fight the demons. But there is also a view that Pururavas' character was tainted by excessive sensuousness and lack of virility.[34]

Urvashi no doubt comes across as a heartless celestial nymph in earthly love, but her character has been considerably improved in Kalidasa's drama as compared to Devi-Bhagawata.[35]. She is not shown to have much motherly love for Ayus, her son and the future King of Haryana, whom she leaves in a hermitage immediately after his birth. It has been said that was perhaps a common trait of nymphal character, because Shakuntala, wife of the Haryana King Dushyanta, had also been abandoned by her mother, Menaka, a nymph. However, Ausinari, the wife of Pururavas and the queen of Haryana, is shown to be an accommodating lady, who, initially fulminated at the unfaithful conduct of Pururavas after the discovery of Urvashi's love letter, but later changed her attitude and agreed to live amicably with any woman whom the king loved.

The Mahabharata which briefly refers to Pururavas and Urvashi in Adi Parva (chapter 75) gives a rather unflattering account of the king's character. It says that Pururavas was born to Ila, who was both his father and mother. He is said to have ruled over thirteen islands.[36]. He kept bad company and quarrelled with the Brahmins from whom he forcibly took away their wealth even as they cried over their plight. Then the Brahmins destroyed him through their curses.[37] Pururavas is said to have lost his conscience as a result of getting intoxicated with his greed and prowess. He had brought from Gandharvalok along with Urvashi three kinds of fire required for performing sacrifices.

Pururavas had six sons, Ayus, Dheeman, Amavasu, Drirhayu, Vanayu and Shatayu. Ayus succeeded Pururavas as the king. In his Vikramorvasiya, Kalidasa mentions the episode of a vulture taking away a precious gem that was to adorn the crown of the queen. Ayus killed the vulture with an arrow on which was inscribed 'Ayus, son of Pururavas". When everybody was lamenting the disappearance of the gem, Ayus appeared there and saw his father Pururavas for the first time. There was great jubilation and in due course Ayus was coronated as king. Kalidasa describes the greatness of Ayus in several verses of Vikramorvasiya:

"First Bard—Glory to the young king.

Like the divine sage Atri of Brahman, or the Moon of Atri, or Budha of the moon, and our King of Budha, so do you be worthy of your father by your qualities which are dear to the people. For in your most exalted family, all blessings have indeed reached their highest pitch.(chapter V, 21).

Second Bard—Now royal glory shines more bright divided as it is between your father, the foremost of the exalted, and yourself whose fortitude is unshakable and who are so upright, like the Ganges whose waters are divided between the Himalayas and the ocean." (chapter V, 22).

Ayus had five sons one of whom was Nahusha, the powerful and virtuous ruler of Haryana, who, according to the Mahabharata [38], had taken good care of his people and suppressed the demons, thus providing a peaceful ambience for the sages' spiritual activities for which, of course, the king exacted a price from them by way of taxes imposed on them! But he had also succeeded in suppressing his own senses and acquiring a remarkable measure of self-control.

It is said that Nahusha was chosen as the ruler of the three worlds ((heaven, earth and the nether region) when Lord Indra went into hiding in the wake of the killing of a Brahmin. This made Nahusha so very powerful that he lost his self-control and began to go down the path of sin. He even thought o seeking the hand of Shachidevi, wife of Lord Indra. He started getting hard manual chores done by the sages, whose curse turned him into a snake. In this incarnation, Nahusha began to live in a forest. After many years, when the Pandavas came to that forest during the period of their exile, this snake was about to bite Bhima. Then Yudhisthira spoke to Nahusha, following which the latter was absolved of the sages' curse and went to heaven.

Yayati, son of Nahusha, who succeeded the latter, had a sizeable kingdom which included the territory of present-day Haryana and Punjab. The Mahabharata (Adi Parva, chapters 75-85) deals extensively with various themes associated with Yayati and his two wives, Devyani and Sharmistha. This subject also finds mention in the Ramayana (Uttarkand). Devyani was the daughter of sage Shukracharya. Though a Brahmin, she had to marry Yayati of the lower Ksatriya caste as a sequel to a curse pronounced by Koch, son of Vrihaspati, the Guru of the gods. And thereby hangs a tale.

The gods had deputed Koch to learn from Shukracharya, Guru of the demons, the modalities of restoring life to a dead person. On coming to know of this, the demons managed to kill Koch. As Devyani had in the mean time come to get attracted to Koch, she made a plea to her father to revive Koch, which was easily done. The demons again killed Koch, who was again brought back to life by Shukracharya on the unctuous plea made by Devyani. The demons killed Koch a third time, burnt him down to ashes and manipulated to get the ashes mixed with wine that was imbibed by Shukracharya. When Devyani again requested her father to restore the life of Koch, the sage came to know through his spiritual powers that Koch was inside his stomach. As Shukracharya moved to revive Koch and bring him out, the latter burst out of the former's stomach causing the death of the former in the process. Koch revived Shukracharya with Mantras he had learnt from the latter.

Now it was time for Koch to go back to heaven. At this stage, Devyani expressed her desire to marry Koch. But Koch turned down her request as he thought that, being the daughter of his preceptor, Devyani was like a sister to him. Enraged by this, Devyani cursed Koch by saying that his knowledge of the art of reviving a dead person acquired from her father would prove infructuous. Koch retorted that his own knowledge might thus lose its utility, but anybody else acquiring this knowledge from him would be able to revive a dead person. Thereafter, Koch pronounced a curse on Devyani that the latter, though herself a Brahmin, would have to marry someone of the Ksatriya caste.It is as a result of this curse that Devyani had to get married to Yayati. Koch went back to heaven and taught the gods the art of reviving dead persons that he had learnt from Shukracharya.

Devyani was an intimate friend of Sharmistha, daughter of Vrishaparva, king of the demons. Once they had gone for a bath together. After her bath, Sharmistha got out of the water first and by mistake put on the clothes of Devyani. This led to a quarrel between them as a sequel to which Sharmistha beat up Devyani and cast the latter into a well. Coincidentally, King Yayati came there on a hunting expedition and went to that well to get some water. He discovered Devyani inside the well and brought her out. Devyani expressed her geatitude to the king with whose physical grace and personality she was charmed.[39]

Returning home, Devyani complained against Sharmistha's conduct to her father, Shukracharya, who was so enraged over this incident that he decided to leave the territory of Vrisaparva, father of Sharmistha. To pacify him, Vrisaparva pacified him and dissuaded him from adopting this course by appointing Sharmistha as a maid-servant to Devyani.

Later, Yayati and Devyani happened to meet again and expressed their romantic feelings towards each other. After securing the permission of Shukracharya, they got married. When Devyani left with the king to live in his palace, she was accompanied by Sharmistha, her maid-servant. At that stage, Shukracharya had told Yayati to show due courtesies to Sharmistha, but never to invite her to his bed! [40] in due course, Devyani bore the king two sons—Yadu and Turvasu.

As Sharmistha also lived in the royal palace, her beauty began to tug at some sensitive strings of Yayati's heart. Sharmistha fully utilized her gift of the gab to seduce Yayati. She disclosed her love for the king and wanted to marry him, but the latter expressed his reservations, saying that Shukracharya had earlier advised him against taking her to his bed. Sharmistha bluntly told the king that he could safely tell a lie about this because, as she said, it was not a sin to lie in certain circumstances such as when one is cutting jokes or one is speaking before a woman or at the time of one's marriage or when one's life is in danger or when all that one has is going to be stolen.[41]

King Yayati said that he was not prepared to resort to falsehood since a king was the symbol of truth for his people and a king who lied would inevitably be destroyed.[42] Sharmistha then said: "There is no difference between the husband of a mate and one's own husband.

Moreover, it is to be understood that I have also been married to my friend Devyani's husband because I am also living in your house along with Devyani. Shukracharya has gifted me as well to you along with her daughter. Here, you are providing for my maintenance, apart from giving me jewels and diamonds even without my asking for anything. All this shows that you are already playing the role of a husband to me. Gifting a son and one's own self are the most difficult of charities. But after one gifts away one's own body, every other gift pales into insignificance. You have announced that as a king, you would anything that anybody may ask for. The why are you rejecting my prayer?" [43]

King Yayati, who was by now sufficiently taken in by Sharmistha's eloquence, asked her what she was asking for to which she replied: "Kindly save me from the path of irreligion and allow me to perform my religious duty by bearing a child to you. So be pleased to take me as your wife." the king then married her and, as desired by her, he had sexual union with her.[44]

In due course, Sharmistha gave birth to three sons namely, Druhyu, Anu and Puru. In protest against Yayati's marriage with Sharmistha, Devyani left the palace and went away to her father's place. Following a curse pronounced by Shukracharya, Yayati lost his youth as old age set in all of a sudden. Later, Yayati's prayers somewhat mollified Shukracharya, who added a rider to his curse by decreeing that the king would have the option of getting back his youth provided someone else was prepared to take upon himself the king's old age

Yayati asked each of his sons to give him the latter's youth in exchange for his old age. All of them except the youngest Puru refused to accede to his request. Puru turned into an old man, while Yayati regained his youth and ruled for many years, enyoying the pleasures of life. Then he gave back his youth to Puru and made him the king, thus ignoring the elder sons. Before retiring to the forest, Yayati gave some words of sage counsel to Puru, which figure among the most quotable quotes from the Mahabharata. Briefly put, his advice was: "Though I have tried for a long time to enyoy the pleasures of youth, I have not been fully satisfied. Like the fire flaring up as a sequel to offerings of clarified butter made to it, one's passion also does not subside as a result of indulgence, but rather gets progressively intensified by it. So, it is desirable to discard worldly pleasures." [45]

In the Ramayana (Uttarkand, chapter 85), Lord Rama is quoted as paying handsome tributes to King Yayati's qualities such as his capcity to forgive and keep his anger under control.

Puru's dynasty came to be known as the Puru Vamsha or the Pauravas. It was in this Puru dynasty (also called the lunar dynasty) that Dushyanta, the famous ruler of Haryana, was born. As we all know, he had married Shakuntala, the daughter of sage Vishwamitra, according to Gandharva rites. The story of Dushyanta and Shakuntala figures in the Mahabharata, Bhagawata-Purana, Padma-Purana and Kalidasa's Sanskrit drama Abhijnana-Shakuntalam.

The Mahabharata (Adi Parva, chapter 68) says that Dushyanta was the ruler of the whole world encircled by the four oceans. Under his rule, the people enjoyed economic prosperity as they did not have to till their lands to get their crops nor did they have to dig the mines to extract the jewels. The people did not commit crimes and were free from fear, hunger and disease. The rains came in time, the crops were good and the world abounded with jewels and all kinds of animals. The Brahmins did not lie even in their dreams. Dushyanta was endowed with great valour with a body as tough as the thunder. He could lift a mountain along with the forests with his hand and cast it across. In valour, he was like Lord Vishnu and as spirited as the sun. The people lived happily in his kingdom.

The Mahabharata describes how Dushyanta went to a forest for hunting and met Shakuntala at the hermitage on the bank of the Malini river of her foster father, sage Kanva. The two fell in love and went through a Gandharva marriage. Their sexual union resulted in the birth of a son, Sarvadamana (later called Bharata). Kanva, who was absent at the time of their marriage, later approved of it. I do not want to go into the details of how Dushyanta subsequently forgot about this marriage and failed to even recgnise Shakuntala and their son, Sarvadamana, and how a voice from heaven reminded the king of his marriage as well as the duty that he owed to his legitimate wife and son.

I would, however, like to mention certain aspects of this story with a view to highlighting some facets of the characters and personalities of Dushyanta and Shakuntala, because they were the king and queen of Haryana respectively. The Mahabharata (Adi Parva, chapter 68) describes Dushyanta as a mighty person with the shoulders of a lion, long-armed, wide-chested, with a very tough physical build and big eyes etc. Shakuntala is described as dark-eyed, charming, young and sweet of speech.[46].

The Mahabharata also gives an account of how Shakuntala's mother, Menaka, the celestial nymph, had seduced sage Vishwmitra at the instance of Indra, who was apprehensive of losing his position as the lord of heaven after Vishwamitra engaged himself in penance. As Menaka met Vishwamitra and stood in a playful pose, the wind blew away her white garment. Gently smiling, Menaka stooped to gather her garment. Seeing the naked form of Shakuntala, who was blushing in shame, Vishwamitra was overpowered by lust and invited her for coition. This led to Shakuntala's birth to Menaka.[47].

It was to this manner of her birth that Shakuntala referred when she reproved Dushyanta for failing to recognize her and accepting her as his legitimate wife. Boasting of her noble parentage, she said that sage Vishwamitra was her father and Menaka, the child of Lord Brahma and a nymph from heaven had come down to earth to give birth to her. She charged that Dushyanta was deserting her just as a woman discarded a son born to her out of wedlock.[48] Shakuntala threatened Dushyanta by saying that if he did not accept her, his head would break into a hundred pieces.[49]. Strong words indeed!

The exchange between Shakuntala and Dushyanta took on a rather undignified colour. Dushyanta minced no words and said that he was not aware that Sarvadamana was born as his son. He said that since women were all liars, he could not accept her claim. He damned Menaka as an unchaste woman, who was also cruel-hearted as she had discarded Shakuntala after her birth at some place on the Himalayas. He expressed his reservations about the greatness of Vishwamitra saying that while he, a Ksatriya, was engaged in penance with a view to becoming a Brahmin, he allowed himself to fall a prey to his lust.[50]. He again said that Menaka was an unchaste woman, who was caught in the grip of lust and had engaged in sexual union for pleasure with someone, thus giving birth to Shakuntala.[51] Shakuntala retorted by saying that her birth was much nobler than that of Dushyanta. She said that if a person did not accept his own son, the gods were sure to destroy his wealth.[52]. It was after a voice from heaven told Dushyanta that Shakuntala and Bharata were his legitimate wife and son respectively that the king realized his mistake and accepted both of them. This led to the happy re-union of Dushyanta and Shakuntala.

Kalidasa's Abhijnana-Shakuntalam takes its theme from the Puranas and the Mahabharata, but heightens the dramatic effect by departing from the latter at many junctures and adding some events and situations that do not figure in these texts. That is why Sir Mortimer Williams made the following observation about this: "No composition of Kalidasa displays more richness of his poetic genius, he exuberance of his imagination, the warmth and play of his fancy, his profound knowledge of the human heart, his delicate appreciation of its most refined and tender emotions, the familiarity with the workings and counter-workings of its conflicting feelings—in short, more entitles him to rank as the Shakespeare of India." the German poet Goethe had composed a poem to describe the beauty of this play. Literally speaking, Abhijnana-Shakuntalam means a play that describes how Shakuntala is recognized.

Kalidasa depicts Dushyanta as a great ruler–valiant, benevolent, righteous and judicious—as well as a passionate lover and an affectionate father. He offers protection to the hermits against the demons who disturbs their sacrifices. Even Lord Indra sought his help in exterminating some demons—so great was his valour. Some of the noble qualities of Dushyanta are brought out by Kalidasa in the following utterances of two bards:

"First Bard: Thou (*i.e.*the King) seekest not thy own happiness, but for the people thou dost toil from day to day. or thus is thy very nature made. For the Tree bears on his head the fierce heat (of day) while his shade allays the fever of those who seek shelter under him.

Second Bard: Wielding the rod of justice, thou bringest to order all those who have set out on bad courses; thou biddest contention cease; and thou preservest thy people. One may have, in truth, a number of kinsmen, when wealth abounds; but in thee the duty of your subjects' kinsmen towards them finds perfection."—Abhijnana-Shakuntalam, chapter V, verses 7&8.

Kalidasa's Shakuntala was a paragon of beauty as brought out in some of the most oft-quoted verses of Abhijnana-Shakuntalam. This becomes evident when King Dushyanta says of her:

"This her youthful body, by reason of the bark garment tied with delicate knots upon the shoulder, and covering the expanse of her twin breasts, does not exhibit its own charms, like a flower enfolded by a pale leaf."

"Truly her lower lip grows like a tender leaf, her arms resemble flexible stalks. And youth, bewitching like a blossom, shines in all her lineaments."—Abhijnana-Shakuntalam, chapter I, verses 19&21.

"Was she delineated in a picture and then endowed with life? or was she moulded in the creator's mind from an assemblage of all lovely forms? When I meditate on the power of the creator and on her lineaments, she appears to me like a matchless creation of the loveliest of women."

"I do not know the person who is destined to marry this perfect beauty, who is like an unsmelt fresh flower, like a sprout unscratched by nails, like an unperforated gem, like untasted fresh honey and like a perfect reward of meritorious deeds." [53]

Shakuntala, the queen of Haryana, was the daughter of a nymph—Menaka known for her proverbial beauty, while another queen of Haryana namely Urvashi—also a ravishing beauty—was herself a nymph. Both these queens of Haryana needed a poetic genius of the stature of Kalidasa to give full expression to their exquisite beauty.

An observation made by Kalidasa in Abhijnana-Shakuntalam in justification of Dushyanta's love for Shakuntala at first sight without knowing anything about her background is said to have become quite popular among students of Sanskrit literature. Dushyanta said: "She should undoubtedly be eligible to be the consort of a Ksatriya for the the simple reason that my noble mind longs for her; for, virtuous persons' dictate of conscience is their final authority in matters of doubt."[54]

As pointed out by Prof. Ram Gopal, Kalidasa delineates the gross and passionate aspect of love between Dushyanta and Shakuntala, but at the appropriate stage he also brings out the nobler aspects of conjugal love between the two.[55]. Kalidasa's concept of true conjugal love finds expression in the words of advice proffered to the couple by sage Maricha, who describes a virtuous wife (Shakuntala), a noble husband (Dushyanta) and good progeny (Sarvadamana) as faith, sacred injunction and prosperity respectively.[56].

When Shakuntala took leave of her foster father Kanva before proceeding to Her husband Dushyanta's palace, the sage counsel given by Kanva to the departing Shakuntala represented the epitome of an ideal wife's conduct and reflected contemporary social mores. As Kanva said: "Pay respectful attention to thy elders; treat thy rivals as thy dear friends; should thy husband wrong thee, let not thy resentment lead thee to disobedience. Be ever courteous towards thy servants, not puffed with pride in thy fortune. By such behaviour, young women become honoured wives; but perverse wives are the bane of a family." (Abhijnan-Shakuntalam, chapter IV, 17).

After Dushyanta, his son Bharata became the King of Haryana. It was after his name that our country came to be called Bharat. The Mahabharata (Adi Parva) has described how Bharata was born and later became the king. As the Mahabharata says: "The great nativity and the life of the Bharatas is called the Mahabharata. Through Bharata is the glory of the Bharatas; and after Bharata is this lineage named Bharata." [57].It was after the Gandharva marriage between

Dushyanta and Shakuntala that the latter gave birth to Bharata. When this child was born, flowers were showered on him from heaven, the drums of the gods rolled and the Apsaras (nymphs) danced.[58] Shakuntala was then told by Lord Indra that her son would in due course become a king endowed with unparalleled prowess and physical charm who would perform the Ashwamedha and Rajsuya sacrifices and donate enormous wealth to the Brahmins. Naturally, this greatly pleased sage Kanva and Shakuntala.

The Mahabharata says that in his boyhood, Bharata had white teeth and his constitution was like that of a lion. There was a sign of a circle on his palm. He was very strong and his head was big. Even as a boy he was so strong that he used to tether the lions, tigers, bears, buffaloes and elephants to the trees of the forest close to the hermitage of sage Kanva. He protected the sages by overpowering the demons and other enemies of the gods.

Once when a demon came rushing towards him, he caught hold of him and pressed him between his hands in such a manner that the demon began to scream aloud and blood started jetting out of his body. Soon the demon's lifeless body fell on the ground. After this incident, the demons never dared to come anywhere near the hermitage. Since this boy suppressed the demons and all other hostile elements, the sages gave him the name 'Sarvadamana' (subduer of all).

When Shakuntala left sage Kanva's hermitage for the palace of her husband Dushyanta, Kanva gave his blessings to Sarvadamana and told him that on reaching the palace, he should make salutation to the king, who would install him as the crown prince so that in due course he would be in a position to nurture the kingdom of his ancestors. But, as already mentioned, Dushyanta failed to recgnise Shakuntala and Srvadamana and it was only after a voice from heaven reminded him of that chapter of his life that Dushyanta realized his mistake and accepted them as his wife and son respectively. Dushyanta expressed happiness over their re-union to his mother, Rathantarya, who told him that his son, Sarvadamana would become the king at the appropriate time.

Now Dushyanta named Sarvadamana as Bharata and made him the crown prince. The Mahabharata mentions the reason why he was called Bharata. Because the voice from heaven told Dushyanta to look after and arrange for the 'Bharana' (meaning maintenance in Sanskrit) of Sarvadamana, he was named Bharata.[59]

Kalidasa's Abhijnana-Shakuntalam paints Bharata as bold and strong, who, even while he was a boy, used to play with lion cubs rather than with toys. Dushyanta is amazed to see Bharata drag a sucking lion cub from its mother and play with it. An ascetic lady tells Dushyanta about the striking resemblance with the latter of the boy who is said to belong to the Puru family from which Dushyanta also hailed. The king is not sure if the boy could be the son of Shakuntala. He picks up a talisman that had fallen off the boy's wrist, two ascetic ladies present there are greatly surprised because if the talisman were to be touched by any person except the boy or his parents, it would have turned into a snake that would have bitten that person. When the king affectionately touches Sarvadamana, addressing him as his son, the latter sternly rejects those gestures and retorts that he is not his father because Dushyanta is his father.

The Vedas refer to the glory of the 'Bharatas' (descendants of Bharata) and to two of their kings—Divodasa and Sudas—who belonged to the Tritsu clan of the Bharatas. Divodasa was succeeded by his son, Pijavana, who does not seem to have been a great ruler.[60] Pijavana's son, Sudas was a powerful ruler to whose greatness there are many references in Vedic literature. He is said to have worsted many ruling chiefs as well as two powerful confederacies of peoples—one of three peoples and another of ten peoples (Dasharajna Yuddha). His victory over the ten confederates in the region of the Ravi river made him the paramount ruler of the whole region including Punjab.[61] Similarly, his victory over the three confederates led by King Bheda helped him in incorporating into his domain an extensive territory below the Yamuna. Sudas was a benevolent ruler and a patron of learning whose fame spread far beyond Haryana. His long reign was notable for the contribution it made to the all-round c prosperity of the people.

The victory of Sudas over the two confederacies had far-reaching significance for the spread of Aryan civilization to the eastern and southern regions of India. Some of the defeated peoples moved over to new areas. For example, a branch of the Yadavas (one of the ten confederates) led by their king Vidarbha went along with sage Agastya, crossed the Vindhyas and occupied some territory further beyond, which even today is called Vidarbha after the name of the Yadava ruler.[62] Thereafter, they proceeded further south as the torch-bearers of Vedic civilization.

It has been suggested that the Bharata rulers, Divodasa and Sudas, fought against certain peoples who practised usury and hoarding and exploited the common man. Their rise and the extension of their territory had, therefore, the support of the ordinary people and represented a new social order.[63]

It has been said that the sites of the Indus Valley Civilisation in Punjab, Haryana and western Uttar Pradesh were urbanized settlements representing a decadent phase of Harappan civilization and perhaps evoked popular resistance on account of the scope for exploitation that it provided. The onslaught by Divodasa and Sudas on the cities and the forts is said to have spearheaded the drive of the local people against the tyranny of the urban people. It has been suggested that the decline of Harappan civilization followed a resurgence of the rural people against the exploitation of the urban classes.[64]

After the demise of Sudas, his successors failed to maintain their position. One Trasadasyu (son of Purukutsu, the Puru ruler of the Saraswati valley, whom Sudas had once vanquished) occupied Haryana, defeating the Tritsu ruler. Several powerful rulers followed Trasadasyu such as Hiranin, Trikshi, Tryaruna and Kurushravana. Their rule was marked by peace, prosperity and the excellence of their manners, language and culture that bore the stamp of Vedic civilization. Gradually, these rulers succeeded in winning the hearts of the defeated Bharatas and in due course the Purus and the Bharatas so seamlessly mixed and merged with one another that they emerged as one people.

During the rule of Shamvarana, a descendant of Kurushravana, the Panchalas attacked and annexed Haryana. Shamvarana moved over to Sind where he enlisted the help of sage Vashistha and of the powerful people known as the Kurus. This enabled him to win back his kingdom in the Saraswati valley. After the death of Shamvarana, the Kurus took over Haryana.

There was a succession of rulers of this dynasty beginning with the celebrated King Kuru and including further down the line such well-known figures as Parikshit I, Shantanu, Vichitravirjya, Pandu and Dhritarastra. During the reign of Shantanu, the Gandharas from the north west attacked Haryana. Shantanu's son, Chitrang led the forces that faced the Gandharas at Kurukshetra on the bank of the Saraswati river. He succeeded in defeating the Gandharas in this battle called the first battle of Kurukshetra, but he himself lost his life.

After the premature death of Vichitravirjya, his younger son, Pandu, became the ruler as his elder brother, Dhritarastra, was blind. Following Pandu's death, Duryodhana, son of Dhritarastra, became the king. It was at this stage that the Mahabharata war was fought—in 1400 B.C., according to most historians—in which Pandu's sons, the Pandavas, were victorious. Haryana came under the rule of the Pandavas, who made Indraprastha—present-day Delhi–their capital.

Dhritarastra's sons, the Kauravas continued to have their capital at Hastinapur. Yudhisthir, the eldest of the Pandava brothers, became the King of Haryana, but after some time, he gave up the throne, paving the way for the assumption of power by Parikshit, son of Abhimanyu and grandson of Arjuna.

Parikshit's extensive domain included three regions namely Kurukshetra and Kurujangal of Haryana and Hastinapur (now in Uttar Pradesh). Though his capital was at Hastinapur, he had a second capital at Asandh near Karnal in Haryana.[65] Parikshit was killed as a sequel to his conflict with the Nagas whose capital was probably located at Taxila. His son, Janamejaya, destroyed the Nagas in a battle described in the Puranas as a snake sacrifice (Sarpastra) in which innumerable snakes (literally meaning Naga) were said to have perished. Janamejaya's territory was more extensive than his father's and included Taxila (now in Pakistan).

Janamejaya's death was followed by a gradual decline in the power of the Pandavas, which resulted in a division of Haryana into two parts *i.e.*Kurukshetra and Kurujangal. This also led to the arrival of several tribes into the Saraswati valley, the most important of whom were, according to Dr. Buddha Prakash, the Abhiras, now known as Ahirs, and the Jats.[66] Soon Haryana faced invasions from the north west.

When Alexander the Great invaded India in 326 B.C. And reached the Beas, he heard of the material prosperity and the military prowess of the people of Haryana. A Greek historian by name Arrian wrote as follows: "It was reported that the country beyond the Hyphasis (Beas) was exceedingly fertile, and that the inhabitants were good agriculturists, brave in war, and living under an excellent system of government; for the multitude was governed by the aristocracy who exercised their authority with justice and moderation. It was also reported that the people there had a greater number of elephants than the other Indians and that those were of superior size and courage. (page 121 of J.W. M'Crindle's 'Invasion of India by Alexander the Great') [67]

Haryana formed part of the Mauryan empire as is evident from archeological finds at Sugh and the pillars of Ashoka at Topa and Hissar and his 'Stupas' at Chaneti and Thanesar. What was the background of Chandragupta, who founded the vast Mauryan empire across north India in 324 B.C.? Various views have been expressed by the historians in this regard. Dr. K.C. Yadav has provided quite some evidence for his view that Chandragupta belonged to the Maurya people of the 'Maur' republic of Haryana.[68] in this context, he has mentioned the reference in the Mahabharata to the 'Mattamayuras', who lived in this region. He thinks that in course of time, this word evolved into 'Maurya'. After Alexander retreated from north west India, Chandragupta took advantage of the chaotic situation to establish his rule in Haryana and Punjab and then extended his territory over north India up to Magadha in Bihar.

Foreign peoples like the Bactricians, Greeks, Parthians, Scythians and Kushanas, who invaded India in the wake of the break-up of the Maurya empire created turmoil in the Haryana region, which led after some time to the rise of the Yaudheyas, an Indo-Iranian tribe, who established themselves as the rulers with their capital at Prakritanak (Naurangabad-Bamla), the other important seats of their power being probably Rohtak and Sirsa.[69]

The Yaudheyas had to fight hard against the Kushanas. The first two Kushana rulers namely Kadphises I and his son, Kadphises II or Wima Kadphises, did not succeed in completely overpowering the Yaudheyas, but the next and the most famous Kushana ruler, Kanishka, was able to defeat them and annex their territory. However, during the time of the Kushana ruler by name Vasudeva, the Yaudheyas joined hands with some other republics and threw out the Kushanas. Among these other republics was the republic of the Agras in the Hisar region with its capital at Agrodak or Agroha. Kunind was another republic whose territory extended over a part of present-day Ambala district.

When the Gupta rulers extended their authority over north India in the 4th century A.D., the Yaudheyas of Haryana accepted their suzerainty and paid tributes to them.. Thus Haryana lost its independence and formed part of the Gupta empire.

In early sixth century A.D., the Hunas invaded India and established their rule over north-eastern India including Haryana and held sway right up to Kaushambi near Allahabad. Some settlements, like, for example, Jaula, which bears the name of the ruling Jau(b)la or Jaula clan, still bears testimony to Haryana's tryst with the Hunas.[70] By about the thirties of the sixth century A.D., the brief eminence of the Hunas came to an end as their ruler, Mihirakula, had to bite the dust after being confronted by two Indian rulers namely Yashodharman of Malwa and Narasimha-Gupta Baladitya, the last great Gupta emperor.

In the latter part of the sixth century A.D., one Pushpabhuti established his rule in Haryana around Thanesar. Haryana was then known as Shrikantha Janapada. Several rulers of this dynasty including Prabhakaravardhana and Harshavardhana extended their domain and emerged as the unrivalled power in north-western India. The greatest of the Vardhana rulers was, of course, Harshvardhana (606 A.D.–647 A.D.), whose territory extended from Punjab to Assam as well as to Sind and Kashmir. Harsha's court poet, Bana Bhatta, who wrote the 'Harshacharita', and the Chinese traveller, Hiu`en Tsang, who visited Thanesar, have left behind fascinating accounts of the contemporary socio-economic conditions of this region, which reflected the all-round prosperity of the people.

Harsha's death in 647 A.D. triggered centrifugal moves in the region, leading to chaos and inviting the attention of the Hunas and Turks. It was towards the end of the seventh century A.D. that a certain measure of stability was restored to Haryana and the adjoining territory on the north-west when King Yashovarman of Kanauj establishing his sway and taking measures to keep the Turks under check. It was around 730 A.D. that Yashovarman took over Haryana without having to face any serious resistance. After a short while, King Lalitaditya of Kashmir marched on Kanauj and defeated Yashovarman, thus bringing the entire region including Haryana within his domain.

Haryana soon faced political anarchy as Lalitaditya's successors failed to assert their authority. Several local powers established their authority in Haryana and the adjoining territory around the beginning of the 8th century A.D. The Khalimpur Copper Plate Inscription mentions these powers as Matsya Madra, Yadu and Kuru.

This Inscription also indicates that Dharmapala (770–810 A.D.), the Pala ruler of Bengal, had held a Durbar at Kanauj to install the King of Kanauj in the presence of the various rulers of the Punjab as well as the chief of the Kuru country (*i.e.* Haryana), who "bowed before him respectfully with their diadems trembling".[71] It shows that Kurudesh (Haryana) had an independent chief at that time and that "the Pala ruler tried to win him to his side to make a show of paramountcy over North India".[72] This issue of an old imperial link between Bengal and Haryana naturally arouses a good deal of curiosity in me because the Pala rulers' capital, Vikrampur (now in Bangladesh), is my native place.

Soon the Pala ruler's dreams came unstuck as the Gurjara-Pratihara King, Nagabhatta II (795 A.D.–833 A.D.) conquered Kanauj, annexing in due course extensive territories including Haryana to his own empire. Haryana achieved considerable economic prosperity and a high level of excellence in art and cultural activities during the Pratihara era as is borne out by the Pehowa Inscription of 882 A.D.

In the post-Harsha period, the Bhadanakas dominated a large part of Haryana comprising Gurgaon, Rewari and Bhiwani as well as parts of adjoining Alwar State. Bhadawasa near Rewari was probably their seat of power.[73] There is a view that the Bhadanakas were identical with the Ahirs. The Bhadanakas are mentioned in the Kavyamimansa of Rajasekhara and also in the Skanda Purana.

The death of Mahendrapala, the Pratihara ruler, in 910 A.D. led to instability in Haryana, taking advantage of which the Tomara Rajputs established their rule here. Anangapal, a Tomara ruler of Haryana, founded the city of Delhi and made it the capital of Haryana. Little wonder, therefore, that the people of

Haryana have always looked upon Delhi as an integral part of their territory.

During the rule of the Tomaras, Haryana had to face a series of attacks from various quarters—the Chauhans, the Ghaznavis and the Lohara rulers of Kashmir. Chandan, the Chauhan ruler of Shakambhari, attacked Peepalrajdev, the Tomara ruler (897–919 A.D.), and defeated the latter. Haryana came under Chauhan rule and Peepalrajdev's successor namely Raghupal Vilhan continued to remain under Chauhan tutelage. Vilhan's son, Gopala, fought with the Chauhans to regain Haryana's independence, but was defeated. His son, Sulakshanpala (997-1015 A.D.) was, however, able to restore Haryana's independent status. He was succeeded by his son Jayapala (1005-1021 A.D.).

Notes

1. "ऋज्रमुक्षण्यायने रजते हरयाणे ।
   रथं युक्तमसनाम सुषामनि ।।
   —Rig Veda, Mandal 8, Sukta 35, Mantra 5, cited in an article by Dr. Bhubaneswar Prasad in the journal of Haryana Studies, Vol. XVIII, Nos. 1&2, 1986, p. 87
2. Haryana by D.C. Verma, p. 13.
3. Article by Dr. Bhubaneswar Prasad mentioned at 1 above.
4. Cited in the article mentioned at 1 above.
5. *Ibid.*
6. तत्रं सुकृतिनो हरिवंशजन्मनः चण्डमहासेनस्य नृपतेः सूनुः मारदत्तो नाम राजा ।
   —Yashastilaka-Champu, Somadeva
7. Cited by Dr. K.C. Yadav in his article 'Hariyana–The Land and the People" in Dr. J, N. Singh Yadav's book "Haryana–Studies in History and Politics".

8. Haryana: Itihas Ebam Sanskriti by Dr. K.C. Yadav, p. 6.
9. देशोस्ति हरियानाण्यः पृथिव्यां स्वर्गसंनिभः
   दिल्लिकारव्या पुरी तत्र तोमरैरस्ति निर्मिता।।
   Cited by Dr. Bhubaneswar in the article mentioned at 1 above.
10. *Ibid.*
11. Glimpses of Ancient Hariyana by Dr. Buddha Prakash in Dr. J. N. Singh Yadav's book "Haryana–Studies in History and Politics", p. 1.
12. "Hariyana—The Land and the People" by Dr. K.C. Yadav in Dr. J.N. Singh Yadav's book "Haryana—Studies in History and Politics", p. 77.
13. Page 9 of Dr. K.C. Yadav's book mentioned at 8 above.
14. Article by Dr. Hari Ram Gupta in Haryana Studies in History and Politics edited by Dr. J.N. Singh Yadav, p. 20.
15. *Ibid*, p. 20.
16. Page 43 of Dr. K.C. Yadav's book mentioned at 8 above.
17. *Ibid*, p. 51.
18. *Ibid*, p. 71.
19. एतद्देशप्रसूतस्य सकाशादग्रजन्मनः।
    स्वं स्वं चरित्र शिक्षरेन् पृथिव्या सर्वमानवाः।।
    —Quoted by Dr. K.C. Yadav at page 4 of his book mentioned at 8 above.
20. *Ibid.*
21. A.D. Pusalker in the History and Culture of the Indian People, Volume I edited by Dr. R.C. Mazumdar, p. 275.
22. Page 82 of Dr. K.C. Yadav's book mentioned at 8 above.
23. सापि तं चकमे कान्तं बुधं सोमसुतं पतिम्
    संयोगस्तत्र संजानस्तयोः प्रेम्ना परस्परम
    —Devi-Bhagawata, chapter 12, verse 28.
    The Ramayana also says:
    तम्यास्तददुतप्रख्यं श्रुत्वाहर्षमुपागतः।। सवैकामीसहतयारेमेचंद्रमसःसुतः।।७।।
    —Uttararkand, chapter 89, verse 7.
24. इति स्तुत्वा महीपालो जगाम शरणं तदा।
    परितुष्टा ददौ देबी तत्र साषुज्यमात्मनि।।५२
    सुदुयम्नस्तु ततः प्राप पदं परमकं स्थिरम्।
    तस्या देवां प्रसादेन मुनीनामपि दुर्लभम्।।५३
    —Devi-Bhagawata, chapter 12, verses 52-53.
25. सुदुयम्ने तु दिवं याते राज्यं चक्रे पुरुरवाः:
    समुणश्च सुरुपश्च प्रजारन्जनततपरः।।
    —*Ibid*, chapter 13, verse 1.
26. तस्य रुप–गुणौदार्य्य–शोल–द्रविण–विक्रमान
    श्रुत्वोर्व्वशी वशीभूता चकमे तं नराधिपम
    —*Ibid*, Chapter 13, verse 6.

27. घृतं मे भक्षणं नित्यं नान्यत् किन्चिन्न पाशनम्
नक्षं त्वाचं महाराज नग्नमत्र मैथुनात्।।६
—*Ibid*, chapter 13, verse 9.
28. *Ibid*, chapter 13, verse 9 cited above.
29. हतास्म्यहं कुनाथेन नपुंसा बीरमानिना।
उरणौ मे गतौ चाद्‌य सदा प्राणप्रियौ मम।
—*Ibid*, chapter 13, verse 21.
30. सदेहोश्यं पतत्यत्र देवि दूरं हृतस्तया
खादन्त्येन बृकाः काकास्त्वया त्यक्तं बरोरु यत्।
—*Ibid*, chapter 13, verse 29.
31. मूर्खोहसि नृपशार्दुल ज्ञानं कुत्र गतं तव।
क्कापि सरथं न च स्त्रीणां वृकाणामिब पार्थिव।३१
न विश्वासो हि कर्त्तव्यः स्त्रोषु चौरेषू पार्थिबैः
गृहं गच्छ सुखं भुक्ष मा विषादे मनः कृथाः।।३२
—*Ibid*, chapter 13, verses 31-32.
32. The History and Culture of the Indian People edited by Dr. R.C. Mazumdar, Vol. I, p. 349.
33. *Ibid*.
34. Works of Kalidasa by C.R. Devadhar, Vikramorvasiyam, p. xxiii.
35. Kalidasa–His Art and Culture by Dr. Ram Gopal, p. 84.
36. Verse 19, chapter 75, Adi Parva, Mahabharata.
37. *Ibid*, verses 20-22.
38. *Ibid*, verses 27-28.
39. तस्य शुक्रस्य कन्याऽहं स मां नूनं न बुध्यते।
एष मे दक्षिणो राजन्पाणिस्ता म्रनखाङ्.गुलिः।।२०
समुद्धर गृहीत्वा मां कुलीनस्त्वं हि मे मतः।
जानामि हि त्वां संशान्तं वीर्यवन्तं यशस्विनम्।
तस्मान्मां पतितामस्मात्कूपादुद्धर्तुंमर्हसि।।२१।।
—Mahabharata, Adi Parva, chapter 78, verses 20-21.
40. इयं चापि कुमारी ते शर्मिष्ठा वार्षपर्वणि।
संपूज्या सततं राजन्मा चैनां शयने ह्वये।।३५।।
—*Ibid*, chapter 81, verse 35.
41. शर्मिष्ठोवाच।
न नर्मयुक्तं वचनं हिनस्ति
न स्त्रीषु राजन्न विवाहकाले।
प्राणात्यये सर्वधनापहारे
पञ्चानतान्याहरपातकानि।।१६।।
—*Ibid*, chapter 82, verse 16.
42. ययातिरुवाच।
राजा प्रमाणं भूतानां स नश्येत मृषा वदन्।

अथकृच्छ्रमपि प्राप्य न मिथ्या कर्तुमुत्सहे।।१८।।

—*Ibid*, chapter 82, verse 18.

43. शर्मिष्ठोवाच।

समावेतौ मतौ राजन्पतिः सख्याश्च यः पतिः।

समं विवाहमित्याहुः सख्या मेऽसि वृतः पतिः।।१६।।

ययातिरुवाच।

दातव्यं याचसि मां कामं ब्रू हि किं करवाणि ते।।२०।।

—*Ibid*, chapter 82, verses 19-20.

44. वैशम्पायन उवाच।

एवमुक्तस्तु राजा स तथ्यमित्यभिजज्ञिवान्।

पूजयामास शर्मिष्ठां धर्मं च प्रत्यपादयत्।।२४।।

स समागम्य शर्मिष्ठां यथाकाममवाप्य च।

अन्योऽन्यं चाभिसंपूज्य जग्मतुस्तौ यथागतम्।।२५।।

—*Ibid*, chapter 82, verses 24-25.

45. नाध्यगच्छत्तदा तृप्तिं कामानां स महायशाः।

अवेत्य मनसा राजन्निमां गाथां तदा जगौ।।४६।।

न जातु कामः कामानामुपभोगेन शाम्यति।

हविषा कृष्णवर्त्मेव भूय एवाभिवर्धते।।५०।।

पृथिवी रत्नसंपूर्णा हिरण्यं पशवः स्त्रियः।

नालमेकस्य तत्सर्वमिति मत्वा शमं व्रजेत्।।५१।।

यदा न कुरुते पापं सर्वभूतेषु कर्हिचित्।

कर्मणा मनसा वाचा ब्रह्म संपद्यते तदा।।५२।।

यदा चायं न बिभेति यदा चास्मान्न विभ्यति।

यदा नेच्छति न द्वेष्टि ब्रह्म संपद्यते तदा।।५३।।

—*Ibid*, chapter 75, verses 49-53

46. वैशंपायन उवाच।

अपश्यमानस्तमृषि तथा चोक्तस्तया च सः।

तां दृष्ट्वा च वरारोहां श्रीमती चारुहासिनीम्।।१०।।

षिभ्राजमानां वपुषा तपसा च दमेन च।

रूपयौवनमंपन्नामित्युवाच महीपतिः।।११।।

—*Ibid*, chapter 71, verses 10-11.

47. तस्या रूपगुणान्दृष्ट्वा स तु विप्रर्षभस्तदा।

चकार भावं संसर्गात्तया कामवशं गतः।।७।।

न्यमन्त्रयत चाप्येना सा चाप्यैच्छदनिन्दिता।

तौ तत्र सुचिरं कालमुभौ व्यहरतां तदा।।८।।

रममाणौ यथाकामं यथैकदिवसं तथा।

जनयामास स मुनिर्मेनकार्या शकुन्तलाम्।।६।।

—*Ibid*, chapter 72, verses 7-9

48. तासां सा मेनका नाम ब्रह्मयोनिर्वराप्सराः।
दिवः संप्राप्य जगतीं विश्वामित्रादजीजनत्।।६६।।
सा मां हिमवतः प्रस्थे सुषुवे मेनकाप्सराः।
अवकीर्य च मां यातां परात्मजमिवासती।।७०।।
—*Ibid*, chapter 74, verses 69-70
49. *Ibid*, chapter 74, verse 36.
50. *Ibid*, chapter 74, verses 73-75
51. *Ibid*, chapter 74, verse 80
52. *Ibid*, chapter 74, verses 97
53. अनाघ्रातं पुष्प किसलयमूलनं कररूहै–
रनाविद्धं रत्नं मधु नवमनास्वादितरसम्।
अखण्डं पुण्यानां फलमिव च तद्रूपमनघं
न जाने भोक्तारं कमिहं समुपस्थास्यति विधिः।।
—Abhijnana-Shakuntalam, II, 10.
54. असंशयं क्षत्रपरिग्रहक्षमा यदायंमस्यामभिलाषि मे मनः।
सतां हि संदेहपदेषु प्रमाणमन्तःकरणप्रवृत्तयः।।
—Abhijnana-Shakuntalam, I, 19. Cited by Dr. Ram Gopal in his 'Kalidasa–His Art and Culture', pp. 112, 118
55. *Ibid*, pp. 139-141
56. दिष्ट्या शकुन्तला साध्वो सदपत्यभिद भवान्।
श्रद्धा वित्त विधिश्चेति त्रितयं तत्समागतम्।।
—Abhijnana-Shakuntalam, VII, 29. Cited by Dr. Ram Gopal in his book at pages 141, 145.
57. भरतानां महज्जन्म महाभारतमुच्यते।
भरताद् भारती कीर्तिर्येनेदं भारतं कुलम्।
—Page 2 of Commentary on Mahabharata (Adi Parva) by Pandit A.M. Srinivasacharar (Uppal Publishing House, Delhi)
58. तस्मै तदान्तरिक्षात् तु पुष्पवृष्टिः पपात ह।
देवदुन्दुभयो नेदुर्ननृतुश्रवाप्सरोगणाः।।
गायन्तो मधुरं तत्र देवैः शक्रोऽभ्युवाच ह।
शक्र उवाच
शकुन्तले तव सुतश्रवक्रवर्ती भविष्यति।।
बलं तेजश्व रूपं च न समं भुवि केनचित्।
आहर्ता वाजिमेधस्य शतसंख्यस्य पौरवः।।
अनेकानि सहस्राणि राजसूयादिभिर्मखेः।
स्वार्थे ब्राह्मणासात् कृत्वा दक्षिणाममितां ददात्।।
—Mahabharata, Adi Parva, chapter 74, verse 3.
59. शाकुन्तलं महात्मानं दौष्यन्ति भर पौरव।
भर्तव्याऽयं त्वया यस्मादस्माकं वचनादपि।।११४।।
तस्माद्भवत्वयं नाम्ना भरतो नाम ते सुतः।

तच्छत्वा पौरवो राजा व्याहृतं त्रिदिवौकसाम्।।११५।।

—*Ibid*, chapter 74, verses 114-115

60. Page 85 of Dr. K.C. Yadav's book mentioned at 8 above. There is a divergence between Vedic and Puranic texts as to the time sequence as well as the relation inter se of these rulers. Also see pages 310-315 in A.D. Pusalker's write-up in the History and Culture of the Indian People edited by Dr. R.C. Majumdar
61. Hariyana Through the Ages by Dr. Buddha Prakash, p. 2.
62. Page 87 of Dr. K.C. Yadav's book mentioned at 8 above.
63. Page 2 of Dr. Buddha Prakash's book mentioned at 25 above.
64. *Ibid*, p. 3.
65. Page 120 of Dr. K.C. Yadav's book mentioned at 8 above.
66. Page 10-12 of Dr. Buddha Prakash's book mentioned at 25 above.
67. *Ibid*, quoted at page 13.
68. Page 126-127 0f Dr. K.C.Yadav's book mentioned at 8 above.
69. *Ibid*, p. 131.
70. "Glimpses of Ancient Hariyana" by Dr. Buddha Prakash vide "Haryana: Studies in History and Politics" edited by Dr. J.N. Singh Yadav, p. 7.
71. Article entitled "Early History and Archaeology of Haryana" by R.C. Agraala in "Haryana Studies in History and Culture" edited by Dr. K.C. Yadav, p. 39.
72. Hariyana Through the Ages by Dr. Buddha Prakash, pp. 27-28.
73. Haryana by D.C. Verma and Dr. Sukhbir Singh, p. 17.

3

Further on Haryana's History : Its Saga of Rebellion and Resistance : the 1857 Struggle for Independence First Started Here : Haryana's Rich Spiritual and Cultural Heritage

In the first quarter of the 11th century A.D., Mahmud of Ghazni launched seventeen attacks on India, destroyed Hindu temples and looted an enormous wealth. His sixth attack on India and the first on Haryana was in 1009 A.D., when he reached Thanesar with a huge army, but in the face of the stiff resistance offered by Haryana's forces, he retreated from Narayangarh in the Ambala district of Haryana.

In 1014 A.D., Mahmud attacked Haryana a second time, which was his seventh attack on India. The Tomara ruler of Haryana issued an appeal to the Hindu rulers of north India to get together with a view to safeguarding the sanctity of Thanesar, an important religious center. But since nobody responded, the people of Haryana fought alone and were defeated by Mahmud, who plundered Thanesar and its temples and destroyed the famous idol of Chakratirthaswami. Thereafter, Mahmud went back, giving up Haryana, but after incorporating Punjab into his territory.

After Mahmud's demise, his successor Masud attacked Hansi, Sonepat and Thanesar in 1030 A.D. Haryana's armed forces fought hard against him but were defeated with the result that Masud gained control over almost the whole of Haryana. After Masud's death, the Haryana people were able to regain their territory. Masud's successor, Madud, launched an attack on Haryana. The Tomara ruler of Haryana appealed to several rulers of north India for help to which the latter responded positively. Therefore, this time around, the Indian forces defeated the invaders, forcing them to retreat. Masud's successor, Ibrahim (1059-1109 A.D.) again attacked Haryana. The then Tomara ruler of Haryana abjectly surrendered before the Ghaznavis and so Haryana passed into the hands of the latter.

It has been said that the Lohara kings of Kashmir tried to annex Haryana at the time when the Ghaznavis were making their inroads into this region. Kalasha, son of the Lohara King Ananta of Kashmir, is believed to have attacked Kurukshetra and conquered the territory up to the Yamuna. This might have compelled the Tomaras of Haryana to patch up with the Ghaznavis.[1] the Kashmir ruler's men withdrew from Haryana when dynastic trouble in Kashmir called for their immediate presence there.

Arnoraja (1133-1151A.D.), the Chauhan (Chahamana) ruler of Shakambhari, annexed Haryana, which then became his feudatory state. The Bhadanakas of south west Haryana also appeared to have accepted Arnoraja's supremacy. After Arnoraja, there was a serious quarrel among his descendants over the throne—a situation that helped the Bhadanakas of Haryana to recapture their power. Around 1156 A.D., the Chauhan ruler, Vigraharaja IV or Visaladeva, finally conquered Haryana including Delhi and the areas held by the Bhadanakas. Some time after the death of Vigraharaja IV, the Bhadanakas regained their independent status. In 1182 A.D., Prithviraja III, the Chauhan ruler, defeated the Bhadanakas and annexed their territory.

However, the Chauhans could not retain their power for long. In 1191 A.D., Muhammad Ghori of Afghanistan, who had been dreaming of establishing the rule of Islam in India, invaded India and was confronted by Prithviraja Chauhan at Tarain near Karnal in Haryana. The brave Chauhans dealt a crushing defeat on Ghori, who himself was badly injured. Smarting under this defeat, Ghori began to prepare himself for his next attack on India and, as he was reported to have said, he gave up seeing his wife and did not even change the dress he had worn at the battle of Tarain till he launched his next attack with a view to realizing his dream of conquering India.

Prithviraja Chauhan did nothing much by way of preparing himself to face the next attack of Ghori. On the contrary, he began to administer pinpricks to the other native chiefs including Jayachandra of Kanauj, whose daughter, Samjukta, he abducted from the Swayamvara held by her father. It is another matter that both Samykta and Prithviraja had earlier come to cherish each other in the light of what they had heard of each other's admirable traits, thus providing the themes of many tales of their romance. It has been said that while

Muhammad Ghori had chosen the path of extreme self-abnegation in order to prepare himself for his next attack on India, Prithviraja, on the other hand, had been engaged in dalliance with the lovely princess Samyukta, whose company was said to have"lulled him into lassitude and obliviousness of the menace hovering in the North West."[2] It has been said—on what basis I do not know—that as a measure of revenge against Prithviraja, Jayachandra offered his help to Ghori and invited him to launch his second attack on Prithviraja.

Muhammad Ghori avenged his defeat of 1191 A.D. by attacking India again in 1182 A.D. And defeating Prithviraja on the same battlefield of Tarain (or Taraori), though the Rajputs had fought bravely. Prithviraja was arrested and ordered to be killed. Thus Haryana and Delhi came under the occupation of the Turks, marking a defining moment of India's history and the advent of Muslim rule in our country.

But the people of Haryana did not readily accept the imposition of Muslim rule and offered resistance to the new rulers, wherever possible, particularly at Hansi, Rohtak, Meham, Rewari etc. The people attacked the Afghans at Rewari and killed the chief of their armed forces. Following this, Qutbuddin Aibak, Commander-In-Chief of Ghori's forces, launched an attack on Rewari and put down the rebels. A similar development took place in the Mewat belt of Haryana, where also the local people killed the chief of the Afghan forces. A big force was sent by Qutbuddin to quell the rebellion. It took quite some time for the Afghans to establish their authority in Haryana.

After the death of Muhammad Ghori in 1206 A.D., his military chief Qutbuddin proclaimed himself as the Sultan of Delhi. This marked the beginning of the rule in India of what was called the Slave dynasty because originally Qutbuddin was a slave in Turkestan. There was not much change in Haryana's political situation during Qutbuddin's rule, but after his death in 1210 A.D., there was turmoil in Haryana following the revolt of his son-in-law, Nasruddin Qubacha, and the attack on Punjab by Tajuddin Yuldoz, the ruler of Ghazni. Qubacha annexed quite some territory around Sirsa in Haryana. But soon, Yuldoz had the better of Qubacha and occupied this territory. Shamsuddin Iltutmish, who had in the mean time sat on the throne of Delhi, had a fight with Yuldoz—again at Taraori near Karnal—on January 25, 1216 A.D. Yuldoz was defeated. Soon, Iltutmish also defeated Qubacha, who had declared his independence from Sirsa and established his rule in Haryana.

After the death of Iltutmish in May 1236 A.D., his son, Rukn-ud-din Feroze's rule was marked by considerable political instability. He was murdered in a palace coup, following which Razia, the daughter of Iltutmish, took over the reins of power. The people of Haryana, particularly the Meos of Mewat, challenged her authority in diverse ways. They adopted guerrilla tactics to harass the Sultan's forces. In fact, she was assassinated at Kaithal in Haryana on October 14, 1240 A.D. The rule of Bahram Shah, Masud Shah and Nasiruddin Mahmud that followed in succession saw widespread rebellious activity in Haryana. According to Minhaj-ud-din, the Meos swooped down on Delhi from places in Haryana, harassed the people and destroyed their houses. The people of Delhi were so scared of Meo attacks that they could not sleep in peace. Businessmen hesitated to venture out of Delhi.[3]

Nasiruddin deputed his army chief and Prime Minister, Balban, to suppress the Mewatis. Though Balban managed to put them down and killed many of them in a couple of expeditions undertaken in 1260 A.D., the latter asserted themselves again and again at opportune moments. After Nasiruddin's death, Balban became the Sultan in 1265 A.D. And gave the first priority to establishing peace in Mewat. The elaborate measures that he took restored a semblance of peace, which, however, did not last very long. Moreover, the number of rebels killed in Balban's operations exceeded a lakh!

The Mewatis of Haryana refused to accept Delhi's authority when Jalaluddin Khalji became the Sultan in 1290 A.D. A story about how Jalaluddin was humiliated in Haryana is sometimes recounted.[4] It is said that before he became the Sultan, he had to fight hard against the Mandhars near Kalayat in Haryana. A chief of the Mandhars inflicted a severe injury on his face. After Jalaluddin became the Sultan, he held a Durbar to which he invited this Mandhar chief with a view to honouring him. When asked about the reason for honouring a person, who had caused him a severe bodily injury, he replied that he had fought many battles, but nowhere had he seen such a brave warrior. Jalaluddin pursued a policy of conciliation towards the people of Haryana.

Jalaluddin's successor, Alauddin switched over to a hard line approach and harassed the people of Haryana by imposing heavy taxes. Mubarak Shah, another ruler of the Khalji dynasty, however, reverted to the moderate policy of Jalaluddin. Ghyasuddin Tughlak, the next Sultan, who set up the rule of the Tughlak dynasty, revived Alauddin's repressive policies. His son, Muhammad-bin-Tughlak (1325–1351 A.D.) adopted harsh measures that led the people of Haryana to revolt. On his death on March 23, 1351 A.D., his son, Feroze Shah Tughlak, sat on the throne and withdrew some of the taxes with a view to pacifying the people. His economic measures benefited the people of Haryana but in religious matters, he displayed extreme intolerance towards the Hindus. In his memoirs, Feroze Shah himself mentioned how he chastised many Hindus, who worshipped idols, and destroyed their idols, besides killing the trouble makers among them. When the Hindus of Haryana rose in revolt, the Sultan himself proceeded with a large army to suppress them. As a sequel to the Sultan's oppression, Hindus in large numbers converted to Islam, particularly in Mewat.

After Feroze Shah's death in September, 1388 A.D., his grandson, Ghyasuddin Tughlak II became the Sultan, but he was assassinated by Abu Bakr, who sat on the throne in February 1389 A.D. Soon, palace intrigues constrained him to flee Delhi, paving the way for Nasiruddin Muhammad Shah to take over as the Sultan in August 1390 A.D. Haryana witnessed widespread disorder at this time. After Nasiruddin's death in January 1394 A.D., Alauddin Sikander Shah (earlier known as Humayun) became the Sultan. Following his sudden death, Nasiruddin Mahmud (1395–1413 A.D.) sat on the throne. But one Nusrat Shah had also taken over as the Sultan at Ferozabad almost simultaneously in December 1394–January 1395 A.D. with the result that there were now two Sultans.

Nasiruddin Mahmud was the last ruler of the Tughlak dynasty and it was during his rule that Taimur, the Turkish ruler of Samarqand, invaded India in 1398 A.D. He ravaged Punjab and marched to Delhi, proceeding from Rajasthan through several places in Haryana such as Sirsa, Hisar, Ferozabad, Fatehbad, Tohana, Kaithal, Assand, Salwan, Saman, Karnal, Panipat etc., indulging in plunder and loot. Taimur did not attack Mewat in view of the strong position and high reputation of a Bahadur Nahir, the Rajput chief of Mewat, who had converted to Islam. Taimur then attacked Delhi on December 16, 1398 A.D. Sultan Mahmud, who was defeated, ran away from Delhi. Taimur captured Delhi where he remained for 15 days during which he looted the city's wealth and killed about a lakh of Hindus. Thereafter, he proceeded towards Meerut and and Hardwar, where also the same orgy of loot and killings was repeated. Before leaving India Taimur also conquered Jammu.

Taimur was in Haryana for about a month when he had to face resistance from the people, thousands of whom sacrificed their lives fighting the invaders. But they failed to stop Taimur's onslaught as they received no assistance from the government in Delhi.

After Taimur's departure from India, Sultan Mahmud, the Tughlak ruler, returned to Delhi, but his rule did not extend beyond the city of Delhi. In Haryana, the people became virtually independent. An independent territory was carved out in the Mewat region of south west Haryana by Bahadur Nahir and his successors, while in north Haryana, Mohan Singh Mandhar of Kalayat set up another independent state. The ruler of the Sayyid dynasty, who replaced the Tughlak dynasty, initially tried to take over these independent states, but as he found it difficult to do so, he entered into some sort of a modus vivendi.

After the death of Mahmud in 1413 A.D., Khizr Khan, a ruler of the Sayyid dynasty, occupied the throne of Delhi. While leaving India, Taimur had nominated him as his Governor in India. The Sayyid dynasty was replaced in 1451 A.D.by the Lodhi dynasty which was able to establish its authority in Haryana.

Bahlul Lodhi (1451–1489 A.D.), the first ruler of the Lodhi dynasty, desisted from interfering with the religious affairs of the Hindus of Haryana. But his successor, Sikander Lodhi (1489–1517 A.D.), was a religious fanatic, who prohibited the Hindus from bathing in the sacred tank at Thanesar in Haryana. His son and the next ruler, Ibrahim Lodhi was no different. Therefore, the people of Haryana were not favourably disposed towards him when Babar confronted him in the First Battle of Panipat in 1526 A.D. Babar defeated Ibrahim Lodhi in April 1526 A.D. And captured Delhi, thus laying the foundation of Mughal rule in India.

Haryana became a part of the Mughal Empire, but the people of Mewat did not accept Mughal rule. It was after defeating the Mewatis and killing their leader, Hussain Khan, in the decisive battle of Khanwa in March 1527 A.D. that Babar could restore order in that region. In 1530 A.D., Babar had to face the revolt of the Mandhar Rajputs at several places in Haryana. The latter defeated an army sent by Babar under the command of the Governor of Sirhind, Ali Quli. Babar then sent a much bigger army, which defeated the Mandhars and killed many of them.

Humayun, who became the Mughal Emperor after the death of Babar on December 26, 1530 A.D., failed to properly handle the situation. As a result, his empire passed into the hands of Sher Shah Suri, an Afghan of the Sur dynasty, after his defeat by the latter in the battles of Chausa and Bilgram in 1540 A.D. Thus Sher Shah, who was born at Narnaul in Haryana in 1486 A.D., became the ruler of Haryana. But after Sher Shah was accidentally killed during the battle of Kalinjar on May 22, 1545 A.D., there was political instability taking advantage of which, Humayun staged a come-back to become the Emperor of Delhi and the ruler of Haryana in 1555 A.D.

Humayun died accidentally on January 26, 1556 A.D., when his son, Akbar, then barely 14 years of age, who was away at Kalanaur in

Punjab, was proclaimed as the Emperor. At this time, Sher Shah's successors were still in occupation of many areas of his territory. After the death in Ocober 1553 A.D. Of Sher Shah's son, Islam Shah, the latter's brother-in-law, Adil Shah, had usurped power. He was a weak ruler, who failed to control the infighting among the Afghans. His ambitious Prime Minister, Hem Chandra, who hailed from Rewari in Haryana, occupied Agra and Delhi and proclaimed himself as an independent kin, assuming the title of Maharaja Vikramaditya. Akbar proceeded with his forces to recapture Delhi. This led to the Second Battle of Panipat in 1556 A.D. In which Himu got killed even as he was almost on the cusp of victory. Akbar occupied Delhi and Agra and established himself as the Emperor of India. His forces succeeded in bringing Haryana under Mughal rule and he adopted a sympathetic attitude towards the Hindus.

Jahangir, who became the emperor in 1605 A.D. after his father's death, maintained the system of administration that Akbar had introduced and also treated the Hindus with sympathy and kindness. He had a great liking for Haryana.

Jahangir's son, Shah Jehan, ascended the throne in 1627 A.D after the former's death. Under his rule also, Haryana continued to enjoy peace and economic prosperity. But with the assumption of power by Aurangzeb in 1658 A.D., Haryana witnessed widespread disorder and revolts. Aurangzeb had to resort to repressive measures to put down the revolt of the Mewatis as well as that of the Satnamis (1672 A.D.), a sect of simple-minded Hindus living in and around Narnaul in Haryana, who protested against his policy of religious intolerance. A large number of the Satnamis were killed under Aurangzeb's orders. Apart from Aurangzeb's religious fanaticism and anti-Hindu measures, a factor that had been stoking the discontent of the people of Haryana was the occurrence of several famines that badly affected their economic condition and resulted in many deaths. Haryana was stalked by severe drought and famine conditions in 1554-1556 A.D., 1572-1573 A.D., 1596 A.D., 1615-1616 A.D., 1636-1637 A.D., 1650 A.D. ad 1658 A.D.

The death of Aurangzeb on March 3, 1707 A.D. marked the onset of the process of disintegration of the Mughal empire. In Haryana, Mughal rule existed only nominally and several local rulers emerged to take advantage of the situation. Among them were Fauzdar Khan of Farrukhnagar, Gopal Singh of Ballabhgarh, Nand Ram of Rewari, Sardar Khan of Hisar and Nazawat Khan of Kunjpura.

During the period from 1707 A.D. to 1857 A.D., there were several Mughal rulers beginning with Bahadur Shah I and ending with Bahadur Shah II. The latter was the last ruler of this dynasty, who joined the struggle against the British in 1857 A.D. And was deported to Rangoon where he died in 1862 A.D. An important development that affected Haryana was the rise of the Sikhs led by Banda Bahadur, who operated from his headquarters in villages Sihiri and Khanda near Rohtak and occupied Sonepat, Kaithal and Thanesar. He then captured Sirhind which he made his headquarters. Thus he came to exercise his authority over almost the whole of Haryana. He continued to launch attacks on the Mughal territory till 1716 A.D. when he was captured during the rule of the Mughal Emperor, Farrukh Siyar. He was given the option of either converting to Islam or facing death. He preferred death to conversion and was put to death after being subjected to inhuman physical torture.

When Muhammad Shah was the Mughal ruler of Delhi, Nadir Shah, a freebooter, who had become the ruler of Persia, invaded India in 1739 A.D. He came up to Karnal in February 1739 A.D., where Muhammad Shah's forces offered feeble resistance to him. In this battle, the then ruler of Rewari by name Rao Balkishan offered his assistance to the Mughal ruler and himself led his men with exemplary courage to fight Nadir Shah's men. Balkishan and 5000 of his men sacrificed their lives, but failed to stop Nadir Shah's onslaught. Nadir Shah defeated the Mughal forces and marched to Delhi where he ordered a general massacre. After spending 57 days in Delhi, he went back with a huge booty that included the famous Koh-I-Noor diamond and the jewel-studded Peacock Throne of Shah Jehan.

Around the middle of the 18th century A.D., the territory of Haryana became the target of attack from several quarters.[5] Surajmal, the Jat ruler of Bharatpur, occupied some areas near Faridabad, Madho Singh, the ruler of Jaipur, captured some areas near Mahendragarh and Narnaul. A local chief of Farrukhnagar established his authority in Gurgaon, Jhajjar and Hisar while some others gained control over Bahadurgarh. Qutb Shah held sway over Panipat and Sirhind and Najawat Khan over some areas near Kurukshetra and Karnal. Muhammad Anur and Hassan Khan captured Sirsa, Rania and Fatehabad. Thus almost the whole of Haryana became independent of the Mughals' authority for all practical purposes.

At this time, the rise of the Marathas introduced a new potent force in the power equation of northern India. In 1752 A.D., Ahmed Shah Durrani, the ruler of Afghanistan, invaded Punjab and captured Lahore. This led Alamgir II, the Mughal Emperor, to enter into an agreement with the Marathas in 1752 A.D. that provided for Maratha protection for Mughal interests against internal and external aggression in lieu of certain financial guarantees to the Marathas and the vesting of a good measure of administrative authority in north India including Delhi in Maratha hands. In October 1754 A.D., Alamgir also ceded Kurukshetra in Haryana to the Marathas as a gesture of goodwill.

But soon, the Marathas had to go back from Haryana in view of certain developments elsewhere. Taking advantage of the situation, Qutb Shah, who had earlier been deprived by the Marathas of his 'Jagir', stepped into the void in Haryana and established his rule in 1754-1755 A .D. The Mughal forces proceeded to Haryana to dislodge Qutb Shah, but in a battle fought at Karnal on Mrch 11, 1755 A.D., the latter defeated the Mughal army. Thereafter, Qutb Shah attacked Sirhind, where Adina Beg, the Subedar of Punjab, defeated him on April 11, 1755 A.D., forcing him to flee. As a result, north Haryana came into the possession of Adina Beg.[6]

After some time, Ahmed Shah Abdali, the successor of Nadir Shah, invaded Punjab, defeated Adina Beg and incorporated north Haryana into his territory. Proceeding further, Abdali occupied Delhi in January 1757 A.D. He had some clashes with the Marathas at Faridabad and Palwal and with the Jat ruler Surajmal's son, Jawahar Singh, near Ballabhgarh. Abdali defeated Jawahar Singh and plundered southern Haryana, besides unleashing an orgy of repression near Mathura. He killed thousands of people and looted the wealth of the people in Delhi before returning to Afghanistan.

After Abdali's departure from India, Ali Gohar, the eldest son of Alamgir II, and another person by name Imad, a nominee of Abdali, vied with each other to gain authority in various parts of Haryana. Ali Gohar went to several places in Haryana such as Jhajjar, Hisar, Farrukhnagar, Dadri etc. And fought with the local chiefs to assert his supremacy. Imad took Alamgir II, the Mughal emperor, with him during his visit to Haryana. The visit to Jhajjar passed off peacefully, but in the Bhiwani-Hisar region, they faced serious problems. In some villages, the peasants fought against them in 1758 A.D. The people of Bhiwani humiliated Alamgir II by looting his belongings right in his presence. The Bhattis of Rania behaved similarly with Imad.[7]

At this juncture, the Marathas came back to the Delhi region. Sadashivrao Bhau, the Maratha army chief, captured Delhi on August 1, 1760 A.D. and installed Shah Alam II as the Mughal Emperor. As the Marathas had no money to pay their army, they took to loot and plunder. They entered Haryana and looted the foodgrain of the peasants. On October 16, 1760 A.D., a big Maratha army launched an attack on Najawat Khan, Nawab of Kunjpura, who was assisted by the Rohilla Afghan leader, Najibuddaula, and Abdus Samad, the Durrani Governor of Sind. In a fierce battle that took place on October 17, 1760 A.D., the Marathas defeated the Afghans and killed about 20,000 men as well as Najawat Khan, his two sons and Abdus Samad Khan. The Marathas destroyed the fort of Kunjpura and plundered the people.

The Marathas now occupied Punjab which had earlier passed into the hands of the Afghans. Realising the seriousness of the situation, the Afghan ruler, Ahmad Shah Abdali reached Panipat along with a huge army on November 1, 1760 A.D. The Maratha army was also camping there. On January 14, 1761 A.D., the Afghans defeated the Marathas in the Third Battle of Panipat.

Ahmad Shah Abdali had to leave India soon after this victory as he had to suppress a revolt that had erupted in his own country in his absence. Before gong back, Abdali installed the Rohilla Afghan, Najibuddala on the throne of Delhi. The result was that the whole of southern Haryana below Panipat came under the rule of Najibuddaula. The Afghans gradually retired from the scene, while the Marathas wilted as their dream of establishing a Hindu empire in India lay shattered. This left the field open for the Sikhs and the Europeans to step in.

With a view to fighting the tyranny of the Mughals and the Afghans, the Sikhs of Punjab had organized themselves into two Dals—the Budha Dal (the army of the elders) and the Tarun Dal (the army of the young). On January 14, 1764 A.D., the two groups joined hands and defeated Zain Khan, the Afghan Governor of Sirhind and divided among themselves the territory of Hryana above Panipat. Many small independent states cropped up in Hryana where the Sikhs were in power. The ruler of Patiala occupied some areas and in pursuance of an agreement, Hansi, Hisar and Rohtak remained with the Mughals. The territory between Panipat and Delhi was in the hands of Najibuddaula, the Afghan chief of Delhi.

The Sikhs indulged in loot all over the territory. They went to Rewari (which at that time was with Nagarmal Khatri, a Jagirdar of the Mughals) and plundered the town. They proceeded to Narnaul and Kannod, which then formed part of the territory of the Maharaja of Jaipur. In 1767-1768 A.D., they entered Panipat and Sonepat and then advanced to Delhi, where they defeated Najibuddaula, forcing him to vacate Delhi. Following dissensions among themselves, the Sikhs withdrew from Delhi, but they continued to maitain their hold on Haryana. They raided Panipat and Karnal in 1770 A.D. And indulged in loot on a large scale. As their position became stronger in the wake of the death in October 1770 A.D. Of Najibuddaula, they kept on plundering the people of Haryana till 1772 A.D.

Following the Third Battle of Panipat, the Jats attained a dominant position in several areas of southern Haryana. One Gokula of Tilpat village, who had organized the Jats on militant lines, died in 1670 A.D. Rajaram, a Jat from Mathura, then took over the leadership of the Jats and fought against Aurangzeb's forces. After his death in 1688 A.D., his nephew Churaman became the leader, who brought under his control a sizeable territory between Delhi and Rajasthan. Churaman was succeeded by his son, Badan Singh, who kept the Jat flag flying. Badan Singh's successor, Surajmal (1755-1764 A.D.) was the ablest Jat ruler and statesman, who has been characterised by Sir Jadu Nath Sarkar, the well-known historian, as the Plato of the Jat tribe. He extended his territory to several areas of Haryana such as Mewat, Jhajjar, Rohtak etc.

Surajmal entrusted his son, Jawahar Singh with the responsibility of overseeing the affairs of Haryana. Jawahar Singh failed to maintain order in Mewat, where some lawless elements were indulging in loot and plunder with the support of the Biloch chief as well as the ruler of Farrukhnagar. Jawahar Singh's military expedition to bring the Biloch chief to book met with failure. But Jawahar Singh was able to defeat he ruller of Farrukhnagar. Some time after Surajmal's death in December 1763 A.D., Najibuddaula, the Rohilla chief, attacked Bubana, a village of Sonepat district, in April 1765 A.D. But his forces were badly defeated by the villagers. Najib's men again launched an attack on the village with a big army, killed a few thousand villagers, took many of them prisoners and set the village on fire.[8]

Thereafter, Najib entered Bhiwani, where again he faced fierce resistance from the people. Here also Najib's men eventually won and repeated the same orgy of repression, killings, arson etc. Gradually, north western Haryana came under Najib's control. Thus the whole of Haryana became free from the control of the Jats. Now Najibuddaula voluntarily laid down the reins of power, handed over all responsibilities to his son and retired to Najibabad, where he died on October 31, 1770 A.D. Then followed a period of widespread lawlessness and chaos in Haryana.[9]

Mughal Emperor Shah Alam, who had left Delhi in the wake of the Third Battle of Panipat and had been living as a virtual refugee in Allahabad, was anxious to return to Delhi. He was able to do so on January 6, 1772 A.D. with the help of the Marathas after an interval of over ten years. Shah Alam was an emperor only in name as the Marathas had taken away from him all administrative powers and military authority.

But soon, the Marathas fell out with one Mirza Najaf, an astute person, who had once worked under the British in Kolkata and had then joined the Mughal forces of which he was regarded as the leader for all practical purposes. Mirza Najaf succeeded in dislodging the Marathas from Delhi and became the administrative head of Mughals' set-up in Delhi. He turned his attention towards Haryana and in due course managed to take over Rewari, Jhajjar and Gurgaon from the Jats, Kannod and Narnaul from the Rajputs, Sonepat, Rohtak, Bhiwani, Hisar and Sirsa from the Bhattis. He also entered into a treaty with the Sikhs that accepted the latter's occupation of Ambala, Kurukshetra and Karnal in return for which the Sikhs gave the Mughals certain rights in these areas, besides agreeing to desist from attacking any territory of the Mughals.

However, after Mirza Najaf's death on April 26, 1782 A.D., the Marathas under the leadership of Mahadji Scindhia returned to Delhi with a huge army in response to overtures from the Mughal Emperor Shah Alam. From 1785 to 1787 A.D., Mahadji Scindhia exercised full control over Delhi. In 1787 A.D., some functionaries of the Mughal Emperor, Rohilla chiefs and Rajputs from Rajasthan joined hands to overthrow Mahadji Scindhia. Soon, the Rohillas started misbehaving with Emperor Shah Alam and the members of his family. In 1789 A.D., Mahadji Scindhia attacked Delhi and drove away the Rohillas. The Mughal Emperor, who felt extremely happy over this, entrusted Mahadji Scindhia with the responsibility of running the government.

Mahadji Scindhia took measures to recover Haryana which had slipped out of Mughal control. He reached an understanding with the Sikhs, who were then in control of Ambala, Karnal and Jind. He deputed a trusted commander, Ismail Beg, to dislodge one Najibullah Khan from Gurgaon, Rewari and Kannod. In November 1789 A.D., Mahadji Scindhia concluded an agreement with Kashi Rao Holkar and gave him the territory of Mewat and Panipat in Haryana, which the latter then occupied.

However, Ismail Beg turned against Mahadji Scindhia and joined hands with the anti-Maratha rulers of Rajasthan. Mahadji Scindhia's commander, Gopal Bhau, launched an attack on Ismail Beg in early 1790 A.D. There was a fight near Rewari in which Ismail Beg's local lieutenant surrendered on July 16, 1791 A.D.[10] Some time later, Najafkuli Khan, who had joined hands with Ismail Beg, expired. Gopal bhau kept on chasing Ismail Beg. At this juncture, Najafkuli Khan's widow, who was residing in the fort of Kannod, wrote a letter to Ismail Beg, appealing to the latter to come to Kannod and take charge of the fort.

Ismail Beg proceeded towards Kannod. As he reached a place about 8 miles from Kannod, he was confronted and defeated by Khande Rao Holkar and his men. However, Ismail Beg kept on moving towards Kannod. When he reached the gate of the fort there, he was told that he was no longer welcome, as the widow of Najafkuli Khan had changed her mind in the mean time after getting a fuller picture of the former's cruel and greedy nature. Chased by the Scindhia's and Holkar's forces, Ismail beg moved towards Madhogarh and then towards Kannod.

At this time, Najafkuli Khan's widow was accidentally killed. She was sitting on the roof and playing chess with her maid servant when a gun shot hit her, killing her on the spot. The fort came under the control of the Marathas. In April 1792 A.D., Ismail Beg was captured and after some time he was killed. Soojn, the Marathas defeated the Bhattis and occupied Fatehabad, Sirsa and Rania. Thus Mahadji Scindhia established his authority over Haryana.

The politico-military instability in Haryana during the 18th century provided a fertile ground for many indigenous and foreign adventurers to seek their fortune here. An important figure that deserves mention in this context is George Thomas, an Irishman, who arrived at Delhi in 1787 A.D. And joined the service of Begum Samru of Sardhana. In 1793 A.D., he was employed by the Marathas. Soon he set himself up as an independent ruler of some areas of haryana with Hansi as his capital. Gradually, he extended his territory to some places in the districts of Gurgaon, Rohtak, Sonepat, Hisar and Bhiwani. In November 1798 A.D., he laid siege to Jind town. After he occupied Jind, the Sikhs mounted an attack on him, forcing him to retreat from the town in 1799 A.D. The Sikhs chased him but were defeated. Peace was restored after the two sides entered into an agreement. After some time, George Thomas was defeated by the Maratha forces and in 1801 A.D., he was permitted to move over from Haryana to the British territory.

As a result of the instability and chaos that prevailed in Haryana over several centuries, the economic condition of the people and the socio-cultural environment suffered a serious set-back.

In 1803 A.D., when Lord Wellesely was the Governor-General of the East India Company, the Marathas were defeated by the British and on December 30, 1803 A.D., the treaty of Sirji Anjangao was signed between the two sides, which ceded the territory of Haryana to the East India Company. The British divided this this region into two parts, the smaller of which comprising areas on the right side of the Yamuna such as Panipat, Sonepat, Samalkha, Ganaur, Haveli Palam, Nuh, Hatheen, Tizara, Bhora, Tapukara, Sohna, Rewari, Indri, Palwal etc. formed what was called the 'assigned territory' that was placed under the control of a Resident, who worked directly under the Governor-General. The rest of the Haryana territory, which was was bigger in area, was distributed among the various local chiefs, who had assisted the British in their fight with the Marathas.

Initially, the Resident administered the assigned territory of Haryana with the help of a few Assistants. In 1819 A.D., this system was modified, entrusting only political powers to the Resident, while all administrative powers were conferred on a new functionary called the Civil Commissioner. The assigned territory was split into three Divisions—the northern Division consisting of Panipat, Sonepat, Rohtak, Hansi and Hisar with its headquarters at Hisar; the central Division comprising Delhi and the surrounding areas with headquarters at Delhi; and the southern Division that included Palwal, Hodal, Mewat, Rewari and Gurgaon with headquarters at Gurgaon. Moreover, the name assigned territory was changed to Delhi Territory. Since this system led to friction as a result of conflicts between the Resident and the Commissioner, it was modified in 1825 A.D. And the Resident was again entrusted with all powers. But in 1829 A.D., when William Bentinck was the Governor-General, the earlier system of bifurcation was re-introduced.

A more radical change was made in the system of administration in 1833 A.D., when the Bengal Presidency that extended from Bengal to the north western India was bifurcated and a new Province called the North West Province was carved out of it with Agra as its headquarters. This new North West Province had six Divisions of which one was the Delhi Division headquartered at Delhi. The Delhi Division, which included Haryana, had five districts namely Panipat, Hisar, Rohtak, Gurgaon and Delhi.

The British authorities simultaneously introduced several measures such as the abolition of Sati, capital punishment etc. And completed the settlement of land.

But the people of Haryana did not readily accept the rule of the British whom they looked upon as usurpers and rose in revolt at many places. The Meos, Gujjars and Ahirs of Gurgaon, the Jats and Ranghars of Rohtak, the Bhattis, Ranghars and Bishnois of Hisar, the Rajputs, Sainis and Sikhs of Ambala, Karnal and Kurukshetra indulged in rebellious activities for the next six to seven years. The British authorities dispatched troops to several places under the command of experienced officers such as Colonel Burn, Edward Gardiner and Colonel James Skinner, who eventually managed to suppress the rebels.

There was widespread discontent in Haryana as a result of the policy of repression and economic exploitation pursued by the British authorities. The people reacted adversely when the British interfered with their old village communities and deprived them of their autonomy. The over-assessment of land revenue and the fall in the prices of agricultural products hit the peasants very hard, forcing many of them to go to the money-lender and even to leave their villages. The import of cheap goods from abroad struck a severe blow to the artisans, traders and townspeople, many of whom lost their jobs. Interference in the religious affairs of the Hindus antagonized the latter.

What aggravated the situation in Haryana was the occurrence of several famines in 1803 A.D., 1812-1813 A.D., 1833-1834 A.D. And 1851-52 A.D., which caused untold suffering to the people to mitigate which the British authorities did not take adequate measures. As a consequence, the people of Haryana fell prey to diseases of all kinds, which broke out in epidemic form in 1841 A.D and 1843 A.D., causing the death of thousands.

All this paved the way for the 1857 uprising against the British in Haryana as in the rest of the country. But even before the final outburst of 1857 A.D., some localized revolts took place at several places in Haryana, which foreshadowed what was to come in 1857 A.D. Dr.K.C. Yadav, a noted historian, has pointed out that the top-notch historians of our country have generally ignored these important revolts of the Haryana people that prepared the ground for the much bigger conflagration.[11]

Dr. Yadav has given a detailed account of these events. At Chhachhroli in the Jagadhri area of Ambala district, following the death of the local ruler, there was a dispute over succession. Taking advantage of the situation, the British dispatched troops in December 1818 A.D. to take over the territory and incorporate it into their own dominion, much against the wishes of the local people, who staged a stiff fight against the former. In 1818 A.D., the British Resident of Delhi asked the Nawab of Rania in Sirsa district to check the lawless activities of the local people who used to indulge in loot and plunder in the near-by British territory. As there was no response to this suggestion, the British sent troops to Rania where the Bhattis offered stiff resistance. Eventually, the British annexed this territory.

In 1824 A.D., the Jat peasants of Rohtak, Gurgaon and Hisar, who had been groaning under the burden of over-assessed revenue, raised the banner of revolt, attacking government buildings and looting treasuries and banks. The British authorities dispatched a big contongent of Gorkha soldiers to suppress the peasants of Haryana, who fought valiantly under the leadership of one Surajmal. At the end, the peasants were subjugated and subjected to severe repression at various places. In Jind, the people stood solidly behind Pratap Singh, son of the local ruler, who staged a revolt in 1814 A.D. In protest against the unwarranted interference of the British authorities in the affairs of that state. The British had to send troops to put down the rebellion. There were several confrontations between the opposing forces, but in 1815 A.D., Pratap Singh was defeated and taken prisoner. The situation in Jind continued to remain disturbed for several years as a result of the people's revolt, which the British eventually suppressed in 1835 A.D. by resorting to repressive measures.

Certain events that took place in Loharu in the 1830's reflected the discontent of the local people. William Fraser, who became the Resident of Delhi in 1830 A.D., had a glad eye and had aroused the ire of Shamsuddin, the ruler of Loharu, who had taken exception to the Resident's misdemeanour towards Shamsuddin's sister. Displeased over this, Wiliam Fraser manipulated to get the Loharu state divided among Shamsuddin and his two brothers, thus drastically reducing the size of Shamsuddin's domain.

Shamsuddin got Fraser killed in Delhi on March 22, 1835 A.D. by one Karim Khan. The British managed to get hold of Shamsuddin and Karim Khan and, after a trial, both of them were hanged to death—Karim Khan on August 28, 1835 A.D. And Shamsuddin on October 10, 1835 A.D. As Fraser had incurred the wrath of the people in view of his cruelty and oppressive ways, the latter thought that he deserved to be killed and that Shamsuddin and Karim Khan had done the right thing.[12]

Shamsuddin was hanged from a scaffold put up at a high place near Delhi's Kashmiri Gate to make an example of him to the people. Clad in green clothes, the Nawab gladly mounted the scaffold before he was hanged. It is said that after his hanging, his face had turned towards the Kaba, which the people took as a pointer to his innocence and his martyrdom. About 8000 persons had reportedly joined Shamsuddin's funeral procession. As some well-wishers of Shamsuddin were anxious to publicise their views on his martyrdom, the first Urdu newspaper of Delhi namely the 'Delhi Akhbar' was published in 1836 A.D. Gradually some more Urdu newspapers came out from Delhi. This was an important fall-out of the murder of Frazer and the hanging of Shamsuddin.[13]

The situation in the Kaithal state of Haryana took an explosive turn in 1843 A.D. after the death of its ruler, Bhai Udai Singh, who had no issue. The British had earlier provided protection to his father, Bhai Lal Singh. The British issued a diktat that when the ruler of a native state that had been given protection died without leaving behind any issue, his territory would pass into the hands of the British. The leading personalities of Kaithal did not accept the British stand and insisted on the mother and the widow of Bhai Udai Singh being vested with all authority.

However, the British directed the Prime Minister of Kaithal and the other functionaries on March 23, 1843 A.D. to hand over the administration of the Kaithal state to them. The latter refused to comply with this order and began to make military preparations. The British organized a blockade of Kaithal and their forces took up positions all around the territory. On April 11, 1843 A.D., the people and the armed forces of Kaithal state attacked the British forces. Following this confrontation, the British sent re-inforcements which were also aided by the forces of Patiala, Nabha and Jind states. The British succeeded in annexing Kaithal and then resorted to inhuman repression on the local people.

Ajit Singh, the Sikh ruler of Ladwa in north Haryana, refused to accept British supremacy and joined hands with the forces of Patiala state during the First Anglo-Sikh War in 1845-46 A.D. to resist the British forces. He was chased and killed in the disturbances that had enveloped the whole region.

Haryana was seething with discontent when India's First War of Independence (the so-called Sepoy Mutiny) broke out in 1857 A.D. The first spark for the conflagration was provided by what has been called the greased cartridge story. A new rifle known as the Royal Enfield was introduced in the Indian Army in 1856 A.D. whose cartridge had a top that had to be removed by the mouth before it could be loaded in the rifle. This led to the circulation of a rumour that the cartridge was greased with the fat of cows and pigs—something that offended the religious susceptibilities of both Hindu and Muslim Sepoys. The soldiers revolted at various places in different parts of India and were soon joined by people from various walks of life, who had been nursing their grievances against the British rulers.

The soldiers of Barrackpore in Bengal refused to use the cartridges and were punished with dismissal and the disbandment of their regiment. Mangal Pandey, who fired at his Sergeant Major on March 20, 1857 A.D., was arrested and executed. Soldiers of the Third Cavalry Regiment located at Meerut, who refused to use the cartridges on April 24, 1857 A.D., were put into prison, besides being disgraced in public. A large number of soldiers of this regiment as well as those of the infantry rose in revolt at Meerut on May 10, 1857 A.D., killed many British officers, released Indian prisoners and then proceeded to Delhi which they captured on May 12, 1857 A.D.

The first cantonment in north west India affected by the uprising was Ambala. Between March 26 and May 1, 1857 A.D., fires broke out at 14 places in different parts of the cantonment, causing a great loss of government property and raising doubts about the complicity of an organized network in these acts of incendiaryism. Then, at about 9 a.m. On May 6, 1857 A.D., the Sixth N.I. rose in revolt at Ambala—about nine hours before the mutiny broke out at Meerut later the same evening. The Sepoys of Ambala seized the arms of the regiment and arrested the English officers. Further disturbances took place and in the districts of Haryana. The uprising spread to Delhi and then to several places of north India. However, the British promptly quelled the disturbances at Ambala.

By the end of May 1857 A.D., the whole of Haryana except Ambala was in the hands of the mutineers, who proclaimed their loyalty to the Mughal Emperor, Bahadur Shah. Administrative arrangements were worked out by the local leaders of Haryana and Emperor Bahadur Shah in the various districts and the territories of the native rulers who had freed themselves from British rule. The administrative system introduced in Rewari under the guidance of Rao Tula Ram came in for praise from Bahadur Shah and even from certain British officials. Communal harmony between the Hindus and the Muslims was seen at its best in the Haryana of those days as a result of the concerted efforts of the Emperor and the local leaders.[14]

Soon, however, the British authorities took the offensive and their armed force put down the rebellion in Haryana after resorting to brutal repression. The Haryana people fought bravely at various places, but were defeated. By November 1857 A.D., Haryana was back under British rule. The leaders of the movement were severely dealt with and some of them were hanged, their properties being confiscated. The people of Haryana expected the rulers of the princely states and the Jagirdars to stand by and lead them in their fight against the British. Some of the latter no doubt provided leadership to them, but simultaneously they remained in touch with the British in order not to antagonize them. Thus they played a double and deceitful game which the British saw through.

It was for this reason that the Nawabs of Farrukhnagar and Jhajjar and the Raja of Ballabhgarh were hanged by the British. Rao Tula Ram had, however, fought valiantly against the British and saved himself by fleeing to Iran and then to Afghanistan, where he eventually died after some years. The rulers of the neighbouring Sikh states, who had joined hands with the British in the crucial battle of Narnaul, were rewarded by the British. Narnaul was gifted to the maharaja of Patiala and renamed after him as Mahendragarh. Ballabhgarh, Bawal and Dadri were given to the Faridkot, Nabha and Jind states respectively. New Jagirs were created at Farrukhnagar and Pataudi.

Many eminent historians have come out with retrospective analyses of the character of the 1857 uprising. Confining myself primarily to Haryana, I agree with the view of Dr. K.C. Yadav[15] that the first organized revolt took place at Ambala rather than at Meerut, as is generally said. Though incidents of a rebellious nature occurred earlier at several places in north India before the 1857 uprising, it was the Sepoys of Ambala, who raised the banner of revolt in an organized manner at 9 a.m. On May 10, 1857 A.D.—nine hours before their brethren did so at Meerut. Dr. R.C. Mazumdar, the well-known historian, to whose notice this fact was brought by Dr. K.C. Yadav, wrote to the latter: "That there was an open revolt of the Sepoys there (Ambala) on the morning of the 10th May (1857) before the outbreak at Meerut is, I confess, a news to me and probably to many others. I congratulate you on bringing this point to public notice." [16]

There is no doubt that the uprising of 1857 A.D. was the consequence of a pre-meditated conspiracy to rise in revolt on May 10 among the Sepoys, if not everywhere, at least at three places Delhi, Meerut and Ambala. This view of Dr. K.C. Yadav differs from that of Dr. S.N. Sen, who had questioned the existence of a prior conspiracy.

The next question to which Dr. K.C. Yadav addresses himself is whether the Sepoys of Haryana, like their counterparts in Meerut and elsewhere, had any prior understanding with the civil populace. He does not think so and draws the conclusion that 'the uprising by the civil populace was spontaneous, spurred on by widespread indignation, quite independent of sepoy influence." [17]

In Dr. K.C. Yadav's view, the uprising in Haryana was widespread, covering the whole region except some small pockets and its leaders drawn from amongst small traders and peasants enjoyed the support of the general masses. He does not find anything on record to substantiate the generalization of Sir Jadu Nath Sarkar, as far as the Haryana leaders were concerned, that 'dispossessed dynasts' had made the 'simple folk their cat's paw in a gamble for recovering their thrones.' [18]

Dr. K.C. Yadav also thinks that Dr. R.C. Mazumdar's generalization that the leaders of the movement were representatives of the 'obsolete aristocracy and centrifugal feudalism of the medieval age' does not hold good in the case of Haryana, where a little over 36% of the leaders belonged to the lower strata. He does not agree, in so far as Haryana is concerned, with the finding of Dr. S.N. Sen that the leaders of the revolt were counter-revolutionaries, 'who would have set the clock back'. Dr. Yadav is of the view that the goal of the Haryana revolt was to root out foreign domination and oppression. He agrees with Prof. Hiren Mukherjee that if the rebellion had not been crushed, 'new ideas and new strength more appropriate to the changing times" would have been generated among the people.[19]

Dr. K.C. Yadav is of the view that the concerted action of the people of Haryana during the uprising gave it the character of "a national effort for independence."

The British authorities punished Haryana not only by transferring parts of its territory to some friendly princely states but also by dismantling the Delhi Territory that included Haryana. In place of the Delhi Territory, they created two divisions—the Delhi or Eastern Division comprising Delhi, Gurgaon and Panipat districts and the Hissar or Western Division with Hissar, Rohtak, and Sirsa districts. All these districts were additionally detached from the North West Province (corresponding to present-day Uttar Pradesh) and added to the territory of Punjab. Steps were also taken to change the administrative pattern in these districts to make them conform to the system in vogue in Punjab. Simultaneously, the administration of the whole country including that of Haryana was transferred from the East India Company to the British Crown.

The foregoing account is an humble attempt at depicting the saga of the Haryana people's heroic resistance to foreign invaders coming across the western borders of the Indian sub-continent as well as of their uprisings against the Muslim and British rulers in different phases of our history. Certain views expressed in a recent publication (The Indus Saga) by the noted author Aitaz Ahsan have a direct bearing on this very issue. The main plank of his thesis is that the Indus Valley was the precursor of and is identical with the post-1947 Pakistani nation as distinct from the Indian nation and that "1947 was only a re-assertion of that reality" (*Ibid*, p. 11).

I do not need to comment on this aspect of Aitaz Ahsan's thesis as it is not directly relevant to the Haryana people's resistance to foreign invaders upon which I have dilated at length in this chapter. I would, however, mention in passing the issue of whether the socio-cultural and spiritual ethos of present-day Pakistan has anything in common with that of the Mohenjodaro-Harappan and Aryan civilizations that once prevailed in the Indus Valley. or is the ethos of today's Pakistan—predominantly or almost wholly loaded in favour of the civilizations of Central Asia and of India after the advent of Islam?

Another view expressed by Aitaz Ahsan that runs directly counter to the theme of this chapter is that "the entire resistance that successive Central Asian expeditionaries met with was confined to the Indus region" and further that "once Panipat was reached, an entire empire lay at the feet of the conqueror." I beg to differ sharply from this assessment. What about the stubborn resistance the invaders faced at Panipat in the course of all the three battles fought there? in the second battle of Panipat (1556 A.D.), Hemu, the hero of Haryana, was at the point of defeating the Mughal army when most unexpectedly an arrow hit him in the eye as a result of which he fell unconscious and the Mughals walked away with victory.

As regards the 1857 uprising against the British, while the Sepoys and the people at large fought bravely against the alien rulers in different parts of India and particularly in Haryana, the response in the Indus region was by and large lukewarm, though at some places the Sepoys did mutiny. Aitaz Ahsan himself says that the Sepoys in the Indus region remained generally indifferent (*Ibid*, p. 2).

Several forces that were at work in Haryana during British rule helped to bring about a sense of national awakening as in the rest of the country. The Arya Samaj movement led by Swami Dayanand Saraswati prepared the ground in Punjab and Haryana for moral and social regeneration. The Indian National Congress that led the movement for national independence had several leaders in Haryana prominent among whom were Lala Lajpat Rai and Pandit Shri Ram Sharma. Sir Chhotu Ram was the tallest of the Haryana leaders, whose Unionist Party based on a programme of agrarian reforms galvanized the masses in Haryana and Punjab.

After India was partitioned in 1947 A.D., Haryana formed part of East Punjab, which was later renamed as Punjab. It was on November 1, 1966 that Haryana came into being as a state of the Indian Union after being separated from Punjab.

No look-see at Haryana's past would be complete without taking due note of its rich spiritual and cultural heritage that dates back to pre-historic times before the advent of the Dravidian and Aryan civilizations. The Siswals belonging to the agricultural community, who lived in Haryana thousands of years ago, must have had some kind of a religion about which, however, nothing much is known. We have some information about the gods and goddesses of the Dravidians and a clear picture of the Vedic religion of the Aryans, who settled down in Haryana. The famous sages of ancient India such as

Jamadagni, Uddalak, Pippalad, Chyavan, Durbasa, Kapil and Vyas had their hermitages in Haryana at places that are now in the districts of Hisar, Mahendragarh, Rohtak, Jind and Kurukshetra respectively. It was here that Vedic culture flourished, that the Mahabharata and the Puranas were composed and the eternal message of the Gita was preached. It was at Pehowa in Haryana that Manu wrote the Manusmriti.

When Hindu religion lost the simplicity of Vedic times as a result of the intrusion of orthodox rituals and the onset of casteism, Jainism and Buddhism made their appearance and in due course spread to Haryana. Unlike at some other places, Jainism came to Haryana later than Buddhism. Lord Buddha visited several places in Haryana and converted some people to Buddhism. Among the places he visited was Kommasadhamma where he delivered several discourses or 'Suttas'. Kammasadhamma has been identified with several places such as Kamaspur (in the Meerut district of Uttar Pradesh), Kaithal, Kamodha and Pehowa (all in Haryana). The most generally accepted view is that Kammasadhamma is identical with Kaithal. Lord Buddha also visited Thullakothita (now identified with Thanesar in Haryana), whose king embraced Buddhism.

It has also been suggested that[20] Lord Buddha had visited a city in the Kuru country where he accepted alms on the banks of the Anolatta lake. This city was probably Kurukshetra. The other places visited by Lord Buddha in Haryana were Agroha [21] and Sughna.[22] Several disciples of Lord Buddha such as Ratnapal, Nandutara and Mittakoli came to Haryana and helped in spreading Buddhism extensively. Buddhism received a boost in Haryana during the reign of Emperor Ashoka when several places including Hisar, Karnal, Topra, Thanesar etc. became important centers of this religion. Ashoka passed through Haryana early in his life at the head of a big army to pacify the rebellious people of Taxila.[23]

The discovery in Haryana of several statues of Buddha, Stupas and stone pillars known as Dharmastambhas testifies to the fact that Buddhism had flourished here in ancient times. It thrived in Haryana during Maurya, Indo-Greek, Saka and Kushana rule. The Pushpabhutis including Rajyavardhana and Harshavardhana also helped the spread of Buddhism in Haryana, but later this region came under the influence of the Brahmanical religion of the Yaudheyas. Hieuen Tsang, the Chinese traveller, who visited Haryana during Harsha's rule, drew attention in his account to the influence of Buddhism there.

Jainism which came to Haryana after Buddhism, was propagated by Bhiksu Lohacharya at Agroha and by Dharma Yaksha at Rohtak. Jainism did not command as much influence in Haryana as Buddhism. However, after the 6th and 7th centuries A.D., when Buddhism suffered some loss of influence, Jainism began to make quite some impact at places such as Hansi, Rohtak, Sirsa etc. Many Jaina images of the medieval period have been discovered at some places in Rohtak, Sonepat, Hisar and Sirsa districts. Unlike Buddhism, Jainism remained alive in Haryana and even now Jains are to be found at some places of this state.

In the post-Vedic era, Shaivism became popular in various parts of Haryana. Karttikeya, son of Lord Shiva, also had his devotees in the 3rd century B.C., particularly among the Yaudheyas, who had thrown out the Kushanas. Rohtak was the main center of Karttikeya worship till the 10th century A.D. Ganapati or Ganesha, the other son of Lord Shiva was also worshipped in various parts of Haryana. Worship of the mother goddess or Devi in several forms was also in vogue in Haryana in ancient times. Vaishnavism spread in Haryana after the first century A.D. Worship of the sun became popular here in the 6th and 7th centuries A.D.

Haryana has an ancient linguistic heritage. The Siswals of Haryana perhaps spoke some language akin to Andamanese. Some time later, this gave way to the language of the people of Sind, perhaps coinciding with the advent of the Indus Valley Civilisation. During the Rigvedic period, the Chhandas language was spoken here, which, despite its being a difficult language, was quite popular. After the Rigvedic period, this language was radically simplified. This new version of Chhandas came to be known as Oudichya, which was some kind of a folk language. By about 500 B.C., Panini, the renowned grammarian, reformed this language by bringing it within the framework of the rules of grammar. This reformed language was known as Sanskrit whose literature in due course became vast in volume and rich in quality.

Gradually, the ordinary people introduced many changes in this refined Sanskrit language. This simplified version of Sanskrit was known as Prakrit. In course of time, Prakrit—evolved into its two forms—the Abhiri Apabhransha and the Sauraseni Apabhransha. The Abhiri Apabhransha gave rise to some dialects such as Rajasthani or Ahirwati, Bagri and Mewati (which are known as western Hindi). From Sauraseni Apabhramsha sprang the sub-languages of Bagru,

Kaurvi and Braj (which are known as eastern Hindi). Sanskrit suffered some decline later on, but came into its own again during the Gupta age with the composition in it of many works including several Puranas.

After the advent of the Muslims in India, three other languages namely Arabic, Persian and Urdu came to be spoken in Haryana in the medieval period. In the latter half of the 18th century A. D., the Punjabi language came into vogue in Haryana. In the medieval period, there were many well-known writers in Arabic and Persian languages in Haryana, the most famous among them being Syed Alauddin Panipati of Panipat (a contemporary of Alauddin Khalji), Shah Jalaluddin Hanswi and Sheikh Qutbuddin of Hansi and Ahmed Thanesari of Thanesar. During the Mughal period, there was a well-known scholar and poet by name Sheikh Abus Qadis at Thanesar. Haji Sultan of Thanesar, who was in touch with Emperor Akbar, was a scholar of Sanskrit, besides Arabic and Persian. As suggested by Akbar, he translated the Mahabharata into Persian. His contemporaries, Sheikh Panipat and Sheikh Abdul of Thanesar, were great scholars.

In the latter part of the medieval age, great strides were made in Urdu literature in Haryana, which, in fact, is regarded as the place where this language was born. The most important figure in this field in Haryana was Muhammad Afzal (1539-1626 A.D.) of Panipat. The other important names in Haryana were Sheikh Jeevan of Jhajjar, poet Mir Atal and Syed Abdul Jalil 'Atal'.

During the medieval period, Haryana produced many scholars of Sanskrit, Prakrit and Apabhramsha. Among them were Thakur Ramchandra of Rohtak and Srigupta of Narnaul. The scholars of Apabhramsha were Pushpadant of Rohtak (10th century A.D.) and poet Sridhar (12th century A.D.). Thakur Pheru of Haryana, who was a contemporary of Alauddin Khalji, was a scholar of Sanskrit, Prakrit and Apabhramsha, besides Arabic and Persian and had authored many books. A well-known Apabhramsha scholar of Haryana was Buchraj (15th century A.D.), whose language was regarded as being an old version of Haryanvi. In the 16th century A.D., poet Vallaha of Haryana also wrote in that language. Jinballabh Suri of Hansi was another Apabhramsha scholar of that period. In the 17th century A.D., the Apabhramsha language gradually receded into the background, its place being increasingly taken by Sanskrit. Many works in Sanskrit began to be brought out in Haryana.

Great advances were made in the field of Hindi literature in Haryana in the medieval period. Chowranginath (13th century A.D.) of Rohtak and Matsyanath (both saints of the Nath Sampradaya),

Ishadas (14th century A.D.), Surdas (15th century A.D.) of Sihi in Haryana, Veershan (16th century A.D.) of Narnaul, Maldev of the Satnami sect, Sundardas (17th century A.D.) of Karnal, Hridayram, Ramdas of Agroha and Rupchand of Kurukshetra are some of the names that deserve mention. Garibdas (1697-1778 A.D.) of Rohtak and Sant Nityanand of Narnaul made important contributions to Hindi literature in Haryana in the 18th century A.D. Some Jain poets such as Ramchandra and Atmaram of Ambala as well as Tulsi of Panipat, Fatehchand of Kalanaur, Gopal Singh of Thanesar, Santokh Singh (1788-1819 A.D.), Vijayanand Suri (1837-1897 A.D.) of Ambala, Ghulam Qadir Jilani (1749-1819 A.D.), a Sufi poet of Rohtak, poet Sadulla of Mewat (author of some famous books on the Mahabharat and the Ramayana), Umadas (19th century A.D.) of Thanesar, Jayram of Kurukshetra, Tau Sangi of early 19th century A.D. and Hiradas deserve mention.

In the medieval age, some literary works in the Haryanvi language were also composed.

In the 19th and 20th centuries A.D., notable advances in Sanskrit, Hindi and Urdu literature came to notice in Haryana. The Arya Samaj and the Sanatan Dharma Sabha helped in promoting the study of Sanskrit. The Sanskrit works of Sant Nischal Das (1791-1863 A.D.) of Hisar, Chhajuram Shastri and Madhavacharya Shastri attracted notice in view of their literary excellence.

The towering proper nouns of Haryana in the field of Urdu literature in the 19th and 20th centuries A.D. were Mir Mahadi Majruh (1833-1902 A.D.) of Panipat, who was a disciple of Mirza Ghalib, Altaf Hussain Hali (1837-1914 A.D.), Khwaja Jafar Hussain Ansari (1837-1915 A.D.), Wahiuddin Salim (1867-1928 A.D.), Bishwambardas Garma Panipati, the composer of Ghazals, Shugan Chand Roshan (1896-1958 A.D.) of Panipat and Anupchand Aftab Panipati (1897-1968 A.D.). In Hindi literature, important contributions were made in the 20th century A.D. by Babu Balmukund Gupta and Madhav Prasad Misra of Haryana.

Haryana has a rich and ancient cultural heritage in such diverse spheres as architecture, sculpture, painting, music and dance. In the medieval period, fine arts suffered a set-back in Haryana as a result of the unsettled conditions that prevailed. However, in the field of music, Haryana produced two great maestros—Surdas of Sihi and Kalla Khan of Rewari, the famous Khayal singer of the post-Mughal period. Haryana's folk music and dances continue to captivate audiences everywhere even today. Many famous Ragas of Hindustani classical music had their origin in the folk tunes of Haryana.

Notes

1. *Ibid*, pp. 32-33.
2. *Ibid*, p. 40.
3. Cited by Dr. K.C. Yadav at page 289 of his book mentioned at 8 above.
4. *Ibid*, pp. 292-293.
5. *Ibid*, p. 344.
6. *Ibid*, p. 346.
7. *Ibid*, p. 349.
8. *Ibid*, p. 364.
9. *Ibid*, p. 366.
10. *Ibid*, p. 379.
11. *Ibid*, Volume ii, pp. 83-100.
12. *Ibid*, p. 95.
13. *Ibid*.
14. The Revolt of 1857 in Haryana by Dr. K.C. Yadav, pp. 83-87.
15. For the views expressed by Dr. K.C. Yadav on the i857 uprising in Haryana, to which references have been made in this and the next few paragraphs, the reader may see pages 129-138 of his book mentioned at 50 above.
16. *Ibid*, p. 137.
17. *Ibid*, p. 131.
18. *Ibid*, p. 133.
19. *Ibid*, p. 134.
20. Journal of Haryana Studies Vols.XXVII-XXVIII, 1995-96, article by Devendra Handa, p. 2.
21. *Ibid*, p. 4.
22. *Ibid*, p. 6.
23. *Ibid*, Vol. XVI, Nos. 1&2, 1984, article by Mrs. Kamla Nehra, p. 18.

4

Getting into My Stride

We started adjusting ourselves to our new life-style at Raj Bhawan as fast as we could. Apart from attending to official business at my office in the Raj Bhawan, I began to receive visitors cutting across the social, political and official spectrum, who wanted to pay courtesy calls on me and my wife, Anita. Several officers of the Governments of Haryana and Punjab as well as of the Chandigarh Administration called on us along with their wives. Many defence services officers followed suit. Senior police officers and their wives took a special interest in building social rapport with us.

Among the callers whom I particularly recall were Lt. Gen. V.K. Nayyar, GOC-In-Chief, Western Command, and his wife. They made a special request to us to attend a cocktail party at their official residence on February 27, 1988 to mark the silver jubilee of their wedding. How very gracious of them to have asked for our company on such a happy occasion! the pleasure of attending this party was entirely ours. Lt. Gen. Nayyar, who had a distinguished career in the Indian Army, became the Governor of Manipur in the early 1990's.

Among several eminent persons with whom we developed close social relations were B.K.Nehru, the distinguished civilian and ex-Governor, and his wife, who used to spend the greater part of the year at their resort in Kasauli, not very far from Chandigarh. They dropped in sometimes at our Raj Bhawan on their way to Delhi from Kasauli or on their return journey to Kasauli. They put up at Raj Bhawan overnight as our guests on some occasions. It was a pleasure to have had the opportunity of knowing them so closely.

An interesting person whom we got to know in Chandigarh and who adorned the city's social landscape was P.L. Verma, retired Chief Architect of the Punjab Government. He had worked with Le Corbousier, the famous French architect, who had designed and built the beautiful city of Chandigarh. Verma, an old man when I came to know him, used to tell me many anecdotes about how the city was built and about the many personages, who had lent a hand in bringing the city into existence. He had a spiritual bent of mind and was a sincere devotee of Ma Anandamoyee. He had deep knowledge about the Geeta and took great interest in all matters pertaining to Kurukshetra and the many pilgrimages in the region.

I recall with great pleasure our association in Chandigarh with R. K. Saboo, an industrialist, and his wife. Saboo was related to the Birla family and hailed from Kolkata, where he had studied in the St. Xaviers College. He and his wife took great interest in a wide range of social activities, particularly in those of the Rotary Club. It was a matter of pride for our country that in the early 1990's, Saboo was elected as the President of the Rotary International. In that capacity, he had to shift to the U.S.A. for a year and to move about all over the globe to discharge his responsibilities in different countries.

Within a few days of our arrival at Chandigarh, we called on S.S. Ray, the Governor of Punjab, and his wife, Maya Ray, who was once upon a time a Member of the Rajya Sabha. We also met there Maya Ray's mother, Smt. Asharani Bhattacharya, an affectionate lady to whom we took immediately. She had settled down in London many decades ago and had come down to Chandigarh to be with her daughter and son-in-law. She and her husband used to work in close liaison with Krishna Menon and the India League in London in the pre-independence era. Before this, I used to meet S.S. Ray officially at meetings in Delhi after he had taken over in 1986 as the Governor of Punjab–a State that needed the special attention of the Centre in view of the rise of terrorism and attendant security-related problems. From now on, our relationship acquired a new social connotation. The fact that we both belonged to Vikrampur of Dhaka district in pre-partition East Bengal (now Bangladesh) was an additional factor that helped to cement our social ties. We both felt proud that the two of us, hailing from the same area of a district in Bangladesh, were now the Governors of two neighbouring States of north India, living in our respective Raj Bhawans in Chandigarh that touched each other at two strategic corners, though the vast expanses of these Bhawans stood in the way of our being within hailing distance!

The Haryana Raj Bhawan located on several acres of land had extensive lawns and gardens with flowers of various kinds in full bloom in the different seasons. Vegetables as well as paddy, wheat, pulses etc. grew in abundance on the premises. There was a fish pond that provided enough fish for our daily consumption. There were orchards whose fruits of different varieties including apples and delicious mangoes in the right seasons more than sufficed for our daily requirement. The frolicking deer and peacocks that swaggeringly pranced about with their distended tail-feathers on the lawns of Raj Bhawan lent colour to the landscape.

Our Raj Bhawan was flanked on one side by the famous Sukhna Lake, which offered facilities for water sports including boating, sailing, ski-ing etc. And had served as one of the centres of water sports for the Asian Games, 1982. On another side, our Raj Bhawan adjoined the Chandigarh Golf Course that spread over several square miles of greenery.

During our drives along the roads of Chandigarh, what impressed us was the meticulous planning of the various sectors and the unique architecture of the houses. Whenever we passed by the Rose Garden, we saw streams of visitors. From Raj Bhawan, we had a clear view of the not-so-distant Shivalik Hills. At night, we saw the twinkling lights of Kasauli that ever seened to beckon us.

In the first week of March, 1988, I paid a visit to Delhi and called on President R.Venkataraman, Vice-President Dr. Shanker Dayal Sharma and Prime Minister Rajiv Gandhi. I also transacted some official business that required my presence in Delhi. I was surprised when one of the dignitaries I met asked me with a mischievous twinkle in his eyes what kind of plan had been given to me by the Prime Minister to get rid of Devi Lal's government. I told him point-blank that the Prime Minister had given me no such task and further that there was no reason for him to think like that as long as I was the Governor of Haryana. I knew that this worthy was not well disposed towards Rajiv Gandhi. He must have thought that, having served as the Director of the Intelligence Bureau, I must have been considered pliable enough to be sent to Haryana as Governor with a pre-conceived plan of overthrowing Devi Lal's government. It was obvious to me that this dignitary did not know me well.

Within a few days of our arrival at Chandigarh, we paid a visit to Chandi Mandir after which the city was named. Soon thereafter, we worshipped at the Mansa Devi temple in the Bilaspur village of Panchkula Tehsil which was located close to Manimajra near Chandigarh. It is a 'Shakti Peeth' where the anterior part of Sati's head had fallen after her body was splintered into pieces by Lord Vishnu in the wake of the big sacrifice that her father, Daksha, had organized. It is generally believed that a person who worships here for 40 days at a stretch is rewarded with the fulfillment of all his wishes.

The temple is said to have been originally located in the Nahan State (now in Himachal Pradesh). A stream which flowed by the temple and provided water to it was obstructed by some people, which deprived it of its water supply. Goddess Mansa is said to have appeared in a dream before the ruler of Manimajra and asked him to build another temple in his territory, which he did in 1815 A.D. References to this temple are found in the Shiva Purana. There two other temples of the goddess here which were built by the Maharaja of Patiala.

According to another account, the Mansa temple got its name from Mahant Mansa Nath, who lived in the Bilaspur village during the time of Emperor Akbar. It is said that the Mughal authorities imposed a tax of a rupee on each visitor to this temple. Mahant Mansa Nath, who incurred the displeasure of the authorities for opposing this tax, was stopped from entering the temple. He, therefore, shifted to a place a little distance away from where the temple is now located and began to worship the goddess there. Later, Akbar withdrew this tax in response to the plea made by the people when he visited Kurukshetra in 1567 A.D. on the occasion of a solar eclipse.

Once we went to the famous Pinjore Gardens near Kalka that was not very far from Chandigarh. Located at the confluence of Kaushalya and Jhajjar rivers. Pinjore is an ancient and holy place as is evident from various archaeological finds such as the remnants of old Hindu temples and idols of Hindu gods and goddesses. It used to form part of the territory of King Birat, a prominent figure of the Mahabharata. During their exile, the Pandavas are believed to have visited this place before proceeding towards the Himalayas. They are said to have spent a full year in Birat's kingdom in disguise along with Draupadi. Because of its association with the five Pandavas, it came to be called Panchpur of which Pinjore is a corrupt version.

Pinjore finds mention in 'Al-Hind' of Alberuni and the "Tawakat Nasiri" of Minhaz Siraj. Iltutmish, the Delhi Sultan, was so impressed by the beauty of this place that he annexed it from the king of Sirmour and destroyed a temple that existed there. Sultan Nasir-ud-Din of Delhi and later Tamerlane plundered the riches of Pinjore. Mughal Emperor Akbar made several abortive bids to annex Pinjore from the Raja of Bhowana, who then held sway over this territory.

It was one Fidai Khan, an illegitimate son of Mughal Emperor Jehangir, who really laid the foundation of this city and put up a terraced garden on the pattern of the Shalimar Garden that Jehangir had created at Srinagar in Kashmir. Enclosed by a wall, the Pinjore Gardens have six terraces at successively lower levels with a stream running down the middle, whose waters cascade gradually from higher to lower level from each terrace. There are lush green lawns, colourful flower beds and fountains, besides the Sheesh Mahal, Rang Mahal and the gateway with a suite of rooms super-imposed on it from which we had a fascinating view of the whole landscape.

Fidai Khan fled from Pinjore in curious circumstances.[1] He had requested the Raja of Bhowana to send his harem over to the Pinjore Gardens for an interview with his wives. The Raja sent to him some of his maid servants, who had their throats swollen with goitre. Fidai Khan's wives felt alarmed thinking that the place bred such a ghastly disease. Fidai Khan left the place in a huff., when the Gardens passed on to the Raja of Bhowana and thence to the Raja of Sirmour. Later, the Maharaja of Patiala bought the place from the Raja of Sirmour for a paltry sum of sixty thousand rupees! Afterwards, it became a part of Punjab and then of the State of Haryana, which spent a lot of money to convert it into an attractive tourist spot and named it as Yadavindra Gardens after the ruler of Patiala.

Not far from Pinjore is Kalka, which I had occasion to pass through not only during my tenures as the Governor of Haryana and Himachal Pradesh, but several times earlier in the course of my trips to Simla from Delhi. I had the opportunity on a couple of occasions of paying obeisance at the well-known temple of Kalka Devi located here. It is a very ancient place and a 'Siddha Peeth', also known as 'Kali Peeth'. The story of how the powerful goddess Mahakali came into being is recounted in the Chandi. Parvati, the consort of Lord Shiva, created goddess Mahakali from the frown on her brow and asked her to kill Raktabeej, the demon, who had been oppressing the gods.

It is said that before the Mahabharata war, the Pandavas had come here and worshipped Adyashakti Kali, who gave them the boon of victory. They had come here again to worship the goddess after their victory in the war.

Centuries ago, Baba Balaknath of the Nath community had worshipped here and was vouchsafed a direct vision of the goddess. In compliance with Emperor Akbar's directive, the local head of the administration had repaired the temple here. Since then, the priest of this temple has always been a member of the Nath community. Ibn Batuta, the well-known Moroccan traveller, who had visited India in the 14th century A.D., had written about this temple in his account. Hazrat Nizamuddin Aulia had also expressed his appreciation of the spirit of devotion with which numerous pilgrims used to travel to this place to worship the goddess.

In early March 1988, I had the pleasure of receiving a visit from Sardar Gurdial Singh, retired Inspector-General of Police, Punjab, and his wife. A very senior officer of the Indian Police, he was a Joint Director of the Intelligence Bureau (in the rank of Inspector-General of Police) in the 1950's, when I had worked under him as a very junior officer. After retirement, he had settled down in Chandigarh. At my suggestion, Haryana Raj Bhawan had sent him an invitation to attend my swearing-in as Governor. I had noticed his absence at the ceremony.

When Sardar Gurdial Singh and his wife called on us at Raj Bhawan, he said that they were extremely sorry to have missed attending the ceremony because they were out of station Then we talked about our old days in the Intelligence Bureau. He also told me about his work as a police officer in pre-independence days at Hissar and Sirsa, which were then in Punjab and from which region Devi Lal, our Chief Minister, hailed. He narrated several anecdotes about how he had dealt with the freedom struggle in that area and, in particular, with Devi Lal, who had been sent to jail.

When our meeting was about to end, my A.D.C. came in and, significantly looked at me and my wife, which meant that, in accordance with the rules of protocol, we should leave the room whereafter Sardar Gurdial Singh and his wife could leave. I thought about the situation and told my A.D.C. that for once I would deviate from protocol in deference to my one-time boss, who was 21 years my senior in service. Then, my wife and I accompanied the honoured visitors to the porch and saw them off. Sardar Gurdial Singh understood the point and thanked us profusely before taking leave of us.

In the mean time, some of the Judges of the Punjab and Haryana High Court had been calling on us along with their spouses. This High Court, as the name implies, has jurisdiction over Punjab, Haryana and Chandigarh. The Governors of Punjab and Haryana performed certain constitutional responsibilities in respect of this High Court and its Judges. We had a role to play in the system then in vogue in regard to the appointment of High Court Judges. Even in such a small matter as the grant of leave to the Chief Justice, each of the two Governors had to accord his approval.

Within a month of my taking over, we hosted a dinner at Raj Bhawan for the Judges of the High Court and their wives. Punjab Governor S.S. Ray and his wife, Maya Ray also graced the occasion. We had many other opportunities later of interacting socially with the Judges. The Chief Justice, Ramaswamy, who later became a Judge of the Supreme Court, came to be known all over the country for reasons

I need not go into. M.M. Punchhi, then a Judge of our High Court became in due course the Chief Justice of India. Some other Judges of this High Court adorned high offices elsewhere including that of the Governor of Kerala.

In March 1988, I had occasion to proceed to Karnal to inaugurate the Haryana State Sports Festival and give the awards at the State Awards Function. Smt. Kamala Verma of the BJP, who was then the Minister for Health and Sports, addressed the gathering, besides welcoming me to the function. The youth of Haryana excelled in various sports and games and displayed great zeal and excitement on this occasion. After delivering my inaugural address, I distributed awards, some of the recipients being the famous Indian test cricketer, Chetan Sharma, wrestler Dharamvir and volleyball player Hanuman Singh.

Apart from reading some books on Karnal, I had also interacted with some knowledgeable persons, who had enlightened me about the historical and cultural background of the district. Karnal derived its name from Karna, an elder brother of the Pandavas, born to Kunti before her marriage and sired by the sun god. He was a rival to Arjuna and joined forces with Duryodhana in the Mahabharata war. Karnal was known in ancient times as Karnalaya or the home of Karna. What it meant was that during the Kauravas' battle with the Pandavas, Karna had made Karnal the centre from which he launched his operations. There is an ancient tank in Karnal, which is known as KarnaTal. Tradition has it that every morning, Karna used to bathe in this tank, worship the sun and then donate in charity gold equivalent in weight to one and a quarter maunds!

In Karnal, there are several old gateways and a fort that once encircled the town, but later fell into ruins. Ibrahim Hussain Mirza, one of the descendants of Timur, who had revolted against Emperor Akbar, had plundered this town in 1573 A.D. This district witnessed the flight of Prince Khusru through it in 1606 A.D. after revolting against his father, Jahangir, the Mughal Emperor. It suffered the ravages of the incursion by the Sikhs led by Banda Bahadur in 1709 A.D. It was here that Nadir Shah, the Persian invader, defeated Muhammad Shah, the Mughal Emperor, in 1739 A.D. And then proceeded to Delhi, where he indulged in large-scale plunder and loot. The ruler of Jind annexed Karnal in1763 A.D., but in 1787 A.D., it was taken over by the Marathas, who handed it over to their protégé—the Irish adventurer, George Thomas. In 1805 A. D., the British annexed it. A more recent fact that deserves mention is that Liaqat Ali, the first Prime Minister of Pakistan, used to live in Karnal in an old historic building known as Shamsad Manzil. Karnal has another distinction—it is here that Asia's biggest grain market is located.

Karnal was the home of many Pirs and Faqirs, famous among whom were Qalandar Sahab, Meera Sahab, Mastgir Baba and Baba Simran Das. Qalandar Sahab lived here in the thirteenth century A.D. It is said that he used to do his unrelenting penance, standing day and night in the waters of the Yamuna on whose bank Karnal was located. He remained unperturbed even as the lower parts of his body were being eaten up by creatures that lived in the water. At the end of his penance, he prayed to the Yamuna to make way for him to get out of the water. The Yamuna accepted his prayer and moved several miles away. This is the mythological explanation for the fact that the Yamuna, on whose bank Karnal was once located had shifted to the east in course of time.

There are several Mazhars of Qalandar Sahab in Karnal and other adjacent districts. The Mazhar near the Qalandar Gate of Karnal was built by Aurangzeb. Each year, 'Melas' are held at these Mazhars where people of all faiths come and pray for the fulfillment of their 'Mannat' (wishes). I understand that in 1999, many gold coins of Mughal Emperor Bahadur Shah (1719 A.D.—1748 A.D.)—each of considerable weight—were discovered accidentally near this Mazhar while someone was digging the earth for constructing a shop.

The Samadhi of Baba Simaran Das is located at Indri Khand in Karnal. It is known as the 'Kachchi' Samadhi (as opposed to a pucca Samadhi), because no brick, stone or mortar was used in its construction. It is said that whenever any attempt was made in the past to raise a pucca Samadhi there, it invariably collapsed, thus signalling the failure of man's attempt to thwart divine dispensation. It is also said that whenever such an attempt was made, a voice was heard to say that no 'Kankar-Patthar' (stone) was to be used there.

There is a famous Shiva temple in Karnal on a small plot of land with a height of 100 feet. It looks like a tower and has 134 spiral steps. It has seven floors on each of which there are idols of various deities of the Hindu pantheon.

Karnal's Chakravarti Lake named after Haryana's famous Governor—the late B.N.Chakravarti—located mid-way between Delhi and Simla provides an idyll of peace for tourists and holidayers. As we were driving from Chandigarh towards Karnal, we saw the road that led to a place called Amin at a distance of a little more than a mile from the Grand Trunk Road. Amin is known as Abhimanyu Khera (Kshetra) or the field of Abhimanyu, because it was here that

Abhimanyu, the warrior son of Arjuna was killed in the Mahabharata war by Jayadratha inside a Chakravyuha, a strategic deployment of the Kauravas' army planned by Dronacharya to trap the forces of the Pandavas.[2]

Proceeding further, we passed through Taraori, about 15 miles from Karnal. In 1191 A.D., Prithviraj Chauhan had defeated Muhammad Ghori at this very place. The next year, Ghori attacked again and defeated Prithviraj. I was told that place was called Azamabad after Aurangzeb's son, Prince Azam, who was born here. Old relics of a mosque, a tank, a wall, a Serai etc. built in Aurangzeb's time were still extant.

Notes

1. Haryana by D.C. Verma, p. 117.
2. The Encyclopaedic District Gazetteers of India edited by S.C. Bhatt, Northern Zone, Volume III, p. 145.

5

In the Holy Land of Kuru

On my way back from Karnal to Chandigarh on March 13, 1988, I made a brief stop-over at Kurukshetra, as I had planned in advance. I felt that it would not be in order for me to pass Kurukshetra by because, ever since my boyhood days, this place had been invested in my mind with a sanctity and significance all its own. It was the cradle of India's ancient culture and civilization and the symbol of the country's religion and spirituality. It was here that Lord Brahma had started the whole process of creation, the Mahabharata war was fought and Lord Krishna had delivered the eternal message of the Geeta.

Kurukshetra's religious importance is underlined by its description as 'Dharmakshetra' in the Geeta. Sanat Kumar, the son of Lord Brahma, dwelt here. The Shatapatha Brahman calls it the land of the gods.[1] It looks as if the Vedic sages used to be present in person while the gods performed sacrifices at Kurukshetra.[2]

The Aitreya Upanishad says that the gods used to reach heaven after performing sacrifices here.[3] The Mahabharata says that a person, who even touches a particle of Kurukshetra's dust, achieves liberation.[4] It has been said that every person should aspire to visit Kurukshetra because the mere sight of this place relieves one of all sins.[5] Even if a person merely expresses the wish to visit Kurukshetra and live there, he is said to be relieved of all sins.[6] A person, who visits Kurukshetra with due reverence, is believed to achieve the merits of Rajsuya and Ashwamedha sacrifices.[7]

The Vamana Purana and the Naradiya Purana have said that the planets, stars and other heavenly bodies might at some time fall from above (*i.e.* get destroyed), but a person who leaves his mortal coil at Kurukshetra never meets such a fate (*i.e.* he gets liberated from the cycle of birth and death).[8]

We have been told that the Naimish Tirth is the greatest on earth; Pushkar is the greatest in the intermediate zone between the heaven and the earth; Kurukshetra is the greatest in all the three worlds.[9] According to Matsya Purana, it is best to pay a visit to Kurukshetra, because it is the holiest of all pilgrimages.[10]

It is said that a stone slab with an inscription made by Maharaja Devnik in the 5th century about the religious significance of Kurukshetra has been discovered in far-off Laos.[11]

According to Vamana Purana, a person may be in a pure or an impure state, but if he recalls the name of Kurukshetra, he becomes purified, both physically and mentally.[12] the Vamana Purana mentions four requirements for securing liberation—knowledge of Brahman, 'Sradh' performed at Gaya, death in a cowshed and living at Kurukshetra. It also says that one who donates something at Kurukshetra gets the donation back multiplied thirteen times for the next thirteen days.[13]

According to our scriptures, the water of the Ganges liberates a person, but so far as Kurukshetra is concerned, not only its water but even its land and air liberate him.[14] It is further said that while people are required to observe fast and get their heads tonsured during visits to other pilgrimages, no such ritual is de rigueur at Kurukshetra.[15]

The Manusmriti has enjoined on humankind to emulate the rules of conduct followed by the Brahmins of Kurukshetra. It says that between the rivers Saraswati and Drishadwati, there is a God-made land named by the pundits as Brahmavarta (which is identical with Kurukshetra). The customs followed by the four 'Varnas' (*i.e.* castes) and others of that land, which have come down as part of the tradition are regarded as the rules of good conduct. Kurukshetra, Matsya, Kanyakubj and Mathura—these places constitute Brahmarsidesha. Brahmavarta (*i.e.* Kurukshetra) is said to be superior to the other three places of Brahmarsidesha. The people of the whole earth have been told to learn their rules of conduct from the Brahmins of all these places (of Brahmavarta and Brahmarsidesha).[16]

It was at Kurukshetra that the ancient sages sang the Vedas on the banks of the sacred Saraswati. Sages Vashistha and Vishwamitra lived, moved and had their being here. The Matsya Purana described it as the most sacred region of the Dwapara age and as one of the sixteen Mahajanapadas of Jambudvipa. There is a view that Lord Buddha had visited this place. The Astadhyayi of Panini mentions this place.

How could I then go straight to Chandigarh from Karnal without getting down at and paying my obeisance to Kurukshetra at the first opportunity that came my way? This time round, I made it a very brief introductory visit, but came back here on many subsequent occasions when I had work to do and more time at my disposal.

I had one more reason for paying such a hurried visit to Kurukshetra this time. It was to return, as soon as I could, a call that the Gandhian leader, Gulzari Lal Nanda had made on me in Chandigarh some days ago. I held Nandaji in high esteem because he was a perfect specimen of a Biblical commodity called the 'salt of the earth'. And the right kind of salt at that—salt that had not lost its savour. He was now the Chairman of the Kurukshetra Development Board which had been set up in 1970 to ensure the general development of the many pilgrimages in and around Kurukshetra. He used to operate from his austere residence-cum-office in Kurukshetra located on the bank of the ancient and auspicious tank known as Brahmsarovar.

One day Smt. Komal Anand I.A.S., Secretary to the Governor, who had been doubling as Secretary to the Kurukshetra Board, told me that Nandaji was in Chandigarh and wanted to call on me, to which I readily agreed. When he actually came calling, I was overwhelmed by the sheer simplicity and frankness of this great man, who, apart from holding important ministerial berths in the State and Central Governments including that of the Union Home Minister, had the unique distinction of having officiated twice as the stop-gap Prime Minister in 1964 and 1968 after the demise of Pandit Jawaharlal Nehru and Lal Bahadur Shastri respectively!

Nandaji was putting up at some guest house in Chandigarh when he met me. I made a request to him—to stay at Haryana Raj Bhawan as my guest, whenever he visited Chandigarh. He reacted by saying that it hardly made any difference to him, because, he said, his needs were simple and were easily met wherever he stayed. I told him that it would be an honour for us and our Raj Bhawan, if he stayed there. From then on, he used to put up at our Raj Bhawan as our honoured guest.

I had known Nandaji for a long time, though not personally, in the initial stages. It was in the summer of 1964, when Nandaji was the Home Minister of India, that I saw him for the first time, though from a distance. I was then an Assistant Director in the Intelligence Bureau, an attached office of the Union Home Ministry. I was based in New Delhi's South Block, where Nandaji's office was also located. As I saw him occasionally flitting into or out of South Block, dressed in immaculate 'Khadi', he exuded an aura of stark simplicity, the hall-mark of a true Gandhian that he was.

B. N. Mullik, the then Director of the Intelligence Bureau, had already served a record 14 years as the country's intelligence chief during Pandit Nehru's stewardship of the nation as Prime Minister. He was an upright officer of outstanding professional ability with the highest integrity and sense of patriotism. It came to be widely known in the Intelligence Bureau that Nandaji and Mullik had hit it off rather well because of the identity of their views on many administrative, socio-political and spiritual questions. Incidentally, I happened to be the son-in-law of Mullik. I had, therefore, the unique opportunity of observing the close interaction and rapport between Nandaji and Mullik, as they worked out their strategies to meet the challenge of the multifarious problems that stared the country in the face. One of their constant endeavors was to curb the canker of corruption that had been eating into the vitals of our nation.

I have digressed a little to bring out why I was so particular about showing all courtesies to Nandaji. Our convoy left Karnal and reached Pipli on the National Highway No.1, where we turned left towards Kurukshetra that was hardly 5 kilometeres away. As I looked out through the car window, I could see Kurukshetra every inch of whose ground, I recalled, was witness to the many events associated with our country's history and culture. I turned over in my mind the opening line of the Geeta, which describes Kurukshetra as 'Dharmakshetra', the land of piety, which I was now seeing with my own eyes, unlike Dhritarashtra who had to rest content with merely visualizing with his mental eye what the place looked like after he was given an account of how the contending forces of the Kauravas and Pandavas stood facing each other on Kurukshetra's battleground to fight out the great war adumbrated in the Mahabharata.

We arrived soon at the Guest House of the Kurukshetra University of which I was the new Chancellor and where I had to register my presence on my first formal visit to the place. There I was introduced to M.K. Miglani, an I.A.S. Officer then acting as the Vice-Chancellor, Dr. Sukhbir Singh, the erudite Collector of Kurukshetra district and several others. After visiting some faculies of the University and the Jawaharlal Nehru Library, I proceeded to the sacred Brahmsarovar in which complex Gulzari Lal Nanda lived and worked in his avatar as the Chairman of the Kurukshetra Development Board. As I alighted from the car, Nandaji embraced me and showed me round the place. Then we sat down for a long chat during which he told me about what work the Board had already done and further plans he had for the development of the numerous pilgrimages located not merely in Kurukshetra city, but in the whole region that was dotted with a large number of temples, holy tanks etc. He presented me with a set of books on Kurukshetra.

Then, along with my wife, I visited Brahmsarovar and drove around it to see the many temples and 'Dharamshalas'.Several scholars and priests, who accompanied us, enlightened us about the spiritual background and significance of Brahmsarovar. This tank was first got excavated by King Kuru before the Mahabharata war. It must have undergone many changes through the ages. It was now 3860 feet in length and 1860 feet in width. Two islands—one small and another big—in the middle of the tank and the bridges which connect them with the banks have enhanced the beauty of the place. The bigger island has some ruins of a castle, which the Mughal Emperor Aurangzeb had built in order to accommodate armed soldiers charged with the collection of taxes from pilgrims bathing in the tank or taking sacred water from it. The charges levied were a rupee for a pot of water and five rupees for a bath—quite exorbitant in those good old days. Those evading the payment of these charges were severely punished and some were even said to have been shot dead!

Lord Brahma is said to have raised a 'Vedi' (altar) for a sacrifice at this place which is known as Samanta Panchaka. That is why this place is called the Uttara Vedi of Brahma. There are four other 'Vedis' (altars) of Brahma—at Prayaga, Gayasiras, Pushkara and Viraja. Lord Brahma had set up a Shiva temple here. In ancient times, this tank was called Brahmasar, but later it came to be known as Ramahrida, as mentioned in the Vamana Purana.[17]

It is also called the lake of Parashurama. The Kshatriyas had killed Jamadagni, the father of Parashurama. In revenge, Parashurama killed so many Kshatriyas that five big pools were filled up with their blood. Then Parashurama did penance to propitiate his ancestors, who blessed him and converted these pools of blood into pools of holy water. It is said that whoever observes the vow of celibacy, bathes here and worships Parashurama becomes very wealthy.[18]

According to Vamana Purana, a person, who bathes in the Brahmsarovar—on Chaturdashi (14th day of the moon) or stays at this place and undertakes a fast on the Ashtami (eighth day) of the dark phase of the moon, attains Para-Brahma (or supreme divinity) and is liberated from the bondage of life and death.[19]

In ancient times, the Brahmsarovar was sometimes referred to as Vayusar, perhaps on account of the fact that the wind used to cause the waves on its water to rise and fall a good deal. It is said that the famous dialogue between Pururavas, King of Haryana and his nymph-spouse Urvashi had taken place here on the bank of Brahmsarovar.[20]

Leaving Brahmsarovar behind, we went to the Sannihit tank in Kurukshetra, which was much smaller than the former. It had a length of 1500 feet and a width of 550 feet.[22] It was much bigger in ancient times, as according to the Vamana Purana, it extended over half a 'Yojana' or about four miles.[23] the same Purana says that the Sannihit Sarovar extended from Vishweshwar to Hastipur in one direction and in another from Vriddha Kanya to Odhvati river.[24] It appears that the Brahmsarovar and the Sannihit Sarovar might have formed one continuous lake in days of yore and might have got separated at a later date.

According to Vamana Purana, the Sannihit tank was the place from which Lord Brahma came into being and then created the whole universe.[25] the Vana Parva of the Mahabharata says that one, who touches the water of the Sannihit tank during a solar eclipse, achieves the virtues of a hundred Ashwamedha sacrifices.[26] the Skanda Purana says that the Pandavas had come here during their exile and set up a Shiva temple on the southern bank of the Sannihit tank.[27]

The spiritual significance of the Sannihit tank derives from the belief that three important gods of the Hindu pantheon—Brahma, Vishnu and Shiva—reside here.

When the Gopis of Vrajabhumi expressed their desire to meet Lord Krishna, who was at Dwarka, the latter sent word to them to meet him at Kurukshetra on the day of solar eclipse. It was on the bank of the Sannihit tank that he met them on arrival from Dwarka. It is said that child Krishna's Mundan (tonsure) was performed here. His mother, Yashoda, brought Krishna to the famous Bhadrakali temple of Kurukshetra for this purpose and then got the water from river Saraswati brought to the Sannihit tank for bathing baby Krishna. At that time, the Bhadrakali temple was located on the bank of the Sannihit tank.

The Puranas say that when King Nala got lost in the dense forest, his wife Damayanti reached the Sannihit tank in the course of her long travels to trace him. She discovered Nala hiding in the Sannihit tank. What a romantic finale to the sacred and eternal love story of Hindu mythology!

It was on the bank of the Sannihit tank that sage Dadhichi sacrificed his life in furtherance of Lord Indra's cause. Dadhichi had his Ashrama here. Each morning, he came to the Sannihit tank to worship Lord Shiva at the temple of Dukhbhanjeswar Mahadev that was located here. At this time, the gods who had been driven away from heaven by Vritra, an Asura, came to learn that the only weapon that could give them victory over the Asura was one that would have to be made out of a particular bone of Dadhichi.

One day, Lord Indra appeared before Dadhichi in the guise of a Brahmin and begged of him to donate that particular bone of his, to which he readily agreed. But Dadhichi laid down a condition that before making this gift, he would like to bathe in the tanks that existed at all the pilgrimages. Upon this, Indra told him that whichever god, goddess or pilgrimage Dadhichi would contemplate would become manifest at that very place on the bank of the Sannihit tank. Since his wish was fulfilled, Dadhichi ended his life through the process of Yoga after which Indra acquired his bone. It was with the weapon made of Dadhichi's bone that the gods defeated Vritra, the Asura.

The Sannihit was one of the five pools at Kurukshetra that had been filled up with blood of the Kshatriyas, who had been killed by Parashurama. It is said that at the end of the Mahabharata war, Yudhisthira, on the advice of Lord Krishna and he sage, offered 'Tarpan' and 'Pinda' as part of the 'Sradh' ceremony performed at the Sannihit tank for his near and dear ones. Many pilgrims visit this place throughout the year to perform 'Sradh' for their ancestors.

I was told about an ancient tank known as Kula Prachin, where Mother Ganges is believed to have taken her bath in order to get purified of all the sins which people committed and with which they defiled the Ganges by bathing inher water. Some people believe that this fact is an indication of the greater sanctity of Kula Prachin and Kurukshetra as compared to pilgrimages like Hardwar, Prayag etc. located on the Ganges. However, I do not know if it is appropriate to make such comparisons.

As the Mahabharata says, gods including Brahma and the sages assemble every month at Sannihit. All the pilgrimages, rivers, lakes, tanks, springs, wells etc. that exist on earth and above converge at this place on the day of each full moon. It is because of this convergence that this is place is called Sannihit'. One who bathes here and drinks its water goes to heaven.[28]

We then visited the Sri Krishna Mueum, where we saw the many archaeological discoveries, sculptures based on the Krishna theme, some fine specimens of miniature painting and manuscripts, besides the tableaux depicting Lord Krishna's exploits. Smt. Komal Anand, Secretary to the Governor of Haryana, and Shri V.N. Shah, Chief Architect, Government of Haryana, along with some others had worked hard to make a success of this project.

It was almost evening when we left Kurukshetra for Chandigarh. After some time, we passed through Shahabad, about 20 kilometres from Kurukshetra and a little before National Highway No.1 crosses the bridge over the Markanda river. At Kurukshetra, I had been briefed about the religious significance of Shahabad by some knowledgeable persons. Shahbad is famous for its Markandeshwar temple about which the Puranas have a lot to say. This temple has been named after Markandeya, son of a sage, Mrikandu. The Mrikandu couple, which had initially no issue, undertook penance for long years, praying for a son. Pleased with their penance, Lord Shanker granted them the boon of a son, but with the stipulation that the boy would have a short life of only 16 years.

The son, Markandeya by name, aware that he had but a few years to live, spent most of his time in worshipping the gods, including Lord Shanker on the completion of 16 years of his age, King Yama, the Lord of death, arrived before him on dot in order to take him away. Terrified by the fearful image of Yama, the boy caught hold of the Shiva Linga before him in a tight grip and let out a loud cry of prayer to Lord Shiva. Trident in hand, Lord Shiva appeared on the scene and warned Yama to let go of his devotee Markandeya, who, Shiva ordained on the spot, would live for ever.

After granting this boon to Markandeya, Lord Shiva vanished. Ever since, the Shia Linga there has been known as Markandeshwar. A new temple of Markandeshwar was built there in 1979. I learnt that discourses on Ramayana had been going on there uninterruptedly for several years.

After I returned to Chandigarh, I managed to get hold of a lot of literature on Kurukshetra and devoted considerable time to a systematic study of this subject. I was able to supplement this study with several visits in course of time to many places in the Kurukshetra region as well as with discussions with scholars and academicians whose knowledge of the subject was encyclopaedic.

Kurukshetra derived its name from the Kuru tribe that inhabited this region. The name of the Kuru tribe as such does not find mention in the Rig Veda, but persons by name Kurushravana and Kaurayana figure in it.[29] the tribe of Kurus appears in the Atharva Veda and in the Brahmanas as people, who not only imparted their name to the place but also converted it into a center of Aryan and Vedic culture. The Atharva Veda speaks of a person Kauravya.[30] The Mahabharata and the Puranas mention the name Kurukshetra for the first time.[31]

Some historians have traced the name of the Kuru tribe to a river called Kuru flowing between the territories of present-day Iran and Azarbaizan to the south of Baku and falling into the Caspian Sea. I do not know how valid this hypothesis is.

The boundaries of Kurukshetra have been described in several ways in ancient Sanskrit literature. According to the Traittrriya Aranyaka, to the south of Kurukshetra was Khandav, to its north Turghna, to its west Parinaha and Moru.[32] Khandav refers to present-day Delhi. Turghna is generally believed to refer to a place called Sugh in the Yamunanagar district of Haryana. Parinaha has not been identified, but Moru is a place that is still to be found to the west of Kurukshetra.

Kurukshetra was located between two rivers—Saraswati and Drishdwati—and living here was believed to be synonymous with living in paradise.[33] In a similar vein, the Narada Purana says that a person living at any place on the bank of the Saraswati achieves knowledge of 'Brahman'.[34]

The Vamana Purana says that the Sraswati took a turn towards the west after providing an ample quantity of water to Kurukshetra.[35]

According to the Puranas, Kurukshetra had an extensive area that formed a circuit of about 160 miles or 20 'Yojanas', which tallies with the Mahabharata's description of this place as 'Samantapanchaka' or five 'Yojanas' on each of the four sides *i.e.*, 20 'Yojanas' in all. Within this circuit of 160 miles, all the pilgrimages of the Kurukshetra region are to be found. In fact, in ancient times, Kurukshetra referred not to one place, but to the whole region.

King Kuru, son of Samvarana and Tapati, brought prosperity to Kurukshetra and imbued its people with the highest principles of spirituality and ethical values. These facts are brought out in myhological language by the Vamana Purana, according to which, King Kuru arrived there in a golden chariot and made out a ploughshare with its gold. He started ploughing the soil of Kurukshetra after taking on loan the bull, Nandi, from Lord Shiva and a buffalo from Yama. Indra, the King of the gods, appeared there and asked Kuru what he was doing. Kuru replied that, through a combination of manual labour and moral conduct, he was preparing the land of Kurukshetra to make it yield the eight virtues of Satya (truth), Tapas (religious austerity), Kshama (forgiveness), Daya (kindness), Shaucha (purity), Yoga (composure), Dana (charity) and Brahmacharya (continence). He explained that the judicious use of his body, hands and head would ensure material prosperity and spiritual progress. On being asked by Indra where he would get the seed of the manifold virtues outlined by him, King Kuru said that he was in possession of the seed. Indra went away laughing at the king.

King Kuru carried on with his cultivation for some time after which Lord Vishnu came to quiz him. Vishnu asked him the same questions and on being told that he had the seed with him, Vishnu asked him to give him the seed so that he could sow it for the king. Kuru thrust forward his right arm, which Vishnu, with the help of his Chakra, cut into a thousand pieces and sowed these into the field. Then King Kuru offered his left arm, his legs and his head to Vishnu for sowing them in the field. Greatly pleased with Kuru, Lord Vishnu blessed him.

Simultaneously, Lord Indra appeared on the scene and told him to ask for any boon. Kuru asked for two boons, the first one being that this place should remain holy for ever and would be named after him. The second boon Kuru sought was that anyone, who died at Kurukshetra would go to heaven irrespective of any sin he may have committed. This Puranic story provides a symbolic explanation as to how Kuru converted Kurukshetra into a region of immense wealth as well as a center of righteousness and sanctity.

It was on the bank of the sacred Saraswati river that King Kuru chose the land for cultivation. Both the Saraswati and Drishdwati rivers between which Kurukshetra was located disappeared in course of time. The Mahabharata mentions the geographical location of this place thus: "Between spots known as Tadrantuka and Arantrika, and between Machakruka Yaksha's temple and Parashurama's pools—this is Kurukshetra, the Samantakapanchaka and Brahma's northern Vedi".

Kurukshetra was described as Brahmavarta by Manu, the Hindu law-giver, who had composed the Smritis here. It is called Brahmakshetra, the land of Lord Brahma. Nardak, another name of Kurukshetra, is perhaps derived from the word Nirdukh, which means a land without sorrow.

In ancient times, Kurukshetra was surrounded on all sides by dense forests, some of which were named in the Puranas as Kamyakavana, Vyasavana, Phatakivana, Aditivana, Madhuvana and Sitavana. It was in the Kurukshetra region that the Aryans started their settled life. From here, they spread out to other places in India, but they had a deep sense of attachment to this place. They did not like to shift from here to far-off places, as is evident from their prayer to the Saraswati mentioned in the Rig Veda:

"Guide us, Saraswati, to glorious treasure. Refuse us not thy milk nor spurn us from thee. Gladly accept our friendship and obedience. Let us not go from thee to distant places."[36]

The Saraswati was once a mighty river flowing into the sea on India's west coast. According to Vamana Purana, there were nine rivers in the Kurukshetra region, which included the Saraswati Vaitarini, Vasu, Drisshdwati, Kaushiki, Hiranyavati etc. Of these rivers, only the Saraswati flowed throughout the year, the others flowing only in the rainy season. Now, of course, there is no trace of the Saraswati. In Haryana of today, only the Yamuna flows all the year round. The Drishdwati is also not traceable. The Vedic sages used to perform sacrifices on the bank of the Drishdwati. The Mahabharata characterizes the Drishdwati as a place of great virtue, on whose bank there were five Ashramas.[37]

Another river mentioned in the Rig Veda along with the Saraswati and the Drishdwati was the Apaga, which was also called the Apaya. This river also cannot be traced any more. The Mahabharata and the Puranas said that a person who performed Sradh on the banks of this river had all his wishes fulfilled.[38]

The Brahmanas disclosed that the Saraswati had vanished into the sands of Kurukshetra at a spot that was called Vinasana. As J.H. Dave observes[39], the Saraswati rose in the outer Himalayan range of Shivalik, its source being described as 'Plaksha Prasravana' (or a river "springing from the Plaksha tree"). The land between the sorce and Vinasana at Kurukshetra was regarded as a sacred place for Saraswati Satra. Manu spoke of Vinasana as the eastern boundary of Madhyadesha. According to Dave, many scholars were of the opinion that the sudden disappearance of such a mighty river was due to a volcanic eruption.

There is so much on record about the Saraswati river that it is worthwhile to devote some space to this subject. In my school days, I had read about the glory of this river in the writings of Rabindranath Tagore. In his Hindu Mela, he wrote: "You have heard the Aryan poet sing with open mind and heart on the bank of the Saraswati." ("Tumi Shuniyachha Saraswatikule, Arya Kavi Gaay Manaprana Khuley"). In his Prakitir Khela, he writes: "On the bank of Saraswati, the poets are joyously singing sweet songs, with open heart." ("Saraswati Nadikuley, Kavira Hriday Khuley, Gaaichhey Harashey Aha Sumadhur Geet").

The late D.C. Verma, author of 'Haryana', had said that the Saraswati did not rise in the hills but in a large depression at Kalawar in the north of the Mustafabad Pargana of Jagadhri (Ambala district of Haryana). For the first 32 kilometres of its course, it is utterly insignificant. It is only after the tributary Chutang joins it at Bhaini that it acquires a continuous channel.

However, in ancient literature, the source of the Saraswati was traced to the Plaksha Prasravana or a Plaksha tree in the Himalayas, more specifically in the Sirmur Hills of the Shivalik range (in present-day Himachal Pradesh). It descended on the plains at Ad-Badri in Ambala district (Haryana).

The Imperial Gazetteer of India (1908) in its Punjab section also observed that the Saraswati rises in the Sirmur State close to the borders of the Ambala district, "debouches on the plains at Adh Badri, a place held sacred by all Hindus. A few miles further on, it disappears in the sand, but comes up again about three miles to the south, at the village of Bhawanipur. At Balchhapar, it again vanishes for a short distance, but emerges once more and flows on in a south-westerly direction across Karnal, until it joins the Ghaggar in Patiala territory after a course of about 110 miles. A District canal takes off from it near Pehowa."

According to some scholars, the Saraswati originated at Brahmasaras or at Badarikashrama (or Badrinath). I have read another account[39], according to which, the Saraswati had two sources, one of which was the Banderpunchh (monkey's tail) massif in the Garwal Himalayas, which now has become the source of the independent river, Tons. The second source of the Saraswai is said to be Kapalshikhar in Tibet near the holy lake, Mansarovar. The river is still there, known locally as Mang Nang Tsangpo and, further downstream, it is called the Saraswati in the map of the Survey of India.

There were many rivers which acquired the name Saraswati, as there were also many by name Ganga in ancient times.[40] Whenever a river was considered sacred, it was called Saraswati and if a sacred river fell into the sea, it came to be known as the Ganga (Sarvah Punyah Saraswatyah, Sarvah Gangah Samudragah). The Mahabharata speaks of seven Saraswatis covering the universe and Kurukshetra is mentioned as being the Saptasaraswata Tirtha. According to O.P. Bharadwaj, a scholar, the important rivers which bore the name Saraswati were the Harkhaiti or Harahvaiti (also called the Arghandab or Helmand in Kandahar or Arachocia), the Arbuda-Saraswati in Gujarat and the Thanesar-Saraswati near Thanesar or Kurukshetra.

The Imperial Gazetteer says that the word Saraswati is the Sanskrit form of the Zend Haragaiti (Archosia) and means 'rich in lakes'. According to it, "the name was probably given to the river by the Aryan in memory of the Haragaiti of Arachosia, the modern

Helmand in Seistan".[41] The argument that the Aryans had invaded India has not found favour with many present-day scholars. O.P. Bharadwaj has in his article also debunked the suggestion that the name Haragaiti or Harkhaiti or Harahvaiti travelled with the Aryans to India, when 'Ha' changed to 'Sa'. On the contrary, Bharadwaj thinks that the word 'Sa' usually changed to 'Ha' as one travelled westward from Madhyadesha, thus justifying his conclusion that the name Saraswati underwent the same process in its westward journey and became Harahvaiti or Harakhaiti in Arachosia.

Bharadwaj then takes up the task of identifying the original Saraswati of the Vedas. He rules out the Arbuda-Saraswati of Gujrat as being the real Saraswati because the association of the word Arbuda suggests that it is of later origin. He regards the Thaneswar-Saraswati as the Vedic Saraswati. He cites several literary references to the Vedic Saraswati in support of his contention—references found in poet Bana's Harsha-Charita, the Mahabharata and the Ramayana. According to Harsha-Charita, Bhairavacharya, who initiated Harsha's father, Prabhakaravardhana, into Tantric rites, used to live in a deserted temple on the banks of the Saraswati. His wife, Queen Yashovati, pre-deceased him by jumping into the fire at at the same river. Describing this scene, Bana says that the seal of King Prabhakaravardhana dropped face downward on the dry mud on the bank of the holy river with the result that his name was imprinted on the soft earth signifying, as it were, 'the stamping of the earth with the single seal of his sole command'.

Bharadwaj cites in support of his view the names of several Tirthas (pilgrimages) mentioned in the Mahabharata as being located on the Adbadri-Thanesar-Saraswati, namely Kapalamochana, Sthanniswara and Prithudaka. He then cites the evidence from the Valmiki Ramayana, which, while describing the return journey of Prince Bharata from Girivraja in Kikaya to Ayodhya, 'refers to his crossing the joint stream of the Saraswati and the Ganga before entering the Bharunda forest in the north of the Kira-matsyas.' As Bharadwaj says, this Saraswati was also the Adbadri-Thaneswar-Saraswati, while its tributary, Ganga, represented a small stream in Kurukshetra named after the holy Ganga.

Further on, Bharadwaj speaks of the reference in the Ramayana to the westward journey of the messengers from Ayodhya to fetch Bharata from his maternal uncle's capital, Girivraja, on the sudden demise of King Dasharatha. After crossing the Prachi Saraswati and passing by the town of Pushkaravati, probably the same as Bilaspur (in the Jagadhri Tehsil of of Ambala district), known as the capital of Shrikanta Janapada (old name of Haryana), the messengers forded the celestial river, Saradanda, which has been identified with the present Saddeni, a tributary of the Markanda river, which joins the Prachi Saraswati near Pehowa. Sometimes, a river Saravati is mentioned, which is the same as the Saradanda, both signifying a river abounding in reeds. Another tributary of the Markanda was the Aruna, now called Run-cho. Bharadwaj thinks that the Saradanda is apparently the same as the Sarawati and that the three sister streams—Saradanda, Markanda and Aruna—shared the same name Saraswati.

The next river which the messengers crossed after the Saradanda, according to the Ramayana, was the Iksumati, which has now been identified with the Ghaggar, flowing by Panchkula near Chandigarh. The Mahabharata describes Iksumati as a river of Kurukshetra. Literally the name signifies a river that is rich in sugarcane or whose belt is noteworthy for its fabulous cane crops. This description is applicable to the present river Ghaggar, which is called Hakra in Rajasthan. Valmiki uses Iksumati only as another name for Saraswati.[42]

Proceeding further, Bharadwaj identifies the Vedic Saraswati with the present-day Ghaggar, which represents the combined streams of several rivers, namely the Iksumati-Ghaggar-Saraswati, the Aruna-Saradanda-Saravati-Markanda-Saraswati and the Kurukshetra-Thaneswar-Saraswati (also known as Prachi or Eastern Saraswati).

Bharadwaj also answers the question as to how the Saraswati, described as a great and mighty river in the Vedas, could be identified with the present moribund river near Kurukshetra. It is true that the Rig Veda describes the Saraswati as a river rushing down right from the mountains to the ocean with a tempestuous roar (Yato Giribhya Aa Samudrat), breaking and carrying down ridges of hills like lotus stems (Sanu Girinang Tavierbhirurmibhih), with a tempestuous roar (Amashcharati Roruvat) and filling the realms of earth and the firmament. It is said to surpass all other rivers in her majesty and glory. It is fierce, swiftest of the swift and the mightiest of her class ('Ghora', Apasamapastama, Asurya Nadinam). It is the best of all rivers, the best of all mothers and the best of all goddesses (Naditame, Ambitame, Devitame). The Mahabharata describes the Saraswati as a river of great virtue adorned with a garland of pilgrimages and having many lakes (Saraswati Mahapunyah Hradini Tirthamalini)

Neither the Markanda-Saraswati nor the Thanesar-Prachi-Saraswati could ever lay claim to this description. It could never have been so big as to inspire the Rigvedic poets to apply the lofty epithets quoted above.[43] As Bharadwaj says, this picture of the Rigvedic Saraswati would at once call to one's mind the 2.6 miles wide bed of the Hakra in Rajasthan and the furious floods of the Ghaggar inundating vast areas.

The Ghaggar must have been once a perennial river to have deseved the Rigvedic description. Even now, although shorn of its pre-historic grandeur it presents a formidable picture at the peak of flood. The richness it bestowed on the soil earned it the epithet of Iksumati from Valmiki and won from the Rigvedic sages several adjectives such as 'possessed of wealth', 'having a golden path', 'possessed of vigour on account of flood' and 'distributing riches to the whole world'. Bharadwaj concludes that the Ghaggar-Iksumati was the original and Rigvedic Saraswati, which had been acknowledged by Valmiki in his use of the adjective 'Pitripitamahi' for this river, which means 'created by God Brahma'.

However, at some point of time between the composition of the nucleus of the Rigveda and the age of the Atharva Veda and the Brahmanas, something happened which led to a drastic reduction in the flow and partial diversion of the waters of the Saraswati.[44] Many stories and anecdotes in ancient literature contain veiled references to this drying up of the Saraswati. The Puranas describe the conveying of Agni-vadavanala to the western ocean at the instance of God Brahma by his daughter Saraswati that flowed underground and surfaced only when she felt exhausted on account of the unbearable heat.[45]

The story is that Brihaspati's wife Tara was seduced and carried away by the moon god. When Brihaspati invoked the assistance of Lord Indra, the moon god sought refuge with the Daityas. This led to a fierce battle between the gods and the Daityas. Peace returned only with the restoration of Tara to Brihaspati. At the end of the war, the gods kept their weapons at the hermitage of sage Dadhichi. After some time, Dadhichi wanted to retire to the Himalayas for undertaking penance, but before that, he washed the weapons and drank the water that was used for it. This had the result of the power of the weapons (or Astrashakti) being drunk up by Dadhichi.

When Lord Indra and the other gods wanted their weapons back, Dadhichi told them to make their weapons out of his bones, for which purpose he gave up his body. Dadhichi's son, Pippalada, was very angry to hear that this had been done in the interest of the gods. He performed penance at Badarikashrama and out of his thigh, he created the Vadavanala (fire, also known as Aurvanala), which began to destroy the gods, eating up one of them daily. At this stage, Lord Vishnu intervened and managed to persuade Vadavanala to go to the ocean and drink only water to satisfy his thirst.[46]

Vadavanala insisted that only a virgin should carry him to the ocean. Lord Brahma told his daughter Saraswati to carry this fire. (According to another view, Saraswati was the wife of Lord Brahma). Saraswati undertook the job, occasionally disappearing and going underground to avoid contact with the sinners.[47] It is said that Vishnu had warned Saraswati that she should not consider herself free from danger while carrying the fire (Vadavanala), as it would drink up the waters of her course. Modern scientists believe that this was a hint that the Saraswati would disappear.

Several explanations have been provided for the disappearance of the Saraswati. One story is that Lord Shiva, who had committed Brahmahatya (killing of a Brahmin), wanted to take a bath in the river. To avoid this, Saraswati vanished. Another story is that sage Utathya had cursed Saraswati and, therefore, the river had to go to Marudesha to become dry.[48]

Another legend is that though Saraswati was the daughter of Lord Mahadeva, the latter once got drunk and in that state approached Saraswat with a view to ravishing her. She ran away from her father, who began to chase her. Whenever she saw her father, Saraswati went underground to save herself, coming out when her father went out of sight.

Why did Saraswati come down to the earth at all? It is said that Saraswati came out of the maw of Lord Krishna's mouth. Charmed by Krishna's personality and beauty, Saraswati insisted on marrying him. Krishna told her that it was not possible because he had no identity different from that of Vishnu into whom he had merged himself. So Krishna told her to marry Vishnu. But this posed a problem for Vishnu, who already had two wives—Ganga and Yamuna.

Despite this, however, Saraswati got married to Vishnu, but she could not get along smoothly with the two earlier wives of the latter. At this stage, Narada, an expert in instigating quarrels, got into the act. As a result, all the three—Ganga, Yamuna and Saraswati—began to quarrel among themselves and ended up cursing one another that each of them would turn into a river on earth. This is how these three rivers came into existence.

The legend in the Skanda Purana (Prabhasa Khanda) is that as the Saraswati proceeded onward after emerging from the Plaksha Prasravana in the Himalayas, a mountain interposed itself on her path, seeking to marry her. Saraswati adopted a clever device to get rid of the mountain. She said that she would like to have a bath before the marriage and asked the mountain to temporarily hold the fire, which she was carrying. This burnt down the mountain. In another age, this fire was born as Aurvanala to a woman of the tribe of Bhrigus, who had been attacked and plundered by the Kshatriyas. The woman was pregnant and escaped, concealing the foetus in her thigh (Uru), which began to consume the earth immediately on its emergence.[49]

There are many versions of the Vadavanala episode in ancient literature, all of which, according to Bharadwaj, point to an important event, 'probably a large-scale tectonic-seismic-volcanic upheaval, rightly described as the Deluge', which was indeed so gigantic that it vastly changed the topography of the Shivaliks and affected the whole region along the Saraswati. According to Bharadwaj, that this event led to the disappearance of the Saraswati is specifically implied in the statement that the river vanished underground on account of the Vadavanala, which it was made to carry to the ocean.[50]

Bharadwaj cites several episodes from the Mahabharata to justify the conclusion that, according to traditional belief, it was the Great Deluge that led to the disappearance about Kalibangan in the sands of Rajasthan of the Rigvedic Saraswati represented by the present Ghaggar river as a result of the diversion of its waters and the loss of its catchment area.

According to Bharadwaj, the episode of the destruction of the Krauncha mountain symbolizes the volcanic aspect of the upheaval. As indicated in the Mahabharata,[51] the gods led by Brahma brought Karthikeya to the holy Saraswati and anointed him as the Commander of their army to fight against the Daityas. With powers given by Agni (fire), Karthikeya rent asunder the Krauncha mountain, from which Bana, son of Bali, harassed the gods. Bharadwaj concludes: 'the involvement of fire in the destruction of the Krauncha mountain near the Saraswati river clearly points to volcanic eruption in the hilly tract about the upper reaches of the river.

Bharadwaj also draws upon the testimony of archaeology to substantiate the traditional belief in the occurrence of the Great Deluge that destroyed the pre-Harappan phase of Kalibangan. Excavations carried out at Kalibangan by the Archaeological Survey of India has thrown light on a catastrophic earthquake, probably accompanied by strong volcanic eruption, that changed the face of this region and led to the drying up of the Ghaggar as a result of the diversion of some of its tributaries. This leads Bharadwaj to observe that Wheeler's sensational theory about the destruction of Harappa and Mohenjodaro by the savage Aryan hordes of India was no more taken seriously.

Bharadwaj also cites the findings of archaeological excavations to show that, as a sequel to major tectonic upheavals, many settlements of the Harappan era, which had been sea ports, were now located as far as thirty miles inland, which mean that the coast-line had risen considerably during the past 4000 years, the initial rise having occurred during the Harappan periods.

According to N.S. Rajaram of the Institute of Indian Studies, Ottawa, the drying up of the Saraswati might have been due to the depletion of ice caps accumulated in the north towards the end of the Ice Age corresponding to 8000 B.C. Rajan mentions the fact that the Panchavimsha Brahmana, which is later than the Rig Veda, had described the Saraswati as being already partially dry. An account of the Saraswati river's course given in the Shalya Parva of the Mahabharata is similar to that of the Panchavimsha Brahmana, but since the Mahabharata came later than the Panchavimsha Brahmana, the account in the Mahabharata shows the Saraswati as having already vanished into the desert and having reappeared at a place Chamsodbhava. After this, the river flowed onward coursing along different branches towards the western sea into which it debouched at several places such as Prabhasa Pattana (modern Somnath), Bhrigukachha (Broach) and Dholavira.

Some time ago, the scientists of the Central Groundwater Board reportedly traced the course of the ancient Saraswati river and discovered the fact that a sub-terranean flow of water was still there. The scientists were believed to be examining the feasibility of reviving the old river, thus opening up the possibility of changing the face of the Thar desert region and making it turn green and fertile. This prospect led the Times of India (July 13, 2000) to editorially recall poet Rabindranath Tagore's famous lines: "Je Nadi Marupathe Haralo Dhara/ Jaani Hey Jaani Tao Hayni Hara" (The river that lost its course in a desert/ I know isn't lost for ever).

Considerable research work has been undertaken over the years to ascertain if the Saraswati river was a myth or if it really existed, and if so what its precise course was. In 1985, the late Dr. V.S. Wakankar, a reputed archaeologist, along with a team of twenty historians, geologists and archaeologists, conducted a survey spanning a distance 3500 kilometres from Adi Badri in the Shivalik hills in Ambala, believed to be the source of the river, right down to Somnath in Gujarat to trace the Saraswati described in the Rig Veda as 'the mother of rivers'.

Dr. Wakankar, who had a deep knowledge of our country's ancient literature, had on that basis chosen the sites for scrutiny along the probable course of the old Saraswati. He had trial pits sunk at different points along the course of the river and tested the chemical properties of the sub-terranean water, which conformed to the accounts given in ancient literature.

A report dated October 10, 1989, circulated by the UNI news agency gave the details of their findings after visiting 150 sites along the course of the Saraswati. They got concrete evidence of a highly developed culture on the banks of the Saraswati and established the scientific validity of the belief about the existence of a big river matching the description of the Saraswati in the Vedas. For this expedition, the team of experts had taken the help of the multi-sectoral scanner (MSS), an equipment widely used in archaeology. The team came to the conclusion that the Sutlej was the main tributary of the Ghaggar (present name of the old Saraswati). Tectonic movements forced the Sutlej to flow in a different direction, leaving the Ghaggar dry. Dr. Wakankar concluded that the Thar desert in north-western Rajasthan was a green belt once upon a time.

Sangam at Prayag near Allahabad is believed to be the confluence of the Ganga, Yamuna and Saraswati. But the team led by Dr. Wakankar was of the view that the Saraswati had never flowed in any course towards Prayag. The UNI report of October 10, 1989 mentions the explanation given in this regard by poet Tulsidas, according to whom, the Saraswati at Prayag is nothing but an eternal, invisible flow of the idea of Brahman. The Saraswati is believed to have dried up over a period of twelve years around 2900 B.C. during the rule of Ashwan Adhaga, the fifth ruler in the line of Parikshit. Some scholars believe that the Saraswati is running at the sub-soil level through the Rajasthan desert. Some say that the river might be in existence in the form of pools as Saraswati means , abounding in lakes or pools.' (Saras means a lake)

Dr. Wakankar believed that the Harappans living on the banks of the Saraswati had their golden age around 3000 B.C. All historians, who followed the track of the Saraswati, are said to be of the view that the Harappans were the Vedic masters living along the banks of the Saraswati and moved away to greener belts when the river began to dry up. This runs counter to Mortimer Wheeler's theory that the Aryans were the masters of the Vedas and had destroyed the Harappans.

Various projects have been undertaken in recent years to trace the course of the ancient river by groups of scientists, hydrologists and scholars with a religious background. The Central Ground Water Board was reported to be co-ordinating a project entitled "The Reconstruction of Palaeo Drainage Network in Western Rajasthan", which was undertaken by the Rajasthan Ground Water Board, Jodhpur. Lending a hand in this project were the Central Arid Zone Research Institute, the Rajiv Gandhi National Drinking Mission, the Space Applications Centre, Ahmedabad, the Physical Research Laboratory, Ahmedabad and the Bhabha Atomic Research Centre (BARC), Mumbai.

The sand dunes over Ghantiyal Ji and some other locations in Rajasthan were chosen as the sites drilling for this project. Water samples taken from the wells at several places pointed to the existence of a uniform channel of sweet water at a depth of 52 to 95 meters, while the water samples taken from either side of the channel were found to be saline. This, according to the scientists, showed that this was the course of the old Saraswati river.

An article entitled "Search For the Saraswati" by Rohit Parihar and Samar Halarnkar in the September 28, 1999 issue of the "India Today' mentioned that it was an English engineer by name C.E. Oldham, who had sparked off the search for the Saraswati about 100 years ago, while riding on horse-back through the dry bed of the Ghggar, he realized that there was no reason why it should have a breadth of 3 kilometres at places unless it was the bed of a big river. After that, many scientists and historians took up the task of tracing the course of the Saraswati river over the decades. Many of them matched the mythological references to the river with satellite images of the underground channel.

The article by Parihar and Halarnkar mentioned the fact that excavations at Indus Valley sites had found 175 sites along the alluvial plane of the Ghaggar as compared to 86 in the Indus area now in Pakistan. According to many experts, this could not have happened unless the Ghaggar was once the mighty Saraswati. It has, therefore, been surmised by one expert that this should be called the Saraswati Valley Civilisation and not the Indus Valley Civilisation. It is believed that part f this cvilisation ended around 1500 B.C., the same time the scriptures speak of the Saraswati's decline.

The India Today article observed that "tectonic movements initially pushed up the old Aravalli hills, cutting off the headwaters of the Saraswati. Forced eastwards, the Saraswati was then progressively robbed of its waters: first by the Yamuna, then by the Sutlej—both rivers, along with the Tons, were once a part of the massive expanse.

A branch of the Chambal cut northwards in a channel deeper than the Saraswati, finally beheading the great river. The new channel became the Yamuna, which migrated eastwards. Similarly, the Sutlej migrated westward. A geological paroxysm in the Aravallis pushed it into a U-turn at Ropar, Punjab, forcing a complete abandonment of the Saraswati, sending the Sutlej into the arms of the Indus ....Betrayed by its two snow-fed sources, the Saraswati was left with the waters of petty streams rising in the puny Shivaliks ....the climate too was changing. Over the years, western Rajasthan, once a green, rich expanse with extensive rainfall, gradually turned into a parched desert land."

The article concluded: "With the Saraswati gone, its place in mythology was taken over by the Ganga. To this day, it is the Ganga that is predominant to India's Hindu consciousness. But the Saraswati, as the drilling rigs at Ghantiyal Ji should reveal, has not disappeared altogether. The greater river might never flow again, its spiritual form might never regain its mythological glory, but its legacies are flooding back all over again."

The late D.C. Verma, author of 'Haryana' did not attach much importance to the phenomenon of the desiccation of the Saraswati river. He thought that this was amply explained by the supposition that in ancient times, the Ghaggar was considered an affluent of the Sraswati instead of the Saraswati being that of the Ghaggar. The Ghaggar, an important river of Punjab, Haryana and Rajasthan, rises in the Himalayan ranges between the Yamuna and the Sutlej, passes by Ambala and enters the Patiala district of Punjab, where it is joined by the Saraswati, Markanda and many hill streams. Then it bends to the west and passes through the Hisar district of Haryana and the Bikaner Division of Rajasthan, where it gets lost. When the ancient writers speak of the Saraswati, they include under that name the united flow of the Ghaggar and the Saraswati.

According to D, C. Verma, the failure in the water supply was easily explained by the greater volume of water drawn off in recent times for irrigation and by the silting up of the river beds caused by dams south of Ambala to direct the water to the fields. He did not think that the supply of water in the sources of these two rivers had permanently decreased. He said that there was no mystery about this. But how do we react to the great mass of evidence that historians, archaeologists and scientists have turned up over the decades about the tectonic movements that resulted in the diversion of the rivers of this region?

The Rig Veda describes the Saraswati as a river, but Saraswati is also often mentioned as a goddess—the goddess of learning. While the Vedas generally project her as a river, the Puranas mostly speak of her as a goddess. There is definitely a connection between these two entities of Saraswati. In fact, her identity as a river gradually evolved into her identity as a goddess. The Aryans, who lived on the banks of the Saraswati, were greatly attached to it and later, when they moved away from it to other territories, they could not get over their nostalgia for the river. So they conceptualized a goddess named Saraswati as the source of all knowledge and learning. From her association with a river, the new goddess was depicted as having a lotus and a swan, which thrived in rivers. Is this how the Saraswat Brahmins, who hailed from the land of the ancient Saraswati river, started worshipping goddess Saraswati adorned with a lotus and a swan? I do not know.

Apart from the antiquity of Kurukshetra, there is also the question of the historicity of the events of the Mahabharata, more particularly, the issue concerning the year in which the Mahabharata war was fought at Kurukshetra. The Mahabharata or the fifth Veda, as it is sometimes called, is a mammoth epic of one lac verses that is several times the combined size of the Greek epics, Iliad and Odyssey, which have 16, 000 and 10,000 verses respectively. Ved Vyasa, the Indian sage, who compiled the Vedas, the 18 Puranas and the Brahma Sutra, also authored the Mahabharata.

It would have been too tiresome a task for Ved Vyasa to write all this in his own hand. So he employed Lord Ganesh as his amanuensis, who took down his marathon dictation, but on the condition that Ved Vyasa would dictate non-stop and without any break. Ved Vyasa accepted this condition, but insisted on Ganesha accepting the stipulation that he would write down everything only after comprehending it properly. If at any stage, Ved Vyasa found that he was unable to think of any matter, he pronounced some difficult verses (called Vyasa Kootas), which Ganesha found it difficult to understand. This clever device gave Ved Vyasa some time to cogitate and then come forward with some new matter for Ganesha to take down.

Whether or not we believe the above legend, we have to accept the fact that the Mahabharata has a lac of verses. Here again, there is no authentic information about how many verses Ved Vyasa's original Mahabharata had. There is no doubt that there have been many interpolations as a result of which the Mahabharata has grown in volume over time. The original known as Jayasamhita had only 8800 verses, while the next version of the Mahabharata known as 'Bharata' had only 24, 000 verses. Historians have, therefore, displayed their reluctance to accept the truth of everything that is contained in the present version of the Mahabharata.

Scholars are also inclined to keep in view the possibility of exaggeration in the recounting of the many events in the Mahabharata. The armies that fought in the Mahabharata war on both sides are said to have numbered 18 Akshauhinis (somewhat like a modern army division). Each Akshauhini consisted of 109350 infantry men, 65610 horses, 21870 elephants and 21870 chariots. Eighteen such formations would have meant the deployment of uncountable numbers of participants in the war, which in those far-off days could have been difficult to mobilize, even after making allowance for the fact that the armies of most of the kingdoms in different parts of the country might have sided with either the Kauravas or the Pandavas and got sucked into the war.

Among the names that figure in the Mahabharata is Hastinapur, the capital of the Kauravas and Varanavata, where the Kauravas had planned to get the Pandavas burnt alive in a house of lac. Hastinapur has been identified with a place in Meerut and Varanavata with Barnwa in Uttar Pradesh. Viratnagar, another name in the Mahabharata is identical with Bairat in Rajasthan. Paniprastha, Sonaprastha, Tilaprastha, Vrikshaprastha and Indraprastha—the five places which the Pandavas had demanded of the Kauravas and which the latter had refused to concede, thus triggering the Mahabharata war—are identical respectively with Panipat, Sonepat (both in Haryana), Tilpat, Baghpat and Indraprastha or where Delhi's Purana Qila stands today.

Historically speaking, a lot of evidence about the events of the Mahabharata and contemporary culture has come to light as a result of excavations at Hastinapur, the discovery of a dice at Ropar, Punjab) and of inscriptions that throw light on the probable date of the Kuru-Pandava war. My own studies undertaken over the years revealed the divergence of views expressed by scholars and historians about the precise timing of this war.

The Aihole Inscription of Pulakesi II, the Chalukya ruler, which was recorded in 634-635 A.D. reveals that 3735 years had elapsed since the Mahabharata war. This would fix the date of this war in 3102 B.C., which, in the view of many historians, marked the beginning of the Kali Yuga according to the astronomical tradition represented by Aryabhatta. However, according to another school of Hindu astronomers represented by Vriddha-Garga, the Bharata war took place 653 years after the commencement of the Kali Yuga era *i.e.*, In 2449 B.C.

According to the view expressed in the History and Culture of the Indian People edited by Dr. R.C. Mazumdar (Volume I, pp. 272-273), the year 3102 B.C. said to represent the beginning of the Kali Yuga, signified some epoch-making event in the traditional history of India. This event may have been the Great Flood recorded in the Satapatha Brahmana and other accounts in which Manu Vaivasvata played the role of the saviour of humanity. The year 3102 B.C. did not represent the year of the Bharata War, as has been made out by some scholars.

The Mahabharata contains references to certain astronomical occurrences and positions of planets on which basis some scientists have sought to fix the date of the Bharata War.[51] But this approach has not led to any unanimous finding. Moreover, the data available in this regard available in the Mahabharata are often contradictory making it difficult to accept any particular statement as a basis for reaching a valid conclusion. For example, Prof. Virendra N. Sharma of the University of Wisconsin Centre, Fox Valley, Menasha, U.S.A., who had presented a paper at an international seminar (January 5-6, 1994) held at the B.M. Birla Science Centre, Hyderabad, referred to a series of planetary positions described by Ved Vyasa, author of the Mahabharata, which foretold a great calamity ahead for the warrior class of the country. On the basis of these planetary positions, he developed models and from them deduced three probable dates of the Mahabharata war—1493 B.C., 2109 B.C. And 3022 B.C.

At the same symposium, another paper was presented by Prof. Anjani Kumar Mehra and Prof. Virendra N. Sharma of the Wisconsin University, U.S.A., who had studied solar and lunar eclipses from 3500 B.C. to 20 A.D., using the latitude and longitude of modern Delhi, which closely approximated the location of ancient Kurukshetra. They looked for the conditions that gave a very rare 'Paksa' or Indian fortnight of 13 days 9 'Tithis') encompassing a solar and a lunar eclipse as mentioned in the Mahabharata. The normal 'Paksa' is supposed to have 14 to 15 'Tithis' with some having 16. They followed the ancient convention that the 'Tithi' changes after sunrise. A solar eclipse just after sunrise followed by a lunar eclipse 14 days later just before sunrise would have only 13 'Tithis' and hence the condition used in their search. It is not possible to have this with the lunar eclipse occurring first. They found three dates—167 B.C., 2290 B.C. And 2919 B.C.—of which they considered 2919 B.C. as the most interesting astronomically.

These different dates bring out the difficulty of finding out a precise date.

One of the calculations, which is based on the timing of a solar eclipse during the Mahabharata war, fixes the date of the war in 1429 B.C. After Abhimanyu, the valiant son of Arjuna, was killed on the thirteenth day of the 18-day war, Arjuna vowed to take revenge by killing Jayadratha, the son-in-law of Dhritarashtra, before the sun rose the next morning. Lord Krishna used his Chakra (disc) to hide the sun till Arjuna had time to fulfill his vow. This action of Lord Krishna has been characterized by historians and scientists as nothing but a solar eclipse. On the basis of an analysis of the eclipses that took place in the pre-Christian era the view has been expressed by some scientists that the war at Kurukshetra occurred in 1429 B.C.—more precisely in the middle of February, 1429 B.C.

Scientists of the National Council of Science Museums, who have done path-breaking work in this field, have found corroboration for their view mentioned above in translations of the Mahabharata by C. Rajagopalachari and Rajshekhar Bose respectively in which the departure from this world of Bhisma during Uttarayana is said to tally with their calculations about the date of the Mahabharata war. Another piece of evidence relied on by them is a Shloka in Vishnupurana, according to which, Parikshit, the grandson of Arjuna, was born while the war was on at Kurukshetra. That was 1015 years before one of his descendants, Mahapadma Nanda, became the king in 413 B.C., according to Greek historians. Calculating backward, the scientists have dated the Kurukshetra war in 1428 B.C.

However, according to the History and Culture of the Indian People, edited by Dr. R.C. Mazumdar (Volume I), Mahapadma Nanda was coronated in 382 A.D., thus yielding 1397 B.C. (1015+ 382) as the year of the Mahabharata war. The broad conclusion that is reached in this book is expressed as follows: 'We may, therefore, take 1400 B.C. as the provisional date for the Bharata War and the event must have taken place between this date and 1000 B.C. In round numbers.' [52]

In the course of my studies about Kurukshetra, I chanced to come across a legend, according to which, it was here that Sita was born. There are several stories about how and where she was born, the generally accepted view being that she was born at Mithila out of a plough used to till the soil. According to the version available in the Ananda Ramayana, Ravana was a tyrant, who used to go about killing the sages and storing their blood in a certain pot. A sage by name Gritsamad did long penance praying for a daughter as accomplished as goddess Lakshmi. As part of the ritual, he used to store in a pot the milk used during his penance. One day, Ravana stole this pot, mixed up the milk with the blood of the sages that he had stored in a pot and offered this concoction to his wife, Mandodari, to drink. Mandodari was very unhappy at this horrific conduct of her husband and wanted to commit suicide by drinking the concoction given by Ravana. However, after she drank it, she did not die, but, on the other hand, became pregnant. She became nervous at this odd happening, took out the foetus and concealed it under the soil at Kurukshetra. It is out of this foetus that Sita was born! [53]

Excavations carried out at several places in Kurukshetra and adjacent districts have thrown fresh light on the ancient history of this region. Daulatpur, Mirzapur and Bhagawanpur in Kurukshetra district and Balu in Jind district are the sites which have revealed the existence of Harappan and pre-Harappan settlements in this region, thus pushing back the antiquity of Indian history. The evidence of juxtaposition and overlap between these cultures has great significance from the point of view of reconstructing a continuous history of the region.

Many references are available in Vedic literature to the names of post-Kuru kings, who ruled over the Kurukshetra region such as Balhika Pratipiya, Parikshit and Janamejaya. There is some confusion about the identity of these successors, particularly with regard to Janamejaya. The accession of Parikshit after the Mahabharata war marked the end of the Dwapara Age and the beginning of Kali Yuga. He is said to have chased away Kali from his kingdom, which means that he was a good and popular ruler.

Parikshit's son Janamajeya succeeded him, but there are references in ancient literature to two 'Janamejaya Parikshitars', causing a lot of confusion. Scholars are mostly of the view that one of these two was an ancestor of the Pandavas, who had performed an Ashwamedha sacrifice. The other Janamejaya Parikshita, who came later, was the son of Abhimanyu and grandson of Arjuna. He had performed a 'Sarpasatra' (snake-sacrifice). According to legend, once during a hunting expedition, Parikshit lost his way in the forest and asked a sage to tell him the way. As he was observing a vow of silence, the sage did not answer him. This infuriated Parikshit, who put a dead snake around the sage's neck and left the place. The sage's son cursed Parikshit saying that in a week he would be bitten to death by Takshak, the king of snakes. And this is what actually happened. In revenge, Parikshit's son, Janamejaya organized a 'Sarpasatra', where innumerable snakes rushed into the sacrificial fire as oblations.

This mythological story has been explained as a genuine historical fact by scholars. It is said that Takshaka, King of the Nagas in Gandhara, marched against Parikshit, the Kuru ruler, who died in the battle that ensued. To avenge this, Janamajeya, son of Parikshit, invaded Takshasila and slaughtered countless Nagas. It was after the intervention of Astika that Janamejaya stopped this massacre. Takshaka escaped safely. The slaughter of the Nagas has been mythlogised into the 'Sarpasatra' (snake-sacrifice) of Janamejaya.[54]

Kurukshetra has passed through many vicissitudes of history since time immemorial and has been in the forefront of the fight against foreign invaders. In the sixth century B.C., it came under the spell of Buddhism. In course of time, the Buddhists built many 'Stupas' in this region. It formed part of the Mauryan empire in the pre-Christian era. In the Gupta period, Kurukshetra was an important center of political power. Thanesar, a part of Kurukshetra, was the capital of Harshavardhana's empire in the seventh century A.D. It was a part of the Pratihara empire in the 9th and 10th centuries A.D.

Kurukshetra bore the brunt of the invasions by Mahmud of Ghazni in the 11th century A.D, by Muhammad Ghori in the 12th century A.D. And by Timur in the 14th century A.D. In between, it eked out a comparatively peaceful existence in the 12th centurt A.D., when the Chauhans brought under their control. The defeat of Prithviraj Chauhan in the battle of Tarain in 1192 A.D. exposed the whole of north west India to Muslim rule. In the 18th century A.D., Kurukshetra again suffered badly during the invasions by Nadir Shah in 1739 A.D. And by Ahmed Shah Abdali between1748 A.D. And 1761 A.D. Many temples in this region were destroyed as a result of all these invasions over the centuries. This area also suffered from chaos and instability in the wake of the devastation caused by the Sikhs and Marathas in the 18th and early 19th centuries A.D.

But in the midst of all the destruction, plunder and killings that Kurukshetra has been witness to, it has preserved its spiritual sanctity that has attracted devotees from far and near. Lord Buddha preached the eternal message of peace and non-violence here. It was here that the great saint of Advaita, Jagatguru Shankaracharya explained his spiritual philosophy to blunt the edge of Buddhist theology and the great Vaishnava saint, Vallabhacharya expounded the Bhagavata Purana. Mughal emperors Akbar, Jehangir, Shahjehan and Aurangzeb came here during solar eclipses. All the ten Sikh Gurus visited Kurukshetra to convey their teachings to the people. All this reflects the great importance the leaders of different religious persuasions have attached to Kurukshetra.

Notes

1. तेषां कुरुक्षेत्रं देवयजनमास। तस्मादाहः कुरुक्षेत्रं देवानां देवयजनमिति।
—Shatapatha Brahman, 14.1. 1-2.
2. कुरुक्षेत्रे अमो देवाः यज्ञं तन्वते।
—*Ibid*, 4.1 5.13, Aitareya Aranyaka 5.1.1, Part I.
3. यतो वा अधिदेवा यज्ञेनेष्ट्वा स्वर्ग लोक मायस्त कुरुक्षेत्रे।
—Aitareya Brahmana 7.35. 30.
4. पांसवोऽपि कुरुक्षेत्रे वायुना समुदीरितः।
अपि दृष्कृत कर्माणं नयन्ति परमां गतिम्।
—Mahabharata, Vana Parva, Shalya Parva.
5. ततो गच्छेत राजेन्द्र कुरुक्षेत्रममिष्टुतम्।
पापेभ्यो यत्र मुच्यन्ते दर्शनात् सर्वजन्तवः।।
—*Ibid*, Vana Parva.
6. कुरुक्षेत्रं गमिब्यामि कुरुक्षेत्रे वसाम्यहम्।
य एवं सततं बूयात् सर्वपादेः प्रमुच्यते।।
—*Ibid*.
7. गत्वा हि श्रद्धया युक्तः कुरुक्षेत्रं कुष्दह।
फलं प्राप्नोति च तदा राजसूया श्वमेघयोः।।
—*Ibid*.
8. ग्रहनक्षत्रताराणां कालेन पतनाद् भयम्।
कुरुक्षेत्र मृतानां च पतनं नैव विद्यते।।
—Vamana Saro 12-16, Naradiya Purana 2.64. 24.
9. पृथिव्यां नैमिषं तीर्थमन्तरिक्षे च पुष्करम्।
त्रयाणामपि लोकानां कुरुक्षेत्रं विशिष्यते।।
—Mahabharata, Vana Parva 83.202-203.
10. कुरुक्षेत्रं महापुण्यं सर्वतीर्थ समन्वितम्।।
—Matsya Purana 22.18.
11. Article by Dr. Amar Singh in the brochure on Kurukshetra brought out by the Kurukshetra Development Board to mark the solar eclipse on September 23, 1987.
12. अपवित्रः पवित्रो वा सर्वावस्यां गतोइपिवा।
यः स्मरेत कुरुक्षेत्रः बाह्मभ्यन्तरः शुचिः।।
—Vamana Purana.
13. भृगुक्षेत्रे महाबाहो यत्किचित्क्रियते नरः
त्रयोदश दिनान्येव त्रयोदश गुणं भवेत्।।
—*Ibid*.
14. गंगाया जले मुक्ति वाराणस्यां जले स्थले।
कुरुक्षेत्रे विधामुक्ति अन्तरिक्षे जले स्थले।।
15. मुण्डनं उपवासं च सर्व तीर्थ स्वयं विधिः।
वर्जीयत्वा कुरुक्षेत्रं विशालं विरजां गयाम्।।

16. एतद्देश प्रसूतस्य सकाशादग्रजन्मनः
स्वं स्वं चरित्रं शिक्षेरन पृथिव्यां सर्व्वमानवाः।।
17. आद्यं ब्रह्मसरः पुण्यं ततो रामह्रदस्मृतः।
—Vamana Purana.
18. J.H. Dave, Immortal India, Volume I.
19. चतुर्मुखं ब्रह्मतीर्थ सरो मर्यादया स्थितम्।
ये सेवन्ते चतुर्दश्यां सोपवासा वसन्ति च।
अष्टम्यां कृष्णमक्षस्य चैत्रे मासि द्विजोत्तमाः।
ते पशयन्ति परं सूक्ष्मं यस्मान्नावर्तते पुनः।।
—Vamana Purana.
20. Article on Brahmsarovar by Dr. Shiv Bahadur Singh in the brochure brought out by the Kurukshetra Development Board to mark the solar eclipse on September 23, 1987.
21. Article by Dr. B.C. Ghosh under the caption "Language and Literature" in the History and Culture of the Indian People edited by Dr. R.C. Mazumdar, Volume I, p. 349.
22. *Ibid.*
23. सरः सन्निहितं ज्ञेयं समन्तादर्धयोजनम्।
24. विश्वेश्वरादस्तिपुरम् तथा कन्या जरद्गवी।
यावदोघवती प्रोक्ता तावत् सन्निहितं सरः।
25. यस्मिन् स्थाने स्थितं हयण्डं तस्मिन् सन्निहितं सरः।
अण्डमध्ये समुत्पन्ने ब्रह्मा लोक पितामहः।।
26. सन्निहित्यामुपस्पृश्य राहुअस्ते
अश्वमेध शतं तेन इष्टं भवति शाश्वतम्।
27. गुप्तचर्या यदायाताः पाण्डवा वनवासिनः
स्थापयामासुस्ते सर्वे लिंग सन्निहिता तटे।
28. ततो गच्छेत धर्मज्ञ तीर्थ सनिहतीमपि।।१६०।।
तत्र ब्रह्मादयो देवा ऋषयश्व तपोधनाः।
मासि मासि समायान्ति पुण्येन महतान्विताः।।१६१।।
तत्र स्नात्वा च पीत्वा च स्वर्गलोके महीयते।
अमावस्यां तु तत्रैव राहुग्रस्ते दिवाकरे।।१६३।।
यः श्राद्धं कुरुते मर्त्यस्तस्य पुण्यफलं श्रणु।
अश्वमेधसहस्रस्य सम्यगिष्टस्य यत् फलम्।।१६७।।
स्नात एव समाप्नोति कृत्वा श्राद्धं च मानवः।
यत् किंचिद् दुष्कृतं कर्म स्त्रिया वा पुरुषेण वा।।१६८।।
स्नातमात्रस्य तत् सर्व नश्यते नात्र संशयः।
पद्मवर्णेन यानेन ब्रह्मलोकं प्रपद्यते।।१६६।।
—Mahabharata, Vana Parva, Ch. 83, verses-190, 191, 196-199.

29. कुरुश्रवणमावृणि राजानं त्रासदस्यवं।
30. कुलायन् कृष्वन् कौरव्यः पतिर्वदति जायया।
31. प्रजापतेरु तरवेदिरुच्यते सनातनं नाम समन्तपञ्चकम्।
प्रकृष्टमेतत् कुरुणा महात्मना ततः कुरुक्षेत्रमितीह प्रपथे।।
32. तेषां कुरुक्षेत्र वेदिरासीत्। तस्यै खाण्डवो दक्षिणार्ध
आसीत्। तूर्घ्नमुत्तरार्ध। परीक्षज्जघनार्धः भरवः उत्करः।।
33. दक्षिणेन सरस्वत्या दृष्द्वत्युत्तरेण च।
ये वसन्ति कुरुक्षेत्र ते वसन्ति त्रिविष्टपे।।
34. यत्र यो वे वसेद्धीर सरस्वत्या स्तरे स्थितः।
तस्य ज्ञान ब्रह्मयं भविष्यिति न संशयः।।
35. कुरुक्षेत्रं समाप्लाव्य प्रयाता पश्चिमां दिशम्।
36. सरस्वत्यभि नो दस्यो माप स्फरीः पयसा मा न आ धक।
जुषस्व नः सख्या वेश्या च मा त्वत् क्षेत्राण्यरणानि गन्म।।
—Rig Veda, VI, 61, 14.37.
37. दषद्वती महापुण्या यत्र ख्याता युधिष्ठिर।
न्यग्रोधाख्यस्तु पुण्याख्यः पाञ्चाल्यो द्विपदांवर।।११।।
—Mahabharata, Vana Parva, chapter 90, verse 11.
38. य तु श्राध्यं करिष्यन्ति प्राप्य तामापगां तटम्।
ते सर्ब काम संपुक्ता भविष्यन्ति न संशयः।।
39. Immortal India, Volume I, p. 16. Vinasana is not generally held to be close to Kurukshetra. For example, O.P. Bharadwaj thinks that Vinasana is identical with Kalibangan in the Hanumangarh district of Rajasthan.
40. Journal of Haryana Studies, Haryana Sahitya Academy. Article captioned "The Vedic Saraswati" by O.P. Bharadwaj.
41. Imperial Gazetteer, pp. 185-186.
42. Article by O.P. Bharadwaj cited above.
43. *Ibid.*
44. *Ibid.*
45. Skanda Purana, Prabhasa Khanda, cited by O.P. Bharadwaj.
46. J.A. Dave, Immortal India, Volume IV, pp. 15-16.
47. *Ibid.*
48. *Ibid*, p. 14.
49. *Ibid*, pp. 15-16.
50. Article by O.P. Bharadwaj, Journal of Indological Studies, Vol. II, Nos. 1-2
51. ततः कुमारमादाय देवा ब्रह्मपुरोगमाः।
अभिषेकार्थमाजग्मु शैलेन्द्रं सहितास्ततः।।५१।।
पुण्यां हैमवतीं देवीं सरिच्छ्रेष्ठां सरस्वतीम्।
समन्तपञ्चके या वै त्रिषु लोकेषु विश्रुता।।५२।।

—Mahabharata, Shalya Parva, pp. 43-51, 52.

बाणो नामाथ दैतेयो बलेः पुत्रो महाबलः।

कौञ्चं पर्वतमाश्रित्य देवसंघानबाधत।।८२।।

तमभ्ययान्महासेनः सुरशत्रुमुदारधीः।

स कार्तिकेयस्य भयात् कौञ्चं शरणमीयिवान्।।८३।।

ततः कौञ्चं महामन्युः कौञ्चनादनिनादितम्।

शक्त्या बिभेद भगवान कार्तिकेयोऽग्निदत्तया।।८४।।

—*Ibid*, pp. 45, 82-84.

52. The History and Culture of the Indian People edited by Dr. R.C. Mazumdar, Volume I, p. 273.
53. Article entitled "Sita" by Purva Sengupta in the Bengali weekly 'Bartaman', Kolkata, dated January 29, 2000.
54. The History and Culture of the Indian People edited by Dr. R.C. Mazumdar, Volume I, p. 324.

6

Governor or Jack of All Trades?

For some days after my return to Chandigarh, my mind remained brimful of thoughts about Kurukshetra and Mahabharata. However, it did not take me long to get inexorably sucked into the web of official, social and cultural activities. An important constitutional task that I had soon to perform was the inauguration of the budget session of the Haryana Legislative Assembly on March 14, 1988. On this occasion, I had to deliver a long formal speech at the Assembly. The speech had been prepared by the Haryana Cabinet headed by Ch. Devi Lal and I was to read it out in the Assembly. I had the option of reading it in either English or Hindi. Since Hindi was not my mother tongue, it would have been easier for me to read the English version of my speech. However, I had decided to read out the Hindi version because this was the primary language of Haryana. Of course, I prepared myself for this by reading the speech several times over in advance.

On the appointed day, I entered the State Assembly in a formal procession. When I started reading out the speech in Hindi, Ch. Devi Lal, the Chief Minister, stood up and suggested that I could read out the speech in English, because, as he implied, that would be more convenient for me. Speaking in extempore Hindi, I thanked him for his suggestion, but asserted that I would read out the Hindi version, whatever my shortcomings, for which I craved the members' indulgence. Upon this, the whole Assembly burst out in spontaneous applause, which continued for some time. This gave a tremendous boost to my self-confidence. Then the cheers subsided and there was pin-drop silence, as I went on with my speech in Hindi that ran into 28 pages! When I concluded after an hour and 20 minutes, I was again greeted with a thunderous applause by the members, who looked extremely pleased with my love for Hindi and the sincere effort I had put in to excel in Hindi language. Reproduced below are some relevant press reports:

The Tribune, March 15, 1988

Haryana Governor's Address

From the Tribune Bureau:

Chandigarh—The Haryana Government has set up an anti-terrorist cell on a regular basis while it is raising a commando force. These are among a number of preventive measures taken by the State Government in the context of the prevailing conditions in the neighbouring State of Punjab.

This was stated by the Haryana Governor, Mr. H.A.Barari, this afternoon during his maiden Address to the members of the State Vidhan Sabha. He spoke for nearly 85 minutes in Hindi.

The Governor said that superior weapons were being provided to the police personnel of the anti-terrorist cell. The wireless network for quick transmission of intelligence reports had been revamped. Additional vehicles and modern equipment was being given and computerization of crime records carried out. The Government was also determined to end crime against Harijans and women and maintain peace in the industrial sector.

Mr. Barari was repeatedly cheered by members during his long Address. Soon after he started speaking, the Chief Minister, Mr. Devi Lal got up and requested him to read out his Address in English if he encountered any difficulty in doing so in Hindi. The Governor thanked the Chief Minister for his plea but said that he would continue to read it in Hindi – the State language of Haryana. At this nearly all Members in the House loudly cheered him.

Even at the end of the Address the Deputy Chief Minister, Mr. B.D.Gupta. and the President of the Haryana BJP, Dr. Mangal Sein, congratulated and thanked the Governor, a Bengali Brahmin, on reading his Address properly in Hindi.

The Tribune, March 16, 1988

In Punjab's Shadow

The Haryana Governor's Address in the Vidhan Sabha on the opening day of the Budget session dwelt on issues of vital import to the State. Of course most of what Mr. H.A. Barari said on Monday was at best in the nature of a "ready reckoner" for those following the recent developments in Haryana. Inevitably. the best part of the speech was devoted to the problems faced by the State because of what was happening in neighbouring Punjab. Even the Governor's insistence on speaking in Hindi carried a hidden message to those who are still reluctant to use Hindi as a language of communication at least at the official level. The proposed move to set up an anti-terrorist cell in the State besides raising a crack commando force to prevent the recurrence of the Lalru and Daryapur types of massacres, will be welcomed. No one would grudge the State Government credit for the firm and tactful handling of the situation particularly after the Daryapur carnage. The killing of 34 bus passengers on July 7, 1987, by terrorists near Daryapur in Hisar district had indeed led to a sudden emotional upsurge and incidents of arson and looting in several towns. Effective action by the State administration helped restore normalcy and prevented a backlash. Looted property worth Lakhs of rupees was recovered and restored to the rightful owners and a large number of rioters and looters were arrested. Lt. Gen J.S. Aurora, MP and President of the Sikh Forum, had nothing but praise for the Haryana Government for its action which included the suspension of a few police officials believed to have shown leniency to the rioters. It is just as well that the Haryana Government is revamping its intelligence network to facilitate speedy transmission of reports and is providing sophisticated weapons and other equipment to the anti-terrorist cell. Daryapur cannot bear repetition.

The demand for the early completion of the Sutlej-Yamuna Link Canal too is linked to developments in Punjab. The State Government's concern over the "repeated slippage of

THE STATESMAN, (Chandigarh, 16-3-1988)

'Unique Steps' for Development

CHANDIGARH, March 14–The Budget Session of the Haryana Assembly started today with the address of the State Governor, Mr. H. A. Barari highlighting the achievements of the State Government in irrigation and power health education and industrial development. The Governor, who belongs to West Bengal, read out his address in Hindi.

As soon as the Governor began his address, the Chief Minister, Mr. Devi Lal, was on his feet to remark; "We request you to go ahead with the remaining part of your address in English." Obviously Mr. Barari was making efforts to read out the address in Hindi. But the Governor announced that he would complete his address in Hindi. He was then lustily cheered by the House. A smiling Mr. Devi Lal also joined in the cheering of the Governor.

The Governor said that in a sort time the State Government had taken several "unique steps" for accelerating the pace of development and improving the lot of the poor sections of society. He mentioned measures like old age pension and remission of co-operative and other loans for the weaker sections taken by the Devi Lal Government.

Referring to the law and order situation in the State, the Governor said an anti-terrorist

He said this was one of the worst droughts of the century and the farmers in Haryana suffered a loss of Rs. 700 crores. In agricultural production alone. The State Government received Central assistance of Rs. 37.22 crores to mitigate the suffering of the drought-affected people which was inadequate, the Governor stressed.

The Governor highlighted the steps taken by the State Government to assist the people affected by the drought including the suspension of luccart loans. The public distribution system has been strengthened to ensure fair and equitable distribution of essential commodities through a network of 6,447 shops." A sum of Rs. 2 crores has been ear-marked for supplementary nutrition for children and bursting and expectant mothers. To help the Landless labourers and poor wage earners, the State Government has provided an additional sum of Rs. 15 crores for creating employment in the drought-affected areas.

Highlighting the State Government's economic policy the Governor said the states has been to increase farm production through a judicious mix of incentives and access to improved agricultural practices and strong theming of the basis infrastructure by increasing the irrigation and power potential."

As was the custom, that evening, a dinner was hosted by me at Raj Bhawan for the Ministers, Members of State Assembly and officials of the State Government. As I went round meeting the guests, many of them congratulated me on my performance in the State Assembly. This also came in for praise in the press, particularly in Haryana and some other Hindi-speaking States.

My activities increasingly brought me in touch with a wide cross section of people in different walks of life. This gave me an opportunity to mingle with people from the highest to the lowest strata of society, to gauge their moods, apprise myself of their problems and feel their pulse. For example, a flower show organized by the Haryana Urban Development Authority, which I inaugurated in the Topiary Garden at Panchkula in the vicinity of Chandigarh on March 12, 1988 gave me a chance to meet the social elite including some leading figures in the field of gardening and horticulture. I was impressed by the wide variety of flowers and cacti that were displayed, particularly by those put up by Smt. Usha Saboo, a leading social activist of Chandigarh.

Some time in March 1988, Navjeevan Khosla, a retired I.A.S. Officer, who was active in Chandigarh's cultural circuit came to call no me. He was a highly cultured person with a special interest in

Indian classical music and dance. He invited me and my wife to attend two cultural programmes at Chandigarh's Tagore Theatre. One of these was a musical programme on the life of Amir Khusro directed by Sheila Bhatia and the other was Sheila Bhatia's play on Mirza Ghalib organized the next evening. We immensely enjoyed the programmes during which we met several well-known musicians and artistes of Punjab and Haryana.

From this time onward, we maintained very close relations with Navjeevan Khosla, who offered us many occasions to enjoy classical music of a high standard at functions, which he and his organization held periodically. He also helped me organize musical programmes at our Raj Bhawan to which I used to invite as many of Chandigarh's aficionados of classical music as the available space could accommodate.

There was an amazing variety of functions that I had to inaugurate or address in my capacity as Governor. I remember delivering the valedictory address on March 17, 1988 at the graduation ceremony of the 11th Commonwealth Diploma Course in Youth and Development, which had been organized by the Commonwealth Youth Centre in Chandigarh headed by one Agiyochi. At this function, I met the trainees, who had come from several Asian countries.

I had occasion to rub shoulders with Chandigarh's academics at the convocation of the famous DAV College on March 29, 1988. After delivering the convocation address, I had the pleasure of meeting the Principal and Professors as well as some students of the college. Talking to them informally was like a breath of fresh air because it was after a long time that I came in touch with the members of the academia. I nostalgically recalled the days when I was a Lecturer in Economics at a Kolkata college way back in 1952. My first of several jobs that I had taken up one after the other before finally settling down to the life of a police officer!

From contemporary reports in the press, I felt that my activities were already drawing favourable comments. I have earlier mentioned the praise showered on me after I had read the budget speech in the State Assembly in Hindi. As will be seen from the write-up reproduced below, shortly after my appointment as Governor was announced and a few days before I was sworn in, the Tribune, a very important English daily of Chandigarh, in an editorial on February 16, 1988, had taken exception to my appointment because I was an ex-policeman and a former Director of the Intelligence Bureau to boot:

Imposed Governors

Haryana's case is an instance apart. Mr. Devi Lal, a believer in "people power," has been an outspoken critic of the Central leadership and is an active leader working for non-Congress unity. A former police officer will replace a former bureaucrat—Mr. S.M.H. Burney–in Haryana. It is somewhat premature to jump to any conclusion about what sort of a Governor Mr. H.A. Brari will make. But the springing of a former Director of the Intelligence Bureau on an unsuspecting State Government does not indicate honourable intentions on the part of Delhi. Mr. Justice Sarkaria must be wondering to what earthly purpose he had been slaving away for the past four days.

It was, therefore, with great pleasure and surprise that I read the following write-up on me in the same newspaper, the Tribune of March 23, 1988, which made quite some positive references to my activities:

The Tribune, Wednesday, March 23, 1988

CHANDIGARH CALLING

Unlike his predeceser the new Haryana Governor is not keen to keep a low profile. Within a week of Mr. Barari's arrival in Chandigarh the message was out : the former Director of Intelligence Bureau does not lead a life shrouded in secrecy any more.

And, like his Punjab counterpart, Mr Barari too is likely to open the hitherto contined precunts of Raj Bhawan, a people from all walks of life. Hardly two months in office, Mr Barari has accepted several invitations to public functions—perhaps already more than Mr. S.M.H. Burney's quota for an entire year—both in Haryana and Chandigarh. He was present on both days at T agore Theatre last week to witness Sheila Bhatia's musical plays to Amir Khusro and Mirza Ghalib.

His desire for communication was made evident elsewhere too: his maiden speech in the Haryana Vidhan Sabha was one hour and

If Mr. Siddhartha Shankar may plays tennis. Mr. Barari has been into yoga. His love for the ancient form of exercise, as Mr Ray's love for tennis, is well known, at least to senior intelligence officers. Even as IB Director, when he had in repute to the ruling every morning, he seldom missed his yoga exercises. Besides helping him to keep trim, yoga has reportedly cured his nasal problem.

Few people are aware that Mr J.F. Ribeiro, Punjab's director General of Police, and Mr Barari are batch mates in the Indian Police Service. It is a coincidence indeed that both IPS officers occupy key and high positions in neighbouring States.

Mr Barari is the son-in-law of Mr. B.N. Mullick, one of India's most famous police officers and a former IB Director, The Haryana Governor has three daughters-all toppers from Delhi University, all working as lecturers and all married to men in the India services.

In between my multifarious activities, I was not neglecting sports. Soon after reaching Chandigarh, I took to tennis, a game I had played in the 1950's and 1960's, but had to keep on the back burner for many years owing to the exigencies of a demanding intelligence career. Now that I had all the time in the world to play any game I liked, I took to tennis again. I saw how S.S. Ray, the Punjab Governor, made time to play tennis in Chandigarh despite his busy schedule. I decided to follow suit and lost no time in getting myself a racquet and joining the company of Chandigarh's tennis enthusiasts. In fact, as I have already mentioned, the press and the tennis-playing crowd of Chandigarh had been anticipating that I would soon try my hand at tennis.

I had played some cricket as well, but had never taken this game seriously. Each year, a friendly cricket match was played in Chandigarh between the teams representing the officials of the Punjab and Haryana Governments respectively. The match for 1988 was fixed for March 13, 1988, a Sunday. S.S. Ray, an ace cricketer ever since his young days and now the Governor of Punjab, was the Captain of the Punjab team. A suggestion was made on behalf of the Haryana officials that I lead their team, which I gladly agreed to do. The Punjab team batted for 45 minutes and piled up a big total of 279 runs. Soon the rains came literally out of the blue and disrupted the match. We had to call it a day. The same evening, I hosted at our Raj Bhawan—a dinner for all the participants and their wives including Governor S.S. Ray and Smt. Maya Ray. The botched match was played again on March 27, 1988 and was won by the Punjab team. It was now the turn of the Punjab Governor to host a dinner at his Raj Bhawan, which we all attended. In retrospect, I think that it was a good tradition to have a sporting event like this as it fostered a lot of goodwill and camaraderie among the officials of Punjab and Haryana.

As the Governor of Haryana, I automatically became the Chancellor of the three universities in the State namely the Maharshi Dayanand University, Rohtak, the Kurukshetra University, Kurukshetra and the Haryana Agricultural University, Hissar. The post of Vice-Chancellor of the Maharshi Dayannd University was lying vacant for some time and was being temporarily held by P.P. Caprihan, I.A.S., a distinguished civil servant of the State.

I decided to appoint a proper Vice-Chancellor for the Maharshi Dayanand University and spoke to Ch. Devi Lal about it. He called on me and suggested the name of a person for this post. In the course of discussions with him, I left him in no doubt that while I would most seriously consider the name proposed by him, I would also try to find out on my own some other persons, who might fill the bill for this post. I explained to him that, according to the law enacted for this purpose, it was the Governor and not the Chief Minister, who had the power to appoint the Vice-Chancellor.

I was aware that the Governments and Chief Ministers of many States were interested in having their own nominees as Vice-Chancellors so that they could control the affairs of the universities.

This naturally politicized the functioning of the universities and adversely affected the standard of higher education.

I lost no time in going into the background of the person whom Devi Lal had recommended for the Vice-Chancellor's job at Rohtak. My enquiries conducted through reliable sources about this person's past activities and academic achievements did not inspire much confidence in me about his suitability. In the mean time, I had requested some of my acquaintances in the academic field as well as the Chairman of the University Grants Commission to suggest some names.

During one of my meetings with Ch. Devi lal, I told him that the candidate he had proposed was not acceptable to me for reasons I have already mentioned. It appeared to me that he had forwarded to me the name that had been suggested to him by his own men in the party or the government and that he himself did not know him for Adams. I took this opportunity to tell him that by suggesting this gentleman's name with a not very palatable background, his men were going to put him in an embarrassing situation. I must say it to the credit of Ch. Devi Lal that he agreed with me.

Then I told Ch. Devi Lal that he had many things to do and many powers to exercise in his capacity as Chief Minister. I told him in all sincerity: "Why should you bother so much about who becomes the Vice-Chancellor of a university, when the law gives me, and not you, the power to appoint this functionary? Can you not trust me to select the right person for the job so that he can bring about an improvement in educational standards, which would benefit the youth of the State and open up better opportunities for them in their lives?"

Ch. Devi Lal was quite frank with me and said that he feared that I might yield to pressure from people in the Central Government and appoint one of their nominees as the Vice-Chancellor. I disabused his mind of such fears and told him that in my long official career I had never succumbed to pressure and that now, when I was holding a constitutional post subject to nobody's control, there was no question of my yielding to pressure. I assured him that I would select a person purely on merit and take Ch. Devi Lal into confidence before taking the final decision. I made it clear that I would not choose a person who was related to me or in whom I was personally interested. I further told him that he was bound to agree with my choice because I would select a person who would be eminently suitable for the job. Ch. Devi Lal agreed with my course of action and told me to go ahead.

After interviewing several candidates in Chandigarh as well as in Delhi, I found that Lt. General (retd.) G.C. Aggarwal, a former Surveyor-General of India, to be the most suitable from all points of view. His name had been suggested by the Chairman of the University Grants Commission. He had a brilliant academic record and considerable administrative experience and in his official capacity, he had attended and presided over international conferences.

When I told Ch. Devi Lal about my choice, he readily agreed because he understood that I had not been influenced by political pressure from Delhi. On my suggestion, he agreed to issue a statement appealing to all concerned to extend their co-operation and support to Lt. Gen (retd.) G.C. Sharma after he was appointed as Vice-Chancellor of the Maharshi Dayanand University. Gen. Sharma did an excellent job at Rohtak and earned the praise of all concerned by virtue of his non-partisan role and the efficient discharge of his responsibilities.

Meanwhile, my wife and I were socializing quite a bit both at Raj Bhawan functions and elsewhere. Some time in April 1988, I, along with wife, went one evening to the Tagore Theatre in Chandigarh to inaugurate a ballet put up by a troupe from the Soviet Union. Here, I met a cross section of Chandigarh's elite and music lovers. Some of them put across to me the idea of hosting programmes of classical music at our Raj Bhawan. My wife was also playing an active social role and attending functions including some organized by the wives of the I.A.S. Officers of Haryana.

At about this time, B. K. Nehru, the doyen of the Indian Civil Service, who had distinguished himself in various capacities including those of Governor and Ambassador, called on us along with his wife, on their way to Delhi from the beautiful hill station of Kasauli, where they had settled down. It was great pleasure making their acquaintance and getting to know them well at the personal plane.

On April 11, 1988, I swore in some new Ministers of Haryana at Raj Bhawan. Some of them had left the Congress Party and joined Ch. Devi Lal's Lok Dal. Those sworn in included three Cabinet Ministers, two Ministers of State and two Deputy Ministers. One of the Cabinet Ministers sworn in was Tayab Hussain, who had resigned from the post of Leader of the Congress Legislature Party. He was known to be pro-Bansi Lal and anti-Bhajan Lal. Congress leaders accused Ch. Devi Lal of encouraging defections by citing the example of Tayab Hussain. Ch. Devi Lal retorted by saying that Tayab Hussain had displayed his political morality by resigning from the State Assembly. He also indicated that Tayab Hussain would contest the by-election form Taoru, the seat vacated by him.

Haryana contributes a large number of its people to the armed forces, the police and the para-military forces. Each village of the State counts among its population a number of serving as well as retired servicemen of all ranks. Over the decades, the Haryana Government has adopted many special measures to safeguard the interests of servicemen, particularly ex-servicemen. There are ex-servicemen's bodies at different levels all over Haryana to look after the welfare of this segment of the State's population that has made a vital contribution to the country's defence requirements. The apex body in this sphere of activity is the Rajya Sainik Board presided over by the Governor of Haryana and including the representatives of the State Government, defence services and ex-servicemen's organizations.

In my capacity as the President of the Rajya Sainik Board, I was to address an ex-servicemen's rally at Jind on April 18, 1988. Leaving Chandigarh on April 17, 1988, I stopped over for a few hours at Kaithal, which at that time formed part of Kurukshetra district. Earlier, when the State of Haryana came into being on November 1, 1966, both Kaithal and Kurukshetra were in Karnal district. In 1973, Karnal district was split and a new district of Kurukshetra carved out of it with Kaithal included in it. On November 1, 1989, a new district of Kaithal was formed with some areas of Jind and Kurukshetra districts.

At Kaithal, I was received by Nar Bahadur Dhanda, the local MLA, whom I had sworn in as a Minister of State a few days ago. The local officials and others from different walks of life, who called on me, told me about the history, culture and religious importance of Kaithal and some near-by places. On my way to Jind, I passed through some of these places. Later, a study of some books on the historical and spiritual background of these places revealed a fascinating picture of Haryana's ancient glory.

The Mahabharata describes Kaithal as a place surrounded by thick forests or 'Vanas'. Yudhistira, the eldest Pandava, is said to have founded this settlement, which, because of its association with Hanuman, the monkey-god, was known as Kapisthala or Kavitala—the abode of the monkeys.

Kaithal was a part of the Mauryan empire and was annexed by the Greeks in the second century B.C. It successively formed part of the Kushan empire (in the first and second centuries A.D.), the empire of the Yaudheyas (in the third century A.D.) and the Gupta empire (in the fourth century A.D.). In the sixth century A.D., the Huns attacked and destabilized this region. Then this place came under the sway of the Vardhana rulers of Thanesar. The Bhoja Pratihara and the Tomara rulers established their rule here in succession. The Kaithal region saw the invasions of Muhammad Ghauri in 1190-1191 A. D. And again in 1192 A.D. after which this place became an appendage of Delhi.

Kaithal witnessed serious political turmoil in the 13th century A.D., and in 1240 A.D., Razia, the Sultan of Delhi, was assassinated here, as has been mentioned earlier in Chapter III. In the 14th century A.D., famine stalked the area and widespread distress led the people to rebel against the authorities. They stopped the payment of their customary tribute to the ruler in protest against the failure of Muhammad bin Tughlak, the Sultan of Delhi, to take ameliorative measures. Towards the end of the 14th century A.D., in the wake of the death of Firoz Shah Tughlak, there was a civil war, following a clash over succession, between rival contenders. Kaithal and in fact the whole region up to Delhi were laid waste as a result of the plunder and pillage unleashed by Humayun, the grandson of Firoz Shah.

Kaithal was a halting station for Tamerlane on his route to Delhi in 1398 A.D. Some say that he had crossed the Ghaggar and Saraswati rivers over bridges at Ghula and Polar and proceeded from Kaithal through Assand, Salwan and Panipat to arrive at Delhi on December 3, 1398. Anarchy and lawlessness stalked this region, which was, therefore, deserted by the local people, who sought refuge at safer places elsewhere.

Kaithal saw better times during Mughal rule. A fortress built here by Akbar still bears testimony to the emperor's effort to give a face-lift to Kaithal. In early 18th century, Guru Govind Singh's acolyte, Banda Bairagi, raised a group of Sikhs, whose revolutionary activities created chaotic conditions in this region. Soon the Sikhs assumed power here and in 1767 A.D., Bhai Desa Singh was in control of the Kaithal region. One of Kaithal's rulers, Bhai Udai Singh, was known for his love of learning and had extended his patronage to Santokh Singh, the Sikh scholar famous for his voluminous work on the Ramayana. In 1843 A.D., the British authorities extended their rule to this area on the pretext that Bhai Udai Singh had died without leaving behind a male issue.

During the 1857 war of independence, the people of Kaithal and adjoining areas rose in revolt against the British and had to face the repression let loose by the latter. Soon this area was amalgamated into Karnal district. While passing along the streets of Kaithal, I was shown several tombs of Muslim saints as also the famous Gurdwara of Guru Tegh Bahadur, where, I was told, there still stood a Neem tree dating back to the time of the Guru. I also had a look at the big Bidkiyar Lake, Bhai Desa Singh's palace and some of the eight gates of the town.

It would be in order to refer here to the ancient history of several places in the Kaithal region. There is, for example, a place Siwan, whose name was derived from 'Sitaban' or 'Seoban', which means the forest of Sita, *i.e.*, a place in the forests where Sita had lived. At this place, Mother earth is believed by devout Hindus to have swallowed up Sita, the emblem of chastity. A temple of Sita is located here. Another place, Guhla, about sixteen miles from Kaithal, figures in the memoirs of Tamerlane, because it was here that he and his army had crossed the Ghaggar river over a bridge, which, I learnt, still existed.

Pundri is another very ancient place near Kaithal, which is an important pilgrimage mentioned in the Mahabharata as Pundrik. The place got its name from the Pindrok Tank, which was excavated during the Mahabharata age. The tank was also known as 'Naghrod', a bath in whose waters was considered to be highly meritorious.[1]

According to the Mahabharata as well as the Puranas, those who bathed in this tank, meditated here and performed 'Sradh' on the tenth day of the bright fortnight of the moon achieved liberation.[2]

Hardly five miles from Pundri is another pilgimage, Pharal, which is believed to be identical with what is mentioned as Phalakiban in the Mahabharata and the Puranas. Near this village is a sacred tank where sage Phalgu had immersed himself in meditation. Phalakiban was believed to have been located on the bank of the ancient Drishdwati river, which later disappeared. The gods are said to have done penance for a thousand years at this place.[3]

A pilgrimage known as Mishrak was located here. It was called Mishrak because sage Vyasa had got assembled here all the pilgrimages for the convenience of the gods It is said that whenever a person remembered this place, his ancestors felt gratified.[4]

It was late in the evening, when, on April 17, 1988, I reached Jind from Kaithal along with my wife, Anita. On arrival, we were received by Parma Nand, Minister, Kulbir Singh Malik, Deputy Speaker of the State Assembly (both of whom belonged to the district) and Ashok Lawasa, I.A.S., the young Collector. In the course of our discussions, they gave me a low-down on Jind district and its ancient as well as more recent history.

On April 18, 1988, I addressed a large gathering of ex-servicemen, dwelling at length on their problems and the ameliorative measures being taken or contemplated by the State and Central Governments. I felt happy that I could make a major speech in Hindi extempore at a large public meeting. As a matter of fact, I delivered all my speeches in Haryana extempore, whether in English or in Hindi. At a lunch party organized on this occasion by the district administration, I was introduced to several retired service officers of various ranks, who apprised me of their problems and their concerns.

My exchanges with ex-servicemen gave me an opportunity of getting to know a lot about them and the martial traditions of Haryana and its people. Some of them told me interesting anecdotes about the habits and life-style of ex-servicemen of subordinate ranks who are called Phojis. Since many of the Phojis had worked with British officers in pre-1947 days, they often tried to show off by imitating the latter's manners. They professed to be strict disciplinarians and insisted on the rural folk observing certain norms of discipline in their day-to-day life.

I recalled these traits of Haryana's Phojis while going through a book 'Wit and Humour of Haryana' written by Rajbir Deswal, a police officer of Haryana. A joke about Phojis narrated by Deswal runs as follows: A Phoji was narrating his experience in the army to his mother, sister and Bhabi (elder brother's wife). He said that his day began with drill. The ladies asked him to explain clearly what drill meant. The Phoji said that he would give a live demonstration to convey the precise meaning of drill. He made them stand in a queue and gave his words of command: "Saamne Dekh (look forward), Harkat Nahin (no movements)". Then looking at his Bhabi, who was pregnant, he said: "Pet Andar (squeeze your stomach), Chhati Bahar (thrust your breasts forward)". The ladies pushed the Phoji out of the house.

There are many folk songs in Haryana that bring out the martial strand of the people's cultural background. One of the songs which a retired Army officer cited in this context would read somewhat like this in English: "My husband, please join the armed forces to vindicate your credentials as a rue warrior. Go and fight the enemy to bring credit to your parents. Fearlessly face the cannons on your bare chest."

During World War I, Haryana contributed a large number to the Jat Regiment of the Indian Army. Many of them distinguished themselves in the war and won laurels and awards. One Deep Chand of Sonepat district, known as the Shakespeare and Kalidasa of Haryana, composed songs belonging to the category called 'Swaang', which brought out his creative genius. His martial songs composed during World War I won him the title of 'Rai Sahib' apart from other awards. One of his many catchy and highly popular martial songs, which helped in securing numerous recruits to the Army ran as follows: [5]

"Bharti holai tara bahar khara rangat
Yaha rakhta madham bana
Milta ha phatta purrana
Vaha milta hai full boat
Bharti ho lai ra ...."

Translated into English, it would read like this: "Come and join the army: the recruits are waiting outside your door: you have old worn-out clothes to wear here, but there—in the army—you will get full boots."[6]

The 'Allah' folklore of Haryana has many popular songs, which dwell on the martial and chivalrous traditions of the people. In one of the 'Allah' songs brought to my notice and which I later traced in a book, [7] the warrior challenges his rival, shouting at him:

"Hum bate hain Rajputan ke, dhar par shish samagta nai, Aisa maroo ka paggi ka dhoonda khog milanga na". (We are sons of Rajputs and don't give a thought to our life).

Reflecting on the martial traditions of Haryana, I detected a close similarity between the thinking of the local people and the teachings of the Gita. Lord Krishna had exhorted Arjuna to fight against the Kauravas, unmindful of what consequences were to follow. I felt happy that the people of Haryana, on whose soil the Gita was preached and the battle of Mahabharata fought, had through the ages continued to abide by the message of the Gita as was clearly reflected in their military traditions and folklore.

Later, I had further occasions to visit several places in Jind and the adjacent districts and to interact with people from various walks of life. This, together with my extensive studies, helped me in getting a comprehensive picture of Jind and its remote as well as its more recent past. Jind is a very ancient place, where the Pandavas had built a temple of Jayanti Devi, the goddess of victory. This place was, therefore, called Jayantipuri, which later came to be known as Jayanti and finally as Jind.

This district has many pilgrimages of the Kurukshetra region. Three of these pilgrimages mentioned in the Vamana Purana are

Somatirtha, Jwalamaleshwar and Bhuteshwara. About seven miles from Jind is Barah, a place which has derived its name from Vishnu's incarnation as Varaha (boar). There are many other pilgrimages in this area such as Ikas, Pindora-Nirjan, Kasoon, Simla, Sanghan, Sajooma, Barta and Mator. This region abounds with old temples. People from far and near come here and throng the pilgrimages and temples during numerous fairs and festivals.

About five miles from Jind is the famous pilgrimage of Ram Rai, a corruption from Ram Hrada, which figures in the Mahabharata and the Puranas. Ram Hrada is said to be one of the four 'Yakshas' (*i.e.* gate-keepers or rather points of entry) on the periphery of the sacred Kurukshetra region. The other three are Tarantuk, Arantuk and Machakruk.[8] Before a pilgrim enters the holy land of Kurukshetra, it is essential for him to pay obeisance to these four gate-keepers.[9]

Given the name 'Kapil Yaksha' in the Vamana Purana 10, Ram Hrada means the 'Lakes of Rama' and signifies the fact that Parashurama had filled five lakes with the blood of Kshatriya kings whom he had slain. One of these lakes was Brahmsarovar in Kurukshetra, as I have mentioned in Chapter V.

Machkruk mentioned above has been identified by Alexander Cunningham, the celebrated archaeologist, as Sinkh, mid-way between Jind and Panipat, which was located in ancient times on the Drishdwati river.

Hatyaharana, Parashurama Tirtha and Surajkunda are some of the other sacred places in and around Jind. An important pilgrimage of this district is Kalyat (which was transferred to Kaithal district in 1989). There is a big tank here, apart from some ancient temples, which were built without mortar. Excavations here have yielded some statues, perhaps dating back to 200 B.C., which are exquisite works of art. According to Puranic accounts, Kalyat was known as Kapil Tirtha because Lord Shiva was believed to have lived here as Kapil Muni.[11] Anybody who had a view of Lord Shiva worshipped by the sages was said to achieve instantaneous liberation.[12]

Safidon, a famous pilgrimage of Jind district finds mention in the Mahabharata as well as in the Puranas. It is believed to be a corruption from the Sanskrit word Sarpadevi or Sarpadadhi or Sarpadamana. Said to have been founded by the Pandavas, Safidon was also known as Nagatirtha in ancient times. According to the Mahabharata, a person paying a visit to Sarpadarvi pilgrimage acquired merit accruing from the 'Agnistoma' sacrifice, [13] while the

Vamana Purana says that anybody having a bath here becomes free from the fear of snakes.[14] Close to Safidon is a village, Hat, where there are several pilgrimages, two of which, namely Panchanada and Koti Tirtha figured in ancient literature.

Captain R.C. Temple has written in his three-volume magnum opus "Legends of Punjab' about two old traditions which revolve around Safidon.[15] According to the first of these traditions, there were three big wells at Safidon which contained Amrita, snakes and locusts respectively. King Basak (or Vasuki) was afflicted by leprosy as a sequel to a curse pronounced by a cow that had been bitten by a snake. It was believed that Basak could be cured with the Amrita from the well at Safidon that formed part of the territory of the Pandava King, Parikshit. The well at Safidon was covered by heavy stones that only Niwal Dai, daughter of King Basak, was in a position to lift with the help of magic.

So Niwal Dai went to Safidon to fetch the Amrita, unmindful of the risk of getting caught. Khvaja Khizar, the god of water, who was anxious to have a look at her beautiful face, managed to depress the level of water in the well to such an extent that Niwal Dai had to lower her head deep inside the well in order to get at the Amrita. The god of water thus had the satisfaction of having a good view of the princess, but, then, the water in the well swelled up, creating a big noise that attracted the notice of the Pandavas. As the Pandavas tried to seize her, she assumed the form of a snake and hid herself inside a platform around the well. After the Pandava King, Parikshit, assured her that he would not touch her, she came out.

Parikshit, however, could not resist his temptation and refused to let her go, saying that her father had earlier betrothed her to him but had not kept his word. Niwal Dai was, however, allowed to leave as she said that she would come back after delivering the Amrita to her father. The Amrita was applied all over King Basak's body except over the thumb with the result that his whole body except the thumb was cured of leprosy. Disregarding the wish of her father, Niwal Dai again went to Safidon the fetch some more Amrita to cure her father's thumb. There, she was seized by Parikshit, who married her.

R.C. Temple described the second tradition on the basis of what was narrated as some sort of a poetic verse by two scavengers of village Babyl of Ambala district. This account is similar in its general outline to the first tradition discussed above except in some minor details. It is said that King Basak once went on a hunting expedition when he was captured by King Parikshit for having strayed into his territory. Parikshit allowed Basak to go after he promised to give his daughter, Niwal Dai, in marriage to him.

Basak did not act on his promise and started preparing for some religious rites to neutralize the sin of breaking his pledge. The priest needed some yak's milk for this purpose, but when this was procured, he refused to take it on the apprehension that the girl, who had been deprived of her share of this milk, would curse him. Basak, who lost his cool upon this, assumed the form of a snake and bit the yaks. The girls, who were thus deprived of the yaks' milk, cursed King Basak, who contracted leprosy as a result. Then Basak's young daughter, Niwal Dai, went to Safidon to obtain the Amrita from the well, as has been described earlier. Then the legend more or less follows the account of the first tradition given above, which brings us as far as the marriage of Niwal Dai with Parikshit.

Angry with Parikshit, Basak mobilized his warriors and kinsmen and made several unsuccessful attempts on the life of Parikshit. Basak's Naga army also invaded Parikshit's territory, but to no avail. Basak then enlisted the help of his nephew, Tatig Naga (also called Takshak Naga), who took the form of a snake and bit Parikshit to death. Finding her husband dead, Niwal Dai approached Parikshit's Guru, Dhanvantar Baid, for help. Dhanvantar failed to cause any harm to Tatig and then sent his disciples to mount Meru to procure some herbs for reviving Parikshit. Tatig, who came to know this, went to Meru and lighted thousands of lamps with the result that Dhanvantar's disciples, blinded by the glow of so many lamps, failed to locate the herbs for which they had gone there. So Parikshit was now finally dead. Dhanvantar told his disciples to cook Parikshit's flesh and eat it because that would make all of them Dhanvantar Baids. Tatig misled he local people by saying that some robbers were eating human flesh. The people came forward and attacked Dhanvantar's disciples, who fled. Parikshit's flesh was left to be preyed upon by crows and kites.

Parikshit's wife, Niwal Dai, was four months pregnant when the former died. A son by name Janamejaya was born to Niwal Dai. When Janamejaya grew up, he heard how is father had been killed by the Nagas.He decided to take revenge. He invited his grandfather, King Basak, to Safidon. The latter was very happy and sent his ambassador, Jado, to Safido with a large retinue along with loads of gifts. Janamejaya killed them by throwing them into a cauldron of boiling oil, though Jado managed to escape. Later, Janamejaya pursued

Tatig and brought him to Safidon. He spared the life of Tatig in compliance with an undertaking given to Holy God not to kill him. However, he branded Tatig by putting a part of his body into the boiling oil before he was allowed to go. It is said that just two and a half families of the Nagas survived the revenge killings by Janamejaya.

In the Puranas and the Mahabharata, the snake sacrifice done by Janamejaya has been described. It has been said that once King Parikshit went to a forest for hunting. He felt thirsty and went to the hermitage of sage Samika and requested the latter for water. But as the sage was engaged in meditation, he did not respond to the King's request, which annoyed the latter. In a fit of rage, the king put a dead snake around the sage's neck and then left the hermitage. The sage's son, Shringi, who learnt about this incident, pronounced a curse as a sequel to which Parikshit was bitten to death by the snake Takshaka. Janamejaya, son of King Parikshit, avenged the death of his father by performing a snake-sacrifice. However, Takshaka escaped death because sage Astika, nephew of King Basak, appeared on the scene and successfully intervened to prevail upon Janamejaya to save the life of Takshaka, besides many other snakes.

The account in the Mahabharata mentions the conquest of Taxila and a snake-sacrifice that was performed there. According to the Bhagavata Purana, the Samika incident had taken place near the Prachi Saraswati and Shringi had cursed Parakshit at a place in the same region. A scrutiny of the two traditions—the local tradition of Safidon and the literary tradition in the Mahabharata and the Puranas—reveals some similarities as well as some differences. O.P. Bharadwaj, who had gone into this matter in some depth, has made some observations, which are worth quoting:[16] "While both agree on the death of Pariksit at the hands of Taksaka Naga and the ultimate large-scale destruction of the Nagas by his son Janamejaya, there are some important points of difference between them. Firstly, the root cause of Pariksit's death is the curse of a young sage in one and the abduction of a Naga princess in the other. Secondly, while the literary sources describe the conflict of Pariksit and Janamejaya with snakes who had the faculty of assuming human form on need, the local tradition depicts their enemies as primarily a tribe of human beings called the Nagas possessing the power of changing themselves into snakes whenever necessary. Finally, the main literary source, the Mahabharata mentions Taksasila as the venue of the snake-sacrifice against which the local tradition places it at Safidon or Sarpadevi."

Bharadwaj thinks that the account in the literary source is thickly covered with a strong layer of mythology while the oral tradition, even while being so, looks more realistic as far as the genesis of the conflict and the presentation of the Nagas as a tribe is concerned. As he observes: "In this connection, Pargiter's view that the Nagas had slain Pariksit II and his son Janamejaya III defeated them and made peace with them would seem to be reasonable although it has yet to gain general acceptance." [17]

The venue of the snake-sacrifice is an issue over which there is a divergence between the Mahabharata and the local tradition. Only the Mahabharata says that Janamejaya had conquered Taxila and performed the snake-sacrifice there. The local tradition mentions Safidon as the place where this was done. As Bharadwaj observes, the stand taken by the Mahabharata not only runs counter to the local tradition but also contradicts its own statement that testifies to the existence of a Tirtha called Sarpadevi, where the goddess of snakes resided and granted the merit of the Agnistoma sacrifice to her visitors. The Vamana Purana also refers to Safidon, which it calls Sarpadadhi, as the venue of the snake-sacrifice. Moreover, the Mahabharata itself speaks of Takshaka as belonging to the Kurukshetra region, besides mentioning the presence of Parikshit near Prachi Saraswati and the pronouncement of the curse by Shringi with the water of the Kaushiki river, which was a tributary of the Drishadwati. In view of this, it seems unlikely that Janamejaya had attacked Taxila or had performed the snake-sacrifice there.[18]

O. P. Bharadwaj feels that probably "the commonness of the first half in the name of Taksasila and the name of the Naga chief Taksaka misled the poet (*i.e.* The author of the Mahabharata) to think of a connection between the two and he could not resist the temptation of inventing a situation which did not appear to him too absurd once the idea was born. ....In the circumstances, we are inclined to believe that Taksasila did not in reality form a part of the kingdom of Janamejaya Pariksita and its association with him is born out of poetic fancy, abetted by a confusion of his identity with an illustrious ancestor who happened to be his namesake." [19]

The more recent history of Jind is also quite interesting and interwoven with the general history of north western India during the 18th and 19th centuries, when, against the backdrop of this region's unsettled conditions, the Muslims, the Sikhs and the British were vying with one another to retain or establish their rule. Jind, Patiala and Nabha were called Phulkian States because they were ruled by the descendants of one Phul. The rulers of Jind were the descendants of Sukh Chain, a grandson of Phul. In 1755 A.D., Sardar Gajpat Singh, the second son of Sukh Chain, annexed a sizeable territory in this region that included Jind, Safidon, Panipat and Karnal, but failed to retain control over these places.

In 1763 A.D., when the Sikhs occupied Sirhind after defeating Zain Khan, the Governor appointed by Ahmad Shah Durrani, the Sikh leaders of the region took over the territory and divided it among themselves. Gajpat Singh became the ruler of Jind and Safidon and set up his capital at Jind in 1766 A.D. Though he paid tribute to Delhi, he secured the title of Raja in 1772 A.D. Soon he annexed some territory including Sangrur from the ruler of Nabha and though he could not retain most of it, Sangrur continued to form part of Jind State. In 1775 A.D., the British tried in vain to get hold of Jind, their move being foiled by the joint resistance offered by the rulers of the Phulkian States.

Towards the end of the 18th century A.D., George Thomas, an Irish adventurer, made a bid to annex this territory, but the rulers of Jind, Kaithal and Patiala joined hands and, with the help of Louis Borquin offered on behalf of the Scindia, succeded in 1802 A.D. In putting paid to his dream. In 1857 A.D., when the people of Haryana, like those in other parts of India, rose in revolt against the British authorities, the rulers of the Phulkian States of Jind, Nabha and Patiala had helped the latter and were later liberally rewarded by the British with the grant of extensive territories. Narnaul was given to the Maharaja of Patiala and was named after him as Mahendargarh. Bawal was given to the Nabha State, Ballabhgarh to Faridkot and Dadri to Jind.

There are some Rajputs in Jind district. The Rajputs of Haryana belong to either of two clans namely the Mandhars and the Chauhans. The Mandhars, who trace their lineage to Lav, the son of Rama, regard Kalyat in Jind district as their stronghold. In this district, there are some Brahmins, who are called Tyagis as distinguished from the Gaud Brahmins. Those Brahmins, who chose agriculture as their occupation in preference to priestly duties, came to be known a Tyagis. They trace their origin to the time when Janamejaya performed the snake sacrifice at Safidon in Jind district.[20] It is said that since there were no Gaud Brahmins in this country at the time, Janamejaya got many of them from beyond the sea. Those who did not accept money accept money as reward for their services were awarded villages. When they decided not to take offerings at a later date, they came to be known as Tyagis. Those who accepted offerings were called Gaud Brahmins. The Tyagis wear sacred threads, but the Gauds do not intermarry with them.[21]

Notes

1. ततो गच्छेत् विप्रेन्द्र नागस्य ह्रदमुक्तमम्।
पौण्डरीके नरः स्नात्वा पुण्डरीकफलं लभेत्।।
(वामन सरो. 15/39)
2. दशम्यां शुक्लपक्षस्य चैत्रस्य तु विशेषतः।
स्नानं जपं तथा श्राद्धं मुक्तिमार्ग प्रदायकम्।।
(वामन सरो. 15/40 महा. 3:81:69)
3. ततो गच्छेत् राजेन्द्र फलकीवनमुत्तमम्।
यत्र देवाः सदा राजन्फलकी वनमाश्रिताः।।
तपश्चरन्ति विपुलं बहुवर्षसहस्रकम्।।
(वामन सरो. 15/45 महा. 3:81:72)
4. मनसा स्मरते यस्तु फलकी वनमुत्तमम्।
तस्यापि पितरस्तृप्तिं प्रयास्यन्ति न संशयः।।
(वामन सरो. 15/39)
5. Haryana by D.C. Verma, p. 145.
6. *Ibid*, p. 146.
7. *Ibid*, p. 150.
8. तरन्तुकारन्तुकयोर्यदन्तरम् रामह्रदानां च मचक्रुकस्य।
एतत्कुरुक्षेत्र समन्तपंचक पितामहस्योत्तरवेदिरुच्यते।।
(महा. वन 3/81/178, शल्य 53/24) (वामन पुराण सरो. 1/14)
(अभिधान, चिंतामणि, श्लोक 950)
9. रन्तुकं च नरो दृष्टवा द्वारपाल महाबलम्।
यक्षं समभिवाद्यैव तीर्थ यात्रा समाचरेत्।।
(वामन सरो. 13/11)
10. कपिलश्च महायक्षों द्वारपालः स्वयं स्थितः।
(वामन सरो. 13/44)
11. तत्र स्थितं महादेवं कपिलवपुरास्थितम्।।
(वामन सरो. 14:25:26)
12. दृष्टवा मुक्ति मवाप्रोति ऋषिभिः पूजितम् शिवम्।
(वामन सरो. 14:25:26)
13. सर्पदर्वी समासा नागानां तीर्थमुत्तमम्।
अग्निष्ठोममवाप्रोति नागलोकं च विन्दति।।
(महा. 3/81/12) (वामन सरो. 13/23) (पद्म पुराण, आदि खण्ड 26/12/13)

14. तत्र स्नानं नरः कृत्वा मुक्तो नागभयाद् भवेत्।
(वामन सरो. 13/24)
15. For a detailed account of these traditions, one may refer to "Janamejaya Pariksita and two ancient traditions of Kuruksetra" by O.P. Bharadwaj in the Journal of Haryana Studies, Vol. XIV, Nos. 1&2, 1982.
16. *Ibid.*
17. *Ibid.*
18. *Ibid.*
19. *Ibid.*
20. Haryana by D.C. Verma, p. 81.
21. *Ibid.*

7

Governor As Patron of NGO's: On Panipat, Rohtak, Pehowa and Other Places

From Jind, I proceeded to Delhi on April 18, 1988 late in the evening because there I was to attend a dinner party being held by the officers of the Intelligence Bureau, my very own organization, in celebration of the completion of the 100th year of its existence. This party was timed to coincide with the annual conference of the Directors-General of Police of the States and the heads of Central Police and para-military forces. It was with great pleasure that I met my old colleagues of the police service, both serving and retired, as well as many bureaucrats and Central Ministers, most of whom I knew intimately because they had something or other to do with the intelligence machinery of the country.

A week after my return to Chandigarh, I presided over a meeting of the Haryana Rural Development Board held at Raj Bhawan, which was attended by Chief Minister, Ch. Devi Lal, several ministers and officials. Several important measures to give a boost to rural development were decided upon. On May 11, 1988, a meeting of the Bharatiya Grameen Mahila Sangh was held at Raj Bhawan, over which I presided. This body, which looks after the problems of rural women, was doing a commendable job, thanks to the voluntary work and zeal of several ladies such as Smt. A. Sehgal, Smt. Singh (wife of Trilochan Singh, an I.A.S. Officer) and Smt. Asha Sharma, I.A.S., Secretary to the Social Welfare Department of the State Government.

I still recall the enthusiasm displayed by the members of Saket, an NGO for the welfare of orthopaedically handicapped persons, at a meeting of its Executive Committee that I chaired at Raj Bhawan in the latter half of May, 1988. Dr. A.K. Chakrabarti, Secretary of the organization, and Smt. Gupta, wife of Shri Banarsi Das Gupta, Deputy Chief Minister of Haryana, took an active part at this meeting.

I was also the President of the Haryana State Council for Child Welfare. S.S. Yadav, a retired Air Commodore, who was its Secretary, used to render yeoman's service. On may 25, 1988, I chaired a meeting at Raj Bhawan of the State Council of this body, which was followed by a meeting of the Executive Committee, which decided on steps towards the implementation of the programmes evolved at the State Council's meeting. The Executive Committee authorized the State Council to place helpless children or orphans for adoption by recognized agencies under the Hindu Adoptions and Maintenance Act, 1956 and the Guardians and Wards Act, 1890, as amended from time to time. It also approved of substantial funds to be provided to Bal Kunj, a children's home at Chhachhrauli, which was doing very useful work.

Towards the end of May, 1988, I presided over a meeting of the State-level Committee for the celebration of the 40th anniversary of our independence and of the centenary of Pt. Jawaharlal Nehru's birth. Chief Minister Ch. Devi Lal, some of his colleagues and many officials assembled at Raj Bhawan for this meeting, which chalked out elaborate programmes for these celebrations. I had a feeling that by requesting me to give the lead in such activities Ch. Devi Lal and his government were increasingly reposing their trust in my non-partisan role.

As Governor of Haryana, I also functioned as the chief of the Red Cross and the St. John Ambulance Corp (SJAC) in the State in the same way as the President headed these bodies at the national level. These important organizations with international networks perform useful functions through a well-oiled hierarchical machinery spread out all over the globe. Dr. A.K. Chakrabarti, Secretary of the Haryana unit of the Saket, was also the Secretary General of the Red Cross and the SJAC for Haryana. The meetings that I chaired at Raj Bhawan some time towards the end of May, 1988, of the executive bodies of the Haryana units of the Red Cross and the SJAC helped me to acquire some basic knowledge about the functioning of these bodies.

Another organization of which I was the President in my capacity as Governor was the State Council of Bharat Scouts and Guides. L. M. Jain, an able I.A.S. Officer, was the State's Chief Commissioner of this body. He briefed me about its functioning in Haryana in advance of the meeting of its general body held some time in the first fortnight of June, 1988 as far as I recall. This organization served the useful purpose of instilling a sense of discipline and a spirit of social service among young boys and girls. It has its own style of drill, which I learnt before presiding over the meeting, where I had to put my newly acquired knowledge into practice by returning the salutes of the members in the manner of a Scout.

There are several other non-governmental organizations of which the Governor of Haryana is the head. How much work a Governor does on these fora depends on his individual disposition and the interest he takes in promoting social causes. There is no doubt that a Governor's active participation in these multifarious activities can go a long way in raising the morale of the social activists in diverse spheres and in the removal of roadblocks in the smooth functioning of the various NGO's through his intercession with the concerned departments of the government.

All round the year, my work on behalf of this multiplicity of organizations involved correspondence, enlisting of office-bearers at various levels, keeping an eye on the implementation of various programmes and maintaining vigilance about the probity of the numerous office-bearers charged with carrying out various tasks at the ground level.

As a consequence of involving myself in a wide variety of activities, my plate was always reasonably full. I was requested on behalf of the medical fraternity of Chandigarh to inaugurate and address a seminar on cancer at the prestigious PGI (Post-Graduate Institute of Medical Education and Research) towards the end of April, 1988. There I mingled with members of the medical profession and social workers, who had come to take part in the seminar. What they told me about their experience in this field was an eye-opener for me and made me aware for the first time of many facts about the unremitting struggle they were carrying on in different parts of the country.

In May, 1988, a campaign was launched in Chandigarh for cleansing up the picturesque Sukhna Lake, which was getting progressively filled up with silt. Surrouded by forests and rocks, it mirrors the blue of the sky and the twinklig stars at night. It is an idyll of bliss and tranquillity, on whose placid waters one could often see the swan float double—swan and shadow—as poet Wordsworth had seen on the waters of river Yarrow. It was a favourite picnic spot and a center of water sports of all kinds.

The person, who took the lead in the 'Clean Sukhna Campaign' was Ashok Pradhan I.A.S., Adviser to the Administrator of Chandigarh, whom I knew rather well from my Delhi days and whom I often met on the tennis lawn in Chandigarh. One day, he called on me and explained to me his programme of getting the Sukhna Lake de-silted by mobilising the voluntary effort of government employees, including the police, para-military forces and the Armed Forces as well as members of the NGO's and the people at large. On May 2, 1988, I, along with the members of Raj Bhawan staff, turned up at the Sukhna Lake and joined Ashok Pradhan and thousands of people in removing the sand and silt. I also spoke to Chief Minister Ch. Devi Lal, who, along with a large number of government employees and members of the public, rendered 'Shramdan' (voluntary labour) at the Sukhna Lake.

I again visited the Sukhna Lake on June 11, 1988 to inaugurate the working of the dredging machinery donated by the Government of Haryana for de-silting operations. Work on the same lines was resumed in 1989 under the leadership of Ashok Pradhan and the Sukhna Lake regained much of its old glory.

In May, 1988, the Sikh terrorists stepped up their activities in Haryana and the adjoining areas of Punjab. Mohinder Singh Pannu, former Press Secretary to Chief Minister Ch. Devi Lal, was attacked by some terrorists at his Chandigarh residence necessitating his admission into the Post-Graduate Institute for immediate medical treatment. When I visited the Institute to look up Pannu, Dr. Wali, Director of the Institute and some other doctors, who received me, told me about the grievous nature of the injuries suffered by Pannu.

Soon after this, the terrorists struck at Panipat on May 7, 1988, killing 14 persons and injuring several others. In the course of my meetings with the top police officers of Haryana, measures for organizing raids on terrorist hide-out were discussed. On May 10, 1988, accompanied by my wife, Anita, I paid a visit to Panipat. I examined the spot where the killings took place and then visited the Civil Hospital to meet the injured persons admitted there. It was ghastly sight that has till today remained embedded in my memory.

I spent a considerable part of my day at Panipat visiting some important spots and meeting local officials, besides a cross section of people from various walks of life. I was aware of Panipat's significance from the point of view of our country's history and it was this awareness that had led me forty years ago, when I was a college student in Kolkata, to pay a visit to this and some other places during the Puja holidays in the autumn of 1948. During the intervening decades, I had occasion to read more about the role that the three battles of Panipat had played in shaping the course of the country's history and its destiny.

Panipat is an ancient place, having been one of the 'Prasthas' or 'Pats' (settlements), which were demanded by Yudhisthira, but were refused by Duryodhana, thus becoming the proximate cause of the Mahabharata war. The discovery of Painted Grey ware by archaeologists at Panipat has led some of them to trace its antiquity to the Harappan vintage. Sir Sayyad Ahmed Khan was of the view that Panipat had been founded by Dandapani in 707 B.C. According to some historians, a king by name Arjuna had built here a castle, which had numerous gates.

It was during the period of Mohammedadan rule in India that Panipat leapt into prominence, having formed along with some other near-by places such as Kurukshetra and Taraori (old Tirawari) the cockpit of Indian history, as someone has said. Even before the three famous battles of Panipat, the history of this place became interwoven with the fortunes of the Tughlak dynasty. Firoz Shah Tughlak, the cousin of Muhammad Tughlak, succeeded the latter and ascended the throne of Delhi in 1351 A.D. Firoz Shah's death in 1388 A.D. resulted in a war of succession among the descendants. Prince Humayun, son of Nasir-ud-din Muhammad Shah and grandson of Firoz Shah, mobilized his forces at Panipat in 1390 A.D. to press his father's claim. His plunder and loot caused untold sufferings to the people of the area right up to Delhi. Abu Bakr, another grandson of Firoz Shah, who was then holding sway at Dehi, took up the cause of his father, Zafar Khan, the third son of Firoz Shah, and dispatched his men to give fight to Prince Humayun, who lost the battle at Passina Khurd, a place near Panipat.

Soon there was a protracted civil war between the two claimants to the throne of Delhi, namely Nasir-ud-din Mahmud Shah, and his cousin, Nusrat Shah. Many of the prominent actors in this drama operated from Panipat, which, therefore, became a hot-bed of military intrigue. Only a small area around Delhi remained under the control of Nasir-ud-din Mahmud Shah, the last Tughlak Sultan of Delhi.

The Turkish chief Timur or Tamerlane invaded India during Sultan Mahmud's rule. Timur, the ruler of Samarqand, who belonged to the Mongol race, arrived at Panipat with his troops on December 3, 1398 and saw that the place deserted as the local people had fled. He is said to have found 16, 000 maunds of wheat at Panipat, which he gladly took into his possession. Then Timur marched to Delhi and took it over as Sultan Mahmud Tughlak had already fled. Having plundered Delhi during his 15-day sojourn, Timur returned to Samarqand with a rich haul of booty.

When the Lodhi dynasty took over the throne of Delhi in the middle of the 15th century A.D., Prince Nizam Khan, son of Bahlul

Lodhi, Sultan of Delhi, gained control over Panipat, but without the approval of his father. From the 16th to the 18th centuries, Panipat held the center stage of the Indian panorama with three battles fought here to decide who the ruler of Delhi was to be. Along with Delhi and other adjacent areas, Panipat suffered untold misery and agony during the invasions of Nadir Shah and Ahmad Shah Abdali in the 18th century A.D.

This was followed by the victory of the Sikhs over Zain Khan, the Governor of Sirhind in 1764 A.D. as a sequel to which Sirhind Province including Panipat came under the rule of the Sikhs, who carried on relentless plunder and pillage in Panipat, Karnal and adjoining areas. Then the Scindias appeared on the scene, but they failed to dislodge the Sikhs or to establish any firm grip in the area. Towards the end of the 18th century, Panipat had for a while passed into the hands of Begum Samru of Sardhana. In 1803, the Marathas' power in this region finally came to an end under the Treaty of Surji Arjungaon and the whole of Karnal district that included Panipat came under British rule.

During the 1857 uprising, Panipat, once described as "the most turbulent district in the North West Province", did not cause much headache to the British forces because, being located on the Grand Trunk Road, over which the British Army constantly marched to and fro, the local people had been kept under effective control. Moreover, the forces of the Phulkian States such as Patiala and Jind, which had extended their helping hands to the British, also maintained vigilance over the area. Still, however, the people in the villages around Panipat were found to be "quite refractory", with the revenue and police officers being 'in the state of flight".

In Panipat itself, the Imam of the shrine of Bu Ali Kalandar gave a tough fight to the British, but ultimately his people were defeated and he was caught and hanged.[1] the Muslim Ranghars of village Bulleh came to the rescue of their Hindu brethren, when they were attacked by a Brtish force led by Capt. Hughes of the First Punjab Cavalry on July 14, 1857.[2] in this fight, about a hundred Jats lost their lives. The British ransacked the area and imposed heavy fines on the people. At village Bala, the people revolted and Captain Hughes, who reached there with his force, failed to subdue them and had to flee. Later, he succeeded in putting down the revolt with the help of re-inforcements from the Nawab of Karnal and the ruler of Patiala.[3]

The situation in Assand, an important town of present-day Panipat district, was said to have been quite bad as the local Ranghars captured the police station. Lieut. Pearson went there with a strong force, but was attacked and pushed back. Later, Capt. Macneil proceeded from Karnal with some force, stormed Assand village and captured it. The village was then plundered and burnt down to ashes! Heavy fines were imposed on the people and the land revenue was raised.

I went along the streets of Panipat to get a feel of the place. The principal monument of Panipat is Dargah Qalandar Shah, the 700 years old tomb of Buali Shah Qalandar, built by the sons of Ala-ud-din Khilji. The touchstone pillars of the tomb were erected during the reign of Mughal emperor Akbar. I could also catch a glimpse from a distance of the tomb of Ali Shah, which attracts visitors from far and near. His parents had come to Panipat from Iraq and he was born here in 1209 A.D. He was an important Sufi saint, who later in life shifted to the Qutb Minar area of Delhi. Behind Ali Shah's tomb is the tomb of his parents.

Another important landmark of Panipat, which I did not have time to visit this time, is the grave of Ibrahim Lodi, who was killed in the First Battle of Panipat in 1526 A.D. There are several mosques and Idgahs at Panipat. Once a place known for many Sufi saints, it became famous in recent times for having been the birth place of the Urdu poet Khwaja Altaf Hussain 'Hali'.

At a little distance from Panipat is Kala Am, where Sadashiv Rao Bhau, leading the Maratha forces during the Third Battle of Panipat, was driven into a corner. On a subsequent date, I had occasion to visit this place, about which more later.

Panipat has made considerable progress in both agriculture and industry. In fact, it is a highly industrialized place famous for its woollen carpets and blankets. There are many small and big industrial units in the district which produce sugar, distillery, fertilizers, steel, soft drinks, industrial gases as well as textiles, which are exported. The National Fertilizer Ltd., an important public sector plant, is located here.

Too much irrigation and excessive rains during some months had in the past affected the health of the local people resulting in migration from some villages to drier areas in the adjoining districts. There is a belief among the local peasants that excessive irrigation caused impotence in men and unfruitfulness in women. The Jats of dry areas, therefore, refused to give their daughters in marriage to men of Panipat and other heavily irrigated places.[4]

In May 1988, we organized a programme of classical music at Raj Bhawan. The opportunity came when Smt. Sulochana Brihaspati, a well-known classical musician, came to Chandigarh from Delhi and called on us, as we knew her quite well. She was visiting her sister, Smt. Kalekar, who was the Principal of the Government Music College, Chandigarh. At our suggestion, the two sisters did a programme at Raj Bhawan on May 14, 1988, which was a great success. We had invited a wide cross section of people to the function and most of them highly appreciated the fare that was served. While thanking us for giving them an opportunity of enjoying good classical music, most of them expressed the hope that it would not be a one-shot affair and that they would look forward to many such programmes at Raj Bhawan in future. I can say with some degree of humility that we did disappoint them.

Echoes of this musical programme were heard at a dinner reception that we hosted at Raj Bhawan on May 24, 1988 in honour of the members of the Finance Commission headed by N.K.P. Salve, who had come to Chandigarh to discuss Haryana's financial affairs with the representatives of the State Government. Many of the invitees from among the city's elite, who had attended our musical programme, spoke effusively about it.

Towards the middle of May, 1988, I paid a visit to Roitakh, generally called Rohtak, the hub of Haryana's social, cultural and political life, where the Jats were the dominant community. The occasion was provided by a seminar on leprosy, which I inaugurated on May 17, 1988 at the Rohtak Medical College, a premier medical institution of our country. The doctors of the college had decided to boycott this function to press some of their grievances. However, they called off this move after I assured a delegation of doctors that their demands would be sympathetically considered by the authorities within a specified time frame. After I spoke at the seminar on the need to educate people about the latest advances in medical science in regard to the treatment of leprosy, several experts delivered speeches, which I found highly instructive.

I utilized this opportunity to pay my first visit to the campus of the Maharshi Dayanand University, Rohtak, where Lt. Gen. (retd.) G.C. Aggrawal, the Vice-Chancellor newly appointed by me had taken over. I went round the campus and then addressed a gathering of the Faculty members. The Vice-Chancellor seemed to have created a good impression among all concerned. As far as I remember, this was the first time that a retired Army officer was appointed Vice-Chancellor of an Indian University. I, therefore, felt happy to see that new experiment was succeeding.

In the afternoon, along with my wife, I visited a model village, Kharak Kalan, on the outskirts of Rohtak and saw how funds provided by the Haryana Development Board were being utilized in various development activities on the ground. A primary health center constructed by a local philanthropist was donated to the village. The Deputy Commissioner of the district told me that almost all the roads of the village had been made 'Pucca'.

In the midst of all these activities, I was getting myself continuously briefed by the professors of the University as well as the local officials about the history and culture of Rohtak district, the heartland of Haryana. Many books were made available to me for study during my leisure hours. I happened to visit a number of places in this district on several subsequent occasions. This, together with my study of the literature given to me, helped to give me some idea about the pivotal role that these places played in the history of Haryana as well as that of our country since time immemorial. This history is fascinating and bears narration.

The old name of Rohtak was Rohtasgarh because it was said to have been built by a king, Rohtas, in ancient times. Two very old sites adjacent to Rohtak known as Khokrakot are still referred to as Rohtasgarh. Some believe that the name Rohtak was derived from the Roherra tree (tecoma undulate), whose synonym in Sanskrit is Rohitak. Rohitaka, the ancient name of this place, is said to have been corrupted to Rohtak. Rohitaka often figures in ancient literature and is said to have been one of the places visited by Lord Buddha.

In the Mahabharata, Nakula, the Pandava prince, is said to have led an expedition to Rohitaka along with many horses, cattle, wealth and crops. He was blessed by Karttikeya and had a bitter fight with the 'Mattamayurakas' (*i.e.*the people of Rohtak). Then he advanced to the other end of the region comprising the deserts and reduced the city of Sirsa (Shairishaka).[5]

From Sirsa, Nakula proceeded to Punjab and fought with the many local clans. Dr. Buddha Prakash thinks that in many respects this account tallies with accounts of Yaudheya courage. From excavations at Khokrakot mound near Rohtak and the coins discovered there, it looks likely that the Yaudheyas had established their rule here after the death of Pushyamitra Sunga. They are said to have been the descendants of Yudhisthira. A Yaudheya coin that has been discovered shows the figure of Kumara Karttikeya, which means that he was their tutelary god. Dr. Buddha Prakash, therefore, presumes that the Yaudheyas had a special regard for the peacock, thus providing the basis for the description of the people of Rohtak as Mattamayura in the Mahabharata. The Yaudheya coins also give the name 'Bahudhanyaka' (land of plenty) to this region.

The Yaudheyas had their seats of power at Sunet and Rohtak. Somadeva, in his 'Yashtilakachampu' written in the tenth century A.D., described the Yaudheya country as "an ornament of the earth, replete with all the requisites of good and happy life." "Its people having all objects necessary for the pursuit of religion (dharma), material gain (artha), bodily pleasure (kama) and spiritual liberation (moksha) lived as it were in a heaven."[6] Its villages were full of cattle-wealth, cows, buffaloes, goats, sheep, camels, horses. Abundance of irrigation works rendered them free from the vagaries of rains (adevamatrika). Their well-watered fields of black soil (Krishnabhumayah), settled by subjects of all eighteen categories were green with harvests and gardens. They yielded such bouncing harvests that the farmers were unable to thrash and stack them properly. The bulk of the people consisted of working classes, artisans and peasants (nakshatradvija), who were hospitable and magnanimous (atithiprarthanamanorathah).

Continuing his eulogy of the Yaudheya country (of which Rohtak was the most important place), Somadeva says that, despite their wealth and prosperity, 'the burden of taxation on them was high, which they had to bear without demur (bhartrikara-sanbadhasahah). Yet, they were devoted to their rulers and were devotees of Karttikeya, the generalissimo of the gods. Their villages and settlements were devoid of rocks and stones and cleared of thorns or bushes and were so near to each other as to be within the reach of cocks (kukkutasampatyah). Their ladies, robust and handsome, laden with ornaments and dressed in tight garments, worked in farms and fields and attracted the notice of the travelers. The peaceful and contented life of the people was proof against social frictions so that the order of castes and callings was quietly maintained and people respected the Varnashrama dharma." [7]

This portrait of the life of the people of Rohtak has not changed much over the centuries. When I visited Rohtak, I could see pictures of Karttikeya riding his favourite peacock painted on the walls of houses in urban as well as rural areas.

After the Tomaras, the Chauhans under Prithviraj gained ascendancy in this region in the 12th century A.D. Muhammad Ghauri, who started raiding India in 1175 A.D., faced defeat at the hands of Prithviraj in 1191 A.D. at Tarain (Karnal district), but the next year, he came back to defeat Prithviraj at the same place. Ghauri wrought havoc in the Rohtak region and virtually laid waste Meham, an important place in present-day Rohtak district, which attracted nation-wide notice in May, 1990 as the worst example of electoral violence during the Chief Ministership of O.P. Chautala, whom I had sworn in just a few months ago.

During the 1857 uprising, Rohtak played a pivotal role as the Jats, who formed 30% of the local population, rose in revolt and were joined by the Ranghars, Muslims of Rajput origin. They succeeded in freeing a sizeable area from British control, but failed to dislodge the British from Rohtak. A turning point in this struggle came with the arrival from Delhi on May 24, 1857 of Tafzal Hussain, the representative of Emperor Bahadur Shah, with a force which Deputy Commissioner Loch failed to subdue. Loch as well as all other British officials had to flee. The office buildings and the bungalows of the British officials were burnt down along with office records and documents by the rebels. Tafzal Hussain returned to Delhi via Meham and Sampla after collecting over a lac of rupees from the Rohtak Treasury. He plundered the Europeans and their followers on his way back and burnt down the European buildings at Sampla.

The 6th N.I., a regiment of Ambala, was now sent by the British authorities under the leadership of Deputy Commissioner Loch to re-capture Rohtak. But the men of this regiment also rose in revolt as a sequel to secret negotiations with the rebels. This forced the European officers to flee.

During the revolt in Rohtak district, various clans of the Jat community engaged in their traditional fights amongst one another. The Dahiyas, Dalals and Ahlawats did not lose any opportunity of settling old scores against their traditional foes. There were villages which fought against the villages of their age-old enemies. But over-all, they kept up their fight against the British. Moreover, there was no communal trouble between the Hindus and Muslims.

The British authorities deputed Lt. R. Hodson with a force to re-capture Rohtak. At Kharkhanda, about 20 miles from Rohtak, the villagers confronted Hodson on August 15, 1857. According to Hodson's own admission, the villagers "fought like devils". As this battle remained indecisive, Hodson left with his force for Bohar and then for Rohtak. The battle at Rohtak also remained undecided, with both parties retreating to their respective positions. Later, narrating his story, Hodson said: "Unfortunately, I had no ammunition left and, therefore, could not without unprudence remain so close to the town filled with matchlock men. We marched quietly to the north of the town and encamped near the first friendly village that we came to." Before returning to Delhi, Hodson left Rohtak in the hands of the ruler of Jind and some local Chaudhuris, who had helped him with money and materials, for which they were later handsomely rewarded.[8]

The British authorities sent Gen. Van Courtlandt, the Deputy Commissioner of Ferozpur, to subdue Rohtak district. The news of Delhi having already come under British control had a demoralizing effect on the people of Rohtak and so the district was reduced to submission without much difficulty and without a gun being fired. By September 26, 1857, the district came under British rule and even the collection of revenue started.[9]

As pointed out by Dr. K.C. Yadav, the rulers of the princely States that now form part of Haryana had behaved in an unpatriotic manner during the 1857 uprising.[10] the rulers of three States that later came to form part of Rohtak district (namely Dujana, Bahadurgarh and Jhajjar) deserve to be mentioned. Hassan Ali Khan, the Nawab of Dujana, was a kind-hearted man, who was liked by his subjects. He did not play any significant role during the 1857 conflict. The British authorities let him go.[11]

Bahadur Jang Khan, the Nawab of Bahadurgarh, played a minor role that was marginally helpful to Emperor Bahadur Shah of Delhi and got off lightly having been awarded a minor punishment by the British authorities. He was deprived of his territorial estates, but was given a nominal monthly pension and packed off to Lahore.[12]

Abdur Rahman Khan, the Nawab of Jhajjar, the biggest State in Haryana, paid for his role in the 1857 uprising with death by hanging. He was a man of taste and ability, but had earned a bad name because of "gross debauchery" and his oppressive behaviour towards his subjects.[13] He no doubt revolted in 1857, but played a double and deceitful role. He helped the British authorities with men, money and material. But at the same time, he was keeping open his line of communication with Emperor Bahadur Shah. The result was that he could please neither the British nor the Emperor. The British felt greatly offended because of an incident in which he first gave shelter to C.T. Metcalfe, Judge of Delhi, and another Englishman and then threw them out of his territory. Emperor Bahadur Shah got infuriated with the Nawab as the latter refused to comply with his repeated requests for money to fight the British.

As Dr. K.C. Yadav points out, the Nawab of Jhajjar had no nerve to take an open stand against the British nor did he dare to displease Bahadur Shah. While he paid lip service to the latter, he extended substantial help to the former—a stance which pleased none. The British in particular viewed him as their enemy. He was tried by a British court, where, in reply to charges framed against him, he put up a strong defence, saying that he was "a staunch and devoted subject and servant of the British Government." Denying that he had extended any help to the rebels, he stated: "Had I really intended to give money, I would have done so without any delay .... I had in possession treasure in gold and silver coins to the extent of 11, 00,000 rupees, as well as stores of ammunition. Had I been in combination with the rebels, I should have given them not promises but the treasure itself."[14]

Obviously, this defence, though quite strong, cut no ice with the British authorities. The testimony of C.T. Metcalfe against him must have weighed heavily with the military court. He was sentenced "to be hanged by the neck until he be dead" and all his properties were forfeited.

A graphic description of his execution is reproduced from Dr. K.C. Yadav's book: "The time of hanging was evening (sahpahar). All the gates of the city were closed. A company of the European band came playing on their musical instrument and stood before the Kotwali (Chandni Chowk). The prince was brought from the (Red) Fort on a wooden cart. He was made to sit on it on his feet (ukarań). His hands were tied on back (mahken kasna) and covered with a piece of cloth. The European spectators sat on all sides. When the prince was brought to the gallows and the plank was removed, and the prince suffered death, the Europeans sitting near by felt jubilant and joyful."[15]

As Dr. K.C. Yadav observes, quoting an eye-witness, a European army officer, the Nawab was humiliated even at the gallows. During such executions, the army officer remarked, 'the Europeans used to bribe the executioners to keep the mutineers a long time hanging since they liked to see the "criminals" dance a "pandies horn pipe", as they termed the "dying struggles of the victims". The Nawab was also a long time dying.[16]

In the post-1857 period, the British administration displayed a spirit of authoritarianism which must have been resented by the ordinary man. The murder of F.E. Moore, the British Deputy Commissioner of Rohtak in August 1877—20 years after the 1857 uprising—by one Amar Singh, aged 40 years, hailing from a Jat family of a village near Rohtak showed that even an ordinary villager was no longer overly scared of the British and could summon the courage to do away with a British officer if he had a grouse against the latter.

The assailant entered the official residence of Moore in Rohtak early in the morning and managed to attack him with a hoe as a result of which he died a few hours later.[17]

Amar Singh was caught on the spot, then tried by J. G. Gordery, the officiating Sessions Judge, who completed al the proceedings in just two days and sentenced him to death. The Chief Court of the Punjab consisting of two British Judges upheld the sentence in less than ten days! Surprisingly, the judges did not go into the motive behind the murder. Dr. K.C. Yadav, the well-known historian of Haryana, who made a special study of this case by visiting the village of Amar Singh and talking to his descendants, came to the conclusion that what had impelled him to commit the crime was his grouse against Moore for having given an adverse decision against his father in a land dispute. As Dr. K.C. Yadav observes, the British administration was so greatly terrorized by this incident that "they forgot all about their laws, rules, regulations, procedures and killed the murderer of the deputy commissioner without going into the full details of the case in a most uncivilized manner. This throws ample light on the real working of the British administrative system, specially their judiciary and the executive in 1870's.................... Perhaps they wanted to strike terror in the hearts of the people by such a savage act."[18]

As I went round Rohtak town, I could see a few dilapidated gates of what was perhaps an old wall around the town, which no longer existed. I saw the minarets of several old mosques including the Adina Masjid. I was told about the archaeological finds at some places of Rohtak district such as the five sandstone images of Hindu gods and goddesses and the Jain architectural remains of Bohar, the sandstone head of Buddha, the famous Bhimeshwari Devi temple of Beri and several temples of Mohanbari and the old images of Hindu gods and goddesses discovered there.

During later visits to this area, I saw some of these places. The territorial configuration of Rohtak district underwent many changes during British rule and after independence, when the princely State of Dujana was incorporated into it. Bahadurgarh State was merged into Rohtak district in 1860. Once while driving through Bahadurgarh, I saw some places of historical interest such as the Qila Mohalla, Nagr Khana etc. I also saw from a distance the old temple of Shyam Baba.

And thereby hangs a tale. According to the story that was narrated to me by a local official, the temple of Shyam Baba was built at Bahadurgarh about 300 years ago by the disciples of the Baba from

Sakhol village after they had an audience with him at village Khatu. On their telling the Baba that they wanted to build a temple in his honour in Sakhol village, the latter told them to go ahead. As they were leaving for their village, they chanced to meet a Brahmin, who, on hearing of their plan to build the temple, gave them a slab of stone and told them to keep it at the very place where they wanted to build the temple.

While on their way back to their village, they stopped for some time at Bahadurgarh by the side of a tank, where they had a bath. They kept the slab of stone at a spot near by as they bathed in the tank. Before leaving the place, they tried to lift the stone from the ground but failed to do so despite repeated attempts. They were unable to do so even after digging up the place to a depth of over 16 feet because the stone appeared to be without any end whatsoever. Then they recalled that the Brahmin had advised them to place the stone at the spot where the temple was to be built. So, it was at that spot in Bahadurgarh that they built the temple of Shyam Baba. Many devotees flock to this temple throughout the year to seek the Baba's blessings.

Jhajjar, which also I once visited, was an ancient place whose site has been discovered a little away from the town. This is said to have been known as Bhagulan. There are seven tombs of prominent personalities outside the town, which looked very impressive. There are several tanks, mosques and Idgahs. I saw the tomb of Shah Ghazi Kamal, who gave fight ot Prithviraj Chauhan and ended up by having his hand chopped off.

In later days, Rohtak district produced one of Haryana's political stalwarts and a leading figure of the freedom struggle—Pandit Shri Ram Sharma. Born in Jhajjar in 1899, he joined the Congress Party in 1920 as a student leader and organized the freedom movement in Haryana. As the editor of the Haryana Tilak Patrika, he played an important role in motivating the youth to join the freedom struggle. Having spent many years in jail, he became a legislator and a Minister after independence.

Gohana in Rohtak district, which I once passed through while going from Panipat to some other place, is an old pilgrimage that was known as Govambhavana. A fort was built here by Prithviraj Chauhan, ruler of Delhi, but it did not survive. However, traces of this fort are now to be found by way of several old gates of the town through which the traffic moves towards Delhi, Panipat, Rohtak and Hissar. Fairs and festivals are held here from time to time. Important among these are the annual fair at the shrine of Shah Zia-ud-din Muhammad, a saint, who had come to India along with Muhammad Ghauri, and an annual festival held at the two Jain temples of the town.

Meham, a Tehsil headquarters of Rohtak district that I visited once is said to be as old as the Mahabharata. Raja Ballu, a Pawar ruler, re-built this town that had been destroyed by Muhammad Ghauri, as I have already mentioned. The Afghans ruled here for a few centuries before it was annexed by the Rajputs led by Durga Dass during Aurangzeb's reign. Among the important landmarks of this town that I still recall are a "Baoli" (a well with several steps) and the Pirzada Masjid built during Humayun's reign, though, according to some, this existed even earlier.

Several visits that I paid to Rohtak district and my studies on the history and culture of the Jats of Haryana left me in no doubt about the many qualities of the people of this community. Any book having anything to do with Haryana would be incomplete without a proper discussion on the role of the Jats. I would, therefore, venture to devote some space to this subject. The Jats constitute the single largest group of people in Haryana, more particularly in Rohtak district and the adjoining region (*i.e.* The districts of Hissar, Karnal, Ambala, Sirsa, Gurgaon, Bhiwani and Sonepat in Haryana, besides some areas of the neighbouring States). This is why this region is sometimes called Jattiana or Jatait and the Haryanvi dialect spoken here is called Jatu.

There is no unanimity among historians over the issue of the origin of the Jats. The Rohtak District Gazetteer says that the Jats believed themselves to be Aryans.[19] Some say that the Huns and Scythians were their progenitors.

A Russian scholar, M.K. Kudryavtsev of the former U.S.S.R., who has made a deep study of this matter, has expressed the view that the origin of the Jats is shrouded in mystery.[20] He is of the view that the Jats spread over Punjab, Haryana, Rajasthan, U.P. And even Jammu and Kashmir belong to a distinct ethnic group. He discusses the facts mentioned by James Tod and Alexander Cunningham in support of their views regarding the likelihood of the Jats having come to India from Central Asia.

Tod suggested that they might have come in the wake of the Scythian invasions from Central Asia at the beginning of the Christian era. Cunningham, who traced references to the Jats in old Greek and Roman literature, identified the Jats with the Zantii or Xantii *i.e.*, Turanians, who belonged to the Central Asian territory between the Oxus and the Yaxarthes. However, Kudryavtsev also mentions the fact that even before the Scythians invaded the country, there were Jats living in Sind. Some speak of a direct association of the Jat chiefs with the heroes of the Mahabharata. Thus, the last word on this subject does not appear to have been said.

The Jats' role during the medieval period is also discussed by Kudryavtsev. They had fought against or otherwise harassed the Muslim invaders as is evident from their battles with Mahmud Gaznavi, Timur and Babur. The Jats also fought against Aurangzeb. They are Hindus, Sikhs and Muslms alike. Kudryavtsev concluded that the Jats had all along been a separate ethnic group and had always played a major role in the ethnic history of northern India as a "large, dynamic and very active population group". Further on, he adds: "It was the Jats who formed the ethnic nucleus of the people now called the Punjabis. The role of the Jats has not, however, been confined to this. In different periods and conditions, they made up an essential ethnic component of the Sindhis, Rajasthanis and other peoples of the Republic of India and Pakistan."

Dr. G.C. Dwivedi[21] has given an account of the many views that have been expressed about the origin of the Jats. One such view is that after the extermination of the warrior class by Parashurama, their daughters prayed to the gods to save their class from extinction. In response to their prayer, their wombs (Jatharas) were "impregnated with seeds. Their sons were called Jatharas, who were the ancestors of the Jats. This view is based on a legend and has no historical basis.

Another view—that the Jats were the descendants of Emperor Yata of the Yadava dynasty—is rejected by Dr. G. C. Dwivedi on the ground that it is 'frivolous' Devasamhita mentions a story that Lord Shiva created the Jats out of his locks (Jata) with a view to punishing his father-in-law, Daksha, who had humiliated him and his spouse by not inviting them to a 'Yagna' (sacrifice). This story is called 'fanciful' by Dr. Dwivedi and is based on the flimsy ground of the phonetic similarity between the words "Jat' and 'Jata'. Nor does Dr. Dwivedi find any ground for accepting the view that the Jats were the offspring of a Rajput king and a Gujar girl whose beauty had attracted him. Similarly, another view that the Jarittakas of the Mahabharata were the ancestors of the Jats is not considered plausible by Dr. Dwivedi because it does not have any leg to stand upon except a superficial verbal resemblance between the two names—Jarittaka and Jat. Dr. Dwivedi finds some substance in the view of the well-known historian, K.R. Qanungo, that the Jats were descended from the 'Jatas' or 'Sujatas', a branch of the Haihaya Yadavas. But he rejects this view as well because it fails to provide satisfactory explanations in regard to some issues that he raises.

After making a close survey of the customs, usages, institutions and habits of the Jats and those of the warrior tribes of ancient Punjab, Dr. Dwivedi finds a remarkable similarity between them. As he observes; "Very significantly, the present-day Jat fraternity displays almost the same preference for equality, kinship and democratic ways, the same adeptness in war and agriculture and the same repugnance to the rigidity of caste, creed and ritual, which were so characteristic of the republicans of the Punjab, Haryana and Sind. These similarities are so crucial that we cannot brush them aside lightly ......" These ancient warrior tribes had republican and democratic governments and were of Vedic stock. After the second century B.C., some foreigners began to pour in and settle down here and gradually some of these elements got absorbed by the local Hindu population. It may, therefore be guessed that the tribes of ancient Punjab, Haryana and Sind were originally descended from the Vedic stock, but in course of time some foreign elements must have melded into them. Yet, as Dr. Dwivedi concludes, "preponderantly, the Aryan line of descent is not inconspicuous among the Jats."

As regards the etymology of the word Jat, Dr. Dwivedi thinks that it may have been derived from the Sanskrit word 'Jata', which means a Samgha or a close combination. After having said all this, he eventually expresses the view that nothing final can be said about the origin of the Jat community in view of the paucity of material, which compels us to make only bold guesses.

Some say that the Jats were the descendants of the Rajputs. On this issue, D.C. Verma, author of 'Haryana', expressed his agreement with Sir George Campbell that the Rajputs and the Jats were once congeners of a common stock, that they both entered India by the same route, that the Rajputs came earlier, becoming more Hinduised and that the Jats followed them a long time later.

The Jats are divided into numerous 'Gotras'. The names of these 'Gotras' are different in the different districts of Haryana. However, they inter-marry. Agriculture is their normal occupation, though they have now established themselves in other occupations as well. Their important role in the country's defence services and the police has earned them high praise.

Sir George Campbell has characterized the Jats as being endowed with great physical energy and high morale. This may be due to the process of miscegenation and the melding of some foreign elements with the local people. Dr. M.S. Randhawa, a noted scholar, has observed that the Jats, being a heterodox people, have avoided some evils of Hindu society such as the rigidity of the caste system and food taboos and married women from all castes. They allow widow remarriage. In Dr. Randhawa's view, "it would be difficult in any country to find a more remarkable combination of cultivator, colonialist, emigrant and soldier".[22]

The Jats are often wrongly described as rough and over-bearing, the fact being that they are conscious of their rights to land, which make them tenaciously assert their rights. They are highly disciplined and well-behaved and, with the spread of education, they have entered the civil services and all segments of white collar jobs in which many have distinguished themselves and made their presence felt.

The Jats have dominated Haryana's political field ever since the State was formed in 1966. Of the three famous Lals, who were Chief Ministers of Haryana—Bansi Lal, Devi Lal and Bhajan Lal—the first two were Jats. O.P. Chautala, son of the late Ch. Devi Lal, was another Chief Minister of Haryana, who is also a Jat. In 2005, Chautala made way for another Jat Chief Minister, Bhupinder Singh Hooda (not to be confused with HUDA, short for the Haryana Urban Development Authority). Hailing from Rohtak, the heart of Haryana's Jatland, Hooda belongs to the oldest Congress family of Haryana, his grandfather having been a freedom-fighter. His father Ch. Ranbir Singh, whose 92nd birthday was celebrated in November 2005, is also a veteran freedom-fighter and the only live member of the Constituent Assembly. Bhupinder Singh Hooda represented Rohtak in the Lok Sabha four times with the added distinction of having thrice defeated the late Ch. Devi Lal, former Chief Minister and Deputy Prime Minister, in the Lok Sabha polls from Rohtak.

But even before the formation of Haryana State in 1966, there were some Jat leaders, who could be characterized as the heroes of Haryana. According to Shri Bhim Sain Tyagi, there were three heroes in the history of Haryana—Hemu, Suraj Mal and Chhotu Ram.[23] Of them, the last two were Jats. About Hemu, I shall have much to say later in this book.

Suraj Mal was the son of Thakur Badan Singh, who became the ruler of Dig in 1723 A.D. after the death of Churaman, the earlier ruler. The Jats, who had revolted against Aurangzeb, the Mughal Emperor, continued their rebellious activities in north west India after the latter's death in 1707 A.D. In a bid to assert their supremacy. Suraj Mal, who became the ruler of Bharatpur after his father, extended his territory over parts of eastern U.P., besides Rohtak and Gurgaon. He was a great ruler, who was characterized by Jadu Nath Sarkar as "the Plato of the Jat tribe". He was an emblem of Jat pride not only in Rajputana and Haryana, but in the whole of north India. But his death in December 1763 marked the beginning of the decline in the power of the Jats.

Sir Chhotu Ram, the other Jat hero, was born on November 24, 1881 A.D. In Gahi Sampla village of Rohtak district. His father's financial status not being very good, he had to prosecute his studies and complete his education at Delhi's St. Stephens College through the generosity of his relations and some philanthropists. He did some odd jobs for a few years and then obtained the Ll. B. degree at Agra, where he did some practice before shifting to Rohtak in 1912 A.D.

He began to champion the cause of the farmers, who had been suffering from the ravages of famines and the oppressive machinations of money-lenders. During the First World War, he called upon the people of Haryana to join the Army. He joined the Congress Party, but when it launched the Non-Co-operation Movement, he left it along with another leader, Fazl-I-Hussain, and then the two formed the Unionist Party, which dominated the political scene in Punjab (that then included Haryana) right till the country's independence in 1947.

Chhotu Ram was a Minister in the Punjab Government during 1924-26. The next several years he devoted to building up the Unionist Party as the most powerful political force in the region. In 1936, he again became a Minister, in which position he continued till his death in January, 1945. Along with the Muslim leaders of the Unionist Party, he tried his best to rid the country of the virus of communalism and fight the divisive forces. He fought against both the Muslim League and the Congress Party , which he accused of being soft towards M.A. Jinnah and the Muslim League and of indirectly helping them in furthering the cause of the country's partition.

The Unionist Party defeated the Congress Party in the elections to the Punjab Legislative Assembly held in 1937 and merged as the most powerful party in the Haryana region. This led to intense rivalry between their supporters. When the Second World War broke out, it was said in some quarters that while, on the one hand, the Congress refused to co-operate with the British war effort, on the other hand the big Zamindars, princes and the Unionist Party led by Chhotu Ram and Hindu Mahasabha workers led by Rao Balbir Singh helped the British in every possible way.[24] When the Congress Party launched a campaign in Haryana to mobilize the masses in order to oppose the

British war effort, the Unionist Party tried to thwart this campaign. This led to considerable political tension and some clashes.

In 1938, Sir Sikandar Hayat Khan, a leader of the Unionist Party, entered into an agreement with M.A. Jinnah known as the Sikandar-Jinnah Pact whereby every Muslim member of the Unionist Party automatically became a member of the Muslim League "to safeguard all-India interests of the Muslim community." This had an adverse impact on the communal situation in Punjab. In 1942, after Sikandar Hayat Khan's death, he was succeeded by Khizar Khan Tiwana as the Prime Minister of Punjab. M.A. Jinnah tried to persuade Khizar Hayat Khan to change the name of his party into the Muslim League, but the latter refused to do so on account of the stubborn resistance of Sir Chhotu Ram. After Sir Chhotu Ram's death in 1945, Sir Khizar Hayat Khan continued to steer the Unionist Party on a secular course for quite some time.

Sir Chhotu Ram was the undisputed leader of the rural masses of Haryana, Hindu as well as Muslim. He espoused the cause of the peasantry and the agrarian reforms introduced by the Unionist Party Government of which he was an important leader had earned the support of the rural people as well as of many leaders of other political parties such as the Congress leader Maulana Abul Kalam Azad and M.N. Roy, the communist leader, who later became a radical humanist. It was in recognition of his stature as the leader of Haryana and his contribution to the welfare of the peasantry that the Haryana Government officially celebrated his birth centenary in 1981.

Sir Chhotu Ram had opposed the suggestion for the formation of a Haryana Province or a Greater Delhi by taking out the Ambala Division from Punjab.[25] This suggestion was contained in a report that was to be submitted to the Simon Commission. The suggestion was withdrawn as Chhotu Ram rejected it outright. If he had supported the idea, Haryana would have become a separate Province in 1935. Why did he oppose it? According to Shri Bhim Sain Tyagi, it was Chhotu Ram's statesman-like political attitude that stood in the way. Two reasons perhaps led him to oppose the separation of the Ambala Division from the Punjab Province.[26] One was the delicate communal balance that prevailed in Punjab at that time. The Indus and the Sikhs, though in a minority in Punjab, would have been reduced to a hopeless minority if the Ambala Division with its Hindu majority areas was taken out of Punjab.

Another reason was that the Bhakra Project was still under study. Its potentialities had been foreseen by Chhotu Ram quite some time in advance. The Haryana region was badly in need of water and power and Bhakra was its only hope. If a separate Haryana Province was created, Chhotu Ram would not have been there in the Punjab Government to press for the execution of the Bhakra Project and for the diversion to Haryana of its legitimate share of water and power. "His most enduring work is the Bhakra Project which he pulled out of the forgotten shelves and whose details he completed as the last act of his life so that the parched lands of Rohtak and Hissar could be irrigated. How would he have felt to see that much of its water had been divertwd to the Punjab where it was causing problems of silting and seepage, while Haryana lands continued to remain as parched as ever?" [27]

The Jats are a proud people with considerable self-esteem, as they belong to the warrior caste equivalent to the Kshatriya caste. Since they occupy a high place in the caste hierarchy, many have questioned the justification for including the Jats in the list of 'Other Backward Classes' (OBC's) for purposes of reservation, as has been already done by the Central Government and some State Governments. However, the fact remains that they are predominantly a farming class and many of these farmers are economically quite badly off. This has been put forward as the ground for including the Jats among the OBC's in Haryana, where a movement over this issue is being spearheaded by the Haryana Jat Aarakshan Sangharsh Samiti.

Rohtak district occupies the center stage in Haryana's history and culture, having been the home of a very rich cultural heritage, both ancient and modern. As in Punjab, the Arya Samaj caught the imagination of the people of Haryana and became very popular among the Jats both in the towns and in the rural areas. This is how a number of schools and colleges came to be established in Haryana, which were named after Swami Dayanand Saraswati, a pioneer of the Arya Samaj movement, who believed that Hinduism based on the Vedas was the true religion because, as he said, no other religion except the Vedas existed 5000 years ago.

Because of the interest that the workers of the Arya Samaj took in social service during floods and other calamities, they were naturally drawn into some political activities, which aroused the ire of the British authorities. The latter got alarmed at the political awakening in Haryana and other areas, which they attributed to the social reform programmes and the spread of education initiated by the Arya Samaj. Accusing the Arya Samaj of having launched what they called a political movement with an anti-British slant, the British authorities sought to curb what they regarded as disaffection among the people by enforcing the Seditious Meetings Act in Rohtak district. There was great consternation among the British rulers in 1905 A.D. that the Jat officers and men of the Jat Regiment recruited from Rohtak and adjoining districts were being infected by the ideology of the Arya ama, which they considered to be seditious. As a preventive measure, many Jat officers and men were removed from service and the recruitment of people to the armed forces from these districts was stopped.

Rohtak remained in the forefront of political and freedom movements in Haryana. It was also the center that spearheaded the spread of education in the State. Several leading social, political and cultural figures of Haryana such as Sir Chhotu Ram, Pandit Neki Ram Sharma, Ch. Lal Chand, Lala Shyam Lal and Pandit Lakshmi Das, the famous hero of Haryana's folk drama hailed from Rohtak. It also played an important role in Haryana's green revolution and industrial development.

Despite the heat and dust of Rohtak's severe summer and the tight schedule I had to go through, I felt quite happy to have been able to visit this important district of Haryana and acquaint myself with the role that its many leading personalities have played in different phases of the State's history. I had further occasions to come to this district from time to time and see more of it.

Some people of Rohtak told me about the literary and spiritual legacy of Hardedas (short for Hridaydas), who lived several centuries ago in the Badli village of Rohtak district. He was a saint whose Guru was one Swami Indraj. He was a social reformer, a poet and a spiritual leader, who preached the greatness of his Guru's ideals and the utter futility of orthodox social customs and religious rites. His philosophical ideas are voiced in his numerous poems whose language clearly reflect the imprint of the language of the Ahirwal region of Haryana as well as of Brajbhasa, apart from Arabic and Persian. Many of his compositions are in circulation in the form of popular folk songs.

Notwithstanding this impressive social, cultural and historical background of Rohtak, and several other Jat-dominated areas of Haryana, people elsewhere do not miss any opportunity of cutting jokes about the alleged crudity and rough and tough ways of these valiant and straightforward people with a no-nonsense attitude towards life. Fun, though mostly of an innocent kind, is often made of certain typical Haryana characters, particularly Jats, who are referred to as Tau (an elderly person) and Taei (Tau's wife), Chhora (a boy), Kaacha Chhora (a small boy), Chhori (a girl or a daughter), Bateu (son-in-law), Gaamris (villagers), Angrez or Shaukeen (a villager who has worn freshly washed clothes) Bajewalas (bands), Geetan-aali (females singing a chorus), Moochhanaley Mards (physically virile persons with an impressive moustache), Dooms and Bhands (musicians singing Raginis and songs of various other kinds, sometimes in a lighter vein), the Naai, usually a very witty person, Pali (shepherd), the Modas (who have renounced the world and ceased to be householders), the Boojh-Bujhakar (a very knowledgeable person who offers easy and quick solutions to the problems of the villager, and of course, the Phoji or the ex-serviceman.

There are some other rural figures of fun such as the Hookah-Bharania (who does all kinds of odd jobs for others), the rustic simpleton who stands out by virtue of what is called Chusarkee, the sound made by sucking in air through the mouth at the time of drinking water or any other kind of liquid and when he is thus identified, he is said to have been Pichhan-gya (recognised), and last but not the least, the rural yesmen who say 'Humbai' (meaning 'yes') to anything that others say or suggest.

When a married woman seeing a doctor about some sexual disorder tells him about her Baat-Cheet with her husband, she does not refer to some inane conversation with her husband, which this Hindi word normally means. In Haryanvi language, Baat-Cheet means sexual intercourse which is what she means to convey to the doctor (Wit and Humour of Haryana by Rajbir Deswal, p. 61). But these occasional forms of verbal suavity cannot take away from the often very rough and blunt overtones of what is called the 'lath-maar' dialect of the Haryanvi language. Some years ago, while on the Internet, I came across the following joke on Haryana, which clearly brings out the roughness of this dialect:

"Once a Tau was walking along the middle of the road. A person driving a car blew the horn. Tau looked back and asked the driver: 'Ya sadak ke tere baap ki sai?' (Does this road belong to your father? the driver replied in annoyance: 'Haa, Tau' (yes, Tau). Tau retorted: 'Aapne baapse keh de sadak thorii choree karva dega' (tell your father to broaden the road as this Tau would not move aside)."

Another joke, which also caught my on the internet, seeks to project Haryanvis as simpletons and runs as follows: Once a Haryanvi thought that he would teach his father a bit of the English language. He started from teaching him from A for apple, B for buffalo etc. Coming to M, he told his father M for mummy. When Tau reached W, he said: 'Yaa kimi jaani phchani lage hai' (it seems that I have seen it somewhere). Recllecting further, Tau said: Haa, naa sai to aapke Ma per yaa ulti kayun hoo rahi sai' (Yes, it is your mother. But, why is she upside down?).

Towards the end of May 1988, my wife and I spent a day at Morni Hills, a hill resort that was coming up quite well. This visit gave me an opportunity to see for myself the development activities and the growth of tourist facilities at this place, which is the only hill resort of the State. Haryana is well known for its 'highway tourism' and its well organized chain of lake resorts, restaurants and bars, but unlike the States of Uttar Pradesh, Himachal Pradesh and Punjab, it has no hill station to boast of. The Morni Hills complex is not a hill station proper, but can be regarded as a hill resort, which tourists can find quite attractive. In fact, we found this to be a haven of peace and tranquility, with plenty of fresh ozone-laden air, a wide variety of flora and fauna, pine trees towering over the rocks and numerous picnic spots for holidayers. It is an ideal place for honey-moon couples.

After crossing the Ghaggar river, we took the zig-zag road along the southern Shivaliks dotted on both sides with thick jungles. We saw peacocks, monkeys, quails and fowls occasionally crossing the road. On arrival at Morni Hills, we were received by Parashar, Deputy Commissioner of Ambala district, Satinder, the superintendent of Police, Joshi, Sub-Divisional Magistrate , Kalka, and several others. By and by, they briefed me about the government's projects for developing this place and converting it into a worthwhile tourist resort. They also narrated to me the legends and historical anecdotes about this place, which prompted me to trace the relevant books and read them in due course.

The Morni and Tapra Hills of Ambala district are lower than the ridges of the Himalayas to their north and constitute a link between Haryana and the Himalayas. The Korah peak on the Nahan border is the highest point (1499 metres). The average height of Morni Hills is 3000 feet, while the Mountain Quail, a retreat at the top of the hills has an elevation of 3980 feet above the sea level, according to the account given to me by the local officials.

Morni Hills, earlier known as Kotaha Hills, was named after a poor peasant girl. And thereby hangs a romantic tale. A young man of high lineage and a poor girl by name Morni hailing from a peasant's family had fallen in love, but, as it happens so often in such cases, they could not get united in wedlock. Their love had a tragic end that is writ large on their graves inside an old and crumbling fort that attract visitors from the adjoining areas all through the year. It is this girl who gave her name to the Morni Hills.

The British Governor-General of India had donated the Kotaha Hills to one Mir Jafar in 1816 A.D. as a reward for the help that the latter had extended to the British authorities during the Gorkha campaign. The land in this area, therefore, belongs to Mir Jafar's descendants, but much of it has now been acquired by the government to develop the forest potential of the place as well as to promote tourism.

Beyond the Morni Hills, the road takes you to the Sherla Taal, a beautiful lake that is a hot favourite of the picnickers. Further beyond are the impressive twin lakes at Tikkar Taal, which, according to legend, had been formed by the impress of the Pandava hero Bhima's knees when he knelt down there. The two lakes are separated by a ridge. From whatever little we saw in the course of our day-long wandering, we thought that there was much more to explore in this sylvan terrain with a multiplicity of forest paths leading to spots of extraordinary natural beauty, which afforded magnificent views of the surrounding hills and the Ghaggar valley.

As we left the place in the evening, the setting sun's rays filtering through the tall pine trees invested the whole scenery with a magic charm. It had started getting dark while we were still winding down the hill road. We could clearly see the lights of Chandigarh and Panchkula glittering at a distance.

My wife and I have very pleasant memories of informal dinner parties held alternately at the Punjab and Haryana Raj Bhawans at intervals of, say, three to four months. At these parties attended only by the two Governors and their spouses, all the formalities of Raj Bhawan dinner parties were dispensed with and the A.D.C.'s and other officers asked to take the evening off. Simply put, these parties gave Shri S.S. Ray, me and our wives an opportunity of indulging in gossip or 'Adda', as it is called in Bengali, and as is the time-honoured habit of true blue Bengalees. Where on earth did you have two Bengalees, both hailing from the same part of a district now in Bangladesh, serving as Governors of two adjacent States and living in Raj Bhawans that touched each other at a particular corner? If, therefore, we occasionally allowed ourselves the pleasure of indulging our passion for 'Adda', we deserved to be pardoned. At these parties, which went on till after midnight, we had the freedom to talk whatever we liked because there was none to overhear and more particularly because we had the fullest trust in one another.

Not that we were not available for urgent official business while attending such informal dinner parties. I distinctly recall that some time in June, 1988, when I had gone to the Punjab Raj Bhawan for such a party, Sardar Buta Singh, Union Home Minister, was on the line from Delhi to tell me about the complaint of some Congress workers of Haryana that they had been harassed by the police and the workers of rival political parties during the by-elections held on June 16, 1988 at Sirsa and Faridabad. The next day, Bhajan Lal, a former Congress Chief Minister of Haryana and then a Central Minister also spoke to me from Delhi about the same complaint. At my request, Ch. Devi Lal saw me, when I brought this matter to his notice. He denied that any excesses had been committed by anybody, but in any case, he promised to ensure that no such incident would take place in future.

At this time, the Sikh terrorists struck at a couple of places in Haryana. On June 19, 1988, a bomb blast triggered by them killed as many as 15 persons and injured several others at Kurukshetra. The very next day, there was another ghastly incident in which 6 persons were killed and some others injured by the terrorists at the near-by sacred town of Pehowa in the some district. On June 20, 1988, I visited the hospital in Chandigarh to look up those injured in the Kurukshetra incident.

These two incidents were viewed with concern by Chief Minister Ch. Devi Lal, who called on me on June 21, 1988 and discussed the situation with me. Soon, he changed the police personnel at the top level. Home Minister Sampat Singh closely monitored the steps the police was taking to bring the culprits to book.

I paid a visit to Kurukshetra and Pehowa on June 22, 1988 and apart from visiting the spots where the incidents had taken place, also discussed with the local officials what preventive steps they had taken. This time round, I did not have time at my disposal, but I managed to snatch a few moments to visit the Brahmsarovar and touch its sacred water. Then I proceeded to Pehowa.

After visiting the spot where the incident of terrorist violence had taken place at Pehowa on June 20, 1988 and discussing the situation with the local officers, I went around some of the holy places of this ancient pilgrimage. In fact, I had heard so much about this pilgrimage that I had already undertaken some study on its history and spiritual background as reflected in the Hindu scriptures and the Mahabharata.

The picture that had emerged from my study and my visit to Pehowa was really fascinating. Pehowa is one of the many pilgrimages dotting the traditional Kurukshetra region. Pehowa is a corruption from the ancient name Prithudaka, which in turn had been derived from Prithu, once a king of this place. Prithu was the son of King

Vena. Prithudaka was located on the left bank of the Saraswati river.Vena was afflicted by leprosy of which he was cured after taking a dip in the Saraswati.

After Vena's death and the cremation of his body, Prithu performed his funeral rites and took his seat by the side of the Saraswati for 12 days in order to offer water to all who came there. The place thus came to be known as Prithudaka or the pool of Prithu. He got a tank dug there and a time came when a visit to Kurikshetra was not regarded as fruitful unless a pilgrim took a dip in this holy tank. It is believed that sage Vishwamitra was elevated to the status of Brahmarshi at Pehowa. It was here that Lord Brahma created the world along with water, air and the sky, as the Vamana Purana says.[28]

About the sanctity of Prithudaka, the Mahabharata says that one should go to that famed pilgrimage of Kartikeya, where, after bathing and worshipping one's ancestors, men and women are relieved of all their sins committed knowingly or unknowingly, secure the merit of an Ashwamedha sacrifice and go to heaven.[29] the same idea of a person ascending the heaven if he does 'Japa' (mutters his prayer) on the left bank of the Saraswati river (*i.e.* at Prithudaka) is conveyed by the Vamana Purana Saro.[30] This pilgrimage is said to be the holiest of all. One who leaves one's mortal coil here after 'Japa-Mantra' (*i.e.* muttering 'Mantras') is not born again.[31] Even a very sinful person is said to go to heaven if he bathes here.[32]

There is an ancient temple of Kartikeya at Pehowa which women do not enter. There is an interesting Puranic legend behind this taboo. It is said that once all the gods and goddesses met and decided that, of the two sons of Shiva and Parvati—Ganesh and Kartikeya—whoever was able to go round the earth and reach Pehowa first should be coronated. Accordingly, Kartikeya sat on his favourite conveyance, a peacock, and began to move from place to place. Ganesh, the elder of the two brothers, however, did nothing of the kind. Their mother, Parvati, advised him to simply go round all the gods and goddesses assembled there, which, she said, would be tantamount to circumambulating the globe which, in her view, was represented by the assemblage of all the gods and goddesses. Lord Shiva felt amused by Parvati's suggestion, but all the gods and goddesses agreed with Parvati and coronated Ganesh after he went around them.

When Kartikeya returned after his round-the-globe trip, he flew into a rage over the stratagem adopted by Ganesh and blamed Parvati for being partial to his elder brother. He said that it was to his mother that he owed his skin and flesh and that, in protest, he was removing his own skin and flesh. He also uttered a curse that whichever woman would see him or his idol in this form would become a widow in seven successive births. The gods and goddesses pacified him by sprinkling him with oil and vermilion—a custom that is still followed by the pilgrims who worship at this temple.

A flame has been kept burning at this temple—for how many centuries nobody knows. It is said that Lord Krishna had got this flame lighted by Yudhisthira, when the latter performed the funeral rites on the bank of the Saraswati at Pehowa of his near and dear ones, who had been killed in the Mahabharata war. The same flame is said to be burning today.

The Mahabharata says that Kurukshetra is sacred, the Saraswati river is more sacred than Kurukshetra and Prithudaka is still holier than the Saraswati.[33]. The same sense is conveyed slightly differently in slightly different words words by the Vamana Purana.

The Vamana Purana also says that Lord Shankara had come down from the Himalayas to Prithudaka to take a dip here in accordance with strict religious rites in order to get rid of all sins.[34]

It is considered meritorious to offer 'Pinda' (oblations) here to one's forefathers in the month of Asadh (June-July) on a special 'Tithi' (a particular lunar day) as Lord Indra had done.[35] It is believed that after the Kurukshetra war, Yudhisthira, the eldest Pandava, had offered 'Pinda' at Prithudaka to all his relations, who had lost their lives in the war.

The Mahabharata and the Vamana Purana tell the story of one Rushangu, who lived at 'Gangadwar' (which stands for Haridwar or any place where the Ganges comes down on earth). At the fag end of his life, he told his sons to shift him to Prithudaka because he felt that continued stay at 'Gangadwar' would not be conducive to his welfare. On moving over to Prithudaka, Rushangu took a dip in the sacred waters there, which endowed him with immortality. This story testifies to the antiquity of Pehowa, apart from the fact that in those days Prithudaka's sanctity ranked higher than that of 'Gangadwar' *i.e.*, Haridwar.

It is believed that by taking a dip in the holy tank at Pehowa, one not only gets rid of all sins, but also imbibes all the virtues of having performed an Ashwamedha sacrifice and, besides, goes to heaven.[36]

Several Sikh religious leaders including Guru Nanak and Guru Govind Singh came to Pehowa for a dip in its tank. There are two Gurdwaras here named after them. Maharaja Ranjit Singh came here to perform the funeral rites of his mother. The Gurdwara in memory of Guru Govind Singh is called Gurdwara Jowda Sahib and is located at village Saiyana Saiyada which is about five miles from Pehowa. The name Jowda Sahib derives from the fact that a pair of the 'Kharaus' (wooden sandals) of Guru Govind Singh are preserved here.

There is a story about how this village came to be known as Saiyana Saiyada. This used to be a village of the Syed Muslims. One of them, Bhikhran Shah, offered Namaj one day, facing the east. Some villagers asked him the reason for this deviation from the normal Muslim practice of offering Namaj with the face turned towards the west. He replied that he had done so because on that day a great soul (meaning Guru Govind Singh) had appeared on earth at a place towards the east (meaning Patna). Saying this, he left on foot for Patna and walked the entire distance in order to see the new-born child. It is said that it was after him that his village began to be called Saiyana Saiyada.

Pehowa now consists of an area that is spread partly over level ground and partly over the ancient ground that has an elevation of 30 to 40 feet. It was a part of he kingdom of Kanauj during the reign of King Bhoja and his successor, Mahendrapala, as revealed by two inscriptions dating back to the end of the 9th century A.D., which were found at this place. One of the inscriptions dated 882 A.D. was on the wall of the Garib Nath temple, while the other dated 895 A.D. was found on the wall of a house in the heart of a market place. These inscriptions reveal that Pehowa was an important pilgrimage during Gurjara-Pratihara rule.

No archaeological excavations have been made into the old mounds in Pehowa. These inscriptions and some old artefacts that have become available here throw considerable light on its old history. The inscription of the time of King Mahendrapala, which is in elegant Sanskrit verse, shows that there were three Tomar brothers at Pehowa by name Gogga, Puranaraja and Devaraja respectively, who were the sons of Jajjuka. They had built a triple temple of Vishnu at Pehowa. This triple temple represented a unique feature of the contemporary architectural style.

The inscription of the time of Mahendrapala contains an invocation to Madhava (or Vishnu), who is shown to be reclining on the ocean of milk. Mihira Bhoja was a devotee of Bhagawati, but had also built a Vishnu temple in his seraglio. All this is a pointer to the fact that Vaishnavism was widely prevalent among the people. The epigraph of Mahendrapala's time refers to the two wives ofJajjuka, which indicates that polygamy was in vogue—an inference which is also corroborated by other contemporary inscriptions discovered elsewhere. This inscription also refers to the Tomars for the first time and speaks of Jaula, an earlier ancestor of Jajjuka, as 'the ornament of the Tomara clan.'[37] This family was ruling Pehowa under the Gurjara-Pratihara King Mahendrapala.[38]

The inscription of the time of Mihira Bhoja mentions a famous horse fair that used to be held at Prithudaka. Tradespeople from far-off places came to this fair. The names of nine places from which these traders used to come are referred to in this inscription. It has not been possible to identify all these places except one, namely Sarankadia, which has been identified as a town called Sharakpur in Pakistan's Lahore district.[39]

Many old idols including those of Vishnu have been found at Pehowa. I saw temples in Pehowa constructed in later years, the important among them being the Shravan Nath and Garib Nath temples.

After the Sikhs established their control in this region in the 18th century, Bhai Kainthal built a palace at Pehowa. This place was forcibly taken over by the British in 1843 A.D. after the death of Bhai Kainthal, who had no issue. During the uprising of 1857 A.D., the people of Pehowa, along with their brethren at other neighbouring places, rose in revolt and drove away the British and their officials, extinguishing all vestiges of British rule. However, in due course the British restored their rule in this region, though after a bitter struggle.

As I entered Pehowa town, I could see numerous persons, who looked like pilgrims and had apparently come there from other places. Every year, in the month of Chaitra (March-April), a big fair is held here, when lakhs of pilgrims from other parts of the country, particularly from Punjab, congregate and bathe in the Saraswati river, before offering 'Pinda' to their forefathers. From what I understood, Pehowa has a significance for the Hindus of north west India that is somewhat similar to that of Gaya for the Hindus in the rest of our country. Pehowa is where most people of north west India come to perform this rite for the simple reason that it is close by and is at the same time highly rated in our scriptures.

While Pehowa can be said to be the Gaya of north west India, there is another place in Haryana *i.e.*, Pharal, whose religious importance is also very great and where also the Hindus offer 'Pinda' to their ancestors. This place of Kaithal district is quite close to Pehowa. In ancient times, it was called Phalakivana or just Phalgu because a sage by name Phalgu lived here. It was one of the seven forested areas of Kurukshetra in days of yore. Both the Pandavas and the Kauravas had performed here the last rites of those killed in the Kurukshetra war. People from far and near come here to attend a very big fair held on a new moon day before Dussehra in September-October provided it is also a Monday (*i.e.* Somavati Amabasya). As it is obvious, an occasion like this comes at intervals of many years. The people gather around a big tank with many well-built 'Ghats' to perform 'Sradh' and offer 'Pinda' to their ancestors.

The Vamana Purana says that if a person performs 'Sradh' at this place on Somavati Amabasya day, he acquires great virtue.[40] It also says that just as 'Sradh' performed at Gaya provides eternal gratification to the forefathers, the same effect is achieved by 'Sradh' performed at Phalakivana.[41]

It is said that even if a person just remembers the name of Phalakivana, his forefathers derive great satisfaction. The Puranic story behind the religious significance of this place, which is quite interesting, runs like this. In ancient times, a sage by name Phalak used to live at Phalakivana (*i.e.* present-day Pharal). At that time, a demon called Gayasur lived at Gaya, the famous Hindu pilgrimage located in Bihar (is it Jharkhand?). Gayasur had three daughters—Soma, Bhoma and Goma. Gayasur had declared that anybody who could defeat him in a fight would be entitled to claim the hands of all his three daughters.

Sage Phalak challenged Gayasur to a fight and defeated the latter, which led to his marriage with the three daughters of Gayasur. Among his new wives, Phalak was particularly fond of Soma to whom he gave a boon saying that 'Pinda' offered during 'Sradh' performed at Phalakivana on a new moon day that fell on a Monday (*i.e.* Soma) would confer much greater benefit than the same rite performed at Gaya. It is said that on such a day, no 'Pinda' is offered at Gaya. From that time onward, Phalakivana started attracting people desirous of offering 'Pinda' on Somavati Amabasya.

I do not know if there is something missing in all this, which, if discovered, would have established a closer link between Phalgu of Haryana and Gaya of Bihar. Both are sacred pilgrimages where the Hindus offer Pinda' to their forefathers. The Vamana Purana Shloka (36/50) mentioned earlier refers to this fact and gives an assessment of their comparative importance from this point of view. The name of the river at Gaya on whose bank the Hindus offer 'Pinda' is Phalgu, which is identical with Haryana's Phalgu, where also the same rite is performed. To my mind, this suggests the possibility of some missing link between the two places.

Pharal is known for its religious significance on other counts as well. It is said that many gods and goddesses used to live in ancient times in the forest known as Phalakivana. Goddess Aditi is said to have engaged in penance at this place for ten thousand years! During this rather long period, she observed silence and lived on a diet of simple air! Pleased with her, God gave her a boon that all her wishes would be fulfilled. A further boon that she was granted was that anybody, who did meditation for three nights at a stretch in this forest, would be rewarded with desired results. Even if a person living at some other place remembered the name of Phalakivana, he would derive great merit. It is further said that anybody, who comes here and feeds one, three or five Brahmins, would achieve liberation.

Very close to Pehowa or rather on its north-eastern outskirts is another pilgrimage, Arunaya. I drove to Arunaya to have a feel of this place (which was located at the confluence of the Aruna and Saraswati rivers in ancient times). I had a view of the very old Sangameshwar Mahadeva temple. It is said that this temple had earlier been located at a slightly different spot near by, where banyan and Peepal trees existed.[42]

One of those far-off days, a wood-cutter came to Arunaya and began to cut the branch of the Peepal tree. The axe slipped from his hand and fell on the head of the Shivalinga, causing a deep mark on it. From that mark, milk started flowing out. The wood-cutter became perplexed at this turn of events. Begging forgiveness of Lord Shiva, he cleared up the place and built a 'Chabutra' around it. Soon people began to pour in there to worship the deity.

It is further said that long years ago, a person by name Baba Ganesh Giri, a great devotee of Lord Shiva, lived in a village of far-away Bihar. One night, he had a dream, in which Lord Shiva told him that if he wanted to have a real vision of Him, he should proceed to Arunaya at the confluence of the Aruna and Saraswati rivers, because there not only had sages Vashist and Vishwamitra had worshipped Him, but even Lord Indra had been absolved of the sin of having killed a Brahmin. So Baba Ganesh Giri proceeded there and after a good deal of search reached the spot indicated by Lord Shiva. He did long penance there and one day Lord Shiva appeared in a dream and told him that He was present at a slightly different spot near by.

Baba Ganesh Giri looked around and saw a mound of earth, which he opened up with his 'Chimta' (a pair of tongs carried by Sadhus).

There came out a beautiful Shivalinga, which he tried to dig out of the earth. Failing to dislodge the Shivalinga from the ground, he sat down there in despair, when a voice from heaven told him that He, Lord Shiva, had been there since eternity and that it was no use trying to remove Him from there. Lord Shiva asked him to renovate the place—task for which in fact He had summoned him there. Baba Ganesh Giri looked at the Shivalinga in reverence and saw that over it was a snake whose head was studded with a bright jewel. He began to make preparations for renovating the place, when the snake disappeared. In this story again, there is seen to be a link between Haryana and Bihar to which I have already drawn attention.

The spiritual importance of Arunaya is mentioned in many Puranas and the Mahabharata. The Shiva temple here is looked after by an organization of some Sadhus. Numerous pilgrims visit the place all through the year. I was told that there are some special customs in vogue at the temple. For example, nobody can spread out a cot on its premises to sleep on nor can anybody use milk here to make curd out of it nor is curd to be distributed among the visitors here.

Notes

1. The Revolt of 1857 in Haryana by Dr. K.C. Yadav, p. 111.
2. *Ibid*, p. 86.
3. *Ibid*, p. 112.
4. Haryana by D.C. Verma, p. 32.
5. Article by Dr. Buddha Prakash in "Haryana: Studies in History and Politics" edited by J.N. Singh Yadav, p. 5. The relevant text in the Mahabharata is as follows:

   ततो बहुधनं रम्यं गवाढ्यं धनधान्यवत्।
   कातिकेयस्य दयितं रोहीतकमुपाद्रवत्।।४।।
   तत्र युद्धं महच्चासीच्छूरैर्मत्तमयूरकैः।
   मरुभूमिं स कात्स्न्र्येन तथैव बहुधान्यकम्।।५।।
   शैरीषकं महोत्थं च वशे चक्रे महाद्युतिः।
   आक्रोशं चैव राजर्षि तेन युद्धमभून्महत्।।६।।
   -Digvijayparva, 32-4, 5, 6
6. *Ibid*, p. 13.

   अस्ति खल्विह भरतक्षेत्रे चतुर्वर्गमार्गणोपकरणप्रसूतः समस्तप्रशस्तमहीवलयालालङ्.करणभूतः सुरलोकमनोरथाभिधेयो यौधेयो नाम धाम सम्पदो जनपदः।
   —Yashastilakachampu of Somadeva.
7. *Ibid*, p. 14.

   निष्कण्टकमहीभागाः विगतोपलसीमानः कुक्कुटसंपात्या सन्ति ग्रामाः।
   क्वणत्कनकमयकङ्.कणाः पीनकुचकुम्भदर्पत्रुटत्ककव्चुकाः शालिवप्रेषु यान्त्यः क्षणं गोपिकाः पान्थसार्थेषु नयनोत्सवं कुर्वते।
   भजन्ति सांकर्यमिमानि देहिनां न यत्र वर्णाश्रमधर्मवृत्तयः।
   —Yashastilakachampu of Somadeva

8. Article by Kapil Chandra Yadav in "haryana: Studies in History and Politics" edited by J.N. Singh Yadav, p. 61.
9. The Revolt of 1857 in Haryana by Dr. K.C. Yadav, p. 112-113.
10. *Ibid*, pp. 88-102.
11. *Ibid*, p. 99.
12. *Ibid*, p. 100.
13. *Ibid*, p. 89.
14. *Ibid*, p. 92.
15. *Ibid*, p. 93.
16. *Ibid*, p. 93.
17. For details, one may read an article "Murder of F.E. Moore: A Reflection on British Justice in 1870's" by Dr. K.C. Yadav in the Journal of Haryana Studies, Vol. XX, Nos. 1&2, 1988.
18. *Ibid*.
19. Haryana by D.C. Verma, p. 74.
20. "The Role of the Jats in Northern India's Ethnic History" by M.K. Kudryavtsev in "Haryana: Studies in History and Politics" edited by J.N. Singh Yadav.
21. "Origin of the Jats' by Dr. Girish Chandra Dwivedi in the Journal of Haryana Studies, Vol. XXI, Nos. 1&2, 1989.
22. Quoted by S.S. Chib in "This Beautiful Haryana", pp. 89-90.
23. The History of Haryana by Bhim Sain Tyagi, p. 48.
24. Haryana: Stydies in History and Politics edited by J.N. Singh Yadav: Article entitled "Political Developments in Haryana, 1928-1947" by Dr. Jagdish Chander.
25. History of Haryana by Bhim Sain Tyagi, p. 61.
26. *Ibid*, p. 62.
27. *Ibid*, pp. 63-64.
28. महा जलं वहिनसमीरमेव खां त्वेवमादो विवमो पृथूदकः।।
    (वामन पु. 23:44)
29. ततो गच्छेत राजेन्द्र तीर्थे त्रैलोक्यविश्रुतम्।।१४१।।
    पृथूदकमिति ख्यातं कार्तिकेयस्य वै नृप।
    तत्राभिषेकं कुर्वीत पितृदेवार्चने रतः।।१४२।।
    अज्ञानाःगा़नतो वापि स्त्रिया वा पुरुषेण वा।
    यत् किंचिदशुभं कर्म कृतं मानुषबुद्धिना।।१४३।।
    तत् सर्वे नश्यते तत्र स्नातमात्रस्य भारत।
    अश्वमेघफलं चास्य स्वर्गलोकं च गच्छति।।१४४।।
30. मसरस्वत्युत्तरे तीरे यसत्यजेदात्मनस्तनुम्।
    पृथूदकं जप्यपरो नूनं चामरतां व्रजेतु।।
    (वामन सरो. 18:20)
31. उत्तमे सर्वतीर्थानां यस्त्यजेदात्मनस्तनुम्।
    पृथूदके जाप्यपरौ नैवं श्वोमरणं भवत्।।२६।।

32. तत्र स्नात्वा यन्ति अति पापकृतो जनाः।
प्रथूदके नरश्रेष्ठ प्राहुरेयं मनोषिणः।।२८।।
33. पुण्यमाहु कुरुक्षेत्रं कुरुक्षेत्रात्सरस्वतीम्।
सरस्वत्याश्च तीर्थानि तीर्थेभ्यश्च पृथूदकम्।।
(महा. 3:81:125)
34. शंकरौऽपि महातेजा विसृज्य गिरिकन्यकम्।
पृथूदकं जगामाथ स्नानं चक्रे विधानतः।।
ततस्तु देवप्रवरो महेश्वरः पृथूदके स्नानमपा स्तम्वः।
35. आषाढ़े मासि मार्गक्षे चन्द्रक्षयतिथिर्हिया।।
तस्यां पुरन्दरः प्रीतः पिण्डं पितृषु भक्तितः।।
(वामन 24:8)
36. तत सर्व नश्यते तस्य स्रातमात्रस्य भारत।
अश्वेधफलं चापि स्वर्गलोकं च गच्छति।।
(महा. 3:81:124, पदम् आदि खण्ड 27:32:33)
37. **"Pehowa Inscriptions of the Gurjara-Pratiharas: A Socio-cultural Interpretation" by Brajesh Krishna in the Journal of Haryana Studies, Vol. XIV, Nos. 1&2, 1982.**
38. *Ibid.*
39. *Ibid.*
40. सोमाक्षये च संप्राते सोमस्य च दिन तथा
यः श्राद्धं मत्यस्तस्य फलं पुण्यं।
(वामन 36:49)
41. गंगायां च यथा श्राद्धं पितृन्प्रीणति नित्यशः
तथा श्राद्धं च कर्तव्य फलकी वन–माश्रितः।
(वामन 36:50)
42. **Though I have heard about and read several accounts about Arynaya's religious significance, here I have mostly gone by the account given in an article by Krishna Dhamija 'Nanha' in the daily Punjab Kesari (Delhi edition) of December 28, 1998.**

8

Visits to Simla, Ambala and Baba Ka Ladhana: Sher Shah, A Haryanvi? The Battles of Panipat: Himu, the Emperor of Delhi and Hero of Panipat

Some time after we returned to Chandigrh from Pehowa, my wife and I paid a visit to Simla, as was the practice of the Governors of Punjab and Haryana in summer. Our eldest daughter, Radha, was already with us along with her 5-year old son, Abhishek, for the summer holidays. We were later joined by our son-in-law, Pinak Ranjan Chakravarti, an officer of the Indian Foreign Service, now our country's High Commissioner to Bangaldesh.

Reaching Simla on June 25, 1988, we spent the next few days going round several old spots, some in the town and some at short distances from it—places we already knew from our visits of earlier years. I specially recall our visit to the famous Kalibari of the Bengalees of Simla, where we worshipped goddess Kali. The priests and many other local Bengalees received us very cordially, as they knew that I, a fellow Bengalee, was the Governor of Haryana. Shri Mukherjee, Chief Conservator of Forests, Himachal Pradesh, and President of Kalibari, showed us round.

The high point of our visit to Simla was a dinner party hosted in our honour by Rear Admiral (Retd.) R.K.S. Gandhi, Governor of Himachal Pradesh, and his gracious wife, at their Raj Bhawan. The other invitees included the Ambassador of Czechoslovakia, besides the late C.S. Jha, a former officer of the Indian Civil Service, and his wife, whom we came to know in Delhi in the 1950's. Among the guests, there were also Sardar G.S. Kahlon, an ex-I.C.S. officer, and his wife. Sardar Kahlon was an officer of the Bengal cadre in the days of the Raj, but had switched over to the Punjab cadre after independence. Smt. R.K.S. Gandhi, our hostess, was the daughter of a former I.C.S. officer of U.P. cadre (if I remember aright) and so she and her Governor husband were acquainted with many ex-I.C.S. officers, some of whom they had invited to this evening's party.

Sardar Kahlon and his wife told us that they were very glad to meet us when I said that we were Bengalees and that I had been an Indian Police Service officer of West Bengal cadre before my retirement a year ago. It was obvious from our conversation that Sardar Kahlon was aware of my having been the Director of the Intelligence Bureau, because he put me some significant questions about his son-in-law, Sardar S.S. Mann, an officer of the Indian Police Service, who had left his job to pursue the cause of Khalistan, and had been nabbed by the police a few years ago while trying to sneak into Nepal from India.

We returned to Chandigarh on June 29, 1988, rather late in the evening, visiting en route Chail, at one time the summer capital of the Patiala rulers, with its salubrious climate and its cricket stadium which is the highest in the world. We also passed through the famous hill station of Kasauli and Parwanoo.

Early next morning, M.S. Mali, D.I.G., C.I.D., Haryana, rang me up to say that in an encounter with Sikh terrorists the previous night, a Sub-Inspector of Police and a Head Constable of Haryana, a Constable of the CRPF and a terrorist had been killed at Samana in the Patiala district of Punjab that adjoins Haryana. The senior police officers of Haryana often spoke to me direct about important matters and Chief Minister Ch. Devi Lal used to request me from time to time to give any direction to the police which I considered necessary.

Soon after the encounter at Samana, an incident of terrorist violence took place in Chandigarh in the early hours of July 18, 1988. The details were communicated to me over telephone early that morning by another senior police officer, R. K. Vachher, who was then my A.D.C. Chaudhuri Devi Lal declared handsome monetary grants for policemen who had suffered in this incident, though they were not on the strength of Haryana police. He did this quite promptly before S.S. Ray, the Punjab Governor, had time to come out with his announcement about similar grants. This was interpreted by some as a political move by Ch. Devi Lal to make a favourable impact on the Jat community (some victims were Jats) and on the Abohar-Fazilka area of Punjab (one victim was from this place).

In July, 1988, I was the chief guest at a function of the Rotary Club in Chandigarh. An official from the headquarters of the Red Cross Society in Delhi came to Chandigarh to brief me about the work of this organization because I was its patron in Haryana.

The ASHI (Association for Social Health in India) was an important organization that was doing a lot of good work in Haryana in the fight against the drug menace. In early July 1988, a function was organized at our Raj Bhawan where I released an informative brochure about this body and then spoke on what was needed to be done on this front. My wife, Anita, who took considerable interest in these activities, was unanimously made the President of the ASHI.

At Ambala, I attended to some work connected with the Red Cross and the Social Welfare Council of both of which I was the patron so far as Haryana was concerned. I was also the chief guest at a function of the Rotary Club of Ambala.

I had visited Ambala from Delhi on several occasions in the past and had in course of time also read some books about this place. In ancient times, Ambala was a part of Brahmavarta where the Aryans had settled down in the second millennium B.C. (as distinguished from the second millennium A. D. that we entered just a few years ago). Ambala was witness to the rule of the Bharatas, Purus and Kurus, the battle of Mahabharata and the rule of the Pandavas and their descendants, the Parikshitas.

Ambala formed part of the kingdom of the rulers of Thanesar namely the Pushpabhutis in the seventh century A.D., who were followed by Rajyavardhana and Harshavardhana. It did not escape the attention of Yashovardhana of Kanauj and Lalitaditya of Kashmir. In the ninth century A.D., Ambala was incorporated into the territory of Pratihara Mihira Bhoja. Mahmud of Ghazni and others plundered Ambala several times in the tenth century A.D. Then came the Chauhans of Delhi in the 12th century A.D. The Mughals annexed Ambala, but after the death of Aurangzeb, it was occupied by Banda Bahadur in 1710 A.D. However, Banda Bahadur was soon defeated by the Mughals. In 1739 A.D., Ambala faced the onslaught of Nadir Shah.

By the beginning of the nineteenth century A.D., the British established a political agency at Ambala, which exercised control over the officers of the many local potentates, whose rule, however, gradually came to an end as they had no male heirs. Their territories were taken over by the British, who constituted the district of Ambala in 1847 A.D. This together with the economic policies pursued by the

British authorities created widespread discontent among different sections of the people of Haryana. Moreover, British rule brought in its wake interference with religious matters and increased activities of the Christian missionaries designed to secure religious conversions.

All this paved the way for the anti-British uprising of 1857, the last straw on the camel's back being provided by the introduction of new rifles in which cartridges greased with cow's fat and lard were used, thus creating a fear in the minds of the Indian sepoys that the Government was bent upon converting them to Christianity. Ambala, being an important military station, was badly affected by the uprising of 1857.

It is generally believed that this uprising was first launched by the sepoys of Meerut on the evening of May 10, 1857. This is, however, not true as it was pointed out some decades ago by Dr. K. C. Yadav, Professor of History at the Kurukshetra University, that the sepoys of Ambala in Haryana were the first to commence the revolt at 9 a.m. on the morning of the same day.[1] This view was also upheld by the well-known historian. Dr. R.C. Mazumdar[2] as I have pointed out earlier in chapter 3.

Dr. K.C. Yadav does not accept the view of Dr. S. N. Sen, another historian, that the uprising of 1857 was not the result of a pre-meditated conspiracy. He puts forward a hypothesis that the sepoys of at least Ambala, Meerut and Delhi had maintained contact with one another and planned a simultaneous uprising that was to culminate in a march to Delhi. However, in the absence of positive evidence to this effect, he has remained reconciled to letting his view remain just a hypothesis.

Dr. Yadav does not agree with the views of Sir Jadunath Sarkar, Dr. R. C. Mazumdar and Dr. S.N. Sen that the leaders of the revolt were reactionary feudal lords and that the ordinary people had no role in it. According to him, at least in the case of Haryana, large numbers of ordinary people fought together against the British, forgetting their communal differences.

However, the British authorities took prompt steps to bring under check the civil population as well as the Indian troops at Ambala. The British officers operating in Ambala district were surprised to see that the local people, including even those who had derived various benefits from them, extended no help or co-operation to them in fighting the rebels. According to the old records of the Punjab Government, the rich bankers of Jagadhari, an important place in Ambala district, "displayed a spirit of disloyalty and close-fistedness unworthy of a class who owe their prosperity to the fostering care and protection of the British Government."[3]

Ambala town is said to have derived its name from Amba Rajput, who laid the foundation of this town in the 14th century A.D. Another story links the name of Ambala with a very old temple of the town – that of goddess Amba, which attracts many devotees. It is also said that the name Ambala is a corruption from 'Ambawala' or the village of mango groves that used to thrive here once upon a time.

While driving through Ambala, I saw a lake that was thronged by many visitors. I was told that there were several Muslim shrines as well as some Gurdwaras, two of which were associated with Guru Hargovind Singh and Guru Govind Singh. I saw the Lakhnaur Sahib Gurdwara located a few miles beyond the Ambala Cantonment Railway Station. It was here that Guru Govind Singh had spent his childhood. The Manji Sahib Gurdwara at Ambala, which also was shown to me from a distance, fondly cherishes its association with Guru Hargovind Singh, who had come here and taken rest while going from Amritsar to Delhi on the suggestion of Emperor Jahangir. Later, Jahangir kept the Guru imprisoned in the fort at Gwalior. At the time of his release from the fort, Guru Hargovind Singh was able to secure the release of 152 rulers, who had also been kept confined at the fort. On his way back to Amritsar, Guru Hargovind Singh had again stopped overnight at the Manji Sahib Gurdwara.

I was told about the observance of Bawan Dwadashi by the people of Ambala, particularly women, who keep fast on this occasion, which coincides with the twelfth day of the bright fortnight of the moon in the month of 'Bhadon' (usually August). The celebration is associated with the name of Vaman, one of the many incarnations of Lord Vishnu. It is believed by the Hindus that anybody taking a dip in the waters at the confluence of rivers on this day is bound to go to heaven after death. A big fair is held at Ambala on this occasion and a procession taken out along the streets. I had several occasions to visit Ambala later, when I familiarized myself with the various facets of its cultural life.

The next day we were at Kaithal, where we attended several functions connected with the wedding of the Haryana Minister, N.P. Dhanda, who had extended an extended an importance to me. My wife and I were quite impressed to see the Minister in the ceremonial costume of a bride-groom. The whole place was swarming with people from all walks of life—virtually a show of the Minister's political strength and an index of his popularity.

As I was seated among the guests, I was introduced to some people, who appeared to be of a religious bent of mind. Ever since my going to Haryana as Governor, I had been thinking of locating a spiritually important place of the State, namely Ladhana, which had the honour of being associated with the name of one of India's great saints—Tota Puri, the Guru, who had initiated Ramakrishna Paramahansa into a particular line of spiritual quest that led to his achieving the final goal that all spiritual seekers aim at. I was delighted to hear from one of the invitees to the Minister's wedding that Ladhana (or Baba Ka Ladhana, as it was sometimes called) was hardly seven miles away from Kaithal. On further enquiries, he told me that in Ladhana, there was a Shiva temple, a Samadhi of Tota Puri and a Dera, where the Sadhus lived.

Had I known earlier that Ladhana was so close to Kaithal, I would have ensured that my programme included a visit to that hallowed place. Since I could not change my schedule at a short notice, what I did was to drive through Ladhana on my way back to Chandigarh. I also decided to read a little more about Tota Puri, his spiritual philosophy and what exactly transpired between him and Ramakrishna Paramahansa. But of that more later.

An important meeting of the Haryana Rajya Sainik Board, of which I was the Chairman, was held at Haryana Raj Bhawan on July 19, 1988, which was attended by several officials of the State Government, the Union Defence Ministry and the Defence Services as well as the representatives of ex-servicemen. Since Haryana contributed a large number of people to the armed forces and since its villages and towns consisted of numerous ex-servicemen's families, some of their problems we discussed at this meeting, had a vital bearing on the lives of many people of the State. Soon after this meeting, I presided over a meeting of the Amalgamated Fund Committee of the Rajya Sainik Board which took some decisions on financial matters.

My other engagements in the month of July 1988 included a visit to Pinjore to inaugurate and address a workshop on communication for health and development jointly organized by the UNICEF and the Inter-Media Publicity Co-ordination Committee, Chandigarh. The workshop focused attention on the need to give priority to the health care of children and expectant mothers.

In the last week of July 1988, Ch. Devi Lal dropped in for a long chat about the general political situation in Haryana. I felt that he was interested in drawing me out on what I thought about the various issues that he raised. I welcomed the discussion because it gave me an opportunity of finding out how the Chief Minister's mind was working in relation to these issues. I got the impression that he no longer held me in suspicion.

This became obvious from Ch. Devi Lal's second visit to Raj Bhawan the same evening to attend a classical music programme. The artiste was the famous Shruti Shirodkar of Bombay, who had come down to Chandigarh at the request of J.N. Khosla's Indian National Theatre and had agreed to perform at Raj Bhawan.

Alongside these activities, I was not neglecting my tennis either. One Beyant Singh, the best tennis player of Chandigarh, coached me up for a few days as I was resuming playing tennis after a long gap of several years. Prof. Marya and Rajan Kashyap, President and Secretary respectively of the Chandigarh Lawn Tennis Assciation took a good deal of interest in organizing a tennis tournament at the Stadium in July-August, 1988. I played in this tournament and was partnered by Naidu, a veteran coach and a good player. Thanks to the latter's support, we reached the final as did Shri S.S. Ray, Governor of Punjab, who had as his partner Beyant Singh, whom I have already mentioned. At the final played on August 3, 1988, we lost to Governor Ray and his partner, who played better tennis.

All these days, the Chandigarh Stadium was pulsating with activity and excitement with people from various walks of life including government and non-government officials, doctors, lawyers and students thronging the place and clapping and shouting appreciatively as the matches were played. Where else in India would you get such sports-loving people to cheer up the Governors of two adjacent States paying tennis (and cricket as well) with each other and vying for honour at the lists in an atmosphere of friendship and camaraderie?

In Chandigarh, I associated myself closely with the activities of the Bharatiya Vidya Bhawan, which made me its patron. On July 30, 1988, while I played a tennis match in the morning, I had another important engagement in the evening—delivering the convocation address at the Bharatiya Vidya Bhawan and awarding the certificates to those who got post-graduate diplomas in management.

In the mean time, I had paid a day-long visit to Panipat on July 28, 1988 to attend a meeting of an organization known as the Battles of Panipat Memorial Society, of which I was the Chairman. Chief Minister Ch. Devi Lal, PWD Minister Shri O.P. Bharadwaj and several officials and leading personalities of Haryana attended the meeting.

Also present there by special invitation were the Rajmata of Gwalior and Sardar Angre, a close associate of the Rajmata. Since the Rajmata belonged to the BJP, which was a constituent of the Devi Lal-led coalition government in Haryana, there was a special rapport between Ch. Devi Lal and the Rajmata. The rationale for the Rajmata's and Sardar Angre's presence at the meeting was the fact that the Marathas were the main force that fought the Afghans during the Third Battle of Panipat in 1761 A.D.

At this meeting, we discussed measures to put up some suitable memorials to honour those who had fought gallantly in the three famous battles of Panipat that decided the political destiny of our country at critical junctures of our history. We also visited the spot at Kala Am (alternatively called Kala Amb) five miles from Panipat, which is closely associated with memories of the Third Battle of Panipat. There was a mango tree at the spot where the battle was fought and it was from this tree that the place derived its name Kala Am (black mango).

The name Kala Am may have originated from the black colour of the mango tree's foliage. But there is another version as well. The mango tree stood as a mute witness to the battle that raged at a place near Ugrakheri village between the armies of the Maratha general Bhau Sadashiv Rao and Ahmed Shah Abdali, the ruler of Afghanistan. Bhau Sadashiv Rao is said to have stood near this mango tree while directing his forces during the battle. The Marathas were defeated and about 20,000 of their soldiers got killed. The general belief is that as the blood of these soldiers seeped into the roots of the mango tree, its colour changed into black, thus leading its being called Kala Am or the black mango tree.

In due course, a person by name Pandit Shugan Chand made two doors out of the wood of this tree. When these doors were given as presents to Queen Victoria, she gave one to King Louis XIV of France, while the second door was kept in the Victoria Hall, a museum at Karnal, which was later named as the Gandhi Memorial Hall. I later learnt that the door was shifted in 2000 A.D. to the museum at Kala Am near Panipat.

I had read so much about the three battles of Panipat that a visit to this place proved very rewarding and helped in getting some of my ideas on this subject clarified in the course of discussions with several learned persons, who happened to be present on the occasion of the meeting of the Battles of Panipat Memorial Society. Later, I had the opportunity of undertaking further studies and going through books on the battles of Panipat that came out subsequently. Many facts about these battles, which I regard as rather interesting, deserve to be mentioned.

As I drove along the roads of Panipat, a certain area was pointed out to me as the place where the historic battles were supposed to have been fought. I got down on the road in order to imbibe a few whiffs of the airn that still blew over this plain land where the storied battles were fought. Is this then the place about which I had been reading and hearing so much since my school days? I could not believe my eyes.

I recalled a fascinating description of this place that I had once read in Frederick Augustus' book, "The Emperor Akbar: A Contribution Towards the History of India in the 16th Century" (pages 74-75). To quote: " The great military road which runs through Hindustan towards north-western Asia, bisects the broad plain of Panipat at a distance of some 45 to 50 miles north-west from Delhi. Panipat is a far-reaching, almost illimitable level tract, broken only by insignificant undulations. Here and there where shallow soil is moistened by some niggardly water-course, grow sparse grasses and stunted thorn bushes but for the most part the eye falls only on a sterile yellowish-grey waste. Empty silence reigns and it would almost seem that this desert had been created by the battle-field of nations. Here, in the course of ages, the most momentous issues have been fought out; here more than once has the fate of all India been decided; here the Mahabharata places the pre-historic battles of her demi-gods and heroes; here the knightly Babur won the sovereignty of Hindustan, in a conflict as stubborn as it was decisive; and here now, thirty years later, the fighting power of the Chagatais was arranged to chase the audacious invader to the dominions of his grandson."

So far as the First Battle of Panipat is concerned, everybody knows that in 1526 A.D. Babar, the Mughal invader, defeated Ibrahim Lodi, the Afghan Sultan of Delhi, in the battle and thus laid the foundation of the Mughal empire in India. But there are many facts about this battle, many sidelights and side-shows, which have not received all the attention that they call for. The Lodis were Afghans, who were playing an important role in the affairs of the Delhi Sultanate by joining the army as well as by rising to become nobles in Muslim society when the Khiljis and Tughlaks were in power. They also served the Sayyids, who later assumed power in Delhi. It was in 1451 A.D. that Bahlul Lodi succeeded in occupying the Delhi throne, thus establishing Afghan rule in our country for the first time. He was succeeded by his son, Sikander Lodi, in 1489 A.D. and in 1517 A.D. and in 1517 A.D., his grandson, Ibrahim Lodi, became the ruler of Delhi.

Apart from the Lodi Afghans, there were also the Suri Afghans, one of whom, Sher Shah, became the ruler, as is generally known. The Afghans had lived long enough in India to become Indianised or naturalized as more or less Indians; the Mughals were new comers and hence regarded as foreigners vis-à-vis the Afghan natives.

Babar, a Chagtai Turk, was a descendant of Timur from his father's side and of Chengiz Khan from his mother's side. Thus, he was in the lineage of two very cruel Mongal invaders, who had plundered north-west India. After conquering Kabul in 1504 A.D., he began to cast covetous eyes on India's territory. As Babar observes in his Memoirs: "As it was always in my heart to possess Hindustan and as these several countries had once been held by the Turks, I pictured them as my own and was resolved to get them into my own hands, whether peacefully or by force." He was encouraged in this venture by one of his nobles, who said to him: "Go on then and possess yourself of the noblest country in the universe. Establish beyond the river Indus the empire which your forefathers have marked out for you. Go and fix your court in the center of Hindustan and prefer the delights of the Indies to the hoar and snow of Tartary..................God and Mohammad engaged you to extinguish the idolatry of the Indians."

Babar invaded India several times between 1512 A.D. and 1525 A.D., but failed to get any toe-hold on our country. Then his real opportunity came in 1526 A.D. The oppressive and unpopular Lodi rulers of Delhi were troubled by the intrigues of their nobles. Ibrahim Lodi's uncle, Daulat Khan, was the Governor of Punjab, but he did not like the former and was anxious to become the independent ruler of Lahore. Though Daulat Khan had initially given some trouble to Babar, later he made up with the latter and, in fact, invited him to invade India and overthrow Ibrahim Lodi. At this time, Rana Sangha, the Hindu ruler of Rajputana, who was rather unhappy with Ibrahim Lodi as a consequence of the conflict between the two over the eastern part of Rajputana, is said to have extended an invitation to Babar to attack Ibrahim Lodi.

Encouraged by the offer of support from two important potentates of India, Babar launched an attack on Punjab in 1525 A.D. and occupied Lahore. Thereafter, Babar turned against Daulat Khan, who now realized his folly and withdrew his support from Babar. Rana Sangha, who had offered to support Babar on condition that the latter would help him against Ibrahim Lodi in getting control over east Rajputana, also changed his mind at seeing Babar's betrayal of Daulat Khan and not only desisted from supporting Babar, but went a step further and joined forces with Ibrahim Lodi. At this stage, Babar had to go back to Kabul for some time to deal with a problem of aggression by the Uzbeks. He returned soon and confronted Daulat Khan, who submitted to the former and in fact passed away after some time.

Babar then marched towards Delhi in April 1526 A.D. Ibrahim Lodi was in high spirits as his astrologers had told him that his victory was certain. He marched to Panipat from Delhi with a large army. On the night of April 19, 1526, Babar's army attacked Lodi's troops, but it was repulsed. This boosted the morale of Lodi's men. In gratification, Ibrahim Lodi held a feast and gave away to the officers and men jewels, pearls and gold, which he had brought with him.[4] When the real fight took place on the plains of Panipat, Babar's men won decisively. Though much smaller in size, Babar's army proved stronger because of the devastating artillery at its command. Ibrahim Lodi died fighting in the field of battle, while Babar chose not to lead from the front, but to stay with the command headquarters at the rear. Ranged against Babar on Ibrahim Lodi's side was the Rajput Raja Vikramjit of Gwalior. After the victory at Panipat, Babar's troops went forward and occupied Delhi and Agra.

This was celebration time in Babar's camp. As pointed out by K.K. Bharadwaj[5], Babar gave seventy lakh dams (20,000 pounds sterling) to his son, Humayun, and rewarded his chief Begs with six to ten lakh dams (approximately 1700 to 2800 pounds sterling). Everyone got his present in gold, silver, cloth and jewels in Farghana, Khurasan and Kashgar. Holy men in Heart and Samarkhand, Mecca and Medina got a substantial reward. To every person in Kabul, a silver coin was sent to commemorate the victory. The wealth of India was squandered quite easily.[6]

Soon after the First Battle of Panipat, Babar defeated the combined forces of Rana Sangha, Sultan Mahmud Lodi and the Rajputs at the historic battle of Khanwa in 1527 A.D. This was a great victory which helped Babar in establishing the Mughal empire in India.

When Babar arrived in India from Kabul, he did not have a particular liking for it. He wrote in his memoirs: "Hindustan is a country that has few pleasures to recommend it. The people are not handsome. They have no idea of the charms of friendly society, of frankly mixing together or of familiar intercourse. They have no genius, no comprehension of mind, no politeness of manner, no kindness or fellow-feeling, no ingenuity or mechanical invention in planning or executing their handicraft works, no skill or knowledge in design or architecture, they have no good horses, no good flesh, no grapes or musk-melons, no good fruits, no ice or cold water, no good food or bread in their bazaars, no baths or colleges, no candles, no torches, not a candle stick.........."[7] What a blatantly biased and one-sided picture! If he is to be believed, there was no ice in India. Obviously, he had not heard of the eternal snows of our Himalayan peaks!

Babar used to feel home-sick and had no intention of staying on in India. He had written to one of his confidants in Afghanistan in 1529 A.D. that the affairs of Hindustan had been brought to some degree of order and that he hoped to return to Afghanistan as soon as possible. He wrote: "How can one like me, who has vowed abstinence and purity of life, possibly forget the delicious melons and grapes of that happy land? The other day, they brought me a musk-melon: as I cut it up, I felt a deep home-sickness and sense of exile from my native land, and I could not help weeping."6 But God had willed otherwise. Babar did not return to Afghanistan. He died in his capital Agra in 1530 A.D., when he was just forty seven years of age! (Ishwari Prasad—History of Muslim Rule in India).

Pursuing my interest in Haryana studies, a few years ago, I went through a book "Hemu, The Hindu Hero of Medieval India" by Sunil Kumar Sarkar, which gives a very interesting account and interpretation of the battles of Panipat. One of his moot points is that the conflict in north west India during this period was a tripartite one, India having been 'a bone of contention among the Hindus, the Afghans and the Turks." "But", he says, "unfortunately historians so far have narrowed down this tripartite conflict into a bipartite one *i.e.*, only the conflict between the Afghans and the Turks."

Proceeding further, Sarkar says that before Babar appeared on the scene, there was a conflict between the Hindus (Rajputs) led by Rana Sangha and the Afghans led by Ibrahim Lodi over eastern Rajputana. The Mughals were the "third force", the other two being the Hindus and the non-Mughal Muslims (*i.e.* the Afghans). In the opinion of Sarkar, the historians have committed a grave blunder by treating the non-Mughal Muslims and the Mughals as a monolithic Muslim bloc, ignoring the differences between the "Afghan natives" and the "Mughal foreigners." He finds fault with the historians for calling the entire period from the time of the Delhi Sultanate to that of the British as "the Muslim period of Indian history, basing the periodization on religion only." He would rther divide the entire period into Afghan rule and Turkish rule. As he says: "Due to the partisan motivation of the historians of the house of Taimur and their object of glorifying the Mughals, the history of the Afghans, who ruled India for about 106 years, has not received due justice of being adequately noticed."

Sarkar's analysis of the differences between the Afghans and the Mughals makes interesting reading. He writes: "The Afghans were self-seekers, quarrelsome, indisciplined, and maintained low ambitions. The Mughals, on the other hand, were disciplined barbarians, blood-hungry, and nursed very high ambitions. The entry of the Afghans into India was slow and almost imperceptible, and as such there was less resistance from the natives against their immigration. And in course of time the Afghans were "Hinduised" (Marx, 30), but the Mughals, till then, remained foreigners, strangers."`9 Sarkar quotes from certain authors to assert that even in the thirteenth century, the Mughals were 'inhuman and beastly", "rather monsters than humans", "thirsting for and drinking blood" and were even "a threat to the existence of Islam."`

Sarkar agrees that there were conflicts between the Hindus and the Afghans, but the tension was not over religion, while, on the other hand, the Mughals "had a religious zeal against the native idolaters, as is evident for instance, in the oratory of Babur, before his troops just on the eve of the first move in the field of Panipat (1526), or as is evident in the purpose of Taimur, the forbear of Babur, in chastising the Hindus for their idolatry and the Muslims of India for their conniving at it. Not only this, the Afghans as well as the Khaljis were always on the alert against the Tartars, the Turks and the Mughals."[10]

Elaborating further, Sarkar says that the historians have so far dealt at low key with the role of the Hindus. According to him, from the very beginning of the Muslim invasions of India starting with the usurpation of Sind by the Arabs in 712 A.D., the Hindus had put up resistance though in vain because of the disunity among themselves. When the Mughals came to India, the Afghans and the Hindus made common cause against the Mughals in order "to obliterate the foreign Mughal Muslims' entry into India." [11] To quote Sarkar again: "Since the capture of Sind by the Muslims, the Hindu power had certainly been diminishing, but still it was looking for an opportunity for revival...............In the north, such strivings were apparent, for example, in the three Hindu leaders—Rana Sangha, who fought against Babur; Himu, who fought against Akbar, as King Vikramaditya of Delhi; and, later on, Shivaji, who fought against Arangzeb, for a Hindu Rajyya."[12]

And this brings us to the Second Battle of Panipat, of which Himu of Haryana was the hero. As has already been mentioned, it is said that there were three leaders, who counted most for the people of Haryana, namely Himu, Suraj Mal and Sir Chhotu Ram. While this is undoubtedly true, it may give a wrong impression to say that Himu was the hero of Haryana alone. The fact is that Himu was the hero of the whole country at a critical juncture of our history. From a very humble beginning, Himu rose to become the Emperor of Delhi, though only for a short while.

Before taking up Himu's role, I would briefly mention the course that the Afghan-Mughal conflict had taken towards the middle of the 16th century A.D., the time by which he appeared like a meteor in the firmament of our country's history, crashing again like a meteor in a very short span of time. After his victory in the First Battle of Panipat in 1526 .A.D., Babar proceeded against several formidable enemies in different parts of the country and established himself as the undisputed ruler of practically the whole of northern India.

But the people of Haryana were still not in a submissive mood and in 1529 A.D., the Mandhar Rajputs of Kurukshetra area (often referred to as Nardak, the land without misery) rose in revolt to put down which Babar sent a big detatchment of troops that resorted to large-scale killing of the rebels and burnt down their houses. Even after all this, he could hardly consolidate his position and when in 1530 A.D. he died prematurely, the Afghans were still trying to create problems for the Mughals. Humayun, who ascended the throne, was not known for any great military skill or administrative ability, failed to consolidate the Mughal position in the country for quite some time. He faced rebellion in Gujarat and his three brothers, who had been appointed by him as the Governors of Kabul, Mewat and Sambhal, proved disloyal to him.

In Bihar and Bengal, Humayun had to fight the Afghans, who, under the galvanic leadership of Sher Khan (later Sher Shah), a Sur Afghan, posed a big challenge. Sher Khan defeated Humayun in 1539 A.D. in the battle of Chausa and then in 1540 A.D. in the battle of

Kanauj, forcing the latter to flee the country and indue course seek refuge in Persia. In "The History and Culture of the Indian People: The Mughal Empire" edited by Dr. R.C. Mazumdar (page 68), Sher Shah has been described as "one of the most striking and redoubtable figures in medieval Indian history", who, from "an humble beginning in life eventually revived the Afghan power in Northern India by defeating and ousting the Mughal emperor Humayun, and gave his newly established empire a well-organised administration, hitherto rare in medieval Indian history."

One of Sher Shah's lasting contributions was the construction of roads or national highways in modern terminology, one of which called the Grand trunk Road connected East Bengal to the farthest point of north west India. This was perhaps the first step taken in our country towards the building of infra-structure. In his "Memoirs of the Races of the North West Provinces of India", W. Crooke highlighted one more important aspect of Sher Shah's contribution by observing that he had attempted to found an Indian Empire broadly based upon the people's will. According to him, Sher Shah had the genius to recognize that the government must be based on popular support and must govern for the benefit of the people and that the Hindus must be conciliated by a policy of justice and toleration. I fully agree with the summing up of Sher Shah's role in "The History and Culture of the Indian People: The Mughal Empire" edited by Dr. R.C. Mazumdar: " Considering from different aspects of his love and sympathy for his subjects, care for the peasantry, liberal outlook, sense of even-handed justice, indefatigable industry, devotion to duty even at the cost of personal rest and comfort, and, above all, his constructive statesmanship, he must be accorded a position much ahead of his predecessors in medieval India and next only to that of Akbar."

I have dilated at some length on Sher Shah's achievements because—and this will definitely warm the cockle of many a Haryanvi heart—according to some historians, he was born on the soil of Haryana. Noted historians, Dr. Ishwari Prasad and Dr. K.R. Kanungo, are of the view that Sher Shah was born in the Pargana of Narnaul, whereas, according to the Makhzan-I-Afghani, he was born at Hissar. As everybody knows, both are places in Haryana. The view about his birth-place being in the Pargana of Narnaul is said to be in keeping with the implication of what Abu-'l-Fazl said in this regard in the Akbar-nama, because it was here that his father and grandfather lived and where Sher Shah in his later years built a mausoleum over the grave of his grandfather.[13] However, there is no unanimity among historians about his birth-place.

It was after Sher Shah's life was abruptly cut short in an accidental explosion on May 22, 1544 A.D. that Humayun considered the situation favourable for his return to India in a bid to recover his lost empire. Following Sher Shah's death, his son succeeded him, assuming the name Islam Shah. He was an able ruler, who made his mark by his military and administrative capability and preserved the integrity of Sher Shah's kingdom. He died as a consequence of fistula on October 30, 1553 A.D., but, according to Abu-'l-Fazl, his death was due to "a malignant ulcer that had formed in one of his lower members owing to the issue of corrupt matter". Another historian says that Islam Shah died on November 22, 1554 A.D. Be that as it may, after his death, his minor son, Firuz Shah, succeeded him, but he was murdered by Mubariz Khan, brother-in-law of Islam Shah, who then ascended the throne, assuming the title Adil Shah.

Weak and indolent, Adil Shah was unable to check the prevailing chaos. He appointed Himu as the Chief Minister in whose hands he left all affairs of the State. Some historians have said that Himu was made the all-powerful Prime Minister or Vakil-i-Alah. Historians have often described Himu as the Samudragupta or the Chandragupta Maurya of medieval India. Some have characterized him as the Napoleon of medieval India, particularly in view of the physical resemblance between the two. Napoleon was a little over five feet in height and so was Himu. Both displayed a remarkable quality of military leadership. Abul Fazl had hurled many invectives at Himu, but even he had observed: "For on none of those former occasions was there a ruler of India possessed of such courage, enterprise and plan (as Himu).[14]

Himu was the first Hindu Prime Minister of the Muslim empire of medieval India. The second such figure was Todar Mal. Both of them reached this position by dint of their intellect and hard work.[15] Himu, the great patriot, was not a Rajput nor did he belong to any of the fighting classes of India and still he gave his life on the field of battle, fighting for the honour of his country.

I have read several books on the history of India, but in most of them, no detailed and connected account is available about the spectacular career of Himu, who, despite his very humble beginning, ended up being the Emperor of Delhi albeit for a brief period. Dr. R.C. Mazumdar, the great historian, was conscious of this shortcoming on

the part of India's historians in general, which led him to add to his book a brief appendix captioned "Himu—A Forgotten Hero" in which he observed: "Neither fate nor historians have been kind to Himu to whom reference has been made above (pp. 94-96). Historians, medieval and modern, have done scant justice to, and failed to show due appreciation of the unique personality and greatness of a Hindu, who, during the heyday of Muslim rule in India, worked his way from a grocer's shop to the throne of Delhi, and, but for an accident in a battle which turned into defeat, might have founded a Hindu ruling dynasty, instead of the Mughals, in Delhi. Although his career is known to us almost exclusively from the writings of historians who looked down upon him as an upstart Hindu and an arch-enemy of their patrons, the Mughal rulers yet enough have been preserved in their chronicles to show that bare historical justice demands that the career of this great Hindu should be impartially reviewed as a whole, separately, as an important episode in the history of medieval India. For, there is no doubt that he furnishes the only shining example of a Hindu, born and brought up as such in a Muslim State, who once dominated the political stage of North India by sheer merit and personality without any advantage of birth or fortune. As no attempt seems to have been made in any general history of India so far, no apology is needed for the short sketch of the life and activities of the great Hindu Commoner, Hemchandra, called by his Afghan followers after his accession to the throne of Delhi, Himu Shah."

One reason for this callous indifference towards this great figure of medieval Indian history is that most of the contemporary historians were Muslims, who were hostile towards a person that did great harm to their cause. Even some basic facts about the life of Himu (variously mentioned as Hemu, Hemchandra or Basanta Rai) such as the date and place of his birth are not known for certain, because the historians have expressed very divergent views about them. The majority of the historians are agreed that Himu's ancestors came from Narnaul and settled down at a small village Qutabpur near Rewari in Haryana, where he was born. But there are others who say that's forefathers came from the south and settled down in Delhi. M.L. Bhargava, who has written a book on Himu in Hindi, mentions Deoti Macheri or Dewli Sazari (*i.e.* south of Delhi) as the birthplace of Himu. Rahul Sankirtyayana is of the view that Himu was born somewhere close to Sasharam (Bihar).

Nothing definite is known about the date of Himu's birth or his caste. Various guesses have been made by historians and all that can be said with some degree of certainty is that Himu was born in the twenties of the 16th century A.D. As regards his caste, the general view is that he belonged to the Dhunsar Bania or Vaisya caste. However, Sir Jadunath Sarkar, the noted historian was of the view that Himu was Himu Bhargava, a Gaud Brahmin.

No authentic picture of Himu is available. A picture of Himu reproduced in some books showing him with a modestly beautiful mien, riding on horse-back, wearing a sword, is not authentic in view of Abul Fazl's statements that Himu had no "beauty of form (surat) nor noble qualities (sairat)" and that he was an "evil-looking one of puny form." Other historians have said that Himu was incapable of horse-riding and that he never carried a sword.[16] Abul Fazl, who had great contempt for him, had observed that Himu had neither rank (hasb) nor race (nasab) nor beauty of form (surat) nor noble qualities (sairat).

Himu was a grandson of Rai Jai Pal, who was a petty trader, though he had earned the title Rai. His father was Puran Das, a highly religious-minded person, who moved about with saints and Sadhus, singing devotional songs. He went to Brindavan in search of a Guru to guide him on the spiritual path. There he joined the Radhavallabh sect led by Hit Harivansha. He traveled to many places to preach the teachings of his sect and is said to have visited a place in Sindh, where he persuaded the local Governor to join his sect in 1535 A.D.

Himu's early education was quite ordinary. Apart from Hindi and Sanskrit, he also learnt Persian and Arabic as was customary in those days. His education suffered on account of his straitened circumstances, which forced him to give up school; and take up the profession of a huckster, who, at a tender age, used to sell salt in the winding streets of Rewari.[17] That is why the historians have variously called him a "shop-keeper" (bakkal) and a "green grocer."

It was his merit and capacity for hard work that attracted the notice of Islam Shah, who appointed him as the Superintendent of the Delhi market (Shahan-I-Bazar) and later as the head of the Departments of Intelligence and Posts. Himu's role as the intelligence chief must have earned him the appreciation of Islam Shah. Then his soldierly qualities prompted Islam Shah to appoint him as the Director-General or Chief of the Army. According to one historian, Himu was in due course appointed as the Minister of Food and Civil Supplies. It has been said that one seer of Sona Moong (the best variety of pulses) and a quantity of fresh rice from Bengal used to be brought for Himu every day, wherever he was, be it the Indus Valley or some other place.

Abul Fazl denigrated Himu by alleging that the latter had made himself known to the ruler by "feline trickery" and "evil-speaking", but even he conceded Himu's "astuteness" and "business capacity". Several historians have said that Himu was a man of no ordinary character, that he had a conspicuous ability for war and civil administration and that he was clever, [18] though not a Rajput.

It was when Adil Shah became the ruler that Himu's career graph showed a sudden rise, because the former had no time for governance. Adil Shah, an indolent and pleasure-seeking ruler, spent much of his time with the inmates of his harem. Hateful of men of learning, he preferred the company of illiterate persons of his own ilk. He opened his treasury on several occasions and "drained it dry". As recorded in contemporary historical works, sometimes he paraded through the streets, shooting golden-headed arrows. Anybody who retrieved such an arrow was rewarded with five hundred tangas (about 200 pounds sterling at 1975 rates).[19]

Confronted with rebellion in several parts of the empire and with palace intrigues, it is no wonder, therefore, that an incompetent and pleasure-loving man like Adil Shah handed over the reins of government entirely to Himu, whom he made the Prime Minister and "generalissimo" in charge of all the portfolios of government. Adil Shah was just a symbol of the State or, in modern jargon, a constitutional figurehead. When Adil Shah became insane for all practical purposes, Himu grabbed all power and began to rule as if he was the king. He distributed "jagirs" at his will and freely spent from the treasuries accumulated by the earlier rulers.[20]

Himu displayed his ability on the battle ground as many of Adil Shah's kinsmen and some Afghan nobles, who were occupying important positions in different parts of the country, rose in rebellion and challenged his supremacy. Sher Shah's empire, which had been preserved with great effort by Islam Shah, now disintegrated and split into four separate piece with Islam Shah, brother-in-law of Adil Shah, capturing Delhi and Agra, Sikander Shah, another brother-in-law of Adil Shah, ensconced in Punab and Samsuddin Mohammad Shah Ghazi proclaiming independence in Bengal, while Adil Shah controlled the territory beyond Agra up to Bihar. It was Himu who helped Adil Shah in stemming the tide of these revolts.

It has been said that Himu had fought as many as twenty two battles on behalf of Adil Shah and won all of them. However, the details of only eleven of these battles are available. Some historians described these battles on the basis of accounts given by Abu-'l-Fazl and Abdul Qadir Badauni. Sunil Kumar Sarker[21] has given detailed accounts of each of these battles, which bring out the intense in-fighting among the Afghans. These accounts make fascinating reading, but I am skipping over these details in order to make way for taking up the Second Battle of Panipat and Himu's role in it.

Feeling encouraged by the spate of revolts against Adil Shah, Humayun, who had in the mean time recovered Kabul, returned to India and, in February 1555 A.D., captured Lahore. Proceeding further, he occupied Delhi and thus re-established the rule of the Mughals. However, on January 26, 1556 A.D., Humayun died of an accidental fall in his library in Delhi. News of Humayun's condition was sent to his son, Akbar, then all of 14 years, who was then at Hariana nearJullundur in Punjab under the tutelage of Bairam Khan.

Since it took time in those days for the news of Humayun's death to reach Akbar, it was kept a secret for a long time, as is the practice even nowadays, because news about the bad health or death of a V.I.P. can sometimes trigger political moves not to the liking of those close to the powers that be. A person by name Mulla Bekase, who was Humayun's look-alike, was made to dress like Emperor Humayun and make public appearances to hide the news of the emperor's death! It was only on February 11, 1556 A.D. that the news was made public, leading to Akbar's enthronement two days later at Kalanpur. Tardi Beg Khan was appointed as the Governor of Delhi.

At this stage, Himu proceeded with a large force along with 50 thousand horses and 5000 elephants via Gwalior and captured Agra, when its Governor, Iskander Khan Uzbeg, fled. He chased the retreating Mughal troops and arrived at Tughlakabad, a few miles east of the Qutb Minar, and confronted Tardi Beg Khan, the Mughal Governor of Delhi, in a battle on October 7, 1556 A.D. One historian has described Himu's large army as consisting of 50 thousand horses, one thousand elephants and many cannons and falconets "as numerous as the locusts and ants of the deserts." [22] According to Sir Jadunath Sarkar, the Mughal forces initially inflicted heavy losses on Himu's army.

Believing that they had already won a victory, the Mughal troops left the place to plunder the city, while Tardi Beg Khan himself stayed behind in the field "very thinly guarded".[23] Himu, who had kept a select group of men with horses and elephants all this time "promptly seized the opportunity and made a sudden charge at Tardi Beg", forcing him and his men to flee. Himu occupied Delhi and distributed among the Afghan soldiers some of the spoils of these battle in order to win their support. He proclaimed himself sovereign and assumed the title of Raja Vikramaditya. As Dr. R.C. Mazumdar observes, Himu asserted his independent status in a practical manner by ascending the throne with the imperial canopy raised over his head and issuing coins in his name.

All historians are not unanimous as to whether Himu became an independent king after the occupation of Delhi or he merely assumed power on behalf and as a representative of Adil Shah. Most of the historians are, however, of the view that Himu became an independent king. The title of Raja Vikramaditya that he assumed meant that he wanted to revive the empire of Hindustan and found a Hindu Raj. According to Lt. Col. H.C. Kar, Himu became "a monarch in his own right, the only Hindu to occupy the throne of Delhi during the medieval history of India." [24]

Himu's glory lasted for a very short while—just for about thirty days—till Akbar defeated him in the Second Battle of Panipat. When Himu captured Delhi, Akbar was at Jullundur. His advisers suggested that he should retreat to Afghanistan in view of Himu's dominating position, but Bairam Khan, Akbar's guardian, over-ruled them and persuaded Akbar to advance and throw a challenge to Himu. As Bamber Grascoigne observes, [25] Akbar and Bairam Khan "indulged in some expensive showmanship" in order to boost the morale of their troops and ordered "fire-works as a treat for the soldiers along with instructions to make an image of Hemu, fill it with gun-powder and set it on fire."

As Akbar and Bairam advanced towards Sirhind, they met those fleeing from Delhi, including Tardi Beg Khan. Bairam Khan stopped them on the way and awarded death penalty to Tardi for fleeing from Himu. It is said that one motive behind this was the religious difference between Bairam and Tardi, the former being an orthodox Shia and the latter a Sunni.[2]6 The cruel murder of Tardi Beg Khan has been denounced by many historians.

Akbar and Bairam reached Thaneswar in Haryana with their troops to face Himu. The Mughal advance guard inflicted a crushing defeat on Himu's advance guard and captured the entire artillery sent with the latter, thus causing a great loss to Himu's forces. Before the final battle at Panipat, another battle took place at "Tillepat which is situated between Panipat and Delhi" [27] On November 5, 1556 A.D. Akbar's and Himu's forces met on the historic battleground of Panipat.

Various accounts have been given by historians about the course of this battle that decided the fate of India at this juncture of our history. Many of these accounts are in conflict with one another, so far as the details are concerned. Sunil Kumar Sarker's book has provided a useful sketch showing the battle formations of the two armies.[28] According to Sir Jadunath Sarkar, Himu's army consisted of 30,000 Rajput and Afghan horsemen and 500 war elephants with musketeers and cross-bowmen on their backs, while the Mughals with a cavalry of ten thousand and "without the help of Babur's profuse fire-arms" were heavily outnumbered. Obviously, to make up for this big imbalance, Bairam Khan tried to tone up the morale of his army by "an inspiring speech to his officers, pointing out that they must conquer or perish and his brave words were supported by the divination of a soothsayer who deduced favourable omens from his inspection of the shoulder-blade of a sheep." [29]

Himu took his seat on his elephant Hawai and personally took pert in the Second Battle of Panipat, while neither nor his guardian Bairam Khan were personally present there. Akbar had been kept at a safe distance in a camp about eight miles away from the field of battle. Describing the battle, Dr. R.C. Mazumdar says that Himu began with a charge on the Mughals whose right and left wings were thrown into confusion. Then, with the help of his war elephants, "he dashed against the enemies' center and, although the fifgt appeared to be in his favour, it continued unabated, when an arrow pierced his eye, making him unconscious. This decided the fate of the day, as his army, considering him dead, fled pell-mell in all directions."[30]

Sir Jadunath Sarkar gives some more details: "He (*i.e.* Himu) made repeated counter-charges with his powerful elephants, overthrowing the Mughals in the direct line of his advance. But the war was taking toll of his strength; two of his bravest lieutenants, Bhagawan Das and Shadi Khan Kakar, were killed before his eyes. The mixed fighting raged most stubbornly for some time, when an arrow pierced his eye. The blood spouting from the wound was seen by the Afghans near him, but he pulled the arrow out, bandaged the eye with a scarf and ordered the fight to go on, after which he fell down on the handa in a faint. The fall of the leader ended the battle and the Afghan-Rajput army broke up in hopeless flight."[31] The consensus among historians is that about 5000 persons were killed in this battle.

Most historians agree that Himu was a valorous king, who was deprived by a sheer accident of victory that was almost certain. There is a divergence of views among historians as to who took the unconscious Himu to Akbar. Abul Fazl describes this event in the Akbarnama in the following words: "Just then Shah Quli Khan and some brave men came up to the elephant on which Hemu was riding. He did not know that Hemu was on the elephant and sought to kill the driver in order that he might make the elephant his spoil. The helpless driver, who had neither the helmet of loyalty nor the cuirass of courage, from fear of his life, pointed out his master. When Shah Quli Khan heard of his great fortune, he blessed his stars and tossed the cap of joy to the skies. He gave quarter to the driver and made him hopeful of a royal reward.....................Shah Quli Khan brought in Hemu bound."

How did Himu's end come? Here again, there is no unanimity. Vincent A. Smith, like some others, is of the view that Akbar himself did not kill Himu. Bairam wanted Akbar to earn the meritorious title of "Ghazi" or "slayer of the infidel" by touching his sword on Himu. Akbar complied with the desire of his guardian and struck Himu on the neck with his sword. "The bystanders also plunged their swords into the bleeding corpse. Himu's head was sent to Kabul to be exposed and his trunk was gibbeted at one of the gates of Delhi."[32]

There are several other historians such as Abul Fazl, Nizamuddin, Badauni and a latter-day historian by name Dashrath Sharma who say that Akbar Akbar, the young prince, refused to kill Himu and then Bairam Khan slew him with his sword.. In his Akbarnama, Abul Fazl says that Bairam Khan tried to persuade Akbar to kill Himu, but Akbar's "lofty spirit did not permit him to slay a captive", because "there was nothing meritorious in such an act." Proceeding further, Abul Fazl writes: "At last Bairam Khan Khan-Khanan .... under the influence of hereditary beliefs which take their place in men from imitation of fathers and teachers, himself became engaged in the acquisition of this fancied merit, and with his sword cleansed the world from the contamination of his existence."

Abul Fazl's account is also corroborated by a contemporary Rajasthani book, Dalpat Vilas, according to which, Akbar refused to kill Himu, saying that he felt an upsurge of pity in his heart. Then, it is said, Bairam Khan from one side and another person by name Wali Beg from the other did Himu to death.

It is obvious that, as many historians have pointed out, Himu's defeat was nothing but providential. If Himu had not been accidentally killed by an arrow at a moment when the tide of the battle ws clearly in his favour, India would have been ruled by his dynasty rather than by Akbar and the subsequent Mughal emperors.[33]

The Mughals then set upon a vengeful course and, after conquering Alwar, they proceeded to the place where Himu's family lived. Pir Muhammad, the steward of Bairam Khan's household, was dispatched to Mewat where Himu's treasure was deposited. After much fighting, Akbar's forces captured Himu's old father, who was a religious recluse, and brought him before the Nasir-al-Mulk, who asked him to change his religion. "The old man answered, 'for eighty years I have worshipped my God, according to this religion. Why should I change it at this tie and why should I, merely from fear of my life, and without understanding it, come into your way of worship?' Pir Muhammad treated his words as if he heard them not, and answered him with the tongue of the sword."[34]

However, the Mughals failed to capture Himu's wife, who had escaped from Delhi to Mewat, taking with her all of Himu's treasure.[35] Nor could anything be known of Himu's nephew, Ramaya, who had been fighting by his side. He might have been killed on the battlefield.[36]

Thus the Afghan dream was shattered in India, particularly after the death of Adil Shah in 1557 A.D. in a battle against Khizir Khan Sur of Bengal. With this also ended for the time being the hope of Hindu revival in India.[37]

Some historians[38] have laid the blame for Himu's failure on a logistic blunder before the main battle at Panipat, namely his dispatch of the whole lot of his artillery without any supporting force with the result that it fell into Mughal hands. Some have attributed Himu's defeat to his excessive dependence on his elephants, which, though bigger in number, could not match the speed and adaptability of the Mughals' horses. Moreover, the Mughals' tactic of subjecting Himu's elephants to barrages of arrows had the result of spreading confusion among the latter.

A factor behind Himu's defeat was what has been characterized as his "ignorance of war strategy and his short-sightedness as military general."[39] It has been said that immediately after his occupation of Agra and Delhi, Himu could have chased the handful of Mughals out of India without much difficulty. But instead of doing so, Himu "indulged in paranoid grandeur" after occupying Agra and Delhi.[40]

But all said and done, there is no doubt that Himu was a military genius, who had won all but one of the 22 wars that he had fought and lost the last one by just an 'accident'. As Dr. R.C. Mazumdar observes:

"Unfortunately Himu's history has been written almost wholly by his enemies, who dreaded him most and, far from doing justice to his greatness, they have tarnished his name with unmerited odium. It is time to resuscitate the memory and give a true account of the life of Hemchandra, really a great hero, whose dreams and achievements have been forgotten by his countrymen."[41]

Some observations made by Dr. R.C. Mazumdar in the Preface to "The History and Culture of the Indian people: the Mughal Empire" indicate the true status of Himu in our country's history in the medieval period and bear quoting: "One of the most characteristic features of this period is a galaxy of great personalities who have left a deep impress upon the political history of India. They are Babur, Sher Shah, Hem Chandra (Himu), Akbar, Chand Sultan, Rana Pratap, Nur Jahan, Shivaji, Baji Rao and Guru Govind Singh, who have secured a permanent niche in the shrine of Indian history and of whom any country might well feel proud."

Sunil Kumar Sarker has made an assessment of Himu from different points of view.[42] Himu achieved the unachieveable in spite of many hindrances. He was short in stature and thin in frame and yet he became the military chief. He was Hindu by religion and yet he commanded an army with a majority of Muslim soldiers. He served a Muslim master, but founded a Hindu kingdom.

Himu's qualities as a general come out clearly from Abu-'l-Fazl's observation that he had fought many battles and that he was "everywhere victorious". The noted historian, K.R. Qanungo has also said of him: "No Hindu had been covered with so many glorious wounds on the field of battle except Maharana Sangha .... No Rajput wielded the sword so bravely against the foreign invaders as this humble Hindu of Rewari did on the battle-field of Panipat." Himu was a good administrator. He was endowed with fellow-feeling and sympathy for the 'Baqqal' community to which he belonged. He was fully conscious of his Hindu nationality.

It has been rightly observed by a historian that he was the only Hindu emperor to occupy the throne of Delhi in the medieval period after 350 years of foreign rule.[43] His achievement symbolized Haryana's perpetual effort to throw out the invaders. It has also been appropriately said that Himu was the first and last Hindu, who assumed the imperial status in north India after the defeat by Ghauri of Prithviraj Chauhan in 1192 A.D. in the second battle of Tarain.

Badaoni, a highly sectarian and communal-minded historian, had in his Tarikh-I-Badaoni painted Himu as a "black-faced Hindu", while hailing Akbar's victory in the Second Battle of Panipat. His verse (as translated into English by Elliot and Dowson) is quite interesting and is quoted below:

"If through treachery, deceit and
fraud great Delhi fell
By Fate's decree, into the hands
Of Hemu Hemuu;
Muhammad Akbar, that Shah
Whose glory reached the sku,
By help of God captured that black-faced
Hindu Hemuu,
Creation's scribe on lasting tablet with
Pen of power
Wrote concerning that day:
He seized Hindu Hemuu"

This portraiture of Himu as an out-and –out Hindu does less than justice to him. Himu was a Hindu all right, but one who was broad-minded and secular in outlook. A story told about Himu by Sir H.M. Elliot and quoted by Sunil Kumar Sarker describes his faith in the lession of the Gita that one should do one's duty to the best of one's ability, leaving the rest to the almighty. Himu no doubt tried to establish the Hindu Raj in India by turning out the Muslim invaders. He was in fact following in the foot-steps of Prithviraj Chauhan, whose dream of establishing Hindu rule in India was shattered by his defeat in the second battle of Tarain near Thanesar in 1192 A.D. at the hands of Muhammad Ghauri. Another example before Himu was that of Rana Sangha, whose confederacy of Rajput rulers lay in ruins after his defeat at the hands of Babar in the battle of Khanwa in March 1527 A.D.

Himu treated his Hindu and Afghan followers as equal partners in his fight against the Mughals whom he looked upon as foreign invaders. He regarded the Hindus and Muslims as his two eyes, both dear to him. At the battle of Panipat, if his right flank was commanded by Shadi Khan Kakar, his left flank was led by his nephew Ramaya.[44] Though a staunch Hindu, Himu showed no disrespect towards any other religion—Islam or Christianity.[45] In fact, both the Hindus and Muslims had fought unitedly against the foreign invaders in many battles. In the first Battle of Panipat, Raja Vikramjit of Gwalior had joined Ibrahim Lodi to fight against Babar; Hasan Khan Mewati had joined forces with Rana Sangha against Babar and in the Third Battle of Panipat, the Marathas and Mughals had fought together against the Afghans.

Dr. R.C. Mazumdar has observed that Mughal historians like Abu-'l-Fazl and Badaoni have painted Himu in the blackest colour and represented him as having won the confidence of Adil Shah by ignoble means. Badaoni has charged Himu with brutality. Dr. Mazumdar thinks that it was natural for these Muslim historians to demonise Himu whom they regarded as the greatest enemy of the Mughals. Moreover, Vincent A. Smith says that the other historians are silent about Himu's brutality.

Considering the fact that not much authentic information is available about Himu's background and his military and other achievements, Sunil Kumar Sarker has suggested the need for adopting a heuristic approach on the part of historians and for further research in order to bring out all relevant facts and resurrect Himu from the limbo of history.

After the death of Himu, the prospect of the Hindus asserting themselves in north India suffered a set-back, as had similar prospects after the death of Rana Sangha, who had challenged the might of Babar. With the rise of the Marathas under the leadership of Shivaji in the 17th century A.D., these prospects looked good for some time. In the wake of Aurangzeb's death in 1707 A.D., the Marathas acquired de facto control over Delhi, though de jure, the weak Mughal Emperor was the sovereign. The Marathas led by the Peshwas carried on the fight on behalf of the Hindus against the Muslims with great patriotic fervour.

Towards the middle of the 18th century A.D., some Muslim invaders wrought havoc in north western India including Haryana and Delhi. Nadir Shah, the ruler of Persia, invaded India in 1739 A.D. and came up to Karnal without any resistance. He defeated Muhammad Shah, the Mughal Emperor, took him prisoner and marched to Delhi, where he indulged in unprecedented orgies of murder and loot. As many as 30,000 persons got killed in Delhi. Before returning to his country, Nadir Shah carried away with him the famous diamond Koh-I-noor and the jewel-studded Peacock Throne of Shah Jahan, apart from rupees 15 crore in cash—not a small sum in those days. Besides, a great grand-daughter of Aurangzeb was given in marriage to Nadir Shah's son!

Nadir Shah's general, Ahmad Shah Abdali, who occupied Afghanistan after the former's death in 1747 A.D., repeatedly invaded and plundered Punjab, Haryana and Delhi. In 1758 A.D., the Marathas invaded Punjab and threw out the Afghan usurpers. This was a severe blow to the ego of Ahmad Shah Abdali, who had given himself the title of 'Durrani' meaning "the pearl of the age". As a riposte, Abdali attacked Punjab in October 1759 A.D. and recovered the territory. The Marathas tried to give a fight to Abdali, but they were defeated at Thanesar in Haryana and their leader, Dattaji Scindhia, was subsequently killed in January, 1760 A.D. in the battle of Barari Ghat close to Luni about 20 kilomtres north of Delhi. (Please note that the place has the same name as I !).

The Marathas, who were acting as the protectors of the Mughal Emperor, Shah Alam II, challenged Ahmad Shah Abdali's forces on the battlefield of Panipat in 1761 A.D. The Marathas failed to enlist the help of the other indigenous rulers for their fight against the Afghans. The Rajputs did not join hands with them. Suraj Mal, the Jat ruler of Bharatpur, , refused to help them as they did not accept his counsel that they go in for guerrilla warfare against the Afghans rather than face them in a direct battle. Later, Abdali succeeded in securing the submission of Raja Suraj Mal.[4]6 The Rohillas and the Nawab of Oudh joined hands with the Afghans.

Thus began what is known as the famous Third Battle of Panipat. The Peshwa Balaji Rao's cousin Sadashiv Rao Bhau and his (the Peshwa's) son Vishwas Rao, all of 17 years, led the Maratha forces. After some initial successes, the Maratha army eventually lost. Both Sadashiv Rao Bhau and Vishwas Rao were killed in the battle The number of those killed was estimated at thousands, while thousands were taken prisoner. The Peshwa Balaji Rao died soon after this, unable to bear the shock of these losses.

Apart from the failure of the Hindu rulers to present a combined front against the Afghans, another reason for the defeat of the Marathas in this battle may have been the lack of solidarity among the local people and their inability to offer a cohesive and determined challenge to the Afghan invaders. Many years later, I read in a newspaper a story, perhaps apocryphal, that on the eve of the Third Battle of Panipat, the Afghan invader Ahmad Shah Abdali had noticed a large number of small fires lit in the Indian camps. He enquired about them and was told that because of caste considerations, the Indians cooked their food separately and did not eat together. Abdali, who led the small force, was said to have declared that in that case, the victory of his army was certain.[47]

A story that I read about the reason for the Marathas' defeat was narrated by Khushwant Singh, the noted journalist, in the Hindustan Times of July 8, 2000. He wrote:

" Astrology is Sheer Bunkum

Not many people are aware that the man responsible for the defeat of the Maratha army in the third battle of Panipat was the Rajya Jyotishi of the Peshwa. It may be recalled that the Marathas outnumbered the Afghans led by Ahmed Shah Abdali by more than two to 10. Abdali was ready to withdraw if the Marathas took the offensive. They did not because the Rajya Jyotishi consulted the stars and opined that they should wait till the auspicious moment arrived. Abdali realized the Marathas were unwilling to fight. He quietly surrounded the Maratha camp and cut off their food supplies. Within a couple of months of inactivity, the Marathas ran out of rations. Finally, the Rajya Jyotishi assured the commander that if he commenced hostilities before the dawn of January 19 (1761) the stars would assure him victory.

A famished Maratha army took on the well-fed Afghans. Within three hours, the Marathas were routed, losing over 30,000 men in an unequal combat. The history of India would have been different if the Maratha commander had used his own brain, not listening to the advice of his sooth-sayer; all sooth-sayers including astrologers are charlatans who feed on the cupidity of the feeble-minded."

To this the BJP leader, K.R. Malkani, retorted as below in a letter to the editor of the Hindustan Times of July 11, 2000:

"Stars foretell

Most people will agree with Khushwant Singh that Astrology is sheer bunkum (July 8). But at times astrologers are right. Cheiro's World Predictions had predicted (vide The Motherland, Jan 26, 1975) that Mrs. Gandhi would declare 'artificial Emergency'. In the same report he had predicted an unnatural death for her.

K.R. Malkani
Delhi"

In fact, both the Afghans and Marathas failed to capture power in Delhi after this battle. The Afghans did proceed to Delhi, but did not have the resources required to establish their rule and advance further south. Abdali, therefore, went back, leaving Delhi to be ruled by the weak Mughals, as before. The Marathas lacked the political cohesion to capture power in Delhi and went back south. It was the Jats and more particularly the Sikhs, who filled the political void for

some time till ultimately the British appeared on the scene and established their supremacy in Delhi in 1803 A.D.

The role of the Marathas in the Third battle of Panipat provides the background against which I viewed the participation by the Rajmata of Gwalior in the meeting of the Battles of Panipat Memorial Society that was held at Panipat on July 28, 1988. Gwalior had also played an important part in the first Battle of Panipat (1526 A..) in which Babar defeated Ibrahim Lodi, the Afghan ruler of Delhi. As historian Sunil Kumar Sarker observes: "It was the first battle of Panipat in which, for the first time, the Hindus came forward to fight against the Mughals. In this battle, Raja Vikramjit of Gwalior fought side by side with Ibrahim Lodi against Babur, the Mughal, and sacrificed his life, as did his about sixteen thousand soldiers. The first battle of Panipat stands out in the military history of India as the first battle in which the united Hindu and native Muslim (Afghan) forces made a common bloc against the Mughals." [48]

Returning to Chandigarh that evening, I felt happy that I was able to visit a place where our country's destiny had been decided several times in the past. After this, whenever I sat down with a book on the battles of Panipat, I could see the images of the battles come alive and flash in front of my eyes. I felt as if history was something tangible.

Notes

1. The Revolt of 1857 in Haryana by Dr. K.C. Yadav.
2. Ibid
3. Ibid, p. 71.
4. Rise and fall of the Mughal Empire by Dr. R.S. Tripathi, p. 33.
5. Hemu, Napoleon of Medieval India by K.K. Bharadwaj, Appendix III, p. 83.
6. Ibid, p. 83.
7. Ishwari Prasad, A Short History of Muslim Rule in India, pp. 228-29.
8. Stanely Lane Poole, Rulers of India Series, p. 195.
9. Himu: The Hindu "Hero" of Medieval India by Sunil Kumar Sarker, p. 15.
10. Ibid, p. 15.
11. Ibid, p. 23.
12. Ibid, p. 23.
13. The History and Culture of the Indian People: The Mughal Empire edited by Dr. R.C. Mazumdar, p. 69.
14. The Akbarnama.

15. Hemu, Napoleon of Medieval India by K.K. Bharadwaj, p. 9.
16. Himu: The Hindu "Hero" of Medieval India by Sunil Kumar Sarker, p. 39.
17. Ibid, p. 39.
18. Ibid, p. 40.
19. Ibid, p. 44.
20. Ibid, p. 46.
21. Ibid.
22. Ibid, p. 52.
23. Military History of India by Sir Jadunath Sarkar, p. 67.
24. Military History of India by Lt. Col. H.C. Kar, p. 283.
25. The Great Mughals by Bamber Gascoigne (page 71) cited in Sunil Kumar Sarker's book, pp. 57-58.
26. Himu: The Hindu "Hero" of Medieval India by Sunil Kumar Sarker, p. 58.
27. A Contemporary Dutch Chronicle of Mughal India by De Lact, cited by Sunil Kumar Sarker in Himu: The Hindu "Hero" of Medieval India. page 59.
28. Ibid, p. 61.
29. Akbar, The Great Mughal by Vincent A. Smith, p. 28.
30. The History and Culture of the Indian People: The Mughal Empire edited by Dr. R.C. Mazumdar, p. 96.
31. Military History of India by Sir Jadunath Sarkar, p. 69.
32. Ibid, p. 39.
33. Hemu, Napoleon of Medieval India by K.K. Bharadwaj, p. 15.
34. Dr. R.C. Mazumdar's book cited above, p. 101.
35. Sunil Kumar Sarker's book cited above, p. 72.
36. Ibid, p. 73.
37. Ibid, p. 74.
38. Ibid, pp. 74-75.
39. Advanced Study in the History of Medieval India (The Mughal Empire 1526-1707) by J.L. Mehta cited in Sunil Kumar Sarker's book, pp. 143-144.
40. Sunil Kumar Sarker's book, p. 75.
41. Book edited by Dr. R.C. Mazumdar cited above, p. 101.
42. Sunil Kumar Sarker's book, pp. 101- 109.
43. A Few Pages From The History of Haryana by Bhim Sain Tyagi, p. 50.
44. Hemu, Napoleon of Medieval India by K.K. Bharadwaj, p. 53.
45. Ibid, p. 54.
46. Ibid, p. 100.
47. Editorial captioned "Urgent Summons" in the daily Times of India, New Delhi, dated June 24, 1999.
48. Sunil Kumar Sarker's book, p. 82.

9

Teej, the Joyous Festival of Home-coming: Bhiwani's Links with Harappan Civilisation: Hissar, the Town of Emperor Feroze Shah Tughlak: the Emperor's Romance With A Peasant Girl: Sher Shah Suri Born At Hissar? 1857 Uprising: Heroic Roles of Hissar and Hansi: Agroha: the Original Home of the Aggarwals

Widespread floods caused by heavy rains and breaches in the Sutlej Yamuna Link (S.Y.L.) canal wrought havoc in several districts of Haryana in July-August, 1988. The Ghaggar river that is believed to be roughly the present-day incarnation of the old Saraswati river remains almost dead for the greater part of the year. But there are years—as it happened in 1988—when it suddenly leaps into life in the wake of heavy rains and the excess water floods the low-lying areas of the districts along its course.

I made aerial surveys of the flood-affected areas of Ambala, Kurukshetra, Karnal and Jind that helped me in getting some idea of the extent of damage. Officials of the Government of Haryana including R.K. Kapoor, Chief Engineer (Drainage), who had accompanied me, apprised me of the various measures that were being taken by the Government to evacuate people from the affected places, provide free shelter, meals and medical help to them, inoculate them as well as the cattle to prevent the spread of cholera and give some financial help to the those whose crops and houses had been damaged. My subsequent talk with Chief Minister Ch Devi Lal showed that he was fully seized of the matter.

In between all this, certain political issues cropped up in the month of August, 1988, which called for my attention. The leaders of the Congress party, at the State as well as Central level, brought to my notice their charge that the their party workers were being harassed by the police and the workers of Ch. Devi Lal's party in different parts of the State. I remember that Bhajan Lal of the Congress party, who was a former Chief Minister of Haryana and was then a member of the Union Cabinet, telephonically informed me about a case of attempted murder registered against him by the the Haryana police and the withdrawal of personal security from Devendra Sharma (Congress), a former Minister.

A few days later, Devendra Sharma and Hardwari Lal, the well-known Haryana leader, who at that time was in the camp of Bhajan Lal, called on me and gave me a memorandum requesting me to urgently look into various issues that adversely affected the functioning of the Congress party in Haryana. When I mentioned all this to Ch. Devi Lal, he, of course, rebutted these allegations, but on my suggestion, he did take some action.

Now it was time for the famous 'Teej' festival. It is celebrated in Haryana, Punjab, Rajasthan, Uttar Pradesh and Delhi on the third day (that is why the name 'Teej') of the new moon in the month of Sawan, when the monsoon reaches its peak. Songs, dances and swings are the special features of this happy and joyous occasion, when one's close relations, who are away from the family for earning their livelihood, return home and meet their near and dear ones. Teej is, therefore, a symbol of love and bonhomie among the members of a well-knit family.

A large number of people from Haryana serve in the army and the para-military forces at far-off places. On the occasion of Teej, they make it a point to come home on leave and join their family members for spending a few days in mirth and merriment, somewhat like Christians all over the world seeking to spend Christmas at home or like the Bengalees taking leave to go home on the occasion of Durga Puja in autumn. The armed forces grant special annual leave during Teej to those, who want to go home, because this is a festival of home-coming and family re-union. The Haryana Government treats the day as a gazetted holiday.

Teej has a special significance for the women of Haryana, who regard it as a symbol of the eternal union of Shiva and Parvati. Women, who are married, observe the fast of 'Hartilaka' on this occasion to seek a long and happy conjugal life. That is why the Haryana I.A.S. Officers' Wives Association celebrated 'Sawan' on the eve of Teej at Chandigarh on August 11, 1988. The lady I.A.S. Officers of Haryana cadre also joined the celebration that took place in beautiful surroundings on the banks of the Sukhna Lake. My wife Anita gladly took part in the celebration as an invitee. Besides the usual features of 'Choori', 'Jhoola' and 'Mehndi' (bangle, swing and henna), there were cultural programmes including songs in which my wife also participated, as she later narrated to me. Boat rides enhanced the thrill of the occasion.

I had been hearing for quite some time stories about Teej in Haryana and its importance in the socio-cultural life of the people. I decided that Teej would be celebrated in our Raj Bhawan—something that was never attempted before. This decision was widely acclaimed. The Raj Bhawan staff and the various Departments of the Haryana Government went all out to make this function the great success that it turned out to be. I invited Ch. Devi Lal to the function well in advance. He not only expressed great jubilation, but ensured that no effort was spared to make the programme as colourful as possible.

So hundreds turned up on the immaculate lawns of our Raj Bhawan on the afternoon of August 12, 1988. Several swings were put up in different parts of the ground. Some people from the villages set up shops to sell 'Mehndi' and 'Choori'. Folk singers from the districts sat in groups singing the typical Teej songs. Ch. Devi Lal, who was present with almost all the Ministers and their wives, took me round, introduced me to some of the musicians and asked them to sing their melodious songs.

Haryana has a very ancient music tradition that is borne out by many literary and archaeological references. Both classical and folk music used to thrive. So far as folk songs are concerned, the people of Haryana are said to have so excelled in it that they had become famous in different parts of our country. According to the author of the Chaturbani, folk musicians from Haryana were in great demand even in places as far as Ujjain.[1] in the words of Banabhatta, author of Harsha-Charita, some of these folk songs called 'Rasaka' could be obscene (Ashlila). Such songs were said to have been sung at the time of the wedding of Rajyashri, sister of Harsha.[2] It is from these songs that the 'Sithanas', so popular in present-day northern India had reportedly originated.[3]

A stalwart of 15th century Haryana's music world was the blind musician Surdas born in the Sihi village of Faridabad district, who had sung over a lakh of verses composed in the Dhrupad and Bhajan styles. In the later Mughal period, the famous Khayal singer Kallan Khan and his sons Hafiz Khan and Basir Khan, who belonged to a village of Rohtak district, were great names in the world of music. Another musician of this period was Mian Achpal of Haryana, who had acquired unparalleled mastery over several styles such as Khyala, Tarana, Trivata, Chaturanga and Sargama.[4]

In the British period, music suffered a great setback in Haryana, a reason for which was the absence of local feudal lords as in Rajasthan and U.P. However, we have a great classical musician in Pandit Jasraj, who is from Hissar in Haryana.

Folk music continued to thrive in Haryana and at places, this gave rise to several Ragas of Indian classical music. As I listened to the songs that were being sung by the artistes from the villages of Haryana, I could clearly see that they had a lot in common with well-known Ragas. While going round and meeting different groups of musicians, it was explained to me how the Ragas of our classical music had evolved from the folk tunes that had been in vogue in the villages of Haryana for centuries. At my request, some simple folk songs were sung which I clearly recognized as having served as the sources from which some particular Ragas of our classical music had originated.

I was also told that some villages of Mahendragarh district and of the Dadri Tehsil of Bhiwani district had names that suggested their association with the famous Ragas of Indian classical music. These villages are Dhanasari, Nandgam, Sarangpur, Bilwala, Brindabana, Todi, Asaveri, Jaishri, Malakosha, Hindola, Bhairavi and Gope Kalyana.[5]

Apart from classical music that is closely interwoven with the lives of the Haryana people, there are some forms of music that are popular in the countryside of Haryana and are based on our legends and mythology. These are sung in various Ragas such as Jai Jai Vanti, Pahari, Bhairavi, Kamod, Kafi Jhinjhoti, Jaijaivanti, Ramakali etc.[6]

The folk singers from different parts of Haryana were sitting in groups on the lawns of our Raj Bhawan and singining Teej songs to the accompaniment of the typical musical instruments of Haryana such as the Iktara, Sarangi, Dhol, Daph, Damru, Ghara, Jhil, Chimta and what have you.. There has been a rich tradition of instrumental music in Haryana since time immemorial as is evident from references to this in Vedic literature. In his Harsha-Charita, Banabhatta describes the march of the Thanesar army as follows; "No sooner than the marching drum had been sounded, musical instruments began to be played. Straightway, the drums rattled, the Nandis rang, the trumpets brayed, the Kahalas hummed, the horns blared."[7]

Banabhatta refers to an auspicious ceremony held on Harsha's birth, when conch shells were blared and drums and trumpets were sounded. He further adds: "Later, harlot women danced to the accompaniment of many musical instruments: tambourines tinkled, strong drums were belaboured, the low gourd lute sang, gently boomed the Kahalas with their brazen sounding bozes."[8] 'Alingyaka', a special elongated drum, Anuttana Alabuvina, a lute with a sound box placed below, Kamsyakoshi, a metallic bell, are said to have been used for musical sounds by ammutracs in their galleries, sweet music reverberated in the streets, and public places of Thanesar.[9] There were many great masters of instrumental music at Harsha's court.[10]

Some of the Teej songs that I heard were reminiscent of Tagore songs and poet Kalidasa's verses in celebration of the rains. The women were dancing in groups. Haryana's famous folk dances represen a tradition that is very old. Banabhatta has given a detailed account of how, on the birth of Harsha, a captivating dance performance took place was put up by the courtesans. "The dancers in their initial pose glided through a hundred graceful steps from all the sides to the king's presence and bowed before him with bent foreheads touching the earth. After this, they stood erect allowing a full view of their beautiful forms, limbs and make-up from head to foot with all the short and long necklaces fully visible in lunate shapes arranged on their breasts. Then they gave playful movement to their tremulous eye brows. This was followed by heaving deep sighs and displaying or swelling breasts so as to produce an atmosphere of rhythm. On so doing, they also seemed to have stretched their intertwined arms in all directions in the form of loop (pasha) next followed vigorous dance-movements displaying their accentuated beauty of their swaying breasts, beautified with Bankula wreaths. The tempo of the dance rose still further and the breasts, the middle-portion and the hips combined to produce more aggressive movements, causing a swaying of the central pendants of their necklaces with their rays flashing all round. After this, they slided into a dance-form involving movements of out-stretched arms creating the effect of graceful embraces. They next turned to a pose of little relaxation. The last item in the dance consisted of rapid bendings of the limbs (anga-bhanga-valanani) of which the different poses were accompanied with gesticulation of cracking fingers of their twined hands resembling a forest of small bows of the god of love."[11]

Bana has also spoken effusively of the court dancers and folk dancers of Thanesar.[12]

Haryana of today boasts a variety of folk dances such as Chhathi, Khoria, Phag, Phog, Loor and Chhari dances, which are performed on different occasions. Teej dances are performed during the Teej festival by young girls in colourful garments as they hold their hands in circles or other formations and sing in a spirit of gay abandon, as I could see them doing at our Raj Bhawan.

The swings put up on this occasion at Raj Bhawan were a great hit with the ladies. Smt. Sushma Swaraj, a Minister, not only sang and danced with the members of the cultural troupes, who gave a captivating performance, but also had a gala time in one of the swings and was obviously enjoying herself. Suddenly, she caught hold of my wife and took her to the swing, which they both mounted before starting to swing together to great heights, forward and backward, as much to their own delight as to that of the assembled crowd.

I awarded a prize of Rs. 5000/-to the best cultural troupe that regaled us with songs of Sawan as well as music from the ballads of Haryana. Seeing the atmosphere that evening, I felt that our Raj Bhawan had shed its insular image of an institution that was far removed from the socio-cultural milieu of the ordinary man of Haryana and had instead become a symbol of that milieu by actively joining in the celebration of the people's collective joy and festivity.

As we were celebrating Teej on August 12, 1988, a ghastly incident took place within the limits of Panchkula Police Station, which marred the joyous atmosphere all around. It was a bomb blast caused by some Sikh terrorists, which killed three persons and injured several others. It was a pathetic sight that I saw the next morning when I went to the PGI Hospital, Chandigarh, to look up those injured in this incident and speak a few words of solace to them.

I had decided to hoist the National Flag and take the salute at the Independence Day parade on August 15, 1988 at Bhiwani, the headquarters of the district of the same name. Reaching Bhiwani a day earlier, I put up at the State Government Rest House there. Bhiwani is a beautiful place with many temples. That is why it is called the second Benares of our country. In 1968, archaeological excavations in Mitathal, a village about 7 miles from Bhiwani brought out old relics of the copper-bronze age of the second and third millennia B.C. that clearly suggested its links with Harappan civilization. The territory of the Bhadanakas, who were a power to reckon with in Haryana in the post-Harsha period, comprised Rewari, Bhiwani, Gurgaon and part of Alwar. Coins of Samudra Gupta, an important ruler of the Gupta dynasty, which have been discovered here indicate that the dynasty's rule once extended to this place. Bhiwani was now a thriving business center with several small–scale industries and textile mills.

In Tosham village of this district, about 15 miles from Bhiwani, there is a hill that emerges from the surrounding sand to a height of about 800 feet and assumes the shape of a camel with its typical hump. This hill which I saw during a drive outside Bhiwani town, impressed me as the most dominating feature of the whole region. There are legends that the Pandavas had come here and that the ancient sages used to do penance here. Many historically important old buildings and inscriptions discovered here by the archaeologists throw abundant light on contemporary history.

I was told about a versatile scholar of medieval India by name Thakur Pheruman, who was born at Kanana village near Charkhi Dadri in Bhiwani district. I later read an account given by Dr. K.C. Yadav,[13] according to which Thakur Pheruman had a deep knowledge of Indian literature and various sciences. He was a Jaina belonging to the Vaishya caste. Emperor Alauddin Khalji (1296 A.D.–1316 A.D.) was said to have been so impressed by Pheru's scholarship that he had given the latter a place of honour in his Darbar. Pheru was closely associated with the treasury and the mint of the Emperor.

Pheru wrote in Prakrit and Apabhramsa languages on a wide range of subjects, which reflected the encyclopaedic sweep of his knowledge. His works important works were (i) Yugapradhanachatushpadika in Apabhramsa, which lists the names of the Jainacharyas beginning with Mahavira; (ii) Ratnapriksha in Prakrit, which deals with gems of different kinds, their values, effects, etc.; (iii) Vastusara a book on architecture in Prakrit; (iv) Ganitasara in Prakrit, which deals with weights and measures, rates of tax etc.; (v) Dhatupatti in Prakrit, which deals with metals of various kinds and certain substances such as Hingul, Sindura, Chandana, Kasturi etc.; (vi) Jyotishasara in Prakrit, a learned treatise on astrology; (vii) Dravyapriksha in Prakrit, which reflects the influence of Apabhramsa and local dialects. This book discusses the various methods of purifying metals like gold, silver, copper, tin, lead etc.[14]

There is another village Kalyana in Dadri Tehsil about 25 miles from Bhiwani, which was believed to have been the capital of one Raja Kalian, who had revolted in 1326 A.D. against the ruler of Delhi, Alaf Khan (a son of Ghiyas-ud-din Tughlak) and was killed in a battle with the army of the latter. There is a hillock in this village, which has the distinction of yielding what is called flexible sand-stone that is also known as Ital-Columite. The only other place in the whole world with a flexible stone rock is said to be in Brazil.

August 15, 1988 was a busy day for me. The various engagements of the day culminated in a big evening reception hosted by me on the lawns of the Govt. Rest House, which was attended by Chief Minister Ch. Devi Lal, his cabinet colleagues, top bureaucrats and members of the public drawn from various walks of life.

The next day, I left Bhiwani for Hissar, a divisional headqueters, where several engagements had been fixed for me by Dr. Harswaroop Singh, Vice-Chancellor of the Haryana Agricultural University located there. This was my first visit to the university of which I was the Chancellor.

Leaving Bhiwani in the morning by car, I made a slight detour to drive for a while around Hansi town, which was just a little away from the highway that led to Hissar. By the time I reached PWD Rest House in Hissar after having a look-around not only in Hansi but also in Hissar town, I was already pondering in my mind over the historical background of so many important architectural landmarks that I had managed to see in such a short time. I had some other occasions to visit Hissar and some of the important towns in the district and had the opportunity of reading up several books on Hissar and the surrounding region.

Hissar has a very ancient history as has been revealed by archaeological discoveries at Rakhigarhi and several other sites. Some scholars have identified Hissar with Aishukari or Isukera, an ancient city of Kuru Janapada. But this view is not generally accepted. Farishta, the well-known Muslim historian, has mentioned 'Warais' as the original name of Hissar. For the time being, I would not go that far into the history of Hissar, but would confine myself to its more recent history that is comparatively better known.

So far as this later history of Hissar is concerned, I have found the account given in the Imperial Gazetteer of India quite succinct and interesting.[15] It is said that Hansi in Hissar district was perhaps a stronghold of the Kushan rulers. At Tosham (earlier in Hissar district but now in Bhiwani district), there is an inscription that seems to commemorate a victory over Ghatotkacha, the second known member of the Gupta line (circa A.D. 305). In the 8th century A.D., the Tomar Rajputs established their rule here. Anagapala, a Tomar ruler, is believed to have founded the Hansi town in the 11th century A.D.

Masud, son of Mahmud of Ghazni, captured Hansi, but was soon defeated by the Tomar ruler of Delhi. The discovery of the coins of the

Tomar rulers at Hansi and some other places is an indication that Hansi had been recaptured by the Tomars from the Ghaznavis. The Chauhans replaced the Tomars in this region, but after the defeat of Prithviraj Chauhan by Muhammad Ghauri in the battle of Tarain in 1192 A.D., Hissar and several places in the region came under the sway of the Muslims. The Khiljis, who ruled here for a short while from the end of the 13th century A.D., yielded place to the Tughlaks in the 14th century A.D.

It was during the rule of Feroze Shah Tughlak that the town of Hissar was founded. He was the cousin of Muhammad bin Tughlak and the son of Nasiruddin Rajab, but his mother was the daughter of the Rajput Hindu chief of Akbar. Feroze's personal background is quite interesting.[16] He had married more than once. His first wife was a Hindu girl with whom he had fallen in love while he was the guest of her brothers at Thanesar. His second wife was the daughter of Qutubuddin Mubarak Shah of the Khilji dynasty, whom he married after he became the Sultan. He had also fallen madly in love with a Gujar girl, but no account is available of his marriage with her. She may have been his keep.[17] Feroze became the Sultan of Delhi on March 23, 1351 A.D. after the death of Muhammad bin Tughlak.

Despite being the son of a Turkish father and a Rajput mother, Feroze had neither the chivalry of a Rajput nor the military capability of a Turkish warrior. His reign was marked by a series of military fiascos. However, he distinguished himself by turning out to be a great "builder" known for his architectural achievements. He established a number of cities that included not only Hissar, but also Fatehabad, Firozabad, Jaunpur and several minor towns. He built many forts, palaces, mosques, Madrasas, hospitals etc. throughout his empire. He had organized a very efficient and well-equipped building department as well as a department to finance architectural projects. The buildings that he got constructed were very functional with attractive designs. Timur, who visited the Jami Mosque at Kotla Feroze Shah in Delhi to offer prayers during his invasion of India in 1398 A.D., was highly impressed by it and decided to build a similar mosque at Samarkhand.[18]

The name of Hissar town was derived from the Arabic word 'Hisar', which means a fort. The town was initially called Hisar Firoza (the fort of Feroze). Feroze personally supervised the construction of the town that commenced in 1354 A.D. As the sandy area chosen for the township was short of water, he took great personal interest in the digging of a canal from the Yamuna river to bring water to this area. It was initially called the 'Rajiwah' canal after his father's name Rajab, but later it came to be known as the Western Yamuna Canal. The prosperity of Hissar and the adjoining areas owed a lot to this canal.

The new fort-city was surrounded by a wall, which again was encircled by a ditch. The fort had four gates—the Delhi Gate leading towards Delhi, the Mori Gate which derived its name from the word 'Mori' (or passage) being used for letting out waste water, the Nagori Gate deriving its name from 'Nagor', a particular kind of bullock, and the Talaaki Gate, which performed a very interesting function, because all women, who were given 'Talaaq' (*i.e.* were divorced) by their husbands, had to pass through this gate! [19]

Hissar became the headquarters of a division that comprised the districts of Agroha, Fatehabad, Sirsa, Salurah and Khizirabad. Hansi, which earlier used to be the divisional headquarters, lost its importance to Hissar because Feroze Shah greatly loved this new town, which, apart from its commercial utility, had great importance for defence purposes as well since the local inhabitants were a turbulent and rebellious lot. Another important reason behind Feroze Shah's decision to build this town was his passion for hunting. Many earlier Sultans, who were also fond of hunting, restricted themselves to hunting birds. Feroze Shah surpassed them all because he hunted wild animals. He was fond of hunting wild ass, deer, Neel Gai (antelope), wild buffaloes, lions and tigers. His stables were said to have been over-crowded with ferocious lions, lynx, dogs, camels and elephants. An idea of the big scale on which all this activity was conducted can be had from the fact that twelve thousand persons were employed in the hunting department. He was extremely fond of elephant-lion combats, which he watched with great zest. Among birds, he liked the hawk.[20]

The Sirmur hills, the Badaun-Ambala region and the Dipalpur-Sirsuti area (modern Sirsa) that included Hissar and adjoining places were the favourite hunting ground of Feroze Shah. One summer, Prince Feroze Malik, as he was then called, came to Hissar on a hunting trip. In the evening, he went to the 'dera' (a small village) of a Sufi saint (perhaps for rest or a drink of water), where his eyes fell on a beautiful Gujar girl with whom he instantaneously fell in love. It is said that the Gujar girl, tired of the day-long chore of grazing her herd of buffaloes, had come there to look for some water to quench her thirst. "Their eyes met, and it was love at first sight. That was the beginning of the romance in the desert".[21] the prince, who had come to hunt, himself became a victim, having been smitten by Cupid's arrow, as is aptly expressed by the local saying: "Shikar karne aaye thaiy, magr khud hi shikar ho gaye."

After ascending the throne in 1351 A.D., Sultan Feroze Shah Tughlak, as he was now known, tried to bring his beloved Gujar girlfriend over to the royal capital of Delhi, but the latter declined, saying that she would not leave her native place, her aged parents and, of course, her herd of buffaloes. The Sultan, not knowing what to do now, sought the guidance of the Sufi saint, widely respected as the wise man of the desert, and then decided to build a palace for his ladylove at the place of her own abode. This is how Hissar came to be built.

While constructing the palace known as Gujari Mahal, Feroze Shah also built a new city around it. Hissar thus represented a town built to commemorate the Sultan's love for the Gujar girl. Had she gone to Delhi to live with the Sultan, Hissar, as we see it today, might perhaps have never come into existence! According to some, Feroze Shah married the Gujar girl, who became the queen. But the generally held view is that their relationship was not converted into marriage. There are many interesting stories about how the milkmaid won the Sultan's heart and how their love blossomed. During the Sultan's frequent halts at Hissar, he used to hold court and discharge many administrative duties. "The Gujar girl, the mistress of the Sultan, though not literate, yet quite intelligent, would help the Sultan in his official work. She was famous for her loving attitude towards her people."[22]

When I saw the Gujari Mahal, all these romantic stories were narrated to me. The palace complex has several buildings—the residences of the Gujar girl and Feroze Shah, Shahi Darwaja, the Diwan-e-Aam, the Baradari with three underground apartments, a Hammam (bath) and a mosque with some pillars. In the construction of these buildings, some materials of Hindu temples were used, a large quantity of which had perhaps been brought from near-by Agroha, which had already lost much of its importance.[23]

The palace had several dark underground apartments with many zig-zag passages, which made it difficult for a stranger to find his way out. There are stories of many persons having lost their way in these labyrinthine passages and spent several days before being extricated by the guards or guides. On one of the pillars of the mosque (known as Laat Ki Masjid), there are some inscriptions in Sanskrit, which were deciphered in due course by Sir Alexander Cunningham, who thought that the original pillar might have been erected by the Maurya Emperor Ashoka. A part of this pillar was believed to have been shifted to Fatehabad by Fateh Khan, the eldest son of Feroze Shah.

The Diwan-e-Aam (or the public court) is a big hall with forty pillars and a throne for the Sultan. According to popular legend, there was a well beneath the throne. If the Sultan gave a judgement sitting on this throne, which was not just, the slab of the throne would break and the person sitting thereon would fall into the well.

The Gujar Mahal was not as beautiful as the Taj Mahal, but they both were memorials to the noble sentiment of love and sacrifice. Feroze Shah had set an example for Shah Jahan to emulate.[24]

Feroze Shah took a great deal of interest in the development of irrigation facilities through the digging of many canals. He has sometimes been called the father of Indian irrigation. At his instance, hundreds of beautiful gardens were laid out. He was a versatile ruler with great literary taste and a patron of learning. He was an orthodox Muslim who upheld the Sunnis and suppressed the Shias. His persecution of the Hindus, imposition of 'Jiziya' (a kind of tax) on the Brahmins and the other Hindus, attacks on Hindu shrines such as the jagannath temple at Puri and the Vaishno Devi temple had made him unpopular among the Hindus at large. He was "soaked in wine and sunk in debauchery".[25]

One Fauzdar Sayeed Nasir, who was the Nawab of Hissar, had captured a descendant of Prithviraj Chauhan, converted him to Islam and given him the name of Kayam Khan. After the death of Sayeed Nasir, Kayam Khan became the Nawab of Hissar and enjoyed great prestige at the court of the Sultan of Delhi.[26] the descendants of Kayam Khan came to be known as Kayamkhanis, who were Muslims, though originally they were Rajput Hindus and descendants of Prithviraj Chauhan. There are many Kayamkhanis in the adjoining areas of Rajasthan.

In 1398 A.D., Timur invaded India and marched through Bikaner, Sirsa and several places of Hissar district such as Fatehabad and Tohana, leaving behind a trail of plunder and massacre. Hissar was captured by the rebels in 1408 A.D., but was soon recovered by Emperor Muhammad Tughlak, who himself led his forces. Khizar Khan of the Sayyid dynasty secured control of the Hansi area in 1411 A.D. And in 1414 A.D., he became Delhi's first Sultan of this dynasty.

Hissar was included in the empire of the Lodhis and one Muhabbat Khan got Hissar as a fief during the rule of Bahlol Lodhi. When Babar arrived at the Ghaggar river on the eve of the First Battle of Panipat in 1526 A.D., he learnt that Hissar was an important military centre of Ibrahim Lodhi from which troops were being dispatched to pose a challenge to him. Babar's son, Humayun, who was sent to meet the challenge of the Lodhi forces, succeeded in routing the latter. Babar rewarded Humayun by handing over the town of Hissar to him. Naturally, Humayun developed a special liking for Hissar as it was here that he had achieved his first military success.

According to some contemporary Muslim historians, Sher Shah Suri was born at Hissar—a view which Dr. K.R. Qanungo also accepted, but with which some other historians did not agree. However, it is known that Sher Shah had lived here for a long time after driving out Humayun from the Indian territory in 1540 A.D. But Humayun recovered this area in 1553 A.D. Hissar became the headquarters of a revenue division of the Province of Delhi during the reign of Akbar and was thus an important place as brought out by Abul Fazl in his Ain-I-Akbari. There was a mint here that turned out copper coins. The "Ghee" of Hissar must have had something special about it and so substantial quantities of it were sent from here to the royal palace in Delhi, as mentioned by Abul Fazl. Even when I visited Hissar, I did not fail to get duly impressed by the quality of Hissar's dairy products including "Ghee".

After the death of Aurangzeb in 1707 A.D., Hissar faced considerable instability and confusion. It became the cockpit of a triangular contest among the Sikhs on the north east, the Bhatti chiefs of Bhatner and Fatehabad and the Muslim chiefs on the south. The Sikhs trounced the combined forces of the Bhattis and the Muslims in the battle of Dharsul in 1757 A.D. The Nazim or the Imperial Governor of Hissar was killed in the battle. The Sikhs penetrated as far as Hissar and sacked it freely.[27] Gradually, the Sikhs took possession of the whole region that included Hissar, Hansi, Tohana, Rania and Sirsa.

In 1781 A.D., the Treaty of Jind was concluded under which Hissar, Hansi, Rohtak, Tosham and Meham were restored to the Delhi empire, Fatehabad and Sirsa went to the Bhattis and the remaining territory already annexed by the Sikhs was retained by them. Then within a couple of years—in 1783 A.D. corresponding to Samvat 1840. San Chalisa Kal or the worst ever famine stalked Hissar and the whole region, causing the death of many human beings as well as numerous heads of cattle. Even the Sikhs left the place!

George Thomas, an Irish adventurer, took advantage of the prevailing confusion to establish himself at Hansi as the ruler of this region and declared himself as the Raja of Haryana. This period of India's history witnessed the rise of several military adventurers such as Gen. Boigne, Gen. Perron, Gen. Samru and Gen. Raymond, but none of them fared as well as Gerge Thomas. Arriving in India as a sailor in 1781 A.D., he left his British masters and joined the army of the Polygars, a tribal community of south India and then switched over to the army of the Nizam of Hyderabad. Thereafter, he came over to north India and took up employment with Begum Samroo of Sardhana. Forced to leave her service as a result of intrigues, he joined the service of the Marathas and served in the armies of several Maratha chiefs such as Appa Khandi Rao, Vaman Rao and Bapu Scindia. He was rewarded for his good work by the grant of some territories in Haryana. However, his differences with Bapu Scindia led to his dismissal from the army of the former, who also took over the control of George's territory in Panipat, Sonepat and Karnal districts which had earlier been granted to him.

Thus, George Thomas was in dire straits and unable to pay the soldiers of his private army, who were, therefore, threatening to revolt. George tried his best to wriggle out of this situation by plundering the towns and villages around Delhi. It was at this time that he decided to carve out an independent State in the Haryana region. He situation in Punjab was in turmoil as a result of the mutual fights among the Sikh rulers and the repeated attacks launched by Abdali's grandson, Shah Zaman.

Taking advantage of the disturbed conditions prevailing in Punjab, George Thomas made a dash towards the adjoining territory of Haryana in 1798 A.D. And launched an attack on the fort of Kanhori that lay in the region of the Bhattis. But the Bhattis repulsed his attack, forcing him to retreat after losing a large number of his men. Geoge Thomas took steps to reinforce his military strength and again attacked Kanhori, which he was able to conquer this time. Gradually, he managed to extend his territory over the rest of Haryana and established his capital at Hansi. George had also established a fort at a place near Rohtak, which came to be known as Georgegarh after him. The fort acquired the name Jahazgarh in due course.

Soon, the Marathas challenged his supremacy by despatching an army led by Lt. General Bourquin that also included the famous James Skinner. According to the Imperial Gazetteer of India (Provincial Series—Punjab—Volume I, p. 242), Skinner, born in 1778 A.D., was the son of a Scottish officer of the East India Company and a Rajput lady. He received his first commission from De Boigne, the "famous Savoyard adventurer", who had organized the Scindia's brigades. After many years' service under the Marathas, during which he fought the Irish adventurer, George Thomas, he joined the British forces under Lord Lake in 1803 A.D. And received the command of 2000 of Peron's

Hindustan Horse. This body served with great distinction under Skinner for thirty years. He rose to be a Lt. Colonel in the British service and received large grants of land in the Delhi territory that included Hissar and Hansi. He settled down at Hansi, where he died in 1841 A.D. Several estates owned by Skinner's descendants existed for many years in Delhi, Haryana and Punjab.

Now back to the story of George Thomas. A fierce battle at Beri between George Thomas and the Marathas near Georgegarh ended indecisively, but he was forced to retreat to Hansi, where Bourquin soon followed him for negotiations. George had to abandon all his territories and retire into the British territory. He died in 1802 A.D.

During the period of George's rule, he had established peace in Hansi and took a number of steps to develop the town. He established a mint and coined his own rupees. He extended his territory over the Haryana region. He improved the functioning of the administrative machinery. Many tanks were excavated and wells dug. He got many roads repaired. His achievements during his short rule won wide acclaim.

Bourquin remained in Hissar district for some time, restored order and rebuilt the towns of Hissar and Tohana.[28] Mirza Ilias Beg was appointed as the Nazim of Hissar district on behalf of the Marathas in 1802 A.D. George Thomas, who was an independent ruler of the Hissar region of Haryana for five years (1797 A.D. to 1802 A.D.) left behind in Hissar the Jahaz Pul and the Jahaz Kothi, his residence, to remind us of his legacy. In 1803 A.D., the British ousted the Marathas from this region and under the Treaty of Surji Arjungaon signed that year, they took over Haryana including Hissar.

At this stage Hansi in Hissar district acquired considerable importance because the British built a fort here and appointed Mirza Ilias Beg as the Nazim of the districts of Haryana. I had occasion to drive through Hansi sometimes during my trips to Hissar and Sirsa. Hansi had a very ancient past about which, however, not much is known. Inscriptions of Prithviraj Chauhan and some literature of the Jains indicate that 'Asika' was the name of the place in the late 12th century A.D. before the Muslims established their rule here. Though it retained its strategic importance during the early stages of Muslim rule, it yielded place to Hissar and Fatehabad, the new towns that came up in the 14th century A.D. I have already mentioned how it regained its importance when Col. Skinner made it the center of his activities and the headquarters of the Skinner's Horse, his famous cavalry unit.

Hansi had other claims to greatness such as its having been an important religious centre. Baba Farid, the great 13th century Sufi saint of our country had spent twelve years at Hansi. He belonged to the order known as 'Chisti' and was the disciple of Bakhtiyar Kaki, who in turn was the disciple of Khwaja Moinuddin Chisti, the founder of the Chisti Sufi order in India. Baba Farid was one of those who had helped in founding the Chisti order in Haryana and had set up a centre of this order at Hansi. He spread the message of love and understanding, devotion to God, purity of the mind, the insignificance and transitoriness of life, avoidance of excessive worldly wealth and the equality of all before the eyes of God irrespective of their caste, creed or religion. He was all for renunciation and asceticism, but what he meant by this was the renunciation of worldly possessions and of sinful ways rather than wandering about in the deserts and jungles. He wanted man to live in society and look inward to find God in his own heart. His sermons were known for their simplicity and straightforwardness.

Baba Farid's full name is Shaikh-ul-Islam Maulana Diwana Baba Fariduddin Ganj-I-shakar Suleman Aujodhani, but he is generally known as Baba Farid. He was born in 1149 A.D. at Khetwal near Multan. His father, Jamuluddin (or Kamaluddin) was a nephew of Mahmud Gaznavi.[29] He wrote poetry in several languages such as Persian, Punjabi, Multani, Hindi and Punjabi. He was one of the first poets of Punjabi literature. Many of his devotional hymns and couplets have found the pride of place in the Guru Granth Sahib. He has a good following among the Sikh masses, particularly rural people, in whose language and idiom he generally speaks. The following couplet of Baba Farid brings out the depth of his spiritual thought:[30]

Farida khak na nindiye, khak jehu na koi
Jiwandian parian tale, moiyan oupar hoi.

(Baba Farid says that there is nothing like the dust and no one should show disrespect to dust, because one walks on it when one is alive and it covers one when one is dead.)

A story—whether true or apocryphal I do not know—that I heard about Baba Farid's meeting with the ruler of Delhi also serves to bring out one of his cardinal messages—that one should give to others rather than beg anything of others, that there is greater joy in giving than in begging. The story goes that once the people of a village met him and urged him to go and meet the ruler of Delhi in order to press their plea for the opening of a Madrasah in their village. Baba Farid repeatedly told them that he had never gone to anybody to ask for anything and that what he had done was to give to others whatever he had. But the villagers kept on pestering him with the result that he eventually proceeded to Delhi.

When Baba Farid was presented before the ruler, the latter was engaged in offering Namaz. Baba Farid saw that at the end of Namaz, the ruler fervently prayed to Allah to grant him more wealth, more property and a more extensive territory to rule over. He thought that what the ruler was doing was straightforward begging before the Almighty. Seeing this, Baba Farid turned about and started to walk away.

At that point, the ruler looked at Baba Farid and asked him why he was going away. Baba Farid replied: "I have never asked anybody for anything. I am all for giving away to others whatever I have. However, at the persistent request of some villagers, I had come to see you and make a plea on their behalf for the opening of a Madrasah in their village. But I just now saw that you were begging of the Almighty to grant you so many things. Since you are yourself a beggar, I do not think it proper to beg you for anything." Then Baba Farid left the place.

An important historical site in Hansi is the Chaar Qutb where the four tombs of the disciples of Baba Farid. The other historical monuments in Hansi are the tomb of Mir Tajarah, the Tughlak Mosque, the Chhatri, where there are two very old graves, the graves of the descendants of Qutb Jamal and the beautiful tombs of James Skinner and his wife. The fort of Hansi has a gate known as the Barsi Gate (built in 1302 A.D.), a specimen of fine architecture, the George Gate complex, the Baradari with pillars on top of a mound and a cluster of some buildings known as Khangah that include the tomb of Sayyid Niamat Ullah, who fell fighting Muhammad Ghauri in the last decade of the 12th century A.D.

Hissar, Hansi and Fa.ehabad were looked upon by the British authorities as centres of turbulence, which caused them much worry during early 19th century. The British forces that included Col. Skinner's cavalry succeeded in putting down the rebellious people of these places in 1810 A.D. Edward Gardener under whose leadership this was achieved established his civil headquarters at Hansi. Though peace was established in the Hissar region, the people were unhappy with the policies of the British authorities that interfered with the autonomy of the old village communities and adversely affected the agriculture of the region, causing great discontent among the peasantry whose lands were over-assessed for revenue. This was the reason why the people of Hissar, Hansi and many other places in Haryana spontaneously joined the uprising of 1857 A.D. against the British.

As pointed out in many books on this uprising, the Jats, Ranghars, Rajputs, Bishnois and Bhattis of Hissar district which at this time also included the present district of Sirsa and most of Bhiwani district, rose in revolt on hearing of the fall of Delhi on May 11, 1857 A.D. There were good leaders to guide the people such as Muhammad Azim, the Assistant Patrol of Bhattu and a young descendant of the royal family of Delhi, who came down to Hissar and proclaimed the end of British rule. At Hansi, the leaders included Hukam Chand, a Jain businessman, his nephew Faqir Chand and a Muslim friend Mirza Munir Beg. Nur Mohamad Khan, the Nawab of Rania, began to rule his erstwhile State. All of them accepted the central authority of Emperor Bahadur Shah. The troops stationed at Hissar, Hansi and Sirsa were affected by this revolutionary upsurge and mutinied. Many British officers fled Hansi out of fear, but the others numbering eleven and including women and children were massacred by the rebels. Their bungalows were set on fire and the town of Hansi was plundered.[31]

At Hissar, a wing of the Haryana Light Infantry and a section of the Dadri Cavalry revolted on May 27, 1857 A.D. The Hissar fort was attacked. Two Englishmen, who came out, were shot down. The rebel troops and some local people joined hands in breaking open the district jail and releasing many prisoners, besides plundering the houses of the Europeans and seizing the district Treasury. They killed Wedderburn, the Deputy Commissioner, and twelve other Europeans.[32] Charles Ball, the author of the "History of the Indian Mutiny", has given detailed accounts of these events. The course of events at Sirsa, then in Hissar district, followed a similar pattern.

By the beginning of June 1857 A.D., the whole of Hissar district had freed itself from British rule. Soon the British launched a counter offensive that saw the restoration of their rule in Hissar district. General van Courtlandt, Deputy Commissioner of Ferozepur, took the lead in this campaign and began the operation at Sirsa. Many British residents of Sirsa, who had got demoralised on hearing the news of the killing of their compatriots at Hissar, had fled to some other places. Some of the British officials met the Sepoys in their barracks and pleaded with them to desist from any rebellious action, but the latter refused to listen to any such advice and told the former to leave. The next day, the Sepoys looted the Treasury and burnt down some buildings including the residence of the Deputy Commissioner. This forced the most of the British officials to flee to places which they considered safe. Two of these officials were killed by the rebels. Some of the British officers were, however, granted asylum by Maharaja Sardar Singh of Bikaner.

Under the leadership of the Nawab of Rania, the people declared their independence. All the leaders of the rebellion acknowledged the supremacy of Emperor Bahadur Shah. In the first week of June, 1857, General van Courtlandt, the Deputy Commissioner of Ferozepur, proceeded with a big force to recapture the Sirsa region. In the fierce battle that took place at Odhan, a village near Sirsa, on June 17, 1857, between the British and the Bhattis led by the Nawab of Rania, over 500 of the Nawab's men fell fighting and Courtlandt won. The Nawab was chased and caught before being condemned to death by hanging.[33] Courtlandt subdued several villages, burnt and plundered them and killed numerous people. He reached Sirsa on June 20, 1857 and stayed there for a couple of weeks to restore British authority. Captain Pearse, who was deputed to Hissar, re-established British rule there in the last week of June 1857 A.D. Courtlandt proceeded from Sirsa via Fatehabad towards Hissar where he reached in the latter half of July 1857 A.D. Many local people were mercilessly slaughtered. The house of Prince Muhammad Azim was plundered and destroyed and his Begum was captured.[34]

After the British forces recaptured Hissar, they spotted out the bones and skulls as well as some blood-stained clothes of the Englishmen and their family members, who had been done to death during the uprising and these were then interred. Close to the Anglican Church in Hissar, I saw a pillar that had been built to commemorate these Europeans.

Courtlandt then advanced to Hansi, where the rebels failed to offer him any resistance. But as soon as he stepped out of Hissar, Prince Muhammad Azim mobilized a big contingent of cavalry and infantry along with some guns and attacked the town. However, before Azim could capture Hissar, Courtlandt swiftly retraced his steps from Hansi to Hissar and chased away the rebel forces, who now made their way to Tosham. The rebels attacked Tosham, killed several government officials and looted the Treasury and the bankers. Then they tried to move towards Hansi, but were checkmated on the way by Courtlandt. After suffering reverses at some other places, Prince Azim moved on to Gurgaon. Thus order was restored in Hissar district under the leadership of Courtlandt.

This was soon followed by severe punitive action against the people such as the confiscation of their proprietary rights to land and the imposition of fines on many villages. Courtlandt was responsible for the hanging to death of 133 persons. Thousands of people fled to distant places fearing reprisals.[35] Some people saved their skin by betraying the rebels and joining hands with the British. The worst examples were those of Hukam Chand, Faqir Chand and Mirza Munir Beg of Hansi, who, after having led the revolt in that town, went over to the side of Courtlandt when he arrived and served him loyally in the revenue department.

But the earlier correspondence of these persons with Bahadur Shah fell into the hands of the British after the fall of Delhi. They were put to death for their duplicity. Lala Hukam Chand was hanged to death in public in front of his house in Hansi. One can see the statue of Hukam Chand outside his house. Hansi is proud of its Lal Sadak, the road that runs through the heart of the town, on which many of the rebels were killed by the British by getting them crushed under road rollers. What a savage way to take political revenge! These killings went on for several days and the blood of the martyrs turned the road red. That is why the name Lal Sadak. An inconspicuous memorial to the martyrs greets the visitor at the entrance into the road.

To deliberately outrage the religious sentiments of the Hindus as well as the Muslims, Hukam Chand was buried instead of being cremated and Munir Beg was cremated instead of being buried.[36] After crushing the uprising, the British authorities detached Hissar and the rest of Haryana from the North West Frontier Provinces (latter-day Uttar Pradesh) and merged them into the Punjab.

This is the story of the brutal repression faced and the sacrifices made by the people of Hissar district during the uprising of 1857 A.D.

Hissar started playing a prominent part in the Arya Samaj movement as well as in the activities of the Indian National Congress towards the end of the 19th century. Swami Dayanand Saraswati had launched the Arya Samaj in Bombay in 1875 A.D. with clear religious, social and political objectives reflected in the slogans "Back to the Vedas" and "India is for Indians". Various social goals such as the abolition of child marriage and untouchability, spread of female education and encouragement to widow re-marriage were sought to be achieved by the movement. In Hissar, a group of Hindus that included Lala Lajpat Rai took the lead in setting up a branch of the Arya Samaj in 1886 A.D. Generally known as the Punjab Kesari, Lajpat Rai, who hailed from the Ferozepur district of Punjab, moved over to Hissar for legal practice and lived here for six years from 1886 A.D. to 1892 A.D.

He contributed a great deal to the Arya Samaj movement as well as to the Congress Party's activities in Hissar district.

In 1918, the Hissar branch of the Arya Samaj established two schools—a high school in memory of Lala Chandu Lal, a prominent leader of the movement, and the Arya Kanya Pathshala for girls. On the eve of the partition of India in 1947, the Arya Samaj played a leading role in organizing the Hindus as well as in driving out the Muslims from Hissar—the town that their ancestor, Feroze Shah Tughlak had founded nearly six centuries ago. This no doubt widened the breach between the Hindus and the Muslims.[37]

Lal Lajpat Rai was a leading member of Motilal Nehru's Swarajya Party, but this did not prevent him from pursuing a non-secular agenda. He joined hands with Pandit Madan Mohan Malviya and campaigned against the Congress. He even become the President of the Hindu Mahasabha in 1925.

The Arya Samaj came to be looked upon by the British as a political outfit because of the political slant in many of its activities. Since a large number of people from Punjab and Haryana, particularly from the Haryana districts of Hissar, Rohtak etc., joined the armed forces, it was suspected by the British authorities that the Arya Samaj movement was likely to inject the political virus into the officers and men of the armed forces. It was widely believed that for some years preceding the First World War, the recruitment to the armed forces of Jats from Haryana, who dabbled in Arya Samaj activities, had been stopped as a precautionary measure.

An important leader of the Congress Party of whom Hissar was justly proud was Dr. Gopi Chand Bhargava. He was born at Sirsa in 1899 A.D., but his family moved over to Hissar soon after his birth. So Hissar was the centre of his political and other multifarious activities. He was a staunch Gandhian in his outlook and a follower of Lala Lajpat Rai. He was the first Chief Minister of Punjab after independence.

Fatehabad, an important place of Hissar district, derives its name from Fateh Khan, son of Feroze Shah Tughlak. It is known for its cotton as well as for its historical monuments including Humayun's Masjid, where Humayun, the Mughal Emperor, had prayed when he passed through this place on a Friday.

At the Haryana Agricultural University, besides holding discussions with Dr. Harswarup Singh, the Vice-Chancellor and the members of the Faculty on academic and administrative issues, I went round the various colleges in the campus and also attended an impressive cultural programme put up by the students.

In between all these engagements, I found time to visit Agroha, a town about thirteen miles from Hissar on the road that leads to Fatehabad. It is an ancient place from which the Aggarwals are said to have originated. Agroha has derived its name from Raja Agra (also called Agra Sain), who used to rule here in the pre-Christian era. Agroha was well known for the democratic and socialist system of government introduced by King Agra Sain, which was a departure from the autocratic and feudal systems that prevailed elsewhere.

It is said that any person who came to live in Agroha from elsewhere was given a brick and a rupee by each resident of the place so that he could build a home for himself. This clearly brings out how King Agra Sain upheld the system of trusteeship in his domain.

He was a powerful and far-sighted ruler, but rather fight with the other rulers, he established friendly relations with them and encouraged the growth of trade and commerce among the various kingdoms. He also went in for marital ties with rulers of other kingdoms as a means of strengthening relations with them. He himself had married eighteen times and had arranged the marriage of his sons and daughters with members of the ruling families of many other kingdoms. He had managed to establish his supremacy by organizing 'Ashwamedh' sacrifices eighteen times. By dint of his intellect and diligence and by the grace of goddess Lakshmi, he succeeded in making Agroha the wealthiest and the most prosperous kingdom.

He ruled for 108 years and then left for 'Vanaprastha' (i. e. retired to the forest) after handing over the reins to his eldest son, Bibhu. For many generations, his descendants ruled in Agroha.

Once a saint named Dhranganath came to Agroha along with his disciple, Kirtinath. He told Kirtinath to light a fire so that he could start his spiritual activity. He also asked Kirtinath to go in search of some food, saying that in a prosperous place like Agroha there would be no dearth of people ready to help them. Dhranganath commenced his religious rites and soon went into a trance while Kirtinath was away on his quest for food. But surprisingly, no householder offered him any food or even water. Hungry and fatigued by evening, he was going to fall down when a potter's wife saw him and obliged him with some food. She also gave him an axe with which he could cut wood in order to make a living. His Guru woke up from his trance after several months when he told him about the unhelpful attitude of the local people.

Dhranganath was so distressed to hear Kirtinath's account that he pronounced a curse by which the whole of Agroha with the exception of the potter's wife was reduced to ashes in 24 hours. One can still see several mounds of varying heights covering an extensive area towards the north-western part of Agroha which are said to represent the old Agroha that had thus turned into heaps of ash.

Some relics of the old glory of Agroha can be seen even today. Remnants of Agra Sain's palace and the ramparts of his fort were shown to me.

Some Greeks who came to India with Alexander the Great during his mission of conquering the world have left behind accounts in which references to Agroha are to be found. Towards the end of the 19th century, excavations had been undertaken to unearth Agroha's old glory, but this work was stopped mid-way. Agroha was known as Agro-daka in ancient times, as is evident from the coins discovered in the course of archaeological excavations. These coins also show that the town had come into existence in the 5th century B.C. The Mahabharata and the Astadhyayi contain references to this place. The various archaeological finds such as coins of the Kushans and Yaudheyas, terracotta plaques, seals and sculptures, an image of Lord Vishnu etc. reveal that Shaivism, Buddhism and Jainism had flourished here in different phases of history.

Muhammad Ghauri had captured and burnt down Agroha in 1194 A.D. after which the Aggarwals spread out all over the country. It regained its prosperity and became an important town during the rule of Feroze Shah Tughlak. However, it was hit by a devastating famine during the rule of Muhammad Tughlak and was deserted by the people. Ibn-i-Batuta has narrated how the Hindu temples in the area were dismantled and their materials used to build the various edifices of Hissar-e-Firoza.

I was taken round the place and shown the many archaeological finds that included earthen jars of various kinds, incense burners, cups, dishes, bangles, terracotta figures and copper artefacts. I saw the many traces of the existence of a flourishing town of an earlier era such as walls of baked bricks, cemented floors and good roads. I paid obeisance at the newly constructed Maharaja Agra Sain Temple and visited the sight where a Mahalaxmi Temple was under construction. I also visited the area where a huge lake spread over 35 acres was coming up, thanks to the funds donated by the prosperous Aggarwal community. On September 24, 1976, the Government of India released a stamp to mark King Agra Sain's birth anniversary.

I did not have the opportunity this time to visit a famous institution of Hissar—the Government Livestock Farm, which is the biggest such institution in Asia. Of course, I had occasion to see it some time later.

I was also unable this time to fully acquaint myself with developments pertaining to the several old Harappan sites and the many archaeological finds brought out in the course of excavations that revealed the links of this region with the pre-Aryan Indus Valley civiliastion. However, I had preliminary discussions on this subject with some academics and archaeologists, who sent me voluminous reports from time to time in Chandigarh for my study. About this, more later.

Notes

1. V.S. Agrawala, Moti Chandra, Chaturbani, p. 168, cited in "Art and Architecture in Haryana Through the Ages: A Survey" by Dr. K.C. Yadav in the Journal of Haryana Studies, Vol. XV, Nos.1 and 2, 1983.
2. *Ibid.*
3. *Ibid.*
4. S.K. Chaube, Sangita Ke Gharoun Ki Charcha, pp. 134-135, cited by Dr. K.C. Yadav in article at 1 above.
5. Haryana by D.C. Verma, p. 97.
6. *Ibid*, p. 27.
7. V.S. Agrawala, cited by Dr. K.C. Yadav in article at 1 above.
8. *Ibid.*
9. *Ibid.* Pages 223-224 of Banabhatta's Harsha-Charita translated into Hindi by Pt. Jagannath Pathaka, Chowkhamba Vidyabhawan, Varanasi–1 may be referred to for further details.
10. *Ibid.*
11. *Ibid.*
12. *Ibid.*
13. "Thakur Pheru: An Introductory Study of the Man and his Works' by Dr. K.C. Yadav in the Journal of Haryana Studies, Vol. VII, Nos. 1-2, 1975.
14. *Ibid.*
15. Imperial Gazetteer of India: Provincial Series: Punjab: Volume I (1908), pp. 228-247.
16. History of Hisar by M.M. Juneja, pp. 28 onward.
17. *Ibid*, p. 29.
18. *Ibid*, p. 31.
19. I*Ibid*, p. 40.
20. This and the next few paragraphs are based on the History of Hisar by M.M. Juneja.
21. Quoted from the Times of India in the History of Hisar by M.M. Juneja.
22. Jansatta dated September 10, 1987, quoted in the History of Hisar by M.M. Juneja.

23. Cited in M.M. Juneja's book from the District Gazetteer of Hissar.
24. M.M. Juneja's book, p. 48.
25. M.M. Juneja's book, pp. 31-33.
26. This account is based on a write-up by Anand Jha in the Times of India, New Delhi, dated December 3, 1999.
27. M.M. Juneja's book, p. 55.
28. *Ibid*, p. 60.
29. Haryana by D.C. Verma, p. 29.
30. Cited by D.C. Verma in 'Haryana' (page 29) from Dr. Shiv Prasad Goyal's 'Haryana Ka Hindi Sahitya Udbhav Aur Vikas' (page 9).
31. The Revolt of 1857 in Haryana by Dr. K.C. Yadav, pp. 65-66.
32. *Ibid*, p. 66.
33. *Ibid*, p. 108.
34. Cited in Dr. K.C. Yadav's book from N.A. Chick's "Annals of the Indian Rebellion, 1857-56", p. 109.
35. Dr. K.C. Yadav's book, p. 110.
36. Cited in M.M. Juneja's book from "The Punjab and Delhi in 1857" by J. Cave-Brown, Volume II, pp. 275-276.
37. M.M. Juneja's book, pp. 95, 98.

10

Sirsa Where Prithviraj was Captured by Mohd. Ghori: Akbar at Kurukshetra During A Solar Eclipse: I Swim Across Sannihit Tank on A Solar Eclipse: Jyotisar Where Krishna Revealed the Gita: the Ancient Temples of Bhadrakali and Katyayani

Floods in the Yamuna and the Ghaggar rivers during August-September, 1988 affected several districts of Haryana. On August 31, 1988, I paid a visit to some affected villages of Karnal district located near the Yamuna along with Sachdev Tyagi, Minister for Irrigation, to study the situation and see what all was being done to help the people.

Soon after this, I paid a visit on September 7, 1988 to Sirsa district, which had been rather badly hit by the floods in the Ghaggar. The State Government plane, which carried me, my wife and a few concerned officials, circled over the affected areas of Sirsa district, which at some places looked like sprawling sheets of water. The pilot pointed out an important tourist spot of the district—Abubshehr, which was lòcated very close to the tri-junction of three States—Haryana, Punjab and Rajasthan. At this point, the Bhakra Canal and the Rajasthan Canal intersected each other.

The Kalateetar tourist resort built on stilts on the bed of the Bhakra Canal near this point was said to provide a beautiful view of the enchanting surroundings that encompassed the not-so-distant Thar desert. There were some other tourist resorts also in this district such as the Shikara at Asakhera and the Surkhab in Sirsa town. After deplaning at Sirsa, I went into a huddle with the local officials to discuss various issues pertaining to the floods. I visited some villages, where I addressed gatherings of the people and assured them of adequate relief.

Even in the midst of the floods that enveloped the whole district, I could feel that Sirsa was a rather hot place, which had also become quite humid now. The terrain was sandy at many places. The excess waters of the Ghaggar had raised the level of the Otu Lake near Sirsa town.

I visited Sirsa again the next month in connection with some official business. Meeting various people and reading up some books that went into the history of Sirsa, I came to learn what an ancient place it was. The town is divided into two halves by the Ghaggar that is regarded as being roughly identical with the course of the ancient Saraswati river of Hindu mythology—a river that is believed to have gone underground.

A few months after I took over as the Governor of Haryana in February, 1988, I was told that many articles including terracotta figurines, coins and inscriptions had been retrieved from a big mound in Sirsa town, which suggested that this was one of the ancient sites of Aryan civilization or Painted Grey Ware civilization.[1] I had the opportunity of seeing some of these specimens, which led me to undertake some studies with a view to comprehending some of the issues involved.

The antiquity of Sirsa is evident from the fact that it is mentioned by Panini, the famous Sanskrit grammarian (who, according to one view, lived in the sixth century B.C.) in his Astadhyayi [2], the name given to Sirsa is Shairishaka, which was derived from the Sanskrit word 'Shirisha' (meaning Acacia Speciosa), a tree that was preponderant in the flora of the region. That is why some of the officials, who briefed me during this trip to Sirsa, said that this area used to have thick forests of the Shirish tree in very ancient times.

The Mahabharata says that Nakula, one of the Pandava brothers, had come here after conquering Rohtak. The name of this place also "figures in the story of Kunala (Kunalavadava), in the Buddhist work Divyavadana (between 200–350 A.D.). Then we hear of it after the lapse of almost a thousand years in the Jaina work Puratana Prabandha Sangraha dated to V.S. 1290–1350."[3] This place was known as Bharat Pattan where the Jain scholar, Laxmi Niwas, the disciple of Ratna Prabh Suri, had compiled three poetical works in 1438 A.D.[4]

Shirishvan (Shirish forest) has been mentioned by Patanjali in his Mahabhashya. As it was located on the bank of the Saraswati river, Sirsa was also known as Saraswati Nagar. Some say that Sirsa got its name from Baba Sarsai Nath, whose shrine is located here, but there is no historical basis for such a view.[5] There is also a view that the name Sirsa was derived from Saras, a king who ruled here and built a fort about 1400 years ago. But no such ruler's name figures in history. A ninth century A.D. inscription of Bhoja, the Pratihara ruler, mentions the construction of a temple of Pashupati (Shiva) at Sirsa. It is said that this is the first time that the name of Sirsa town has been mentioned.[6]

Archaeological discoveries here include coins of the Yaudheyas and the Kushanas and also a stone slab containing the last five of the eighteen verses of a eulogy to a certain king, whose name is not known and is perhaps assignable to the 5th or 6th century A.D. While driving through Sirsa, several ancient mounds were pointed out to me. In the medieval period, the Ghaggar river here was famous for "its fabulous sugarcane crops, with which the forces of Saltan Masand, son of Mahmud of Ghazni, used to fill up the moat for storming the fortress."7 in the medieval period, Sirsa was known as Sarsuti and Prithviraj was said to have been captured here after his defeat by Mohammad of Ghori in 1192.

A few decades ago, a historian by name Devendra Handa had obtained from one of the ancient mounds at Sirsa a small broken sculpture—a female figure flanked by Krishna and Baladeva that was identified as a deity named Ekanamsa in the Brihatsamhita and Vishnudharmottara. It has been surmised on the basis of this discovery that the cult of Ekamansa was prevalent in this region once upon a time.[8]

Sirsa was captured by Timur in 1398 A.D., when its inhabitants fled before his arrival and during the reign of Sher Shah, it became for some time the headquarters of Rao Kalyan Singh of Bikaner. But soon the Jodhpur house gained control over it. In the 18th century, it became a stronghold of the Bhattis. In 1783 A.D., the place was virtually depopulated by a severe famine. In 1818 A.D., it was annexed by the British and in 1838 A.D., Captain Thoresby laid out the present Sirsa town, which remained the headquarters of Sirsa district between 1858 A.D. And 1884 A.D. Later, it formed part of Hissar district.

I visited Sirsa again after a month to make a further assessment of the ravages of floods. About that, more later.

I had the opportunity of paying one of my many visits to Kurukshetra again along with my wife on September 10, 1988 in order to take a dip in some of the sacred tanks there on the important occasion of a solar eclipse that came off the next day. I reached there a day in advance to see what arrangements had been made by the police and the local authorities to handle the mammoth crowds that had already begun to converge there not only from all over Haryana but also from many far-off places in the rest of the country. Going round the place along with the top police officers, I saw how beautiful the Brahmsaovar and Sannihit tanks and the numerous temples looked at night when they were all illuminated.

The Gurdwaras of Kurukshetra, which were also illuminated, were thronged by many Sikh pilgrims, who had come to take a dip in one or the other of the holy tanks. All except one of the ten Sikh Gurus had visited Kurukshetra. Guru nanak's visit here is commemorated by Gurdwara Sidhbati near the Brahmsarovar. Close to the Sannihit tank stands the Gurdwara in memory of Guru Hargovind. There are Gurdwaras in memory of some other Sikh Gurus as well. It was a joy to see the display of religious fervour by both Hindu and Sikh pilgrims on this holy occasion.

I found time during this trip to Kurukshetra to visit some holy spots in and around the town. One was the Chandra Kupa, a well on an island in the Brahmsarovar tank. After the Pandavas' victory in the Kurukshetra battle, Yudhisthira was believed to have built a victory pillar at this spot, which, however, no longer exists. Then we went to Ban Ganga or Bhisma Kund in a village, which is a little away from the town on the road to Pehowa. Bhisma, who lay on his bed of arrows here felt thirsty and called upon Arjuna to offer him a drink of water. Arjuna pierced the earth with an arrow and there at once gushed out a spring with whose water Bhisma assuaged his thirst. There is now a tank here in which the pilgrims take a dip.

Then we visited another Ban Ganga located in a village called Dayalpur, not very far from the Brahmsarovar. There is a holy tank here, which was created by Arjuna by shooting an arrow into the ground in order to provide drinking water to the horses drawing his chariot during his encounter with Jayadratha, a famous figure of the Mahabharata. We also visited the Sarveshwara Mahadeva Temple by going over a bridge on the Brahmsarovara.

Before paying this visit to Kurukshetra, I had gone through some of the available literature, old and new, pertaining to solar eclipses that had taken place at Kurukshetra through the centuries. A fact that stands out is that, since time immemorial, people in large numbers from all over the country have been visiting this place during solar eclipses and taking dips in one or the other of the tanks here, obviously to gain religious merit or at least to secure mental or spiritual bliss that this confers on them.

The Vedas do not mention solar eclipses, but the Mahabharata does. There was a solar eclipse on the day the Mahabharata war began, which, according to Udyog Parva, was the day of Jyestha Amavasya, 15 years after Yudhisthira had performed the Rajasuya Yagna. There is a reference in the Vana Parva to the religious merit of taking a dip in the holy Sannihit tank of Kurukshetra on the occasion of a solar eclipse.

The Matsya Purana also refers to the virtue one earns by taking a dip here on such an occasion. The Bhagavata Purana mentions the assembly of people from all over the country at Kurukshetra on the eve of a solar eclipse. "They are extremely anxious to attain Punya; and so they observed fast, had their bath at Kurukshetra and distributed garlands and cows among the Brahmanas. The great assembly at Kurukshetra on this occasion included even the rulers of various states and countries *i.e.*, Matsya, Usinara, Kosala, Vidarbha, Kuru, Sanjaya, Kamboja, Kekaya, Madra, Kunti, Anarta, Kerala etc. Besides this, they had their relations too with them."[9]

Varahamihira, the great Indian astronomer, referred in the Vrihat Samhita to the effects of a solar eclipse at Kurukshetra and some other places in these words: "If an eclipse should occur in the lunar month of Shravana, the people of Kashmira, Pulindas, Chinese, Yavanas, those born in Kurukshetra and Gandharva, those living in the central tract, Kambojas and all whole-hoofed animals and also grains of the autumnal season will suffer damage and perish."[10]

To quote Varahamihira further: "With the exception of those stated above, all those living elsewhere shall be happy and live in peace."[11]

Varahamira also says: "When a malign Ketu eclipses or touches the star Citra, people in the know should declare the exit from the world of the Chief of Kurukshetra."[12]

Further on, Varahamihira says: "If the star in question be Svati, the two kings of Kashmir and Kamboja will cease to exist."[13]

During the Sultanate period (1206–1526 A.D.), taxes were imposed on the pilgrims visiting Kurukshetra.[14] During the reign of Aurangzeb, Hindu pilgrims had to pay a tax of a rupee for a small pot of water of the holy tank of Kurukshetra and five rupees for a dip in it (eka rupaya lota aur pancha rupaya gota).[15]

Mughal Emperor Akbar was in Kurukshetra in 1567 A.D. during a solar eclipse,[16] when there was a big assemblage of people. There was a quarrel between the followers of the Puri and Kuru sects, which gave rise to the apprehension of a fight. According to Muslim historians, Abul Fazl and Nizamuddin Ahmad, the quarrel began over the possession of gold, silver, jewels and other valuables, which had been thrown into the water by the people or bestowed as gifts upon the Brahmins. Akbar went there personally to settle the dispute. When persuasion failed, he allowed the two sects to fight out the issue. Bows and arrows, swords and stones were fully used in the fight. The Puris were fewer in number and so the fight was unequal. Then Akbar lent some of his soldiers smeared with ashes to assist them. This enabled the Puris to kill the Mahant of the rival sect. There were many casualties on both sides. The event appeared to the emperor to be a gladiators' sport and he had hearty laugh over it.[17]

The Akbarnama referred to the tank in Kurukshetra as a miniature sea, which historians have identified with the Brahmsarovar, the biggest tank of Kurukshetra.

According to the account of Francois Bernier, a French traveller, who had visited India during the reign of Shahjahan, a solar eclipse had taken place in 1666 A.D., when more than a lac and a half people had assembled at "Tanaiser" (*i.e.* Thanesar) from all parts of the country, its waters being considered more holy and meritorious than those of the other rivers on the day of an eclipse.[18]

Why does a solar eclipse attract such big multitudes of people to Kurukshetra? Is there any scientific reason for it? Some scholars have suggested[19] that the importance of Kurukshetra during a solar eclipse might be traceable to its central position for astronomical calculations. In his masterpiece on astronomy, 'Siddhantashiromani', Bhaskaracharya mentions a straight line passing through Kurukshetra, which divides the earth. This line used for astronomical calculations passed from Sri Lanka to Meru through Ujjain, Rohtak, Kurukshetra, Mathura and Himavat (Himalayas).

The Haryana Government makes elaborate police and other administrative arrangements during solar eclipses in view of the large number of pilgrims, who turn up at Kurukshetra. In 1987, the State Government had got a whole new tank of the same size as the Brahmsarovar excavated at Kurukshetra, which was filled up with the waters of the Brahmsarovar so that the pilgrims would have an alternative tank to bathe in. This was a wise move as this helped in reducing the big rush of people at the main Brahmsarovar.

On the morning of September 11, 1988, the day of the solar eclipse, my wife, Anita, and I were escorted to the Sannihit Tank for a dip. Pilgrims estimated at about five lakh had turned up for the holy occasion. Normally, a million or two converged on Kurukshetra on such occasions. But the spectre of terrorism had cast its shadow on Kurukshetra this time, resulting in a much lower turn-out.

We had our dip at the special 'Ghat' made for us. Then slowly but steadily, I started swimming across the tank. I reached the other side of the tank quite comfortably and swam back to the place from where I had started. My wife was noticing my antics quite coolly, because she knew that swimming was great fun for me, though I had not done any swimming during the previous decade. Of course, policemen as part of their security drill, had been going alongside me in a boat, ever ready to come to my rescue in case they saw that I was drowning!

After I came up and changed into a fresh set of clothes, H.S. Brar, the Director-General of Police, who was keeping a sharp eye on me all this while, told me that he had heaved a sigh of relief on seeing me back ashore. The next day's newspapers commented on his aspect of my Kurukshetra trip. The daiy Tribune of Chandigarh (12.9.1988) wrote as below:

The Tribune, dated 12.9.1988

Lakhs take dip in sarovars

From Y.P. Gupta

KURUKSHETRA, Sept. 11 – Lakhs of devotees had a holy dip in Sannihit Sarovar and Brahm Sarovar here today on the occasion of the solar eclipse. As soon as the eclipse started at 7.49 a.m. the melodious sounds of bells and "shankhas" rent the air from temple situated around the tanks.

However, terrorism did cast its dark shadows of the eclipse fair. Hardly one-third of the expected 15 lakh pilgrims turned up here to participate in the fair. It was surprising especially because the next solar eclipse would occur after seven years on October 24, 1995.

It seems that the recent terrorist activities in Kurukshetra district, particularly the bomb blast which claimed 15 lives of Ramayan viewers here, dampened the enthusiasm of the pilgrims.

Even the number of nagas, who have the first right to take a dip in the holy tank, was less than in the past.

Twelve-year-old Munish, son of Mr. Hanuman Parshad Aggarwal of Ellenabad in Sirsa district, was drowned in the Sannihit Sarovar. Divers saved two lives each in Brahm Sarovar and Sannihit Sarovar.

Three persons were injured, one of them seriously, when they fell from a running train between Paldarsi and Thanesar stations.

The Haryana Governor, Mr. H.A. Barari, and his wife, Anita, were among the first to take a dip, in Sannihit Sarovar as soon as the eclipse started. Mr. Barari gave anxious movements to the security forces when he went across the safety ring and started swimming in the 17-foot-deep tank. The S.P., Mr. Resham Singh, immediately posted two divers to escort the VIPs in the water. The Governor reached the other side of the tank and came back to the VIP ghat by executing flawless back strokes.

Welcoming the pilgrims to the fair on behalf of the Haryana Government, the Food and Supplies Minister, Mrs Sushma Swaraj, said the State Government had made elaborate arrangements to help the devotees.

Among other prominent persons who visited the fair were Mr. Ranjit Singh, a son of Mr. Devi Lal, several Ministers and MLAs.

About 6,000 men of the security forces, including seven companies of the BSF, were on duty. Besides black cat commandos were posted at strategic points. The dog squad and a bomb disposal squad were kept in readiness.

The police and the Home Guards restored around 300 children, aged men and women, lost in the crowds to their families.

The railways and the Haryana Roadways operated special services for the pilgrims to and from Kurukshetra.

The Nav Bharat Times, a Hindi daily of Chandigarh (12.9.1988), wrote:

कुरुक्षेत्र के पवित्र सरोवरो में पाँच लाख यात्रियों ने स्नान किया

कुरुक्षेत्र 11 सितम्बर (निस) । सूर्यग्रहण में यहा के प्रसिद्ध सन्निहित सरोवर, ब्रह्म सरोवर में लगभग पाँच लाख यात्रियों तथा श्रद्धालुओं ने स्नान किया सूर्य के खंड ग्रास होते ही सन्निहित सरोवर पर स्नान करने वालो में हरियाणा के राज्यपाल श्री हरि आनन्द बरारी और उनकी धर्मपत्नी श्रीमती अनीता बरारी ।

श्री बरारी लगभग 10 मिनट तक सन्निहित सरोवर में नहाए तथा तैरते रहे उन्होंने रैलिंग को पकड कर 17 फुट गहरे सरोवर में कूद तैरना शुरू किया तो सुरक्षा अधिकारी सकते में आ गए । श्री बरारी को सन्निहित सरोवर के बीच तैरते तथा गोता–खोरी करते देखकर कुरुक्षेत्र पुलिस अधीक्षक और दो तैराक पानी में उतार दिए। श्री बरारी तैरते हुए सरोवर के दूसरी किनारे तक जा पहुँचे और फिर आराम से तैरते हुए वापस वी.आई. पी. घाट पर आ गए । बाद में वे ब्रह्म सरोवर में स्नान करने चले गए।

We then moved over to the Brahmsarovar for a dip. We also went about in a motor boat, accompanied by some officials, to greet the pilgrims taking their dips on all sides of the Brahmsarovar. Looking at their beaming faces, I thought that they had full faith in what the Matsya Purana had said, namely that by having a bath in the tanks of Kurukshetra during a solar eclipse, one earns great merit.[20] As I have mentioned earlier, the Mahabharata also says: one taking a dip in the Sannihit tank during a solar eclipse earns the virtues of having performed a hundred Ashwamedha sacrifices.

It is said that Lord Krishna had come to Kurukshetra on the occasion of a solar eclipse and met here his father, Nanda, his mother, Yashoda, and some of his Gopi friends after a long interval.

The Vana Parva of the Mahabharata says that whoever—man or woman—takes a dip in a tank in Kurukshetra has all his sins neutralized and reaches Brahmalok.[21]

Further, if there is a solar eclipse on a new moon day, a person, who performs Shradh here and then takes a dip in the Sannihit, secures the virtue of having performed a thousand Ashwamedha sacrifices.[22]

The Skanda Purana says that a person, who properly feeds a single Brahmin here secures the merit of having fed one crore persons.[23]

It further says that whoever performs 'Homa' here earns the merit of a crore of sacrifices.[24]

The Puranas say that Sradh performed at Kurukshetra on a full moon day achieves ever-lasting merit and a person, who worships his forefathers here is relieved of all the debt that he owes to them.[25]

According to the Bhagavata Purana, a solar eclipse had occurred at Kurukshetra at the end of the Kalpa (*i.e.* a day in the life of Lord Brahma, which is equivalent to 432 crore years of ordinary mankind!) People in large numbers had come here from far and wide at that time to seek spiritual merit.[26]

Through the ages, many people have visited Kurukshetra on the occasion of solar eclipses. From the writings of Kahlon, the Kashmiri author of Rajatarangini, the prince of Kashmir had visited Kurukshetra during a solar eclipse on July 23, 1134 A.D.—a date on which a solar eclipse took place and was visible from Kurukshetra.[27]

I paid several more visits to Kurukshetra and each visit gave me an opportunity of learning a little more about the place and its history and culture. In the last week of September, 1988, I undertook another trip to Kurukshetra, the occasion this time being the 15th Junior National Swimming Competition held at the swimming pool of the Kurukshetra University, where I distributed the prizes. I had plenty of time to go round and visit some spiritually important places.

One of these places was Jyotisar, where Lord Krishna had delivered the eternal message of the Gita to Arjuna on the eve of the Mahabharata battle. There I saw the 5000 years old banyan tree, which is known as the 'Akshay Bat' and is believed to be the only surviving witness to the fact of Lord Krishna's expostulation of the Gita to Arjuna. It was under this tree that the chariot of Arjuna stood still between the rival armies of the Pandavas and Kauravas on the battleground of Kurukshetra, while Lord Krishna preached the message of the Gita. Many years ago, the Maharaja of Darbhanga had got a 'Chabutra' constructed around this banyan tree.

The place has been called Jyotisar (meaning the pool or stream of knowledge) because Lord Krishna imparted true knowledge to Arjuna here. There is an old tank here which is regarded as very sacred, A new lake which has been excavated at Jyotisar by the Kurukshetra Development Board is 1000 feet long and 500 feet wide. I saw here a Shiva temple and another temple of Adi Shankaracharya built in 1967 by the Shankarcharya of Kamakothi Peetham. Gita Jayanti is celebrated here every year during the month of Agrahayana (November-December) for a fortnight beginning on the eleventh day of the bright moon.

I also went with my wife to pay obeisance at the holy Bhadrakali temple in Kurukshetra. It is also called 'Devi Kupa', which is one of the four sacred wells of Kurukshetra. I have earlier mentioned the Chandra Kupa temple on an island in the Brahmsarovar tank. Devi Kupa is one of the 51 famous Peethasthanas of India, each of them representing a place where some part or the other of Sati's body had fallen as a sequel to a big sacrifice arranged by King Daksa, the father of Sati. At Devi Kupa where the Bhadrakali temple stands, it was the heel of the right foot of Sati that had fallen. According to Tantrachudamani [28], the heel of Sati's foot exists here; Sthanu (*i.e.* Lord Shiva) and Savitri (the symbol of Shakti) manifested themselves here.

The Puranic story about King Daksa's sacrifice , which led to all this, is like this. The king did not invite to this sacrifice his son-in-law and Sati's consort, Lord Shiva. Sati attended the sacrifice organized by his father, but was horrified to hear the abuses hurled by Daksa at Lord Shiva. Unable to tolerate this, Sati gave up her life voluntarily. On hearing this, Lord Shiva rushed there and out of anger, he started tearing off the matted tissues of his hair and throwing them around. Out of these tresses arose Birbhadra and Bhadrakali, who started wreaking havoc and dismantling all the arrangements that had been made for King Daksa's sacrifice. Lord Shiva then took up the corpse of Sita on his Trishul (trident) and began to rotate it with great speed. Brahma, Vishnu and Shani vanished through the power of Yoga, entered Sita's body, tore it off to pieces and cast them around over various places on earth. Each of these places became a sacred Peethasthan or Shaktipeeth, where Sati began to be worshipped by her devotees.

The Bhadrakali temple at Kurukshetra stands at the site of a Peethastha, as I have already stated. The deity inside the temple is similar to one of the several forms of goddess Kali that is worshipped all over our country. It is dark-complexioned and has four arms—two on the right side held out in the pose of offering blessings to the devotees and two on the left side, one of which holds a scimitar, while the other holds the severed head of a man. Her red tongue is protruding. She wears a garland of human heads around her neck. The image of Lord Shiva lies under her foot. On the right side stands the image of fair-complexioned Parvati, another form of goddess Bhadrakali.

Bhadrakali is a particular form of Durga and Kalika and figures in Kalika Purana as well as in the Tantras. In the Puranas, Bhadrakali has the likeness of Durga, while in the Tantric literature, Badrakali resembles Kali. In Kalika Purana, demon Mahisasura is found to be a devotee of Bhadrakali.

Once Mahisasura had a dream in which a 16-armed goddess chopped off his head and drank his blood. He realized that this dream was sure to come true because of a curse pronounced on him by sage Katyayana. This sage, who had his Ashrama in the Himalayas, had a disciple by name Rudrashiva. Once when Rudrashiva was deeply immersed in meditation, Mahisasura took the form of a charming damsel to distract him. As Rudrashiva looked at this beauty, he got derailed from his austere path of penance. This enraged Katyayana, who cursed Mahisasura by saying that since the latter had assumed the form of a woman to distract Rudraksha, a woman would one day kill him. Thus Mahisasura thought that he was bound to get killed by a goddess as his dream had now indicated.

Mahisasura commenced an austere penance in order to please Devi (or Shakti). After several months, Devi appeared before him when Mahisasura told her about her premonition that he was going to be killed by her. He prayed to the Devi for a boon that from then on he should get a part of all offerings made at 'Yagnas' (sacrifices) that her devotees were to hold by way of worshipping her Devi told him that this was not possible because, under a previous arrangement, all these offerings were to be shared by her with some others. However, she assured him that as long as Durga, Ugrachanda and Bhadrakali were worshipped by the devotees, would Mahisasura would also be worshipped along with them. Thus assured, Mahisasura now reverted to his earlier oppressive ways!

Goddess Bhadrakali also figures in Srimadbhagavata. When Devaki and Vasudeva were cast into the prison by Kansa, Bhadrakali Yogamaya was born to Nanda Gopal and Yashoda in the form of a girl. In compliance with the direction received through a voice from heaven, Vasudeva took the new-born son of Devaki (*i.e.* infant Krishna) to Yashoda for safe-keeping and brought with him the just-born to the prison. Learning that a child was born to Devaki, Kansa came to the prison to kill it. But Kansa failed to carry out his mission, as the girl slipped out of his hand and flew into the sky, assuming the form of Bhadrakali and sounding the warning to Kansa that his end was near as the one (meaning Krishna) who was to kill him had already been born.

In the Ramayana too, the name of Bhadrakali is mentioned as the goddess worshipped by Ravana. In this capacity, she used to protect the city of Lanka on behalf of Ravana. When Hanuman tried to enter Lanka in search of Sita, it was goddess Bhadrakali who stopped him. But Hanuman cleverly managed to please Bhadrakali, who gave her blessings to the former, thus allowing Hanuman the much-needed access to Lanka.

At the Peethasthan in Kurukshetra, the Pandavas had worshipped Bhadrakali on the eve of the Mahabharata battle, praying for victory. Arjuna had chanted the 'Durga Stotra' to please Bhadrakali. After their victory in the Mahabharata battle, the Pandavas came here with Lord Krishna and presented a horse to Bhadrakali. Since then the custom of offering a hose here on the fulfillment of a person's wish has been in vogue. In course of time, people started offering horses of gold or silver. Now people rest content with offering earthen horses—a pointer to the impact of inflation on the observance of religious rites.

Lord Krishna had a special relationship with Bhadrakali because she was the tutelary deity of the Yadava dynasty to which the former belonged. It was here that the 'Mundan' ceremony of child Krishna and his brother Balarama was performed. There is a banyan tree in the Bhadrakali temple complex under which the devotees sit and pray to the goddess. It is believed that this tree had been planted by Lord Krishna! There is a sacred tank to the south of the temple, which is called Devital. On the north-western side of the tank, there is the temple of Dakseshwar.

My wife and I sat inside the Bhadrakali temple and worshipped there, observing the elaborate rites.

The Varadaraj temple of Kurukshetra, which we saw from a distance, also deserves mention. This is the only temple of Lord Vishnu in north India, though there are several Vishnu temples in south India. Varadaraj is one of the names of Vishnu and in the 'Vishnusahasranama' (which mentions the thousand names of Lord Vishnu), the word 'Varada' (giver of boons) figures 330 times. It is said that Bhisma had advised Yudhisthira to chant the thousand names of

Vishnu and to pray in particular to Varadaraj, who confers immense wealth and happiness on his devotees. Dussehra and Diwali are observed at the Varadaraj temple with great enthusiasm. On the eleventh day of the moon after Diwali, some special religious rites are performed here because this is the occasion when Lord Vishnu is believed to wake up from his eternal sleep with a view to playing his role as the protector of the universe. The Vaishnavas celebrate this occasion with great devotion.

Near Kurukshetra, there are a few other Devi temples with deities that are different manifestations of Shakti. Two of these temples that I visited on different occasions along with my wife are the Katyayani temple and the Devi temple at Hathira, a village about seven miles from Kurukshetra. The Katyayani temple is located on an island called Purushottambag in the midst of Brahmsarovar. This deity, the emblem of Adi Shakti, has been worshipped through the ages—by maidens praying for good husbands, by Sita before her marriage with Lord Rama and by Rukmini before her union with Lord Krishna. Katyayani is the sixth of the nine forms of Durga (Chhathi Durga), who had manifested herself in the hermitage of sage Katyayana.

And thereby hangs a tale. In days of yore, a demon by name Raktabeej conquered heaven and drove away the gods from there. The gods went in a procession with Brahma at its head to meet Lord Vishnu and place their grievances against Raktabeej. They found Shiva also seated with Vishnu. On hearing the gods' litany of woes, Shiva and Vishnu became very angry with Raktabeej. Their anger, which was very great, was joined by the anger of all the gods, who had come as members of the procession. This combined anger of Shiva, Vishnu and al the other gods assumed the dimensions of a virtual mountain and reached the hermitage of sage Katyayana, whose anger now joined that of all the other gods. This combined anger equalled the splendour and heat of thousands of suns.

Then there appeared a big-eyed resplendent goddess, Katyayani, embodying all this energy and brilliance. The different parts of her body reflected the power of the limbs of different gods and goddesses: her face reflected Lord Shiva's power, her three eyes the power of fire, her hair the power of Yama, her breasts the power of the moon, her feet the power of Brahma and so on. This powerful goddess, Katyayani, killed demon Raktabeej and disappeared at the feet of Lord Shiva, assuring the gods that she would appear again and again, when the need arose. It is this goddess that is worshipped at the temple that I visited in Purushottambag.

There is also an old Shiva temple in this complex. Local tradition has it that Kunti, mother of the Pandavas, had done penance here before the Mahabharata battle and thereby pleased the Sun God. Lord Krishna had meditated upon goddess Katyayani before this battle, whereupon the goddess appeared in the sky and offered her blessings saying that his side would be victorious. Various religious functions are held at the Katyayani temple, particularly during Navaratri.

As I have already said, I also visited the Devi temple at Hathira in the vicinity of Kurukshetra, which is another centre of Shakti worship. It is said that when the Pandavas and the Kauravas failed to arrive at a settlement of their dispute, thus making the battle of Mahabharata a certainty, Arjuna went to see Lord Krishna to seek his guidance. Krishna learnt through the power of Yoga that the battle was going to take place soon. He went with Arjuna in his chariot to find out the place where the battle would be fought. They arrived at Kurukshetra when Krishna told Arjuna that it was here that the Pandavas and the Kauravas would fight each other. Then Krishna told Arjuna to worship at that place the eight-armed goddess Durga so that his side could win the battle. And this is what Arjuna did. The goddess blessed him and offered him the boon of victory in advance.

The temple of Devi at this place is a very ancient one and had remained under the ground since the time of the Mahabharata. It was discovered and brought overground as a result of excavations after many centuries. The priest of the temple belongs to a family hailing from Pune in Maharashtra. It is his ancestors, who had initiated the process of excavation to unearth this temple. It is said [2]9 that about 500 years ago, an ancestor of this priest, who resided at Pune, had resolved to build a temple of Devi. The same night, he had a dream in which Devi appeared and told him that her temple already existed at the site in Hathira near Kurukshetra. He was directed by Devi to go there and bring the temple out from under the ground. He proceeded to Hathira and with the help of some local people managed to reclaim the temple and take out some idols. When I visited the temple, I saw many pilgrims, who had come from far and near. I was told that big fairs were held there during Navaratri in spring and autumn every year.

Notes

1. "The Antiquity of Sirsa Town" by Dr. J.K. Gupta in the Journal of Haryana Studies, Vol. XXI, Nos.!&2, 1989.
2. For much of the information figuring in this and some other paragraphs of this chapter, I have drawn upon the Encyclopaedic

District Gazetteers of India, Volume III, edited by S.C. Bhatt, Gyan Publishing House, New Delhi.

3. *Ibid.*
4. Article by Dr. J.K. Gupta mentioned at 1 above.
5. *Ibid.*
6. *Ibid.*
7. Source mentioned at 2 above.
8. Article entitled "An Ekanamsa Relief From Sirsa" by Devendra Handa in the journal of Haryana Studies, Vol. X, No. 2, 1978, published by the Kurukshetra University, Kurukshetra, Haryana.
9. Quoted by Harihar Panda in his article "Kurukshetra and the Solar Eclipse" in the brochure brought out by the Kurukshetra Development Board to mark the solar eclipse on September 23, 1987.
10. हन्यात् कुरुक्षेत्रकान् मध्यदेश सहितान् दृष्टो ग्रहः श्रावणे।।
11. Harihar Panda's article cited above.
12. पश्चात् संध्याकाले संवर्तो नाम घूखताभ्रशिखः।
    नक्षत्रे भवति वधो येषां राज्ञां प्रवक्ष्ये तान्।
    चित्रासु कुरुक्षेत्राधिपस्य मरण समादिशेत ज्ञः।।
13. Harihar Panda's article cited above.
14. *Ibid.*
15. *Ibid.*
16. *Ibid.*
17. *Ibid.*
18. *Ibid.*
19. *Ibid.*
20. कुरुक्षेत्रे माहपुण्यं राहु ग्रस्त दिवाकरे।
21. स्नात एव समाप्नोति कृत्वा श्राद्धं च मानवः।
    यत्किंचिद् दष्कृतं कर्म स्त्रिया वा पुरुषेण वा।।१९८।।
    स्नातमात्रस्य तत् सर्व नश्यते नात्र संशयः।
    पद्मवर्णेन यानेन ब्रह्मलोकं प्रपद्यते।।१९९।।
    —Mahabharata, Vana Parva, 81, 118-119
22. अमावस्या यथा चंव राहुग्रस्ते दिवाकरे।
    अश्वमेधसहस्रस्य सम्यगिष्टसथ यत्फलं
    स्नात एव तदाप्नोति कृत्वा श्राद्धं च मानवः।।
23. यस्तत्र भोजयेद विप्रं षड्रसं विधिपूर्वकम्।
    एकेन भोजितेनव कोटिभंवति भोजिता।।
24. यस्त्र कारयेव् होमं सन्निहित्यां समीपतः।
    एकैकाहुति दानेन कोटिहोम फलं लभेत्।।
    —Skanda Purana
25. उक्तमेवाक्षयं श्रद्धं धर्मराजनिषेवितम्।
    श्रद्धं दतमआवस्यां विधिना च यथाक्रमम।

पंसः सन्निहित्यां तु कुरुक्षेत्रे विशेषतः।
अचार्ययित्वा पितृस्तत्र स पुत्रस्त्वनृणों भवेत्।

26. सूर्योपराग सुमहानासीत् कल्यक्षये यथा।
स्यमन्तपज्चकं क्षेत्रं ययुः श्रेयो विधित्सया।
महत्मां तीर्थं यात्रायां तत्रागम भारती प्रजाः।
ययुर्भारत तत्क्षेत्रं स्वमघं क्षपयिष्णवः।।
27. Dr. Amar Singh's article in the brochure brought out by the Kurukshetra Development Board to mark the solar eclipse of September 23, 1987.
28. शर्वाणी देवता तत्र कुरुक्षेत्रे च गुल्फतः।
स्थाणुनीम च सावित्रो मणिवेदिकदेशतः।।
29. Article by Krishna Dhamija 'Nanha' in the Punjab Kesari, new Delhi, dated March 29, 1999.

11

Thanesar, the Place of Lord Shiva, Harshavardhana and Sufi Saints, Sheikh Chilli and Qutb Jalaluddin

Adjoining Kurukshetra is Thanesar, which also my wife and I visited during our Kurukshetra trip in September, 1988. Its old name is Sthanvishvara, which was derived from the word 'Sthaṇu', another name of Lord Shiva. It is said that the Shiva temple in this city is the oldest in our country. In ancient Buddhist and Jain literature, mention is made of a village of Brahmins by name 'Thuna' located to the west of Madhyadesa.

Scholars have identified this village with Thanesar. The Mahabharata refers to this place as 'Sthanutirth' of which Lord Shiva himself had laid the foundation.[1] It is after 'Sthanutirth' that this place has been named as Sthanvishvara or Thanesar [2]. The name given to it in the Matsya Purana is 'Sthaneshvar'.[3]

There is a tank in Thanesar (the Sthaneshvara tank) whose water is so sacred that by simply taking a dip in it, King Vena got cured of his leprosy. Legend has it that the king, who was being carried in a palanquin, halted at this spot when he saw a dog cross the river Saraswati, stop near the palanquin and shake itself. He was astonished to see that "each spot thus wetted immediately became whole".4 the king at once plunged himself into the stream and came out entirely cleansed of his leprosy.

The other landmark of great religious significance in Thaner is the Sthanvishvara Mahadeva temple, which my wife and I made a point of visiting. It was built by an ancestor of King Harsha, who had established his capital at Thanesar.

An interesting account of the great religious significance of this Shiva temple is given in the Vamana Purana. Sages Sanaka and

Valkhilya, who were the spiritual sons of Lord Brahma, constantly kept themselves immersed in meditation, penance and other spiritual activities, but still did not succeed in pleasing Lord Shiva. When asked about this by his consort Uma, Lord Shiva said that these sages neither knew what true religion was nor were they devoid of passion (Kama) and anger (Krodha). In fact, Shiva branded them as foolish—an unparliamentary word, no doubt.

So saying, Lord Shiva proceeded to the hermitage of these sages, taking the guise of a beggar and asked for alms. The wives of the sages made no secret of the fact that they were charmed by Shiva's appearance. This enraged the sages, who started chasing Shiva with sticks and stones in order to beat him up. At this point, Lord Shiva disappeared from the scene, leaving behind the 'Linga' that was his alternative form. As a sequel to Shiva's unhappiness over the conduct of the sages, the people on earth began to suffer in various ways. Feeling greatly concerned, the sages approached Lord Brahma, who rebuked them for having invited their misfortune by showing disrespect to Lord Shiva. Along with the sages, Lord Brahma then proceeded to meet Lord Shiva in order to seek a way out of the difficult situation. They all first reached the Kailash mountain and offered their prayers and eulogies to Shiva.

Shiva was pleased and directed them to proceed to a forest where there was a Linga. They were told to take the Linga to Sthanutirth, set it up there and worship it, which alone would help them in achieving their objective. Accordingly, the sages went to the forest and discovered the Linga there. But unfortunately, the ages and even the gods could not move the Linga from that place. The sages again met Brahma and, along with him, went to Shiva to tell him of their discomfiture. They requested Shiva to lend his hand in moving the Linga to Sthanutirth. Shiva now accompanied the sages to the forest and assumed the form of an elephant which lifted the Linga with its trunk and placed it on the bank of the sacred Sthanishvara tank. In great jubilation, the gods and sages sang in praise of Lord Shiva, who now gave up the guise of an elephant and entered the Linga. That explains the great spiritual importance of this Linga.

The Vamana Purana has dilated upon the diverse aspects of this Linga's spiritual significance. There is a banyan tree near this place, the very sight of which rids a person of all sins.5 Each day, at noon, the seas, rivers and lakes converge at Sthanutirtha.6 Whoever has a view of the banyan tree here is relieved of all sins. Under the influence of Sthanutirtha, sins committed, knowingly or unknowingly, by any person—a man or a woman—are eliminated. It is said that a person, who sees the 'Linga' at Sthanutirtha or touches the banyan tree there, is liberated and achieves his goal by taking a dip in its waters. Even by simply remembering the name of Sthanvishvara's Sthanu, one is believed to be liberated from all sins.[7]

It is said that anybody, who bathes in the Sthaneshvara tank on the 14th day of the dark fortnight of the moon in the month of Chaitra (March-April), derives great virtue. The Pandavas are believed to have come here along with Lord Krishna on the eve of the Mahabharata battle, worshipped Sthanvishvara Mahadev and received blessings for their victory. Maharshi Dadhichi worshipped this deity, which endowed him with a body as strong as the thunderbolt and made it possible for his bones to be used as thunderbolt. On the eastern bank of the Sthaneshvara tank, sage Vishwamitra is believed to have done penance. The idols of many Hindu deities have been put up in the Sthanvishvara Mahadev temple complex making it easy for the pilgrims to worship most of their deities. Near the Sthaneshvara tank, we saw the beautiful Gurdwara built to commemorate the visit to this place of the ninth Sikh Guru Tegh Bahadur.

Thanesar was an important centre of the worshippers of the sun-god as is evident from the names of some members of the Vardhana dynasty such as Aditya Vardhana and Prabhakara Vardhana and their title 'Paramaditya-bhaktas'. In fact, Surya (i. e. The sun) is one of the several 'Adityas' that are mentioned in the Vedas, Puranas, Brahmanas and Visvakarmashastra. The Adityas are said to be eternal beings with an inner core of celestial light, who protect men from distress and also give them offspring, prosperity and wealth.[8]

Several years ago, an image of Aditya-Surya was found at Thanesar and was kept in the museum of the Kurukshetra University. This image, which is believed to belong to the 10th or 11th century A.D., testifies to the fact that sun-worship was quite popular during the rule of the Vardhanas and the Pratiharas and later as well. The image has some unique features, in view of which a scholar has described it as "a remarkable piece of sculpture in the domain of art and iconography."[9]

In Thanesar, I was shown some traces of an old fort probably built by King Dalip, an ancestor of Kuru, which was now totally in ruins. Close by was a big mound known as Harsha Ka Tilla where recent excavations are reported to have revealed many old relics of our history.

Thanesar and the adjoining territory once formed part of the Magadhan empire as becomes amply clear from the discovery here of an Ashokan Stupa. In due course, this region witnessed considerable political chaos and confusion as a result of invasions by foreign peoples such as the Bactrians, Greeks, Parthians, Scythians and Kushans. This paved the way for the Guptas to establish their rule here.

Thanesar's historical importance derived from its position as the capital of King Harsha Vardhana, who ruled in the 7th century A.D. After the break-up of the Gupta empire in the 6th century A.D. there were signs of political disintegration reflected in the rise of several independent States in northern India. One of these was the kingdom of Thanesar, which for some time in the 7th century A.D., under the leadership of Harsha Vardhana, brought back a limited measure of political solidarity that was somewhat reminiscent of what the imperial Guptas had achieved. Thanesar was the capital of the kingdom founded by Pushpabhuti in what is now called Haryana (then known as Shrikantha Janapada by virtue of its association with a Naga chief, Shrikantha).

Harsha's court poet, Banabhatta, has given the names of several rulers of this dynasty in his Harsha Charita such as Naravardhana, Rajyavardhana and Adtiyavardhana, whose power received a boost after his marriage with the sister of one of the later Gupta kings. It was Adiyavardhana's son, Prabhakaravardhana, also known as Pratapashila, who waged successful wars against the Hunas, extended his territory, established his rule over Punjab and the North West and spread his influence over Gandharva. His position improved further after he gave his daughter Rajyashri in marriage to Grahavarmana, the Maukhari prince of Kanauj. In fact, he received substantial help from the Maukhari dynasty of Kanauj in his fight with the Hunas.

In Bana's Harsha-Charita, many epithets have been used to describe Prabhakaravardhana's qualities as a warrior: "a lion to the Huna deer, a burning fever to the king of Sindhu, a troubler of the sleep of Gurjara king, a bilious fever to that scent-elephant, the lord of Gandhara, destroyer of the skill of the Latas, an axe to the creeper which is the goddess of fortune (or sovereignty) of Malava".[10] However, all said and done, his kingdom comprised nothing more than the territory of present-day Haryana and eastern Punjab.

Prabhakaravardhana died on account of sudden illness, when his eldest son, Rajyavardhana had gone on an expedition against the Hunas. Rajyavardhana rushed back to Thanesar post haste to find his father already dead. Prabhakaravardhana's wife, Queen Yashomati, had burnt herself on the bank of the Saraswati to avoid widowhood—perhaps an instance of the custom of 'Sati'. Rajyavardhana offered kingship to his brother, Harsha, but the latter declined.

It appears that Rajyavardhana became the King of Thanesar in 605 A.D. But tragedy struck as he received the news that soon after the death of Prabhakaravardhana, Deva Gupta, King of Malwa, assisted by Shashank, King of Bengal, had advanced against Kanauj, captured the city, killed Grahavarman, King of Kanauj (brother-in-law of Rajyavardhana) and imprisoned Rajyashri (wife of Grahavarmana and sister of Rajyavardhana). Rajyavardhana marched against the King of Malwa and defeated the latter, but he himself was treacherously killed by Shashank, the King of Bengal, who was an ally of the King of Malwa. (Dr. R.C. Mazumdar, the noted historian, does not accept the view that Rajyavardhana's murder was accomplished by treachery)

Harsha, then all of sixteen years of age, reluctantly became the King of Thanesar in 606 A.D. And swore vengeance against the King of Gauda. He went in search of his sister, Rajyashri, who had, after the death of her husband, managed to get her release from prison and proceeded to the Vindhya forests, where she was wandering about aimlessly, refusing to take any food. Harsha was able to locate her just at the time she was about to commit 'Sati' by throwing herself into the fire. Then, at the suggestion of Rajyashri, Harsha brought about the union of the kingdoms of Thanesar and Kanauj and transferred his capital from Thanesar to Kanauj. However, before achieving all this, Harsha had to get rid of the brother of Grahavarmana, who had perhaps been installed as the King of Kanauj in place of his brother, presumably at the instance of Shashank.

Harsha extended his empire from Valabhi (Gujarat) and Malwa to Mithila (Bihar) and Utkal (Orissa). However, his efforts to subdue Shashank of Bengal did not meet with any conspicuous success.[11] But it is quite possible that he had for some time been the suzerain power in Bengal [12], perhaps after the death of Shashank. But many historians including Dr. R. C. Mazumdar have pointed out that Harsha's empire was not as extensive as that of the Guptas before him or that of the Pratiharas, who followed him. Some have attributed the excessive importance given to Harsha to the eulogies of Banabhatta and the Chinese traveller, Hiuen Tsang.

Having said all this, we must at the same time take note of the fact that Harsha was a great ruler and military leader, besides being a patron of art and literature and a highly religious person. Notwithstanding all the difficulties that confronted him at the time he ascended the throne of Thanesar as virtually a young lad, he soon converted the small kingdom of Thanesar into the most powerful one in northern India.

E.R. Cowell and F.W. Thomas, who have provided an authentic English translation of Banabhatta's Harsha-Charita, have called Harsha the Akbar of the 'Hindu period' of Indian history in whose regime of tolerance, the adherents of the contending religions—Brahmanism and Buddhism—seemed to forget their rivalries in a common feeling of loyalty, just as the Rajputs and Mohammedans served Akbar with equal devotion. According to these authors, the only difference was that while Akbar's reign was presented to the world by full contemporary narratives such as those of Abul Fazl and Abul Kadir Badauni, Harsha's reign came to be known only through passing allusions made by the Chinese traveller Hiuen Tsang.

Hiuen Tsang's Account of His experiences in India Given in his Book Si-Yu-Ki (or Record of the Western World) provides a fascinating portrait of Harsha's personality, religious outlook and greatness, besides the state of administration, life-styles, religious beliefs and social customs in different parts of India. I do not wish to go into al that since it does not have a direct bearing on Haryana. A fact that deserves mention in this context is that some of his observations gave a somewhat negative account of life in the Sthanvishvara region.[13] He found the soil here fertile, the climate warm and the crops abundant. But the rich families vied with each other in indulging in extravagance. The manners and customs of the people were said to be 'illiberal". The people were greatly devoted to magical arts and highly prized outlandish accomplishments. The majority pursued trade and few were given to farming. This assessment of Hiuen Tsang may have been based on what he saw in the cities only. There were three Buddhist monasteries with 700 professed Buddhists, all followers of Hinayana. There were also over 100 Deva (Brahmanical) temples and the non-Buddhists were very numerous. Harsha's capital, Sthanvishvara, was surrounded by a district called the "Place of Religious Merit", which referred to Kurukshetra, known as 'Dharmakshetra'.

While Hiuen Tsang's account deals with the country at large, Banabhatta's account in Harsha-Charita is more Haryana-specific. Bana gives a vivid picture of the country called Shrikanta (which broadly stood for the territory of present-day Haryana) and of Thanesar (or Sthaneswara), the capital of that country. Though Bana's language is full of rhetoric and hyperbole, I consider it worthwhile to fully reproduce what he has said about both Shrikanta and Thanesar. About Shrikanta, he says: [14]

"Listen. There is a certain region named Crikantha, peopled by the good, a heaven of India, as it were, descended on earth, where the laws of caste usage are ever unconfused and the order of the Krita age prevails. Owing to the number of its land lotuses the ploughs, whose shares uproot the fibres as they sear the acres, excite a tumult of bees, singing, as it were, the excellencies of the good soil. Unbroken lines of Pundra sugar-cane enclosures seem besprinkled by the clouds that drink the Milky Sea (by reason of their sweetness). On every side its marches are packed with corn heaps, like extemporized mountains, distributed among the threshing floors. Throughout it is adorned with rice crops extending beyond their fields, where the ground bristles with cumin beds watered by the pots of the Persian wheel. Upon its lordly uplands are wheat crops variegated with Rajamasa patches ripe to bursting and yellow with the split bean pods. Attended by singing herdsmen mounted on buffalos, pursued by sparrows greedy for swarms of flies, gay with the tinkle of bells bound to their necks, roaming herds of cows make white its forests, revelling on Vaspachedya grass (literally means 'to be cut with tears', *i.e.*, grass that is very tender) and dropping milk as if the Milky Sea had been drunk by the bull of Civa and then divided up by him into many portions through fear of indigestion."

"Like eyes let fall by Indra when blinded by the smoke of its divers burnt sacrifices, thousands of spotted antelopes dot the districts. Regions, pale with the dust of Ketaki beds emitting white pollen gleam like the approaches of Civa's City when made grey by the sprinklings of the Prámathas. Pot-herbs and plantains blacken the soil around the villages. At every step are groups of young camels. The exits are made attractive by vine-arbours and pomegranate orchards; arbours ablaze with Pilu sprays, besmeared with the juice of hand-pressed citron leaves, having flower bunches formed of spontaneously gathered saffron filaments and travellers blissfully sleeping after drinking the juice of fresh fruit, very hostels, as it were, with wood-nymphs dispensing ambrosia: orchards, where the fruit, ripe to bursting, seems coloured by the beaks of the parrots attacking the seeds, and the flowers are tinged by the cheeks of climbing monkey tribes."

"There are lovely groves where woodrangers taste the cocoa-nut juice, where traveling folk plunder the date-trees, monkeys lick sweet-scented date juice, and partridges tear the Aruka to pieces with their beaks. Not barren are the sylvan hollows of forest pools, refuge of myriad travellers, encircled with avenues of tall Arjuna trees and turbid at the edges through the descent of herds of kine. Troops of camels and flocks of sheep form in hordes under the guardianship of camel boys. Wandering droves of mares, besmeared with the sap of crushed saffron beds, where they roll as if to seduce the steeds of the sun's chariot, visit the land, roaming like the deer of the Maruts at will, with snorting nostril and uplifted heads drinking in the air, as it were, to beget speed in the young lying in their wombs."

"Seen like wild geese amid the dusk of ever-smoking sacrifices, the reeds are white upon the earth. The land's vast resources sound through the animate world like peacocks wild at the sound of drums in concert. Good men, in conduct spotless as the moon's rays, adorn it like pearls. It has the attraction of all-welcoming hosts, like huge trees whose rich fruit is plundered by hundreds of voyagers. Great men are its bulwarks, clad, like the feet of the Himalaya, with the hair of deer, bearing the fragrance of civet. Graced is it with ponds like Visnu's navel, where fine birds are seated upon lotuses with tall stalks. Its regions are filled with wide ranches, which, like the turmoil of the churning of the Milky Ocean, wash the lands with torrents of churned milk. Such is the land of Crikantha".

"There did false doctrines fade away, as if washed out by a rain of tears due to the smoke of the Triple Fire. Sinful ways vanished, as if consumed by the burning of the bricks for altars. Demerit was scotched, as if cleft by the axes which fashioned sacrificial posts. Caste confusion ceased, as if cleansed by a rain from the smoke clouds of oblation fires. Sin fled, as if gored by the horns of the many thousands of presented oxen. Disasters were cut away, as if excised by numerous axes chiseling stones for temples. Calamities sped afar, as if routed by the tumult of munificent rites. Disease was dissipated, as if consumed by myriad blazing sacrificial kitchens. Sudden death came not near, as if alarmed by the sharp beat of holy drums stuck at bulls' wedlocks. Plagues departed, as if deafened by the never-ceasing noise of hymns. Overwhelmed, as it were, by the rule of law, mishap did not arise."

As regards Thanesar, Bana's account runs as follows: [15]

"In such a country is a certain district called Sthanvicvara, blessed, like the world's first youth, with sweet fragrance of lovely flowers, in divers pleasances; bedecked, like the road to Dharma's gymnaeceum, with many myriads of buffalos stained from rolling in saffron; whitened at its borders, like a part of the celestial realm, with yak-tail flappers shaken by the winds; blazing to all the ends of heaven, like the encampment of the Krita age, with thousands of flaming sacrificial fires; allaying all inauspicious signs, like the Brahma-world's first descent, by the meditation of Brahmarsis seated in the posture of thought; thronged, like a rival to the Northern Kurus, with hundreds of great rivers uproarious with tumult; surpassing Tripura, as it were, in having all its people unacquainted with the devastating might of Civa's arrow; bright, like a replica of the moon world, with rows of white houses plastered with stucco; like a claimant to the name of Kuvera's City, oppressing the world with clanking ornament of wine-flushed beauties."

"Sages entitled it a hermitage, courtesans a lover's retreat, actors a concert hall, foes the city of death, seekers of wealth the land of the philosopher's stone, sons of the sword the soil of heroes, aspirants to knowledge the preceptor's home, singers the Gandharvas' city, scientists the Great Artificer's temple, merchants the land of profit, bards the gaming-house, good men the gathering of the virtuous, refugees the cage of adamant, libertines the Rogue's Meet, wayfarers the reward of their good deeds, treasure-seekers the mine, quietists the Buddhist monastery, lovers the Apsaras' City, troubadours the festival congress, Brahmans the stream of wealth." [16]

About the women of Thanesar, Bana observes:

"There are women like elephants in gait, yet noble-minded; virgins, yet attached to worldly pomp; dark, yet possessed of rubies; their faces are brilliant with white teeth, yet is their breath perfumed with the fragrance of wine; their bodies are like crystal, yet their limbs are soft as acacia flowers; they are unattainable by paramours, yet robed in bodices; wide are their hips, yet are they possessed of thin waists; lovely are they, yet honeyed in speech; they trip not, yet have a bright and captivating beauty; they are without curiosity, yet wedded."

"Their eyes are a natural mundamala wreath, the garlands of lotus leaves are a mere burden. The images of their curls in the convex of their cheeks are ear-pendants that give no trouble; Tamala shoots are a superfluity. The talk of their dear ones forms happy ear-ornaments; rings and the like are but affectation. Their cheeks alone give a perpetual sunshine; for pomp only have they jeweled lamps by night. Tribes of bees attracted by their breath are their beauteous veils, the duty of noble women their hair-nets. Their voices alone are their sweet lutes, harp-playing is but an irrelevant accomplishment. Laughs are their exceeding fragrant perfumes; needless is camphor powder. The gleam of their lips is a more brilliant cosmetic; saffron unguent is a worthless blot upon their loveliness. Their arms are the softest of playfully smiting wands [17]; purposeless are lotus stalks. Drops of the sweat of youthful warmth are their artful bosom ornaments, necklaces but a burden. Their laps are broad squares of crystal slabs for their lovers; jeweled couches in their mansions a needless means of repose. Bees clinging in greed for such lotuses are their resonant foot-ornaments; useless are anklets of sapphire. Domestic kalahamsas, summoned by the tinkle of their anklets, are the unfailing companions of their walks; attendants are but the accidents of greatness."

A very pleasing description of the women of ancient Thanesar indeed!

Some other observations made by Bana should greatly please the people of Thanesar and of Haryana as a whole. It has been said that the people in those days used to voluntarily deposit their taxes and that the officials of the government never harassed the ordinary people. The houses of Thanesar looked clean as they used to get regularly white-washed.

According to Bana, nothing evil or ominous happened to those who lived in Thanesar. That is why this place was the best replica of Brahmalok.[18]

Bana also describes Thanesar as a veritable Alaka, the land of Kuvera, the lord of all riches and wealth, because the whole world used to resound with the tinkle of ornaments worn by women here.[19]

Bana's observations on the women of Thanesar bring to my mind what several. other Sanskrit poets, particularly Kalidasa, wrote on the beauty of women. Kalidasa's verses on the beauty of Shakuntala, Uma and Urvashi are well-known. But what particularly led me to recall the name of Kalidasa in this context was the fact that he has dilated on the glory of Kurukshetra region in his Meghdoot. There, he suggests to the Cloud Messenger to proceed to Brahmavarta, where Arjuna had shown his valour in the battle of Kurukshetra. Kalidasa also advises the Cloud Messenger to purify himself in the sacred waters of the Saraswati river. I quote here from R.H. Wilson's English translation of the Sanskrit text of Meghdoot:

"Hence to the land of Brahma's favoured sons,
O'er Kuru's fatal field, thy journey runs.
With deepest glooms hang o'er the deadly plain,
Dewed with the blood of mighty warriors slain.
There Arjuna's wrath opposing armies felt,
And countless arrows strong Gandiva dealt,
Thick as thy drops, that, in the pelting shower,
Incessant hurtle round the shrinking flower.[20]
O'er Saraswati's waters wing your course,
And inward prove their purifying force;
Most holy, since, oppressed with heaviest grief,
The ploughshare's mighty Lord here sought relief;

No longer quaffed the wine cup with his wife,
But mourned in solitude o'er kindred strife.[21]

The 'land of Brahma's chosen sons" or 'Brahmavarta', the abode of Brahma, is described in Manu Samhita in the following words: Between the two rivers, Saraswati and Drishadwati, lies the tract sages have named Brahmavarta, because it was frequented by the gods. In his description of Brahmavarta, Kalidasa has managed to give a brief account of the battle of Kurukshetra, highlighting Arjuna's bravery. He has also brought in the role of Balarama, the eldest brother of Krishna, whose hallmark was his weapon, a ploughshare, with which he used to pull his enemies, thrown off their horses, so that he could then despatch with his club. Krishna had sided with the Pandavas in the Mahabharata war, but Balarama did not join any of the two sides and retired into a life of seclusion, settling down on the bank of the Saraswati river, as he was unhappy with the turn of events that led to the battle of Kurukshetra fought by rival kinsmen. Out of grief, Balaram gave up his favourite liquor, which in normal times he used to drink, sitting in the company of his wife Revati, who shared her consort's joy and the sparkle of whose eyes was reflected by the liquor that he drank. There are definitely shades here of Omar Khayyam!

Poet Kalidasa highlights the spiritual value of the Saraswati river on which he bases his plea to the Cloud Messenger to proceed to this river as a means of securing inner purification.

What kind of king, queen, prince and princess did the ruling family of Shrikantha or ancient Haryana have? Here again Bana is at his eulogical best. From Pushpabhuti, the ruler of Shrikantha, there issued a line of kings "free from the stain of violating Dharma, as living beings came from the commencement of the golden age; dominating the world by their splendour, like the rays from the source of light; thronging the regions with their armies in array, like the hills sprung from Brahma; strong to support the world, like the sky elephants born from Brahma's hand; rising in might to guard the oceans, like clouds from the season of rain; bestowing the fruits of desire, like trees of Paradise from the Heavenly Garden ...."[22]

Prabhakaravardhana, a king of this dynasty and father of Harsha also receives his share of praise from Bana. He is described as a "king of kings", "famed far and wide under a second name Pratapacila, a lion to the Huna deer, a burning fever to the king of the Indus land........In the seraglios of slain rivals, his valour was, as it were, materialized in the form of the five elements, fire in the women's hearts, water in the hollows of their eyes, wind in their sigh, earth upon their forms, ether in the vacant solitude."

Prabhakaravardhana's queen, Yashovati was, as Bana says, "noble as Cankara's Parvati, but remaining Sati in another incarnation, holding the heart fast like Vishnu's Lakshmi, with sparkling, glancing eyes like the moon's Rohini, mother of all her people. Prajapati's Buddhi .... endowed with the gait of a hamsa, the voice of a cuckoo, the answering love of a ruddy-goose, the full bosoms of the rainy season, the laugh of wine ..... She was honey in converse, ambrosia to those who sought delight, rain to her servants, beatitude to her friends, bamboo-like to her elders ...."

Rajyavardhana, the first son of Pravakaravardhana is described by Bana as "a prince composed as it were of lightning atoms to quell the cabals of all kings, capable of supporting the whole world's weight, as if endowed with the mechanism of Cisa's hood; heart-shaker of all kings, as if constructed with the limbs of sky elephants. His birth was a birth of joy to the people, who became, as it were, dancing incarnate. For each month, which seemed a day, the king held a great festival, innumerable blown horns noisily sounding, hundreds of beaten tom-toms merrily booming, a world filled to overflowing with the burden of deep-rumbling drums, the hearts of all mankind ravished in a madness of delight."

Then was born a second son, Harshavardhana, to Prabhakaravardhana, about whom the royal astrologer, after making the necessary calculations, predicted: "the son now born to your majesty shall be coryphaens of the Seven Emperors, bearer of the Seven Imperial Signs and the Great Jewels, lord of the Seven Oceans, performer of all the sacrifices of Seven Forms, the peer of him of the Seven Steeds."[23]

Then the celebrations began. As Bana says: "Instantly unblown horns rang out spontaneously loud and sweet. Unbeaten boomed the consecration drum deep as the roar of ocean in turmoil. Unstruck the auspicious tabors pealed .... So proceeded the great birth festival, the order of the royal household gone, the pretence of the chamberlains laid low, the mace-bearers robbed of their maces, entrance to the harem in no wise criminal, master and servants reduced to a level .... Drunk and sober not to be distinguished, noble maidens and harlots equally merry, the whole population of the capital set a-dancing .....There drunken slave women allured the favourites, while the monarch himself looked on with a secret smile ..... In this place and that, harlot-women danced to the accompaniment of instrumental music ...... Whispering softly, like cuckoos, in low passionate tones, they sang the words of vulgar mimes, ambrosia to their lovers' ears.......As if possessed, they were surrounded by throngs of princes ..... Adding passionateness to passion itself, a glow of love, a joy to joy ...... All womankind being thus set dancing, the earth crimsoned by trickling lac from their feet, seemed rosy with the flush of love. Their round gleaming bosoms made the festival like a mass of auspicious pitches."

Then a third child was born to queen Yashomati. It was a girl—Rajyashri, who, in the words of Bana, "added to the two sons, formed a further ornament, like the line of a necklace above her two bosoms."

Bana gives a highly flattering account of Harshavardhana, the Emperor, in the following words[24]: "This then is Emperor Cri Harsa, that union of separate glories—noble in birth and of well-chosen name—the lord of the field bounded by the four oceans—the enjoyer of all the fruits of Brahma's pillar—the surpasser of all the victories won by all the kings of ancient times. Through him the earth does indeed possess a true King! His youthful exploits, unlike Krisna's, transgress not right; his freaks of power cause no offence to the man of refinement as did those of Civa; his boasts lead to no destruction of families as did those of Indra to that of the cowpens; unlike Yama, he is not too fond of wielding the rod of punishment; unlike Varuna, his treasure-houses are not guarded by thousands of pitiless sea-monsters; unlike Kuvera, seeking an interview with him is never fruitless; unlike Jina, the sight of him is never without solid result; unlike the Moon, his glories do not wane. Wonderful is his royalty, surpassing the gods! His liberality cannot find range enough in suppliants, nor his knowledge in doctrines to be learned; his poetical skill finds words fail, as his valour lacks opportunities to exercise it; his energy wants scope and his fame sighs for a wider horizon; his kindly nature seeks in vain more hearts to win; his virtues exhaust the powers of number, and all the fine arts are too narrow a field for his genius."

"Under this monarch are found only the cloths worn by devotees in meditation, and not forged documents; the royal figures of sculptors and not the vulgardisputes with kings; only bees quarrel in collecting dews (dues); the only feet ever cut off are those in metre; only chessboards teach the positions of the four 'members'; there is no cutting off the four principal limbs of condemned criminals; only snakes hate Garuda, the king of bird (dvija-guru); no one hates Brahmans or gurus; and the followers of the Mimansa alone have to ponder problems in administering justice (adhikarana), while they examine the several adhikaranas or 'cases for discussion' in their system."

Giving an account of the people's religious beliefs and practices, Bana has said that in most houses, Lord Shiva was worshipped. There is no doubt that Thanesar was the city of Lord Shiva, as its very name was derived from 'Sthanu', one of the many names by which he is known. Shiva was worshipped in accordance with strict religious rites. It is said that since the bull is regarded as the vehicle of Lord Shiva, some big bulls used to be let loose in ancient Thanesar in the evenings. The Pashupat Shaivites, who smeared their bodies with ash, were the dominant religious sect here. They were very popular in the Haryana region, as is evident from the many references to them made by Hiuen Tsang in his account and by Bnabhatta in his Harsh-Charita, Banabhatta mentions the various rites performed by the Pashupatas, which seemed to be similar to those of the Kapalikas. The monastery of Mattamayura near Rohtak and Sirsa were important centres of the Pashupata sect.

Many old idols and artifacts dating back to the Sunga, Gupta, Kushana and Gurjara-Pratihara periods have been discovered at Thanesar. During archaeological excavations at Daulatpur, about ten miles from Thanesar, some old seals were found with the Sanskrit word "Sthaneshvarasya" inscribed on them in Brahmi script, with an oblique line drawn below it, which was perhaps meant to symbolize a snake or the river Saraswati. The seals may have been those of the priest of the Shiva temple of Thanesar.

Perhaps I have strayed a bit too far. A fact that struck me during my visits to this region is that much of what Banabhatta has said about the economic scene in the Thanesar region holds good even today. While at Thanesar and other places near by, I often tried to compare the modern face of these places with the picture depicted by Bana. I felt that many things had remained unchanged despite the lapse of so many centuries.

As has been pointed out by an author,[25] after a perusal of Bana's Harsha-Charita, a question that arises in one's mind remains unanswered. Both Thanesar and Kurukshetra exist cheek by jowl, justifying the nomenclature of a twin city. Yet, nowhere does Bana mention the name of Kurukshetra in his work. How could he have ignored Kurukshetra so completely?

After the death of Harshavardhana in 647 A.D., confusion engulfed Thanesar region. Harsha's empire practically vanished into the thin air and several small kingdoms cropped up on the ruins of his empire.

Visiting several p[laces in and around Thanesar on different occasions, I got an insight into the ancient legends as well as the historical certitudes that are woven around this region. There are places like Kshirahi and Vasa, where the water of the Saraswati is said to have turned into milk (Kshira) to assuage the thirst of the fatigued Pandavas. There is another place, Asthipura, to the west of Thanesar and south of Aujas Ghat, where the bodies of those killed in the Mahabharata battle were said to have been cremated or buried. The Chinese traveler, Hiuen Tsang, who visited this place, had observed: "The bodies of those killed in the battle were strewn about in confused masses, so great was the number of the slain, and the huge skeletons of those heroes still cover the district, which popular tradition calls the Place of Religious Merit."[26]

My wife and I also visited the holy tank, Kamal Nabh, where Lord Brahma, the creator of the universe, was said to have been born out of a lotus (Kamal) that grew out of the Nabhi (navel) of Bhagwan Vishnu, when he was reclining in the ocean of milk. Then Brahma commenced his penance at Brahmsarovar in Kurukshetra in order to have a vision of Vishnu. Soon after this, at the suggestion of Vishnu, Brahma commenced the process of creation of the universe.

Once we visited the Haveli of Baba Shravan Nath built in the 17th century A.D. that was later being looked after by the Maha Nirvani Akhra. According to tradition, Baba Lachhman Giri had once visited this place and sought some milk. The disciples of Baba Shravan Nath went on pouring huge quantities of milk from his Kamandal (a saint's or devotee's water-can), but, wonder of wonders, neither the Kamandal became empty nor did Baba Shravan Nath's can get filled up! the two Babas now recognized each other's supernatural powers and greeted each other in a warm embrace. Inside the temple here, we saw the beautiful marble statues of the Pandavas and some Hindu deities.

We saw the famous Valmiki Ashram located opposite the Thanesar Railway Station on the road to Pehowa. This called to our minds the story of the Ramayana and served to highlight the fact that this region not merely provided the stage for the enactment of the Mahabharata drama, but had also figured in the chain of many events of the Ramayana. Inside the complex, there is a temple of Maharshi Valmiki with a beautiful statue of the Maharshi. Close by is the temple of Sati Mata Annapurna.

There is an interesting story about how the Sati Mata Annapurna temple came up at this place. It is said that once the gods became displeased with goddess Annapurna for some reason and threw her out of heaven. After wandering about for a considerable length of time,

Annapurna arrived at the place where the present-day Valmiki Ashram is located. She met goddess Sati, who used to live here and who offered her refuge. Once there was a serious failure of crops on earth for more than a couple of years at a stretch, which caused great distress to the people. The gods, who felt concerned over the people's sufferings, requested Lord Vishnu to initiate action for bringing relief to them. Vishnu came to the place where Sati had given refuge to Annapurna. In order to enlist Annapurna's help in relieving the distress of the people, Vishnu urged her to return to heaven. But Sati did not approve of this suggestion and asked what guarantee there was that Annapurna would not be thrown out of heaven again. Upon this, Vishnu directed Annapurna to proceed to heaven, after asking the moon and sun gods to be witnesses to this event. Since then, during lunar and solar eclipses, offerings of grains are made at Kurukshetra because this earns great religious merit.

There is also a story about the circumstances in which Maharshi Valmiki arrived at this place in Kurukshetra. When Lord Rama decided to banish Sita because of the persistence of popular suspicion about her chastity, Lakshmana , acting under Rama's orders, accompanied Sita to the forests in order to leave her there. Deserted by all, Sita proceeded to the hermitage of Valmiki located at Badur because earlier, during her exile along with Rama, she had visited this place and had immensely liked its environment as well as the orderliness that obtained there. Valmiki welcomed her gladly and began to address her as 'Van Devi' (goddess of the forests).

It is said that while living at Valmiki's hermitage, Sita used to reflect on the events of her life. She thought that it was on her account that Ravana, a Brahmin versed in all the four Vedas, and his numerous followers had got killed. Maharshi Valmiki, who noticed Sita's grief over these events, consoled her saying that it was none of her fault because everything had happened as ordained by fate. At this stage, Sita once told Valmiki that she longed to meet the great sages and saints of the country and to seek their advice and guidance. Valmiki suggested that she should visit Dharmakshetra Kurukshetra that was inhabited by many great sages including Pulastya, the elder brother of Ravana, whose hermitage was located on the bank of the sacred Saraswati river. She readily agreed and this was how Maharshi Valmiki arrived at Kurukshetra along with Sita and some of his disciples. First of all, Valmiki took Sita to the hermitage of Pulastya of whom she wanted to beg forgiveness for the chain of events that had led to Ravana's death.

Thereafter, they visited Siwan, a village about six miles north of Kaithal. Siwan is a corruption from 'Seoban' or 'Sitaban', the forest home of Sita. There is an old shrine of Sita at this place, whose architecture is unique and impressive. During Muslim rule, a part of the shrine had been thrown into the near-by tank. According to local tradition, this was the place where mother earth had opened up to draw Sita into herself in response to her appeal when she could not accept the ignominy of taking an oath for the second time, in the presence of all and sundry, to vindicate her chastity. This, however, looks like a local folk tale, because in the Ramayana, it is said that this event had taken place at Ayodhya.

When Sita arrived at Valmiki Asram, she was already pregnant. It was here that she gave birth to her twin sons—Lava and Kusha, whose features had a striking resemblance with those of their father—Rama. When Sita was living at this hermitage, Rama performed the Ashwamedha sacrifice at Ayodhya to establish his supremacy across the globe. Under the rules of this sacrifice, Rama's horses were sent out to the various kingdoms in all directions. If any king or person wanted to challenge Rama's authority, he had to get hold of one of these horses and stop it from going back to Rama. In that event Rama would have to have a fight with that person and subdue him as a token of his supremacy. No one stopped any of these horses or challenged Rama's authority, according to the original Sanskrit version of Valmiki's Ramayana.

However, in the Bengali version of Ramayana, authored by Krittivasa, on which we were weaned in Bengal, there is an important deviation from the account given in the Valmiki Ramayana. In the account of Krittivasa, Rama's horse was stopped at Valmiki Ashrama by the young twins—Lava and Kusha. Valmiki had then gone away to Chitrakoot, leaving the Ashrama in charge of the boys and asking them to ensure its protection. The boys posed a serious challenge to the authority of Rama, who did not know that they were his sons, because their identity had been kept a secret all this time. The Ramayana of Krittivasa gives a fascinating account of the series of fierce battles that the brave boys fought with Shatrughna, Bharata, Lakshmana and eventually Rama himself and of how they defeated their uncles and father, how all the latter as well as Hanumana and Jambuvana, the devotees of Rama, fell down unconscious in the course of these battles. When Sita heard of all this, she came running to the field of battle and began to cry thinking that Rama and the others had all been killed by her sons, who would thus be tarnished by the sin of patricide.

At this stage, Valmiki, who was at Chitrakoot, learnt about all that was happening back home through his supernatural powers and rushed post haste to his Ashrama. Taking charge of the situation, he instantaneously secured the sacred waters from a particular tank and had them sprinkled over the bodies of all the fallen heroes as well as the millions (according to the text of the book) of horses, elephants and soldiers. And hey presto, all of them stood up, hale and hearty, as if nothing had happened! Then Rama and party went to back to Ayodhya to complete the Ashwamedha sacrifice and establish Rama's supremacy.

After this, Lava and Kusha were taken by Valmiki to Ayodhya to sing the song of Ramayana composed by Valmiki and also set to musical Ragas by him. This was, of course, a very impressive and virtuoso performance. This part of the story figures in both Valmiki Ramayana and Krittivasa Ramayana. Nobody in the august gathering knew at that time that Lava and Kusha were the sons of Lord Rama, Highly pleased with the superb music of the two boys, Rama directed that some precious gifts including gold be given to the boys. But the latter refused to accept the gifts saying that they lived in the forest, eating fruits etc. And needed no gold or silver for their living![27]

We had the opportunity once of visiting Amin, a very ancient village situated on a high ground very close to Thanesar. The name of this village is a corruption from 'Abhimanyu', the son of Arjuna, who had successfully penetrated the 'Chakravyuha', a tactical battle formation, arranged by Dronacharya on behalf of the Kauravas, but had got killed after having failed to come out of the trap. Even today, this place is called Abhimanyu Kera. It was at this place that Aditi, wife of sage Kashyap, had undertaken long penance lasting over ten thousand years to achieve her objective of getting some of the gods born to her.

Another sacred place that we once passed through in this region is Kamodha at a distance of about 9 miles from Thanesar. In ancient times, it was part of Kamyakvan, an extensive forest on the bank of the Saraswati river, where the Pandavas had lived for quite some time (Yayo Saraswati teere Kayakang Nama Kananam—Mahabharata–3: 37: 37).

In Kamyakvan, there was a pilgrimage called Kameshwar. There is a temple of Kameshwar Mahadev here and a Mutt. A small brick-built room in this complex is known as Draupadi's 'Bhandar' (store). Legend has it that Draupadi had cooked food here for the Pandavas. Should this place be treated as identical with Kammasdhamma of

Buddhist literature, as some have claimed, then its antiquity should date back to the pre-Christian era. In that case, Lord Buddha had preached his religion among the people here.

After Harshavardhana, Thanesar was never the same again, at least politically. However, its importance as a pilgrimage never declined. In 1014 A.D., Thanesar was sacked by Mahmud of Ghazni, though it was later recovered by the Hindu Raja of Delhi. In the month of April, 1567 A.D., Akbar had viited this place on the occasion of a solar eclipse. Mullan Ahmad, a Muslim writer, alleges that in Akbar's time the Hindus had demolished a mosque standing in the Thanesar tank and replaced it with a temple. Prof. Sukhdev Singh Chib, author of 'This Beautiful India: Haryana", refutes this charge saying that Thanesar had been a holy place of the Hindus much before the arrival of the Muslims and that there might have been a Hindu temple in this tank, which the Muslims might have replaced with a mosque in their hey day. As he argues, the Hindus might have wreaked vengeance by replacing this mosque with a temple. Aurangzeb demolished the Thanesar temple and built a castle there allegedly as a strategic point to shoot the Hindu pilgrims.[28] It is still known as the Mughal Island. The Sikhs occupied the place in 1764 A.D. And the British took it over in 1850 A.D.

Adverting to Aurangzeb's destruction of the Thanesar temple and his harassment of the Hindu pilgrims, it is of interest to recall that the Emperor was specially fond of Gangajal (water of the Ganges). It is said that his daily food was cooked in Gangajal. It was obviously not out of any religious motive that he preferred this, as Hindus generally do. It must have been for purely earthly reasons such as the extraordinary efficacy of Ganges water that contained many beneficial chemical ingredients. It is said that many other Muslim rulers of India such as Muhammad Tughlak, Akbar and Tipu Sultan used to share this liking for Ganges water. Akbar was known to carry this water during his travels for drinking and cooking purposes!

A fact that deserves mention is that Thanesar-Kurukshetra emerged as an important centre of Sufism during Muslim rule.[29] It was at Thanesar that the famous Sufi saint Qutb Jalaluddin lived. Emperor Akbar had visited him several times and during one visit Abul Fazl was also present when the discourse centred round the 'meaning of existence' and 'cure for melancholy'. Haji Sultan Thanesari, another learned man of Kurukshetra, had translated the Mahabharata from Sanskrit into Persian. It was here that other famous personalities such as Hajrat Miraji and Darvesh Yade Moula lived. Another name deserving mention is that of Sheikh Chilli Banmuri, whose mausoleum built with marble and red stone I had occasion to see.

During one of my visits to Thanesar, I saw the mausoleum of Sheikh Chilli, a friend of Dara Shikoh and son of the Mughal Emperor Shah Jahan. Built by Emperor Shah Jahan, this marble tomb stands out prominently and is visible from several miles away. There is no other marble monument in the whole of Punjab and Haryana which is as impressive as this mausoleum. Sheikh Chilli was a Sufi saint from Iran, who had come to Thanesar during the reign of Emperor Shah Jahan to meet Hazrat Qutb Jalaluddin. Shah Jahan, who was a great admirer of Hazrat Qutb Jalaluddin on account of his spiritual powers, had got this mausoleum built for the latter at Thanesar. But Sheikh Chilli, who came to Thanesar, was doing his physical exercise one day, when he suddenly died. He was laid to rest in the mausoleum that was meant for Hazrat Qutb Jalaluddin. In Thnesar, there is a Madrasa named after Sheikh Chilli. Two mosques—Pathar Masjid and Chini Masjid—are the other landmarks of Thanesar that were shown to me during a visit.

Notes

1. यत्रेष्ट्वा भगवान् स्थाणु पूजियित्वा सरस्वतीम्।
   स्थापयामास तत्तीर्थ स्थाणु तीर्थमिति प्रभो।।

   (महा॰ शल्य ४२/६)
2. कुरुक्षेत्रे तु देवर्षे स्थाणुर्नाम महेश्वरः।
   तदेवतीर्थमभवतः स्थानेश्वरमिति स्मृतम्।।

   (वामन सरो॰ महो॰ २३/१५)
3. स्थानेश्वरे भवानी तु (मत्स्य पुराण १३:१३)
4. 'Haryana' by D.C. Verma, p. 6
5. स्थाणुतीर्थ ततो गच्छेत सहस्रलिंगशोभितम्।
   तत्र स्थाणुवटं दृष्ट्वा मुक्तों भवति किल्विषैः।।

   (वामन सरो॰ २१/३०)
6. अहन्यहनि तीर्थानि आसमुद्रसरांसि च।
   स्थाणुतीर्थ समेष्यन्ति मध्य प्राप्ते दिवाकरे।।

   (वामन सरो॰ २४/४)
7. स्थाण्वीश्वरे स्थितो मस्मात स्थाण्वीश्वरस्वतः स्मृतः।
   ये स्मरन्ति सदा स्थाणुं ते मुक्ता सर्वकिल्विषैः।।

   (वामन सरो॰ मा॰ २३/१४/१५)

8. For a detailed study, one may refer to an article "Aditya-Surya and His Rare Image From Kurukshetra" by Dr. Sheo Bahadur Singh in the Journal of Haryana Studies, Vol. XX, Nos. 1&2, 1988, pp. 1–5.
9. *Ibid.*
10. The History and Culture of the Indian People edited by R.C. Mazumdar, Volume III, p. 97.
11. *Ibid*, p. 107.
12. *Ibid*, p. 108.
13. "On Yuan Chwang's Travels in India" by Thomas Watters, p. 314.
14. As translated by E. B. Cowell and F.W. Thomas.
15. As translated by E.B. Cowell and F.W. Thomas.
16. यः तपोवनमिति मुनिभिः कामायतनमिति वेश्याभिः, संगीत–शालेति लासकैः यमनगरमिति शत्रुभिः, चिन्तामणिभूमिरिति अर्थिभिः वीरक्षेत्रमिति शस्त्रोपजीविभिः, गुरूकुलमिति विद्यार्थिभिः, गन्धर्वनगरमिति गायनैः, विस्रकर्ममन्दिरमिति विज्ञानिभिः, लाभभूमिरिति वेदेहकैः, दयूतस्थनमिति वन्दिभिः, साधुसमागम इति सदिभ् वजपव्जरमिति शरणगतैर्विटगोष्ठीति विदग्धैः, सुकृतपरिणाम इति पथिकैः, असुरविवरमिति वातिकैः, शावयाश्रम इति शमिभिः, अप्सर पुरमिति कामिभिः, महोत्सवसमाज इति चारणैः, वसुधारेति च विप्रैः अग्रह्यत।
17. प्रमदानां चक्षुरेव सहजं मुरडमालामण्डनं भारः कुवलयदलदामानि। अलकप्रतिबिम्बान्येव कपोलतलगतान्यक्लिष्टाः श्रवणावतंसाः... कपोल एव सततमालोककारकाः... वाणयेव मधुरतरा वीणा... अधरकांतिबिसर एबोज्ज्वलतरोऽड.गरागो निर्गुणो लावण्यकलंकः कुंकुमपंको, बाहव एव कोमलतमाः परिहासप्रहारवेत्रलता निष्प्रयोजनानि मृणालानि।
18. प्रथमोऽवतार इव ब्रह्यलोकस्य।
19. भूषणरव–भरित–राख्यो–
    भुवनो नामामिहार इव कुबेर नगास्य, स्थाण्वीश्वजनपद विशेषः।
20. ब्रम्हावर्त जनपद्मघश्र्छाययया गाहमानः
    क्षेभं क्षचमधनपिशुनं कौरवं तद् भजेथाः।।
    राजन्यानां शितशरणतैर्यघ गाराडीवधन्वा
    घारापातैस्वमिय कमलान्यभ्यषिघ्द्रन्मुर्खा।।
    —Megha Duta, Purva Megha
21. हित्वा हालामभिमतरसां रेवतीलोचनादक्।
    बन्धुप्रीत्या सभरविमुखो लाड़ली यारिमपेवे।।
    कृत्मा तासामभिगममपां सौम्य सारस्वती।
    सन्तः शुयस्तवमपि भविता वर्णमाचेण कृष्ण।।
    —Megha Duta, Purva Megha

22. The Harsha-Charita of Bana translated by E.B. Cowell and F.W. Thomas, pp. 100-101.
23. *Ibid*, p. 110.
24. *Ibid*, pp. 64-65.
25. Article by Dr. Amar Singh in a brochure brought out by the Kurukshetra Board on September 23, 1987.
26. On Yuan Chwang's Travels in India (AD 629 645) by Thomas Watters MRAS, p. 315.
27. दीयमानां सुवर्ण तु नागृहीतां कुशीलवौ।
    ऊचतुश्र महात्मानौ किमनेनेति विस्मितौ।।२०
    वन्येन फलमूलेन निरतौ वनवासिनौ।
    सुवर्णे्न हिरण्येन कि करिष्यावहे वने।।२१
    —Ramayana, Uttarkand, chapter 94, verses 20-21.
28. This Beautiful India: Haryana' by Sukhdev Singh Chib, p. 101.
29. Article by Dr. H.A. Phadke in the brochure brought out by the Kurukshetra Development Board on September 23, 1987.

12

Rewari and Rao Tula Ram: Haryana's World Class Cricketers: Annual Governors' Conference in Delhi: Prime Minister Helps Flood-afected Haryana, Punjab: Ch. Devi Lal's Pre-election Political Moves: Gurgaon, the Village of the Guru: The Revolutioaries of Mewat

Soon I had to visit Rewari to address an ex-servicemen's rally (Sainik rally) there on September 27, 1988. Rewari was the headquarters of the Mahendragarh district in the south-western extremity of Haryana adjoining Rajasthan. Mahendragarh, the town that had given its name to the district, was, however, not its headquarters. A year later, Rewari district was bifurcated into two—Rewari and Mahedragarh districts. While Rewari became the headquarters of the district of the same name, Narnaul was chosen as the headquarters of the Mahendragarh district, primarily because accommodation for offices was more easily available there. In my account here, I shall cover all these places, as they formed part of the same district when I paid my visit in September 1988. A year later, I had visited several other places in this region.

En route to Rewari, I visited Dharuhera, which had a very good tourist resort of the Haryana Government called Jungle Babbler. This place had a distinctive architectural style with a meandering Jallie work.

At Rewari, I was briefed by the office-bearers of the Rajya Sainik Board and the officers of the defence services as well as the State

Government about the problems of the ex-servicemen and the various measures being taken to sort them out. In my address at the Sainik rally, I dilated on these problems and the ameliorative measures that were to be initiated by the various agencies. The importance of these rallies of ex-servicemen and their family members in Haryana derived from the fact that about 11% of the Indian Army's personnel came from Haryana. Every village of Haryana had a fair sprinkling of ex-servicemen.

In the course of my discussions with several persons, who had considerable knowledge of Haryana's history and culture, I could form in my mind a rough outline of the stages through which this important part of our country's territory had evolved to its present-day social, economic and cultural status. As I understood, Mahendragarh used to be known as Kanaud in ancient times since it was generally inhabited by Brahmins of the Kannaudia clan. In Mughal days, it was a Pargana of Narnaul. There was a time when Mahendragarh was usurped by the ruler of Jaipur, but he was later overthrown by a Nawab, who was a Minister under Shah Alam, the Mughal Emperor of Delhi. Some time later, a feudatory of the Scindias ruled over this area including Rewari. Then the British annexed this territory.

Narnaul, now the headquarters of Mahendragarh district, is an ancient place that figures in the Mahabharata, its name at that time being Nar-Rashtra. Sahdev, the youngest of the Pandava brothers, is said to have ruled over this place. According to local tradition, this area was located in the midst of a thick forest, which had to be cleared before it was founded. As this forest abounded with lions, this place was called 'Nahar-naul' (the fear of lions) and sometimes Nahar-haul (the abode of lions). These names evolved into 'Narnaul' in course of time.

There is another story that is recounted by the local people about how this place came to be called Narnaul. It is said that while the work of founding this place was in progress, a 'Nag' (snake) and a 'Neol' (mongoose) appeared on the scene and attacked each other. Hence the name 'Nagneol' from which 'Narnaul' was a corruption. Another story has it that this place derived its name from Naunkar, the ruler of Bikaner, who is said to have founded this place. Still another story is that this place was established by a certain king Laukaran after whose wife it was named 'Nar Laun', of which 'Narnaul' is a corruption.

Narnaul was initially inhabited by the Jogis, who were known for the many miracles that they performed. The Rathores, a Rajput clan, then ruled in this area. In the 12th century, Hazrat Turkman, a Muslim saint, came and settled here. The Rathores fought the followers of Turkman, who got killed in 1137 A.D.[1] He is looked upon as a martyr by the Muslims and his tomb in Narnaul attracts many Muslim pilgrims.

Ibrahim Khan, the grandfather of Sher Shah Suri, came and settled here as Narnaul together with the adjoining territory that was given to him by the government as a means of meeting the expenses of maintaining his forty horsemen. After his death, his son Hassan Khan (father of Sher Shah Suri) became the Jagirdar of Narnaul. Akbar gave this Jagir to Shah Quli Khan Mehram after the Second Battle of Panipat in recognition of the latter's help in arresting Himu, the hero of Haryana, who got accidentally killed by an arrow that hit him in the eye just as he was about to win the battle.

During Akbar's time, there was a mint at Narnaul. Akbar had visited Narnaul along with Todar Mal to see how the work of the mint could be improved. Birbal, one of the nine jewels of Akbar's court, also used to visit Narnaul and Birbal's Chhatta that can still be seen there is a constant reminder of his association with this place.

The communal scene at Narnaul got disturbed during Aurangzeb's rule when the Satnami Sadhus revolted against the Muslim Jagirdar's oppression and occupied the place after killing the Muslim Fauzdar. Aurangzeb had to personally come down to Narnaul to put down the rebellion.

There are many historical monuments at Narnaul which are mostly relics of the Muslim period. The discovery of a Jain temple beneath a mosque during archaeological excavations is an indication that perhaps during the rule of Aurangzeb the Jain temple got buried underground and mosque was built at the place. The Dhosi hillock about five miles west of Narnaul has a saucer-shaped surface at its top, which is strewn with the ruins of a fortress that had been built by King Naunkar of Bikaner. There is also a temple here of the Vedic sage Chyavana, who is said to be the progenitor of the Bhargava clan, which is known as 'Dhosar' in Haryana. Himu, the hero of the Second Battle of Panipat, was a Dhosar Bania.

Rewari, which is now the headquarters of the Rewari district, was once upon a time a part of the Bhadanaka kingdom to which references are found in the Kavyamimansa, Skandapurana and Mahabharata. According to Prof. Dasharatha Sharma, the Bhadanaka territory perhaps comprised a tract that included the present district of Gurgaon, a part of Alwar State and the Bhiwani Tehsil. Their seat of power was probably located at a place called Bhadavasa, five miles to the south of Rewari. The Bhadanakas were at one time an important power in Haryana.[2]

As regards the identity of the Bhadanaka people, there is no unanimity of opinion among scholars. Prof. Dasharatha Sharma thinks that they were Ahirs. It is a fact that Rewari is a stronghold of the Ahirs whose concentrations are also found in Mahendragarh, Gurgaon and Jhajjar. But, as Dr. Buddha Prakash observes, the mere fact that the Bhadanakas lived in and near Ahiravati (from which Haryana perhaps derived its name) cannot be a basis for the inference that they were Ahirs. According to him, the Bhadanakas were obviously identical with the ancient Bhadras, whom the Mahabharata bracketed along with some other segments of Haryana's population such as the Rohitakas and Agreyas (people of Rohtak and Agroha) as well as the Malavas (people of Malwa lying between the Ghaggar and Sutlej rivers). Dr. Buddha Prakash is of the view that these people *i.e.*, The Bhadras were identical with the Madras mentioned in the Mahabharata and were perhaps a branch of an Indo-Iranian tribe. The Bhadanakas leaped into prominence by virtue of the many encounters they had with the Chauhans. Eventually, they were engulfed in the Chauhan empire of Prithviraja III.[3]

The original site of Rewari is located a little distance away from the present town and is called Badli or Bur Rewari, whose foundation is said to have been laid by Raja Karan Pal, a nephew of Prithviraja. The present town was founded in 1000 A.D. by one Raja Rao or Rawat, who named it after his daughter Rawati. This in course of time became Rewari. This place had in different phases of history formed part of the territory of the Mauryas, Guptas, Pushpabhutis and Gurjara-Pratiharas. In the Muslim period, the various ruling dynasties of Delhi down to the Mughals established their control over Rewari. Then came the Marathas followed by the ruler of Bharatpur. The British extended their rule here in the first decade of the 19th century.

The general discontent against British rule among the people of this region found expression in the uprising of 1857 A.D., which took a serious turn in Rewari and Narnaul. Rao Tula Ram and his cousin, Gopal Dev, descendants of the Raos of Rewari, whom Aurangzeb had granted a Jagir, led the fight against the British. In 1803, when the Marathas fought the British here, Teja Singh, the Rao chief of Rewari, had helped the former and so the British had later dispossessed the Raos of their Jagir. The 1857 uprising against the British provided Rao Tula Ram, the grandson of Teja Singh, with an opportunity to take it out on the British.

Rao Tula Ram, who was born in 1825 A.D., was the Istamaradar of the Rewari Jagir when the revolt against British rule in India started in 1857 A.D. He launched his campaign against the British in response to a request for help that came to him from Emperor Bahadur Shah. He proceeded to the Tehsil headquarters at Rewari on May 17, 1857 along with about 500 followers and deposed the Tehsildar and the Thanedar. They seized all the cash and other government property and proclaimed their rule under the authority of Emperor Bahadur Shah of Delhi over Rewari and the adjoining region.

They established their headquarters at Rampura village (which, incidentally, I saw), a mile to the south west of Rewari, with Rao Tula Ram as Raja and Gopal Dev as Commander-in-Chief. Rao Tula Ram established his rule, enforced law and order, collected taxes, raised a force and set up a unit for manufacturing guns and ammunition. This was acknowledged by the then British Deputy Commissioner of Gurgaon district, who, in a communication to the British authorities, said: "I should respectfully bring to the notice of the Government the great benefit which the town of Rewari and its neighbourhood derived from the attitude assumed by Rao Tula Ram, since the plundering Mewattees were thus kept at a distance and life and property reserved and order preserved on the Jeypur border.' He admitted that "society received many benefits even when this rebel was in arms against the Government."[4]

Rao Tula Ram extended all possible help in cash and kind to Emperor Bahadur Shah and the rebel forces in their fight against the British, but, alas, Delhi fell to the British on September 20, 1857! on October 6, 1857, the British forces led by Brigadier-General Showers reached Rewari and captured the fort of Rampura. Foreseeing this eventuality, Rao Tula Ram had by then left the place and moved over to Jaipur territory. Shortly, Brigadier-General Showers left Rewari and returned to Delhi. Taking advantage of Showers' absence from Rewari, Rao Tula Ram re-occupied Rewari with the help of the Jodhpur Legion.

Taken by surprise over the rebels' return to Rewari, the British authorities deputed a sizeable force led by Lt. Col. Gerrard to recapture Rewari from Rao Tula Ram. On hearing this, Rao Tula Ram moved over to Narnaul, about 30 miles west of Rewari, on strategic considerations. As the British forces reached a place called Nasibpur on their way to Narnaul, there were several battles between them and the rebels, in which their respective fortunes fluctuated from time to time. Then suddenly Lt. Col. Gerrard was killed by a musket ball from the rebels' forces, which demoralized the British forces. The rebels immediately attacked and overpowered the British forces.

The British authorities then sent Major Caujfield to fight the rebels. Now the artillery of the British forces resorted to heavy bombardment of the Indian troops. Soon the British forces reached Narnaul, where a decisive battle was fought on November16, 1857 between them and the rebel forces jointly led by Prince Azam Muhammad Azam of the Delhi royal family, Rao Tula Ram, Raja Nahar Singh of Ballabhgarh, Nawab Samad Khan of Jhajjar, Rao Shahmat Khan and Rao Krishna Gopal of Mewat. Despite all the valour with which they fought, the rebel forces lost to the British, who were superior in numbers and in artillery. Several hundred rebels including many of their important leaders got killed. The British lost about seventy of their men and some British officers as well. At Narnaul, heaps of corpses were seen after this battle.[5] Rao Tula Ram escaped to Rajasthan.

Some documents that have been found recently by a Russian scholar, Prof. Aleixi V. Raikov, at the Leningrad Archives in Russia have thrown new light on Rao Tula Ram's hitherto unknown mission of seeking the help of the Russian Tsar for India's freedom movement.[6] These documents show that Rao Tula Ram met the rulers of Jodhpur, Bikaner and Jaipur with a view to persuading them to work for India's freedom and to seek the help of the Russian Government towards that end. At his instance, these rulers wrote letters to the Tsar saying that their intermediary, Rao Tula Ram, would explain their case to him.

Rao Tula Ram also went to Kalpi, a centre of rebel activity, and attended a freedom-fighters' meeting, which was chaired by Tantya Tope. This meeting had decided to seek the assistance of Afghanistan in India's freedom movement. Towards the end of 1859 A.D., Rao Tula Ram proceeded to Bombay and then left the country with the purpose of enlisting the help of Afghanistan, Iran and Russia in India's fight against British imperialism. Disguised as a Marwari businessman, he went by ship to Iran. However, he got no response to his plea for help from the authorities in Tehran. He then went to Rasht, conducted negotiations with the Russian Embassy and wrote letters to the Russian Government seeking their help. Since he did not get any response from the Russian Government, he moved over to Afghanistan in 1862 to seek the help of Dost Muhammad Khan, the Amir of Kabul. No help came from this source either.

In 1863 A.D., Rao Tula Ram fell seriously ill and then on September 22, 1863 A.D., he breathed his last when he was only 38 years of age. He was the first Indian to plan the overthrow of the British imperialists from India with foreign help.[7] Rao Tula Ram's Samadhi in Kabul bore testimony to his martyrdom in the cause of our country's freedom.

The British rewarded the native States adjoining Narnaul and Rewari for their help in the fight against the rebels. The Maharaja of Patiala got Narnaul district as his reward and its name was changed to Mahendragarh, Bawal in present-day Rewari district was given away to the Raja of Nabha State.

In Rewari, I saw several temples and historical buildings as well as a memorial to Rao Tula Ram. A couple of miles away from Rewari is a place known as Gokalgarh, which has a fort that was built by Rao Gujar Mal, the ruler of Rewari, during the time of Aurangzeb. He had built another fort at Gurwada, about 12 miles away from Rewari, where the relics of some temples and idols of the medieval period have been discovered. Rao Gujar Mal had minted coins at Gokalgarh known as Gokal Sicca, which were still in circulation at Farrukhnagar on the eve of the 1857 uprising. I took time off to visit the palace of Rao Tula Ram at Rampura on the outskirts of Rewari, where a fair is held every year in the month of September to commemorate the death anniversary of this great martyr. There is also a memorial to him that has been built by the government.

I still remember that some time in October, 1988, Chetan Sharma, the famous test cricketer of our country, who belongs to Haryana, came to call on me. He is a very pleasant person to talk to and, in the course of our conversation, he told me a lot about his life-style and the strict regimen he used to follow every day in order to keep fit. He gave an account of how he reached the top in the game of cricket. It was very refreshing to hear one of our country's top cricketers speak so frankly about is own field of activity. I knew that just a year ago he had become the first cricketer in the world to claim a hat-trick by bowling out Ken Rutherford, Ian Smith and Ewan Chatfield at Nagpur in the Reliance World Cup. More recently—in June 1999 when the Pakistani off-spinner Saqlain Mustaq became the second bowler in the world to claim a hat-trick in the World Cup match against South Africa at the Oval, I recalled my meeting with our very own speedster Chetan Sharma more than a decade ago. Haryana has reason to feel proud of cricketers of the ilk of not only Chetan Sharma, but also Kapil Dev, the 'Haryana Hurricane', the hero of India's World Cup victory in 1983 and the holder of the world record for taking the maximum number of wickets.

The annual conference of the Governors of States that I attended at the Rashtrapati Bhawan in Delhi on October 10 and 11, 1988 was a grandiose affair, thanks to the number of parties including dinners and get-togethers hosted by the President, the Vice-President and the Governors of some States at the Bhawans in Delhi of the States concerned. The discussions on the subjects of the agenda of the conference and the conclusions reached acquired some importance from the fact that they represented the collective wisdom of the country's elder statesmen to which the political leadership of the country was expected to pay the most serious consideration. But I was not very sure of what all this meant in terms of practical implementation.I remember that I had made some critical observations against the delay in the completion of the SYL canal, which had adversely affected Haryana's agriculture by stopping the supply of the much-needed water for irrigation. The matter still rests at the same stage as then.

In October 1988, floods in the Ghaggar river and some rivulets had badly affected some districts of Haryana and Punjab and damaged the crops and properties of the local people. The Sirsa district of Haryana was particularly affected. Prime Minister Rajiv Gandhi chalked out a programme of visiting the affected districts of Haryana and Punjab and also some places in Himachal Pradesh on October 13, 1988, making aerial surveys where necessary. Later in the evening, he was to hold discussions on the flood situation and necessary ameliorative measures at separate meetings with the Governor, the Chief Minister, other Ministers and officials of Haryana as well as with the Governor and concerned officials of Punjab (which was under President's rule). These meetings were to be held at the Haryana and Punjab Raj Bhawans respectively.

When I met Prime Minister Rajiv Gandhi at the Governors' Conference in Delhi, he informed me of his decision, which, he said, had already been communicated to the Governments of Haryana and Punjab. He told me to take my gum boots out of the closet and meet him at Sirsa.

So on October 12, 1988, I left Delhi in the morning by car in the morning en route to Sirsa. I reached Hissar and, since Fatehabad in this district was under water, I made a detour to reach Sirsa by mid-day.

I was not particularly happy to skip Fatehabad about which I had heard and read a lot. This was a Tehsil town of Sirsa district that had been founded in 1352 A.D. by Feroze Shah Tughlak in the name of his son, Fateh Khan. I was told about the Idgah of Fatehabad at the center of which stands a monument, the lower part of which is made of yellowish sandstone very similar to a part of a pillar that stands in front of a mosque in Hissar. There is a view that these parts of the monument in Fatehabad and the pillar in Hissar once constituted a single pillar that had been built by Asoka. The epigraph on the Ashokan pillar is said to have been rubbed off to make room for an inscription that records Feroze Shah Tughlak's geneology. I had also read about the famous Humayun Ki Masjid of Fatehabad. While fleeing from Amarkot after his defeat by Sher Shah, Humayun arrived at Fatehabad on a Friday and prayed at this mosque.

After reaching Sirsa in the afternoon, I went about visiting some of the flood-affected villages, meeting the people and listening to what they had to say about their problems and their requirement of assistance. I addressed groups of people in the villages to raise their morale.

Ch. Devi Lal and Virender Singh, Minister for Irrigation and Power, reached Sirsa and called on me in the evening, when we discussed various issues pertaining to the floods and also the arrangements for the Prime Minister's visit the next morning. Ch. Devi Lal was somewhat cool about the Prime Minister's visit perhaps out of a feeling that it was a propaganda gimmick. I used all my powers of persuasion to convince him that; whatever his motive, the Prime Minister was definitely going to announce substantial assistance for Haryana and Punjab, which would benefit the people and help ameliorate their distress.

Next morning, I was glad to see Ch. Devi Lal play ball, when the Prime Minister landed at Sirsa. After visiting several flood-affected place of Punjab and Haryana, Rajiv Gandhi flew down to Chandigarh and attended two high-level late-night meetings—one at the Punjab Raj Bhawan and the other at Haryana Raj Bhawan—to take stock of the situation and then to provide considerable assistance to both the States for mitigating the sufferings of the people. Later, Ch. Devi Lal expressed his gratitude to me for extending my assistance to him during the discussions at the meeting with the Prime Minister and thus helping the cause of Haryana. I greatly appreciated his frankness and gratefulness to me. I told him that my role as Governor, as I saw it, was to remove misunderstanding between the Centre and the State.

With the next parliamentary elections due a little over a year later, the various political parties in Haryana had begun at this time to work upon their respective vote-banks. Both Ch. Devi Lal and Bhajan Lal of the Congress Party started wooing the Gujjars. Bhajan Lal had organized a successful rally of the Gujjars at Samalkha in early October, 1988, where Rajesh Pilot, the late Gujjar leader of the Congress Party was projected as a leader of the community and presented with a purse of Rs. 43 lakh. To counter this move of the Congress Party, Ch. Devi Lal inducted a Gujjar leader, Avtar Singh Badhana, who had earlier left the Congress Party, into his ministry as a minister of State on October 15, 1988. After I administered the oath of office and secrecy to Badhana at our Raj Bhawan, in response to questions from pressmen, Ch. Devi Lal conceded that he had made Badhana a Minister to give representation to the backward community of Gujjars, but refuted the suggestion that his action reflected his concern over the successful Congress rally at Samalkha. He denounced Rajesh Pilot as a 'rootless' leader, who posed no threat to his party in Haryana.

I still recall what a hectic day October 16, 1988 turned out to be following a telephone call from Ch. Devi Lal early in the morning to tell me that he would like to see me at 5 p.m. that day with a view to tendering his own and his government's resignation. As word spread about this move on the part of Ch. Devi Lal, all kinds of rumours and political speculation gave rise to considerable excitement not only in Chandigarh but all over Haryana and, of course in Delhi and in political circles in the rest of the country. Naturally, a spate of telephone calls from the highest echelons of the Central Government kept me busy the whole day.

This development made V.P. Singh and some of the important leaders of the opposition camp rush to Chandigarh and confabulate with Ch. Devi Lal. After seeking an appointment with me, Ch. Devi Lal came to call on me in the evening along with two of his cabinet colleagues, namely K.R. Punia and Virendra Singh, and explain what had happened and tell me that he was after all not resigning! Even before he told me about this, I had come to know that, on the persuasion of V.P. Singh and the other leaders, Ch. Devi Lal had changed his mind before coming to see me. I knew that Ch. Devi Lal had for some time been toying with the idea of dissolving the State Assembly and going for fresh election. In fact, he had broached the subject to me some time ago, though he did not appear to have made up his mind at that stage. I guessed that his intention at that time was to induct his son, O.P. Chautala, as the Chief Minister of Haryana in the wake of fresh elections, which, he thought, his party was likely to win in view of the favourable political climate that prevailed at the time. But his party colleagues and particularly Central leaders like V.P. Singh thought that it wa still too early to plunge Haryana into a state of political uncertainty, because it was worth waiting for the country-wide Parliamentary election that was just over a year away.

With all this turmoil coming to an end, I had now plenty of time to turn my attention to Durga Puja, which had just begun. The leaders of the local Bengalee community had invited me and my wife to the Puja ceremony and a cultural programme held in the evening at Tagore Theatre. It was with great pleasure that we mingled with the devotees on this occasion. On October 17 and 18, 1988, we were at Kali Bari and at the Bengalee Association's Durga Puja in Chandigarh to worship the goddess. On October 18, 1988, we later drove to Delhi to be able to attend a function at Gurgaon the next morning. This made it possible for us to attend some functions organized on the occasion of Durga Puja at Vasant Kunj in New Delhi.

On October 19, 1988, I presided over the annual function of the Haryana Welfare Society for Speech and Hearing Handicapped. I was associated with this and several other voluntary organizations in my capacity as the Governor of Haryana. These bodies helped in enlisting the co-operation of government as well as non-government agencies and members of the public in providing various facilities to those who needed assistance.

I also took this opportunity of my visit to Gurgaon to go round some places of historical and religious importance. I had earlier visited some of these places during the long years I had spent in Delhi as a bureaucrat. Gurgaon, the name of the town and of the district of which it was the headquarters, is derived from the word 'Guru-Gaon' or the village of the 'Guru' (preceptor). This village is said to have been gifted by Yudhisthira, the eldest of the Pandava brothers, to their preceptor, Dronacharya, who had imparted instructions in archery to them. A tank on the western side of the road to the near-by railway track was shown to us as the one that had been dedicated to Dronacharya. It was here that Dronacharyais believed to have given training to the Pandavas as well as to the Kauravas. I still recall that during one of my earlier visits to this place, the guide, while narrating this story of the Mahabharata, had raised a very pertinent point about what he called the pro-upper caste bias of Dronacharya and his discrimination against the low-caste Ekalavya, from whom Dronacharya extracted his (Ekalavya's) right thumb as 'Guru-Dakshina' (preceptor's fee), when Ekalavya said that he had all along looked upon Dronacharya as his Guru. Needless to say, this deprived Ekalavya of his right thumb without which he lost the capacity to match Arjuna's skill in archery. Dronacharya's act of favouritism towards Arjuna, my guide had told me, was meant to help Arjuna in establishing his claim to superiority over Ekalavya in archery.

While at Gurgaon, I recalled my earlier visits from Delhi to Sohna, famous for its hot spring, the beautiful Damdama Lake and the bird sanctuary at Sultanpur. A bath at Sohna's hot spring is believed to cure a person of skin diseases and ailments arising from abnormal blood pressure. This was once upon a time a thickly forested area and the present settlement at Sohna had been initially set up by Maharshi Sonak. Some say that one Sawan Singh was the King of Sohna centuries ago. An old fort still exists here.

It is said that a trader by name Chaturbhuj was once passing this way, his goods being carried by some animals. A dog, which was also in his company, appeared to be thirsty, but there was no trace of water anywhere near by. The dog roamed about all over the place in search of water and after some time it came, looking satisfied, because it appeared that it had got some water to drink and had even managed to have a bath at some near-by spot. Chaturbhuj traced the spring and got some work done at his own expense to make its water usable and easily accessible to the local people.

There is a place called Atta near Sohna, where one can see many specimens of the art and architecture of the Gurjara-Pratihara period as well as a beautiful icon of Adinath, the first Tirthankara of the Jains. Once I had passed through Pataudi, which had been founded during the reign of Jalal-ud-din Khilji by a ruler of Mewat by name Pata, who called it Patodhi of which the present name Pataudi is a corruption. The Nawab's palace is impressive and has a cricket ground that reminds a visitor of this family's signal contribution to cricket.

I had once visited a place called Nuh on the road to Alwar, which has a beautiful masonry tank and the tomb of Sheikh Musa with its shaking minarets. An important landmark of Nuh is a Shiva temple called the Baba Bhuteshwar temple that had been built about 350 years ago. A religious-minded and philanthropic trader of Nuh by name Chuhimal played a significant role in the construction of this temple. It is said that one night he had a dream in which he had a vision of a Shivalinga that looked like being buried under the ground at a spot near the cattle shed of a Muslim peasant of village Salhedi located about two miles away.

Next morning, out of sheer curiosity, Chuhilal went to this village to verify if what he had seen in his dream was true or not. He reached the spot seen in his dream and got it dug up. He was astonished to see that a Shivalinga really existed there. He decided to take the Linga to

Nuh and get it installed in a temple. After securing the consent of the Muslim peasant, Chuhilal placed the Linga on a bullock cart and proceeded towards Nuh. When he reached a certain spot outside Salhedi village, the bullock cart suddenly stopped. Despite all efforts, he failed to make the cart move. Then, with the help of the local people, Chuhilal got a temple built at that very place and had the Shivalinga installed in it.

On another occasion, I had paid a visit to Farrukhnagar, which derived its name from Emperor Farrukhsiyar. The Nawab of Farrukhnagar had participated in the 1857 uprising and so his estate was confiscated by the British. Among the fine specimens of architecture in this town are Sheesh Mahal, Jami Masjid with slabs having inscriptions of the time of the Delhi Sultan Ghiyas-ud-din Balban, Baradari, a Baoli or well octagonal in shape and a shrine of Budho Mata a few miles away from the town, where fairs are regularly held.

During my visit to Gurgaon on October 19, 1988, my convoy passed through an area from where the famous temple of Masani was not very far off. I could not visit the temple this time, but I recalled a visit I had paid there some years ago. Masani, the goddess of small pox, is highly venerated by the local people as they believe that she protects them against the scourge of small pox. This temple is said to have been constructed by a local Jat by name Singha some time in the 18th century after he received a directive from the goddess in a dream. A very big fair is held here in the summer every year.

In Gurgaon, there is also the famous temple of goddess Chhoganan Mata, who is said to be the younger sister of Masani. The local sweepers built this temple as they resented being denied entry into the Masani temple. Fairs are held here all round the year. A big fair held here in the rainy season is exclusively thronged by snake charmers and the Sansis, who belong to the lower castes.

Nuh and some other places of Gurgaon district that I had occasion to visit earlier form part of the bigger Mewat region that comprises parts of Gurgaon and Faridabad districts and the neighbouring tracts of Alwar and Bharatpur in Rajasthan. The Meos, who predominate in this area, regard themselves as the descendants of the Rajputs, who converted to Islam during the reign of Qutb-ud-din Aibak. But this claim is not conceded by many scholars. According to Sir Herbert Risley, author of "The People of India", the Meos are the descendants of the Bhils, who lived in the dense forests of Mewat. There is also a view that the Meos and the Minas are inter-related and that those

Minas, who were converted to Islam for some reason or the other, were called Meos. They observe many customs of the Hindus. It is said that they are neither Hindus nor Muslims, but are a happy blend of the two. Many Meos migrated to Pakistan after partition, but soon most of them came back to Mewat as they could not adjust themselves to the environment there. Their language is Mewati, which is akin to the language spoken in adjoining Rajasthan. Mewat is economically and educationally backward and considerable effort has been made by the authorities to improve their lot.

The Meos, like the Jats and Ahirs, are a daring people, ever asserting their spirit of independence. Since the medieval period, the Meos have not allowed any government in Delhi to enjoy peace and have never recognized any outside authority to interfere in the affairs of Mewat. Two chiefs of Mewat of that period, namely Bahadur Nahir Mewati and Hassan Khan Mewati, deserve special mention because they carried with them all sections of the local people in asserting their independence and in opposing the Sultan and the Mughal Emperor of Delhi. A Meo Kshatriya of the Khan-zada clan, Hassan Khan Mewati was closely related to Sultan Ibrahim Lodhi as they were the sons of two sisters, both daughters of one Aazam Humayun Sarwani. Hassan Khan was a very powerful potentate with an army of about 10,000 Mewatis, whose territory extended over Mewat, Narnaul, parts of Kannod and some areas adjacent to Alwar. He was a staunch supporter of Maharana Sangram Singh of Mewar.

In 1526 A.D., Hassan Khan Mewati joined hands with Sultan Ibrahim Lodhi in resisting Babar in the first Battle of Panipat. Babar won and Ibrahim Lodhi was killed. Hassan Khan managed to escape from the battlefield, buthis son, Nahar Khan was injured and captured by the Mughal army. With Nahar Khan in his custody, Babar tried to put pressure on Hassan Khan Mewati with a view to winning him over to his side because he was perturbed over the growing strength of Maharana Sangram Singh of Mewar. In making his moves for a rapprochement with Hassan Khan Mewati, Babar also stressed the fact that they both were followers of Islam. But Hassan Khan refused to oblige the Mughal Emperor and asserted that both he and Maharana Sangram Singh belonged to the same nation and that their patriotic duty was to defend the country against foreign invaders like Babar.

Hassan Khan Mewati was among the chief commanders of Maharana Sangram Singh when they faced Babar on the battlefield of Khanwa in March 1527 A.D after proclaiming their espousal of Mahmud Lodhi, son of Ibrahim Lodhi, as the Emperor of Delhi. Babar won the battle in which Hassan Khan Mewati lost his life. Hassan Khan's body was taken to Tizara in Mewat where his cemetery inside a mosque still attracts visitors.

After the advent of British rule in India, the Meos, Ahirs and Gujjars of Gurgaon continued to display the same rebellious spirit and defied the new rulers, compelling the British to dispatch troops to Gurgaon (as well as to Rohtak and Karnal) to subdue the people and establish law and order.

Never did the turbulent spirit of the people of Gurgaon come into sharper relief than during the 1857 uprising. The rebels from Delhi and Meerut launched a sharp attack on Gurgaon on May 13, 1857, forcing W. Ford, the Deputy Commissioner, to flee to Mathura along with all the customs officers in the region, thus wiping off all vestiges of British authority in the district. The struggle of the rebels was more fierce in Mewat whose people conveyed to Bahadur Shah their recognition as the Emperor of Hindustan. However, in the urban areas of Mewat, the people by and large continued to avow their allegiance to the British authorities. Groups of people from rural Mewat attacked these urban centers and indulged in considerable plunder and destruction. British forces were sent to subdue the Mewatis were badly roted.

Major W. F. Eden, the Political Agent at Jaipur, who made a move to pass through Mewat on his way to Delhi, met with stiff resistance, though he managed to destroy many villages. He halted at Sohna for a few days and was joined by Deputy Commissioner Ford and thirty other European officers, but finding the going tough, he returned to Jaipur in August 1857. Though Delhi fell to the British in the latter half of September, 1857, the situation did not show any improvement in Gurgaon district. Brigadier-General Showers arrived there in October 1857 with a big force equipped with artillery and was also joined by Clifford, Assistant Collector of Gurgaon. Clifford's sister was said to have been stripped naked at the Palace (Delhi), tied in that condition to the wheel of a gun carriage, dragged up in Chandni Chowk or Silver Street of Delhi and then cut to pieces.[8] Believing that his sister had been outraged by the rebels before being killed, Clifford took revenge by burning village after village. In his own words: "He had to put to death all he had come across, not excepting women and children."9 But soon he was killed by the Meos.

Brigadier-General Showers, assisted by Captain Drummond, burnt down many villages of Gurgaon district and indulged in savage oppression, killing numerous people, though at some places the Meos offered stiff resistance and killed many Sepoys fighting for the British. Recounting his experience, Brigadie-General Showers had said: "From the time I entered the Gurgaon district, I was in enemies' country, that in all encampments and during every march, I was exposed to the attacks of the enemies' horsemen .... I had to be continually on the alert against an enemy ...."[10] After putting down the revolt in Gurgaon district, the British authorities burnt down many of the affected villages and confiscated the property of several villages. Many villagers were hanged and many were sentenced to long-term imprisonment. Heavy fines were imposed on many villages and individuals.[11]

This gruesome story of blood and gore should not leave one with the impression that the people of Gurgaon do not have a softer cultural and artistic streak in their nature. Who has not heard of the famous Dhamal dance, the favourite pastime of Gurgaon's Ahir community, that dates back to the Mahabharata era? It reflects the emotional make-up of these people, who usually perform it on moon-lit nights during spring in open air going round and round in the formation of a circle singing and dancing to the rhythmic beat of the drum. I have heard some of these famous songs that bring out the joys and sorrows and the hopes and fears of Haryana's village folk.

Notes

1. For this and the next two paragraphs, I have drawn upon "This Beautiful India: Haryana" by Sukhdev Singh Chib, pp. 104-105.
2. "The Bhadanakas of haryana" by Dr. Buddha Prakash in "Haryana: Studies in History and Politics" edited by J.N. Singh Yadav, p. 29.
3. *Ibid.*
4. Dr. K. C. Yadav's article "A Rebel Prince: Life and Work of Rao Raja Tularam" in the Journal of Haryana Studies, Vol. XVIII, Nos.1&2, 1986.
5. *Ibid.*
6. "Rao Raja Tula Singh Bahadur's Mission To Russia, 1859" by A.V. Raikov in the Journal of Haryana Studies, Vol. XVIII, Nos. 1&2, 1986.
7. Dr. K.C. Yadav's article in the Journal of Haryana Studies mentioned above.
8. C.J. Griffiths, Siege of Delhi.
9. *Ibid.*
10. Quoted from File R/91 by K.C. Yadav in "The Revolt of 1857 in Haryana", p. 115.
11. The Revolt of 1857 in Haryana by Dr. K.C.Yadav.

13

Kunti, Karna and Karnal: Karva Chauth, Dhan Teras and Diwali: Sonepat or Swarnprasth of Mahabharata: Sos Village, Faridabad: Surdas, Blind Poet of Sihi

On October 20 and 21, 1988, I was at Madhuban and Karnal. Madhuban is virtually a police colony as it accommodates the headquarters of Haryana's armed police battalions and the Police Training College. I had visited this place as well as near-by Karnal several times in the past during my stint in the police service. This time round, I took the salute at the Police Commemoration Parade and placed a wreath at the Police Martyrs' Memorial at Madhuban. This function is simultaneously held by the police forces all over the country to pay homage to those policemen, who had been killed by the Chinese Army while patrolling our borders in Ladakh on October 21, 1959. The names of all policemen killed on duty throughout the country in the preceding year are also read out at this function and tributes paid to them.

During this trip, I took the opportunity of visiting some places of Karnal district which I had not seen so far. This, together with my earlier visits to Karnal and other places in the district helped me to acquaint myself with the history and culture of this region. In the past, I had often stopped at the Oasis tourist resort and visited the Karna Lake (renamed as Chakravarti Lake after the late B.N. Chakravarti, one of Haryana's famous Governors). A place where I had once stopped for a while is Gharaunda on the Grand Trunk Road to the north of Karnal. There is a beautiful Serai here built in Emperor Shah Jahan's time, which, though dilapidated, has some fine specimens of Mughal architecture and two big gates that had been built by two different persons—Mamu and Bhanja—but were similar in design, despite the fact that they had neither seen each other's work while in progress nor compared notes before undertaking their construction work!

Once I had visited Vyasasthali, which is now known as Basthali. About 15 miles from Karnal on the road to Kaithal, this place is of enormous religious significance because sage Vyasa, author of the Mahabharata, used to live here. It is said that the Ganges used to flow underground to reach his well here so as to obviate the need for his going all the way to the sacred river for his daily bath. He had left his loin cloth and 'Lota' (a small pot) at the river which used to flow along with the water up to his well so as to leave no doubt that the water had really flowed from the Ganges. According to the Mahabharata, Vyasa had once decided to give up his life after being overwhelmed with grief on the death of his son. Then the gods interceded with him and dissuaded him from any such action.[1] It is generally believed by the local people that whoever visits Bastali does not have to suffer the pangs of his son's death.

Close to Basthali is village Gondar where sage Gautama had worked upon and created the philosophy of Nyaya. The other names by which he is known are Gotama and Akshapada, while the Mahabharata calls him Medhatithi. The Skanda Purana says that Gautama was the husband of Ahalya, in which case he might not have lived in the territory of present-day Haryana. According to the Ramayana, Gautama's Ashrama was located in the forests close to Mithila.

About seven miles west of Karnal is Bahlopur, which is famous for its Parashar Tank. It is said that the eldest Kaurava, Duryodhana had gone into hiding here after facing defeat in the Mahabharata war. He came out after being worked up over Lord Krishna's taunting remarks and then got ready for a fight. There is a place called Gummala Kheri near Pehowa where Duryodhana was killed by Bhima in a one-to-one duel.

Now about Karnal itself. It has derived its name from its founder, Karna, who had been born to Kunti before her marriage with Pandu. Both Kunti and Karna are highly revered figures of the Mahabharata. Devout Hindus remember the names of five great women the first thing in the morning in order to get liberated from all sins.[2] They are Ahalya, Draupadi, Kunti, Tara and Mandodari. It is a different matter, as some people point out by way of criticism, that all these venerable women had more than one husband or had relationships with persons other than their husbands.

The point to note is that their virtues were so very great that, despite whatever these critics say, they were or rather are even today considered worthy of being remembered in the morning as a means to securing redemption from all sins. In fact, they are placed even higher than Sita and Savitri in this sense. A point to remember in this context is that in the good old days, the standards for making value judgments were different from those of today.

The circumstances of Kunti's case bear recounting in the context of Karnal. Kunti, daughter of Surasena, was gifted away to her putative father, Kuntibhoja. Sage Durvasa, who once came to stay as Kuntibhoja's guest, was highly pleased with Kunti's devotion and hospitality and gave her as a boon a 'Mantra' (incantation) that had the power of bringing down before her any god she wanted.

To test the effectiveness of this 'Mantra', Kunti once remembered the Sun God, who appeared before her instantaneously. Her relationship with the Sun God resulted in the birth of a son to her, who later emerged as the famous Mahabharata hero—Karna. She discarded the child by setting it afloat on the waters of Ashva river. The child was reared by Adhiratha, a charioteer, and his wife, Radheya, who were quite low in the Hindu caste hierarchy. By the social mores of those days, there was nothing morally wrong in Kunti's conduct.

After Kunti's marriage with Pandu, the latter lost his capacity to father a child as a sequel to a Brahmin's curse. It was Pandu, who permitted Kunti to give birth to children by invoking the help of others through what was known as 'Niyoga' (some kind of levirate). It was then that she successfully invoked, by virtue of the power conferred by sage Durvasa, three gods, namely Dharmaraja, Vayu and Indra, unions with whom gave her three children *i.e.*, Yudhisthira, Bhima and Arjuna. (Pandu's other wife, Madri, had also enlisted the help of Kunti's 'Mantra' to invoke the Ashwinis, enabling her to give birth to Nakula and Sahadeva, the other two of the five Pandava brothers). Niyoga was a perfectly valid and socially acceptable custom in those days and Kunti had no reason to nurse any guilt complex about the way the Pandava brothers were ushered into the world.

Karna was a tragic hero, who suffered from the misfortune of having had to face a series of adverse circumstances all through his life. Abandoned by his mother at birth, he had to grow up as a 'Suta-Putra' (a charioteer's son), though in fact he was the eldest of the Pandavas. On the ground of his supposedly belonging to a low caste, he was denied the opportunity of learning the 'Brahmastra' by Dronacharya, the training Guru of the Pandavas and the Kauravas. Eventually, he imbibed this from Parashurama by falsely posing as a Brahmin. When Parashurama came to learn that Karna was not a Brahmin, he cursed the latter that his skill would fail him at the critical moment.

Draupadi refused to marry Karna on the ground that he was a lowly charioteer's son. When Karna challenged Arjuna to a duel, he was denied the right to fight because of his so-called low birth. It was at this point that Duryodhana came forward to stand by his side and made him the King of Anga, which gave a tremendous boost to his amour-propre and social standing.

Kunti and Lord Krishna disclosed to Karna the fact of his high birth, but the latter had no use for it. He preferred to cling to his status of a 'Suta-Putra' and to achieve greatness through his own effort rather than on the strength of his high birth. As he famously said: "Birth in a high caste is in the hands of God; valour is in my own hands" (Daivayattam Kule Janma, Madayattam Pourusam).

Thus Karna declined to join the ranks of the Pandavas, though he could have claimed the whole kingdom in his capacity as the eldest Pandava, which he really was. Lord Krishna as well as Kunti had urged him to throw his weight behind the Pandavas. In return, Lord Krishna had offered him the kingdom of Hastinapur as well as the hand of Draupadi, but Karna declined these offers. He remained a steadfast ally of Duryodhana out of a sense of gratitude to the latter, though this alliance sullied his image a good deal. He told Kunti in so many words that her plea to him to join hands with the Pandavas was nothing but a ruse to ensure that he did not cause harm to Arjuna. But he kept his word given to Kunti not to cause harm to the four Pandava brothers—Yudhisthira, Bhima, Nakul and Sahadeva. His ire was directed only against Arjuna with whom he put up a great fight. And it was at the hands of Arjuna that he was killed, when he became the commander of the Kaurava forces for two brief days. As has been pointed out by a scholar: "Karna met with his end not because he was beaten nor on account of his being inferior to Arjuna in any way, but he was the victim of his own greatness, and destiny was always against him." [3]

Karna is known as 'Danveer' (one with a great charitable disposition). A supreme example of this quality of his was the prmptness with which he handed over his protective armour and ear-rings to Indra, when the latter asked for them, though the Sun God had earlier cautioned him against such a request from Indra, who was interested in saving Arjuna.

A supreme example of Karna's charitable disposition was provided when he was desperately trying to extricate the wheels of his chariot that had got stuck on the battleground owing to a curse pronounced by Parashurama. As Arjuna showered him with arrows, he fell on the ground and was on the point of death. At this very stage, Lord Indra appeared there in the guise of a poor Brahmin and thrust forward a begging bowl, imploring Karna to offer him alms. Karna told him that he had nothing to give then except his flesh, which he offered to the Brahmin.

The Brahmin said that Karna could still give him something else, namely the gold that encrusted his two teeth. Karna readily agreed and asked the Brahmin to take out the gold after breaking the teeth with the help of a piece of stone. The Brahmin refused to do so, saying that this would be tantamount to committing a sin. He asked Karna to himself break his teeth with a stone and then offer the gold to him. With great difficulty, Karna managed to get at a stone, broke his own teeth and offered the gold to the Brahmin. The latter refused to accept the gold because it was unclean and smeared with blood. Karna washed the gold with some water that was kept in a pot lying close at hand. As Karna offered the gold to the Brahmin, Lord Indra revealed himself and begged Karna's forgiveness, saying that he was really a 'Danveer'!

It has been rightly said that Karna occupies a high position among the galaxy of India's epic heroes and that his real worth has not been fully appreciated on account of the prejudice arising from his close association with Duryodhana. As has been observed by the a scholar: "He is indeed a unique hero who should be admired for his magnanimity, unflinching devotion to the cause he championed, valour, skill and truthfulness." [4]

This then is the story of Karna, who gave Karnal its name and heritage. Even today, one can see a tank in this town, which is known as Karna Tal and a gate that is called the Karna Gate. There are many ancient sites in and around Karnal, which are associated with the events and personages of the Mahabharata.

Once upon a time, this whole region consisted of forests of which the well-known were 5 Kamyakavana, Aditivana, Vyasavana, Phalakivana, Suryavana, Madhuvana and Sitavana, whose names correspond respectively to modern Kamoda, Amin, Vyasasthali (Basthali), Pharal, Sajuman, Mohana and Sivana. I do not know if Madhuvana figuring in this list that is said to be represented by present-day Mohana had anything to do with Madhuban, where the police complex is located.

In the last week of October 1988, I got associated with the Senior Players' Tennis Championships held at Chandigarh, which I inaugurated. I also played in this tournament in a doubles match, which we lost. Players from some foreign countries, who participated in the meet, included some Italian players, who were gracious enough to present a few mementoes to one of the clubs of Chandigarh. The local press highlighted the events of this tournament every day. In this context, a write-up in the Indian Express of October 31, 1988 is reproduced:

Elders at Play

Chandigarh witnessed an unusual sight last week, which could perhaps be unique in the country. The occasion was the Senior Players Lawn Tennis Championships of India and there on Wednesday playing matches on adjoining courts at the Chandigarh Club were the three leading citizens of the city. The Punjab Governor, Mr. Siddhartha Shankar Ray, the Haryana Governor, Mr. H. A. Barari, and the Adviser to the Administrator of Chandigarh, Mr. Ashok Pradhan (affectionately called Chhota Governor by one of the tennis fans). All three had sportingly turned out to make the event a great success, though Mr. Ray had to withdraw because of the passing away of his mother-in-law, after he was virtually assured of a place in the finals in his age group. His game has certainly improved in the last one year, thanks to the court in Raj Bhavan.

The tournament attracted participants from all over the country, including such far-off places as Guntur, Tirupathi and Pune. There were even a few foreigners including Ritzenberg from the USA who dethroned the previous 60-65 year category title holder, Mahinder Singh (popularly known as Kanwar Sahib and the spirit behind the tournament),

Stagchowitch from Austria was another outstanding player, while the Indian honours went to M.K. Naydu from Andhra and at present one of the coaches of the CLTA-Garib Das from Amritsar and Ravi Kathpalia from Delhi. Naydu won in the 50-55 category while Das triumphed in the 45-50 group.

On a lighter vein Kanwar Sahib had an appropriate speech ready for the closing function which could not be delivered since Mr Ray could not be present but part of it were the famous lines of Noel Coward : "In Bengal, to move at all is seldom if ever done, but mad dogs and Englishmen go out in the noonday sun." Both Mr. Ray and Mr. Barari are, of course, from Bengal.

On October 26, 1988, I again visited Kurukshetra, to address a rally of ex-servicemen at the Dronacharya Stadium. On this and on some later occasions, my wife and I drove around some places of this region, which are known for their religious significance. One such place was Pawanawa, references to which made in the Mahabharata, Padmapurana and Vamanapurana testify to its sanctity as well as to its antiquity. This place is associated with the name of Pawan, the Wind God, and Marut, which stands for forty nine gods under the control of Pawan. This was, therefore, also known as Pawan-Hriday.

According to Padmapurana, this place was associated with sage Dadhichi, who had voluntarily courted death and donated his bone to Lord Indra, who converted it into a thunder-bolt, the weapon with which he killed Britra, the demon, who had oppressed and driven away the gods from heaven. The Puranas narrate the story of how Pawana, the Sun God, who was overwhelmed with grief over the loss of his son, hid himself in a tank at this place and how Lord Brahma and some other gods pleaded with him and succeeded in bringing him out. Whoever takes a dip in the tank that still exists at Pawanawa and then worships Lord Shiva here is said to get liberated from all sins and blessed with a place at the feet of Shiva.6

A holy place less than a mile to the north west of the Kurukshetra University is Narkatari village or Anarak, which figures in the Mahabharata and the Puranas. According to Vamanapurana and the Mahabharata, to the east of this place is Lord Brahma, to its south is Maheshwara, to its west is the wife of Rudra and to its north is Padmanabha (or Vishnu); at the center of the three worlds is Anarak.[7] the Mahabharata says that if a person approaches the wife of Rudra, he does not have to face any adversity.[8] Whoever has a 'Darshan' of Lord Shiva at the south of Anarak is said to be liberated from all sins.9 Whoever has 'Darshan' of Padmanabha is believed to secure a place in 'Vihnuloka' (heaven). A dip in the waters at Anarak on the sixth day of the moon in the month of Baishakha (April-May), if it happens to be a Tuesday, is said to liberate a person from all sins.[10]

There is a sacred tank here, which is known as Ban Ganga or Bhishma Kund. It was here that Bhishma Pitamaha lay on his bed of arrows and asked Arjuna to give him a drink of water, as he felt thirsty. Arjuna pierced the earth with is arrow and a spring gushed out whose water helped to quench Bhishma's thirst. Whoever bathes in the holy waters of this tank earns great merit. There is another Ban Ganga at village Dayalpur near Kurukshetra, which was created when Arjuna shot the ground with his arrow in order to bring forth water for the horses of his chariot at the time of his fight with Jayadratha.

Another holy spot in the Kurukshetra region I once visited is Koul, which many scholars identify with Kulongpun of the Mahabharata or Kulontaran mentioned in the Vamanapurana, according to which, Lord Vishnu had established it for safeguarding the system of Varna-Ashrama (caste system).[11] A dip here is said to enable the followers of the four 'Varnas' (castes) to secure space at the feet of Lord Vishnu.[12]

Once I passed through a place known as Apaga, a name that figures in the Mahabharata. It is mentioned as Apaya in the Rigveda. In ancient times, there used to be a small rive, here between the Saraswati and Drishadwati rivers. It was on the banks of these rivers that the ancient sages created the verses of the Vedas.[13] According to the Mahabharata, a person who takes a dip in the waters of Apaga and worships Maheshwara achieves supreme merit and the liberation of his family.[14] A person, who offers 'Shyamak' rice (a particular variety of rice) along with 'Ghee' (clarified butter) to the Brahmins here has all his sins destroyed. By feeding a single Brahmin here, he is said to achieve the merit of feeding crores of Brahmins.[15] A person who offers 'Pinda' (offerings to one's dead ancestors) here in the month of Bhadra (August-September) on the 14th day of the dark fortnight of the moon at noon achieves liberation.[16]

It is difficult to correctly identify the spot where this holy place was once located. The place that was pointed out to me is some distance away from the Kurukshetra University to its south west. It said to be close to the spot known as Karna Ka Tila. The whole place is in ruins and not much trace exists of the ancient place, which was so sacred once upon a time.

By this time, the spirit of festivity was already in the air because Diwali, the most important festival of Haryana, was round the corner. An occasion that formed part of the series of observances connected with Diwali was provided by Karva Chauth. Also known as Kartik Chauth or Karak Chauth, it was widely celebrated in Haryana and the other States of north west India. The wives of the I.A.S. Officers of Haryana cadre informally put across a suggestion to me and my wife to organize a get-together at our Raj Bhawan in celebration of Karva Chauth. No such function was ever held at our Raj Bhawan, but I saw on objection to accepting this very welcome suggestion.

And so on the evening of October 28, 1988, the halls of Raj Bhawan resounded with the tingle of bangles and the hearty laughter of a gaggle of venerable ladies—wives of I.A.S. Officers and lady I.A.S. Officers—who turned up on the invitation of my wife Anita. Besides being the hostess for the occasion, my wife also participated in the observance as whole-heartedly as the guests. Though I did not attend the function, the report that I got in due course on the observance of this solemn occasion made me feel quite happy that the assembled ladies had indeed a great time together.

The legend behind Karva Chauth is quite interesting. It is said that once when Arjuna went to the Nilgiris to do penance, Draupadi felt somewhat concerned over the many dangers that, she thought, he would have to face from his enemies. This was her threat perception about Arjuna, a V.I.P. Of the Mahabharata era! She expressed her concern to Lord Krishna and sought his guidance as to what steps could ensure Arjuna's welfare and security. Upon this, Lord Krishna narrated to her what advice Lord Shankar had given to Parvati, who was faced with a similar situation. In this context, Shankar had told Parvati about the story of Karva Chaturthi, which goes somewhat as follows.

Once upon a time, there lived in Shukraprasthapur (an ancient name of Delhi) a wise Brahmin by name Ved Sharma, who had a wife named Leelavati. They had seven valiant sons and an extremely beautiful daughter by name Veervati, who was given away in marriage to a Brahmin well versed I the scriptures. Veervati observed several 'Vratas' (ceremonies for fulfillment of vows) including Karva Chauth on the fourth day of the dark fortnight in the month of Kartik, on which occasion, she along with her brothers and sisters-in-law observed day-long fast and worshipped various gods and goddesses. By evening, Veervati felt hungry and fatigued and fell into a swoon. All her relatives were deeply concerned over this development.

One of Veervati's brothers looked at the night sky and saw a glow on the horizon, which, he thought, was an indication that the moon was rising. The rites of Karva Chauth required a lady to break her fast after moon-rise. Since Veervati's brother disclosed that he had seen the moon, she made the requisite offerings to the gods and goddesses and partook of some food. According to another version of the story, her brothers, out of their genuine concern for her, created the illusion of the moon by making a big ball of fire behind a hillock and interposing in front of it a screen with fine holes as in sieve. Veervati thought that it was the moon that she had seen and so had her meal Soon after this, her husband suddenly expired, the reason being that she had taken food on the night of Karva Chauth before seeing the moon.

Veervati worshipped Lord Shiva, keeping fast for one whole year! As her husband's body had been pierced with 365 nails, she removed a nail everyday. A slightly different version of the story says that she had fasted for the next seven years! At the end of this period, she and her sisters-in-law again observed Karva Chauth in accordance with all the rites. That night, many goddesses including Indrani came down to earth to observe Karva Chauth and sat by the side of Veervati. Then Veervati ascertained from Indrani the appropriate rites of Karva Chauth. She enquired why her husband had expired even though she had observed Karva Chauth. Indrani explained that this was due to the fact that Veervati had not observed Karva Chauth properly and had taken food before moon-rise. She advised Veervati to observe all the rites of Karva Chauth properly and assured her that she (Indrani) would bring her husband back to life.

And that is what happened! Veervati's husband, Ved Sharma, sprang back into life and the two led a long and happy life thereafter. Hearing this account given by Lord Krishna, Draupadi started observing Karva Chauth as a sequel to which the Pandavas succeeded in defeating the Kauravas in the Mahabharata war.

Another version of the legend of Karva Chauth is that a woman by name Karva, the devoted wife of her husband, was once bathing when she was suddenly attacked by a crocodile. She managed to tie up the crocodile with a rope and then approached Yama, the Lord of the dead, with the plea that the crocodile be sent to hell. As Yama declined to oblige her, she threatened to pronounce a curse upon him. Yama now relented and despatched the crocodile to hell. He also rewarded Karva's husband with long life.

It is in pursuance of this tradition that the women of Haryana and some other Sates observe fast on the day of Karva Chauth between star-down and moon-rise. Most of them manage to eat a substantial meal (Sargi) very early in the morning before sunrise. They eat again at night after performing Puja and offering the 'Arghya' of flowers and fruits to the moon in a 'Karva' (*i.e.* an earthen pot with a spout). The daughter-in-law offers to the mother-in-law a 'Karva' made of sugar candy and seeks her blessings for the well-being and long life of her husband.

A ritual observed during the Puja in the evening is the exchange of Karvas among the ladies. An idol of Gaur Mata or Parvati, the consort of Lord Shiva, is placed at the place of the Puja. A prescribed couplet seeking the blessings of Gaur Mata for the long life of the husband is repeated by the ladies. One of the elderly ladies, usually the mother-in-law, narrates the story of Karva Chauth to the other ladies. The ceremonies end with a feast.

The deeper significance of Karva Chauth lies in the emphasis it lays on the spirit of conjugal love, which is the bedrock of social harmony. It is an occasion for giving expression to 'Strishakti' or women's power of achieving their goal through sacrifice, as is brought out in the legend about Karva's success in making Yama accede to her demand for punishing the crocodile and granting a long life to her spouse. Karva Chauth is an ancient custom that finds mention in the Vishnu Purana and in Tantric literature. The cardinal message of Karva Chauth is that the husband and the wife are expected to play respectively the roles of Shiva and Shakti, whose union lies at the root of the creation of the universe, as has been explained by many ancient seers, notably Shankaracharya, who, in his Saundayalahari, has given the name 'Chaitanya Lahari' to the 'cool breeze' that flows in the wake of this union, bringing in good health and well-being.

Here again, the initiative lies with Shakti, because it is she, who, as Kundalini Shakti, lies at the Muladhara Chakra, coiled like a serpent, wakes up and moves from one Chakra to another, ultimately reaching the thousand-petalled Sahasrara Chakra, where Shiva, the Supreme Purusha, resides and awaits her. The union of Shiva and Shakti leads to bliss and liberation. The dynamic role of Shakti in actualizing this union explains why in our ancient tradition women were accorded a place of pre-eminence and venerable figures like Radha and Sita often took precedence over their spouses namely Krishna and Rama respectively. The importance of Strishakti symbolized by Karva Chauth is in consonance with this tradition.

Ganesha, the guardian angel of the Muladhara Chakra, who plays the vital role of the remover of all obstacles by effectuating the Shiva-Shakti union, is also worshipped on the occasion of Karva Chauth.

The Vishnu Purana says that the sixteenth Karva Chauth in the life of a married woman is the most important because it is at that time that she looks her best and radiates feminine charm, grace and, above all, power. The Tantras also assign considerable importance to the number 16, which is reflected in the worship of 'Sodoshi' endowed with 16 graces. The Sri Yantra, a powerful tool of Tantra Sadhana, has 16 lotus petals.

Over the years, Karva Chauth has come to be observed as the husband's day and become quite hip with specially designed greeting cards sold in the market. Riding the wave of consumerism, fashion stores now aggressively sell items of jewellery, Mangalsutras etc. while beauty parlours thrive and Mehndiwalis and Churiwalis do brisk business during Karva Chauth.

There are several other customs that are observed in Haryana as a prelude to Diwali. For example, there is the ceremony of 'Hoi' that is observed seven days before Diwali *i.e.*, On the eighth day of the dark fortnight of the moon. On this occasion also, women fast the whole day, seeking the blessings of the elders for the prosperity and longevity of their husbands. Two 'Gharas' (earthen pots), one slightly bigger than the other, are filled with water and decorated with flowers etc. And are installed in the house. These pots are preserved till Diwali. The eldest lady of the family *i.e.*, usually the mother-in-law or, in her absence, the eldest daughter-in-law wears a silver necklace with some round coin-like silver pieces that look like medals. There are as many of these pieces in the necklace as the number of the family's male members. The necklace is proudly flaunted by the lady wearing it as an emblem of the family's glory. Is it also a symbol of the family's male chauvinism?

This gender bias still prevails all over our country. In Bengal, during Durga Puja, even now we offer 'Anjali' (*i.e.* flower and 'Bel' leaves) to the goddess chanting a prayer: "Dhanang Dehi, Putrang Dehi, Yasho Dehi" (give us wealth, son and glory). A daughter does not figure in the wish-list!

Another custom associated with Diwali is 'Dhan Teras' observed two days before Diwali. I overheard a conversation among some members of our Raj Bhawan staff, which revealed when and where they were planning to go to buy new utensils on this occasion. Buyers throng utensil shops a few days before Diwali. The general belief is that goddess Lakshmi showers her blessings and riches on these utensils.

Many observe this occasion as 'Dhanvanari Jayanti', Dhanvantari being the physician of the gods. It is said that Lord Vishnu once proceeded along with her consort, goddess Lakshmi, towards 'Mrityulok', the abode of Yama (the Regent of Death, somewhat like the Greek Pluto and Minos). He told Lakshmi not to follow him as he made his move towards the south. However, Lakshmi did not oblige him, but followed him and, after some time, entered a field. She began to eat the sugar cane that grew in the field. When Lord Vishnu saw her there, he got angry and pronounced a curse upon her, saying that she would have to render service for thirteen years to the cultivator, who owned the sugar cane field. Lakshmi then went to the house of the cultivator and offered him her blessings that included riches of various kinds. At the end of the stipulated thirteen years, Lakshmi wanted to leave the place, but the cultivator was unwilling to part with her. The cultivator prayed to Lord Vishnu, seeking his intervention to ensure that Lakshmi would never leave her house. Upon this, Lord Vishnu handed over a few 'Cowries' (shells of small gastropod) to him, advising him to take a dip in the Ganges and then to cast the "Cowries' into the river. However, the cultivator did not act on this advice.

At this stage, Lakshmi told the cultivator that, as Dhan Teras was to come off the next day, he should clean up his house and light an earthen lamp in order to keep the place illuminated the whole night. As the cultivator complied with this suggestion, Lakshmi showered various riches on his house. Lord Vishnu realized that it was Lakshmi who had blessed the cultivator. Every year, the cultivator observed this custom, keeping his place clean, illuminating his house and buying new utensils on the occasion of Dhan Teras, which prompted Lakshmi to keep on rewarding him with wealth and prosperity. Following his example, the local people began to observe this custom each year on the day of Dhan Teras. Thus, the practice of buying new utensils on this occasion came into vogue.

Another legend says that, according to the horoscope of the son of King Hima, the former was pre-destined to die of snake-bite on the fourth night of his wedding. That night, his wife illuminated their bed-room with numerous lights and put up a heap of gold coins and ornaments at their door-step. She also sang songs and narrated many captivating stories all through the night. Yama, the god of death, who arrived there, was blinded by the dazzle of the lights and the glow of the gold coins and ornaments. He spent the whole night there, enthralled by the music and the stories and left the place in the morning. The prince's life was saved and Dhan Teras came to be known as Yamadeepdan (gifting of lamps to Yama).

The festival of Diwali that came off on November 9, 1988, was celebrated all over Haryana with traditional gaiety. We organized a function at our Raj Bhawan on this occasion and distributed sweets and fireworks to the children of the ASHI (Association for Social Health in India), an NGO based at Chandigarh. We also celebrated Diwali with the members of the staff of our Raj Bhawan.

At about this time, we attended a few programmes of classical music at the Tagore Theatre, the artistes including such top names as Kumar Gandharv and Ashwini Bhide.

On November 1, 1988, we celebrated Haryana Day, the day on which the State of Haryana came into being in 1966. A big reception followed by a cultural function were organized at our Raj Bhawan to mark the occasion.

In the first week of November, 1988, I paid a visit to Sonepat, which had been carved out of Rohtak as a district in 1972. L.M. Salins, District Collector, and Hari Singh Ahlawat, Superintendent of Police, briefed me about the affairs of the district. I went round some places and met people from various walks of life to acquaint myself with their problems and with the history and culture of this region. Some say that Sonepat is identical with Swarnprasth—one of the five 'Prasthas' or places, which the Pandavas had asked for from the Kauravas as the basis of a settlement—a demand which the Kauravas turned down, thus paving the way for the Mahabharata war. Some say that Sonepat derived its name from its founder, Raja Soni, who was a descendant of Arjuna. It is not known whether there is any basis for these views.

What is known for sure, however, is that Sonepat finds mention in the Ashtadhayi of Panini, which testifies to its existence at least around the sixth century B.C. Some semi-circular coins of the Graeco-Bactrians recovered in Sonepat in the 19th century A.D. point to its antiquity. The unearthing here of a large number of coins of the Yaudheyas are an indication that Sonepat formed part of their territory. This is in consonance with the fact that the Yaudheyas' territory extended from Rajasthan on the west to Yamuna on the east. Between the second century B.C. And the fourth century A.D., Sultan Masud Dipal Har, who was the Governor of Sonepat, was defeated by Sultan Masud of Ghazni in 1037 A.D. While in Sonepat, I had a view of the Dargah Mamu Bhaanza, the old Muslim shrine , which accommodates the tomb of Hazrat Imam Nasimuddin.

There are several important towns in Sonepat district such as Ganaur, where the Bharat Steel Tubes Ltd., the largest such plant of our country is located. Another town is Murthal, which literally means the abode of peacocks, and derives its name from the fact that it used to abound with peacocks and other colourful birds. There is another place called Kundli, whose people rose in revolt during the 1857 uprising. Another place—Akbarpur Barota—has an impressive gate called Akbar Darwaza dating back to the 16th century A.D. At Rai in this district, there is the famous Motilal Nehru Sports School, which is run like a public school and combines liberal education with high class training in sports and athletics. I was formally associated with this institution in my capacity as the Governor of Haryana. Sonepat is a thriving industrial centre of Haryana known for the Atlas Cycles, a leading cycle manufacturing plant of our country.

Sonepat is famous for having sired two outstanding personalities in the cultural field. One is Dip Chand Bahman of Sheri Khanda, who made innovative contributions to Swaang, a form of musical folk drama, by laying a good deal of emphasis on the modulation of the voice and the use of the emotional element to smoothen the rough edges of old stage-craft, imbuing it with a great deal of sophistication. The other great son of Sonepat is Pandit Lakshmi Chand, who opened a new chapter in the style of Ragini singing. A popular singer as well as a composer, he was responsible for staging many Swaang operas with a variety of themes. One Hardeva, a disciple of Dip Chand, introduced some changes in the Swaang by giving considerable importance to the Raginis in preference to earlier musical styles.,

Another form of folk drama that is popular in Haryana is the Ramlila based on the Ramayana that is performed around the time of Dussehra. The Ramayana of Jaswant Singh, a folk poet from Tohana in Hissar district, usually provides the dialogues and songs of Ramlila in Haryana. The Swaang is, however, performed all through the year. Its popularity as a form of folk entertainment owes a lot to the genius of Krishan Lal Bhat, who lived around 1730 A.D. In course of time, the Swaang achieved a measure of professional excellence to be able to replace other professional shows like the Nakkals and the Vaishyas. The story of the Swaang is usually drawn from some myth or an event of one of some epic or the life of some historical figure or folk hero. Verses known as Raginis are sung to the accompaniment of typical instruments like the Sarangi, Dholak, Tabla, Khartal, Chimta etc. It is an open air show performed an a platform made of ordinary wooden cots around which the villagers sit on the ground to provide the audience. The leader of the Swaang artistes is called the Sangi, who initiates the show usually with a brief introduction. From what I learnt about Swaang in Haryana, I got the impression that it had a lot in common with the 'Yatra' or folk theatre of Bengal.

Some time in the first half of November, 1988, Chief Minister, Ch. Devi Lal, called on me and requested me to give my consent to his proposal for the grant of pardon to and stay the execution of Daya Ram, who had been convicted in the case pertaining to the murder many years ago of Pratap Singh Kairon, the famous Chief Minister of Punjab. I had my own reservations about letting off a person, who was guilty of such a heinous crime. But I was aware of the constitutional position that, if the Chief Minister formally put forward such a proposal, I, as Governor, was bound to sign on the dotted line. Still, I tried to dissuade him from adopting such a populist measure. There were doubts in my mind about certain legal issues that arose from the peculiar circumstances of this case. On my suggestion, Ch. Devi Lal agreed that I could have the matter referred to the Attorney-General of India through the Union Home Ministry. Naturally, it took some time to get this matter sorted out, as the opinion of the Attorney-General was not forthcoming. This continued to hang fire for a long time and no action could be taken in the matter as long I was the Governor of Haryana. After I laid down my office in February, 1990, I learnt that Daya Ram was granted pardon.

In the second week of November, 1988, I visited Faridabad district in connection with a few engagements. One of these was to address and interact with the officers of the State Government at the Rajhans Hotel, Surajkund. My next engagement was to visit, along with my wife, the famous SOS Children's Village in Greenfields, Faridabad., of which J.N. Kaul was the moving spirit. I announced a grant for this village, which is a unique institution, functioning as part of a global organization that provides 'home' to orphans and homeless children in many counties.

The first such Village had come into being as the brain-child of Dr. Herman Gmeiner in 1949 in Austria. The movement later spread all over the world. The first SOS Village in India came up at Greenfields in 1964. When I visited this place in November 1988, I was glad to see that J.N. Kaul , a man of 65 years, was a popular figure, highly respected by the inmates of the Village as their 'Papaji' (dear father).

While driving through Faridabad and adjacent areas, I recognized them well because I had visited them or passed through them quite a number of times in the past. I recalled the historical and cultural background of most of these places. It was in 1607 A.D. that Sheikh Farid, an official of Emperor Jehangir's administration, had laid the foundation of this town, giving it a fort and a mosque. Close to Faridabad, on the road to Agra is the town of Ballabhgarh, which is believed to owe its name to one Ballabh Singh, its founder. And thereby hangs a tale. He is said to have been the son of a poor cultivator. One day, his mother carried some lunch consisting of just bread and onions to his father, who was working in the field. Before walking up to his father, his mother put Ballabh Singh (who was a small child) down on the ground under a tree.

When she came back after handing over the food to her husband, she saw to her consternation a black snake that had spread its hood over the child. As she raised an alarm, some men came to deal with the snake. However, a Sadhu, who was also there, stopped them from causing any harm to the snake, saying that it was a good omen and that the boy would one day become a king. And that is what happened in due course.

One day, after Ballabh Singh had grown up, he saw two donkeys walk into his house, carrying loads of gold Mohurs. Thus he became rich and ruled over Ballabhgarh and the adjoining territory. During the time of his successors, many buildings, gardens and tanks came up, which still constitute the important landmarks of Ballabhgarh. Nahar Singh, the last ruler of this dynasty, was executed by the British for his role in the uprising of 1857.

There are some places in this area, which are very ancient. For example, Chhainsa, about 12 miles south east of Ballabhgarh, which is close to the Yamuna, is said to have been associated with the Pandavas. Tilpat near Faridabad was one of the five places, which Duryodhana refused to concede to the Pandavas, thus making the Mahabharata war inevitable.

Sihi is another place, which is well known because it is here that Surdas, a great poet of Brajbhasa, was born. Traces of painted grey ware, which are believed to be relics of the Harappan civilization, have been discovered here as at several other places in this region.

There is some controversy over the exact place where Surdas was born. One view is that he was born at Runkta in U.P. On the Agra-Mathura Road.[17] According to some, he was born at Mathura, while some others have suggested Gwalior and Lucknow. However, Sihi is the generally accepted place of his birth. Similarly, there is no unanimity about the date of his birth. After evaluating the available information in this regard, Dr. K.C. Yadav, the well-known historian of Haryana, mentions Vaisakha Krishna 11, VS. 1535 (1478) as the date of his birth.[18]

There are several views about the caste of Surdas. His caste has been variously mentioned as Bhatt, Dhadhi, Jat, Saraswat Brahmin etc. Considering all the evidence, Dr. K.C. Yadav comes to the conclusion that he was a Saraswat Brahmin. Surdas was the fourth son of his parents, who were extremely poor. He was born blind and did not have even eye-lids. This naturally brings to one's mind the name of the blind English poet, Milton.

In his magnum opus, Sagara, Surdas has given a brilliant description of the imaginary world of his childhood. Leaving home at the age of six, Surdas went away to a village a few miles from Sihi and spent 12 years there. Dr. K.C. Yadav, who made enquiries in this regard at some near-by villages, came to the conclusion that this village was Manjhavali, about 12 kilometres from Sihi, where he lived for 12 years under the care of his Guru, whose name is not known.

Various view have been expressed about the religious sect to which Surdas belonged at this stage. Dr. K.C. Yadav does not attach much importance to views that Surdas was then a Ramanandi or a Shaivite. He is inclined to think that Surdas was a Harivanshi when he lived at Manjhavali. Surdas was initiated into musicology early in life by a Sadhu of the Haridas order at a village not far from Sihi.[19]

In 1496 A.D., at the age of 18, Surdas renounced the world and left Manjhavali with just a piece of cloth on his body and holding a staff. He marched with some of his followers and reached Vishrantaghat in Mathura. Then he proceeded to Gaughat, a small village on the road to Agra. He lived there for 12 years, composing and singing hymns in praise of Lord Krishna. His melodies were so popular that thousands of people became his disciples.

Around 1510 A.D., Vallabhacharya, a leader of the Sudhadvaita school, visited Gaughat after defeating many learned pundits of Mayavada in north and south India. Surdas met him and sang two of his hymns, which were marked by a note of deep penitence. Vallabhdas advised Surdas to adopt a more positive approach and display a spirit of fellowship with God. Surdas accepted him as his Guru and was initiated into the Vallabhacharya Sampradaya. He began to compose songs which were close to Vallabhacharya's teachings. He sang them with such devotion that Vallabhacharya felt extremely pleased.

Soon, he proceeded to Gokul with Vallabhacharya. There, he threw himself on the ground and began to sing verses about Krishna's 'Bala-lila' (child-sport). Thereafter, Vallabha took Surdas to the temple of Shrinathji at Govardhan, the most sacred place of the Vallabhacharya Sampradaya. As advised by Vallabhacharya, he spent the rest of his life here as the Keertanacharya of this temple. This was the most creative period of his life, as he composed thousands of hymns while he was here. His Dhrupads and Bhajans occupied the border-line between classical music on the one hand and tribal or folk music on the other.[20]

Except for brief visits to Mathura and Gokul, Surdas remained at Govardhan. It was during this visit to Mathura that Surdas met Emperor Akbar. It is said that one day when Tansen sang a song composed by Surdas, Akbar was so deeply moved that he was eager to meet Surdas. His wish was fulfilled one day in 1569 A.D. when he had the opportunity of hearing Surdas sing his compositions.

Akbar was moved by the very first song sung by Surdas in praise of Krishna. He said: "Shri Bhagawan has given me the power to rule and every man of talent has sung of my glory. You are also a talented man and, therefore, you should also sing of my fame. If you wish to get something from me (in return of this), you need only ask for it." Sur gave a sharp retort to Akbar in a 'Pada':

"There is no room in my heart for anyone else,
For here lives Krishna, the son of Nanda ...."

Akbar, who was pleased to hear this, wanted to give Surdas a few villages and considerable wealth, but the latter declined to accept anything. At last, Akbar said: "Baba Sahib, give a command at least." Sur's command was typical of a Sannyasi: "From now on, never again summon me or come to meet me." That was the moral fibre of Surdas.[21]

Surdas died in 1583 A. D. at the ripe old age of 105 years.

Surdas got the inspiration for his 'Padas' from the Bhagavata Purana. He had composed a lakh of 'Padas', but hardly a tenth of his output is available now.

Faridabad, as I saw it towards the end of 1988, had still an agricultural economy, but the dominant leitmotif was the industrial development that had taken place there. Faridabad and Ballabhgarh presented the most industrialized face of Haryana, thanks largely to the contribution made over the decades since the partition of the country by the refugees from Punjab and the North West Frontier Province, who came and settled down here, set up their small industrial units to eke out a living and gradually converted them into bigger thriving enterprises. The support provided by the State Government and proximity to Delhi were contributory factors that helped the industrialization of this region.

Notes

1. ततो व्यासस्थली नाम यत्र व्यासेन धीमता।
   पुत्रशोकाभितप्तेन देहेत्यागार्थनिश्चयः।।
   कृतो देवैश्रच राजेन्द्र पुनरुत्थापितस्तदा।।

   महा. ३:११:८२, वामन सरो. १५:५८:५६
   (पदम, आदि खण्ड २६:८८)
2. अहल्या द्रौपदी कुन्ती तारा मन्दोर तथा।
   पंचकरप्याः स्मरेन्नित्यं महापातक नाशनं।
3. A.D. Pusalker in the History and Culture of the Indian People edited by Dr. R.C. Mazumdar, Volume I, p. 304.
4. *Ibid*
5. Article captioned "Glimpses of Ancient Haryana" by Dr. Buddha Prakash in "Haryana: Studies in History and Politics" edited by J.N. Singh Yadav.
6. पवनस्य ह्रदे स्नात्वा दृष्टवा देव महेश्वरं।
   विमुक्ताः कलुषैः सर्वै शैवं पदमाप्रयात्।।

   (वामन सरो. १६:१)

7. यत्र पूर्वे स्थितो ब्रह्मा दक्षिणे तु महेश्वरः।
रुद्र पत्नी पश्चिमतः पद्मनाभोत्तरे स्थितः।
मध्ये अनरक तीर्थ त्रैलाकस्यापि दुर्लभम्।।

(वामन सरो. २०:२४:२५)

(महाः वनः ८१:१४६:४८)

8. अभिगम्य च तां देवीं न दुर्गतिमवाप्यु मात्

(महा. वनः ८१:१४८)

9. अभिगम्य महादेवं मुचयते सर्वकिल्विषैः

(महा. वन. ८१:१४६)

10. वैशाखे च यदा षष्टी मंगलस्य च दिनं भवेत्।
तदा स्नानं तत्र कृत्वा मुक्तो भवति पातकेः।।

(वामन सरो. २०:२६)

11. कुलोत्तारण नामानं विष्णुना कल्पितं पुरा।
वर्णनामाश्रमाणां च तारणाय सुनिर्मलम्।।

(वामन सरो. १५/७४/७५)

12. ब्राह्मणाः क्षत्रियाः वैश्या शूद्रा ये च तत्परायणा।
स्नाता भक्तियुक्ताः सर्वे पश्यन्ति परमं पद्म।।

(वामन सरो. १५:७७)

13. दृषद्वत्या मानुष आपयायां सरस्वत्यरिवदग्ने दिदीहि।

(ऋग्वेद ३:२३:४)

14. आपगायां नरःस्नात्वा अर्चयित्वा महश्वरम्।
गाणपत्यमवाप्रोति कुलं चोद्धरते स्वकम्।।

(महा. वन. ३:८१)

15. श्यामकाभोजनं तत्र मः प्रयगच्छति मानवः।
एकस्मिन भोजिते विप्रे कोटिर्भवति भोजिता।।

(महा. ३:८१:५६)

16. नभस्य मासि सम्प्राप्ते कृष्णपक्षे विशेषतः।
चतुर्दश्यां च मध्याहने पिण्डदो मुक्तिमाप्रयाद।।

(वामन सरो. १५:६)

17. This and the next few paragraphs on Surdas are based on Dr. K.C. Yadav's monograph on Surdas published in the Journal of Haryana Studies, Vol.XI, Nos. 1&2, 1979.
18. *Ibid.*
19. *Ibid.*
20. Article entitled "Art and Architecture in Haryana Through the Ages: A Survey" by Dr. K.C. Yadav in the journal of Haryana Studies, Vol. XV, Nos. 1&2, 1983, p. 43.
21. Dr. K.C. Yadav's monograph mentioned at 17 above.

14

Haryana's Torch-bearers of Vedanta: Gaudapada, Teacher of Adi Shankaracharya's Teacher: Totapuri, Baba of Ladhana, Guru of Sri Ramakrishna

A few months after I took over as the Governor of Haryana, I was presented with a copy of a book "Haryana Ki Vedanta-Parampara" authored by Vaidya Banamali Dutt Sharma. I went through this book with great interest and came across two very important observations made by the author. One of these was that Baba Totapuri, who had initiated Sri Ramakrishna Paramahansa in Vedanta Sadhana and successfully led him to attain Nirvikalpa Samadhi, was a man from Haryana—to be precise—from Ladhana, now in the Kaithal district of Haryana. The author's other observation was that another intellectual stalwart from Haryana, namely Acharya Gaudapada was the teacher of Govinda Yati, who in turn was the teacher of Adi Shankaracharya, the high priest of Advaita Vedanta. Naturally, all this aroused my curiosity and led me to undertake deeper studies into Haryana's Vedantic tradition.

Let me deal with the second name first because Gaudapada had preceded Totapuri by at least a millennium. Since the Vedas and the Vedanta had been first revealed on the bank of the Sarasawti river in Haryana, it is not surprising that some renowned exponents of Vedanta should have hailed from its soil. Vaidya Banamali Dutt Sharma has mentioned in his book that Gaudapada was a son of Haryana. It is said that he was born in a village of Gaud Brahmins near Kurukshetra located on the bank of the Hiranyawati river, which, like the Saraswati river, has also disappeared.[1]

Gaudapada is a well-known figure of the world of Vedanta. Though Badaranarayana had expounded the doctrine of the Brahman as the central reality in his Vedanta Sutra (also called Brahma Sutra) before the Mahabharata was composed, yet, it was Gaudapada, who, in the words of Dr. S. Radhakrishnan, [2] was the first to come forward with a systematic exposition of Vedanta. He lived at the end of the 7th or the beginning of the 8th century A.D. His works Karika and Uttaragita have given a masterly exposition of Advaita philosophy with reference to such themes as the identity of Brahman and Atman, Maya and the importance of wisdom as the means of achieving liberation. His writings bore the distinct imprint of Buddhism, which held extensive sway when he lived and whose doctrines he generally accepted 'when they were not in conflict with his own Advaita'.[3] It is not my intention here to provide a full account of Gaudapada's philosophical ideas. Suffice it to say that there were many differences between his and Adi Shankaracharya's interpretation of Advaita.

Now to Totapuri. Vaidya Banamali Dutt Sharma's book was the outcome of his long and sustained research work that was backed up by visits to many places such as Ladhana, Allahabad, Nagpur, Akola, Bhar, Karnali, Kolkata etc. where he managed to gain access to many old and valuable documents and gathered whatever information was available about Totapuri and his religious order. Karnali near Akola on the bank of the Narmada had a temple and an Akhara which was a branch of the Mahanirvani order. Many Sadhus of Totapuri's religious order used to live here. It was here that Totapuri had done his Sadhana. In fact, centuries ago, Govinda Yati, the Guru of Adi Shankaracharya, had also done his penance here under the guidance of Acharya Gaudapada, the Vedantist from Haryana.[4]

A study of Vaidya Banamali Dutt Sharma's book, which clearly brought out Totapuri's roots in Haryana, whetted my appetite for taking a closer look at this matter. I had occasion to read a little about Totapuri in the course of my studies about Sri Ramakrishna.[5] But it was after I visited Kaithal in July 1988 and learnt about Ladhana being very close by that I began to hold discussions with some learned men as well as local people who were associated with the spiritual world. Later, I had several occasions to visit Kaithal and to see Ladhana as well. I particularly recall my visit to Kaithal in the month of November, 1988.

On the night of November 22, 1988, there was a ghastly incident of terrorist violence at Kaithal (now a district, but then a part of Kurukshetra district). I was rung up by a senior police officer late at night and informed that Sikh terrorists had killed 22 persons and injured 40 innocent persons. The next day, I paid a visit to Kaithal for an on-the-spot assessment of the law and order situation. Sampat Singh, Home Minister and N. P. Dhanda, another Minister, who belonged to the area, were also present there along with some high officials to discuss the situation with me.

In the course of this trip as well as on a later occasion, while driving through Kaithal region, I saw Ladhana that was located on the road towards Warwana at a distance of about seven miles from Kaithal. This place used to be in Karnal district, but was later transferred to Kurukshetra district. When Kaithal became a separate district, Ladhana formed part of it.

Ladhana's fame as a spiritual centre derives from the fact that that the monastery of the Dashnami Sampradaya of Adi Shankaracharya's lineage is located here. The Sannyasins following Adi Shankaracharya's tradition were divided into ten sub-sects, namely Giri, Puri, Bharati, Vana, Tirtha, Aranya, Parvata, Sagara, Ashrama and Saraswati. The Puri Sannyasins of Ladhana traced their origin to the Sringeri Mutt, that was one of the four that had been set up by Shankaracharya at four corners of our country, the others being the Govardhan Mutt at Puri, the Jyoti Mutt at Joshmath and the Sarada Mutt at Dwaraka. The Naga Sannyasins living at the Ladhana monastery were committed to Advaita Vedanta (the non-dual path) of which Adi Shankaracharya was the torch-bearer. It was at Ladhana that the great Vedantist saint Totapuri, the Guru of Ramakrishna, lived. In the 16th century A.D., under the leadership of Swami Madhusudan Saraswati, the Naga Sannyasins of this order started carrying weapons, presumably in reaction to attacks by the Muslims.

Ladhana village came into existence more than 800 years ago.[6] How did it acquire the name Ladhana? and thereby hangs a tale.[7] One Baba Balaknath used to do penance here. He got two wells bored for the local Banjaras. Soon a village cropped up there. The Banjaras used to engage in trade here for which they loaded and unloaded their goods ('Ladana' in Hindi). Thus this place came to be called 'Ladana'. In his write-up on the Mutt of Baba Totapuri in the 'Udbodhan', [8] Swami Alokananda has referred to a severe famine in the Kaithal region caused by lack of rains. When the Nawab of Kaithal approached Baba Rajpuri to help in getting rains, the latter gave him a positive response and also told him to rush back to Kaithal as otherwise he might be faced with some serious problem. No sooner had the Nawab reached Kaithal than the rains came and flooded the whole region. Pleased with this turn of events, the Afghan rulers gifted Ladhana village to the Baba and called it Ladhana Baba.

What has surprised me all these years is that not many people are aware of the name of Totapuri or of his status as the Guru of Sri Ramakrishna or of the fact that this exalted Guru was from Haryana or even of the existence of a place called Ladhana that is known among the local people as 'Baba Ka Ladhana'. To put it the other way round, one could say that Totapuri was the Baba of Ladhana (Ladhana Ka Baba)!

The general lack of awareness about Ladhana is evidenced by the fact that even Swami Saradananda, a direct disciple of Sri Ramakrishna and the author of the Bengali masterpiece 'Sri Ramakrishna, the Great Master" (translated into English by Swami Jagadananda) has stated in his book that Totapuri's Math (monastery) was located at Ludhiana! It was Swami Alokananda of the Ramakrishna Mission, who paid an exploratory visit to Ladhana and disclosed in his article in the November 1977 issue of the 'Prabuddha Bharata' (or awakened India) that Totapuri's Ashrama was at Ladhana, now in the Kaithal district of Haryana.

Swami Alokananda has written in this article about the big reservoir at the entrance to Ladhana and the two monasteries located on its banks, namely Baba Sital Puri's Math and Baba Raj Puri's Math. The latter Math, which is Totapuri's Math, was dilapidated and in a state of utter neglect and disrepair. There were five temples inside the Ashrama complex of which one was meant for 'Dhuni' or keeping fire. The fire was kept burning round the clock because the sect of Naga Sannyasins to which Totapuri belonged highly revered fire. One of these temples was built on the 'Samadhi' of Totapuri. There were more than thirty 'Samadhis' of saints in the Ashrama complex. Swami Alokananda could not ascertain the exact name of Totapuri's Guru. When he visited the Ashrama, one Badri Puri, then about seventy years of age, was its head. To quote Swami Alokananda:

"The name of the Founder-Guru of this class of monks was Marhi Bhagawan Puri, from whom this sect of sannyasins has originated;

therefore, in Hindi language, his lineage is termed as 'Marhi', which signifies house or the source of its origin. Below is given a list of names according to the descending order of Gurus-cum-disciples: Marhi Bhagawan Puri, Jagmohan Puri, Janged Puri, Hardwar Puri, Mansa Puri, Saraswati Puri, Raj Puri, Siddha Puri, Bhandar Puri, Dalel Puri, Aan Puri, Tota Puri, Chaitanya Puri, Hazari Puri, Gopal Puri, Kedar Puri, Badri Puri and Shyam Puri. Beyond this, nothing more could be known about the sacred Ashrama where once Srimat Totapuri lived."

A fair is held at Ladhana every year on the Navami day during Durga Puja. According to the account given by Swami Alokananda, Baba Raj Puri, the founder of Totapuri's monastery, used to be quite intimate with the Nawab of Kaithal and the two sometimes played dice at the latter's palace. An interesting incident narrated by Swami Alokananda runs as follows:

"One day when they were playing at dice, suddenly Puriji began to laugh, and, just after some moments, began to weep bitterly. Being surprised, Nawab Saheb asked Puriji Maharaj the reason of such rapid changes in his temperament. To this Puriji replied: 'In the Delhi royal court one beautiful damsel was entertaining the audience by her superb dancing, and the audience being charmed were regaling at the enchanting performance; therefore, I was also laughing being highly pleased. But suddenly, that dancing girl collapsed and died; and the hearts of those present were gripped by intense remorse at this most tragic incident. That is why I was also weeping, sharing in their grief.'

"The Nawab Saheb immediately dispatched messengers to Delhi in order to verify the statement of Puriji and came to know that the incident was absolutely true. As a result, the reverence of Nawab Saheb for Puriji became all the more intensified. Later, the Nawab Saheb himself got that vast Monastery and the water-reservoir constructed near Ladhana village, and gave vast lands as a gift for its maintenance. Another famous personality, Amar Singh Rathor, had also a share in the erection of the Monastery." the close relations between the Nawab and Puriji were a pointer to their secular outlook. Adi Shankaracharya was an ardent follower of the principle of 'Sarva Dharma Samanvaya'.

Now from clairvoyance to alchemy. Totapuri had told Sri Ramakrishna that he believed in and had practised alchemy, converting on some occasions copper and other baser materials into gold. The ancient monks of his community used to inherit this knowledge lineally. But this knowledge was used not to serve one's selfish interest or to live a life of luxury, but to enable the holy men to meet the expenses of their travel, food and the bare necessities of life, if the need for money arose in certain circumstances.[9]

According to the account given by Totapuri to Sri Ramakrishna,[10] the former was taught Vedanta in his boyhood by his own teacher, the head of the community of monks. Totapuri had lived with him for a long time, studying scriptures and doing Sadhana. There were seven hundred monks in that community, who daily engaged themselves in meditation and other exercises as part of their Vedantic Sadhana. Initially, they learnt meditation, sitting on cushions; then they sat on a piece of skin or on the bare ground. In due course, they were taught to go about naked as part of the exercise to give up the "fetters of shame, hatred, fear, egoism." They had to go out and travel from one place of pilgrimage to another. The monks elected as Mohanta or President one amongst themselves, who had attained the true state of a Paramahansa."

Itinerant Totapuri,[11] who belonged to Raj Puri's Math of Ladhana, had spent a long time in central India on the banks of the Narmada and kept himself fully pre-occupied with his spiritual activities. There he had acquired the knowledge of Brahman by following the path of Vedanta and reached the Nirvikalpa plane of consciousness. Thereafter, he had gone to Puri and had the vision of Lord Jagannath. He then reached Dakshineswar after visiting Gangasagar en route. His plan was to return to Ladhana. But, as Swami Saradananda observes, he did not then understand that "in Her inscrutable sport", the mother of the universe had brought him there to complete his own knowledge and to make Her own child (*i.e.* Sri Ramakrishna) practise Vedantic discipline with his help.

Totapuri was a strong and hefty person and went about completely naked. (Sri Ramakrishna used to call him 'Nangta', the naked one.) Visiting the Kali temple at Dakshineswar, Totapuri saw Sri Ramakrishna sitting in a corner. He at once realized that Sri Ramakrishna was no ordinary person. The year was 1865. Sri Ramakrishna was about 29 years of age, his face beaming with radiance. Totapuri thought that here was one who was fit for undertaking the Vedantic path to achieving Nirvikalpa Samadhi. He asked Sri Ramakrishna: "Vedanta Sadhana Karogey?" (Will you practise Vedantic discipline?) Sri Ramakrishna replied that he was unable to commit himself to anything without getting the permission of his mother. Totapuri asked him to go and seek his mother's permission. Sri Ramakrishna went before goddess Kali, his Mother, and sought her permission, which was instantaneously given.

When Sri Ramakrishna told Totapuri that his Mother had given him the requisite permission, the latter understood that what he meant by his Mother was not his own mother but the image of goddess Kali in the temple. Totapuri had no faith in the idea of a personal god like Kali, which he regarded as a delusion. What he treated as the ultimate reality was Brahman of Vedanta on which alone one was expected to concentrate for achieving one's spiritual goal and God-vision.

Totapuri did not try to disabuse Sri Ramakrishna's mind of ideas about personal God, thinking that the true knowledge of Brahman would in due course make him give up such notions. A problem which Sri Ramakrishna had mentioned to Totapuri as a likely impediment on the path to his initiation into Sannyasa was the fact that he was married. Totapuri brushed it aside, saying that it did not matter at all. He stressed that a person, who had his mind fixed on Brahman, would be in a position not to deviate from the path of renunciation and detatchment, despite his wife being with him. And this was the case with Sri Ramakrishna. Totapuri then proceeded to initiate Sri Ramakrishna into Sannyasa and in the path of Vedanta Sadhana. He asked the latter to give up his sacred thread and the tuft of hair on his head. Sri Ramakrishna complied, but did all this privately with the consent of Totapuri since otherwise this might cause grief to his mother. Then he performed 'Sradh' offering 'Pinda' to his ancestors. Thereafter, he offered 'Pinda' to himself. All this meant that before his initiation into Sannyasa, he renounced any right to the three worlds of 'Bhuh', 'Bhuvah' and 'Swah'.

It is said that at the time of Sri Ramakrishna's initiation, Totapuri gave him the name 'Ramakrishna' by which he later came to be known. But many do not accept this view and believe that it was Mathuranath, the great devotee of Sri Ramakrishna, who had first called him by that name—a view which Swami Saradanda considers reasonable.

Then, at the auspicious moment called 'Brahma-muhurta' *i.e.*, two hours before day-break, Totapuri and Sri Ramakrishna met in a hut in the Panchavati (a secluded garden) of Dakshineswar. The Homa-fire was lighted. Totapuri, the Guru, started chanting the Mantras.

The various rites performed included Viraja Homa that concluded with many oblations.[12]

"Tota, a knower of Brahman, now encouraged the Master (*i.e.*Sri Ramakrishna) to practise the contemplation of "Not this", "Not this", a well-known discipline in the Vedanta and remain identified with Brahman Itself." [13]

Totapuri's efforts to make Sri Ramakrishna attain Samadhi initially encountered some difficulties, as whenever he sat for meditaion on the nameless and formless Brahman, "the intimate form of the universal Mother consisting of the effulgence of pure consciousness" appeared before his mind, making him "quite oblivious of the renunciation of names and forms of all description." Totapuri scolded him severely and still Sri Ramakrishna made no progress."

Swami Saradanda continues: "He (Totapuri) then looked about in the hut, and finding a broken piece of glass, took it in his hand and forcibly pierced my forehead with its needle-like pointed end between the eye-brows and said: 'Collect the mind here at this point.' With a firm determination I sat for meditation again, and as soon as the holy form of the Divine Mother appeared now before the mind as previously, I looked upon knowledge as a sword and cut the form mentally in two with that sword of knowledge. There remained then no function in the mind, which transcended quickly the realm of names and forms, making me merge in Samadhi." [14]

Totapuri sat for a long time by the side of Sri Ramakrishna and then came out of the room, locking it behind him. Sri Ramakrisna remained in that state of Samadhi for three days. Then Totapuri opened the lock, entered the room and saw Sri Ramakrishna seated in the same posture in which he had left him three days ago. His face was effulgent and his mind was merged in Brahman. Totapuri touched Sri Ramakrishna, but there was no response, so wholly he was merged in Brahman. It perfectly fitted the classical description of Samadhi: When the upper, middle and lower parts of the being are completely filled with the consciousness of Atman—this is the sign of Samadhi.[15]

This account of Sri Ramakrishna completely losing himself in Brahman is so captivating that I have considered it worthwhile quoting from Swami Saradananda's book in extenso. Seeing Sri Ramakrishna in that state, Totapuri could not believe his own eyes. He was amazed that Sri Ramakrishna had realized Brahman in a day, something he had himself achieved after forty long years of austere Sadhana! He exclaimed in joy: "Oh, the divine Maya! It is indeed Samadhi—the Nirvikalpa Samadhi, the ultimate result attained through the path of knowledge spoken of in the Vedanta! Ah, how strange is the Maya of the Divine!" [16]

Totapuri brought his disciple back to his consciousness of the external world by repeatedly chanting the Mantra "Hari Aum".

Sri Ramakrishna had thus mastered the technique of moving over to the Nirvikalpa plane of consciousness. At a later stage, when Totapuri left Dakshineswar, Sri Ramakrishna had decided to dwell in this state of oneness with God or the state of 'non-duality' for a continuous period of six months. In this state, he forgot all ideas of "I" and "You" and was not even conscious that he had a body. He described Samadhi as a state of "bliss and bliss alone ......a. state beyond all states, which the scriptures speak of as a sport of the Self with the Self. The Master (*i.e.* Sri Ramakrishna) was always experiencing such an indescribable state without any break." [17]

As mentioned by Swami Saradanda, Sri Ramakrishna had narrated an incident to bring out Totapuri's fearlessness.[18] Once, at dead of night, when it was very calm all around, Totapuri made the 'Dhuni' (fire) bright and prepared to sit for meditation. Suddenly, the branches of the trees in Panchavati (Dakshineswar) shook and a tall human form came down, looking steadfastly at Totapuri, walked up to the Dhuni and sat down. Asked who he was, he said that he was a Bhairava (a demi-god), who resided on the tree there in order to protect that holy place. Totapuri was not at all afraid and told him: "You and I are the same being, you are one manifestation of Brahman, and I am another. Come, sit down and meditate." the Bhairava laughed and vanished into the thin air. Quite unperturbed by this event, Totapuri turned to meditation. Totapuri narrated this incident to Sri Ramakrishna, who said that he had also seen him many times. According to Sri Ramakrishna, this Bhairav had predicted certain future events to him.

As Sri Ramakrishna said: "At one time the Company (Government of India) tried to acquire the whole plot of the Panchavati for the purpose of building a powder magazine. Hearing of the proposal, I was much worried lest I should lose the opportunity of sitting and calling on the Mother in this place away from the noise and turmoil of the world. Mathur instituted a case against the Company on behalf of Rani Rasmani to prevent the acquisition of the piece of land. At that time, one day I saw the Bhairava sitting on the tree. He said to me, by a sign, that the Company would not be able to acquire the land; they would be defeated in the case. It actually came to pass."[19]

Sri Ramakrishna had several spiritual instructors in different phases of his life, but he had mentioned only three of them, namely Bhairavi Brahmani, Totapuri and a Muslm—Govinda. Totapuri no doubt imparted the knowledge of Vedanta to Sri Ramakrishna, but, like the other Gurus, Totapuri also learnt something from Sri Ramakrishna before he left Dakshineswar. He used to move from place to place "like the eternally free wind without any restraint" and like the wind, he remained "untouched by the good or evil of the world." [20] He did not usually stay more than three days at a place. But at Dakshineswar, he lived for eleven months at a stretch because of Sri Ramakrishna's great attraction.

Sri Ramakrishna often expressed to his disciples at Dakshineshwar his appreciation of the spiritual lessons which Totapuri used to convey to him by narrating many anecdotes based on incidents mentioned in ancient religious books. Totapuri had told Sri Ramakrishna that often at dead of night, he heard what was known in spiritual language as 'Anahata Shabda'—a kind of sound that was nothing but divine music, something that ordinary people could not hear. (Sri Sri Ramakrishna Kathamrita by Mahendra Nath Gupta cited by Vaidya Banamali Dutt Sharma in his "Haryana Ki Vedanta-Parampara Aur Baba Totapuri").[21]

Totapuri kept by his side nothing more than a pair of tongs and a water pot, which he used to polish everyday to the point of imparting them a shine. Sri Ramakrishna asked him one day why he practised meditation daily since he had already realized Brahman. Totapuri pointed to the water pot and said that it looked very bright because it was polished daily and that if it was not polished everyday, it would lose its lustre. Similarly, he said, the mind would accumulate dirt if it was not polished by the daily practice of meditation. Upon this, Sri Ramakrishna asked him what would happen if the water pot was of gold. Totapuri agreed that a pot made of gold would not lose its shine. Totapuri learnt from Sri Ramakrishna the truth that the latter's mind was like gold which never lost its brightness. "Thus from the very beginning a kind of interchange of ideas between the teacher and the disciple used to take place".[22]

Elaborating further on how Totapuri learnt some important spiritual lessons from Sri Ramakrishna, Swami Saradananda states

[23] that Totapuri had been brought up under the affectionate care of his teacher right from his childhood. In north western India, there was a custom of issueless couples taking a vow that they would make a Sannyasin of their child if one was born. Swami Saradananda infers from what he heard from Sri Ramakrishna that Totapuri was one such child offered to his teacher.

As pointed out by Swami Saradananda, [24] Totapuri had lived life in very favourable spiritual circumstances. He never had to experience sufferings arising from the many pitfalls of the senses and vicious tendencies. He "was quite ignorant of the influence of the beginningless Avidya Maya, the power of Brahman that was difficult to overcome." He was capable only of a 'hard-hearted aversion" to man's failings rather than "any sympathy for him in his helpless predicament in life." It was only after coming in touch with Sri Ramakrishna that Totapuri understood this aspect of the spiritual problem, as explained below.

An adept at attaining Brahman through the austere path of renunciation, Totapuri did not realize that love, affection and devotion could also teach a man to gradually renounce everything including his own happiness and lead him ultimately to realize God and that devotion, Japa, "glorifying the excellences of the Lord in songs and praises, chanting His name" were not to be scoffed at. As a result, "a loving conflict" of views sometimes arose between Totapuri and Sri Ramakrishna.

An instance of such a conflict is mentioned by Swami Saradananda. Sri Ramakrishna often clapped his hands and danced, while in a highly devotional mood and chanted aloud: "Call on Hari, call on Hari. Hari is the Teacher, the Teacher is Hari." One night when Sri Ramakrishna was doing this, Totapuri felt amused that a person, who had attained Nirvikalpa Samadhi, should continue with such practices of the cult of Bhakti, which, he thought, were meant for men at the lowest rung of the spiritual ladder. He sarcastically asked Sri Ramakrishna if by clapping his hands, he was fashioning Chapatis , as people in north west India did. Sri Ramakrishna laughed in response and said: "What foolishness! I am taking the names of God and you say I am fashioning Chapatis!"[25]

The conflict between the two also came out on another occasion mentioned by Swami Saradanada.[26] One evening, while they were engaged in conversation sitting near Totapuri's Dhuni, a servant, anxious to smoke the hookah, picked up a piece of burning wood from the Dhuni and put it into the bowl of the hookah. Seeing this, Totapuri flew into a rage, called the servant names and threatened him with his pair of tongs. Sri Ramakrishna burst into a laughter and exclaimed at this behaviour of Totapuri: "Ah, wretchedness! Ah, forgetfulness!" Saying this again and again, he rolled over on the ground. Totapuri asked him why he was doing that and if he had not realized that the servant had done something wrong.

Sri Ramakrishna's answer was highly illuminating: "Yes, that is true; but I see at the same time the depth of your knowledge of Brahman! Just now you were saying, "There is nothing except Brahman and all things and persons in the universe are merely its manifestations.' But forgetting all that, the very next moment, you are ready to beat a man! This is why I laugh, thinking of the omnipotence of Maya." Totapuri became serious and, after remaining silent for a while, said: "You are quite right. Under the influence of anger, I forgot everything indeed! Anger is surely very reprehensible. I give it up this very moment." Since that day, Totapuri was never seen to be angry again.

Sri Ramakrishna used to say that none can secure liberation till the grace of the Mother descends on him. Totapuri had received the grace of the Mother of the universe right from his birth and, therefore, it had been easy for him to go forward on the spiritual path, attain Nirvikalpa Samadhi and realize God. He knew that all this was possible only by the grace of the Divine Mother. Now, something happened that enabled him to detect "that mistake of his mind."

Totapuri had a robust physique and could digest whatever he ate. Once he fell seriously ill at Dakshineswar as the water and the humid climate of Bengal told upon his health. He had a severe bout of blood dysentery which caused him acute bodily pain for some days. One night, his pain became unbearable and he felt that he could bear it no more. He decided to get rid of it by drowning himself in the Ganges. He got down into the water and moved further and further, but despite all the effort he made, he failed to get to any place where the water was deep enough for drowning. Totapuri was surprised.

Then suddenly, he felt as if someone from within pulled off the veil over his intellect. His mind was dazzled by a bright light and he saw the Mother of the universe. Here I can do no better than to quote extensively the inimitable words of Swami Saradanada. "Mother, the unthinkable Power! Mother in land and Mother in water! the body is Mother and the mind is Mother; illness is Mother, and health is Mother; knowledge is Mother and ignorance is Mother; life is Mother and death is Mother; everything I see, hear, think or imagine is Mother. She makes 'nay' of 'yea' and 'yea' of 'nay'! As long as one is in the body, one has no power to be free from Her influence, no, not even to die, till She wills! .... That One whom Tota has so long been realizing as Brahman, to whom he has been offering his heart-felt love and devotion, is this very Mother! Shiva and Shakti are One, ever existing in the form of Hara-Gauri—Brahman and Brahma-Sakti are one and the same![27]

Totapuri walked back to the shore and sat near the Dhuni in the Panchavati for the rest of the night, his mind full of bliss. As soon as it was morning, Sri Ramakrishna came to enquire about his health and found him a completely different person. Totapuri described to him all the events of the night and said: "It is the disease that has acted as a friend to me. I had a vision of the Mother of the universe last night and am freed from the disease by Her grace. Ah! how ignorant I was so long! Well, you please persuade your Mother now to allow me to leave this place. I am now convinced that it was She who had kept me confined here somehow or other in order to teach me this Truth."[28]

Sri Ramakrishna said: "Well, you did not accept the Mother before and argued with me saying that Sakti was unreal! But you have now seen Her yourself, and direct experience has now got the better of your arguments. She has convinced me already of the fact that just as fire and its burning power are not different, so, Brahman and the power of Brahman are not different, but one and the same."[29]

Then the two great saints walked up to the temple of goddess Kali and prostrated themselves before the holy image. Both felt in their hearts that the Mother was pleased and had given permission to Totapuri to leave. A few days later, Totapuri took leave of Sri Ramakrishna and left Dakshineswar, walking towards the west. He did not come there again.

Totapuri realized that Brahman and Shakti were identical and that both 'Nirakara' Brahman and 'Sakara' God stood for the ultimate reality—a truth that Sri Ramakrishna had all along been trying to convey to Totapuri. In his book on Totapuri, Vaidya Banamali Dutt Sharma has sought to bring this out by citing some analects from the Upanishads. The idea of 'Niarakara' Brahman comes out clearly in the following line quoted by him from the Kathopanishad(1/3/9): Ashabdamashparshamarupamavyayam Tatha Rasam Nityamagandhavachcha Yat. (That which is without sound, touch, form, sap and smell and is indestructible and eternal—that is the nature of Brahman).[30]

About 'Sakara' God also, Vaidyaji cites several passages, one of which is the following from the Taittriyopanishad (2/6/4): Sohakamayata | Vahu Syam Prajayeyeti | Sa Tapohtapyata | Sa Tapastaptva Idam | Sarvamasrijata Yadidam Kim Cha | . It means: the Parameshwara thought that he should reveal himself and become many. He did penance and created everything that can be seen or comprehended. He created this entire universe.[31]

By his association with Sri Ramakrishna, Totapuri was able to appreciate the truth of the latter's spiritual line that made no distinction between Brahman of the Vedanta and his concept of "God as a Person" whom he knew as Divine Mother or goddess Kali.

The concept of Brahman is similar to the idea of the ultimate reality of the universe. Aldous Huxley, author of 'The Perennial Philosophy', says that the world is a manifestation of a single "Eternal Ground". This view is called "monism" by the philosophers. "Religious monism" is the view that everything in this universe has "the same Ultimate Ground of Existence, God." [32] Adi Shankaracharya can be said to be one of the foremost exponents of religious monism. This school of thought denies the ultimate reality of various phenomena including "Gods as Persons", whom it regards as "Maya" or illusion. Totapuri, a follower of Shankaracharya's line, did not, therefore, initially see any point in Sri Ramakrishna's devotion to Personal Gods like Lord Krishna or Mother Kali. But later, he changed his perception, as has been already explained.

Sri Ramakrishnạ, a devotee of goddess Kali, undertook intense Sadhana to have a direct vision of the Divine mother. And eventually, he succeeded. "..........suddenly, I had the wonderful vision of the Mother .... I did not know what happened then in the external world ..... But in my heart of hearts, there was flowing a current of intense bliss, never experienced before, and I had the immediate knowledge of the light, that was Mother ..... And what I saw was a boundless infinite conscious sea of light! However far and in whatever direction I looked, I found a continuous succession of effulgent waves coming forward, raging and storming ...." [33] Sri Ramakrishna said that he immediately recognized this light as the Mother. Did he have the vision of a woman? According to some scholars, he did see the Divine Mother or Mother Kali i. e. God, who is a Person. Some say that what he saw was Brahman.[34]

In Sri Ramakrishna, we see the epitome of both Jnana Yoga and Bhakti Yoga. A Jnana Yogi discriminates between the real and the unreal and seeks to acquire the knowledge of Brahman, which alone is real. Sri Ramakrishna's realization of Brahman through Nirvikalpa Samadhi was in pursuance of the path of Jnana Yoga. His vision of Mother Kali, who symbolizes both the ultimate reality and God as a Person, by following the path of emotional devotion marked him out as a master practitioner of Bhakti Yoga. For him, both paths were equqlly valid and led to the same goal. As he said: "For the bhakta, he assumes forms. But he is formless for the Jnani." [35] Totapuri imbibed all these lessons from Sri Ramakrishna before he left Dakshineswar.

There is a view that Sri Ramakrishna's spiritual line has a lot in common with Sikhism. The basic formulation of Sikhism, while accepting the Ultimate Reality, does not regard external phenomena as unreal. As pointed out by Prof. Kapoor Singh: "The world of phenomena is no longer a dream and a phantasmagoria in the minds of the gods, to be by-passed and shunned. It is as real, in fact as the Ultimate Reality, but the perceiving human mind is beset with limitations that must be transcended and cut asunder before it can be seen thus. It is this that made it possible for Sikhism to lay down that the highest religious discipline must be practiced while remaining active in the socio-political context, and not by worldly life." [36] (An echo of this idea can be heard in the practical application of Sri Ramakrishna's spiritual line by the Ramakrishna Mission in the field of social service.)

This principle of Sikhism repudiates the basic concept of Hinduism known as the doctrine of Maya, "which is postulated as the illusory power which createth appearances and ignorance." [37] This, however, is very similar to what Sri Ramakrishna used to say. Though this view was not exactly identical with what Totapuri initially believed in, yet it has to be remembered that he is also said to have been a Sikh ascetic—a Udasi Sikh. Those who belong to this sect may hail from various castes and communities, but believe in the tenets of the Granth Sahib. Sri Ramakrishna's most illustrious disciple, Swami Vivekananda often uttered and introduced into his writings the Sikh mystic formula, Waheguru.

After taking leave of Sri Ramakrishna in 1865 A.D., Totapuri went to Puri and then returned to Ladhana. According to the account of Vaidya Banamali Dutt Sharma, [38] Totapuri was the Mahant of the monastery at Ladhana in 1871.

At a later date, Totapuri seemed to have moved over to Benares, Puri and, maybe, to other places. He appears to have stayed mostly at Puri. He preferred to remain unknown and some instances of his attempt to keep his identity under wraps have been revealed in Vaidya Banamali Dutt Sharma's book.[3]9 One such instance was mentioned by Mahamahopadhyaya Dr. Gopinath Kaviraj. He used to see a Naga Sannyasin at Benares many years after he had left Dakshineshwar. He seemed to be living somewhere between the Dashashwamedh and Darbhanga Ghats of Benares. Dr. Gopinath Kaviraj met him daily at one of the Ghats to attend his religious discourse. This Sannyasin was never seen to eat anything. He always remained cheerful and never took any money or articles of food from anybody. Endowed with great wisdom, he appeared to have attained the ultimate spiritual goal. Some knowledgeable people thought that he was none other than Totapuri, though he never disclosed his identity. The second such instance figuring in Vaidya Banamali Dutt Sharma's book was narrated by Dr. Bhagawati Prasad Sinha of the Gorakhpur University. According to him, a great Yogi who had appeared at Puri in the autumn of 1949 was Totapuri, though he evaded all questions about who he really was.

Totapuri got rid of his mortal coil at Puri on August 14, 1961. This was about 97 years after he had met Sri Ramakrishna at Dakshineswar. He must have been quite old at the time of his demise. Even if we assume that he was at least 20 years of age when he began his forty-year-long Vedanta Sadhana, he must have been sixty years of age by the time he turned up at Dakshineshwar in 1864 A.D. to initiate Sri Ramakrishna in Vedanta. Therefore, when he passed away in 1961, he would have been over 157 years of age! in fact, he must have been much older than that. There is nothing very strange about this since several spiritual leaders are known to have enjoyed that kind of longevity. Two great saints from Bengal, namely Hitlal Misra and the Brahmachari of Barodi lived much longer, as brought out in my book 'In Sun and Shower'.[40]

Totapuri lies buried in his monastery in Ladhana.

Notes

1. Haryana Ki Vedanta-Parampara Aur Baba Totapuri by Vaidya Banamali Dutt Sharma, Foreword by Dr. Rajdeo Sinha of the Himachal Pradesh University, Shimla. Page 18. Also p. 21.
2. Dr. S. Radhakrishnan's Indian Philosophy, Volume Two, p. 452.
3. *Ibid*, p. 453.
4. Vaidya Banamali Dutt Sharma's book cited at 1 above, p. 64.
5. Books and literature I consulted in giving this account about Totapuri included: (a) Sri Ramakrishna, the Great Master (original in Bengali) by Swami Saradananda (translated into English by Swami Jagadananda;
   (b) Ramakrishna and His Disciples by Christopher Isherwood;
   (c) Sri Sri Ramakrishna Paramahansa (in Bengali) by Shrish Chandra Motilal;
   (d) Thakur Ramakrishna (in Bengali) by Brahmachari Akshaychaitanya;
   (e) Sri Sri Ramakrishna Punthi (in Bengali verse) by Akshay Kumar Sen;
   (f) Param Purush Sri Sri Ramakrishna (in Bengali) by Achintya Kumar Sengupta.
   (g) Sri Sri Ramakrisnakathamrita by M, a pseudonym for Mahendra Nath Gupta, a disciple of Sri Ramakrishna.
   (h) The Gospel of Sri Ramakrishna by Swami Nikhilananda (an English translation of (g) above.
6. Vaidya Banamali Dutt Sharma's book cited at 1 above, p. 42.
7. *Ibid*.
8. *Ibid*, p. 43.
9. Sri Ramakrishna, the Great Master by Swami Saradanananda (translated by Swami Jagadananda from Bengali into English), Volume I, p. 562.
10. *Ibid*, pp. 551-552.
11. Haryana Ki Vedanta Parampara Aur Baba Tota Puri by Vaid Banamali Sharma and Dhruv Sharma, Haryana Sahitya Sadan.
12. Swami Jagadanda's English version of Swami Saradanda's book, pp. 288 onward.
13. *Ibid*, p. 289.
14. *Ibid*, p. 290.
15. ऊर्ध्वपूर्णमधः पूर्णां मध्य पूर्णां यदात्मकं,
    सर्वपूर्णां स आत्मेति समाधिस्थस्य लक्षणम्।
    —Vide Param Purush Sri Sri Ramakrishna (in Bengali) by Achintya Kumar Sengupta, Volume I, p. 126.
16. Swami Jagadananda's English version of Swami Saradananda's book, p. 291.

17. *Ibid*, p. 407.
18. *Ibid*, pp. 549-550.
19. *Ibid*, p. 550.
20. *Ibid*, p. 549.
21. Vaidya Banamali Dutt Sharma's book cited at 1 above, pp. 153-154.
22. Swami Jagadananda's book cited at16 above, p. 548.
23. *Ibid*, p. 552.
24. *Ibid*, p. 553.
25. *Ibid*, p. 556.
26. *Ibid*, p. 556.
27. *Ibid*, pp. 560-561.
28. *Ibid*, p. 561.
29. *Ibid*, p. 561.
30. अशब्दमस्पर्श मरूपमव्ययं तथा रसं नित्यमगन्धवच्च यत्।

    (कठोपनिषद् १/३/६)

    —Vaidya Banamali Dutt Sharma's book cited at 1 above, p. 132.
31. सोऽकामयत। बहु स्यां प्रजायेयेति। स तपोऽतप्यता
    स तपस्तप्त्वा इदं ँ सर्वमसृजत यदिदं किं च।

    (तैतिरीयोपनिषद् २/६/८)

    —*Ibid*, p. 133.
32. Science Without Boundaries—A Synthesis of Science, Religion and Mysticism, Chapter 9, Copyright by Arthur J.D. Adami.
33. *Ibid*.
34. *Ibid*.
35. *Ibid*.
36. Essentials of Sikhism by Sirdar Kapoor Singh, National Professor of Sikhism, p. 2.
37. *Ibid*, p. 1.
38. Vaidya Banamali Dutt Sharma's book cited at 1 above, p. 53.
39. *Ibid*, pp. 186-191.
40. 'In Sun and Shower' by H.A. Barari, chapter 25, pp. 275-294.

15

I Take to Golf: 1857 Uprising: Raja Nahar Singh's Double Game: the Surajkund Crafts Mela: Plight of Bonded Labourers: Relics of Indus Valley Civilisation Unearthed in Haryana: Vedic Civilisation Pre-harappan? Aryan Invasion of India A Myth? Aryan Roots of the Persians: Vedic Mathematics: Excavations at Rakhigarhi and Other Harappan Sites in Haryana: Indus Valley or Saraswati Valley Civilisation? Was Lord Rama Born at Banwali in Haryana?

In December 1988, I started learning golf for which opportunities were provided to me by the Chandigarh Golf Club, thanks to the generosity of its Secretary, Sudhir Verma. Ajoy Johal, an outstanding golf player of our country, used to coach me up on a part of our Raj Bhawan lawns, where some kind of mini-golf course was improvised for me. Later, I played regularly—all by myself—at the Chandigarh Golf Course, which was located next to Raj Bhawan. Ajoy Johal accompanied me while I played there and put me through my paces. Occasionally, I also met there his brother, Amandeep Johal, an accomplished golf player, who in due course acquired great name and fame, both in our country and in the international golf circuit. Simultaneously, I was playing tennis as well. Looking back, I feel that it was a wise move on my part to take to golf in Chandigarh because it is a wonderful game that I have continued to play in Delhi.

Some time in the second week of December 1988, I went to Kolkata along with my wife and put up at the Raj Bhawan there as the guests of Nurul Hasan, Governor of West Bengal. During this visit to Kolkata that I had the pleasure of meeting Jyoti Basu, Chief Minister of West Bengal, at his official residence located on the premises of the Raj Bhawan. Of course, I had met him earlier at official meetings in Delhi when I was the Director of the Intelligence Bureau, Government of India. But this was my first meeting with him on a one-to-one basis. There is no doubt that he has a certain personal charm, which, apart from many other factors, must have contributed to his gradual rise to the position that he came to occupy in due course in the country's political firmament.

This was my first visit to Kolkata after I became the Governor of Haryana. So I took this opportunity to meet all my near and dear ones including, of course, my old and sick mother, who was so overjoyed that tears began to roll down her cheeks. In less than a year, she was no more.

My wife and I also paid a visit to Shantiniketan, where we were put up as the guests of the Vishwabharati University. The late Dr. Nemai Sadhan Bose, the then Vice-Chancellor, took very good care of us. We spent a whole day going round the campus and attended a cultural programme in the evening that the authorities were gracious enough to organize for us. This was followed by a dinner party which the Vice-Chancellor and the Members of the University's Executive Council very kindly hosted for us. A visit next day to Sriniketan was a highly rewarding experience, as it encapsulated poet Tagore's vision of rural development.

Back to Chandigarh in the third week of Decenber 1988, I again got sucked into vortex of social, official and political activities. In the first week of January 1989, I proceeded to Bhiwani where I inaugurated the 13th All-India Yoga Competition. On January 17, 1989, I went to Surajkund near Faridabad and presided over a meeting of the Executive Council of the Battles of Panipat Memorial Society. Apart from Ch.

Devi Lal, Chief Minister, several Ministers and Government officials of Haryana as well as many historians and architects also attended the meeting. Also present were Vijay Raje Scindia, Rajmata of Gwalior, and Sardar Angre in view of the special role that the Marathas had played in the Third Battle of Panipat. We decided on several steps to be taken for building a suitable memorial to the heroes of the battles of Panipat.

In the afternoon, I visited some near-by places of Faridabad and Gurgaon districts, one of which was Badkhal, a tourist spot with a lake. I was told that the name Badkhal had its origin in the Persian words 'Be Dakhal', meaning a place free from hindrance of any kind *i.e.*, a place where one can move about without any obstacle—a sine qua non for any place from the tourism point of view. Another place I visited was Sohna, which derived its name from 'Sona' or gold, the reference here being to the fact that in the past, gold dust was often found here deposited on the beds of the waterways after the rains. The hot springs here famous since ancient times were patronized by Emperor Akbar.

On January 20, 1989, I visited Karnal to be the chief guest at a programme of Odissi dance by Swapna Sundari that had been sponsored by the SPIC MACAY—Society for the Promotion of Indian Classical Music and Culture Amongst Youth. The wife of an I.A.S. Officer, Swapna Sundari had already made an impact at the national plane and had a great presence, which, together with her virtuoso performance, charmed the predominantly young audience. The SPIC MACAY, which had been functioning since 1977, was doing a wonderful job in the sphere of promoting awareness among the youth and students of the country about Indian culture, particularly classical music and dance.

On January 23, 1989, I presided over the meetings of the Executive Committee and the General Body of the Haryana Hind Kusht Nivaran Sangh held at Raj Bhawan. Thanks to the sincerity and commitment of Smt. Suman Duggal, Honorary General Secretary of the organization, and her devoted band of activists, a good deal of work was being done on the anti-leprosy front. The meetings held Raj Bhawan gave me an opportunity of coming in touch with a large number of grass-roots level workers such as doctors, government servants and representatives of NGO's, who had first-hand knowledge of the problems in this field of work.

Haryana has a long tradition of anti-leprosy work that commenced formally with the setting up of the Leprosy Mission at Ambala as early as in 1874 by W.C. Bailey, an Irish teacher and missionary. Having arrived in this country in 1869 at the invitation of his brother, Christopher, who was already here, young Bailey had the shock of his life when he saw leprosy-affected people and launched his anti-leprosy project. What has become generally known by now is that leprosy is neither the result of a divine curse nor hereditary nor contagious nor incurable. There is, therefore, no reason to treat the victims of leprosy as social outcasts or to even call them "lepers". The most appropriate thing to do is to call them "leprosy patients".

Now a sure remedy for leprosy is available, which is known as the multi-drug therapy (MDT). Any skin patch, white or red in colour, attended with loss of sensation, could be a symptom of leprosy. Early detection and treatment with a single dose of MDT cures it completely. However, delay in detection and treatment could prolong the course of treatment and might even result in deformity. Reconstructive therapy has often proved successful, thus putting paid to earlier notions of "non-healing flesh". It is necessary in this country of Mahatma Gandhi to bring about a change in society's attitude towards the patients of leprosy.

Soon after this, on January 30, 1989, the anniversary of Gandhiji's martyrdom, I inaugurated the Anti-Leprosy Seals Sale Campaign at the Haryana Raj Bhawan.

Before this, on January 26, 1989, I had been to Faridabad to take the salute at the Republic Day Parade held at the Nahar Singh Stadium. The name of the stadium rang a bell in my mind about the role played by Nahar Singh, the Raja of Ballabhgarh adjoining Faridabad, in the 1857 uprising against British rule. Dr. K.C. Yadav, a well-known historian, has not projected a very favourable image of Nahar Singh, whom he has described as "timid and weak-minded".[1] Nahar Singh did not think it proper to rise against the British power, but since his State was close to Delhi, the center of the uprising, and its people had risen in rebellion, he joined the camp of Emperor Bahadur Shah and extended some assistance to the latter. But he avoided meeting Bahadur Shah in Delhi, despite several requests from the latter.

Raja Nahar Singh played a "safe game", which was also a "double game", because he extended his help to the British as well. He allowed the British the use of his territory in their fight against the rebels, besides sending them horses, elephants, bullocks, guns etc. He also wrote a series of letters to the highest British officials including the

Lt. Governor of Agra, the Commander-in-Chief of the British forces and Lord Canning, Governor-General of India, informing them that he had occupied the Parganas of Palwal, Pali and Fatehabad on behalf of the British Government, professing "extreme loyalty" to the British Government and even conveying intelligence to the British authorities about the state of affairs in Delhi.

Eventually, when Delhi fell and the rebellion collapsed, the British authorities did not spare Raja Nahar Singh as they were aware of his double dealing. He was arrested, brought to Delhi and tried for treason and waging war against the British. The Raja's statement in his defence gives a vivid account of his treachery against the country's patriotic movement. His attorney gave an account of the Raja's efforts at saving the lives of Europeans and Christians, how he had apprehended and sent to the British authorities a large number of rebels along with their chiefs. It was pointed out that the Raja had not sent any help to Emperor Bahadur Shah but had, on the other hand, provided intelligence to the British.

This defence did not impress the British authorities, which sentenced Raja Nahar Singh to death by hanging and forfeited all his properties. He was hanged to death on January 9, 1858 at Kotwali in Delhi's Chandni Chowk. As Dr. K.C. Yadav observes, the Raja was not at heart a traitor to the British Government. It was "vindictiveness and hasty judgement" that led to the "unjust" loss of the life and property of "an ally of the British".[2] Ballabhgarh was merged in Faridkot State.

Raja Nahar Singh is treated as a martyr in the light of what is generally looked upon as the injustice meted out to him by the British authorities. It is generally believed that he had organized the Sarva Khap Panchayats to fight against the British. It was in the month of Kartik (October-November) that he was said to have revolted against the British and taken over several villages in the area. For fighting the British, he had reportedly held secret meetings during the Kartik Mela with the Maharaja of Gwalior, Tantiya Tope and Mangal Pande, who attended the Mela. They evolved a strategy for the 1857 uprising.[3]

Several years later, I heard that at the instance of the Congress High Command, the party's Haryana unit had observed January 9, 2000 as the 142nd anniversary of Raja Nahar Singh's martyrdom at a function held at Faridabad. Raj Kumar Tiwatia, a great grandson of Raja Nahar Singh was one of the organizers of this function.

The 1989 Republic Day Parade at the Nahar Singh Stadium was followed by a reception in the evening hosted by me at the famous

Rose Garden of Faridabad. Chief Minister Ch. Devi Lal, almost all the Minister of Haryana, top officials of the State Government and a number of local people from various walks of life attended the reception.

On February 10, 1989, I was the chief guest at the ITF Junior Tennis Tournament held at the Chandigarh Lawn Tennis Association Stadium. The next day, I had the opportunity of seeing Leander Paes, then a very junior player, in action against Pakistan's Usman Rahim, Paes looked to be full of promise.

On February 12, 1989, I visited Surajkund in Faridabad district, where the famous annual Crafts Mela was in progress. This event had started in 1987 and the next year, I had visited the Mela from Delhi just a few days before I took over as the Governor of Haryana. It was, therefore, quite interesting for me to visit the Mela the next year and see it through the eyes of the Governor of the State. It had by then become a tourist hit with people from Delhi and adjoining areas as well as foreign tourists making a bee-line to it each of the 15 days from February 1 to 15 every year when it used to be held. The show was organized by the Surajkund Mela Authority with the active co-operation of the Haryana Government's Tourism Department and the Ministry of Tourism, Government of India.

The day I visited the Mela in my capacity as Governor came to be known as the Haryana Day of the Mela from that year onward. From then on, it also became a convention to choose a particular State of our country as the 'theme State' and to exhibit and specially highlight the crafts and cultural excellence of that State at the Mela. As far as I remember, Andhra Pradesh was the theme State of the 1989 Mela, when I visited it. My wife and I thoroughly enjoyed being at the Mela, as the whole place was resounding with the rhythmic beats of songs and dances put up as parts of various cultural programmes. We went round the Mela, expressing our appreciation of the numerous crafts of Haryana and many other States. There were magic shows, monkey tricks and displays by snake charmers.

The local officials told us many tales about Surajkund. It is a place whose past is steeped in an interesting amalgam of both history and legend. This amphitheatre-shaped sun pool of the shape of an amphitheatre was built in the tenth century A.D. by King Suraj Pal of the Tomar dynasty, who was a devotee of the sun god. Hence the name Surajkund. The king, being a victim of leprosy, was in a dejected mood and one day, while going on horse-back by the side of the sun pool, he came across a bird that was suffering from a particular disease.

The bird took a dip in the waters of the pool and, when it came out, it looked fully cured of its disease. Taking a cue from the bird, Suraj Pal also bathed in the pool and was miraculously cured of his leprosy! in gratitude, he renovated the sun pool and built a sun temple there. When I visited the Mela in February 1989, the temple was still in existence, but was in a dilapidated condition.

A prime attraction of the Mela was the captivating folk dances and music from the different States of our country, including, of course, Haryana. Reshma, the well-known musician from Pakistan, who once belonged to India, gave an enthralling performance in the evening in the fan-shaped open air theatre at the Mela ground. We relished every bit of it. Born at Bikaner in India, she moved over to Faisalabad in Pakistan in the wake of the partition of our country, when she was just six months old. She is an untutored musician, having had neither formal education nor formal training in music. When she sang at some shrines in Pakistan in the 1960's, she was picked up for songs over the radio. Later she flowered into a top-notch musician and in due course she became a disciple of the famous Indian musician Naushad.

Called the nightingale of the desert, Reshma has earned wide acclaim for her songs in several Hindi films, though her forte is her folk numbers in Rajasthani, Punjabi, Urdu and Pushto. Her fans are spread across both India and Pakistan. She regularly visits India to sing at Ajmer Sharif and the Dargas of Nizamuddin Aulia and Hazrat Bakhtiyar Kaki in Delhi. During our visit to the Surajkund Crafts Mela in February 1989, Reshma's Ghazals and folk numbers from Rajasthan drew repeated applause.

The next morning, I played golf at the Surajkund course, which was coming up nicely. S.K. Sharma, an I.A.S. Officer, who was then the Secretary to the Tourism Department, Government of Haryana, met me on the golf course and told me about the plans to improve the course. I used to play golf there whenever I visited Surajkund.

While travelling in this region, I became aware of some of the environmentally hazardous developments that were taking place. The Peacock and Badkhal Lakes faced threats from the construction activity going on in their vicinity. Another lake in the Dhauj village of Faridabad district was getting dry as it was being systematically drained out by the mining and land mafiosi interested in colonizing in the dry basin. Prof. Robert Chambers of the Institute of Development Studies, Sussex (England) and his wife, who had visited this picturesque area in the

1980's, had studied the local flora and fauna, including the numerous species of birds and how all this was being steadily destroyed as a result of quarrying by the mafia. The Indian Mountaineering Foundation had in the early 1980's protested against these depredarions as the Dhauj lake area had the most suitable rocks for climbing exercises, which were both nationally and internationally popular.

A related issue was the employment of bonded labourers for quarrying in the Surajkund area. The other issues were minimum wages and housing for them. The Bandhua Mukti Morcha and its President, Swami Agnivesh, were fighting for the rights of the bonded labourers and had in 1983 gone up to the Supreme Court, which had issued directions to the concerned agencies, most of which remained unimplemented for years.

On February 14, 1989, I proceeded to Hissar in connection with several engagements. Besides inaugurating a school here for hearing and speech handicapped children, I also went round the new building of the District Bal Bhawan and apprised myself of the various measures that were being taken to promote the welfare of children. The next day, in my capacity as the Chancellor of the Haryana Agricultural University, Hissar, I conferred the degree of Doctor of Science on Ch. Devi Lal and a retired I.A.S. Officer for their contributions to agricultural development. On this occasion, about a thousand students were awarded degrees in the disciplines of agriculture, veterinary science, home science, sports etc. Dr. Har Swaroop Singh, Vice-Chancellor of the University, read out the annual report of the University and Dr. L.D. Swindale, Director-General of the International Crop Research Institute for Semi-Arid Tropics (ICRISAT), Hyderabad, delivered the key-note address.

By now, I had paid several visits to Hissar district that had given me an opportunity of studying developments pertaining to the discovery in this region of several sites, which bore under their soil relics of the Indus Valley Civilisation. Names like Mohenjodaro and Harappa, which were now in Pakistan, and Kalibangan in the desert sands of Rajasthan in India, had become famous for the light that excavations at these places had thrown on varios facets of Indus Valley Civilisation. But for some time past, I had also been hearing the names of some places in Haryana, which were said to have been Harappan sites in the hoary past.

The most important of these places—all in Haryana—are Mitathal, Banwali, Kunal and Rakhigarhi. Mitathal is in Bhiwani district and the other three are in Hissar district. Some officials of these districts told me about various relics such as potteries, jewelleries etc. which the local people had stumbled upon in the normal course of their daily life, suggesting the possibility that these places were Harappan sites once upon a time. In fact, I was shown some of these relics during visits to these districts. This had led me to read some books on the Indus Valley civilization as well as reports on the latest excavations at various sites in western India including Haryana. This gave me some idea about the discovery of sites such as Manda in Jammu and Kashmir, Dholavira in Gujarat, Kaliabangan in Rajasthan, Daimabad in Maharashtra and Hulas and Alamgirpur in Uttar Pradesh and also at several places in Pakistan, Afghanistan and even as far as in the Central Asian territory of the former Soviet Union.

The excavations at Mithatal in the Bhiwani district of Haryana are said to have provided rich data for the reconstruction of Haryana's and India's ancient history. About seven miles north east of Bhiwani, Mithatal leaped into prominence when in 1913, coins of Samudra Gupta were found here. Many years later, copper implements and beads were found here in the mid-1960's Excavations undertaken soon thereafter at two mounds of this place brought a number of bangles, terracotta articles, ivory, copper and bone objects, which, according to historians, indicated clear evidence of habitation from pre-Harappan to post-Harappan eras spanning at least a thousand years.

Excavations had also been made at Banwali about nine miles from Fatehabad, which was earlier in Hissar district. A mound there revealed the habitation of some chalcolithic people in the third millennium B.C., who were followed by some other people of Haryana in the next millennium. The excavations unearthed a fort-town where the people lived in brick houses. They wore beads and bangles for ornaments. Pottery and articles of copper, stone, bone etc. were discovered. Jars, goblets and cups of various kinds found at the site reflected the level of the civilization that had flourished here. Several kinds of seals with pictures of animals which were discovered were probably used for sealing packages of goods sent to other places.

I went through an interesting article entitled "Prelude to the Indus Cvilasation" by S.P. Shukla in the Journal of Indological Studies, Haryana Sahitya Academy (Spring 1987), which was sent to me. This sought to interpret the findings of the excavations at many of the Harappan sites. Adverting to the different types of urban settlements developed during the period of the Indus civilisation, he said that while at Harappa, Mohenjodaro and Kaliabangan there existed a 'Citadel' and a fortified 'Lower City' separately, at Banwali there was a closely knit 'Citadel' and 'Lower Town (Annexe)'

About the finds at Banwali, Prof. S.R. Rao, formerly of the National Institute of Oceanography and a great authority in this field of work, observed that both kiln-fired and sun-dried bricks were used here by the pre-Harappans for constructing houses in a planned manner. They knew copper, produced ornamental pottery and used a large variety of beads made of shell terracotta, faience, gold etc. According to Prof. Rao, the brick altars built for fire worship and animal sacrifices at sites like Banwali, Kaliabangan etc. were reminiscent of Vedic rites. The late Harappan writing discovered at Banwali and Dholavira in Kutch was in a script from which the Brahmi script appeared to have evolved.

Kunal, a pre-Harappan site on the bank of the old Saraswati river in Haryana, which was discovered some years ago, was characterized by N.S. Rajaram of the International Institute of Indian Studies, Ottawa, as "the most dramatic" of the pre-Harappan sites, which is evidence that Vedic civilization was mainly pre-Harappan. Commenting on the discovery of silver ornaments at Kunal, Rajaram observed that this showed an advanced stage of the development of metallurgy. Unlike gold, silver never appears in pure form and has to be extracted by separating it from other metals like copper. In Rajaram's view, the date of Kunal was definitely earlier than 3000 B.C., probably 3300 B.C. or earlier.

But the discovery of silver ornaments at Kunal showed that it was still later than the society described in the Rig Veda, which did not know silver. As Rajaram observes: "The oldest Sanskrit word for silver is rajatam hiranmayam—literally white 'gold'—and it is mentioned for the first time in the Yajurveda."[4] According to him, Saraswati sites like Kunal found so far were pre-Harappan, but in all likelihood post-Rig Vedic. The Rig Veda knew gold, but not silver. "Thus both literally and figuratively, the Rig Veda belongs to the Golden Age that ended just before the dawn of the Silver Age".[5]

Considerable progress was made during the last several years in implementing programmes of excavation at Harappan sites in different parts of our country. The Dholavira site in Kutch had been discovered some years ago, but excavation began there only in 1990. During the last decade, many historians, archaeologists and scientists have adopted an inter-disciplinary approach to probe the chronology and relative ancientness of the different phases of early Indian history and civilization. Apart from archaeological excavations, hydrological and ecological data, information obtained from satellite imagery, data from ancient Indian astrology, Vedic mathematics, analysis of the Indus script and language and computer technology have all been harnessed in a co-ordinated endeavour to arrive at acceptable conclusions about the course of India's ancient history. Needless to say, the result of this collaborative effort has brought to the fore the need to re-assess the ancient history of our country that had been wrongly projected by foreign historians on an a priori basis and on which we all had been brought up all these decades.

In an earlier chapter, I have discussed the contribution made by the late Dr. V.S. Wakankar to tracing the course of the Vedic river Saraswati through archaeological excavations undertaken at sites that he had charted out on the basis of his deep study of ancient literature. In the light of the discovery of several pre-Harappan sites on the banks of the old Saraswati river, he concluded that Vedic civilization was pre-Harappan and discarded the idea of an Aryan invasion of India as a pure myth.

In January 1994, I had occasion to visit Hyderabad for some days, when I learnt that top-notch scholars from India and abroad were participating in an international symposium on "Ancient Indian Chronology" at the B.M. Birla Science Centre. I was able to lay my hands on the many learned papers read and presented there and after going through them, I could form some idea about what the consensus was among the experts on the chronology of old civilizations that once flourished in India. The scholars, who participated in the symposium, generally discounted the conventional view 19th century Western historians such as Max Muller and Monier Williams that the Aryans came from Central Asia, invaded and destroyed the Dravidian civilization of the Indus Valley in north west India and pushed the Dravidians to south India.

According to David Frawley, Director, American Institute of Vedic Studies, who attended the symposium, the Puranas showed the spread of Vedic/Hindu religion from the center of India, the Ganges-Yamuna-Saraswati region to the west and the east, with an overflow out of India to the west of Indo-Aryan peoples. Thus the Puranas were said to have totally contradicted the Aryan invasion theory and shown the movement of peoples in the opposite direction. Initially, the Vedic or Indo-Aryan people and the Persians lived together in India, with the

Zoroastrian religion of the latter closely resembling the Vedic. The original land of the Persians appeared to be Kashmir and later they shifted to Punjab and the western mountain region of India.

Then a split is said to have occurred between the Indo-Aryans and the Persians in the later Vedic age, the former moving east and the latter west to Persia. But the split is held to have occurred inside India. According to Frawley, the Vedas do not speak of an original homeland outside India. The Saraswati was the ancient homeland of the Vedic Aryans. As Frawley observes: "One of the most important Vedic battles is thus between the Purus of the Saraswati region (*i.e.* Vedic people) and an alliance, which is dominated in the west of India by Indo-Iranian people, the Anus and Druhyus, who were close kins of the Purus, deriving from both the same father and mother. The battle is not of intruding invaders from Afghanistan, but rather of central against western peoples. The result was not the Aryan conquest of India, but a division among the Aryans into western and eastern peoples, the former moving yet further to the west."

In Frawley's view, there were two great Aryan civilizations, both deriving from the Vedic. The earlier Vedic culture later divided into (1) late Vedic and (2) Zoroastrian (Persian). The Vedic civilization was dominated by the Purus, first from the Saraswati region and later from the Ganges-Yamuna region, where the Purus shifted after the Saraswti went dry. The Zoroastrian derived from north west India (regions of Anu and Druhyu predominance) and later shifted its center to Persia. The other regions of India have historical records going back as far as the Vedas and generally call themselves Aryan, even if not regarding themselves as Vedic or Brahmanical. Both Buddhists and Jains consider themselves Aryan, though non-Vedic, just as Zoroastrians do. This, according to Frawley, suggests several ancient civilizations in India:

1. Vedic civilization of the lunar dynasty on the Saraswati, later shifting to the Ganges-Yamuna.
2. An Indo-Iranian civilization first centred in north-west India, then shifting west to Iran.
3. An eastern Indo-Aryan tradition to the east of the Ganges and in Orissa with proto-Jain and Buddhist elements.
4. A southern Indo-Aryan tradition with a Dravidian predominance.

Aryan culture in ancient India encompassed a number of religions, racial and language and language groups from Vedic times. The term

Aryan was never identified in ancient India with a particular race or language. There may have been other Aryan peoples in western China and Central Asia, who may have had contemporaneous civilizations to the Vedic and from whom the Europeans may have derived.

According to Frawley, the Mahabharata war and the story of Shri Krishna marked the end of the Vedic Age. At the end of the Mahabharata, Dwaraka, the city of Krishna, which was built on land reclaimed from the sea, went under water. The remains of this city recently excavated by marine biology and scientifically dated to 1500 B.C. goes to prove the historicity of the Vedas and the Mahabharata. If the Indus is Vedic, then the Mahabharata of the mid-second century B.C. would be post-Vedic, as the Vedic era came to an end around 1900 B.C. with the drying up of the Saraswati.

Prof. S.R. Rao, formerly of the National Institute of Oceanography, who delivered the key-note address at the Hyderabad symposium in January 1994, stressed the importance of under-water excavations being undertaken at Dwarka in order to fill the gaps in our knowledge of ancient Indian history. He cited the evidence gathered from archaeological excavations, religious practices of the Harappans, study of the language of the Harappan seals and the contribution made by ancient mathematics and astronomy that the people of the Indus Valley were none other than the Aryan-speaking Vedic people living in the Saraswati-Sindhu region. On the basis of his analysis of the compound signs of the Indus script, Prof. Rao concluded that the Indus language showed signs of affinity to the language of the Vedas, which is also known as old Indo-Aryan.

So far as the Dravidian family of languages is concerned, the basic alphabet at the earliest stage of the Indus language has a lot of common ground with the early Dravidian alphabet. The three major contemporary language families of the world, namely Dravidian, Semitic and Brahmi, evolved out of Indus language, which was close to the Rigvedic Sanskrit. All this goes to show the identity of the Vedic people and the people of the Indus Valley.

Prof. S.R. Rao dismisses the earlier view that the Dravidian family of languages is entirely unconnected with the Indo-European or Semitic languages. This view was premised upon the existence of a Dravidian race that was invaded and displaced by the Aryans. The anthropological grounds for the existence of a Dravidian race have been found to be fictitious. Dravida means only the 'Dravida Desha' or a region covered by present-day Tamil Nadu.

N.S. Rajaram of the International Institute of Indian Studies, Ottawa, whose learned paper was presented at the Hyderabad symposium, dismissed the western historians' Aryan invasion theory that was based on the linguistic similarities found between Indian and European languages. He cited the results of archaeological, mathematical and ecological studies to show that the Vedic Aryans were present in India no later than 4000 B.C. And that the Harappan civilization was a continuation of Vedic society and was post-Vedic in the sense that it belonged to the late Vedic age of the Sulba-sutras or Vedic mathematics. The Harappan sites have revealed 'Yajnashalas' or sacrificial facilities with Vedic texts belonging to the Sutra period with detailed instructions for the design and construction of Vedic altars of different kinds. This leads to the conclusion that the great cities of Harappan civilization were made possible by the mathematics, especially the geometry, found in the Sulba-sutras.

Rajaram cited the works of the late American mathematician, A. Scidenberg to show that all ancient mathematics from Greece to Old Babylonia to Egypt were derivatives of the ritual mathematics of the Sulbas. The early Sulba-sutras, like those of Boudhayana and Apastambha must be placed well before 2050 B.C. Of the Egyptian Middle Kingdom (2050–1800 B.C.) on the basis of this comparison alone. The use of pyramidal structures a funeral edifices was traceable to the Baudhayana Sulba.

According to Rajaram, what ended the Harappan world and with it the Vedic age was not the invasion by the Aryans, but an ecological event—the onset of aridity. The Saraswati river became dry by 1900 B.C., perhaps as a sequel to a volcanic eruption. In Rajaram's view, one reason for the drying up of the Saraswati could have been the depletion of the ice caps that had accumulated to the north towards the end of the last Ice Age (8000 B.C.). There are references in the Rig Veda to the cracking of the melting of ice caps. The legend about the killing of Vritra by the solar god Indra probably originated with this phenomenon. The Vedic Age was the beneficiary of an abundance of water, which must have made north India a veritable Garden of Eden. Rajaram concluded that the date of early fourth millennium BCE for the closing of this age was entirely in agreement with the latest archaeological and satellite data. He thus formulated the following chronology:

8000 BCE—Ending of the last Ice Age.
3750 BCE—Ending of the Rig Vedic Age.

3100 BCE—Ending of the Vedic Age: Mahabharata War.

3000 BCE—Beginning of the Harappan-Sutra period.

2700–2200 BCE—High Harappan-Sumerian civilization.

2200 BCE—Drought begins; the beginning of the end of Harappan and Akkadian civilization.

2200—1900 BCE—End of the ancient world.

Rajaram's conclusion: "In summary, the Vedic age and more particularly the Rig Veda were the product of a unique age of abundance brought about by the unique climatic conditions prevailing in the millennia that followed the ending of the last Ice Age. The end of this idyllic Golden Age was also brought about by nature in the form of gradual desiccation and global climatic change that climaxed in a severe drought in 2000 BCE that lasted some three centuries .... The Veda belongs to a world before the rise of the civilizations of Egypt, Sumeria and the Indus Valley. It was a world before the dawn."

Another scholar, Dr. B.G. Sidharth, Director of the B.M. Birla Science Centre, drew upon the ancient astronomical data to fix the dates of the various phases of our ancient civilization. He thought that the antiquity of the Vedic literature and civilization had been grossly underestimated. Ancient Indian literature showed a continuing tradition of astronomy from the earliest Vedic times *i.e.*, about 10,000 B.C. or earlier to the period of the Jyotish Vedanga, that is, about 1350 B.C. According to Dr. Sidharth, most of the ancient myths of India were allegorical descriptions of very precise and well comprehended astronomical phenomena. He referred to several ancient legends to bring out their hidden astronomical meaning.

One of these legends mentioned in the Ramayana was about King Trishanku of Ayodhya, an ancestor of Rama. Trishanku ascended heaven as a Chandala or hunter, the winter solstice being the gateway to heaven. As Dr. Sidharth pointed out, even in the present era, Vaikuntha Ekadasi is celebrated around the winter solstice. Around 10,000 B.C., Rohini, also called Indra, who was at winter solstice, refused to let in Trishanku. Upon this, sage Vishwamitra began creating a duplicate universe with another Indra.

This had a reference to the star Jyeshtha, also called Indra, which at that time was at the diametrically opposite summer solstice. Both Rohini and Jyeshtha are very similar red stars. Thereafter, Trishanku was allowed to hang mid-way. Trishanku with the three pegs was once again Orion, the hunter, all of which referred to the epoch 10,000 B.C. In that epoch, all this happened interestingly in the southern sky as mentioned in this legend. Dr. Sidharth pointed out that, apart from this myth, there were other explicit astronomical references in the Vedas, which independently confirmed that these existed in 10,000 B.C.

The very fact that the Vedic personalities like Vashishtha, Vishwamitra and Agastya figure in the Ramayana showed that this epic belonged to the Vedic period unlike the post-Vedic Mahabharata. One of the Vedic events was the battle between the gods (Devas) and demons (Asuras), which took place at the termination of the 'Yuga' and was mentioned in the Rig Veda. The battle ended with a solar eclipse, which took place in the lunar asterism Tisya or Pushya (Delta Canceri) around 7300 B.C. The presiding deity of this asterism was Brihaspati, the preceptor of the gods.

Dr. Sidharth was of the view that all this conformed very well to several facts of Rama's life. Rama lived as the Treta Yuga ended and the Dwapara Yuga began. The battle between the gods and demons took place in his time. Further, there was a solar eclipse in his time, again in the same Pushya asterism and with the conjunction of planets associated with the termination of the Yuga. There are other references in the Rig Veda, which also yield the date 7300 B.C. Several references point to the Ashwins, that is, the lunar asterism Ashwini in the constellation of Aries being at the winter solstice at the same time.

Dr. Sidharth mentions several other archaeological and historical facts to conclude that ancient Indian literature and civilization could be roughly divided into the following four period:

(a) The early Vedic period with Rohini or Aldebaran at the winter solstice around 10,000 B.C. And in fact earlier.

(b) The middle Vedic period with Ashwini or Alpha and Beta Arietis at the winter solstice around 7300 B.C., which is the period of the Ramayana and Dwapara Yuga.

(c) The late Vedic period with Krittika or Pleides at the vernal equinox, around 2500 B.C., which is the period of Satapata Brahmana and the Indus Civilisation.

(d) The post-Vedic period around 1400 B.C., which is the period of the Mahabharata and Kali Yuga.

Another scholar, Prof. Subhash Kak, a computer scientist at the Lousiana State University, U.S.A., who participated in the Hyderabad symposium , examined an astronomical code stored in the Rig Veda, particularly in connection with fire altars. Information about solar, lunar and planetary movements found in the Rig Veda when analysed indicated that some Rig Vedic hymns talked about epochs which were 7000 to 8000 years old. His conclusion was that the Aryans had arrived in India at least 9000 years ago, though his view did not offer any definitive evidence as to whether the Aryans had migrated from Central Asia and Europe. Prof. Kak's computer analysis of the Indus script also showed that it was 'Sanskritic'.

Prof. Banka Behari Chakravorty from West Bengal presented a paper at the Hyderabad symposium in which he dismissed the notion that the composition of Veda-mantras had begun earlier and then came the Puranas after a long gap. His view was that the Puranas had begun earlier and the Vedas followed. There was a synchronous development of both until the Mahabharata period, when composition of new Vedic Mantras stopped. But the composition of the Puranas, being of 'Itihasa' nature, continued for some centuries. He was of the view that Vedic civilization could have begun in the vicinity of 12, 5000 B.C. And that India's civilization was still older because the Vedas came later than the Puranas.

Some months after I studied these papers presented at the 1994 Hyderabad symposium, I laid my hands on an interesting novel, "Return of the Aryans" by Bhagawan S. Gidwani, which, though written as a work of fiction, was in fact based on considerable research work done not only in India but also in several other countries. Gidwani debunks the theory that the Aryans had come from outside India and claims that India was the original home of the Aryans, who had gone out in groups to different lands to leave there the imprint of their culture and their language, Sanskrit.

In Gidwani's view, the Vedic Aryans, the Dravidians and the creators of the Indus Valley civilization were the same people. The prodigal sons *i.e.*, The Aryans returned to India when they found that their own land was better than the others. Gidwani relies for his thesis on many oral songs not only of India, but also of many other countries such as Lithunia, Seythia, Russia, Germany, Egypt, Turkey etc., which all refer to the 'coming' of the Aryans. This meant that the Aryans had gone to these countries from India.

In recent years, Rakhigarhi, a Harappan site in the Hissar district of Haryana has hogged a lot of limelight. Several studies and surveys had been in progress in Rakhigarhi since 1963, but it wa only in 1997-98 that excavation actually began here. It is about 20 miles from Hansi on the Hansi-Jind road and 50 miles east of Banwali. The river Saraswati once flowed by the south of Rakhigarhi from east to west. It is the most extensive Indus Valley site in India, the two biggest ones, Mohenjodaro and Harappa, being in Pakistan.

Five mounds of Rakhigarhi village were taken up for excavation and the Harappan finds here included terracotta bangles and beads, a chess board, a seal, mud brick constructions and copper fishing hooks and woven nets, which indicate the existence of a river and a fishing community. There are fossils which provide evidence of the rearing of cattle by the Harappan people, who were quite prosperous, judging from the number of golden beads, silver ware and semi-precious stones that have been discovered. The word 'Rakhi' in Hindi means 'protection', suggesting that the place was probably fortified. This seems quite plausible because a strong and thick wall has been found around the site of excavation.

Excavations at Rakhigarhi have revealed something unique *i.e.*, The burial site covered with brick walls resembling a tomb. Only at Mehergarh in Pakistan, a burial site like this has been discovered. Animal sacrifice pits have been found at Rakhigarhi.

I have heard that some excavation was also done at another site, Siswal in Hissar district. The river Drishadvati perhaps flowed close by this place. Harappan relics including ceramics, pottery, bangles, beads etc. have been discovered here.

A recent survey conducted by the Archaeology Department of the Government of Haryana in two villages–Daksha Khera and Khedua–located near Meham in Rohtak district has reportedly yielded surface indications of the existence of what are believed to be Harappan sites. The local people have discovered here relics of Harappan civilization such as bits of pottery, utensils, bones, skeletons etc. The discovery of skeletons conforms to our knowledge that the Harappans buried their dead. They also believed in life after death which probably explains the discovery of utensils supposed to have been kept by them for the use o the dead in their after-life. A complete picture should emerge after full-scale excavations are undertaken at these sites.

There has been a lot of excitement among archaeologists and historians about the finds of the excavations conducted so far, particularly at the Rakhigarhi site, as they feel that these may lead to a revolutionary change in our conception of ancient Indian history. Many of them are of the view that the recent excavations have highlighted the need to shift the focus from the Indus Valley to the other regions of India. They say that the Rakhigarhi site can easily match the Indus Valley sites in dimension as well as its significance from the point of view of history. This, according to them, might lead to the re-writing of India's ancient history.

The long-held view that the Indus Valley civilization flourished around 2500 B.C. may have to be given up because the discoveries made at Rakhkgarhi put this date to around 3500 B.C., thus pushing back this civilization by about 1000 years. Since Rakhigarhi was located on the bank of the Saraswati river, the earlier view that this civilization existed only on the banks of the Indus river is obviously not true. The Saraswati being a river that figured in the Rig Veda, the conclusion that follows is that the people of the Indus Valley and the Vedic people thrived at about the same time.[6] This would imply that the Vedic Aryans and the Harappans were the same people. Aryan culture fits in with the description of Harappan culture.

The discovery at Rakhigarhi of 'Hakra Ware' culture (typical of settlements dating back to a period before the early phases of the Indus Valley civilization) implies that the site dates back to about 3500 B.C. to 4000 B.C. This, as has already been observed above, causes the date of the Indus Valley civilization to recede by a thousand years or more. S.P. Gupta, an expert on Harappa sites now thinks that the Indus Valley civilization pre-dates the period historians assign to it.[7]

Some historians have been heard to say that we should speak of the Saraswati Valley civilization rather than the Indus Valley civilization. Amrendra Nath, former Director of the Archaeological Survey of India, and the main excavator at Rakhigarhi, was of the view that Rakhigarhi was the genesis of Indus civilization. According to him, all that made Indus so special was present at Rakhigarhi too. However, some others thought that Nath's hypothesis was a "cooked up theory" in the absence of a complete excavation report.[8] Prof. D.N. Jha of the Delhi University observed that such an assumption based on a few findings at a site was just a step on the road to cultural nationalism. S.S. Bisht, the excavator of Dholavira also considered it premature to reach any conclusion in this regard.

According to reports in the press that I read, the decision of the National Museum to re-name the Indus Valley Civilisation Gallery as the Indus-Saraswati Bronze Age Civilisation of South Asia Protohistoric Gallery had given rise to controversy.9 Prof. Shireen Ratnagar of the Jawaharlal Nehru University, Delhi, was said to have observed: "There is an ongoing attempt to suggest that the Indus civilization was Vedic, thereby creating a lineal descent of Hindus from that time onwards. By showing the Saraswati river as the cradle of Indus civilization, an attempt is being made to downgrade the Mohenjodaro and Harappan findings, especially since, after Partition, they are perceived to belong to Muslims. These attempts to project our findings as being more relevant than theirs is pathetic. For some time now, there have been attempts to claim that the origins of Indus civilization have been found in Dholavira, Saurashtra. Dholavira is a unique Saurashtrian site, but that does not make Mohenjodaro irrelevant." [10] Several charges and counter-charges have been made by the academicians ranged on the two sides over this issue. I do not want to repeat them primarily because they are of a rather technical nature.

With reference to the alleged attempt to re-write Indian history by playing up the importance of the Saraswati river and the Rakhigarhi site in Haryana, some experts have suggested the need to publish complete reports of excavation projects so that a dispassionate analysis could be made by historians and archaeologists.

A breakthrough in the interpretation of the data acquired from excavations would depend on our ability to decipher the Harappan script, which has remained a mystery for several decades. The message of the terracotta seals with Harappan inscriptions that have been discovered at the Indus Valley sites have not yet been deciphered. What do they say about the life-style of those days? We do not know. The experts are looking for cylindrical seals with a bi-lingual script, because it is these which would enable them to decipher the script. Till a few years ago, only two cylindrical seals were said to have been found, but these were not considered sufficient for a proper decipherment.

Excavations done at several other places in Haryana such as Bhagawanpura and Mirzapur have thrown up relics of ancient times. Very interesting evidence has come from excavations at Bhagawanpura in Kurukshetra district, which is located on the bank of the Saraswati river. Various finds such as pottery objects, painted designs, burial sites, peculiar oval-shaped structures meant for religious functions etc. have revealed an overlap between the late Harappan and Painted Grey Ware cultures, which is quite significant for a reconstruction of the continuous history of Haryana from the middle of the second millennium B.C. [11] Excavations at another place, Daulatpur in the same district located near Pipli, have similarly revealed a relationship between the late phase of the Harappan and Painted Grey Ware cultures. Various relics have been discovered here as also in several villages of this region.[12]

Several Painted Grey Ware sites have also been found in Faridabad district. Aharwan village in Palwal Tehsil has yielded Painted Grey Ware and early historic and late medieval remains. Sondhad, another village in the same Tehsil, which, according to local tradition, had been founded in the Mahabharata era, has yielded Painted Grey Ware, besides several images and figurines of the Gupta period.[13]

Off and on, relics of old history are stumbled upon by people in different parts of Haryana. Some years ago, I had read an account of the chance discovery of earthen pottery of the Kushana period in Begoa village of Bhiwani district by a farmer, when he was leveling his field for cultivation. This led the local people to dig deeper and discover many more pieces of pottery.[14]

In recent times, the controversy over the sequence in time of the Indus Valley and Vedic civilizations has led the protagonists of the so-called secular and saffron camps to take up fiercely antagonistic positions. Some BJP Ministers of the erstwhile NDA Government at the Centre had chalked out elaborate plans of tracing the ancient course of the Saraswati from Adi Badri in Haryana to the western sea coast together with excavations of several Harappan sites along this course. Their idea was to establish the Vedic foundation of the Indus Valley civilization and the unity of the Indus Valley and Vedic civilizations.

Murli Mohan Joshi, Human Resources Development Minister in the NDA Government, was reported to be of the view that there was a civilization in pre-historic India that flourished along the Saraswati river long before the advent of the Aryans—a civilization that was more advanced than the Harappan civilization. His argument ran as follows. The Saraswati river finds mention in the Vedas and since the Saraswati disappeared before the Aryans settled along the Indus, the Vedas must be older than the Aryans, though our historians credit them with writing the scriptures. According to Joshi, the Vedic civilization or the Saraswati Valley civilization pre-dates the Harappan civilization.

Another BJP Minister in the NDA Government—Shri Jagmohan—had suggested that the Indus Valley civilization should more appropriately be called Sraswati or Saraswati-Indus civilization. He debunked the theory of the Aryan invasion of India and cited in his support Swami Vivekananda's observation that there was not one word in our scripture to show that the Aryans came from anywhere outside

India. Under the direction of Shri Jagmohan, the Archaeological Survey of India undertook a well-planned search to trace the course of the Saraswati river, zeroing on a 800-metre belt starting from Adi Badri in Haryana to Dholavira in Gujarat. This formed part of the Saraswati Heritage Project that reflected the Minister's vision for tourism in India and aimed at developing 15 hubs which were to become destinations for tourism and research.

Several anti-saffron scholars such as Shireen Ratnagar, Romila Thapar and Irfan Habib have challenged these views. Some have even alleged that N.S. Rajaram had manipulated the Indus Valley seals to create images of horses in order to prove the Vedic orientation of the Indus Valley civilization. They also expressed their strong disagreement when, in a brochure published by the Archaeological Survey of India on the occasion of an exhibition on Harappan civilization held in 2002 at the National Museum, it was claimed that the Harappans worshipped Lord Shiva, used fire altars and horses and wrote from left to right in the same way as the Rig Vedic Aryans did.

It is true that Swami Vivekananda and Shri Aurobindo had both spoken against the theory of an Aryan Invasion of India that had been propounded by Western scholars including Sir Mortimer Wheeler, head of the Archaeological Survey of India. I do not mean any disrespect to these spiritual leaders of our country, if I say that what they had said might perhaps have been intended to establish the spiritual greatness of Hindu religion, but, considering all that has been discussed in the foregoing pages, a final conclusion in this matter may not have been reached as yet.

Dr. Buddha Prakash, Head of the Department of Ancient History, Kurukshetra University, had in the 1960's gone into this matter at some depth and come to the conclusion that the Harappans and the Aryans were the same people. As far as I know, he was not communally biased, but was a neutral scholar, who had expressed his views which were based on his scientific study.

The last word on this controversy has probably not yet been said. What is needed is further research accompanied by excavations of the many relevant sites. The most important key to this mystery lies in the decipherment of the Harappan script.

The excavations at Banwali in Hissar district that I have already mentioned are said to have thrown up evidence that this place was the birth-place of Lord Rama, no less! I have earlier referred to the mythological story about Kurukshetra being the birth-place of Sita.

This, together with the fresh evidence about Haryana having sired also Rama would make this State the center-stage of the Ramayana, apart from the other epic, Mahabharata, which revolves around Kurukshetra located in Haryana.

I read an article in the Hindustan Times of July 15, 1998 by Rakshat Puri cited the view expressed in this regard by V.N. Krishna Rao, a veteran archaeologist and a pioneer in deciphering the Indus Valley script. Rao's paper on 'Ram and Ravana in Indus Seals' published in J.P. Joshi Felicitation Volume 15 challenged the view that Ayodhya was the birth-place of Rama. It is by interpreting the Indus Valley seals found at Banawali in Haryana that Rao arrived at his conclusion that Ram Janmabhoomi was somewhere there on the banks of the Saraswati river and not at Ayodhya on the banks of the Saryu. According to him, Ramachandra is the Rama Sana of the Indus Valley seals, who is identical with King Ram Sin of Larsa in Sumer. Incidentally, the Indus Valley had a wide expanse covering not only areas in today's India and Pakistan, but also ancient Sumer, Elam, present-day Iran Afghanistan and beyond. Ram Sin ruled over the entire area of Sumer, Indus Valley, modern Iran, Afghanistan etc. He had assumed the title of "King of All Lands" and engaged in a long war with King Hammurabi. According to Rao, the seals found at Banawali suggest that Hammurabi was killed in the war. One of these seals has a legend which reads "Ravana Dami" meaning the vanquisher of Ravana and leading to speculation about Hammurabi's identity.[16]

Notes

1. Dr. K.C. Yadav: the Revolt of 1857 in Haryana, pp. 95–98. The account given in the next few paragraphs is based on this book.
2. *Ibid.*
3. Article by R.Nair in the *Hindustan Times* City, New Delhi dated November 12, 1999.
4. Article captioned "Shattering a myth" by N.S. Rajaram in the Sunday *Hindustan Times*, New Delhi, dated May 15, 1994.
5. *Ibid.*
6. Article by Vimmy Sahay in the Sunday Supplement of the *Hindustan Times*, New Delhi, February 21, 1999.
7. Article by Maneesh Pandey in the *Times of India*, New Delhi, July 18, 1999.
8. Article by Maneesh Pandey in the *Times of India*, New Delhi, July 4, 1999.
9. Rashme Sehgal's write-up in the *Times of India*, New Delhi, August 8, 1999.

10. Quoted in Rashme Sehgal's article cited above.
11. The Encyclopaedic District Gazetteers of India, Northern Zone, Volume III, p. 156.
12. *Ibid*, p. 91.
13. *Ibid*, p. 91.
14. Report in the *Hindustan Times*, New Delhi, August 1, 1998.
15. J.P. Joshi was a former Director-General of the Archaeological Survey of India and V.N. Krishna Rao was a Deputy Superintending Archaeologist.
16. Article by Rakshat Puri in the *Hindustan Times*, New Delhi, July 15, 1998.

16

Seminar on the Gita: A Preceptor Blesses his Pupil: Cricket Match between Punjab and Haryana: 40th Anniversary of our Independence: Hindu Scriptures and Qoran–Similarity of their Spiritual Concepts: Yamunanagar, Sugh, Kalesar, Bilaspur, Kapal Mochan: Tajewala and Firoz Shah's West Yamuna Canal: Motilal Nehru School of Sports, Rai: Generals as Vice-chancellors of Universities: Teej Again: Kaithal and the Pandavas: Kalayat and Sage Kapil

On February 21, 1989, the opening day of the Haryana Legislative Assembly. I delivered my inaugural address, speaking in Hindi as I had done on the same occasion the previous year. I stuck to the text that had been provided to me by the Ch. Devi Lal Government and drew attention to the slow pace of work at the Sutlej Yamuna Link Canal (SYL) and the delay on the part of the Punjab authorities in completing the project. The position on the ground in respect of this project has not changed till today, even though some political parties, which have been in power in Haryana during this long period, have been on friendly terms with the parties in power at the Centre as well as in Punjab.

All this while, the parties in power in Haryana have been mouthing the slogan for early completion by the Punjab authorities of the SYL Canal project, knowing fully that nothing was going to be done in practice. The reason for this hypocrisy is what has come to be known as 'vote bank politics' as nobody is willing to displease Punjab, which has in fact nothing to lose if this canal is completed, allowing the excess water to flow into Haryana and thus helping in boosting its agricultural production. In the event, all that is happening is that the excess water of the Sutlej river goes waste and falls into the Arabian sea!

From this time onward, my wife and I had the pleasure of attending several programmes of music and dance. Notable among these was the All-India Bhaskar Rao Dance and Music Conference, which was organized by the Pracheen Kala Kendra, Chandigarh, headed by Smt. K.Atma Ram. The top-notch artistes, who performed there, included Amjad Ali, Swapna Sundari and Parveen Sultana and her husband, Dilshad Mohd. Khan. The Tribune of March 1, 1989 commented on our fixation with dance and music in the following words:

The Tribune, March 1, 1989

CHANDIGARH CALLING

Thanks to the Pracheen Kala Kendra, Chandigarh experienced that very unusual occurrence of a packed auditorium for performances in classical music and dance. Artistes of such high stature as sarod maestro Amjad Ali Khan, Kuchipudi pioneer, Swapna Sundari and the inimitable Parveen Sultana were in the city to give glimpses of their skill and genius.

Each of the artistes left his or her impress on the minds of art lovers in the city. That such high-priced artistes were brought to display their wares for no fee at all redounds to the credit of the Pracheen Kala Kendra and its guiding spirit, Mr. M.L. Koser.

The three-day festival was memorable in many ways. It was a surprise to see Governor Hari Anand Barari and his wife in the role of art, music and dance lovers sitting unobtrusively through the performances on all three days. It was at Mr. Barari's request that Amjad played Raga Durga tracing to its folk origin.

Amjad incidentally, captured the heart of everyone when he received the garland meant for him in hand and put it on the bronze dancing Nataraja and then took another and placed it at the feet of the photograph of Pandit Bhaskar Rao.

Praveen Sultana was, of course, expected to cast a spell on her audience, but she admitted to the audience casting a spell on her by their dignified and extremely appreciative responses.

Among the audience was Prof. Mehta from Amritsar, a septuagenarian who loves plants and music. On his coat was a fresh rose, the stem of which was immersed in a bulb carrying water stitched to the coat. The Kosers treated him as a VIP, seated him in the front row and allowed him to record parts of the concerts.

At this music conference, some activists of the SPIC MACAY including Piyush Singh met me and followed this up by calling on me at the Raj Bhawan soon thereafter and submitting to me a memorandum asking for some help towards ensuring the promotion of fine arts and music in Haryana. I assured them of all possible help and interceded with the authorities of the Government of Haryana to do whatever was possible in this regard. A few days later, we hosted a programme of classical music at Raj Bhawan, where several well-known musicians such as Prof. M.R. Gautam, Ustad Yunus Hussain Khan and Prof. Sher Singh treated us and the large number of guests to scintillating performances. These musicians also discussed with me and some others what steps could be taken to give an impetus to classical music in Haryana.

On March 15, 1989, I, along with my wife, paid a visit to Kurukshetra, where I inaugurated a four-day seminar on the Gita and its relevance to in modern times in the Bhadavatgita Sadan of the Kurukshetra University. It was organized by the University's Department of Sanskrit, Pali and Prakrit and was sponsored by the University Grants Commission in collaboration with the Kurukshetra Development Board. The last such seminar had been held 15 years ago. A large number of distinguished scholars, professors and spiritual leaders from different parts of the country attended the seminar, which was presided over by the noted Gandhian leader, Shri Gulzari Lal Nanda, who was then the Chairman of the Kurukshetra Development Board. Among those present were Swami Chidananda of the Divine Light (Shivananda) Mission, Rishikesh, Prof. Gauri Nath Shastri, a former Vice-Chancellor of the Benares Sanskrit University, Dr. Vachaspati Upadhyaya, Dr. A.P. Misra, Dr. Arabinda Basu, Dr. (Ms) A. Saha and several well-known personalities active in the spiritual world.

A couple of weeks before this seminar was held, Dr. D.B. Sen Sharma, Head of the Department of Sanskrit, Pali and Prakrit, Kurukshetra University, had called on me in Chandigarh and requested me to inaugurate it and also address the gathering. On the appointed day, my wife and I were introduced to the dignitaries present at the seminar. One of them, as I have already mentioned, was Dr. Gauri Nath Shastri, the very fair-complexioned octogenarian scholar, whom my wife and I at once recognized. He was a famous professor of the Presidency College, Kolkata, of which I was a student in the late 1940's.

I had studied Sanskrit for a couple of years after school, but not at the under-graduate level at the Presidency College. Therefore, I was not a student of Prof. Shastri, but since he was a professor of this college when I was a student of Economics (Honours) there, I naturally looked upon him as one of my college teachers.

Moreover, my wife and I had met him on a couple of occasions many years ago when he had visited the New Delhi residence of her father, the famous B.N. Mullik of the Indian Police, with whom Dr. Shastri shared a common interest in certain religious and spiritual projects. So, when we met him at Kurukshetra on the occasion of this seminar, we both touched his feet and introduced ourselves—I as his ex-student and my wife as the daughter of the late B.N. Mullik. Upon this, he expressed great happiness and showered his blessings on us.

After I delivered a long, extempore inaugural address at the seminar, there was a prolonged applause. After some time, when Dr. Shastri was requested to speak, he complimented me for what he considered a very illuminating talk and said that what gave him great satisfaction was the fact that I was at one time his pupil at the Presidency College, Kolkata. He said that he failed to comprehend how I could find time in he course of my professional career and then as the Governor of a State to undertake such a deep study of the Gita.

As Dr. Shastri said: "The Governor says that he was a student of mine at the Presidency College, Calcutta long years back. Now, look at his performance. This is the kingship of the Vedas. My pupil has spoken here. Is he an ordinary dignitary? He is the right person to address a gathering like this. Eulogising the "merit and quality" of my performance, he observed: "What shall I say? the Chancellor has covered a long, long ground. He has practically exhausted all the points that should attract our attention in the course of our study of this text. .... There is a saying in Sanskrit: "defeat at the hands of a son or disciple is regarded as victory in all respects" (*i.e.* defeat at the hands of one's son or disciple is regarded as victory in all respects). I am very happy (applause). I am particularly indebted to Prof. Sen for the opportunity he has afforded to me to associate myself with this performance of one of my ex-pupils. I did not know at that time when he was probably in the college that he would develop int such a personality."

Shri G.L. Nanda, Swami Chidananda and Prof. D.B. Sen Sharma also spoke at the inaugural session. A couple of months after this seminar, the Indian Express, Chandigarh, reported:

INDIAN EXPRESS,
CHANDIGARH,
FRIDAY, MAY 19, 1989

Teacher and Pupil

The national seminar on "The message of the Bhagwad Gita and its relevance in modern times" held at Kurukshetra University last month not only brought out the scholar in Mr. H.A. Barari, the Governor of Haryana and Chancellor of the university, but also brought together a teacher and his pupil.

The audience at the inaugural ceremony of the seminar was held spell-bound by Mr. Barari with his in-depth knowledge of the Gita. His understanding of the message of the Gita in all its aspects including the metaphysical, the intellectual and the spiritual, was superb. Even his teacher and the main speaker at the seminar, Pandit Gauri Nath Shastri, a renowned Sanskrit scholar, was impressed by the 45-minute extempore address by the Governor. He gave expression to his feelings in the keynote address when he said that he was happy to see his pupil surpassing him in the knowledge of the Gita. Mr. Barari was his student at the Presidency College, Calcutta.

The audience as well as the participants were moved when Mrs. Anita Barari, wife of the Governor, touched the feet of Pandit Gauri Shastri when she was introduced to him after the ceremony.

Contributed by O.N. Garg,
Ashwini Dutta and
Vijay Sabharwal.

My wife and I invited Dr. Gauri Nath Shastri to be our guest at the Raj Bhawan in Chandigarh, which he was scheduled to visit soon. He hesitated, saying that at our Raj Bhawan, it might not be possible for him to stick to certain rules in regard to his food etc., which he followed very meticulously. He said, for example, that he would not like his food to be cooked in the already used pots and pans of the Raj Bhawan nor would he take any food cooked or served by a non-Brahmin. My wife assured him that new pots and pans would be bought for cooking his food and that she would herself cook for him and also serve food to him on new utensils! Now Dr. Shastri looked quite happy. He became our guest in Chandigarh on March 19-20, 1989. Dr. Shastri is no more. We still cherish his memory.

Sports and games occupy an important place in the life of the Haryana people. The Haryana Government's Department of Sports holds an annual State Sports Awards Presentation function to give awards and prizes to the distinguished sportspersons of the State as a means of providing encouragement to them. On March 27, 1989, this function was held at the Haryana Raj Bhawan in Chandigarh, when I gave the awards. The topmost award, namely the State Sports Award, went to two players—Jagdish Chander, the renowned volley-ball player, and Kuldip Singh, a wrestler, who had taken part in the Seoul Olympic Games. More than 180 players, 8 coaches and 42 others associated with sports received awards and cash prizes. Sita Ram Singla, sports Minister, announced a 3% job reservation in the State Government's services for outstanding sportspersons and pension for veteran players.

Towards the end of March 1989, the Devi Lal Ministry underwent several changes. On March 27, 1989, on the advice of Ch. Devi Lal, I relieved Tayyab Hussain, Agriculture, of his responsibilities as Agriculture Minister. This came as a sequel to the Minister's perceived role in the by-election to the State Assembly from the Nuh constituency in Gurgaon district that had taken place the previous day. His brother, Hamid Hussain, had contested the election as an independent candidate against Hassan Mohammad, the candidate of the ruling party. Chief Minister, Ch. Devi Lal probably suspected that Tayyab Hussain had worked for his brother against the interests of the ruling party's nominee. A couple of days later, I accepted the resignation of A.S. Badhana, another member of the Devi Lal Ministry.

On March 30, 1989, I swore in five Ministers at a function held at the Raj Bhawan. Three of them, who became Cabinet Ministers, were Dr. Mangal Sein, the State BJP President, Ranjit Singh, a son of Ch. Devi Lal, and Dr. Maha Singh. There were two new Ministers of State, namely Hassan Mohammad, the newly elected MLA from Nuh, and Manphool Singh. Some existing Ministers were elevated in rank: Subhash Katyal, Minister of State, to Cabinet rank and Deputy Ministers, Sachdev Tyagi and Lachman Kamboj to the rank of Minister of State. Dr. Mangal Sein was made the second Deputy Chief Minister along with Banarsi Das, who was already designated as such. Ranjit Singh's appointment as a Cabinet Minister was interpreted in political circles as a balancing act on the part of Ch. Devi Lal, whose eldest son, O.P. Chautala M.P. had been appointed some time ago as the President of the Haryana Janata Dal.

Some time in the last week of March 1989, Sardar H.S. Chatha, Speaker of the Haryana Legislative Assembly, called on me on the eve of his departure for his native village in Pakistan. He told me that his village was in the Gujranwala district of Pakistan and that he was feeling very excited at the prospect of visiting it, since he had last seen it as a child when leaving for India at the time of Partition in 1947. He knew that I had also left my village in East Bengal before Partition. I could, therefore, appreciate his feelings. He saw me again on April 20, 1989 on his return from Pakistan and told me how warmly he had been welcomed by the people of his village, who knew that he had become the Speaker of the Haryana Legislative Assembly.

I recall what a great fun it was for the Government employees of Haryana and Punjab to play a cricket match in Chandigarh on April 1, 1989. The teams of the Punjab and Haryana Governors were led respectively by Shri S.S. Ray and me respectively. A few days before that, I started net practice at an improvised pitch on the grounds of our Raj Bhawan, where some officers of the State Government also joined me. Eventually, the Punjab team won the limited overs match having scored 301 runs as against Haryana's 152.

I was asked to bowl when Shri S.S. Ray, Punjab Governor batted. It was my good luck that I managed to get him out! Two of the Punjab batsmen scored centuries. For the Haryana side, the highest individual score was 24 runs, while I was the second highest scorer with just 18 runs. S.M. Sharma of the Punjab team was the man of the match and I was declared the best all-rounder. We received prizes from Smt. Maya Ray, the wife of the Punjab Governor. Several newspapers carried reports on this match the next day. A sample:

The Tribune–April 2, 1989

Punjab Governor XI Retain cricket title

By Our Sports Reporter

CHANDIGARH April 1 – Punjab Governor XI beat Haryana Governor XI in their 13th One-Day Limited Over Cricket Match to retain the B.N. Chakravarti Trophy here today.

Unbeaten centuries by S.M. Sharma (100) and A.S. Dogra (103) helped Punjab Governor XI to pile up 301 in 45 overs. Vikas and Kaushik took two wickets each for Haryana. H.A. Barari, Haryana Governor, claimed the wicket of Punjab Governor S.S. Ray.

In reply to the Punjab score, Haryana Governor XI could make just 152 runs. Vijay was the top scorer for Haryana with 24, followed by H.A. Barari, who scored 18 runs.

For Punjab, the bowling honours went to Sarvesh Kaushal and S.M. Sharma who claimed three and two wickets respectively.

S.M. Sharma was declared "Man of the Match".

Mrs. Maya Ray gave away the prizes.

Several official engagements kept me pre-occupied in the first fortnight of April 1989. One of these was the convocation of the Maharshi Dayanand University, Rohtak, held on April 5, 1989. Prof. Yash Pal, an eminent scientist and Chairman of the University Grants Commission, who addressed the gathering, suggested the need for changing the concept of education to bring it in tune with the changing times, while at the same time preserving our country's traditional mores and values.

The Haryana Sahitya Academy organized a seminar at our Raj Bhawan on April 17, 1989 on the subject: "Nehru: the man and his vision". This formed part of the celebrations to commemorate the 40th anniversary of India's independence and the birth centenary of Pt. Jawaharlal Nehru. I delivered the inaugural address at the seminar, which, as I could guess from the thunderous applause, was highly appreciated by the audience that included, apart from Haryana Ministers, Smt. Sushma Swaraj and Ram Bilas Sharma, also several top-notch intellectuals such as Dr. Mulk Raj Anand, Dr. Moonis Raja, Vice-Chancellor of the Delhi University, Prof. Bipan Chandra, Dr. Namvar Singh, Prof. Ravinder Kumar and Dr. Indranath Choudhury, Secretary, Sahitya Academy of India.

Towards the end of April 1989, Prof. Satyadev Verma, a great Sanskrit scholar, and husband of Smt. Kamla Verma, Health Minister of Haryana, called on me and presented to me a copy of his work "Sanskrita Quranam", which was a masterly translation into Sanskrit of the Qoran. Translating the Qoran from its original text in Arabic into Sanskrit requires a deep knowledge of both these languages, which Dr. Satyadev Verma undoubtedly possessed. We discussed various matters and at the end I was left with the definite impression that he was a great scholar indeed. He also gave me a few issues of 'Hitsadhika', a fortnightly in Sanskrit published from Yamunanagar of which he was the editor.

In the foreword to his Sanskrit version of the Qoran, Dr. Satyadev has analysed the similarities between several spiritual concepts that figure in the Qoran on the one hand and in the Vedas and Upanishads on the other. He has quoted several passages from the Qoran and the Hindu scriptures to bring out their common faith in the almightiness of God and in the view that there is only one God.[1] His book also quotes some passages from the Qoran (in Sanskrit) and the Hindu scriptures to show that they both believe in the doctrine of re-birth.[2]

This kind of analysis undoubtedly helps in highlighting the message of inter-religious harmony and goodwill. A similar attempt at translating a holy book in one language into another language came to my notice when one Ashu Ram Arya, a great Sanskrit scholar, called on me on August 8, 1989. He had translated the Vedas into the Urdu language. He presented to me some specimens of his work for which I expressed great appreciation.

During a visit to Gurgaon in the second week of May 1989, I had the opportunity of seeing the fast pace of industrial development that was taking place all around. One of the factors that helped the process of development was the close proximity of Gurgaon to Delhi, which gave it easy access to the vast market in Delhi. On May 12, 1989, I inaugurated the third computer centre of the Haryana Electronic Development Corporation (Hartron) at Gurgaon on the lines of similar centers at Ambala and Chandigarh. There, I was briefed about the steps being taken to ensure the rapid progress of computerization all over the State. I was also shown around the electronics complex in Gurgaon and a few units manufacturing electronic components and systems. The scope for further development in this field looked mind-boggling.

All this time, I was regularly playing tennis as well as golf in Chandigarh. One day, while playing at the Chandigarh Golf Club, I chanced to meet Shri and Smt. Johl, the parents of Ajoy, my golf coach and his younger brother, Amandeep, who had also occasionally lent a hand in giving me some tips about playing golf. The proud parents told me that Amandeep had finished fourth in an international golf tournament held in Scotland. In fact, several young golfers of Chandigarh were doing very well in the national as well as international golf tournaments. For example, Chiranjeev, son of the “flying Sikh”, Mikha Singh, was shaping into a top-notch golf player. To celebrate Amandeep's and Chiranjeev's successes in international golf, I hosted a dinner Party at the Raj Bhawan in their honour on June 13, 1989. Apart from these two outstanding players, several up and coming young golfers and their family members attended the party. The Raj Bhawan reverberated with the care-free chatter of the young guests, some of whom have in later years evolved into famous golf players in the international circuit.

In the mean time, the political situation in the State was getting transformed in the context of developments at the national plane. On June 26, 1989, Chief Minister Ch. Devi Lal called on me and discussed with me the emerging political scenario. His view was that the Congress Party was losing political support and yielding place to the Janata Dal and the allied political parties of which he, V.P. Singh and Chandrasekhar were fast emerging as the leaders. He discussed with me the question of having the State Assembly dissolved so as to have the elections to it held along with the Parliamentary elections due after some time. Probably it was a ploy by him to see how I reacted to his suggestion. I gave no clear-cut answer and ultimately he made no such move.

In the first week of July 1989, my wife and I visited some places of Ambala district, which a few months later were grouped together to form a new district—Yamunanagar. These places with their forests looked beautiful after the first tentative monsoon showers. Yamunanagar's antiquity is evidenced by the discovery of several ancient sites in the course of excavations that have been undertaken.[3] the ancient literature of our country contains references to several places of Yamunanagar district. The Aryans are believed to have settled down in this region on the banks of rivers that included the Yamuna. Once upon a time, this territory formed part of the kingdom of the Pandavas and the Parikshitas.

The earliest literary reference to this territory occurs in the Taittriya Aranyaka, which mentions a place, Trughna, said to be identical with Shrughna or Sugh. Panini's work also mentions this territory. It is situated in the bed of the old Yamuna river about three miles east of Jagadhri. During the sixth century B.C., this area had come under the influence of Buddhism. Hiuen Tsang, the Chinese traveler, gave detailed accounts of this place as it was in the first half of the seventh century A.D. He said that Lord Buddha in one of his previous births had preached the law here. According to him, there was a monastery and an Ashokan Stupa at this place. It was the capital of a kingdom that existed on both sides of the Yamuna adjacent to the Shivalik ranges. The archaeological finds at Sugh include pottery and terracotta figurines, one of which has a plaque with writings whose alphabets belong to the Sunga period.

The ruins where Sugh was once located are believed to suggest that it was a naturally formed stronghold in a triangular form with a large number of projecting citadels on all the three angles. According to Alexander Cunningham, the well-known archaeologist, the city covered an area of 12 square kilometers and included Jagadhri and Chaneti on the west and Buria and Dayalgarh on the north. It lay on the important routes of northern India, connecting the upper Punjab with the Gangetic plain via Ambala, Saharanpu and Meerut. It was a great center of trade. Some old coins along with those of Tomara andChauhan rulers have been excavated here. The place seemed to have fallen into decline after the 12th century A.D.[4]

Yamunanagar formed part of the Mauryan empire as indicated by several archaeological finds. It was an important place during Ashoka's time as revealed by the Topra edict and the Stupas at Sugh and Chaneti. The Topra edict that stood on the Yamuna in the Topra village of Jagadhri Tehsil was removed by Firoz Shah in 1356 A.D. And fixed at Kotla Firoz Shah in Delhi. The discovery of the coins of Applodotus and Antimachus at Amadalpur in Jagadhari Tehsil and of Stratou and Menander at Chhoti Krori and Sadaura as well as several coins of Menander at Sugh shows that this area formed part of the Indo-Greek kingdom of the north-west.[5]

Kushana bricks found at several places indicate that Yamunanagar was at one time a part of the Kushana empire. Several coins of Amoghabhuti, a chieftain of the famous Kunindas, found at Buria, Sugh and Jagadhri are a pointer to the fact that Yamunanagar and the adjacent places were in their territory. Settled between the Satluj and the Yamuna, the Kunindas had collaborated with the Yaudheyas in throwing out the Kushanas beyond the Sutluj.

At one time, Yamunanagar was a part of the territory of Samudragupta. In the 7th century A.D., it formed part of the Srikanta Janapada of the Pushpabhuti rulers of Thanesar. Rajyavardhana and Harshavardhana had marched through this region to meet the challenge of the Hunas. It later fell prey to the impeial ambitions of Yasovarman of Kanauj and Lalitaditya of Kashmir. It was a part of the empire of Pratihara Mihira Bhoja in the 9th century A.D. Mahmud of Ghazni and his successors raided this region several times in the 10th century A.D. The Chauhans of Delhi ruled over the area in the 12th century A.D. In 1192 A.D., the victory of Shihab-ud-din Ghori over Prithviraja III brought the area under the former's rule.[6]

In the 14th century, Firuz Tughlak constructed a canal from the Yamuna to Hissar. The depredations caused during Timur's invasion in 1398 A.D. And his departure caused confusion in this region. In 1450 A.D., Bahlol Lodi brought the area under the control of the Lodis, which lasted till 1526 A.D., when Babar, the Mughal adventurer from central Asia wrested it. The Buria town is said to have been built in Humayun's time, while Shahjahan built the Rang Mahal, an edifice with stone arches.

Banda Bahadur, a disciple of Guru Govind Singh, launched an attack on this area in 1709-1710 A.D. But in 1710 A.D., the Mughals defeated him in a fierce fight at Sadaura. After Banda's defeat, Khidmat, a Mughal official, governed this area till 1739 A.D. The rulers of the newly founded principalities of Mustafabad, Arnauli, Buria, Jagadhri, Damla, Chhachhrauli and Bilaspur of the present Yamunanagar district continued to exist as independent potentates. The arrival of the British changed the scenario and in 1847 A.D. Ambala district was formed with these principalities merged into it. In October 1989, the Yamunanagar was carved out of Ambala district with the two Tehsils of Jagadhri and Chhachhrauli.[7]

During the two days that I spent in Yamunanagar district, I visited or passed through several places. About 6 miles outside Yamunanagar is Amadalpur village, where the old temple of Suryakund is located. Adjoining the temple is an ancient tank called Suryakund. The account given in the Bhagavata Purana about this tank testifies to its antiquity. It is said that in the Treta Yuga, a king of the Suryavansa by name Mandhata performed the 'Rajsuya Yagna' on the bank of the Yamuna river with the help of sage Somu Somri, who acted as the priest. The king then got a tank excavated at this place, which he named as Suryakund after the name of his dynasty.

Now about the temple that is also known as Suryakund. Towards the end of the Dwapara era, Sumitra, the last king of the Suryavansa, did penance near the tank called Suryakund and pleased Surya Narayana, the deity of his dynasty. Then, in order to perpetuate the name of his dynasty, he built a beautiful temple adjoining the tank and named it as the Suryakund temple.

Some historians have dated this temple to the time of the Mahabharata. According to them, the Pandavas came here during the time they spent in disguise. It was at that time that Arjuna went to Kailas to obtain the invincible Pashupat weapon from Lord Shiva. After pleasing Lord Shiva through his penance, Arjuna requested him to give him something, which could be regarded as Shiva's symbol. Lord Shiva gave Arjuna a 'Linga', which he installed inside a temple that he constructed near the Suryakund tank at Amadalpur. It is believed that the Pandavas had built this temple in the course of just one night!

According to the Bhagavat Purana, Lord Krishna and Arjuna once came near the bank of the Yamuna while wandering about in the forest. There, they saw a girl who was immersed in deep penance. On enquiry by Lord Krishna, the girl introduced herself as Kalindi, the daughter of Surya Narayana. She further said that she had engaged herself in penance with the object of getting Lord Krishna as her husband. Thereupon, Krishna married her. It is also said that Adi

Shankaracharya had come and spent some time here. During the rule of Mughal Emperor Aurangzeb, the old Suryakund temple had been vandalized. It was in March 1983 that the people of this village re-built the temple.[8]

There are two triangles on the industrial map of Haryana—one big and another small—which encompass 75 to 80 per cent of the industrial centres of the State.9 the big triangle has Panipat, Ballabhgarh and Hissar as its three points with most of the industrial towns of Haryana falling within it. The small triangle has Ambala, Jagadhri and Yamunanagar as its three corners. This scenario is fast changing with the emergence of Gurgaon and Faridabad as thriving industrial centers.

Jagadhri, an important industrial town of Haryana was earlier known as Yugandhari or Yugandhar, a name that was derived from a tribe of this name that inhabited the area. Jagadhri is famous all over the country for its brass utensils.

Another place, Sadaura, which I passed by was the camping ground of the 'Sadhus' in ancient times on their way to the Ganges in the east. It is a corruption from the original name, 'Sadhu-Rah'. A fair held here every year is reported to have been started by Bairam Khan in 1556 A.D.

Chaneti to which I have already referred is a small village near Jagadhri where there is a huge ancient brick mound that figures in the writings of Hiuen Tsang and from which one concludes that the mound is a remnant of an Ashokan Stupa.

On July 5, 1989, my wife and I drove to Tajewala in Yamunnagar district, leaving Chandigarh early in the morning. Tajewala is located about 12 miles from Paonta Sahib. The sacred Yamuna river, called Kalindi in Sanskrit, enters Haryana below Paonta Sahib, the place where Guru Govind Singh, the tenth Sikh Guru, had fought heroic battles against the hill rulers, who had taken the side of the Mughal Emperor Aurangzeb. The headworks of the Western Yamuna Canal are located at Tajewala. This is the oldest canal in this whole region, having been excavated in 1356 A.D, during the rule of Firoz Shah III for allowing the water to flow to the royal gardens at Hissar and Hansi. Re-excavated by Akbar in 1568 A.D. And yet again in 1626 A.D. by Ali Mardan Khan, the engineer of Emperor Shahjahan, this famous canal continues to irrigate extensive areas in the districts of Ambala, Karnal, Kurukshetra, Rohtak, Hissar and Sirsa, besides some parts of Patiala (Punjab), Rajasthan and Delhi.

We went round the Tajewala Headworks and also visited the site of the Hathnikund Dam. We had lunch with the officers of the Irrigation Department at the beautiful Guest House of the Haryana Government's Tourism Department at Hathnikund. At this place, I happened to go through some old inspection reports of pre-independence days recorded by British officials, who used to come there for official work. They made fascinating reading. Their observations about social mores and local conditions hold good even today.

The same afternoon, we proceeded to Kalesar, which is an extensive hilly area with forests in the north eastern corner of Jagadhri Tehsil. We were received there by the top brass of the Department of Forests. I planted 'Bakul' saplings at the Forest Rest House. I was very happy to see that this species of plant thrived as much in Kalesar area as it does in my native Bengal. At this place, river Yamuna flows very fast through the huge boulders. We went about the local forests in jeeps, studying the flora and fauna. Then we reached the highest point of the hillock where there was a beautiful concrete platform. We sat there for a while, sipping cold drinks as exotic birds chirped in various tunes. When we returned to the Rest House at Kalesar, Aslam Sher Khan, the local Congress MLA called on me. We had a long chat about local problems as well as about the historical background of several places in the district.

Next morning, my wife and I proceeded to Chhachhrauli located about seven miles to the north east of Jagadhri. Earlier, it was the headquarters of the princely State of Kalsia and, therefore, has several prominent buildings including an old palace. At Chhachhrauli, I visited Balkunj, a children's home, opened a new wing of the building and laid the foundation stone of another building. I also discussed with the office-bearers of the Haryana State Council for Child Welfare various steps for looking after orphans and abandoned children.

During our trip to Chhachhrauli, I was introduced to some persons, who were from Sugh, near Jagadhri, to which I have already referred. They told me about several significant archaeological discoveries, which threw light on its past history. My subsequent studies brought home to me the importance of this ancient place references to which are found in Vedic and Pali literature.It has been identified by Cunningham with an ancient place, Shrughna, which figures in the account of Hiuen Tsang, the Chinese traveller, who had come here in the 7th century A.D.

After leaving Thanesar, Hiuen Tsang proceeded in a north west direction to reach Shrughna.[10] According to Hiuen Tsang, Shrughna was the capital of a kingdom bounded on the east by the Ganges, and on the north by mountains, and through which river Yamuna flowed. Its climate and natural products resembled those of Thanesar. The people were said to be honest and with a religious inclination. There were five Buddhist monasteries and over 1000 Buddhist ecclesistics, the majority of whom were Hinayanists. There were 100 Hindu temples, the non-Buddhists being "very numerous".[11]

Hiuen Tsang had seen an Ashokan Stupa at Shrughna, apart from several Stupas containing the relics of Sariputra, Mudgalaputra and other great Arhats. In the post-Buddha era, Buddhism was said to have been on the decline in this region. Hiuen Tsang had spent one full winter and half the following spring to hear religious discourses on Buddhism here. According to him, Lord Buddha had visited Shrughna in a previous birth. What a holy place indeed!

Leaving Chhachhrauli, as we drove towards Bilaspur, we saw a place known as Basatianwala, which is famous for its Hanuman temple. It has a huge idol of Hanuman with a face having five different images.

Bilaspur in the Jadadhri Tehsil, which we reached at mid-day, is a very ancient place. Its present name is a corruption from Vyaspur, the original name of the place, which is derived from its association with sage Ved Vyas, the author of the Mahabharata. About two kilometers north of Bilaspur is the sacred tank of Gopal Mochan, which is generally referred to as Kapal Mochan. In days of yore, this tank is said to have been located on the bank of river Saraswati in the ancient tract of Sindhu Van in the sacred land of Brahmavarta that lay between the rivers Saraswati and Drishadvati (the present Pathraali or Drakshi stream).[12] Every year, a very big fair is held around the Kapal Mochan tank. It is a very ancient fair that is held in the Vikram month of Kartik (October-November) for five days from the eleventh day of the bright fortnight of the moon. The Skanda Purana says that one who bathes in the Kapal Mochan tank on this occasion and worships the Shiva Linga achieves eternal bliss.

There is a legend 13 about how the Kapal Mochan tank came to be regarded as so very sacred. It is said that once goddess Saraswati was being chased by Brahma. In order to rescue the goddess, Lord Shiva struck off Brahma's head. Lord Shiva was left holding a tuft of

Brahma's hair and his body was blackened. He was unable to get his body cleansed for a long time. One night, while resting in a cow-shed, Lord Shiva overheard a conversation between a cow and her calf. The calf said that it was going to kill its master, a Brahmin, to avoid being castrated. The cow tried to dissuade the calf from committing this sin. The calf reassured the cow by saying that it knew of a tank where it was possible to cleanse oneself of the sin of killing a Brahmin. Shiva followed the calf the next day and saw the calf kill its master. The bodies of the cow and the calf got blackened, but they soon managed to cleanse themselves by bathing in the holy tank of Kapal Mochan. Lord Shiva followed their example and was cleansed. Ever since, the Kapal Mochan has retained this power of purification.

It is said that Lord Rama had come to Kapal Mochan on his way back from Lanka where he had gone to do away with Ravana. Since Ravana was a Brahmin, Rama cleansed himself of this sin of killing a Brahmin by coming to this place.

While we were at the Kapal Mochan tank, the process of de-silting it was in progress at the instance of the district administration. We joined the thousands of worker, who were engaged in 'Kar Seva' (voluntary labour). Addressing the large gathering, I expressed my appreciation of the work that wa being done. We went round Bilaspur and some near-by places and visited several temples and sacred tanks. We also paid obeisance at the holy Kapal Mochan Gurdwara, where a 'Saropa' was presented to me. This Gurdwara had been erected by Maharaja Ranjit Singh in honour of Guru Govind Singh at the spot where the Guru had stopped over in 1688 A.D. to celebrate Guru Nanak's birthday.

A couple of days after our return to Chandigarh, we had an evening of classical music at our Raj Bhawan, thanks to the effort put in by the sponsor organization, the Indian Nationa Theatre and its guiding spirit—N. Khosla. As usual, the elite of Chandigarh were invited to this programme. Dr. Suhasini Koratkar, Director (Music) of the All-India Radio, was the main artiste, who sang 'Malhars' in several variations. Her Guru, T.D. Janonkar, was also present on the occasion. The music in raga Malhar was superb, which, many thought, had something to do with hastening the monsoon that lashed Chandigarh within a few days. This is what the daily Tribune of Chandigarh wrote in its issue of July 19, 1989 in this regard:

Tribune, July 19, 1989

CHANDIGARH CALLING

Monsoon continues to play hide and seek with the people. Chandigarh and its surroundings had their worst sultry spell and everyone was giving up hope. At one stage the weatherman said that the monsoon clouds were weakening over the region.

And then came an evening of "malhar" in Chandigarh. Dr. Suhasini Koratkar from Bombay sang malhar at a concert at Haryana Raj Bhavan on a Saturday evening. It was organised by the Indian National Theatre at the initiative of the ever dedicated Navjivan Khosla. And the music loving Bararis willingly played the gracious hosts.

Call it coincidence or what you will within three days of the malhar evening, the city had its rain – a heavy downpour. Many would call it a coincidence. Not so Mr. P.L. Varma, Le Corbusier's associate in the building of Chandigarh. He was among those who heard Suhasini elaborate mian-ki-malhar with exquisite skill and sweetness. Here's how he describes his feelings.

"The music started with a rather dull sonorous start, but it was a precursor to what was coming. Though I am not a musical-minded person, I found it unusually absorbing and thoughts repeatedly came to me that the ancients had stated that malhar can bring rain.

As these thoughts were passing in my mind. I realised that the malhar feast at Raj Bhavan could move rain-bearing clouds and bless the earth with rain. The music brought to one's mind the sound of rain falling on leaves and on the earth together with the occasional gurgling noise. During the entire two hours of the recital I saw complete absorption and attention from those who understood and were capable of appreciating classical music. As for me, I felt the kinship between the music of the rain and the verbal tunes in the song. As the music ended one could see the ecstasy in the eyes and expressions of the audience."

In July 1989, I was the chief guest at the installation ceremony of the Rotary Club, Chandigarh. I used to associate myself with the functions of the Rotary and Lions Clubs, which were quite active in Chandigarh and the districts of Haryana.

The PHD (Punjab, Haryana and Delhi) Chamber of Commerce and Industry had been taking considerable interest in the problems arising from the excessive growth of our country's population. At the request of this body's office-bearers, I delivered the valedictory address on July 22, 1989 at a workshop on family welfare in the organized sector sponsored by the PHD Family Foundation. I have no intention of going into what all I said on this occasion. I may, however, mention that my speech made a great impact that led the participants to give me a standing ovation when I finished speaking. That evening, when I went to a local hotel to attend a dinner party held on the occasion of this workshop, I had the opportunity of rubbing shoulders with many industrialists, who had come to Chandigarh from different parts of the country. The Secretary to the Gujarat Chamber of Commerce and Industry, who was present at this party, complimented me on my speech at the workshop and requested me to visit Ahmedabad and address the local Chamber. I eventually did go there after a few months and address them. But about that, more in due course.

In July 1989, I visited the Motilal Nehru School of Sports at Rai in Sonepat district in my capacity as its ex officio Chairman. It was a residential school run on the lines of a public school and was somewhat unique in the sense that it combined general education with professional training of a high order in sports and games. Y.P. Bharadwaj, Principal of the school, briefed me about the activities of the school. Chief Minister Ch. Devi Lal had once discussed the affairs of this school with me and indicated his intention of taking greater interest in its management. I took part in various programmes chalked out for me by the school authorities during the two days I spent there. I also presided over a meeting of the Special Board of the school, which took several decisions towards improving the facilities available to the students.

In the last week of July 989, there was a minor Ministerial crisis in Haryana that arose from a decision of the Punjab and Haryana High Court disqualifying Dharamvir, a ruling party M.L.A., from the membership of the Vidhan Sabha. Soon thereafter, the Supreme Court stayed the High Court's verdict. At this stage, Ch. Devi Lal wrote to me proposing the re-induction of Dharamvir as a Minister of State. The next day, when Ch. Devi Lal saw me at my instance, I advised him against this course on moral grounds. But Ch. Devi Lal insisted and I had to accept his suggestion, which was constitutionally binding on me.

I, therefore, swore in Dharamvir as a Minister of State. Hardly any Minister turned up at the swearing-in ceremony at Raj Bhawan, reportedly in protest against the re-induction of Dharamvir, a disqualified member of the Vidhan Sabha, as a Minister. This annoyed Ch. Devi Lal, who asked some of the Ministers to tender their resignations from the Ministry. Seven Ministers including four of Cabinet rank promptly put in their papers on July 28, 1989. They included Ranjit Singh, son of Ch. Devi Lal. However, Ch. Devi Lal tided over this crisis by managing to get the disgruntled Ministers to withdraw their resignations.

The next day, Ch. Devi Lal saw me at my request and told me that he had sorted out the problem arising from the resignations of some of his Ministers. I then told him that I was soon going to appoint a new Vice-Chancellor of the Kurukshetra University, as the post had been lying vacant for over a month. I informed him that I had consulted various agencies and interviewed a number of persons from different parts of the country with a view to selecting someone who was suitable. When I disclosed that the person I had chosen was Lt. Gen. (Retd.) K. Balaram, a former Vice-Chief of Army Staff, he enquired about the qualifications and the general background of the new appointee. I told him that Gen. Balaram was from Tamilnadu and that he held several degrees of Indian as well as foreign universities, judging by which, he was academically superior to many of those who were in the academic field.

Ch. Devi Lal agreed with me and said that there were many in the defence and police services of our country, who were academically brilliant, contrary to the generally held view in this regard. He also agreed with me that, being an outsider, he would be neutral as between the groups vying for supremacy in the university's affairs. This, he agreed, would help in getting over the endemic problem of factionalism in the university. Another point on which he agreed with me was that, with his Army background, the General would be able to enforce discipline which was a prime requirement of the situation created by a host of factors such as indiscipline, caste politics and nepotism. Ch. Devi Lal thanked me for having made a good choice and wished all success to the new Vice-Chancellor.

In fact, Ch. Devi Lal issued a public statement lending his support to the appointment of Lt.Gen.(Retd.) K Balaram. I remember that he had extended similar support to Lt. Gen. (Retd.) G.C. Sharma, whom

I had appointed a year ago as the Vice-Chancellor of the Maharshi Dayanand University, Rohtak. After realizing that I was trying to bring about some genuine improvement in the functioning of the State's universities, Ch. Devi Lal never interfered in their affairs. He must have been aware that I would not like any such interference.

The reaction in the press to these appointments was generally favourable. A few samples:

Several engagements kept me busy in July-August, 1989. One of these was the programme of Ghazals by a Delhi artiste, Satish Babbar, at our Raj Bhawan organized by the Haryana Urdu Academy on July 31, 1989. The music was highly appreciated by the guests who included several Ministers, many intellectuals and a cross section of Chandigarh's elite. At the outset, I welcomed the artiste and the guests in a speech that contained many Urdu words—something for which I was complimented by the lovers of Urdu.

This was followed on August 4, 1989 by a function at Raj Bhawan to celebrate Teej, as had been done the previous year. Many Ministers, senior officials and their wives and people from different walks of life joined the celebration that was marked by spontaneous gaiety. The guests were welcomed by 'Rastja' singers from Faridabad, 'Jogis' and 'Damroo' beaters from Jind and other groups of folk singers from various parts of Haryana. Music and dances by youthful artistes dressed in traditional attire—boys in Dhoti and Kurta along with the turban and girls in Ghagra, Kurta and Chunri—created a colourful atmosphere.

'Kanwar' bearers carrying holy Ganges water in pitchers re-created the picture of pilgrims from Haryana bringing Ganges water on foot all the way from Hardwar and offering it to lord Shiva in the temples all over Haryana in the belief that this would wash away all sins and help in the fulfillment of all their wishes. 'Churi' shops set up on the lawns of Raj Bhawan sold bangles of various colours to the ladies. Many ladies took their turn to get their hands decorated with 'Mehandi' patterns

On August 14, 1989, my wife and I reached Jind because the next morning I was to take the salute at the Independence Day parade there. We attended a dance recital by the well-known Kathak artiste, Uma Sharma, and her troupe at the local Government College. After the parade and cultural programmes organized the next morning, I hosted a big reception in the afternoon, which was attended by a large number of invitees that included most of the Chief Minister Ch. Devi Lal and most of the Ministers, officials, many social activists, leading members of the public and a cross section of people from different walks of life.

Late in the evening on August 15, 1989, my wife and I visited the local Bhuteshwara temple and worshipped there. This is a very ancient place and is one of the three pilgrimages mentioned in the Vamana Purana, namely Somanatha, Jwalamaleshwara and Bhuteshwara.

Next day, we visited the famous Pandu Pindarni, a very old temple where the Pandavas had offered 'Pinda' (oblations to ancestors). It is from here that they commenced their journey to heaven. We were very happy to be able to see this place and offer 'Puja'.

Leaving Jind on August 16, 1989, for Chandigarh, we stopped en route at Kaithal, where we were met by Ram Bilas Sharma, a Minister of Haryana, Banarasi Dass, the MLA from Kalayat, and some other prominent persons of that region with whom I discussed various matters pertaining to Kaithal and Kalayat.

Kaithal is a very ancient place where there are over a hundred Shiva temples, the biggest of which is the Rudra Shiva temple. It was at this temple that Arjuna had worshipped Lord Shiva at the time of the Mahabharata war. Pleased with Arjuna, Lord Shiva had granted to him the invincible Pashupat weapon.

There are nine old tanks in Kaithal known as Navagraha Kundas. It is believed that after the Mahabharata war, the Pandavas had a 'Yagna' for peace (Shantiyagna) on the banks of these tanks. Kaithal is also known as 'Chhoti Kashi' (small Benares). Chinese travellers, Hiuen Tsang and Fa Hien, have referred to the importance of Kaithal in their memoirs.

Kaithal, as I saw it in 1988 and 1989, was faced with the problem of decadence, which cried for attention. The old fort of Kaithal was in urgent need of repairs. It was originally built by Bhai Desu Singh and was the chief residence and administrative center of the Bhai Sikhs, who ruled over this area in the 18th and 19th centuries. It is located at the highest point of the town on the banks of a lake that encircles the town. It dominates the whole scenario, which, however, looked dismal, when I saw it, thanks largely to the lack of repairs and the growth of water hyacinth and various weeds in the lake. The police station of the city was accommodated in a part of the fort that had been declared unsafe and due for demolition!

I could appreciate the feeling among the local people in favour of a separate district of Kaithal—a demand that was met in October 1989, when a new Kaithal district was formed together with some areas of Kurukshetra and Jind districts.

Near-by Kalayat is another ancient place of Kaithal district located on the road to Narwana. It was called 'Kapil Had' in Vedic literature. It was here that sage Kapil did his penance and composed the Sankhya that is regarded as the precursor of the Gita.

The Rajputs of Haryana belong to two main clans, namely the Mandhars and the Chauhans. The Mandhars are said to be the descendants of Lav, son of Lord Rama, while his other son Kush, who ruled over Kashmir, was the progenitor of the Kachwaha and Narban clans. Lav is believed to have founded the Lahore city, now in Pakistan. The Mandhars are 'Surajbanshis', hailing from Ayodhya. Kalyat in Kaithal district is their principal stronghold in this region.[14] Kalyat is well-known in Haryana and the adjoining region for its famous folk theatre form of Swaag and for its troupe of women Swaag performers led by Sardari.

At Kalayat, there are two terracotta temples with beautiful carvings which were built in the seventh century A.D. One of these is the Shiva temple built with bricks of a special kind without mortar which is an exquisite specimen of architecture. According to legend, Raja Salivahana, who got cured of his skin disease at Kalayat got seven temples built of which only two survived. The Kapil Sarovar here with its many 'Ghats' covered with floral designs provides an impressive view. The artistically designed ornate 'Havelis' of Kalayat speak of its old glory.

Steps to preserve Kalayat's heritage were urgently called for. In 1983, the Shiva temple was declared a protected monument. But in 1988, there were reports of damage caused to the temple as a result of the seepage of rain water through the cracks in its walls. Its 'Shikhara' (top) was said to have fallen down during heavy rains. The load-bearing capacity of its foundation had reportedly become weak because of water-logging. Thus the temple began to sink. It was slightly tilted towards the tank on which it stood. I was happy to see that several experts of the Central and State Governments devised measures for the preservation of the temple.

The INTACH (Indian National Trust For Art AND Cultural Heritage) was doing a commendable job in creating awareness of the need for preservation of old monuments and cultural heritage. Some units of the INTACH had been set up in Haryana to take up this work that included Kalayat town and the temple.

On August 26, 1989, I went to Palwal and further on to Hathin in Faridabad district and inaugurated the Lok Adalat organized by the District Legal Service and Advice Committee jointly with the State Government's Department of Justice Administration. The utility of this experiment became evident from the statement of Justice G.C. Mittal, Chairman of the State Legal Service and Advice Committee, that about 70,000 cases had been sorted out during the preceding four years in Haryana by the Lok Adalats.

I went around some of the near-by places, one of which was Hodal located on a hill a few miles beyond Palwal by the side of the road to Agra. Atank and a copse here known as Pando Ban are highly venerated by the local people.

Palwal is believed to be identical with Apelava that formed part of Indraprastha during the Mahabharata era. A little to the south west of Palwal is a village Aharwan , which is situated on a high mound. When this place went into decay, King Vikramaditya is said to have restored it. In Palwal, there are many old architectural sites, one of which is a tomb of Roshan Chiragh. It was built in 1661 A.D. by saint Roshan Chiragh by levying a tax of one stone on every cartload that passed from Bharatpur to Delhi for the construction of Emperor Shahjahan's palace.[15]

Hathin, where the Lok Adalat was held, is said to have been founded by a king in the midst of a jungle inhabited by many elephants (Hathi in Hindi). It is from its association with elephants that this place came to be called Hathin. Relics of the Sunga period discovered at this place point to its antiquity.

On September 23, 1989, we were treated to a scintillating programme of classical music at our Raj Bhawan, thanks to the well-known classical musicians—Rajan and Sajan Misra—who responded to a request from the North Zone Cultural Centre. My readiness to host the function—as I was ever willing to do—led to our Raj Bhawan being the venue. Among the guests were E.S. Venkataramaiah, Chief Justice of India, who was on an official visit to Chandigarh, and many Judges of the Punjab and Haryana High Court including its Chief Justice, apart from many other distinguished persons.

The Misra brothers opened the evening's programme with a pice in Raga Hamsadhwani at my request, which was an instant hit. It was followed by a piece in Raga Bageshwari and then by a devotional piece "Vighna Hare Gajanan" (May Lord Ganesha remove all hurdles). Their songs in Raga Jog and Raga Kamod brought out the subtle nuances of their music which tugged at the heart-strings of the audience.

In the first week of October 1989, I had several engagements in Mahendrgarh district. Some days after my visit to the district, it was bifurcated into Rewari and Mahendragarh districts. The new Rewari district was carved out with the Rewari Sub-division, some parts of Mahendragarh Tehsil and some areas of Rohtak district. In an earlier chapter, I have discussed the historical and cultural background of several places in these two districts—Rewari and Mahendragarh.

My first engagement was on October 6, 1989, when I inaugurated a Bal Bhawan at a place called Bawal, a Tehsil headquarters of the newly created Rewari district. It had been built by the Haryana State Council for Child Welfare for the benefit of destitute children. Bawal, located about ten miles from Rewari, had been founded by Rao Sainsmal, a Chauhan Rajput from a place in Alwar. He gave the name Bawal to this place as his family priest belonged to the Bawalia 'Gotra' (clan). It had been merged in Nabha State after the 1857 uprising. At Bawal, I saw a fort.

In the evening, I proceeded to Narnaul, the headquarters of the Mahendragarh district. There, my wife and I were enthralled by a Kuchipudi dance programme put up by the renowned artiste Swapna Sundari and her troupe. The next day, we went around some places in and around Narnaul. Some of the historical monuments we aw were fine specimens of Pathan and Mughal architecture. One of these, the mausoleum of Ibrahim Khan, was a perfect example of the square tomb built in the typical Pathan style by Sher Shah Suri about 450 years ago in memory of his grandfather, who had served at Narnaul as n officer of the Lodhi rulers. The tombs of several members of his family are located in these premises.

We also visited the famous Jal Mahal that had been built as a pleasure house with a big tank and kiosks in 1591 A.D. by Shah Quli Khan, the Jagirdar of Narnaul. The Jal Mahal was in perfect working condition when we saw it, but the tank was dry and in place water, it had only sand! We also visited the historical Chor Gumbaj, which Jagmal Khan had built in his life-time in his own memory! We went round a lace called Birbal Ka Chhata that had been constructed during the reign of Akbar by Rai Mukand Dass of Narnaul. It is said that whenever Akbar and Birbal visited Narnaul, a 'Durbar' used to be held here.

Before returning to Chandigarh, we stopped by in Delhi for a day, which gave us the opportunity of joining the Durga Puja celebrations at a few places. It was in Delhi that I heard with deep sorrow of the passing away at Rohtak of Pt. Sri Ram Sharma, the veteran freedom-fighter, who had courted imprisonment several times during the country's struggle for independence. He had joined the Congress Party as a young boy at the time of the first Non-Co-operation movement in 1920 and played a leading role in organizing the party in Haryana.

On my way back to Chandigarh on October 9, 1989, I dropped in at Sonepat and laid the foundation stone of a welfare centre for the hearing and speech handicapped—a project that was undertaken by the District Child Welfare Council. Subhash Katyal, Welfare Minister, who spoke on the occasion, outlined the various measures taken by the State Government for the welfare of the handicapped children.

A few days before this, Chief Justice V. Ramaswamy of the Punjab and Haryana High Court was appointed as a Judge of the Supreme Court of India. Another legal luminary of Chandigarh, namely Sardar Kuldip Singh was also appointed a Judge of the Supreme Court. Simultaneously with all this, the appointment of Justice Dewan as the Chief Justice of the Punjab and Haryana High Court was also announced. A few days later, it was discovered that my concurrence in my capacity as the Governor of Haryana with this appointment had not been taken before this announcement was made. This was an oversight because the matter had earlier been discussed with me. This led Sardar Buta Singh, Union Home Minister, to ring me up from Delhi and to seek my approval, which I gave. Since this was done verbally, some papers were expeditiously put up to me for my signature, which formalized the order of appointment.

Notes

1. अल्लाहस्य सर्वगुणसम्पन्नता एकेश्वरवादश्च
कुराणम् २ सूक्तम १०७ आयातः
वित्थ किन्नैव राज्यानां व्योम्नामुव्यस्तिथैव च।
स हि सर्वशिताऽल्लाह इत्यादिः।
२.२५५
ईड्योऽल्लाहं विना नान्यस्सजीवश्शाश्वतोऽप्यसौ।
न तन्द्रा न पुनर्निद्रा बाधते तं कदाचन।।
२६.६१
अनुयुंक्ष्व त्वमेमतान् को धरित्रीं वियतस्तथा।
सृष्टवान्, कर्मयुक्तौ कस्सोमसूयो तथाऽकरोत्।।
तेऽनिवार्यं प्रवक्ष्यन्ति ह्यल्लाहस्सृष्टवानिमान्।
११.१२३
परोक्ष यद् धरित्र्याञ्च यद् वियत्सु च तिष्ठति।

अल्लाहस्यैव तत् सर्वम्।

२८.८८

नाल्लाहेन समं त्वन्यं प्रतीष्टं त्वञ्च गायतात्।

प्रतीष्टो नेतरस्तस्मात् इत्यादिः।

यजुर्वेदः, २३.१

हिरण्यगर्भस्समवर्त्तताग्रे,

भूतस्य जातः पतिरेक आसीत्।

स दाधार पृथिवीं द्यामुतेमाम्,

कस्मै देवाय हविषा विधेम।।

ऋग्वेदः, १०, १२, १६०

सूर्याचन्द्रमसौ धाता यथापूर्वमकल्पयत्। दिवञ्च पृथिवीञ्चान्तरिक्षमथा स्वः।

यजुर्वेदः, ३२.३

न तस्य प्रतिमाऽस्ति यस्य नाम महद्यशः।

2. १६, ६५

गतप्राणां धरां पश्चात् प्राणैस्तावदयोजयत्।

१६, ६७

स्मृति याति न किं नरः, सृष्टोऽसौ प्राक् किलास्माभिर्यदाऽऽसीन्न स किंचन?

वृहदारण्यकोपनिषद् षष्ठे चतुर्थं ब्राह्मणम् २५

भूस्ते दधामि, भुवस्ते दधामि, स्वस्ते दधामि भूर्भुवः

स्वः सर्वं त्वयि दधामीति।

भगवद्गीता, २, २२

वासांसि जीर्णानि यथा विहाय नवानि गृहणति

नरोऽपराणि। तथा शरीराणि विहाय जीर्णान्यन्यानि

संयाति नवानि देही।

3. For the historical and cultural background of Yamunanagar and other places mentioned in this book, the author has drawn upon the Encyclopaedic District Gazetteers of India, Northern Zone (Volume III), edited by S.C. Bhatt.
4. This account is based on 'Haryana' by D.C. Verma, pp. 79-80.
5. The Encyclopaedic District Gazetteers of India edited by S.C. Bhatt.
6. *Ibid.*
7. *Ibid.*
8. For this and the two preceding paragraphs, I have drawn upon my study of the Puranas as well as upon what I was told during my visit to the area. These facts were nicely brought out in an article on the Suryakund temple by Munish Bhatia in the Punjab Kesari of March 20, 2000.
9. 'This Beautiful India: Haryana' by Sukhdev Singh Chib, p. 75.
10. Yuan Chwang's Travels in India (AD 629–645) by Thomas Watters MRAS, p. 317.

11. *Ibid*, p. 318.
12. Encyclopaedic District Gazetteers of India, North Zone, Volume 3, edited by S.C. Bhatt, p. 71.
13. 'Haryana' by D.C. Verma, p. 95.
14. *Ibid*, p. 77.
15. The Encyclopaedic District Gazetteers of India edited by S.C. Bhatt, North Zone, Volume 3, p. 91.

17

In Gujarat, the Land of Pilgrimages

In the mean time, arrangements for my going to Ahmedabad on an official visit had been finalized. I have earlier mentioned the fact that in July 1989, I had addressed a workshop on family welfare in the organized sector held under the auspices of the PHD Chamber of Commerce and Industry. After hearing me, the Secretary of the Gujarat Chamber of Commerce and Industry had personally requested me to visit his State and address the Gujarat Chamber. He had followed this up by formally writing to me and renewing his invitation. I forwarded this letter to the President of India, who saw no objection to my going to Gujarat.

So, on October 11, 1989, my wife and I reached Ahmedabad in accordance with a programme earlier chalked out by the Gujarat Chamber of Commerce and Industry. We put up at the Raj Bhawan in Gandhinagar as the guests of Shri R.K. Trivedi, Governor of Gujarat. The next day, I addressed the members of the Gujarat Chamber, the subject being: "Challenges and Opportunities of the Business Community". Later, I also addressed a gathering of women entrepreneurs on the subject: "The Role of Women Entrepreneurs in the Emerging Scenario". I do not want to go into the details of my speeches here. Apart from a lunch party held by the Gujarat Chamber, there was also a dinner party in my honour hosted by the Governor of Gujarat at the Raj Bhawan, where I met many Ministers (some of whom I knew), high officials and members of the intelligentsia. Dinner over, my wife and I were taken to another part of the Raj Bhawan, where a cultural programme to mark Navaratri was held. The main item of the programme was, of course, the famous Garba dance of Gujarat.

Though I had visited Gujarat several times in the past in connection with my official work, during this visit, I went round many of the important landmarks of Ahmedabad and Gandhinagr to refresh my memories of these places. Known as the Manchester of India by virtue of its textile industry, Ahmedabad is a place where the very old and the very new co-exist cheek by jowl. Located in the Anarta region between the Arbuda mountain and the Sabarmati river, it is a very ancient place, which is evident from the references to it found in the Nagarkhand of the Skanda Purana. It is mentioned as Svabhra (area around the Sabarmati river) in the Junagadh rock inscription of Rudradaman.[1]

The Sabarmati river on which Ahmedabad is located is alternatively called Svabhravati or Sabhramati or Chandana. It divides the territory of Gujarat into two halves—Saurashtra and Kutch on the north and the rest of the State on the south. The Padmapurana traces the origin of the name Sabarmati to the word 'Sambhrama', which means agitation and alarm mixed with excitement.[2] It is said that once sage Vashistha, while engrossed in meditation, saw sage Vishwamitra with his powerful eyes. Vashistha's penetrating vision pierced the earth, boring two holes from which came out two rivers—the Saraswati and the Sabarmati. The explanation for the name of the Sabarmati river was that Vashistha's glance towards Vishwamitra was mixed with great 'Sambhrama', *i.e.*, considerable reverence.

The region around the Sabarmati river has been the cradle of India's ancient civilization. Recent excavations have disclosed evidence that the old Harappan culture thrived here once upon a time. It was here that King Karnadev of the Solanki dynasty of Anhilwadpatan had eatablished the city of Karnavati in ancient times. It was also called Srinagar or Rajnagar.

The city of Ahmedabad was founded in 1411 A.D, by Ahmed Shah in accordance with the wishes of his spiritual mentor, Saint Shaikh Ahmed Khattu. It was acquired by Akbar in 1573 A.D. And then taken over by the Marathas in the 18th century. It witnessed the tussle for its control between the Peshwas and the Gaekwads and in 1817, the British stepped in here.

The Padmapurana says that the Khadgatirtha was situated on the bank of the Sabarmati river. There is a temple of Khadgadhareshwara here. Close by are the 'Ghat' of Dudheshwar and the temple of Dudheshwar Mahadev. It is said that the milk of the heavenly cow, Kamadhenu, was poured at this place. It is believed that the faithful can sometimes see milk shooting up in the dark on the waters of this river. It is said that near this place was located the hermitage of sage Dadhichi, who had donated to Indra his bones with which the gods made the 'Vajra' (thunderbolt) in order to destroy a demon by name Vritra.

After paying a visit to the Sabarmati Ashram, we went to call on Shri Gulzari Lal Nanda, who was recuperating from his illness at the Ahmedabad residence of his daughter. We thought it fit to look him up because we had come to know him rather well at Kurukshetra in Haryana, where he had been guiding the activities of the Kurukshetra Development Board. He was very glad to see us and, despite his indisposition, he held forth from time to time on his plans of doing a host of things for the development of several places in the Kurukshetra region so that the country's spiritual heritage and history could be preserved for posterity.

On October 13, 1989, we proceeded to Veraval to worship at the holy shrine of Somnath. On the way, we stopped for a while at Limbdi and were met by some officials with whom we exchanged notes about the background of this and many other places of Gujarat. A Taluka of Surendranagar district, Limbdi was earlier a princely State that was merged along with other States to constitute the State of Saurashtra after independence. It then formed part of Zalawad district, which was renamed as Surendranagar in 1956 after its merger with Maharashtra. This district later formed part of Gujarat ater the bifurcation of the bi-lingual Bombay State on May 1, 1960. The Limbdi rulers traced their ancestry to Harpaldev, from whom the rulers of Dharangadhara also claimed their descent. Limbdi is a beautiful place.

We stopped for lunch at Rajkot, where we were met by senior officers of the I.A.S. And I.P.S. Some of these officers whom I knew previously told me a few things about Rajkot and other places in this region. As is generally known, Rajkot was a princely State before independence that had come into being during the chaos in the post-Aurangzeb period. It was merged as a district of Saurashtra State of which it also became the capital after independence. It formed part of the Bombay State after 1956 and then in 1960, it became a district of Gujarat State when the Bombay State was bi-furcated.

The importance of Rajkot is also traceable to the fact that it was the seat of the Agent to the British Governor-General and later of the Resident and Crown Representative. Jetpur in this district is regarded as a holy place because it was here that Swami Sahajananda, the founder of the Swaminarayana sect, was enthroned. Another place in this district, Tankara, is the birth-place of Swami Dayanand Saraswati. Vavania, also in this district, is a holy place of the Jains because the Jain saint and philosopher, Shrimad Rajchandra, was born here. From him, Mahatma Gandhi is said to have imbibed some of his ideas.

As we proceeded towards Junagadh in the afternoon, we saw en route a place known as Virpur, which is an important pilgrimage. We saw many small groups of pilgrims moving along the roads, chanting aloud; "Jalaram Bapu Ki Jai" (victory to Jalaram Bapu). The story of Jalaram Bapu, as narrated to us by an officer travelling with us is somewhat like this. One day God decided to test Jalaram's religiosity and appeared before him in the guise of an emaciated Sadhu. He told Jalaram that as he was sick, he needed the services of his wife, Veerbai.

Upon this, Jalaram promptly told his wife to accompany the Sadhu and serve him to the best of her ability. So the Sadhu left the place along with Veerbai. As they were going through a forest, the Sadhu asked her to wait at a particular spot, as he was going a little off the track to make water. So the Sadhu disappeared, leaving behind his walking stick and 'Jholi' (a satchel for carrying things that is slung from the shoulder). Even today, in the beautiful temple of Jalaram Bapu, the stick and the 'Jholi' are preserved. The local people say that Jala and God are identical (Yo Jala So Allah).

We stopped for a while at Junagadh, where also, the officers who met us, told us about the place and its history. We were given a bundle of books and pamphlets about Gujarat and its important places, which we browsed through from time to time. Junagadh was known as Sorath in ancient times. It was ruled by the Chudasama Rajputs since the 7th or 8th century A.D. Then came the numerous invasions by the Muslims, who in due course established their rule here after the defeat of the Hindu ruler by Mohamed Begada. Muslim rule in Junagadh ended in November 1948 as the people rose in revolt against Nawab Mohabbat Khan, the last ruler, who had plotted to accede to the new State of Pakistan. Eventually, unable to face the wrath of the people, the Nawab fled to Pakistan, after which Junagadh joined the Indian Union.

Junagadh, together with some other princely States, became a district of Saurashtra State. It subsequently became a district of Bombay State in 1956 and then a district of Gujarat in 1960. Junagadh and many other adjacent places abound with relics of the past as well as several shrines considered sacred by the Hindus and Muslims. Junagadh has derived its name from a near-by old fort known as Uparkot. There are two old step-wells in this fort built in the 11th and 15th century A.D. respectively, which were named by the rulers after their maid servants. The Ranak Devi Mahal inside the fort is said to be a tourist attraction. Narsinh Mehta Chaura is a place in Junagadh where the great soul Narsinh Mehta used to sit and sing devotional songs in the 15th century A.D. Many shrines of the Hindus, Jains and Muslims in this district are constantly thronged by pilgrims.

The famous Shiva temple of Bhavanath attracts a large number of devotees during Shivaratri. The Linga in this temple is said to be 'Swayambhu' *i.e.*, it came out of its own and was not installed by anybody. According to local tradition, once Brahma and Vishnu quarrelled with each other over the issue of who was the greater of the two. Each claimed to be greater than the other. To resolve this dispute, Lord Shiva appeared on the scene and began to beat up Brahma. At this stage, Vishnu interposed himself between the two and started explaining the greatness of Shiva whom he extolled as the greatest of all. After this, Brahma also sang the praise of Lord Shiva. Pleased with their eulogies, Lord Shiva decided to reside there in the form of a Shiva Linga, which came to be known as Bhairavnath Mahadev. It is believed by devout Hindus that whoever has 'Darshan' of Bhavnath gets liberated from all sins and is freed from the cycle of birth and death.

There are several reservoirs or Kunds in Junagadh which are regarded as sacred by the Hindus. One of these is the famous Damodar Kund, whose name is a combination of the two words—'Dam' meaning a rope and 'Udar' meaning the belly—the reference being to Lord Krishna who, as a child, had been tied with a rope around the belly to prevent him from playing his naughty pranks. The devout Hindu believes that several holy rivers such as the Ganges, Yamuna, Saraswati, Narmada, Sindhu, Kaveri, Kshipra, Charnanyavati, Godavari etc. co-exist in this holy 'Kund'. All the gods are also believed to be present in this tank. Here is a local saying:

"Adhsath Tirth Karne Par Bhi Yatra Purn Hoti
Damodar Kun Nahaate Nahin"

(Even after visiting 68 holy places, the pilgrimage is not complete until one comes to Sorath and takes a dip in the Damodar Kund.)

Now about Girnar, the pilgrimage on a hill adjacent to Junagadh whose name in ancient times was Ujjayant or Urjayant or Raivatak. Later, it came to be known as Girinarayan and finally as Girnar. A flight of stairs leads up to Girnar, which has five peaks. The first peak is known as Amba Mata.

There is a story about how Girnar and Amba Mata came into existence. When Himalaya decided to give his daughter Parvati in marriage to Lord Shankara, the bride's brother Giri was placed in charge of looking after the many guests expected on this big occasion. Lord Vishnu, one of the important guests, was very pleased with the way Giri took care of him at the time of the wedding and gave him a boon, according to which, Giri would be regarded as the most important of all the mountains and from then on, all the gods would live on the Giri mountain. Further, according to the boon, all sages doing penance on the Giri mountain would achieve their goals without any difficulty. Lord Vishnu also gave Giri the name Girinarayana. Girnar is a corruption from Girinarayana.

It is said that in ancient times, mountains used to have wings and could fly about, causing harm to living beings. Once the earth god ordered Lord Indra to cut off the wings of the mountains. At this stage, mountain Giri fled for fear of his life and took refuge under the waters of the sea. His sister, Parvati, began to cry over the disappearance of her dear brother, Giri. So her consort, Lord Shankara, and Lord Vishnu launched a thorough campaign of search for her missing brother. They came to know that Giri was inside the sea.

All the gods unitedly offered prayers to the sea god, who, being pleased with them, told them to ask for any boon they wanted. The gods requested the sea god to release Giri from under the water and also to shift from the land mass to the extent of five 'Yojanas'. (One Yojana is equal to eight 'Kosas' and one Kosa is equal to two miles.) As the sea thus receded, Giri revealed himself. To rid Giri of all fears and to protect him, goddess Amba decided to reside on top of that mountain. It is believed that whoever has 'Darshan' of Ambaji is emancipated from the accumulated sins of all previous births.

A scenic place near Girnar is Tulshi Shyam, which is famous for its hot springs and a temple of Kunti and her son, Bhim. It is situated deep inside the forest and attracts a number of pilgrims and tourists. The name of this place is a corruption from Tal Swami. And thereby hangs a tale, which is as follows.

After Lord Nrisimha killed Hiranyakashipu, the King of the demons, the latter's son, Tal Daitya (*i.e.* Tal, the demon) became the King. One day, the great sage Chyavan told Tal about the beauty of Tapt Kund, a water reservoir on earth. Tal went to Tapt Kund and had a refreshing bath. Then he went to Triveni, a confluence of sacred rivers, had a dip there and sat down, engrossed in spiritual thoughts. At this stage, Lord Hari Narayana appeared before him. Tal Daitya paid obeisance to him and sang his praise. Pleased with him, Hari Narayana told him to ask for a boon. Tal Daitya asked for the Lord's forgiveness and a boon that would always keep his mind immersed in Hari Narayana and would give him the opportunity of rendering service to the latter.

The Lord said: "So be it" and also ordained that from then on Tal Daitya would be worshipped by the people. In course of time, Tal Daitya came to be known as Tal Swami. Then Tal Swami got corrupted into Tulsi Shyam. It is generally believed that a pilgrim who visits Tulsi Shyam and worships at the Tapt Kund acquires the same 'Punya' or merit as one who goes round the world, performs 'Sradh' at Gaya or undertakes pilgrimages to Prabhas, Vrindavan and other holy places.

Near Girnar is a place Satadhar, which is associated with the hallowed memory of Gigla Pir. Cows are worshipped here. There was a buffalo here, when I visited the place in October 1989. It is said that the buffalo was once sent to Bombay to be slaughtered. Somehow or other, nobody succeeded in getting it killed. So the buffalo was sent back to its owner in Satadhar. It was a sturdy and healthy buffalo, which every visitor made it a point to see. So this buffalo was as much a worth-seeing fixture of Satadhar as anything else. Of course, when I was at Girnar, I heard many stories about the famous lions of Girnar.

Not far from Girnar is a place Bilkha that was known as Balishnath in days of yore Legend has it that once Lord Shiva appeared before a person here and asked him to chop off the head of his only son and smash it in order to make a meal of it for him. When this person unhesitatingly complied with his command, Lord Shiva restored his son to life. Since then, this place has acquired a holiness that has attracted pilgrims through the ages.

We reached Veraval, the sacred sea-side town, a little before evening. We promptly proceeded to visit some of the holy places in the region. One such place was Bhalka Tirth that is situated between Veraval and Patan. It was here that Lord Krishna, who was taking rest under a Pipal tree, was suddenly struck in the leg by the arrow of a Bhil hunter by name Jara, who mistook him for a deer. Lord Krishna entered the state of Yoga Samadhi and passed into eternal divinity. There is a tank here known as Bhalka Kund, a dip in which confers great merit on a devotee. Explaining why Lord Krishna chose this place for leaving the mortal coil, the Skanda Purana says that Prabhasa is a place that is imbued ith the essence of the Trinity of Hindu gods—Brahma, Vishnu and Shiva. The Pipal tree under which Lord Krishna was sitting while the hunter's arrow hit him is said to still and was shown to us.

Then we were shown the place where Krishna was cremated—a place which is very sacred to all Hindus and particularly to the Vaishnavas. It was at Triveni or the confluence o the three rivers—Saraswati, Hiranya and Kapila. The cremation took place on the bank of river Hiranya. This place is also called Dehotsarga, to which references have been made in the Skanda Purana and Bhagawat Purana. A Gita Mandir has been built here and on its marble slabs, the verses of the Gita have been inscribed.

And then to the sacred Somnath temple, which is one of the twelve 'Jyotirlingas' situated in different parts of our country.[3] It is to be noted that Somnath is mentioned first in this list of Jyotirlingas, thus highlighting its importance as a Shiva temple.

Somnath or Prabhasa Tirtha, as it is alternatively called, is located on the sea in southern Saurashtra. It is said to be the very essence of Anarta, the ancient name of Gujarat. It is as old as creation. The seventh Khanda of the Skanda Purana known as the Prabhasa Khanda is devoted to a description of Prabhasa Tirtha, Mount Girnar, Arbuda or Mount Abu and Dwaraka. According to Prabhasa Khanda, Lord Shiva has resided here since eternity and would do so till eternity. The universe has witnessed the coming and going of a succession of Brahmas in different ages. The current Brahma, the seventh in the series, is known as Satananda, while Lord Shiva, who coexists with the seventh Brahma is known as Somnath. In the eras of the six earlier Brahmas, Lord Shiva, who resided at Prabhasa Tirtha, was successively known as Mrityunjaya, Kalagnirudra, Amritesha, Anamaya, Krittivasa and Bhairavanatha. The eighth Brahma will be Chaturvaktra and the corresponding Lord Shiva at Prabhasa Tirtha will be known as Prananatha.[4]

The antiquity of this shrine is evident from a verse of the Rigveda which means:[5] "Make me immortal at the place where the three rivers Ganga, Yamuna and Prachi Saraswati meet and where there is Lord Somnath. O Moon! Shower nectar for Indra."

This shrine was worshipped in Vedic times. It is a well-known fact that several thousand years ago, Lord Shiva was worshipped in the Indus Valley.

The verse from the Rigveda quoted above shows that Prabhasa stood close to the old Saraswati as well as the Ganga and the Yamuna, which in fact referred to two local rivers, *i.e.*, Hiranya and Kapila. This Saraswati river originated in the Plaksha Prasravana in the Himalayas, as indicated in the Vana Parva of the Mahabharata: (Plakshad Deva sruta Rajan Mahapunya Saraswati). 633

Then the Saraswati flowed through the territories now known as Haryana, Rajasthan and Gujarat and fell into the sea near Prabhasa Tirtha or Somnath:

Eka Chetat Saraswati Nadinang, Shuchiyeto Giribhya Aa— Rigveda, 7-95 2).

Prachi Saraswati mentioned in the Rigveda flowed east near Somnath, while it flowed west in its earlier course from the Himalayas downward.

There is a legend which explains how the shrine of Somnath got its name. It is said that Daksa Prajapati had 27 daughters all of whom were married to the moon god (Soma). Of them, Rohini was the most beautiful and so the moon god was partial towards her. The other wives, who resented this, complained to their father, Daksa, who intervened and told Soma to behave even-handedly with all his wives. But Daksa's advice fell on deaf ears and he pronounced a curse on Soma saying that he would wane as a result of being a patient of consumption. So the moon began to wane. As a consequence, vegetation ceased to grow and herbs lost their taste. Concerned over this, the gods approached Daksa and persuaded him to withdraw the curse on Soma, but on the conditions that Soma would treat all his wives equally, take a dip in the holy waters of the sea at Prabhasa Tirtha and then worship Lord Shiva. If Soma fulfilled these conditions, he would wane during one half of a month, but would wax during the other half, as the following verse says:

"Samudrang Pashchimamang Gatwa 634
Aaradhayatu Deveshang Tatah Shanti Avapsyati"

—Shalya, 36-33

(Let the moon go to the western sea where river Saraswati meets the sea and worship Devesha. Then alone will the Moon-God regain his light.)

So Soma came down to Prabhasa along with Rohini and worshipped Somnath. After Soma's penance lasting 4000 years, Lord Shiva was pleased with him and gave him the strength to wax and shine in the bright fortnight. As the moon regained its light, it came to be known as Prabhasa (Pra = Punah *i.e.*, again and Bhasa = Prakash, *i.e.*, light). As the moon god or Soma worshipped the Shiva Linga here, the place is called Somnath.

Lord Brahma helped Soma and Rahu in establishing the Somnath temple. Brahma cleft the earth open, showing them the Swayambhu Sparsa Linga of Shiva. It was covered with honey and.Darbha grass. On it was placed the Brahmashila over which was established by Brahma Himself the great Linga of Lord Somnath. It was worshipped with Vedic Mantras.[6]

The Prabhasa Khanda of the Skanda Purana describes the Linga of Somnath as being endowed with great prowess, as bright as the disc of the sun, encircled by a serpent, of the size of the egg of ahen, called the Sparsa Linga and situated underground.

There are five 'Sakaras', which are said to stand for the attributes of Somnath and bring out its merit: Saraswati river, Samudra (sea), Soma (the Lord with his consort Uma), Somagraha (the moon) and the 'Darshana' (view) of Lord Somnath.

Somnath is believed to be located 300 bow-lengths from the Kritasmara Mount. It is said that this mountain wanted to marry river Saraswati and sought to touch her even while she was impure. She asked him to temporarily hold the fire which she was carrying till she became pure after a bath. On catching hold of the fire, Kritasmara was reduced to ashes and his bones were used thereafter by masons for the purpose of building temples.[7]

Whoever dies in the vicinity of Somnath is believed to have an eternal abode with the Lord. Visiting Somnath on a moonless Monday night, undertaking a fast there, a dip in the Saraswati where it meets the sea and 'Darshan' of Somnath confer on the devotee the merit of numerous religious sacrifices. A sea-bath at Prabhasa is said to ensure one's place in heaven. It is believed to be the favourite spot of Indra and Surya. The Pandavas as well as Krishna and Balaram are said to have come here. Janamejaya Parikshita is also believed to have visited this place.

In the Adi Parva of the Mahabharata, Arjuna's visit to Prabhasa is described. Arjuna met Krishna here. Then the two went to the Raivataka mountain where they greatly enjoyed attending a big festival that was being celebrated. At this stage, Arjuna's eyes fell on Subhadra and it was love at first sight. Subhadra, daughter of Vasudev and Krishna's step-sister, was attractively dressed and surrounded by her mates. Krishna understood Arjuna's weakness for Subhadra and asked him what he was up to. Arjuna said: "Duhita Vasudevasya Cha Swasa, Rupena Chaisa Sampanna Kamivaisa Na Mohayet"—Mahabharata, Adi Parva, [18]. (She is the daughter of Vasudeva and the sister of Vaasudeva (*i.e.* Krishna) and endowed with beauty. Is there a man who is not charmed by such a beautiful woman?)

Empathising with Arjuna, Lord Krishna said that a Kshatriya girl could choose 'Swayambara' as a means of marrying a person. But Krishna did not recommend this path, saying: "Swayambarah Kshatriyanang Vivahah Purusasarbha, Sa Cha Sangshayitah Partha Swabhavasyaanimittatah"—Mahabharata, Adi Parva, 21, 218. (Oh Partha, the great, the marriage of a Kshatriya through Swayambara is possible, but that is a doubtful path because of the uncertainty about the choice of a woman (*i.e.* it is not sure whom the woman would choose.)

Then Lord Krishna suggested a path that could be regarded as open incitement to abduction: "Prasahya Harananchaapi Kshatriyanang Prashasyate, Vivahahetuh Shuranamiti Dharmavidoh

Viduh"—Mahabharata, Adi Parva, [22]. (Knowers of religion say that for the brave, it is praiseworthy to marry a woman after taking her away.)

Further on Krishna said: "Sa Twamarjuna Kalyaning Prahasya Bhagining Mama, Hara Swayamvare Hyasyah Ko Vai Veda Chikirsaitam"—Mahabharata, Adi Parva, [23]. (Oh Arjuna, carry off my good sister by force at the Swayambara because whom she would choose is not known.)

The eldest Pandava, Yudhisthira, who was then at Indraprastha, was informed of the resolve of Krishna and Arjuna and he promptly approved of it. On the appointed day, Arjuna carried away the gently smiling Subhadra in his chariot to the utter disappointment of the hundreds of suitors, who spoke of their desire to give chase to Arjuna. (Lord Krishna himself had carried away Rukmini and married her.) in fact, Arjuna did not have to use force to to take away Subhadra, as the latter was smiling when Arjuna accomplished this feat!

In the Vana Parva (Mahabharata), sage Pulastya is mentioned as having described to Bhisma the greatness of the various pilgrimages and the fact that Prabhasa is an abode of the sages where Agni or fire stays eternally: ("Tato Gachchhet Rajendra Prabhasang Tirthamuttamam, Yatra Sannihito Nityang Swyameva Hutashanah"—56.)

Further on, the other attributes of Prabhasa are described by sage Pulastya: "Devatanang Mukhang Veera Jwalanohanilasarathih, Tasmingtirthe Narah Snatwa Shuchi Prayatamanasah, Agnistomatiratrabhyang Phalang Prapnoti Manavah, Tato Gatwa Saraswatyah Sagarasya Cha Sangamam, Gosahasraphalang Tasya Swargalokancha Vindati, Tirthe Salilarajasya Snatwa Prayatamanasah Triratramusitastra Tarpayet Pitridevatah, Prabhasate Yatha Somah Sohashwamedhancha Vindati—Vana Parva, Mahabharata, [60].

(Oh valorous greatest of kings, then go to the great Prabhasa Tirtha, where, like the mouth of the gods, always present is the fire god, who has the wind as his charioteer and whose image is always burning. One who with a pure and restrained mind has a bath there deserves the merit of performing Agnistom and Atiratra sacrifices. Then, going to the confluence of river Saraswati with the sea, one who takes a dip, deserves the merit of making a gift of a thousand cows and goes to heaven. One should go with a restrained mind and bathe at the confluence of the Saraswati and the sea, live there for three days, worship the gods and perform the 'Shraddha' of one's father. If one does so, one becomes as handsome as the moon and derives the virtue of performing an Ashwamedha sacrifice..................).

In the Mahabharata (Vana Parva), Tirthas are described as 'Prabhasadini Tirthani" (*i.e.* Tirthas beginning with Prabhasa). Yudhisthira came here, performed the 'Shraddha' of his father and did penance, bathing each day and each night, lighting up a fire around him all the time, fasting for 12 days and living on only air and water. Draupadi also joined him in this austerity. Lord Krishna and Balaram met Yudhisthira here.

In the Vana Parva of the Mahabharata, it is said that river Saraswati vanished near Vinashana and re-appeared near Chamsodbheda in Saurashtra. To quote: "This is the beautiful, divine and swift-flowing Saraswati and there is the vinashana Tirtha.. Oh valorous one, this Vinashana is like the gateway to the country of the Nishadas, because of which blemish, the Saraswati entered the earth (*i.e.* disappeared) here so that the Nishadas could not know it. Here is Chamasodbheda, where the Saraswati is visible again. It is here that all the sacred sea-going rivers have met." [8]

The Mahabharata (Vana Parva) also says that on the sea-shore near Prabhasa, Lopamudra met and married sage Agastya: "Oh thou vanquisher of the enemy, it is that Tirtha close to the sea where Lopamudra came and chose Agastya as her husband".[9]

Once the Yadavas had come to Prabhasa for a holiday. They drank wine and engaged in an internecine fight that led to the destruction of the entire Yadava race. Only Krishna, his brother, Balarama, and two others, namely Babhru and Daruka (Krishna's charioteer) survived.

The Prabhasa Khanda of the Skanda Purana describes Somnath as 'Hamsa', which means the union of Soma or Shiva with Uma or Shakti.[10] the Brihajjabala Upanishad says that the whole Universe is a combination of Agni and Soma—Agni representing the luminous aspect of Shiva and Soma the aspect of Shakti or Uma.[11] It further says that there is nothing in the universe which is not pervaded by Shiva and Shakti.[12]

There are other verses in the Brihajjabala Upanishad which bear quoting: "How can there be death when one is touched with the Virya of Shiva and Amrita of Shakti?" Bhasma is said to be the Virya of Agni or Shiva and, when mixed with water, it is believed to symbolise the Amrita of Shakti.[13]

Another verse of this Upanishad says: "He attains immortality who with Yogic practices burns his body with the fire of Shiva and is sprinkled over with the nectar of Shakti Soma." [14]

There are many legends about the union of Shiva and Shakti. One of these is that after being insulted by her father Daksha, Sati threw herself into the fire and wa reborn as Uma. Sati is identified with Soma or the moon and Shiva or Agni with the sun. On Amabasya day, Sati or the moon merges with or is burnt in the sun (Shiva or Agni) and emerges as the New Moon or Uma.[15]

According to the Prabhasa Khanda of the Skanda Purana, the Acharyas and Siddhas of the Pashupata cult performed the religious rites in the temple of Somnath. This fact is corroborated by historical and epigraphical evidence available at several places.[16] the founder of this cult was Lakulisa, who lived in the second century A.D. In village Karavan (or Kayavarohana) near Baroda. He came to Prabhasa and preached the Pashupata Darshana. The Pashupata cult was in vogue in Gujarat at least till the 14th century A.D. with Somnath as its principal seat.

Over the centuries, the Somnath temple had acquired vast wealth, much of which was repeatedly looted by the Muslim invaders. J.A. Dave, the great Sanskrit scholar, has described its prosperity in these words: "The prosperity of the Somnath temple is described by Mohamedan historians. Water came daily for the Lord from the Ganges and flowers from Kashmir. About 10,000 villages were endowed for the maintenance of the temple. This was the most sacred and biggest temple in India in the days of Mahmud of Gazni. On every eclipse day lacs of pilgrims gathered there. Richest presents were offered to the Lord. A thousand Brahmins were engaged in the daily worship. Three hundred barbers used to shave the pilgrims. About 350 dancing girls were engaged for dancing and music. The Garbhagriha was lighted by jeweled lamps and the huge bell was rung with a chain of gold of 200 maunds in weight. In the treasure room, there were numerous subsidiary images and equipment of gold, silver and jewels. The temple had 56 pillars all studded with gems."[17]

The generally accepted view is that the Somnath temple may have been built at the beginning of the Christian era. It was built a second time in 649 A.D. In 722 A.D., the Arabs turned their attention to India. In 725 A.D., the Muslim Governor of Sind sent armies to invade western India, which defeated the Kings of Saurashtra and Vallabhi. Is it possible that the temple of Somnath was again destroyed at this time? in any case, by about 800 A.D., this temple appeared to have been built a third time. In 1025 A.D., Mahmud of Ghazni invaded and destroyed the temple. About 50,000 Indian warriors were said to have laid down their lives, fighting the invaders, but they failed to save the temple. Mahmud of Ghazni occupied the temple, broke the sacred Shiva Linga into pieces, looted its treasures and burnt down the edifice.

The temple was soon re-constructed by Bhima, the ruler of Gujarat, and King Bhoja of Malwa. This must have been the fourth shrine of Somnath. Subsequently, the temple was repaired and extended with new additions from time to time. In 1300 A.D., Ala-ud-din Khilji's general, Alaf Khan, launched a campaign of destroying many towns and temples of Gujarat including the Somnath temple. The temple was repaired by Mahipala, the Chodasama King of Junagadh and the Linga was installed by his son, Khengar, some time between 1325 A.D. And 1351 A.D. It was destroyed several times thereafter by the Muslim invaders and for the last time during the rule of Aurangzeb in 1701 A.D. Queen Ahalyabai of Indore built a new temple a little distance away from the old temple and, as a protective measure, had the Linga placed in a secret underground shrine below the upper one.

After our independence, the Somnath shrine was re-constructed, largely on the initiative of Sardar Vallabhbhai Patel. Dr. Rajendra Prasad, President of India, installed the Jyotirlinga of Somnath on May 11, 1951 on the same Brahmashila on which the many earlier temples had been built.

I was shown an arrow made of stone near the temple, which pointed in a particular direction. I was told that, along the direction of the arrow, between the Somnath shrine and the South Pole, there was no land mass whatsoever. This means that one could sail from Somnath to the South Pole in a straight line without having to touch any country. On Kartika Purnima night, the moon and the Rohini star stand vertically above the Somnath shrine in a straight line. Rohini, it may be recalled, was the favourite wife of Soma or the moon. On Kartik Purnima day each year, a big fair is held at the Somnath temple, which is thronged by pilgrims from many parts of the country.

My wife and I felt supremely happy to go round this temple, watch the religious rites in progress and worship the Linga. As I looked intently at the Linga, I felt that what stood before my eyes was something that had existed since time immemorial and was going to last till eternity. I was reminded of a verse (No. 39) of Somastavaraja[18], which, translated into English, should read as follows: "It is the same Garbhagriha (or inner chamber) and the same Brahmashila (the stone on which the Jyotirlinga is installed), as they were for the last two or three thousand years. Above the lower layer now shines the new glory and greatness of the Lord of Ancient Manifestation."

I was presented by the local officials with a large volume of literature on Gujarat and its many pilgrimages, which took me several months to go through and comprehend. On October 14, 1989, we left for Porbandar en route to Dwaraka. After traveling for some time on this road, we were told about a place on the west coast called Madhavpur, which had a temple where Lord Krishna and Rukmini had entered into wedlock. The divine couple's romantic escapades are depicted through songs and dances by the men and women of Saurashtra's handsome and virile Mer community, particularly during the Madhavi Fair at Madhavpur held in the month of Chaitra (March-April).

At Porbandar, the birth-place of Mahatma Gandhi, we went round some places associated with the Mahatma's life. This place has a claim to fame in the fact that it was called Sudampuri once upon a time because it was here that Lord Krishna's poor but very intimate childhood companion, Sudama, lived. Krishna and his brother, Balarama, used to study here at the Pathshala of sage Sandipani. Sudama was their class-mate at this Pathshala. In course of time, Krishna became the King of Dwaraka, while Sudama continued to be as poor as ever. Sudama lived in a dilapidated cottage with his wife, Sushila, and two children. They did not have enough food to eat nor did they have the barest minimum of clothes. One day, Sushila persuaded her husband, Sudama, to go to Dwaraka and meet Krishna just for old times' sake. But she warned him not to ask Krishna for anything. Sudama left for Dwaraka, carrying with him as a present for his boyhood friend, Krishna, a handful of flattened rice tied in a piece of cloth, which his wife had obtained from a neighbour.

As Sudama proceeded towards Dwaraka, he fainted on the way because of weakness and fatigue. Lord Krishna came to know of this through his divine powers and ordered Garuda to go to where Sudama was lying unconscious and bring him to Dwaraka. After some time, when Sudama regained his consciousness, he learnt that he was very close to Dwaraka. In Dwaraka, he saw Krishna's imposing palace, went up to the gate-keeper and told him to inform Krishna that his boyhood friend, Sudama, wants to meet him.

On being informed of this, Krishna came out running and warmly embraced Sudama. Krishna took Sudama inside the palace, made him sit down and asked him about news of his family. Seeing the wealth and prosperity of Krishna, Sudama thought that it would be improper for him to give Krishna the modest present he had carried with him—a handful of flattened rice. He tried his best to conceal this humble gift he had brought, but Krishna understood everything about Sudama's economic status. Sudama did not ask Krishna for anything. Moreover, this was the day of 'Ayachak Vrat', when one was not expected to request anybody for a gift or present.

Lord Krishna took the flattened rice from Sudama and ate it with great relish, which made Sudama feel very happy. This also marked the end of Sudama's economic plight, as Fortune smiled on him. After spending some days with Krishna, he returned to Porbandar, where he saw that a big building now stood in place of his old and dilapidated hut. As he was taken inside by his wife, Sudama, he saw many articles that signified their new-found economic prosperity.

However, Sudama continued to live in his old humble way. There is a big temple of Sudama in Porbandar, which we visited.

On October 14, 1989, we left Porbandar for Dwarka. On the way, we were told about the famous Harshad Mata temple (not to be confused with the Indian stock market's Big Bull, Harshad Mehta) located near Miyani on the hills. It is said that after Krishna killed Kansa, the latter's father-in-law, Jarasandha, attacked Mathura eighteen times to destroy the Yadavas, but he failed to achieve his goal because of the leadership Krishna provided to the latter. Then the Yadavas worshipped Lord Krishna and Shakti, praying to them to deliver them from the fear of the 'Asuras'. Shakti destroyed the 'Asuras' and Bhima, the second Pandava, killed Jarasandha. Then Krishna built a beautiful temple of Shakti Mata there. Since the people expressed joy (Harsh) over the killing of the 'Asuras' and Jarasandha, the temple came to be called Harshad Mata temple. Many tales about the miracles performed by Harshad Mata are in circulation among the local people.

In Dwaraka, we went round several temples. We also worshipped at the holy Shiva temple at Nageshwar, about eight miles from Dwaraka, which is one of the twelve Jyotirlingas: "Nageshang Darukavane" (Nagesha in Drukavana or Dwaraka). Later, we made a trip by sea to the sacred island of Bet Dwaraka, where we visited the Dwarkadheesh temple as also the Ashrama of Sitaramdas Omkarnath, a great saint of Bengal.

Dwaraka and Bet Dwaraka are very sacred pilgrimages of the Hindus, where the Yadavas under the leadership of Lord Krishna had migrated from Mathura and Vrindavan after killing Kamsa.[19] Krishna established his kingdom at Dwaraka and lived here along with his wife, Rukmini. Initially, Krishna settled down at Kushasthali on the coast of Saurashtra, which had been built by Kakudmin Raivata, a Yadava ancestor. Later, he extended its territory and called it Dwaraka. It is said that at Krishna's command, Vishwakarma had built this city in just one night! It was from here that Krishna went to Kurukshetra on the eve of the Mahabharata war. Excavations by marine archaeologists have provided evidence to support the general belief that Dwaraka had been swallowed by the sea.

A seal discovered during underwater exploration is said to corroborate the use of seals as identity cards by the citizens when Dwaraka was attacked by Salva, King of Subha. These seals were also believed to indicate the existence of trade and cultural contacts with Bahrain.[20] An inscription on a votive vessel is said to confirm that the people of Dwaraka were literate and spoke Sanskrit. Underwater exploration has revealed the existence of a well-fortified port city at the mouth of river Gomati. Whatever has been traced is said to conform to the description of Dwaraka in the Mahabharata.[21] Marine archaeology has conclusively proved that the existence and submergence of Dwaraka by the sea in the second millennium B.C. referred to in the Mahabharata.[22] It has been claimed that with the scientific investigation of submerged Dwaraka, the man-God personality of Krishna ceases to be a myth and stands established as a fact.[23]

References to Dwaraka found in the Skanda Purana (Prabhasa Khanda), Bhagavat, Mahabharata, Harivansha, Varaha, Vishnu and Vayu Puranas testify to the antiquity of this place. When Krishna went to live and reign in Dwaraka, the people expressed their jubilation and welcomed him by saying: "In You, we have our best leader and guide. We are fortunate that we are in a position to come close to You, who are all kindness, whose face is beaming with radiant affection and smiles, particularly when looking at Your divine height, Your very sight is difficult to be had even by gods."[24]

The old Dwaraka of Lord Krishna was located close to the Raivataka mountain. According to legend, Manu's son Yayati had a son by name Anarta (old name of Gujarat), whose son was Revata. Revata ruled over Anarta from his capital at Kushasthali, which is said to be identical with Dwaraka or Dwaramati. Revata's son, Raivata, had a daughter by name Revati. Raivata consulted Lord Brahma about a suitable groom for his daughter. Brahma told him that in the course of their conversation, several ages had passed by (!) and that, in the light of the circumstances then prevailing, Revati should be married to Balarama, the elder brother of Krishna at Dwaraka.[25]

As mentioned earlier, Arjuna had carried away Subhadra from the Swayanbara ceremony at Prabhasa with a view to marrying her. It was at Dwaraka that this wedding took place (Dwarakayamrjuna-Subhadrayorvivaha—Mahabharata). After this, Arjuna spent a year at Dwaraka (Nivrittascharjunastatra Vivahang Kritavan Prabhuh, Usitwa Tatra Kaunteyah Sangvatsaraparah Ksapa—Mahabharata, Adi Parva, 13–220).

In the Vana Parva of the Mahabharata, it is said that at Dwaraka in Saurashtra resides the living image of Sanatana Dharma known as Puranapurusha (*i.e.* Vishnu) and Adideva (*i.e.*Vishnu).[26]

Scholars are not unanimous about where the old Dwaraka of Lord Krishna was located. Some say that present-day Dwaraka on the western coast in the region of Okhamandal and on the bank of the Gomti river is identical with Krishna's Dwaraka. There are others who say that the original Dwaraka was somewhere else—maybe near Somnath or Junagadh or the Girnar hill. According to the Puranas, Krishna's Dwaraka sank into the sea. It is said that when Lord Krishna abandoned his body, the city of Dwaraka dipped into the sea with the waters closing in over it forever. Archaeological excavations have indicated that the Dwaraka of today is the sixth city near this site, the earlier five having got submerged into the sea.

Janmastami, the birthday of Lord Krishna, is the biggest festival of Dwaraka celebrated in the month of Shravana (July-August). My wife and I visited the Dwarkadheesh temple of Dwaraka and worshipped the deity known as Dwarkadheesh or Ranchhordai seated on a silver throne. The story behind the epithet 'Ranchordai' is that Krishna had come away to Dwaraka giving up the fight when, after his killing of Kamsa, King Jarasandha of Magadha and his allies mounted a combined powerful attack on Mathura.

On the precincts of the Dwarkadheesh temple is the Sarada Peetha—one of the four temples established by Adi Shankaracharya in the 8th century A.D. In the four corners of India to spread the message of our country's spiritual unity.

There is a also a temple of Ranchhordaiji in a town of this region known as Dakor. And thereby hangs a tale. It is said that a man by name Bodhano, who was a great devotee of Dwarkadheesh. As he became too old to travel to Dwaraka for pilgrimage, one night, the Lord appeared before him in a dream and, as instructed by him, Bodhano stole the Lord's idol from Dwaraka in order to bring it to Dakor. When the Brahmins in charge of the temple gave him a chase, he put them off by offering them gold equaling the weight of the idol he had stolen. The greedy Brahmins fell for the bait. At this stage, the Lord reduced his weight to that of the tiny nose-ornament of Bodhano's wife. The Brahmins were then told by the Lord to go back and install at Dwaraka another idol to be had from Savitri Vav. This is popularly believed to have happened in 1156 A.D., but there is no historical evidence behind this story.[27]

According to the Skanda Purana, one may not go to Kashi, Kurukshetra, Prabhasa or Pushkara, but one must go to Dwaraka and see the face of Lord Krishna. The Skanda Purana also says: "In Dwaraka dwells the world-embodied Hari, the giver of happiness and liberation, in all his sixteen Kalas and twelve murtis. This is the best place of pilgrimage, the highest spot, it is blessed Dwaraka where abides Madhusudana. Here Krishna is seen with four arms bearing the Conch, Discus and Mace in His hands. In this Kali age, the faithful obtain salvation by a visit to this place." [28]

Dwaraka was the kingdom of Lord Krishna, whose clansmen were known as Vrishnis. The Bhagawata Purana gives a vivid description of how the Vrishnis destroyed themselves as a result of a fatricidal war in the course of which they killed one another after getting drunk on an intoxicant called Maireyaka. Soon Balarama expired and then Lord Krishna also chose to follow suit after being hit by an arrow shot by a hunter while resting under a tree. All this was believed to have followed as a sequel to a curse of the sages and Gandhari, mother of the Kauravas, who had a grouse against Lord Krishna for having sided with the Pandavas against the Kauravas during the Mahabharata war.

A holy place near Dwaraka is Pindaraka (or Pinda Taraka), which finds mention in the Mahabharata (Vana Parva) : "Then go to Dwaraka Tirtha. There, after taking a vegetarian meal once a day and observing other rules, one who takes a dip at Pindaraka Tirtha, acquires considerable wealth in the form of gold. Oh fortunate vanquisher of the enemy—(here sage Pulastya is addressing Bhisma)—even today at that pilgrimage many gold coins marked with foot prints are to be found, which is very strange indeed! Oh great man and scion of Kuru dynasty, gold lotuses with marks of the trident are to be found. So Mahadeva resides close to that place."[29]

This place has got its name from a Kund or tank called Pinda Taraka, where 'Pinda' or a rice ball floats on the water. It is said to be a very ancient place that existed even before Dwaraka and that Agastya and other sages resided here. The Pandavas had come here on pilgrimage to propitiate the Devi and get liberated from the sin of killing their own kinsmen. On the advice of sage Durvasha, they bathed in the tank here and offered 108 rice iron balls which floated on water! Upon this, Durvasha gave a boon that rice balls offered here as 'Pinda' would hereafter float in this tank. Thus Pindaraka became a holy place for performing 'Shraddha'.[30]

We had a very enjoyable trip by steamer to Bet Dwaraka, an island in the Bay of Kutch, about 30 miles from Dwaraka and near the Okha port. This is also an ancient pilgrimage, which does not figure in the Mahabharata, but finds mention in many of the Puranas such as the Skanda, Vishnu, Vayu and Bhagavata. This is an important center of the Vallabha Sampradaya. Here, we visited the Ranchhodraiji and Sankhoddharji temples. About the latter temple, it is said that in the Satya Yuga, demon Sankha, who had become a menace to the sages, was crushed by Lord Vishnu in his incarnation as Matsya (or fish). Vishnu had also transformed the demon's wife Tulsi into the holy basil plant and made the leaves of this plant indispensable for the worship of Vishnu.

Another mythological story about the Sankhoddhara temple brings out the spiritual prowess of a sage. It is said that a sage by name Trit once came on pilgrimage to Okha. Seeing a beautiful lake there, he took a refreshing bath in its waters and then sat down for meditation. A disciple of his saw the Guru's beautiful conch lying beside the latter, who was engrossed in meditation. Unable to check his temptation, the disciple stole the conch and walked away. Later, finding that his conch was missing, the Guru became angry and pronounced a curse that the person who had stolen it would himself be reduced to a conch shell.

So the disciple became a conch shell. After his long and sustained penance, he was pardoned by the Guru, who said that the disciple would get back his normal human form if he constantly invoked the name of Lord Krishna while he remained under water. The disciple in the form of a conch shell remained under water for a very long time, constantly remembering the name of Lord Krishna. Then Krishna appeared and relieved him of the curse, restoring him back to his original human form. From this episode, the island came to be known as Bet Sankhoddhara.

As in the case of Dwaraka, there are different views about where ancient Bet Dwaraka was located. Some plump for the present location, but there are some, who suggest other locations. There is a view that old Bet Dwaraka was near Veraval or Somnath, because numerous conch shells were unearthed there during excavations. This does not seem to be a valid ground for such a conclusion because similar conch shells are found at many other places on the sea.

Dwaraka and Bet Dwaraka have been important centres of Shakti worship since the time of Lord Krishna, when Bhagawati Durga was worshipped at Dwaraka. The Buddhists and Jains had also established their institutions at Bet Dwaraka many centuries ago. The Chinese traveller Hiuen Tsang, made a special reference in his account to the spread of Buddhist religion and culture in this region.

In 1804 A.D., some inhabitants of Bet Dwaraka had looted a British commercial vessel that came here and thrown a British couple into the sea. In 1916, the British forces attacked Bet Dwaraka and destroyed the fort there. His led to a fight. At this time, the local people had carried away the idols of some temples for hiding them in safe places. Later on, the British handed over the control over Dwaraka and Bet Dwaraka to the Gaekwad of Baroda.

The pottery from a section of a rubble wall on the east coast of Bet Dwaraka was subjected to Thermoluminiscence dating method and the date obtained was said to be 3528 years, which confirmed that the wall belonged to the generally accepted date of the Mahabharata.[31]

Our trip to Gujarat was abruptly cut short as we were informed of the death in Kolkata of my wife Anita's mother on October 14, 1989. We hurried back to Chandigarh and then Anita proceeded to Kolkata. When I joined her in Kolkata on October 23, 1989, to attend the Sradh ceremony of my mother-in-law, my own mother, very old and suffering from various ailments, passed away. I was lucky to have been able to see her alive just before she breathed her last. After a couple of days, we returned to Chandigarh, where I performed my mother's Sradh ceremony on November 2-3, 1989. Thus we both lost our mothers in the short span of nine days. I had to cancel many official engagements in Haryana in view of these bereavements.

Notes

1. The Encyclopaedic District Gazetteers of India edited by S.C. Bhatt, Western Zone, Volume 7, p. 101.
2. For this Puranic account about Sabarmati and Ahmedabad, I have drawn upon 'Immortal India' by J.A. Dave, Volume IV, pp. 92–98.
3. श्रीगणेशाय नमः।। सौराष्ट्रे सोमनाथं च श्रीशैले मल्लिकार्जुनम्।।
उज्जयिन्यां महाकालमोंकारममलेश्वरम्।।१।। परल्यां वैद्यनाथं चडाकिन्यां भीमशंकरम्।। सेतुबंधे तु रामेशं नागेशं दारुकावने।।२।। वाराणस्यां तु विश्वेशं त्र्यंबकं गौतमीतटे।। हिमालये तु केदारं घुसृणेशं शिवालये।।३।। एतानि ज्योतिर्लिंग्ड.ानि सायं प्रातः पठेन्नरः।। सप्तजन्मकृतं पापंस्मरणेन विनश्यति।।४।।
4. Immortal India by J.A. Dave, Volume II, p. 2.
5. यत्र गड.्गा च यमुना यत्र प्राची सरस्वती।
यत्र सोमेश्वरो देवस्वत्र मामगतं कृधीन्द्रायेन्दो सुरिखव।।
Rig Veda, Khila 20–5–At the end of the 9th Mandala.
6. Immortal India by J.A. Dave, Volume II, p. 4.
7. *Ibid*, p. 3.
8. एपा सरस्वती रम्या दिव्या चौघवती नदी।
एतद् विनशनं नाम सरस्वत्या विशाम्पते।।३।।
द्वारं निषादराष्ट्रस्य येषां दोषात् सरस्वती।
प्रविष्टा पृथिवीं वीर मा निषादा हि मां विदः।।४।।
एष वै चमसोद्रेदो यत्र दृश्चा सरस्वती।
यत्रैनामभ्यवर्तन्त सर्वाः पुण्याः समुद्रगाः।।५।।
—Mahabharata, Vana Parva, chapter 30
9. एतत् सिन्धोर्महत् तीर्थे यत्रागस्त्यमरिंदम।
लोपामुद्रा समागम्य भर्तारभवृणीत वै।।६।।
—Mahabharata, Vana Parva, chapter 30.
10. हंसौ तौ पुम्प्रकृत्यारुयौ हं पुमान् प्रकृतिस्तु सः।
—Saradatilaka, 15-51.
11. अग्नीषोमात्मकं विश्वम्।
—Cited in J.A. Dave's book.
12. तदित्थं शिवशक्तिभ्यां नाव्याप्तमिह किञ्चन।
—Brihajjabala 2-12. Cited in J.A. Dave's book.
13. Cited in J.A. Dave's book, p. 8.
14. शिदाग्निना तनुं दग्ध्वा शक्तिसोमामृतेन यः।
प्लावयेद् योगमार्गेण सोऽमृतत्वाय कल्पते।।
—Brihajjabala 2-19. Cited in J.A. Dave's book.
15. *Ibid.*
16. *Ibid.*
तस्येव पूर्वदिग्भागे लकुलीशस्तु मूर्तिमान्।
स्वयं तिष्ठति देवेशि कृत्वा घोर तपः पुरा।

संस्थितः पापशमने तत्र स्थाने तलोपरि।
कार्तिक्यां कृत्तिकायोगे यस्तं पूजयते नरः।।
स पूज्यते महादेवि सर्वै रपि सुरासुरैः।।
—Prabhasa, 177–1 to 3.

17. *Ibid*, p. 13.
18. तदेव गर्भस्य गृहं च सा शिला यथातथं दित्रिसहस्रवत्सराद्।
अघस्तनस्योपरि यत्र नूतनः पुराणमूते गरिमा प्रकाशते।।
—Verse No. 39 of Somastavaraja
19. Article captioned 'From Dwarka to Kurukshetra' by Dr. S.R. Rao of the Marine Archaeology Centre, National Institute of Oceanography, Goa, brought out in December 1994 by the Geeta Kendra, Kurukshetra Development Board, Kurukshetra, Haryana.
20. *Ibid*.
21. *Ibid*.
22. *Ibid*.
23. *Ibid*.
24. अहो सनाथा भवता स्म यद् वयं
त्रैविष्टपानामपि दूरदर्शनम्।
प्रेमस्मितस्निग्धनिरीक्षणाननं
पश्येम रूपं तव सर्वसौभगम्।।
—Bhagavata 1-11-4
—Cited in Immortal India by J.A. Dave, Volume I, p. 53.
25. *Ibid*, p. 53.
26. पुण्या द्वारवती तत्र यत्रासौ मधुसूदनः।
साक्षाद् देवः पुराणोऽसौ स हि धर्मः सनातनः।।२४।।
—Mahabharat, Vana Parva, Chapter 88, 24.
27. Immortal India by J.A. Dave, Volume I, page57.
28. *Ibid*, p. 60.
29. ततो द्वारवतीं गच्छेन्नियतो नियताशनः।
पिण्डारके नरः स्नात्वा लभेद् बहु सुवर्णकम।।६५।।
तस्मिरतीर्थे महाभाग पद्मलक्षणलक्षिताः।
अद्यापि मुद्रा दृश्यन्ते तदद्भुतमरिंदम।।६६।।
त्रिशूलाङ्.कानि पद्मानि दृश्यन्ते कुरुनन्दन।
महादेवस्य सांनिध्यं तत्र वै पुरुषर्षभ।।६७।।
—Mahabharat, Vana Parva, verses 65-67.
30. Immortal India by J.A. Dave, Volume I, p. 59.
31. Article by Dr. S.R. Rao mentioned at 19 above.

18

A New Political Dispensation

Meanwhile, important political developments had been taking place in our country. The non-Congress parties upped the ante against the Congress Government by demanding the resignation of Prime Minister Rajiv Gandhi over the Bofors issue. On November 1, 1989, I received a message from Delhi asking me to see the Prime Minister the next day. I sent a reply that as I was to perform the Sradh ceremony of my mother on that day, I would see the Prime Minister a day later. I was in Delhi on November 4, 1989, as scheduled earlier, but by then the Prime Minister had already left Delhi for the election campaign.

On November 16, 1989, there was some excitement in Chandigarh following speculation in political circles that some Ministers might resign from the Devi Lal Ministry, which could reduce it to a minority in the State Assembly. In the evening something did happen. Four Ministers—K.R. Punia, H.K. Saini, Lachman Singh Kamboj and Parmanand—tendered their resignations from the Devi Lal Ministry and issued a statement expressing their disenchantment with the policies of Ch. Devi Lal's Ministry, which, they alleged, had promoted casteism, nepotism, corruption and lawlessness. I accepted their resignations but their action did not affect the Devi Lal Government as it continued to enjoy a comfortable majority.

Some days before the Lok Sabha election that began on November 22, 1989, K. R. Punia, Parmanand and Kamboj, who had resigned from Ch. Devi Lal's Ministry, saw me along with Muna Lal, MLA, to express their lack of confidence in the Ministry. But their number constituted no effective threat to the Government.

By the evening of November 26, 1989, the results of the Lok Sabha election started pouring in. As the Congress Party failed to get a majority in the Lok Sabha, Prime Minister Rajiv Gandhi tendered the resignation of his government on November 29, 1989.

Ch. Devi Lal had called on me on November 27, 1989 and had a free and frank discussion with me about the new political scenario. He told me that he was now in a position to become the Prime Minister of India. He sought my advice as to whether he should accept the Prime Minister's job, which was there for him for the asking. I told him that I felt very happy that my Chief Minister had been catapulted to a position in which he could now become the Prime Minister of the country. However, I advised him against becoming the Prime Minister because this job required a certain background of education which he did not have. The reasons, I explained to him, were known to all. Rather than pursue higher studies in his adolescent years, he flung himself instead heart and soul into the country's freedom struggle. I told him all this in a manner that did not displease him. What I told him was that rather become the King, he should become the King-maker and the power behind the throne. After a long discussion, I had the feeling that he agreed with what I told him. I also got the impression that he had reservations about the two other likely Prime ministerial candidates—Chandrasekhar and V.P. Singh.

Now the scene of Ch. Devi Lal's activity shifted to Delhi, where he remained most of the time. There was an element of drama in the way V.P. Singh was elected the leader of the Janata Dal Parliamentary Party in Delhi on December 1, 1989. At the very beginning, it was Ch. Devi Lal who was elected leader by the Parliamentary Party. Sitting at the Raj Bhawan in Chandigarh, I was monitoring these developments over the radio, television and the teleprinter channel of the PTI. The first news to reach me through the ticker of the teleprinter was that Ch. Devi Lal had just been elected leader of the Janata Dal Parliamentary Party.

I got a little confused because, after my discussions with Ch. Devi Lal in Chandigarh a few days ago, I was under the impression that he had accepted my suggestion not to stand for this post. But a minute later, another ticker came, which cleared the confusion in my mind, because it said that Ch. Devi Lal, immediately after being elected leader of the Parliamentary Party, had retired in favour of V.P. Singh, who, therefore, became its leader and was to be the Prime Minister! This fitted in with the impression that Ch. Devi Lal had given me during our discussions in Chandigarh. This, incidentally, was perhaps the first example in India's parliamentary history of a political leader renouncing, for whatever reason, the Prime Ministership of our country after having been elected to the post.

In this episode, there was another secret drama that came out into the open almost immediately. This concerns Chandrasekhar, who had never accepted any Ministerial position during his long political career. It was being rumoured that Ch. Devi Lal and Chandrasekhar had secretly agreed to join forces to make Chandrasekhar the Prime Minister, thus keeping out V.P. Singh. It was believed by many that Ch. Devi Lal's relinquishing the crown and offering it to V.P. Singh meant a let-down for Chandrasekhar. Yet, such is the weird world of politics that in a few months' time when Ch. Devi Lal, Deputy Prime Minister in the new dispensation, was thrown out of the Ministry by V.P, Singh and Devi Lal brought down the latter's Ministry by withdrawing his support, it was Chandrasekhar whom Ch. Devi Lal helped in becoming the Prime Minister, of course, with the outside support of the Congress Party.

Ch. Devi Lal became the Deputy Prime Minister in V. P.Singh's Ministry on December 1, 1989. And thereby hangs a tale. Ch. Devi Lal's voluntarily opting out the Prime Ministership created a problem in Haryana. In this new situation, O.P. Chautala, the eldest son of Ch. Devi Lal, emerged as an important figure. It became evident that if Ch. Devi Lal continued as the Chief Minister of Haryana, Om Prakash Chautala's chances of becoming the State's Chief Minister would get blocked. The impression in the public mind was that under political pressure that was brought to bear upon Ch. Devi Lal, he asked V.P. Singh to make him the Deputy Prime Minister. This cleared the way for Chautala to become the Chief Minister of Haryana! on a nod from Ch. Devi Lal, Chautala was elected the leader of his party's legislative wing. This is how Ch. Devi Lal ended up becoming the Deputy Prime Minister after refusing to become the Prime Minister.

This automatically rendered vacant the post of Haryana's Chief Minister and cast upon me the responsibility of swearing in a new Chief Minister. Ch. Devi Lal requested me to swear in O.P. Chautala, the new leader of the ruling party's legislative wing in the Haryana State Assembly, as Chief Minister. He suggested that I could have the swearing-in ceremony at the Haryana Bhawan in Delhi.

On my telling Ch. Devi Lal that I would like to swear in Chautala at Chandigarh and that I had to satisfy myself about the number of MLA's supporting him, he pointed out that on some earlier occasions, the Chief minister of Haryana had been sworn in at places other than Chandigarh and that on the last such occasion, he himself had been given the oath of Chief Ministership in Delhi two years ago by S.M.H. Burney, the then Governor of Haryana. He indirectly hinted that because a non-Congress Government had just taken over at the Centre, I was adopting an obstructive posture. I checked on the facts mentioned by Ch. Devi Lal and found them to be correct. I also consulted some constitutional experts who saw no hurdle.

So I agreed to swear in Chautala in Delhi and proceed there on December 2, 1989. When Chautala called on me in Delhi, I told him that I would like to see the signatures of at least 46 of the 90 members of the Haryana Legislative Assembly, who had agreed to support him. I could clearly see that there was some difficulty in this regard because the signatures of the BJP MLA's with whose support Chautala had staked his claimed to form his Ministry were not available. I requested Shri Chautala to sort this out.

It was at this stage that Smt. Sushma Swaraj, a BJP Minister of the Haryana Goernment led by Ch. Devi Lal, and Atal Behari Vajpayee, the veteran BJP leader, sought an appointment with me and then called on me to say that their party MLA's in Haryana would support the Government to be formed by Chautala. I told them that, constitutionally speaking, I was required to be shown a resolution to that effect passed by the legislature party of the BJP in the Haryana State Assembly. I was told that it would be difficult to arrange a meeting of the legislature party at such a short notice. However, I told them that it had to be done before I could administer the oath to Chautala. I assured them that I would wait for them to complete this formality and put off the swearing-in ceremony. They left immediately, contacted the party MLA's, who held a meeting and passed the requisite resolution whose copy was promptly sent to me.

So the stage was set for swearing in Chautala as the Chief Minister of Haryana late in the evening on December 2, 1989 at a glittering function held at the Haryana Bhawan in Delhi. Among the many important political leaders present at he ceremony was Atal Behari Vajpayee.

When I retired to my suite after the swearing-in ceremony, I was informed by my A.D.C. that Atal Behari Vajpayee wanted to see me again, to which I agreed. He came and met me for a few minutes. He said that he had come to meet me in order to convey his satisfaction at the meticulous manner in which I had discharged my constitutional responsibility, leaving no scope for anybody to come out with allegations about any impropriety in the swearing in of the new Chief Minister of Haryana. How very graceful of him to have done that! Politicians generally forget a person immediately after their work has been done. I thanked Vajpayee for his generosity before he left.

Subsequently, I was told by several eminent people of Haryana that my decision to administer the oath to Chautala in Delhi had gone down well with many people of the State. The reason for this, they said, was both geographical and historical. Geographically speaking, Delhi was surrounded on all sides except the east by the territory of Haryana. So the people of Haryana generally think that Delhi is virtually a part of their territory.

Historically speaking, Delhi has been the capital city of the Haryana territory for centuries. It was in the 8th century A.D. that the Tomar rulers made Delhi the capital of an independent kingdom comprising the territory adjoining it, which for all practical purposes meant the territory of Haryana. In the12th century A.D., Prithviraj Chauhan ruled over this territory as well as parts of the present State of Rajasthan from Delhi as his capital. After his defeat in 1192 A.D. at the hands of Mohammed Ghauri, the control over Delhi as well as Haryana passed into the hands of the Muslim rulers for the next several centuries. But Haryana's umbilical links with Delhi remained intact over all these centuries, because Delhi continued to be the capital from which it was ruled.

Following the 1857 uprising against British rule, in which the people of Haryana played a major role, the British punished Haryana by downgrading it along with Delhi and merged them with the territory of the Punjab Province. Even then, Haryana's link with Delhi was preserved, because most of the districts of present-day Haryana became parts of the Delhi Division of Punjab Province. It was only in 1911 that Haryana got disjoined from Delhi, which was then chosen as the new capital of British India in preference to the earlier capital Kolkata. But despite this physical separation, the Haryanvis continued to look upon Delhi as their pristine capital with which it shared a common historical past. According to one author, the Haryanvis form a majority of the population of Delhi, though I am not sure if this is still true.[1] I thought that it was those without a proper knowledge of past traditions and historical facts who were critical of my decision to hold the swearing-in ceremony at Delhi.

On December 5, 1989, I swore in a 20-member Ministry led by Chautala at a function held on the lawns of the Raj Bhawan in Chandigarh. Apart from many political leaders, a big crowd of about 5000 attended the ceremony. Banarsi Dass Gupta, Deputy Chief Minister in Ch. Devi Lal's Minstry, retained that position. The BJP group supported the Ministry from outside. The swearing-in function was a very lively affair, as brought out in some newspapers:

हिन्दूस्तान– 6–12–1989

चौटाला मत्रिमंडल ने एक को छोड़ हिन्दी में शपथ ली

(हमारे कार्यालय संवादाता द्वारा) चंडीगढ़ 5 दिसम्बर । चौटाला मंत्रिमंडल के एक सदस्य को छोड़ कर दूसरे सभी सदस्यों ने आज हिन्दी में पद तथा गोपनीयता की शपथ ली । केवल राज्य मंत्री अजमत खां ने उर्दू में शपथ ली । शपथग्रहण के मौके पर आज उस समय बड़ा दिलचस्प वाक्य सामने आया, जब अजमत खां उर्दू में शपथ ले रहे थे । बंगला भाषी राज्यपाल हरि आनन्द बरारी ने सही उच्चारण के मामले में उनको कई बार टोका । कई बार तो श्री खां कुछ का कुछ पढ़ गए और तब राज्यपाल को उनसे कहना पड़ा कि वह केवल शब्दों को ही दोहराए। आखिर तक आते-आते हाल यह था कि राज्यपाल को अपनी ही प्रति से श्री खां को शपथ दिलानी पड़ी । इस दौरान पूरे समारोह में कई बार हंसी के जोरदार फुहारे छुटे। खुद राज्यपाल महोदय भी अपनी हंसी नहीं रोक पाए ।

आज जिन मंत्रियों के हिन्दी में शपथ लेने पर सभी को आश्चर्य हुआ, उनमें से कैबिनेट मंत्री वीरेन्द्र सिंह और राज्यमंत्री रघुवीर कादियान थे । ये दोनों इससे पहले हमेशा अंग्रेजी में शपथ पढ़ते रहे हैं ।

NATIONAL HERALD

(06-12-1989)

Mr. Azmat Khan took the oath in Urdu but had a tough time even reading it. Mr. Barari helped him at various occasions to complete the minute-long oath. He fumbled at least thrice and a strong crowd of over 3,000 persons burst into laughter at

Indian Express – 11.12.1989

The swearing-in ceremony at Haryana Raj Bhawan on Tuesday last was an event that everyone present there enjoyed thoroughly. There was not a dull moment in the programme that lasted a little more than an hour. It was by all accounts Mr. Hari Anand Barari's day.

The Governor would size up every MLA who went up to the dais. When Mr. Jagan Nath went up; Mr. Barari made it obvious that he was seeing him for the first time and wanted to know which part of the state he came from.

Mr. Azmat Khan had apparently opted to take the oaths in Urdu. The Governor read out the text fluently while Mr. Khan tumbled and faltered before meandering off to the Hindi version. Mr. Barari interrupted, and told him to continue to Urdu and hesitant Mr. Khan did so. When it came to the oath of secrecy, the gathering burst into a peal of laughter. The Governor was reading the Urdu text and Mr. Khan the Hindi version. Mr. Barari interrupted again, the embarrassed Mewat leader pointed out that the text given to him was in Hindi. "Never mind, you just repeat. I will read it slowly" the Governor said and, went on to administer the oath at dictation speed.

Everyone in the audience was keen to see how the newly sworn ministers would greet their new Chief Minister, who is certainly not the patriarch that Mr. Devi Lal is. Mr. B.D. Gupta who had driven with Mr. Chautala from Delhi did not greet him apparently because they had already spent a lot of time together.

दैनिक ट्रब्यून–6.12.1989

शपथ समारोह की झलकियां

हमारे प्रतिनिधि द्वारा शपथ ग्रहण समारोह में इतनी अधिक भीड़ हो गयी कि हरियाणा राजभवन में लगा विशाल शामियाना छोटा पड़ गया । समय के पाबंद अनेक अधिकारी ऐन मौके पर आये और तब तक उनके लिये आरक्षित कुर्सियों पर इस सरकार के समर्थक विराजमान हो गये थे । व्यवस्था संभाल रहे कर्मचारियों ने अनेक अधिकारियों को तो कुर्सियाँ खाली कराकर बैठा दिया लेकिन कई ने पत्रकार दीर्घा में जा कर शरण ली। सचिव स्तर के दो अधिकारियों को खड़ा पाकर गुप्तचर विभाग के डी. आई.जी. महेन्द्र सिंह मलिक उन्हें पत्रकार दीर्घा तक छोड़ गये ।

बीस मंत्रियों को एक–एक करके शपथ दिलाना राज्यपाल के लिये मेहनत का काम था । समारोह के बीच एक बार पानी पीते हुए उन्होनें कहा–आज तो मैं बहुत मेहनत कर रहा हूँ। श्री अजमत खान को छोड़कर सभी मंत्रियों ने हिन्दी में शपथ ली। अहिन्दी भाषी (बंगला) होने के कारण राज्यपाल हरि आनन्द बरारी को हिन्दी बोलने में उन दिनों वाकई दिक्कत पेश आती थी जब वह हरियाणा में नये–नये आये थे लेकिन आज जिस तरह से वह धाराप्रवाह हिन्दी बोल रहे थे उससे तो लगता हैं कि उन्होनें इन दिनों हिन्दी सीखने पर काफी जोर दिया है ।

श्री अजमत खान ने उर्दू में शपथ ली। राज्यपाल संभल-संभल कर शुद्ध उर्दू बोल रहे थे । लेकिन श्री खान शुरू से ही अटकते रहे । गोपनीयता की शपथ लेते हुए तो कमाल ही हो गया । लगता हैं कि श्री खान का शब्द बदल गया क्योंकि राज्यपाल कुछ बोल रहे थे, और श्री अजमत खान कुछ और । सभी के मध्य राज्यपाल ने उनसे कहा, वह लिखे कि ओर ध्यान न दे और उनके पीछे बोलते रहे । श्री खान को यहां तक कह दिया कि मैं हिन्दी में शपथ ले लेता हूँ लेकिन राज्यपाल बोले नहीं उर्दू में ही जारी रखो । जैसे तैसे उनकी शपथ पूरी हुई तो राज्यपाल ने राहत की सांस ली।

By this time, various rumours began to be heard about the appointment of new Governors of States in place of those appointed during the Congress regime. On December 6, 1989, Punjab Governor S.S. Ray rang me up at night and said that he was going to Delhi the next morning to submit his resignation to the President of India. That is what he did the next day and then returned to Chandigarh late in the evening. My wife and I called on him and Smt. Maya Ray that night to say good-bye and to tell them how much we would miss them.

On December 8, 1989, I proceeded to Kurukshetra to participate in the Gita Jayanti celebrations held annually on the banks of the sacred Brahmasarovar. There, I inaugurated a programme of Bharatanatyam dance performed by the renowned dancer, Lila Samson, who kept the audience enthralled. The next day, I went to a place called Bhanu and inaugurated the West Zone Tournament of the All-India Police Games.

Returning to Chandigarh, I heard that N.K. Mukerji, well-known retired I.C.S. Officer, had been sworn in as the new Governor of Punjab in place of S.S. Ray. I rang up the new Governor and congratulated him.

On December 17, 1989, I hosted a big dinner party at our Raj Bhawan. The occasion was provided by the first visit to Chandigarh of Ch. Devi Lal after his taking over as the Deputy Prime Minister. Besides Ch. Devi Lal, and Chautala and his Ministerial colleagues others who attended the party included the film star Shatrughna Sinha, who had emerged as an important leader of the anti-Congress forces.

On December 19, 1989, I left for Shimla along with my wife, because I was appointed to hold additional charge of the Governor of Himachal Pradesh in order to keep the seat warm for Vice-Admiral (Retd.) R.K.S. Gandhi, Govrnor of Himachal Pradesh, who was going on leave for a month. We spent a peaceful night at the Himachal Pradesh Raj Bhawan in Shimla where Vice-Admiral (Retd.) Gandhi and his wife had left meticulous instructions to the staff to ensure our every comfort.

The next day, I was sworn in as the Governor of Himachal Pradesh at a simple ceremony at the Raj Bhawan by Chief Justice P.C. Balakrishnan of the Himachal Pradesh High Court. Several Ministers as well as Smt. Vidya Stokes, Speaker of the State Assembly and senior officials were present on the occasion. Smt. Stokes belongs to the family of the famous American missionary, Samuel Stokes, who had come to India in 1904 to serve the people. He had settled down at Kotgarh village and married a local girl. He joined our country's freedom struggle led by the Congress and went to jail. He converted to Hinduism and adopted the Indian name Satyanand Stokes. A contribution for which he is remembered by all even today is the manner in which he improved the cultivation of apples, changing the life-style and the economic status of the people of Himachal Pradesh. It is claimed by some that Kotgarh is the richest village of Asia.

At the tea party that followed my swearing-in, I exchanged pleasantries with several Ministers and the other guests. Some of them complimented me on my ability to speak good Hindi. As we were enjoying our tea, we saw through the glass panes of the hall that flakes of white snow were falling softly on the lawns and the trees outside. It was a wonderful sight the like of which I had never seen before. Smt. Stokes walked up to me and, drawing my attention to what she called the season's first snow-fall, said that it was a good omen and the harbinger of the State's economic prosperity. She said that my swearing-in as the Governor of Himachal Pradesh had brought good luck to the State.

The next day, we had a busy schedule, as many Ministers and officials including several police officers, whom I had known for a long time, came calling. We took some time off to visit the tourist complex at Wild Flower Hall at a distance of ten kilometers from Shimla. There we again saw fresh snow falling.

We returned to Chandigarh after a few days and on December 25, 1989, the day of Christmas, we had an enchanting musical programme for almost three hours before mid-day on the lawns of our Raj Bhawan under the open sky in the pleasant winter sun. The artiste was Pandit Hari Prasad Chaurasia, whose fingers worked magic on his flute and kept the audience spell-bound. Even the peacocks and the deer of our Raj Bhawan that always roamed about free on the lush green grass now came close to the venue of the programme, stood still and soaked up the divine fare that was being served. In between, while this programme was on, my wife and I quietly slipped away, went to the Punjab Raj Bhawan and wished Merry Christmas to Governor N.K. Mukerji and Smt. Mukerji. Being Christians, they had kept an open house on this occasion so that guests could drop in informally to wish them. After spending a few minutes with them, we took leave of them, telling them that we had to go back to our Raj Bhawan because Pandit Hari Prasad Chaurasia's programme was on. They thanked us for our visit and expressed their appreciation of the unique manner of our celebrating Christmas.

When we came back to our Raj Bhawan, we saw the audience sitting enthralled, just as we had left them before our visit to the

Punjab Raj Bhawan. We quietly resumed our seats making sure that we did not break their spell.

N. Khosla, a retired I.A.S. Officer and a great patron of music and fine arts, wrote the following piece on this programme in the Daily Tribune of December 26, 1989:

Tribune, December 26, 1989

Echoes from divinity

By N. Khosla

Chandigarh: The specious grounds of Haryana Raj Bhavan made lush by the recent rains, a spotless white marquee decorated with restraint covering the small stage, clouds floating overhead, the time 11 o'clock and Hari Prasad Chaurasia, the man for all four seasons playing the flute as only he can and one could repeat.

"And ever against eating Lap me in soft Lydian airs".

The music lovers of Chandigarh owe deep thanks to the Haryana Governor and his gracious wife for hosting concerts of rich music every now and then. The flute wizard after charming his audience at Harballabh had come down to keep his promise to play morning "ragas" at Haryana Raj Bhavan on Christmas day. This was a boon.

He played "gujari todi" said to have been employed by a old master in honour of a Gujar lady of a potentate's harem. The mood was pensive and it is to Chaurasia's credit that he invests each "raga", each piece with grace and beauty of a high order. After an elaborate "slap" and "jor" came a seven beat "gathu". When he concluded the deer and peacocks often adjoining zoo had been standing nearby listening to the echow from divinity for a long times true to the iconography of "todi".

It was mid-day and Chaurasia played "shudh sarang" which is a "raga" appropriate to that time of the day.

The last piece was a devotion tune much favoured in Bengal and had the 500-strong audience swaying.

Talking to Pandit Hari Prasad Chaurasia after the programme was over, I learnt certain facts of his life, which greatly enhanced my respect for him. He said that he hailed from a family of wrestlers and that his family had not expected him to become a musician. He became a wrestler initially and then a typist in which capacity he earned Rs. 85/-a month. But he started learning the flute secretly and, by virtue of sheer determination and will power, he acquired proficiency with the flute. Then he joined the All-India Radio in Kolkata as a staff artiste. When he was transferred to Bombay in 1962, he came in touch with the film industry, which opened up vast opportunities for him.

On December 31, 1989, my wife and I hosted a tea party at our Raj Bhawan to bid farewell to Daryao Singh Chaudhary, on his retirement from the post of Comptroller, Governor's House (or CGH, as we used to call him). He had worked in that capacity for many years with great devotion, always upholding the highest standards, be it food served at Raj Bhawan parties or the discipline of the Raj Bhawan staff or the general upkeep of the Raj Bhawan.

The same night, we hosted a big dinner party at Raj Bhawan in honour of Justice D.D. Dewan, who had retired from service as the Chief Justice of the Punjab and Haryana High Court. N.K. Mukerji, Governor of Punjab and his wife also graced the occasion.

On January 3, 1989, we went to Shimla in connection with some work I had to attend to in my capacity as the Governor of Himachal Pradesh. Our daughter Radha, son-in-law Pinak and grandson Abhishek were in our party. In Shimla, some elderly Bengalee gentlemen associated with the Kalibari of Shimla called on us and expressed their happiness that a Bengalee had taken over as the Governor of the State, though for a short term. They requested us to visit Kalibari, which we did on January 4, 1989. In the evenings, I played billiard at the Raj Bhawan with Pinak and my A.D.C., Captain Ravi Bhatia.

Returning to Chandigarh, I got a message that Giani Zail Singh, the former President, would come and stay at our Raj Bhawan for a few days. I had known him before and so when he came on January 13, 1990, we discussed many things. I found him to be his old jovial self. He discussed with me the issue of the impending removal of Governors and in his own not so subtle manner tried to probe the chances of my continuing as the Governor of Haryana about which, I told him, I had no clue whatsoever.

It was on January 15, 1990 that the first official indication of my removal reached me. Smt. Komal Anand I.A.S., Secretary to the Governor, saw me and told me that I should submit my resignation in writing, as had been suggested to her over the telephone from Delhi by an official in the Secretariat of the President, Shri R. Venkataraman. On my seeking some clarification, Smt. Anand told me that the President had verbally asked an officer in his Secretariat to convey this message to my Secretary. I told Smt. Anand that the President of India should send a written communication in this regard to me so that I could act accordingly. I told her that I could not take such a step merely on the basis of a verbal suggestion said to have been made by the President to one of his officials, who telephonically conveyed it to my Secretary.

After Smt. Anand conveyed to the President's Secretariat what I had told her, a formal letter from the President of India came to me the next day. I called my Private Secretary in two minutes, dictated my letter of resignation and sent it off to the President through a special messenger so as to reach him the same day.

Earlier on January 15, 1990, I addressed the State Legislative Assembly on the opening day of its session. That evening, I hosted a dinner party for the MLA's, Ministers and senior officials at the Raj Bhawan. There, I could see that most of the guests were aware of my impending departure from the Raj Bhawan, though many of them indirectly hinted at their unhappiness over such an eventuality.

Despite the uncertainty about my continuance as Governor, I continued to discharge my day-to-day responsibilities. On January 20, 1990, many eminent figures of the world of Urdu literature came to our Raj Bhawan from different parts of the country to attend a function under the auspices of the Haryana Urdu Academy. They included Jilani Baus of Hyderabad, Mahabir Prasad Jain , Balkrishan Muztar of Kurukshetra, Azim Zaidi of Azamgarh (who had settled down at Faridabad), Bawa Krishan Gopal Maghmoom, Musavvir Sabzwari and Habib-ur-Rehman. I presented the awards of the Haryana Urdu Academy to some of these men of letters. On this occasion, three well-known musicians namely Pamila Singh, Jyotsna Rana and Ratnika Tiwari sang the Ghazals of Shamim Jaipuri, Shakil

Badauni, Amir Qazalbash and Meer, which were highly appreciated by the audience. K.L. Zakir, the ever active Secretary of the Haryana Urdu Academy and some others addressed the gathering.

The television news of that night announced that I had tendered my resignation. This triggered a spate of telephonic enquiries for the next few days from Chandigarh and elsewhere as to whether my resignation would be accepted.

A few days later, O.P. Chautala, Chief Minister of Haryana, publicly praised my qualities as a man and as an administrator and said that it was for the Central Government to take the decision about the removal and appointment of Governors. However, he said that if his opinion was asked, he would indicate that he had nothing against me. The press widely reported these observations by Chautala, giving rise to speculation that my resignation would not be accepted. A few of these press reports are reproduced:

Times of India, 23.1.1990

Chautala all praise for Barari

Times of India News Service

CHANDIGARH, January 22: Haryana Chief Minister Mr. Om Prakash Chautala today said that Mr. Barari, the state Governor, was good as a man and as an administrator.

These remarks were made during an informal chat with reporters after laying the foundation stone of a Panchayat Bhawan for the state in Chandigarh. Answering questions, Chautala said that if his opinion about the Governor was sought by the Centre, he would say that Mr. Barari was good as a man and the relations between him and the government were good.

Mr. Barari had sent his resignation last week on the advice of the President.

Mr. Chautala's statement today has fuelled some speculation here that Mr. Barari may be retained as the Governor of the state. He had given a similar "hint" to a correspondent of a Chandigarh daily in Delhi yesterday.

Hindustan Times, Jan. 23, 1990

CHAUTALA ALL PRAISE FOR GOVERNOR

CHANDIGARH, Jan. 22 (HTC)

Chief Minister Om Prakash Chautal today described Haryana Governor H.A. Barari as a good man and stated that it was for the Centre to decide about his appointment.

Mr. Barari has already resigned from his post and is continuing till alternative arrangement is made.

Talking to newsmen here after laying the foundation stone of Panchayat Bhawan, the Chief Minister clarified that he had good relations with Mr. Barari and that there was no problem in running the administration.

The Tribune, Jan. 23, 1990

Haryana to stick to claim on city: CM

From The Tribune Bureau

CHANDIGARH Jan 22 — Mr. Om Prakash Chautala, Haryana Chief Minister, asserted here today that there was on change in Haryana's claim over Chandigarh.

Mr. Chautala was talking to newsmen after laying the foundation stone of the Rs. 130 crore Haryana Panchayat Bhavan in Sector 28-A here.

Replying to a question about the retention of the present Haryana Governor, Mr. H.A. Barari, who had already resigned, Mr. Chautala said he was a good person as well as a good administrator. He had always tried to keep "cordial relations'. Mr. Chautala said even though the Centre was having a Congress(I) Government when he took over as Governor, he never created any misunderstanding between the Centre and the State Government. However, he said it was for the Centre to decide about the appointment. But if his opinion was sought, he said he had nothing against him.

The Tribune, 22.01.1990

Barari May Continue

From Harish Gupta
NEW DELHI: January 21

Mr. H.A. Barari, is likely to continue as Governor of Haryana.

An indication to this effect was given by Mr. Om Prakash Chautala Chief Minister of Haryana to this correspondent at an informal meeting.

Mr. Chautala said that Mr. Barari was a fine person and there was perfect harmony between the Government and the Governor. However it was for the Union Government to take a decision in this matter, he added

Meanwhile, informal sources say that the services of Mr. B.S. Ojha, Principal Secretary to the Chief Minister, would be placed at the disposal of the Union Government.

Mr. Ojha among 13 IAS officers to move out of the State in a few weeks. It is also learnt that Mr. Kalyan Rudra would take over as Director-General of Police, Haryana shortly.

दैनिक ट्रब्यून–22.01.1990

बरारी राज्यपाल बने रहेंगे

दिल्ली कार्यालय द्वारा

नयी दिल्ली, 21 जनवरी श्री हरि आनन्द बरारी हरियाणा के राज्यपाल बने रहेंगे । इस तरह का संकेत हरियाणा के मुख्यमंत्री श्री ओमप्रकाश चौटाला ने दिया है ।

इस बीच जानकार सूत्रों के अनुसार मुख्यमंत्री के मुख्य सचिव श्री बी.एस. ओझा की सेवाऐं केन्द्र सरकार को सोपी जायेगी । यह भी पता चला है कि श्री कल्याण रूद्र जल्दी ही पुलिस महानिदेशक का पद संभाल लेंगे ।

On January 25, 1990, I went to Delhi and the next morning, I proceeded to Faridabad to take the salute at the Republic Day parade. In the evening, I hosted a big reception there, which was attended by Chautala, his Ministers, high officials and members of the public from different walks of life.

On January 31, 1990, I inaugurated a musical programme in celebration of 'Vasant' (spring) presented by the famous Singh Bandhus at the Tagore Hall. It was arranged by the Department of Culture, Government of Haryana. Since it was a morning programme, we were entertained to some delightful morning 'Ragas'.

It was on February 1, 1990 that the evening television news announced the acceptance of most of the resignations tendered by the Governors including mine. My place was to be taken by Dhanik Lal Mandal.

In the mean time a spate of articles had appeared in the press in different parts of the country, which questioned the wisdom of the V.P. Singh Government in deciding to remove almost all the Governors. Some specimens are reproduced below:

The Tribune, January 16, 1990

CLUMSY HANDLING

There is nothing unusual about Governors being eased out and ambassadors being recalled when there is a change of Government at the Centre. But what is unusual is the alternately cavalier and hamhanded fashion in which the National Front Government is going about either job. There is indeed a discreet and dignified way of doing it which, however, has not commended itself to the new rulers. The circumstances in which Mr. S.S. Ray had to quit Punjab Raj Bhawan are too well known to need repetition. But it can bear recapitulation that the Union Home Secretary was considered a high enough official to deal with him. Rightly or not, Mr. Ray interpreted that as a kind of slight to him and resigned as Governor. Again, one-day Deputy Prime Minister Devi Lal makes a public announcement that the Governor of Jammu and Kashmir; Gen K.V. Krishna Rao, is about to be "removed" and, on Sunday, the Governor tenders his resignation! It would have added more than a cubit to the stature of the National Front Government if, instead of its representatives publicly declaring its marked men, the Prime Minister, Deputy Prime Minister or the Union Home Minister had summoned the political appointee and politely told them that the new Government needed new persons as Governors to implement new or even old policies and, therefore, the incumbents should quit. There are, God knows, any number of political misfits occupying Raj Bhawans, and no tears would be shed over their removal. But even in their cases, the Government can act with dignity. That such decorum is not being observed is bad enough. But what is worse is Mr. Devi Lal's statement in Pune on Sunday that if such Governors go voluntarily, it will be good "but others will have to be removed". Should Governors learn from newspapers that they are on the hit list of the present Government? Hardly a day passes without one newspaper or another speculation about which Governor is next to be axed. And the speculation is sometimes so wild and to say that even such non-controversial Governors as Mr. H.A. Barari in (who are also not political appointees) might be replaced. Such reports may not necessarily be planted by the Government, but their source cannot but be some Central Minister or bureaucrat and their effect is to instill a sense of insecurity in the minds of the incumbents and devalue them in public esteem.

The treatment of some Indian ambassadors has been more shabby. Again, Indian ambassadors resigning when there is a change of Government in Delhi is not unprecedented. The present Foreign Minister, Mr. I.K. Gujral, had resigned as Ambassador to Moscow when the Janata Party came to power in 1977, but the then Prime Minister, Mr. Morarji Desai, had the grace to ask him to stay put. Similarly, Mr. Nani Palkhivala had resigned as Ambassador to Washington when Indira Gandhi returned to power in 1980. But now it looks as though the Government has launched a sort of witch-hunt against such ambassadors as are believed to have been close to the previous Government. It does not seem to have occurred to the Government yet that the ambassadors represent the country and not the party in power in it at a given time. That much is proved by the tone and tenor of the letter of resignation submitted by Dr. Karan Singh. According to it, he could not get an appointment with the Prime Minister to whom he wanted to submit his resignation personally. This shows that Mr. Rajiv Gandhi was not the Prime Minister who remained inaccessible to all but his coterie. Among, the other envoys for whose scalps some in the Government reportedly screaming is Mr. M.K. Rasgotra, High Commissioner to the U.K. That he is a former Foreign Secretary and, therefore, brings to bear on his present office the insight gained earlier looks irrelevant to the present Government. Does he forfeit the right to continue simply because he was appointed by the previous Government? Are his special qualifications for the job of no consequence? Even so, nobody questions the right of the National Front to sack Governors and Ambassadors but, surely it can handle the job less clumsily if not with greater dignity.

THE TRIBUNE, January 18, 1990

GOVERNORS AS SHADOWS

It is far from clear what overcame the National Front Government but there is no doubt that it has reduced Governors to mere shadows moving in a shadow show. According to one view, the National Front wanted to be selective in the sacking of the Governors. President R. Venkataraman, according to this view, thought that such a course of a action would be discriminatory. Thereupon, the Government agreed to make all Governors tender their resignations so that the acceptance of those of a few of them might not look politically motivated. Even if this interpretation of the Government's action (which otherwise defies comprehension) is accepted, it will leave a host of questions to be answered. Foremost among them is if there is any method in this apparent madness and if any criterion, of course other than political tit-for-tattery, is being adopted. It will be readily conceded that over the years mostly such politicians belonging to the ruling party as had been routed in an election, or such others as could not, for whatever reason, be "kicked upstairs" were packed off to various Raj Bhavans. It will not be denied, either, that most, if not all, of those immured in the gilded cages called Raj Bhavans during the long rule of the Congress, even in its later incarnation of Congress (I), were politicians. But not all of them converted Raj Bhavans into playfields of politics. Vice-President S.D. Sharma, though a Congressman all his life, made, on becoming Governor of Andhra Pradesh, the Telugu Desam Government virtually worship the ground he walked on. Again, Mr. B.K. Nehru, no politician but an eminent diplomat and administrator, refused to carry out the palpably unjust order of the Centre to dismiss the Farooq Abdullah Government and preferred to be transferred from the Raj Bhavan in Srinagar to that in Ahmedabad. The point is that while all Governors are appointed by the President on the advice of his Council of Ministers, not all of them prove to be wire-pulled jacks-in-the box. And since the National Front Government too is likely to replace some Governors with politicians of its own choice, what is there to choose between the present Government and the previous one?

When the Sarkaria Commission laid down the mode of appointment and dismissal of Governors, many of those who are now in the Government had vociferously demanded (as, for instance, in the Rajya Sabha on November 28, 1988) acceptance, among others, of this recommendation. But, once in office, the same persons are violating this very recommendation. For instance, the Commission had said "The Governor's tenure of office of five years in a State should not be disturbed, except very rarely and that too for extremely compelling reasons. The Governor whose tenure is proposed to be terminated before the expiry of the normal term should be informally appraised of the "grounds of the proposed action and afforded a reasonable opportunity for showing cause against it." Has the National Front Government, cared to inform the Governors "of the grounds of the proposed action"? No just a letter has gone to them from Rashtrapati Bhavan asking them to submit their resignations. It is one of the small mercies for which the nation will be duly grateful to him that Prime Minister V.P. Singh, after making Governors look like balls tossed on the bagatelle board, clarified that not all the resignations would be accepted. Then why did his Government decide on what looks like political vendetta? Governors like Mr. H.A. Barari of Haryana and Dr. Gopal Singh of Nagaland have scrupulously kept themselves out of controversy, while others like Mr. P. Venkatasubbiah of Karnataka, Ms.Kumudben Joshi of Andhra Pradesh and Mrs. Ram Dulari Sinha of Kerala did act as agents not only of the Centre but of the party in power there. To club the two categories of Governors and ask them allied to resign is to reduce Governors to the level of Ministers and party functionaries who can be hired, fired and reshuffled at will.

Many questioned the validity of the new Home Minister Mufti Mohammed Sayeed's contention that whenever there was a change in the Central Government, the Governors of the States should put in their resignations. This view ran counter to the constitutional provision that the Governor of a State was an independent constitutional entity not subject to the control of any other authority. This constitutional position has been re-iterated over the decades by several authorities. In 1971, a high-power committee headed by the late Bhagawn Sahay made a expressed the view, later accepted by the Governors' Conference, that the Governor as the head of a State had his functions laid down in the Constitution and that he was not the agent of the President of India in any sense—not even when the State was under President's Rule.

The same view was generally re-iterated by the famous Sarkaria Commission by whose report all political parties in India swear, at least for propaganda purposes. This Commission had clearly said in its report: "The Governor's tenure of office of five years in a State should not be disturbed except very rarely and that too for some extremely compelling reason"

A full bench of the Supreme Court had in its judgement in 1979 in the case of Raghukul Tilak, a former Governor of Rajasthan, observed: "His is an independent constitutional office, which is not subject to the control of the government of India." the Supreme Court bench presided over by Chief Justice Chandrachud had clearly said: "The office of a Governor of a State is not an employment under the Government of India and it does not, therefore, come within the prohibition of Clause (d) of Article 319. The employment can be said to be under the Government of India, if the holder or incumbent of the employment—it is impossible to hold that the Governor is under the control of the Government of India vis-à-vis such employment—it is impossible to hold that the Governor is under the control of the Government of India." the judgement said that the Governor was not answerable to the directives of the Government of India nor was he answerable to it for the manner in which he carried out his functions and duties.

Taking into account the weight of this constitutional verdict, for the Union Home Minister to say that the Governors should be changed the moment there is a change in the Government at the Centre betrayed his ignorance of what all these eminent authorities had pronounced on this issue. Often, it is not that the politicians do not know the correct position; they simply do what suits their convenience.

As Sunanda K. Datta-Ray, a former editor of the Calcutta Statesman said in an article (January 22, 1990), Governors appointed by the Central Government on the basis of what the Union Home

Minister said would be nothing but hatchet men and would cease to be non-partisan and objective. Datta-Ray also said in his article that one of the reasons why V.P. Singh had purged the Governors was that he had to 'find jobs for the boys', who included a host of 'unemployed luminaries' and journalists.

It was generally believed that the V.P. Singh Government had initially wanted to secure the resignations of only a few Governors whose conduct it had reason not to particularly like. President Venkataraman reportedly pointed out that this selective treatment would be discriminatory and urged instead that all the Governors be asked to submit their resignations so that the Central Government would have the option of asking some of them to resign and retaining the others. In fact, by offering the resignation letters of all the Governors on a platter to the V.P. Singh Government, President Venkataraman helped the new regime to end up removing more Governors than had been originally thought of.

Many people thought that the President's action had set a wrong precedent, which had no constitutional sanction behind it. Where is the constitutional provision that authorizes the President of India to seek the resignation of all the Governors in the event of a new government taking over at the Centre? in fact, some political analysts posed the question whether the President of India should also have been asked to resign on the ground that the Lok Sabha, which, along with several other bodies, had elected him, had changed its political complexion. Even the Rajya Sabha and the State Legislative Assemblies, whose members participate in the election of the President of India, come to acquire different political complexions at different times after elections to them are held. It could be argued that just as the Governors that had been replaced were the nominees of the Congress Party, President Venkataraman, once a Congress leader, had also been sponsored by this party for the post of the President of India. If some members of the V.P. Singh Government raised the demand for President Venkataraman's ouster on the ground that the political complexion of the electorate for Presidential election had changed, would he have obliged by tendering his resignation?

The formal letter from the President of India saying that my resignation had been accepted reached me a few days later. In between, I had rung up Dhanik Lal Mandal and congratulated him on his appointment as my successor. We mutually agreed that I would leave Chandigarh on February 6, 1990 so that he could come there the same day to be sworn in.

I had still a few engagements to fulfil in Chandigarh. Rajan Kashyap, a senior I.A.S. Officer of the Punjab cadre, who had contributed a lot to the cause of tennis in Chandigarh, had personally requested me to lend my presence at the Lawn Tennis Stadium on February 2, 1990 and preside over the Satellite International Masters Tennis Final. I did this with great pleasure.

Now it was farewell time. For the next few days that I was in Chandigarh, many persons, mostly with their wives, came to meet me and my wife to personally say good-bye to us. This memory is something that we still cherish.

The prevailing mood in Chandigarh was very well reflected in an editorial in the Tribune of February 3, 1990, which said:

The Tribune, February 3, 1990

A BAD PRECEDENT

It is difficult to expunge the thought that the National Front Government may have followed at least in some instances of gubernatorial appointments, the same old Congress (I) line. Of course, the Rajiv Gandhi regime touched the limits of diversity of foisting activist politicians as Governors on what were then called non-Congress (I)-ruled States. The latest group of appointments to Raj Bhavans too smacks of political considerations. In extenuation, it can be said that none of them is really an active politician. Even those like Mrs. Chandravati, Mr. Yagya Dutt Sharma, Mr. Krishna Kant and Mr. B.Rachaiah, all of whose political allegiances are clearly identifiable, are not in the thick of murky party politics. As Mr. Krishna Kant said, appointment of politicians as Governors cannot be opposed per se. one should actually look at the kind of politics pursued by the individual concerned, as also his or her image and record in public life. Applying this yardstick, the nominees of the President in the list of 14 announced on Thursday night are unexceptionable. Whether it is Mr. Yagya Dutt Sharma or Dr. Sarup Singh or Prof. D.P.Chattopadhyaya or Mr. Yunus Saleem, everyone of the new Governors has had an impeccable political record. Admittedly, there may have been felt political compulsions in assigning Dr. Sarup Singh to Kerala and Mr. Rachaiah to Himachal Pradesh. The Government must be particularly congratulated on the choice of Mr. C.Subramaniam who is in the position of an elder statesman. Admiral Tahiliani's appointment fits in with the recent convention of drawing upon the ranks of outstanding retired officers from the defence forces to constitutional offices. In short, the list of political appointees can be faulted on motives but not on the quality of the people. There is, however, one exception to this assessment. It is incomprehensible that an unknown and nondescript lawyer, Mr. Swaraj Kaushal, has been deemed fit to be a full-fledged Governor of a State.

If the sins of commission are few, the sins of omission are quite glaring. A lot of people in this region have reason to be upset and angry about the removal of two Governors who conducted themselves with dignity and grace, Mr. Hari Anand Barai (Haryana), despite the fact that he came to Raj Bhavan from the Intelligence Bureau, showed himself to be a person of high stature and dignity. Neither Mr. Devi Lal nor his son-successor, Mr. Om Prakash Chautala, had any complaint against him. Similarly, Vice-Adm R.K.S.Ghandhi, besides being a non-political Governor, was a stickler for rectitude and procedure. In all their years in Haryana and Himachal Pradesh, respectively, Mr. Barari and Vice-Adm Ghandhi had never dragged themselves into any controversy and, given the choice, all the parties would not like them to leave. In fact, the National Front Government's exercise on Governors may have done a lot of damage in bundling all the Rajiv regime appointments into one whole instead of separating the grain from the chaff. Few tears need to be shed for the exit of such willing accomplices of the previous regime as Mrs. Kumudben Joshi, Mr. Ram Dulari Sinha, Mr. T.V.Rajeswar, Mr. S.K.Bhatnagar and MRs. Serla Grewal. The National Front Government must be extremely myopic in not visualizing the consequences of its action. By the wholesale removal of Governors, it has set a totally indefensible and unsavoury precedent. A future Government is bound to do to its appointees what it has done to its predecessor's appointees. The tragedy is all the more when a Government seeks to appoint worthy persons as Governors and subject eminent personalities to the indignity of political victimization.

On February 3, 1990, I hosted a farewell tea party for all members of the Raj Bhawan staff and security personnel including Class IV staff and sweepers. There were a few emotional speeches. This was the first time that such a party was hosted by a departing Governor.

The next evening, Chief Minister O.P. Chautala hosted a farewell dinner for me and my wife at his residence, which was largely attended. After Chautala complimented me for my role as a Governor, I gave a reply, expressing my gratitude to all for their co-operation and my hope for a bright future for the people of Haryana. I reminded the audience that there existed a lasting bond between me and Haryana that was symbolized by my very name—Hari Ananda Barari—whose first seven letters stood for the name of the State—Hariana or Haryana. I asked: "Had my father ever thought before giving this name to me in my childhood—decades before the State of Haryana was even conceived of—that I would some day become the Governor of a state whose name would form part of my own name?" I, therefore, said that I might go away from Haryana, but Haryana would ever remain an integral part of my name and of my very being. There was a thunderous applause accompanied by many wet eyes.

One of those evenings, my wife and I took a stroll around our Raj Bhawan's lawns and gardens, the fish tank and the poultry sheds. We looked at the peacocks and the deer and fed them, as we sometimes used to do. I recalled the picture depicted in poet Kaldasa's Abhijnan Shakuntalam of Shakuntala taking leave of the deer and other pet animals before leaving sage Kanva's hermitage for the place of her royal spouse, Dushyanta.

On the evening of February 5, 1990, quite a number of officials and others including people from the worlds of music and sports called on us , most of them with their wives. Many got photographed with us.

We left Chandigarh for Delhi on February 6, 1990 forenoon. Before that, a big farewell ceremony was held for us on the lawns of the Raj Bhawan. I took the salute at a farewell parade by the police and the Home Guards. Ministers, high officials, people from various walks of life and all members of Raj Bhawan staff had turned up to bid us adieu. Many shed tears. We got into the gubernatorial Mercedes car that drove us to Delhi. The same afternoon, R.K. Vachher, A.D.C. to the Governor of Haryana, rang me up in Delhi to say that Dhanik Lal Mandal had been sworn in as the new Governor.

That night and from time to time during the next few days, many officials of the Haryana Raj Bhawan rang me up to say how much they missed me and my wife. I told them that we also missed them equally. Even a few members of the Raj Bhawan's Class IV staff rang up to express similar sentiments.

When I woke up in Delhi on February 7, 1990 morning (*i.e.* The morning after I had relinquished my charge as the Governor of Haryana), a high official of the Central Government in Chandigarh rang me up and said that he was very happy to see a write-up on me and my wife in the Daily Tribune of that morning. He sent me a copy of the write-up, which I received a few days later. I would remain ever grateful to whoever had written this piece, a kind of my gubernatorial obituary, reproduced below, which had quite a few good things to say about us:

TRIBUNE, CHANDIGARH—7.2.1990

CHANDIGARH CALLING

In fewer than three months, two Governors from West Bengal who have in their own ways endeared themselves to the people of this region had left the city. It is a pity that the exit of both the Governors was engineered rather than normal and constitutional. Both Mr Siddhartha Shankar Ray and Mr. Hari Anand Barari became victim of 'the same political process by which they entered the office. The two were poles apart in their styles of functioning, in their personalities and their impact on the people. While the former saw his office as an instrument, the latter was an adornment to the office. The Rays were: flamboyant outgoing and charmingly exhibitionist. The Bararis, on the other hand, were graceful, away from the limelight and content with responding to events rather than seeking to direct their course.

Both Governors were very effective as Heads of State - Mr Ray was a bit too effective to the liking of all people. Punjab was indeed a terribly difficult assignment and perhaps needed an extrovert and political Governor. Haryana called for tact and diplomacy. Mr Ray considered his assignment as a challenge; Mr Barari saw his as a sacred duty. Naturally, when the Bararis left Raj Bhavan on Tuesday, many eyes were moist.

Culture and grace have the hallmarks of the Baran couple. Even as Mr Barari struck an excellent working relationship with Mr Devi Lal and later with 'Mr Om Parkash Chautala, he left neither in doubt that he could not be forced to do the wrong thing. The Congress (1) Government in Delhi too realised this. Mr Barari was always the persuader and not the persuaded

It was primarily because of his sweet reasonableness that the somewhat unnatural, but by hindsight meaningful, appointment of former military officers as Vice-Chancellors of universities could be achieved without much ado or controversy.

Mrs Anita Barari, daughter of the former Director of Intelligence Bureau, Mr B.N. Mullick, acted the perfect complement to her Governorhusband. Both were ardent -music lovers and were on their way to becoming patrons of all that is aesthetic in Chandigarh when the National Front Government has done its graceful act.

Mr Barari took keen interest in the development of Kurukshetra as a seat of higher learning in culture, Sanskrit and spiritual affairs. Perhaps the Haryana Government can partially redeem itself and repair the damage by making Mr Barari the Chairman of the Kurukshetra Development Board so that the good work initiated and sustained 'by him as Governor might be continued from wherever he settles down.

Chandigarh will be poorer by the departure of the Bararis.

Note

1. A Few Pages From the History of Haryana by Bhim Sain Tyagi, p. 20.

19

Haryana on the Road to All-round Progress

Today, when I think of Haryana, certain basic facts stand out such as its cultural and spiritual heritage, its social, economic and political milieu and the character and life-style of its people. Elsewhere in our country, people harbour some wrong notions about the people of Haryana whom they look upon as a rough and rowdy lot and as the votaries of the political culture of 'Aya Ram, Gaya Ram'. These are misconceptions, which betray their ignorance.

The culture of political defection is more endemic in some other States of India. While sharing some deficiencies of character and outlook with the rest of the country, the people of Haryana have certain qualities which are not to be found in many other States. The average Haryanvi is tough and hard-working and earns his bread by the sweat of his brow. Haryana is less infected by the communal virus than many other States. There is much less political unrest and violence in Haryana and fewer crimes are committed here than in many other parts of our country.

The average Haryanvi is a modest person, but he asserts himself when his rights are violated. Haryana's history has been marked by many vicissitudes, trials and tribulations, chief among which were the numerous foreign invasions and the orgies of plunder and loot unleashed on its people by hordes of foreign freebooters. Despite all this, the people of Haryana have retained their basic character and traditional values that represent a mixture of the diverse cultures of the many races which got absorbed into the mainstream of Haryana's population. By and large, the people of Haryana stuck to their Hindu faith without succumbing to overtures from the votaries of Islam, Christianity and even Sikhism. Later, the Arya Samaj movement came to Haryana, but as compared to some other States, this influenced the people of Haryana to a lesser degree.

We have a doll in our house—the idol of a typical village belle of Haryana colourfully dressed and balancing a water vessel on her head, which correctly brings out the beauty as well as the sturdiness of Haryana's women. Apart from performing all household chores, they also work in the field. I have seen many of them plying tractors and other mechanical devices for purposes of cultivation. Their attitudes are also fast changing, as Haryana girls now go in for education in increasing numbers and are thronging the institutions of higher learning in different parts of India and even in other countries of the world.

A straw in the wind is the case of Kalpana Chawla, a girl from Karnal, who obtained a doctorate in aerospace engineering from the University of Colorado (U.S.A.) in 1988 and then emerged on the world scene as a top-notch astronaut at the NASA (U.S.A.). But tragedy struck and she, along with several others, who had flown into space on board their shuttle Colombo, perished 16 minutes before scheduled landing on February 1, 2003. The whole world was shocked and paid handsome tributes to these explorers, who had sacrificed their lives in pursuit of their mission of unravelling the mysteries of space with a view to making life better on earth. Naturally, Haryana, nay India as a whole, feels proud of Kalpana. Haryana, in particular, gratefully remembers 21st century's Kalpana as much as Mahabharata's Kunti, both of whom were from Karnal.

There was a time when the birth of a boy in a Haryana village used to be announced by beating a metal plate. Now this is also being done in the event of the birth of a girl! the gender bias used to come out in the names earlier given to girls such as Bhateri (enough), Sukhni (thin), Rukri (stop being born), Mooli (radish) etc. This has now yielded place to names like Indira (after Indira Gandhi), Kiran (after Kiran Bedi, the first lady I.P.S. Officer) and others.

The Haryana Government is reported to have adopted several measures to improve the lot of women. The women's development programme in the villages picks up socially or economically disadvantaged girls and gives them training and education so as to enable them to stand on their own feet. Many Haryana girls have now discarded the 'Ghungat' in favour of the comparatively more modern 'Dupatta'. From recent reports in the press, I understand that now girls even in the villages perform on the stage without the familiar 'Ghungat' and openly declare that they are not inferior to boys. Mallika

Sherawat, the girl from Rohtak, whose mother still clings to her Ghungat, has set Bollywood on fire by her provocative dare-all roles in hot movies. She has acted in international films and also made a splash by her appearance at the Cannes film festival in 2005. She symbolizes the new face of the Haryana girl out to take on the world at large.

The fast pace of economic development that the State has achieved in the short span of time since it came into being on November 1, 1966 is something that takes one's breath away. This is a tribute to the dynamism and industrious disposition of the people of Haryana as well as to the stewardship of some of its leaders, the most important among them being Ch. Bansi Lal, who did for Haryana what Sardar Pratap Singh Kairon did for Punjab. He worked very hard for the development of Haryana, though he had to face criticism for the unorthodox methods that he sometimes adopted as the means to achieve his goal. The various measures he took contributed to accelerating the pace of development and brought Haryana on the tourism map of India.

Agriculture has thrived in Haryana as a result of the green revolution. Irrigation facilities have been extended to the parched lands through the execution of lift irrigation schemes. All towns and villages of Haryana have been electrified. Industrialisation has received an impetus and many industrial centres have come up. Small-scale industries and handicrafts have made considerable progress. All villages are now connected by metalled roads. Dairy development has registered phenomenal progress. Haryana is famous for its cattle wealth. The Haryanvis take great pride in consuming pure milk and 'Ghee' and in substantial quantities at that. No wonder that they excel in manly sports and games like Kabaddi and wrestling. Bee culture is widely practised in Haryana. It may aptly be said that Haryana overflows with milk and honey. I never saw a beggar in that State. Haryana's per capita income is second only to that of Punjab.

Of course, many shortcomings and bottlenecks are still to be overcome. Female literacy has to be increased. Haryana's rural society is still case-ridden. However, a redeeming feature of the State's caste scenario is that, despite their consciousness of their caste identities, the rivalry or friction among them is not as acute or intense as in many other States. By and large, there is peace and social understanding in the villages of Haryana.

Paucity of water and electricity for agriculture are serious problems. The problem of salinity has been aggravated by improved irrigation facilities. Rohtak used to be the centre of dry land research in the 1930's, but now it is affected by the supply of saline water, which is unsuitable for irrigation. The introduction of transgenic crops made possible by the advances in the field of bio-technology has to be considered. Unless water is allowed to flow into Haryana through the SYL canal, its agriculture cannot realize its full potential. Tapping of solar energy is necessary, if power shortage is to be tackled. An important problem faced by the farmers is the diversion of farm land to residential and other uses through the process of acquisition by the Government.

Haryana should have a capital city of its own at a place located near the centre of the State.

The recent moves for the construction of national highways in Haryana should accelerate the pace of development in the State. Faridabad and several other places are fast emerging as the new centers of rapid economic development. The way Gurgaon is seeking to replicate the life-style of the richest cities of the world shows that Haryana is going to be the trend-setter for our country in the matter of urban development.

I am sure, a glorious future beckons Haryana and its people.

Index

11th Commonwealth Diploma Course, 123
1857 Struggle of Independence, 53
1857 Uprising, 154

A

Abdul Qadir Badauni, 197
Abdur Rahman Khan, 154
Abdus Samad, 62
Abhijana, Shakuntalam, 38-39
Abhimanyu, 44, 86, 113, 270
Abhimanyukera, 270
Abhiras, 44
Abohar-Fazilka, 180
Abul Fazal, 258
Abul Kadir Badauni, 258
Acharya Bhagawan Dev, 22
Acharya Gaudapada, 313
Acharyas, 395
Ad-Badri, 100
Adda, 168
Adhiratha, 293
Adi Shakti, 249
Adi Shankaracharya, 313
Adil Shah, 194
Adina Beg, 61
Adina Masjid, 156
Aditivana, 26, 295
Aditya Vardhana, 255
Adity-Surya, 255
Advaita Vedanta, 313
Agastha, 346, 402
Agnistoma, 137
Agra Sain, 232
Agraha, 45, 232
Ahalya, 292
Ahalya, Draupadi, Kunti, Tara and Mandodari, 292
Ahirs, 67
Ahmad Shah Abdali, 115, 148, 205
Ahmad Shah Durrani, 61, 139
Ahmedabad, 383
Ain-I-Akbari, 223
Aitaz Ahsan, 73
Ajay Johal, 331
Ajit Singh, 69
Akbar, 59, 242, 277, 309
Akbari, 271
Akshapada, 292
Akshay Bat, 245
Alaf Khan, 218
Alaka, 262
Alamgir II, 61
Alauddin Khalji, 76
Alauddin Sikander Shah, 57
Alexander Cunningham, 158
Alexander the Great, 44, 233
Alharava Veda, 96
Ali Gohar, 61
Ali Khan, 154
Ali Shah, 149
Allah Folklore, 133
Altaf Hussain Hali, 77
Amadalpur village, 367
Amalgamated Fund Committee, 184

Amandeep Johal, 332
Amar Singh, 317
Amba Mata, 387
Amba Rajput, 182
Ambika, 27
Amin, 270, 295
Amir Khusro, 123
Amrendra Nath, 349
Ananda Bazar Patrika, 16
Ananda Ramayana, 113
Anangapal, 47
Anarak, 298
Anti-Bhajan Lal, 128
Anupchand Aftab Panipati, 78
Apabhramsha, 23
Apaga, 99, 299
Apelava, 379
Apsaras, 29
Arjuna, 44, 113
Arjuna's skill, 285
Arnoraja, 54
Arrian, 44
Arti of Brahman, 33
Arunaya, 175
Arya Samaj, 73, 164
Aryabhatta, 111
Aryans, 25
Asakhera, 238
ASHI, 304
Ashok Lawasa I.A.S., 132
Ashok Pradhan I.A.S., 145
Ashu Ram Arya, 364
Ashwamedha, 28
Assand, 149
Astadhyayi, 90, 238
Asthipura, 267
Astika, 137
Atal Behari Vajpayee, 409
Atta, 286
Aurangzeb's, 59, 93, 159, 277
Avidya Maya, 322
Avtar Singh Badhna, 284
Aya Ram, Gaya Ram, 425

B

B.K. Nehru, 79, 128
B.N. Chakraborti, 86, 291
B.N. Mullik, 15, 92
Baat-Cheet, 166
Baba Balaknath of the Nath Community, 82
Baba Farid, 226
Baba Ganesh Giri, 175
Baba Ka Ladhana, 184
Baba Lachhman Akhra, 267
Baba Rajpuri's Math, 316
Baba Sarsai Nath, 239
Baba Shravan Nath, 267
Baba Simran Das, 86
Baba Sital Puri's Math, 316
Baba Totapuri, 313
Babar, 58
Bactrians, 256
Badan Singh, 63
Badarikashrama, 29, 100
Badayun Inscription, 23
Badripuri, 316
Baghpat, 111
Bahadur Nahir Mewati, 288
Bahadur Nahir, 57-58
Bahadur Shah, 60, 230
Bahadur Shah, 70
Bahadurgarh, 157
Bahlul Lodhi, 58, 187
Bahram Shah, 56
Bahudhanyaka, 22
Balarama, 263
Balban, 56
Balhika Pratipiya, 114
Balkunj, 144
Ballabh Singh, 307
Ballabhgarh, 307

Ban Ganga or Bhisma Kund, 240
Ban Ganga, 298
Banabhatta, 22, 46, 256
Banarsi Dass Gupta, 410
Banda Bahadur, 85, 366
Banda Bairagi, 130
Banderpunchh, 100
Bandhua Mukti Morcha, 338
Banjaras, 315
Bansi Lal, 128
Basthali, 295
Battles of Panipat Memorial Society, 332
Bawal, 379
Bawan Dwadashi, 183
Bay of Kutch, 402
Beant Singh, 185
Beas, 44
Begum Samru of Sardhana, 65, 148
Bet Dwaraka, 402
Bet Sankhoddhara, 402
Bhadanakas, 217, 277
Bhadanakas, 54
Bhadrakali temple in Kurukshetra, 245
Bhadrakali temple, 94
Bhadras, 278
Bhagawan S. Gidwani, 347
Bhagawanpura and Mirzapur, 350
Bhai Desa Singh, 130, 371
Bhai Kainthal, 173
Bhai Udai Singh, 130
Bhairavi Brahmani, 321
Bhajan Lal, 212
Bhakra canal, 237
Bhakra Project, 164
Bhakti Yoga, 326
Bhal Lal Singh, 69
Bharat Pattan, 239
Bharata War III, 112
Bharata, 40, 42
Bharatiya Vidya Bhawan, 185
Bharatpur, 278
Bhargava clan, 277
Bhateri, 426
Bhattis, 61, 67, 224
Bhawanipur, 100
Bhiksu Lohacharya, 75
Bhima, 34, 396
Bhimeshwari Devi Temple of Beri, 156
Bhishma Kund, 298
Bhiwani, 216
Bhrigukachha, 106
Bhupinder Singh Hooda, 161
Bhuteshwara temple, 376
Bidkiyar Lake, 131
Bilaspur, 101
Biram Khan, 199
Birbal, 277
Birbal's Chhatta, 277
Bishnois, 67
Bishwambardas, 77
Boojh-Bujhakar, 166
Boudhayana, 344
Brahma Sutra, 110, 314
Brahma, 38
Brahmakshetra, 98
Brahmalok, 244
Brahmarsidesha, 90
Brahmasar, 93
Brahmastra, 293
Brahmavarta, 25, 90, 98
Brahmavedi, 26
Brahmosarovara, 30
Brigadier-General Showers, 279, 290
Brihaspati, 346
Bu Ali Kalandar, 148
Buali Shah Qalandar, 149
Buchraj, 77
Buddhism, 74
Budha Dal, 62

C

C.S. Jha, 179
C.T. Metcalfe, 154
Captain Ravi Bhatia, 17
Captain Viswanathan, 17
Cauhans, 377
Century of Pt. Jawaharlal Nehru's birth, 144
Ch. Devi Lal, 126-28
Ch. Ranbir Singh, 161
Chaar Qutb, 227
Chail, 180
Chakravyuha, 270
Chamsodbhava, 106
Chandan, 47
Chandi Mandir, 81
Chandigarh Golf Club, 80, 331, 364
Chandigarh Lawn Tennis Association Stadium, 336
Chandra Kupa, 240, 245
Chandragupta, 44
Chandrasekhar, 406
Chaturbhuj, 286
Chauhans, 47, 152, 278
Chetan Sharma, 85, 281
Chhachhrauli, 144
Chhathi Khoria, Phag, Phog, Loor and Chhari, 216
Chhoganan Mata, 287
Chhojuram Shastri, 77
Chhotu Ram, 161
Chiranjeev, 364
Chisti, 226
Chitrakoot, 270
Chitralekha, 31
Chowaraginath, 77
Chudasma Rajputs, 386
Chunimal, 286
Churaman, 63, 161
Chutang, 99
Chyavan, 74
Clifford Assistant Captain Drummond, 289
Cloud Messenger, 262
Colonel Burn, 67
Colonel James Skinner, 67
Cricket match, 126
Cunningham, 369

D

Dadhichi, 94
Daksa Prajapati, 391
Damdama, 286
Damodar Kund, 387
Dandapani, 147
Danveer, 294
Dara Shikoh, 272
Darayo Singh Chaudhary, 414
Dargah Qalandar Shah, 149
Daryao Singh, 17
Dasharajna Yuddha, 42
Dashrath Sharma, 201
Dasyus or Dasas, 25
Daulat Khan, 188
DAV Colleges, 123
Daya Ram, 306
Dayalpur near Kurukshetra, 298
Dayalpur, 240
De-Boigne, 225
Delhi Territory, 72
Delhi's Purana Qila, 111
Deshnami Sampradaya, 315
Devaki and Vasudeva, 247
Devendra Hand, 239
Devendra Sharma, 212
Devi Kupo, 245
Devi-Bhagawata Purana, 26
Devyani, 34, 35
Dhan Teras, 303
Dhanvanari, Jayanti, 303
Dharamvir, 85
Dharmakshetra, 92

Dharmapala, 46
Dharuhera, 275
Dhauj, 338
Dhramgranth, 232
Dhritarastra's, 44, 113
Dhuni, 316
Dhunsar Bania, 195
Dilshad Mohd. Khan, 356
Divodasa and Sudas, 42
Diwan-e-Aam, 222
Dost Muhammad Khan, 280
Dr. A.K. Chakrabarti, 144
Dr. B.G. Sidharth, 345
Dr. Buddha Prakash, 23, 44, 352
Dr. D.B. Sen Sharma, 357
Dr. Gopi Chand Bhargava, 231
Dr. Guy E. Pilgrim, 24
Dr. Hari Ram Gupta, 24
Dr. Herman Gmeiner, 307
Dr. Indranath Choudhury, 363
Dr. K.C. Yadav, 24
Dr. M.S. Randhawa and Devi Shankar Prabhakar, 22
Dr. M.S. Randhawa, 161
Dr. Moonis Raja, 363
Dr. Mulak Raj Anand, 363
Dr. Namvar Singh, 363
Dr. R.C. Mazumdar, 112
Dr. S.A.Q. Hussain, 24
Dr. S.N. Sen, 182
Dr. Suhasini Koratkar, 371
Dr. V.S. Wokankar, 106-107
Draupadi, 294, 300
Drishdwati, 97
Dronacharya, 270, 285, 293
Dujana, 156
Dukhbhanjeswar Mahadev, 94
Dupatta, 426
Durbasa, 74
Durga Puja, 285
Durvasha, 402
Duryodhana, 43, 147
Dushyanta, 37
Dwarka, 94, 398
Dwarkadheesh temple, 400

E

E.R. Cowell and F.W. Thomas, 258
East India Company, or William Bentinck, 66
Ekalavya, 285
Emperor Alauddin Khilji, 217
Emperor Ashoka, 75
Emperor Bahadur Shah, 153, 279, 335
Emperor Jahangir, 183

F

Faqir Chand, 230
Farghana Khurasan, 189
Faridabad, 307
Farishta, 218
Farrukh, Siyar, 60
Farrukhnagar and Jhajjar, 71
Farrukhsiyar, 287
Fateh Khan, 283
Fatehabad, 231, 232
Fauzdar Khan, 60
Fazal-I-Hussain, 162
Female Ila, 26
Feroze Shah Tughlak, 57, 219, 282
Fifth Veda, 110
Firoz Shah, 130

G

Gaekwad of Baroda, 403
Ganaur, 305
Gandharas, 43
Gandhari, 401
Gandharva Marriage, 37
Ganga, Yamuna and Saraswati, 104

Gangadwar, 171
Gangasagar, 318
Gaud Brahmins, 139, 313
Gaur Mata or Parvati, 301
Gautama, 292
Gaya, 90
Gen. Boigne, 224
Gen. Perron, 224
Gen. Raymond, 224
Gen. Samru, 224
Gen. Van Courtlandt, 154, 229
George Thomas, 65, 85, 139, 223
Ghaggar, 100, 102
Gharaunda, 291
Ghaznavis, 47, 54
Ghungat, 426
Ghyasuddin Tughlak, 57
Giani Zail Singh, 414
Girnar, 387
Goddess Kali, 318
Gopal Dev, 278-79
Gopal Maghmoom, 415
Gopal Sicca, 281
Gopal Singh of Ballabhgarh, 60
Gopalgarh, 281
Gopi friends, 244
Gotras, 160
Govardhan Mutt, 315
Govardhan, 309
Governor of Himachal, 411
Govinda Yati, 313-14
Graeco-antiquity, 304
Grahavarmana, 256
Grand Trunk Road, 291
Great Deluge, 105
Great Master, 316
Gritsamad, 113
Gujarat Chamber of Commerce, 373
Gujari Mahal, 221
Gujjars, 284
Gulzari Lal Nanda, 91
Gurjara-Pratihara King Mahendrapala, 173
Guru Govind Singh, 183
Guru Granth Sahib, 226
Guru Hargovind Singh, 183
Guru Nanak, 172
Guru T.D. Janonkar, 371
Guru Teg Bahadur, 131
Guru-Gaon, 285

H

H.M. Brari, 16
H.S. Brar, 243
Ḥai, 303
Haihaya Yadavas, 160
Haji Sultan of Thanesar, 76, 272
Hajrat Miraji, 272
Hakra in Rajasthan, 103
Hamsi, 227
Hansi town, 218
Hanuman Singh, 85
Hara-Gauri, 324
Harahvaiti, 101
Harakhaiti, 101
Harappa and Mohenjodaro, 24
Harappa, 105
Hardedas (short for Haridaydas), 165
Hardwari Lal, 212
Hari, 323
Haridas, 308
Hari-dhanyaka, 22
Harshacharita, 46
Harswaroop Singh, 218
Haryana Hind Kusht Nivaran Sangh, 333
Haryana I.A.S. Officers Wives Association, 213
Haryana Jat Aarakshan Sangharsh Samiti, 164

Haryana ki Vedanta-Parampara, 313
Haryana Reshma, 337
Haryana Rural Development Board, 143
Haryana Sahitya Academy, 363
Haryana State Council for Child Welfare, 144
Haryana Urban Development Authority, 123
Haryana Urdu Academy, 376, 415
Haryana Welfare Society for Speech and Hearing Handicapped, 285
Hasan Khan Mewati, 204
Hasan Khan, 60
Hastinapur, 44, 111, 294
Hathira near, 250
Hatyaharana, 134
Hazrat Nizammuddin Aulia, 83
Hazrat Qutb Jalauddin Shah Jahan, 272
Hazrat Turkman, 277
Hem Chandra, 59
Hemchandra, 195
Hemu, 161
Hieuen-Tsang, 75
Himu, 191
Hindu Mahasabha, 231
Hiradas, 77
Hisar Firoza, 219
Hit Harivansha, 196
Hitlal Misra, 328
Hiu'en Tsang, 46, 257, 365, 369, 403
Hodal, 378
Hookah-Bharania, 166
Hukam Chand, 228, 230
Humayun, 192, 197
Hunas, 256
Hussain Khan, 58

I

Ibn Batuta, 83
Ibrahim Khan, 277
Ibrahim Lodi, 149, 187s
Iksumati, 102
Indian Mountaineering Foundation, 337
Indian National Congress, 73
Indra, 294
Indraprastha, 111
Indus Valley, 24
Islam Shah, 59
Ismail Beg, 65

J

J.F. Rebeiro, 18
J.N. Kaul, 307
J.W.M. Crindle's Invasion, 44
Jagadhri and Chhachhrauli, 367
Jahangir, 59
Jal Mahal, 380
Jalaluddin Hanswi, 76
Jamadagni, 74
Jamaluddin, 226
Jambudvipa, 90
James Skinner, 224
James Tod, 158
Janamejaya, 114, 136
Janamejaya's death, 44
Janana Yoga, 326
Janmastami, 400
Jat Regiment, 133
Jats, 67
Jattiama or Jatait, 158
Jawahar Singh, 61
Jayachandra, 54
Jayadratha, 113, 299
Jayapala, 47
Jayram of Kurukshetra, 77
Jhajjar Rao Shahmal Khan, 280
Jinballabh Suri, 77

Jind is Barah, 134
Jind, 131, 133
Junagadh, 385
Jyoti Basu, 332
Jyotisar, 245

K

K.R. Malkani, 206
K.R. Punia, 284
K.R. Punia, H.K. Saini, Lachman Singh, 405
K.R. Qanungo, 160
Kaacha Chhora, 166
Kabaddi, 427
Kadphises, 45
Kahlon, 245
Kaithal, 129, 269, 292, 313
Kala Am, 149, 186
Kalasha, 54
Kalateehar tourist, 237
Kalayat, 377
Kalibangan, 105
Kalibari of the Bengalees, 179
Kalidasa, 33, 262
Kalika Purana, 246
Kalinjar, 59
Kalka Devi, 83
Kalla Khan, 78
Kalpa, 245
Kalpana Chawla, 426
Kaluwar, 99
Kalyat, 139
Kamadeva, 29
Kamal Nabh, 267
Kamdyakavana, 26
Kamleshwar, 271
Kamoda, 270, 295
Kamyakavana, 295
Kamyakvan, 271
Kanaud, 276
Kankar-Patthar, 86
Kannaudia clan, 276
Kanva, 37
Kapal Mochan, 370
Kapalamochana, 101
Kapalshikhar, 100
Kapil Dev, 281
Kapil Yaksha, 134
Kapil, 74
Karak Chauth, 299
Karak Kalan, 151
Karim Khan, 68
Karna Katila, 299
Karna, 292
Karnali, 314
Karnavati, 384
Karthikeya, 105
Kartik Chauth, 299
Karttikeya, 151
Karva Chaturthi, 300
Karva, 301
Kashi Rao Holkar, 64
Kashyap, 270
Katyayana, 247, 249
Kavyamimansa of Rajasekhara, 47
Kavyamimansa, 277
Kayam Khom, 222
Kayamkhanis, 222
Keertanacharya, 309
Khalji dynasty, 56
Khandar, 97
Khizar Hayat Khan, 163
Khizir Khan Sur of Bengal, 201
Khizr Khan, 58
Khokrakot, 151
Khushwant Singh, 206
Khwaja Altaf Hussain Hali, 149
Khwaja Jafar Hussain, 77
King Basak, 135
King Bhoja of Malwa, 396
King Daksa's sacrifice, 246
King Dalip, 255

King Hammarabi, 353
King Harish Chandra, 22
King Harsha, 253
King Karnadev, 384
King Kuru, 93
King Nala, 94
King Suraj Pal, 336
King Vena, 253
King Virat, 82
King Yashovarman, 46
King Yayati, 35
Kirtinath, 232
Koh-I-Noor, 60
Kolkata's Presidency College, 21
Kotaha Hills, 167
Koti Tirtha, 135
Koul, 299
Krishan Lal Bhat, 306
Krishna Menon, 80
Kritlivasa, 269
Kruancha, 105
Kula Prachin, 94
Kulbir Singh Malik, 131
Kulongpun, 299
Kulontaran, 299
Kumar Gandharv, 304
Kunala, 238
Kundli, 305
Kunti, 249, 426
Kuntibhoja, 293
Kuru tribe, 96
Kurudesh (Haryana), 46
Kurujangal, 44
Kurukshetra Development Board, 245
Kurukshetra University, 298
Kurukshetra, 21, 26, 89, 94
Kushanas, 239

L

Lachman Kambhoj, 361
Ladakh, 291
Ladhana ka Baba, 316
Ladhana, 184, 313
Lakshmi, 304
Lal Sadak, 230
Lala Lajpat Rai, 73, 231
Lava and Kusha, 269
Laxmi Niwas, 239
Le Corbousier, 80
Leelavati, 300
Leprosy Mission at Ambala, 333
Liaqat Ali, 86
Lodhi dynasty, 58
Lodhi, 148
Lohara King Ananta of Kashmir, 54
Lohara ruler of Kashmir, 47
Lok Adalat, 378
Lord Brahma, 89, 254
Lord Hari Narayan, 388
Lord Indra, 98
Lord Jagannath, 318
Lord Krishna, 22
Lord Lake, 225
Lord Shiva, 253
Lord Vishnu, 98
Lord Wellesely, 66
Louis Borqun, 139
Lt. Col. Gerrard, 280
Lt. Gen. V.K. Nayyar, 79
Lt. General Bourquin, 224
Lt. R. Hodson, 153

M

M.A. Jinnah, 162
M.K. Kudryavtsev, 158
M.K. Miglani, 92
M.M. Punchi, 85
M.N. Roy, 163
M.S. Mali, D.I.G., 180

Machkruk, 134
Madhav Prasad Misra, 78
Madhavacharya Shastri, 77
Madho Singh, 60
Madhuban and Karnal, 291
Madhuvana, 26, 295
Madhyadesha, 101
Madud, launched, 53
Maha Nirvani Akhra, 267
Mahabharata and the Geeta, 21
Mahabharata, 93
Mahabhashya, 239
Mahadji Scindhia, 64
Mahalaxmi Temple, 233
Mahanirvani, 304
Mahant Mamsa Nath, 81
Mahapadma Nanda, 113
Mahapurana, 22
Maharaja Agra Sain Temple, 233
Maharaja Devnik, 90
Maharaja Krishna, 23
Maharaja Ranjit Singh, 172
Maharana Sangram Singh, 288
Maharishi Dayanand University, 126, 363
Maharshi Valmiki, 268
Mahatma Gandhi, 397
Mahendra Nath Gupta, 321
Mahendragarh, 275, 379
Mahisasura, 246
Mahmud of Ghazni, 53, 159, 181, 226, 239, 271
Major Caujfield, 280
Major W.F. Eden, 289
Malavas, 278
Male Ila, 26
Mandhar Rajputs, 58, 192
Mandhars, 139, 377
Mandodari, 114
Mangal Pandey, 70
Mangal race, 147
Manjhavali, 308
Manji Sahib Gurdwara, 183
Mansa Devi, 81
Manu, 74
Manu-Bharja, 292
Manusmriti, 90
Markandeshwar Temple, 96
Masani, 287
Mastgir Baba, 86
Masud attacked, 53
Masud Shah, 56
Masud, son of Mehmud of Ghazni, 218
Mathura, 90
Matsya Kanyakubi, 90
Matsya Purana, 90
Matsyanath, 77
Mattamayurakas, 151
Mattamayuras, 45
Maulana Abul Kalam Azad, 163
Maur, 45
Mauryan Empire, 44
Maya Ray, 80
Maya, 314
Mayavada, 309
Meera Sahab, 86
Meham and Sampla, 153
Menaka, 37
Meos of Mewat, 56
Mewat, 55, 286, 288
Middle Stone Age, 24
Mihira Bhoja, 173
Milkha Singh, 364
Minas, 288
Minhaj-ud-din, 56
Mir Mahadi Majruh, 77
Mirza Ilias Beg, 225
Mirza Najaf, 64
Mishrak, 131
Mitathal Banwali, Kunal and Rakhigarhi, 339
Mithila, 113
Mitravaruna, 29

Mittakoli, 74
Mohana, 295
Mohenjodaro, 106
Mohinder Singh Pannu, 146
Morni Hills, 167
Mortimer Wheeler's, 107
Moru, 97
Motilal Nehru Sports School, 305, 373
Motilal Nehru's Swarajya, 231
Mrikandu, 96
Mubarak Shah, 56
Mufti Mohammed Sayeed's, 420
Muhammad Afzal, 76
Muhammad Anur, 60
Muhammad Azim, 229
Muhammad bin Tughlak, 130
Muhammad Gauri, 54, 115, 152
Muhammad Shah, 85, 205
Muhammad Tughlak, 147
Muhammad-bin-Tughlak, 56
Muladhara Chakra, 302
Mulla Bekase, 198
Mullan Ahmad, 271
Munir Beg, 228
Murli Manohar Joshi, 351
Murthal, 305

N

N.K. Mukerji, 411
N.K.P. Salve, 150
N.P. Dhanda, 315
N.S. Rajaram, 106
Nadir Shah, 60, 148, 205
Nagabhatta, 46
Nagarkhand, 384
Nagarmal Khatri, 62
Nagas, 44
Nageshwar, 398
Naghrod, 131
Nagneal, 276
Nahar Singh Stadium, 334
Nahar Singh, 280, 307
Nahar-naul, 276
Nahusha, 33
Naimish Tirth, 90
Najawat Khan, 62
Najibuddaula, 62-63
Najubullah Khan, 64
Nakula, 22, 151
Nand Ram of Rewari, 60
Nandi, 97
Nandutara, 74
Nar Bahadur Dhanda, 129
Narada, 28
Naradiya Purana, 89
Narasimha-Gupta Baladitya, 45
Narayana, 29
Nardak, 98
Narkatari, 298
Narnaul, 26, 275, 380
Nar-Rashtra Sahdev, 276
Narsingh Mehta, 386
Nasibpur, 279
Nasiruddin Mahmud, 56
Nasir-ud-din Muhammad Shah, 57, 147
Nasruddin Qubacha, 55
Nasurat Shah, 57
National Herald, 19
National Highway, 428
National Museum, 349
Naunkar of Bikaner, 277
Navaratri, 383
Navjeevan Khosla, 123
Nawab Kaithal, 315
Nawab of Bahadurgarh, 154
Nawab of Rania in Sirsa, 68
Nawab of Rania, 228
Nemai Sadhan Bose, 332
New Stone Age, 24
Nischal Das, 77

Niwal Dai, 135
Niyoga, 293
Nur Laun, 276
Nur Mohammad Khan, 228
Nurul Hasan Governor of West Bengal, 332

O

O.P. Chautala, 153, 284, 406, 416, 423
Old Stone Age, 24
Oudichya, 76

P

P.E. Moore, 155
P.L. Verma, 79
Padma Purana, 29
Painted Grey Earthenware Civilisation, 25
Painted Greyware civilization, 238
Palam Cacli Inscription, 23
Panchananda, 135
Panchavati, 319
Panchavimsha Brahmana, 106
Pandavas, 34
Pandit Hari Prasad Chaurasia, 412
Pandit Neki Das, 165
Pandit Shri Ram Sharma, 73, 157
Pandit Shugan Chand, 186
Pandu, 293
Pandu's death, 43
Panini, 76, 238
Panipat Memorial Society, 185
Panipat on May of, 146
Parashurama, 93, 293
Parashuramal Tirtha, 134
Parikshit, 44, 114
Parinaha, 97
Parma Nand, 131
Parveen Sultana, 356
Pashupal Shaivites, 266
Pashupati, 239
Passina Khurd, 147
Pawan, 298
Pawanawa, 298
Pawan-Hariday, 298
Peacock Throne of Shah Jehan, 60
Peepalrajdev, 47
Peethasthanas of India, 246
Pehowa, 169
Perennial Philosophy, 325
Persian Wheel, 259
Phalaki Vana, 174
Phalakiban, 131
Phalakivana, 26, 295
Pharal, 131, 174, 295
Phojir, 132
Phulkain states, 139
Pichhan-gyu, 166
Pinda Taraka, 401
Pinjore Gardens, 82
Pipli, 92
Pippalad, 74, 103
Plaksha Prasravana, 99
Plato of the Jat tribe, 63, 162
Police Commemoration Parade, 291
Police Martyrs Memorial at Madhubani, 291
Porbandar, 397
Post-Graduate Institute of Medical Education and Research, 145
Prabhakara Vardhana, 255
Prabhakaravardhana, 46, 101
Prabhasa Pattana, 106
Pracheen Kala Kendra, 356
Prakrit, 76
Prakritanak, 45
Prasthas, 304
Pratap Singh, 68, 306
Pratihara empire, 115
Pratihara Mihira Bhoja, 366
Prayaga Gayasira, 93
President, R. Venkataraman, 81

President, Smt. R. Venkataraman, 415
Prime Minister, Rajiv Gandhi, 81, 282
Prince Azam, 86
Prince Humayun, 147
Prithudaka, 101, 170
Prithuvana, 26
Prithviraja, 54-55, 152
Prof. Aluxi V. Raikov, 280
Prof. Anjani Kumar Mehra, 112
Prof. Banka Behari Chakravorty, 347
Prof. Bipan Chandra, 363
Prof. Dashratha Sharma, 277
Prof. Gauri Nath Shastri, 357
Prof. Marya, 185
Prof. Ram Gopal, 40
Prof. Ravinder Kumar, 363
Prof. Sher Singh, 357
Prof. Shireen Ratnagar, 349
Prof. Subhash Kak, 346
Prof. Virendra N. Sharma, 112
Pt. Sri Ram Sharma, 380
Pulakesi II, 111
Pundari, 131
Pundarik, 131
Puran Das, 195
Puranas, 26
Puratana Prabandha Sangraha, 238
Puri and Kuru sects, 242
Puru refused, 36
Puru Vamsha, 37
Puruavas, 93
Pururavas, 27
Purushottambag, 248
Pushapdant, 22
Pushkar, 90, 93
Pushkaravati, 101
Pushpabhuti, 45, 263
Pushpadant of Rohtak, 76
Pushyamitra Sunga, 152

Q

Qalandar Sahab, 86
Queen Victoria, 186
Queen Yashomati, 256
Qutb Jalaluddin, 272
Qutb Shah, 60-61
Qutbuddin Aibak, 55

R

R.C. Temple, 135
R.H. Wilson's, 262
R.K. Saboo, 80
R.K. Vachher, 17
R.K.S. Gandhi, 179
Rabindranath Tagore, 99
Rabindranath, 106
Radhavallabh, 195
Radheya, 293
Ragini Singing, 305
Rahlopur, 292
Rahul Sankirtyayan, 22
Raj Jai Pal, 195
Raja Kalian, 218
Raja Karan Pal, 278
Raja of Balabhgarh, 71
Raja of Bhowana, 82
Raja Sali Vahana, 378
Raja Vikramjit of Gwalior, 189
Rajagopalachari, 113
Rajan and Sajan Misra, 379
Rajan Kashyap, 185
Rajan Kashyap, 421
Rajaram, 63
Rajasthan canal, 237
Rajasuya Yagna, 241
Rajatarangini, 245
Rajayavardhana, 75
Rajiv Gandhi, 15
Rajmata of Gwalior, 185
Rajshekhar Bose, 113
Rajya Sainik Board, 129

Rajyashri, 213, 256
Rakhigarhi, 347
Raktabeej, 249
Ram Bilas Sharma, 363
Ram Hrada, 134
Ram Rai, 134
Rama Krishna, 184
Ramachandra, 77
Ramayan, 26, 201
Ramayana of Jaswant Singh, 306
Ramdas of Agroha, 77
Ramlila, 306
Rampura village, 278
Rana Sangha, 188, 190, 204
Ranghars, 67
Rao Balbir Singh, 163
Rao Balkishan, 60
Rao Kalyan Singh of Bikaner, 239
Rao Krishna Gopal of Mewat, 280
Rao Tula Ram, 70, 278
Rasaka, 213
Ratanpal, 74
Ratna Prabha Suri, 239
Ravana, 114
Rawati, 278
Rayavardhana and Adityavardhana, 256
Razia, 56
Rear Admiral, 179
Rehowa, 100
Rewari, 275
Rigveda, 25
Rohit Parihar, 107
Rohitaka, 151
Rohitakas, 278
Rohtak Medical College, 150
Rohtasgarh, 151
Rose Garden, 81
Roshan Chiragh, 379
Rotary Club, 80, 181, 372
Rudraksha, 247
Rudrashiva, 247
Rukmini, 249
Rukn-ud-din, Feroze's, 56
Runkata, 308

S

S.K. Sharma, 337
S.S. Ray, 19, 80
S.S. Yadav, 144
Sabarmati river, 384
Sachdev Tyagi, 237
Ṣadashiv Rao Bhan, 149
Śadashivrao Bhau, 62
Safidon, 134
Sagara Surdas, 308
Sage Durvasa, 293
Sage Phalak, 174
Sahachidevi, 34
Saiyana Saiyada, 172
Sajuman, 295
Saket, 143
Samadhi, 320
Samana, 180
Samanta Panchaka, 93
Samantapanchaka, 26, 97
Samar Halarnkar, 108
Samgha, 160
Sampat Singh, 169
Samvarana and Tapati, 97
Samykta, 54
Sanaka and Valkhilya, 254
Sanaka, 27
Sanatan Dharma Sabha, 77
Sankhoddhara, 402
Sannihit tank, 94, 244
Sannyasa, 319
Sanpat Singh, 315
Sansis, 287
Santokh Singh, 130
Sapta-Sindhu, 26
Saqlain Mushtaq, 281

Saradanda Markanda and Aruna, 102
Saradanda, 102
Saraswat Brahmin, 308
Saraswati and Drishadwati, 24
Saraswati Nagar, 239
Saraswati river, 238
Sardar Buta Singh, 15
Sardar G.S. Kahlon, an ex-I.C.S. Officer, 180
Sardar Gajpat Singh, 139
Sardar Gurdial Singh, 84
Sardar H.S. Chalha, 361
Sargi, 301
Sarkaria Commission, 420
Sarpadevi, 138
Sarpasatra, 114
Sarva Dharma Samanvaya, 317
Sarvapanchaka, 26
Satapatha Brahmana, 112
Sati Mata Annapurana, 268
Satyanand, 412
Sayyid dynasty, 58
Sayyid Niamlullah, 227
Sayyids, 187
Scythians and Kushanas, 45
Seoban, 131
Shah Alam II, 62, 64, 276
Shah Jehan, 59, 291
Shah Quli Khan Mehram, 277
Shah Quli Khan, 200
Shahabad, 96
Shaikh-ul-Islam Maulana, 226
Shairishaka, 238
Shakti Peeth, 81
Shakti, 302
Shakuntala, 37
Shamsuddin Iltutmish, 55
Shankaracharya of Kamakothi Peetham, 245
Shankaracharya, 302
Shantanu, 43
Shantiniketan, 332
Sharmistha, 34
Shasrara Chakra, 302
Sheikh Abdul of Thanesar, 76
Sheikh Abus Qadis, 76
Sheikh Chilli Banmuri, 272
Sheikh Jeevan of Jhajjar, 76
Sheila Bhatia's, 123
Sher Shah Suri, 58, 223, 277
Sher Shah, 187
Sherawal, 427
Sheri Khanda, 305
Sherla Taal, 168
Shirisha, 238
Shirishvan, 239
Shiva and Parvati, 213
Shiva Temple of Bhavanath, 387
Shiva, 27
Shri Aurobindo, 352
Shri Banarsi Das Gupta, 144
Shri Bhim Sain Tyagi, 163
Shri Gulzari Lal Nanda, 357
Shri Jagmohan, 351
Shri R.K. Trivedi, Governor of Gujarat, 383
Shridhar, 23
Shrikanta Janapada, 102
Shrikanta, 258
Shrimad Rajchandra, 385
Shrimantha Janapada, 46
Shrushna, 370
Shugan Chand Roshan, 77
Shukracharya, 34
Shukraprasthapur, 300
Shut Singh, 143
Sihi, 214
Sikander Lodhi, 58, 187
Sikh Guru Tegh Bahadur, 255
Simla, 179
Sindhu Van, 370
Sir Chhotu Ram, 74, 165, 191
Sir George Campbell, 161

Sir Herbert Rislay, 287
Sir Jadunath Sarkar, 23
Sir Mortimer Williams, 38
Sir Sayyad Ahmed Khan, 147
Sir Sikandar Hayat Khan, 163
Sirhind Ali Quli, 58
Sirmur Chills, 220
Sirmur, 100
Sirsa town, 238
Sirsa, 151
Siswal Civilization, 24
Sita and Savitri, 293
Sita Ram Singla, 360
Sita, 131, 249, 268
Sitaban, 131
Sitavana, 295
Sithanas, 214
Sivana, 295
Siwan, 268
Skanda Purana, 22
Skinner, 225
Slave dynasty, 55
Smt. A. Sehgal, 143
Smt. Asha Sharma, 143
Smt. Asharani Bhattacharya, 80
Smt. Kalekar, 150
Smt. Kamala Verma, 85
Smt. Komal Anand I.A.S., 17, 91
Smt. Maya Ray, 411
Smt. Suman Duggal, 333
Smt. Sushma Swaraj, 216, 409
Smt. Usha Saboo, 123
Sodoshi, 302
Sohna, 286
Somadeva, 152
Somnath temple, 390
Sonepat, 304
SOS Children's Village, 307
Sri Ramkrishna Paramahansa, 313
Sri Ramkrishna, 316
Srigupta of Narnaul, 76
Srihind, 139
Srikanta Janapada, 366
Sringeri Mutt, 315
St. John Ambulance Corp., 144
State Council of Bharat Scouts and Guides, 144
State Sports Awards Presentation, 360
Sthaneshvar, 253
Sthanniswara, 101
Sthanutirth, 253
Sthanvishvara Mahadeva temple, 253
Sthanvishvara, 253
Stupas, 75
Subhadra, 392
Subhash Katyal, Welfare Minister, 380
Sudama, 397
Sudhir Verma, 331
Sudyumna, 27
Sufism, 271
Sugh, 369
Sugh, 44
Sukhna Lake, 145, 213
Sukhni, 420
Sulakshanpala, 47
Sulba-sutras, 344
Sulochana Brihaspati, 150
Sultan Mahmud Tughlak, 147
Sultan Mahmud, 57-58
Sultan Masud Dipal Har, 305
Sultan Nasir-ud-din, 82
Sunanda K. Datta Ray, 420
Sundardas, 77
Suraj Kunda, 134
Suraj Mal, 161
Surajkund, 307, 332
Surajmal, 63, 191
Surdas of Sihi, 78
Surdas, 214
Suri Afghans, 187
Suryakund, 367

Suryavana, 26, 295
Suta-Putra, 294
Sutlej Yamuna Link, 211
Swami Alokananda, 315
Swami Dayanand Saraswati, 73, 164
Swami Indraj, 165
Swami Jagadananda, 316
Swami Sradhananda, 316
Swami Vivekananda, 352
Swapna Sundari, 333, 380
Swayambhu, 391
Swayamvara, 54
Syed Abdul Jalil Atal, 76
Syed Alauddin, 76
SYL Canal Project, 356

T

Tadrantuka and Arantrika, 98
Tafzal Hussain, 153
Taittriya Aranyaka, 365
Tajewala in Yamunanagar, 368
Takshika, 115, 138
Tamerlane, 82
Tantiya Tope and Mangal Pandey, 335
Tantras, 246
Tapra Hills, 167
Tara, 103
Tarain in 1192 A.D., 115
Tarain, 153
Tardi Beg Khan, 198
Tarikh-I-Zillah Rohtak, 23
Tarun Dal, 62
Tatig Naga, 136
Tau Sangi, 77
Tau, 166
Taxila, 44
Tayab Hussain, 128
Teej festival, 212
Teja Singh, 278
Tennis enthusiasts, 126
Tennis Tournament, 336
Thakur Badan Singh, 161
Thakur Pheru of Haryana, 76
Thakur Pheruman, 217
Thakur Ramachandra of Rohtak, 76
Thanesar, 253
Thaneswari of Thaneswar, 76
The ASHI Pratihara Mihira Bhoja, 181
The Katyayani temple, 248
The Khalimpur Copper Plate Inscription, 46
The PHD (Punjab, Haryana and Delhi) Chamber of Commerce and Industry, 372
Third Battle of Panipat, 149, 186
Three famous Lals, 161
- Bansi Lal, 161
- Devi Lal, 18, 161
- Bhajan Lal, 161

Tilpat, 111
Timur or Tamerlane, 147
Timur, 222
Todar Mal, 194
Tomar rulers, 410
Tomaras, 152
Topa, 44
Topiary Garden, 123
Topra, 75
Toshans, 217
Training College, 291
Treaty of Jind, 223
Treta Yuga, 346
Trishanku, 345
Tritsu, ruler, 43
Tsangpo, 100
Tyagis, 139

U

Uddalak, 74
Uma Lord Shiva, 254

Uma Sharma, 376
Unionist Party, 162
University Grants Commission, 127
Urvashi, 28, 94
Ustad Yunus Hussain Khan, 357

V

V.N. Krishna Rao, 353
V.N. Shah, 94
V.P. Singh, 284, 364
Vadavanala, 103
Vaishnavism, 173
Vaivasvata, 112
Vallabhacharya, 309
Valmiki Ashram, 267, 269
Valmiki, 102
Vamana Purana, 89
Vanaprastha, 232
Varadaraj temple, 248
Vashishtha Vishwamitra, 345
Vashistha, 90
Ved Sharma, 301
Veda-Dharatala, Varu raja, 22
Vedanta Sadhana, 313
Vedanta Sutra, 314
Vedi, 93
Vedic Civilization, 24
Veervati, 300
Ven. Saddhananda Thera, 15
Vice President, Dr. Shankar Dayal Sharma, 81
Vichitravirjya, 43
Vidya Banamali Dutt Sharma, 313
Vigraharaja IV or Visaladeva, 54
Vijay Raje Scindia Rajmata of Gwalior, 333
Vikramorvasiya, 31
Vikrampur, 46
Vinasana, 99
Viraja, 93
Viratnagar, 111
Virender Singh, 283-84
Vishnupurana, 113
Vishrantaghat, 309
Viswamitra, 37, 90
Vrajabhumi, 94
Vritra, 94, 344
Vyasasthali, 292, 295
Vyasavana, 26, 295

W

W. Ford, 289
Wahiuddin Salim, 77
Warwana, 315
Wedderburn, 228
Western Yamuna Canal, 220
William Fraser, 68
Wima Kadphises, 45

Y

Yadavas, 394
Yama, 96, 301
Yamunanagar, 97, 365
Yashoda, 94, 244
Yashodharman, 45
Yashtilakachampu, 152
Yaudheyas, 22, 151
Yayati, 34
Yudheyas, 239
Yudhisthir, 44
Yudhisthira, 34, 94
Yuldoz, 55

Z

Zafar Khan, 147
Zain Khan, 62, 148
Zantii of Zantil, 159
Zend Harogaiti, 100
Zoroastrians, 342